DIETRICH BONHOEFFER WORKS, VOLUME 10

Barcelona, Berlin, New York: 1928–1931

This series is a translation of
DIETRICH BONHOEFFER WERKE
Edited by
Eberhard Bethge†, Ernst Feil,
Christian Gremmels, Wolfgang Huber,
Hans Pfeifer, Albrecht Schönherr,
Heinz Eduard Tödt†, Ilse Tödt

This volume is dedicated
to the Abyssinian Baptist Church in Harlem,
where Dietrich Bonhoeffer found
"the gospel of Jesus Christ, the savior of the sinner, . . .
really preached and accepted
with great welcome and visible emotion."

This volume has been made possible through the generous support of the Lilly Endowment, Inc.; the Thrivent Financial Foundation for Lutherans; the New England Synod, ELCA; the Bowen H. and Janice Arthur McCoy Charitable Foundation; the Lutheran Theological Seminary at Philadelphia; and the gifts of numerous members and friends of the International Bonhoeffer Society.

DIETRICH BONHOEFFER WORKS, VOLUME 10

DIETRICH BONHOEFFER

Barcelona, Berlin, New York

1928–1931

Translated from the German Edition
Edited by
Reinhart Staats and Hans Christoph von Hase
in cooperation with
Holger Roggelin and Matthias Wünsche

English Edition
Edited by
Clifford J. Green

Translated by
Douglas W. Stott

FORTRESS PRESS MINNEAPOLIS

DIETRICH BONHOEFFER WORKS, Volume 10

Originally published in German as *Dietrich Bonhoeffer Werke,* edited by Eberhard Bethge et al., by Chr. Kaiser/Gütersloher Verlagshaus in 1992: Band 10, *Barcelona, Berlin, Amerika: 1928–1931,* edited by Reinhart Staats and Hans Christoph von Hase with the assistance of Holger Roggelin and Matthias Wünsche; 2nd edition, 2005. First English-language edition of *Dietrich Bonhoeffer Works,* Volume 10, published by Fortress Press in 2008.

The publication of this work was subsidized in part by a grant from the Goethe-Institut Inter Nationes, Munich.

Jacket design: Cheryl Watson
Cover photo: Dietrich Bonhoeffer, UTS Class Photo, 1931, UTS Records, Series 18, The Burke Library Archives at Union Theological Seminary, New York. Copyright © The Burke Library Archives at Union Theological Seminary, New York. Used by permission.
Photo editing: GJ Schultz, Studio LightPlay, 2007
Internal design: The HK Scriptorium, Inc.
Typesetting: Ann Delgehausen, Trio Bookworks

Library of Congress Cataloging-in-Publication Data

Bonhoeffer, Dietrich, 1906–1945.
[Barcelona, Berlin, Amerika, 1928–1931. English]
Barcelona, Berlin, New York, 1928–1931 / Dietrich Bonhoeffer ; translated from the German edition edited by Reinhart Staats and Hans Christoph von Hase in cooperation with Holger Roggelin and Matthias Wünsche ; English edition edited by Clifford J. Green ; translated by Douglas W. Stott.
p. cm.—(Dietrich Bonhoeffer works ; v. 10)
Includes bibliographical references and index.
ISBN-13: 978-0-8006-8330-6 (alk. paper)
1. Bonhoeffer, Dietrich, 1906–1945—Correspondence.
2. Theologians—Germany—Correspondence. 3. Theology. 4. Lutheran Church—Sermons. 5. Sermons, German—Translations into English. I. Green, Clifford J. II. Title.
BX4827.B57A4 2008
230'.044092—dc22
[B]

2007049780

The paper used in this publication meets the minimum requirements of American National Standard for Information Sciences—Permanence of Paper for Printed Library Materials, ANSI Z329.48-1984.

Manufactured in the U.S.A.
12 11 10 09 08 1 2 3 4 5 6 7 8 9 10

CONTENTS

Part 2
Essays and Lectures

General Editor's Foreword to Dietrich Bonhoeffer Works

The German theologian and pastor Dietrich Bonhoeffer has become one of the most influential Christian thinkers of all time. Barely twenty-seven years of age when the Nazi regime came to power in Germany, Bonhoeffer emerged immediately as a radical Protestant voice against the ideological cooptation of his church. He was one of the earliest critics of the Nazi regime and an outspoken opponent of the pro-Nazi "German Christians." From 1933 to 1935, he served as pastor of two German-speaking congregations in England, leading them to join the Confessing Church—the faction within the German Protestant church that opposed the nazification of the Christian faith. He returned to Germany to become director of a small Confessing Church seminary and, after the Gestapo closed it, continued to work illegally to educate Confessing clergy. Throughout the 1930s he attended ecumenical meetings, effectively becoming the voice of the Confessing Church throughout the European and American ecumenical world. In 1939, his ecumenical friends urged him to accept a position in New York. Rejecting the security of a life in exile, Bonhoeffer chose instead to join the ranks of the German conspiracy to overthrow the regime, like his brother Klaus and his brothers-in-law Hans von Dohnanyi and Rüdiger Schleicher. He was arrested and imprisoned in April 1943 and executed in the Flossenbürg concentration camp in April 1945.

In a eulogy published shortly after Bonhoeffer's death, his former professor and friend Reinhold Niebuhr wrote that Bonhoeffer's story "is worth recording. It belongs to the modern acts of the apostles. . . . Not only his martyr's death, but also his actions and precepts contain within them the hope of a revitalised Protestant faith in Germany. It will be a faith, religiously more profound than that of many of its critics; but it will have learned to overcome the one fateful error of German Protestantism, the complete dichotomy between faith and political life."[1]

In the ensuing decades, Niebuhr's prescient insight that Bonhoeffer's life and work offered lasting insights for modern Christian experience and witness has been more than fulfilled. Bonhoeffer wrote hundreds of letters, sermons, and biblical reflections in addition to his published theological works. After 1945, Bonhoeffer's former student and close friend Eberhard Bethge worked with publishers to reissue and translate the books Bonhoeffer had published in his lifetime. In translation, these works—*Discipleship, Ethics,* and *Letters and Papers from Prison*—became classics, finding a wide readership among Christians throughout the world.

Yet there was a growing sense that these works should not stand alone—a realization of the significance of the biographical and historical context of his thought. Bonhoeffer's papers included lecture notes that had been made by his students, documents from the German Church Struggle and ecumenical meetings, circular letters that were sent to his seminarians, sermons, extensive correspondence with theologians and religious leaders in Europe and the United States, and prison writings. Bethge published several early compilations of some of these documents (*Gesammelte Schriften* and *Mündige Welt,* vol. 5) and incorporated additional material into his magisterial biography of Bonhoeffer, which first appeared in English in 1970 and then, in a revised and unabridged edition, in 2000.

Bethge and leading Bonhoeffer scholars in Germany decided to publish new annotated editions of Bonhoeffer's complete theological works, together with most of the documents from the literary estate, including historical documents and correspondence to Bonhoeffer. The *Dietrich Bonhoeffer Werke* series was published by Chr. Kaiser Verlag, now part of Gütersloher Verlagshaus. The first German volume, a new edition of Bonhoeffer's dissertation *Sanctorum Communio,* appeared in 1986; the final volume, Bonhoeffer's complete prison writings, appeared in April 1998. The seventeenth volume, an index for the entire series, appeared in 1999; this volume also includes documents discovered after their respective volumes had been published. Whenever possible these documents are integrated into the appropriate volumes of the English edition; documents that continue to be discovered are published in the *Dietrich Bonhoeffer Yearbook,* a series published by Gütersloher Verlagshaus.

[1.] Reinhold Niebuhr, "The Death of a Martyr," *Christianity and Crisis* 5, no. 11 (1945): 6–7.

Discussion about an English translation of the entire series began as soon as the first German volumes appeared. In 1990 the International Bonhoeffer Society, English Language Section, in agreement with the German Bonhoeffer Society and Fortress Press, undertook the English translation of the German *Dietrich Bonhoeffer Werke.* The project began with an initial grant from the National Endowment for the Humanities with Robin Lovin serving as project director, assisted by Mark Brocker. An editorial board was formed for the *Dietrich Bonhoeffer Works,* English edition, staffed by Wayne Whitson Floyd Jr. as general editor and Clifford J. Green of Hartford Seminary as executive director. Wayne Whitson Floyd Jr., at that time director of the Dietrich Bonhoeffer Center at the Lutheran Theological Seminary in Philadelphia, served as general editor from 1993 to 2004, overseeing publication of the first seven volumes as well as volume 9. Victoria J. Barnett, director of church relations at the U.S. Holocaust Memorial Museum, joined the project as associate general editor in 2002 and became general editor in 2004, joined by Barbara Wojhoski, a professional editor who prepared the manuscripts of the final volumes for publication.

The *Dietrich Bonhoeffer Works,* English edition (*DBWE*) is the definitive English translation of Bonhoeffer's theological and other writings. It includes much material that appears for the first time in English, as well as documents discovered after the publication of the original German volumes. *DBWE* is a significant contribution to twentieth-century theological literature, church history, and the history of the Nazi era. Particularly in their portrayal of the daily implications of the Protestant Church Struggle in Nazi Germany and the response of Christians outside Germany, these volumes offer a detailed and unique glimpse of Bonhoeffer's historical context and its great challenges for the churches and for all people of conscience.

The translators of the *DBWE* volumes have attempted throughout to render an accurate and readable translation of Bonhoeffer's writings for contemporary audiences, while remaining true to Bonhoeffer's thought and style. Particular attention has been paid to the translation of important theological, historical, and philosophical terms. Bonhoeffer's language and style is often reflective of his age, particularly with regard to gendered language, and this is reflected in the historical and church documents. Nonetheless, in the translations of the early volumes of his theological writings (*DBWE* volumes 1–7), the decision was made to use gender-inclusive language, insofar as this was deemed possible without distorting Bonhoeffer's meaning or unjustifiably dissociating him from his own time.

Each volume includes an introduction written by the *DBWE* volume editor(s), footnotes provided by Bonhoeffer, editorial notes added by the German and the *DBWE* editors, and the original afterword written by the editor(s) of the German edition. Additions to or revisions of the German editors' notes are enclosed within square brackets and initialed by the editor of the respective volume. When any previously translated material is quoted within an editorial note in altered form—indicated by the notation [trans. altered]—such changes should be assumed to be the responsibility of the translator(s). Where available, existing English translations of books and articles in German and other languages are cited in the notes.

Bonhoeffer's own footnotes—which are indicated in the body of the text by plain, superscripted numbers—are reproduced in precisely the same numerical sequence as they appear in the German critical edition, complete with his idiosyncrasies of documentation. In these, as in the accompanying editorial notes, the edition of a work that was consulted by Bonhoeffer himself can be determined by consulting the bibliography at the end of each volume.

Each volume contains a list of abbreviations frequently used in the editorial notes. Bibliographies at the end of each volume provide complete information for each written source that Bonhoeffer or the various editors have mentioned in the current volume. Each volume also includes a chronology of important dates relevant to that volume, an index of scriptural references, an index of persons with biographical information, and an index of subjects.

Bonhoeffer's literary estate—the archives, collections, and personal library of materials that belonged to him and survived the war—was cataloged by Dietrich Meyer and Eberhard Bethge; this catalog has been published as the *Nachlaß Dietrich Bonhoeffer.* Most of the documents cited in the *Nachlaß* are collected in the Berlin Staatsbibliothek; some documents remain in other archives. All documents listed in the *Nachlaß*, however, have been copied on microfiches that are now at the Staatsbibliothek in Berlin and in the Bonhoeffer collection at Burke Library, Union Theological Seminary, New York. References to any of these documents are indicated within the *DBWE* by the abbreviation *NL*, followed by the corresponding catalog number. Books in the bibliography from Bonhoeffer's own library are indicated by the abbreviation *NL-Bibl.*

Volumes 1–7 of the English edition, which contain only Bonhoeffer's own writings, retain his original organization of the material, either as chapters or as sections or unnumbered manuscripts. Volumes 8–16 contain collected writings from a particular period of Bonhoeffer's life, including correspondence from others and historical documents. With the exception of volume 8, these final volumes are divided into three sections, with the documents in each section arranged chronologically: (1) Letters, Journals, Documents; (2) Essays, Seminar Papers, Papers, Lectures, Compositions; (3) Sermons, Meditations, Catechetical Writings, Exegetical Writings. Documents are numbered consecutively within the respective sections. In editorial notes these items are labeled by the *DBWE* volume number, followed by the section number, document number, and the page and/or note number; for example, *DBWE* 9 (1/109), p. 179, ed. note 1, refers to the English edition, volume 9, section 1, document 109, page 179, editorial note 1.

The *DBWE* also reproduces Bonhoeffer's original paragraphing; exceptions are noted by a ¶ symbol to indicate any paragraph break added by the editors of the English edition or by conventions explained in the introductions written by the editor(s) of specific volumes. The pagination of the *DBW* German critical edition is indicated in the outer margins of the pages of the translated text. Where it is important to give readers a word or phrase in its original language, a translated passage is followed by the original, enclosed in square brackets. All biblical citations come from the New Revised Standard Version (NRSV) unless otherwise noted. Where versification of the Bible used by Bonhoeffer differs from the NRSV, the verse number in the latter is noted in the text in square brackets.

The publication of the *Dietrich Bonhoeffer Works*, English edition, would not have been possible without the generous support of numerous individuals and institutions. The verso of the half-title page of each volume provides a list of supporters of that particular volume. The series as a whole is indebted to many individual members and friends of the International Bonhoeffer Society and to family foundations, congregations, synods, seminaries, and universities. Special thanks are due the following foundations and donors for major grants: the National Endowment for the Humanities; the Lilly Endowment, Inc.; the Thrivent Financial for Lutherans Foundation; the Aid Association for Lutherans; the Stiftung Bonhoeffer Lehrstuhl; the Bowen H. and Janice Arthur McCoy Charitable Foundation; and Dr. John Young and Ms. Cleo Young. The Lutheran Theological Seminary at Philadelphia and its former Auxiliary provided space and ongoing support. Particular thanks go to our publisher, Fortress Press, and its ever-helpful and skilled staff, particularly its editorial director, Michael West, and his predecessor, Marshall Johnson.

The existence of this series in English and other languages is testimony to the international community of those who have found Dietrich Bonhoeffer to be a profoundly important companion in their own journey. That community would not exist without the wisdom, generosity, and dedication of Eberhard Bethge (1909–2000) and his wife, Renate. Bethge was himself a pastor in the Confessing Church. After 1945, he was convinced that the future of a living church in Germany depended on its addressing its failures under Nazism and in a new understanding of Bonhoeffer's lasting question, Who is Christ for us today?

The editors of this English edition are particularly grateful to the original editorial board of the German edition—composed of Eberhard Bethge†, Ernst Feil, Christian Gremmels, Wolfgang Huber, Hans Pfeifer, Albrecht Schönherr, Heinz Eduard Tödt†, and Ilse Tödt. As liaison between the German and the English editorial board, Hans Pfeifer has given steadfast and congenial support to his colleagues on both sides of the Atlantic. The editors of the individual German volumes have been generous with their time and expertise. As work on the *DBWE* has proceeded, a new generation of Bonhoeffer scholars in Germany has assisted us as well: Christine Kasch, Andreas Pangritz, Holger Roggelin, Christiane Tietz, and Ralf Wüstenberg.

We remain grateful to those whose original translations of Bonhoeffer's words introduced most of us to his work. It is only fitting, however, that this English edition be dedicated, finally, to the remarkable group of scholars who over the years have devoted their time, their insights, and their generous spirit to the translation, editing, and publication of these volumes. That dedication should begin with a special acknowledgment of the capable editorial leadership of Wayne Whitson Floyd Jr., who brought eight volumes to publication, and to Clifford J. Green, whose steady hand has guided the project throughout its existence and ensured the financial foundation for its completion.

The translators who have brought Bonhoeffer's words to new life in these volumes are Victoria Barnett, Douglas Bax, Claudia and Scott Bergmann-Moore, Isabel Best, Daniel W. Bloesch, James H. Burtness†, Lisa Dahill, Peter Frick, Barbara Green, David Higgins, Nick Humphrey, Reinhard Krauss, Peter Krey, Nancy Lukens, Mary Nebelsick, Marion Pauck, Martin Rumscheidt, Anne Schmidt-Lange, Douglas W. Stott, and Charles West.

Since its inception, the following people have served on the *DBWE* Editorial Board: H. Gaylon Barker, Victoria Barnett, Mark Brocker, Keith W. Clements, Wayne Whitson Floyd Jr., Peter Frick, Clifford J. Green, John W. de Gruchy, Barry Harvey, Geffrey B. Kelly, Reinhard Krauss, Michael Lukens, Larry Rasmussen, H. Martin Rumscheidt, and Barbara Wojhoski. The following served on the Advisory Committee: James H. Burtness†, John D. Godsey, Barbara Green, James Patrick Kelley, Robin W. Lovin, Nancy Lukens, Paul Matheny, and Mary Nebelsick.

In September 1943, Dietrich Bonhoeffer wrote his parents from prison: "In ordinary life we hardly realize that we receive a great deal more than we give, and that it is only with gratitude that life becomes rich. It is very easy to overestimate the importance of our own achievements in comparison with what we owe others."[2] Everyone who has worked on this project will, I believe, find meaning in those words and feel gratitude for Bonhoeffer's life and witness. It is a privilege to have been part of this long, deep, and rich conversation with Bonhoeffer's thought and to extend that conversation to the readers of these volumes.

Victoria J. Barnett

[2.] *LPP*, 109.

Abbreviations

AFL-CIO	American Federation of Labor and Congress of Industrial Organizations
DB-ER	*Dietrich Bonhoeffer: A Biography* (Fortress Press, rev. ed., 2000)
DBW	*Dietrich Bonhoeffer Werke,* German edition
DBWE	*Dietrich Bonhoeffer Works,* English edition
EKG	*Evangelisches Kirchengesangbuch*
EZA	Evangelisches Zentralarchiv, Berlin
GS	*Gesammelte Schriften*
KJV	King James Version
Lic.	Licentiate
LPP	*Letters and Papers from Prison* (Simon & Schuster, 1997)
LW	*Luther's Works,* American edition
NAACP	National Association for the Advancement of Colored People
NL	*Nachlaß Dietrich Bonhoeffer*
NL-Bibl.	Restbibliothek Bonhoeffers in *Nachlaß Dietrich Bonhoeffer* (supplement to the literary estate of Dietrich Bonhoeffer)
NRS	*No Rusty Swords* (Collins; Harper & Row, 1965)
NRSV	New Revised Standard Version
PAM	*Predigten—Auslegungen—Meditationen* (Chr. Kaiser, 1984–85)
RM	reichsmarks
RSV	Revised Standard Version
TF	*A Testament to Freedom* (HarperSanFrancisco, 1995)
WA	*Weimarer Ausgabe* (Weimar edition), Martin Luther
WA.Br	*Weimarer Ausgabe, Briefe*
WA.DB	*Weimarer Ausgabe, Die Deutsche Bibel*
WA.Tr	*Weimarer Ausgabe, Tischreden*
YMCA	Young Men's Christian Association

Clifford J. Green

Editor's Introduction to the English Edition

The years 1928 to 1931 were formative for Dietrich Bonhoeffer, both personally and theologically. A decade later he wrote to his church superintendent Max Diestel in Berlin that this period "set my entire thinking on a track from which it has not yet deviated and never will."[1] If Bonhoeffer had already established his academic credentials with a doctorate summa cum laude in 1927, in the years covered by this volume he laid the foundations for his future work in the university and the church, and even—though Hitler was not yet chancellor—set out on the path that made him an outspoken voice in the Confessing Church and eventually led him to participate in the anti-Nazi coup.

First, a brief overview of the years documented in this volume; almost all of its writings appear here in English for the first time. Bonhoeffer finished his doctoral dissertation, *Sanctorum Communio,* in 1927, and it was approved by the theological faculty in July; in December he defended his doctoral theses in the traditional public debate, and the degree was awarded by the Friedrich Wilhelm University, Berlin.[2] In January 1928, he completed his first theological examination, one of two required by the church as steps toward ordination. In February he took up a position as vicar in Barcelona, assisting in the care of the German congregation. Here he had his first extended experience with preaching and pastoral work, including special efforts on behalf of the youth. Alongside his parish ministry, he revised his doctoral dissertation for publication and began work on his postdoctoral dissertation; he also gave a series of three lectures to the congregation.

[1.] Letter of November 5, 1942, *DBWE* 16, 1/207.

[2.] Today it is called Humboldt University.

After returning to Berlin in February 1929, he took up his position in the summer semester as academic assistant in systematic theology to Wilhelm Lütgert at the university. Work on *Act and Being*, the postdoctoral dissertation that would qualify him for university teaching, continued and was completed in March 1930. The month of July that year was intensely busy: for ordination he took his second theological examination; to complete his qualification for university teaching, he delivered a trial lecture on July 12; and on July 31 the newly qualified university lecturer delivered his inaugural lecture, "The Anthropological Question in Contemporary Philosophy and Theology."

After a well-earned August vacation at the family country home in Friedrichsbrunn in the Harz Mountains, Bonhoeffer prepared for his journey to Union Theological Seminary, New York, to take up the Sloane Fellowship for a year of postdoctoral study. His first book, *Sanctorum Communio,* was published on September 2, and on September 5 he set sail on the *Columbus* for New York.

At Union Seminary he worked energetically at his courses, as was his custom, immersed himself in the African American community, especially Abyssinian Baptist Church in Harlem, and made important lifelong friendships with American and European companions at the seminary. He was in demand as a speaker and was a critical observer of the church scene and theological education. He also traveled a good deal, first to Philadelphia to visit relatives, and then to Washington to learn about the Federal Council of Churches and Howard University. At Christmas he visited Havana and preached to the German congregation, and at the end of the academic year he traveled to Mexico by car with his French friend Jean Lasserre, accompanied part of the way by the American theologian Paul Lehmann and the Swiss pastor Erwin Sutz. On June 20, 1931, he took the ship from New York and returned to Europe.

Looking a little beyond the years covered in this volume, after returning home Bonhoeffer spent three weeks in Bonn in July 1931, attending the lectures of Karl Barth and meeting with him, the first personal visit with the theologian who had initially impressed him in 1925 and had greatly influenced his theology. In late August and early September of 1931, Bonhoeffer's official ecumenical career began when he attended in Britain conferences of the World Alliance for Promoting International Friendship through the Churches, of which he was elected a youth secretary. In October he began his ministry as student chaplain at the Technical College in Berlin–Charlottenburg, and the next month he took on a confirmation class for several months in the tough working-class suburb of Berlin-Wedding. Also in November the semester began at the Friedrich Wilhelm University in Berlin,[3] and Bonhoeffer launched his career as a lecturer in the theological faculty with a lecture course, "The History of Twentieth-Century Systematic Theology," and a seminar, "The Concept of Philosophy and Protestant Theology."[4] From his appointment as the assistant for systematics,[5] he had a modest income but a lot of freedom. On the fifteenth of November 1931, Dietrich Bonhoeffer was ordained in the St. Matthias Church in Berlin.

These events trace Bonhoeffer's course over four eventful years—at least the public, outer course. A much more thorough account of these years can be found in Eberhard Bethge's biography, which devotes three substantial chapters to Barcelona, Berlin, and New York. Those chapters are essential reading in parallel to the primary sources in this volume.

Another resource is the extensive afterword to this volume written by Reinhart Staats, the primary editor of its German edition. First, it highlights various themes in Bonhoeffer's writings—youth, peace, politics, the church, education, friendship—that relate to the culture of the period, the waning years of the Weimar Republic. Second, it discusses Bonhoeffer's various experiences with the church—his home church and its officials in Berlin, the congregation in Barcelona, and the churches of America, the white church described so critically, and the black church so affirmatively—as well as his ecclesiology and his early ecumenical experience. In the third section of his afterword, Staats discusses the theologians and philosophers Bonhoeffer engaged—in Berlin the Ritschlian professors of the faculty, especially Harnack, but also Holl and Seeberg—and of course Karl Barth, as well as American pragmatism, the existentialism of Heidegger, and the dialogical philosophy of Grisebach. In his final section Staats explores possible connections between Bonhoeffer's early overseas experience and themes of his later writing. Among the themes mentioned are humanistic theology, the Sermon on the Mount, the ecumenical understanding of the church, grace, the critique of an ethic of principles, Jeremiah 45, and death.

Yet a third resource to accompany the primary texts in this volume comes from a special contemporary of Bonhoeffer in these years, his own cousin Hans Christoph von Hase. Like Bonhoeffer, he too took a doctorate in theology and, two years after his cousin, experienced a similar year of study at Union Theological Seminary. A coeditor of the German edition of this book,

[3.] *DBWE* 11:177.

[4.] *DB-ER*, 211. The seminar surely drew on *Act and Being* and his inaugural lecture; cf. 2/7. But note the change of orientation in the courses for the summer semester 1932 on the nature of the church and on Christian ethics.

[5.] *DB-ER*, 169.

he brings personal memories as well as a unique individual perspective to the commentary in his memoir, "'Turning Away from the Phraseological to the Real': A Personal Recollection."[6]

Given these essential resources, the purpose of this introduction is not to repeat or summarize the work of others. Rather, it must try to find the thread, both personal and theological, that clarifies Bonhoeffer's development in these years and for the decade ahead. This means that in the process of introducing Bonhoeffer's letters and sermons, his academic essays and lectures, we must discover and interpret several statements from this period and even from the Tegel letters more than a decade later—statements in which Bonhoeffer himself describes the significance of these years for his own sense of vocation and his theological development. His cousin Hans Christoph von Hase chose to highlight one of these statements that Bonhoeffer made in Tegel prison in 1944 about the course of his life: "then a turning away from the phraseological to the real ensued."[7] This poses several pertinent questions: "turning away" from what—what does "phraseological" describe? And what is the "real" that ensued? Keeping these questions in mind, we will return to them at the end with evidence assembled in the following pages.[8]

Barcelona: February 1928–February 1929

Four months after he arrived in Barcelona to take up his position as vicar, Bonhoeffer wrote to Max Diestel, his church superintendent and mentor in Berlin, thanking him for suggesting a year in the parish: "Let me thank you for thinking of me so graciously on that November morning and thus helping me along into this period, which will certainly be important for my entire life. I still remember how I wavered back and forth at the time, but not for a single moment have I regretted coming; and I owe that to you."[9]

Bonhoeffer arrived in Barcelona on February 15, 1928. The German colony in the city, mainly business people, numbered some six thousand, of whom about three hundred were members of the Protestant congregation; a good attendance at a Sunday service would be fifty. The pastor was Fritz Olbricht, and initially Bonhoeffer got on very well with him. But as the vicar's

[6.] See pp. 591–604.

[7.] Letter of April 22, 1944, *LPP*, 275 (translation by Isabel Best as in the forthcoming *DBWE* 8).

[8.] Especially suggestive for interpreting the evidence of this period, and particularly the New York stage, is the essay by Hans Pfeifer, "Learning Faith and Ethical Commitment in the Context of Spiritual Training Groups." Forthcoming in the *Dietrich Bonhoeffer Yearbook 3*.

[9.] Letter of June 18, 1928, 1/28, p. 104; see also his diary, 1/5, p. 57.

popularity increased, particularly with the young people and their parents, Olbricht became jealous and stopped announcing the preacher for the following Sunday. Bonhoeffer commented at the time that Olbricht's "main reading material is nationalist literature and newspapers."[10] The centennial booklet of the congregation has a photo of Olbricht that probably dates from 1933 or 1934, wearing a swastika badge on his lapel.[11] But there is no record of a clash over politics between Bonhoeffer and Olbricht, and at the end of Bonhoeffer's term, the pastor wrote a very positive report of his vicar to the church authorities in Berlin. Bonhoeffer's portrait of his supervisor, however, is less flattering.[12]

Parish ministry was not hectic for Bonhoeffer in Barcelona. He had time to launch new activities of his own, such as building up the children's service, putting on a Christmas pageant, proposing a plan for religious instruction in the church school, and initiating a discussion group for older adolescents. He was also able to meet regularly with a Spanish companion to practice the language, make music in the choral club, play the organ, socialize with parishioners, and even attend bullfights. He traveled around Spain for nearly three weeks with his brother Klaus in April and May 1928, and when his parents visited in the autumn for several weeks, he entertained them during their visit and traveled with them for a week through southern France in October. He had time for some academic work too, revising his dissertation for publication, preparing a series of three lectures that were delivered to the congregation, and beginning to work on his postdoctoral dissertation.

In addition to preaching, Bonhoeffer spent mornings in the office of the German relief organization that was located at the church, since the pastor was its treasurer. Here he met a different class of people from his middle-class parishioners. Away from "the masquerade of the 'Christian world,'" he wrote, "I'm getting to know new people each day, . . . people with passions, criminal types, small people with small goals, small drives, and small crimes—all in all people who feel homeless in both senses, people who thaw a bit when you speak to them in a friendly manner—real people. I can only say I have the impression that precisely these people stand more under grace than under wrath, but that it is precisely the Christian world that stands more under wrath than under grace."[13] These words are revealing, since they anticipate Bonhoeffer's association with other marginal groups in the future, such as African Americans in New York.

[10.] 1/75.

[11.] *Deutschsprachige Evangelische Gemeinde Barcelona, 1885–1985*; see p. 12.

[12.] 1/75.

[13.] 1/40.

While Bonhoeffer makes many observations about the Spanish people, and while he compares the Germans of the colony with the people back in Berlin, it is notable that he makes no comment about the political situation in Spain during his sojourn. It was the time of Primo de Rivera, the general who mounted a coup in 1923, dissolved the Cortes, and ruled as a military dictator. The constitution and civil liberties were suspended. Though the military dictatorship ended in 1925, Primo de Rivera continued as a civilian dictator, surviving a failed revolt by liberal forces in 1929, until his resignation over economic failures in 1930. We hear nothing of this from Bonhoeffer; only Klaus mentions that they once sat near Primo de Rivera at a bullfight. At this time politics was not in the forefront of his mind. (In 1932 he was embarrassed at having used the word "disinterestedness" to his friend Rößler in relation to political issues.)[14]

In the summer, parish activities slowed to a minimum, the pastor was away, and services were reduced. In 1928 Bonhoeffer was in charge for three months, and he preached every other Sunday.

A detailed analysis of the sermons is not possible here, but a few observations contribute to the larger picture. Bonhoeffer's sermons were based on biblical texts, all chosen from the New Testament except one on Psalm 62:2 and one from the Song of Songs. Written out, they sometimes read like lectures, with many long sentences; but we know that on occasion Bonhoeffer memorized a sermon and used notes to deliver it extemporaneously.[15] Illustrations are drawn from classical mythology, from ancient and recent philosophy, from old Teutonic legends, from Schiller and Goethe, from paintings and sculpture, from music and architecture, and from martyrs of the early church. Stories are rare, but one in a children's service on Remembrance Sunday about two dying soldiers—one of them only a youth—is particularly moving, alluding as it does to the death of his brother Walter in World War I.[16] With considerable regularity, impersonal abstractions appear as interruptions—"the eternal," "the infinite,"[17] "divine things,"[18] "the spirit of the divine,"[19] "the idea of God in Christianity."[20] Such phrases sound like a young preacher, an academic, who is still seeking his natural pastoral language. Bonhoeffer does not shield the congregation from modern bibli-

---

[14.] *DBW* 12 (1/22), p. 41; *DB-ER*, 165. See Rößler's letter of February 22, 1931 (1/164, p. 283) in which he called Bonhoeffer "unpolitical" by his very nature.

[15.] Cf. 3/3, pp. 489–90.

[16.] See 3/16, pp. 539–40.

[17.] 3/2, p. 481–82; 3/18, p. 547.

[18.] 3/3, p. 486.

[19.] 3/5, p. 496; 3/9, p. 515.

[20.] 3/2, p. 484.

cal criticism, speaking candidly of the "Old Testament myth" of Adam and Eve,[21] while emphasizing its serious theological point. In the theology of the sermons, the love of God is a recurrent note: Christ is "God's love among human beings," the cross is a "sign of divine love,"[22] it is "where God dies in love for human beings."[23] One of the more fervent sermons on the church as the body of Christ draws heavily on *Sanctorum Communio.* It stresses self-giving sacrifice, intercession, and forgiveness of sins as the threefold form of love between the members of the body.[24] And it equally stresses the church as an ecumenical community, "a people extending over the entire world . . . whose members love one another," a people who transcend the pride and animosity of nationalism.[25] In three different sermons Bonhoeffer quotes Augustine's famous sentence from the beginning of the *Confessions*: "You have made us for yourself, and our heart is restless until it rests in you."[26]

One sermon invites particular attention. On August 12, 1928, Bonhoeffer preached on a text from the Sermon on the Mount, Matthew 5:8: "Blessed are the pure in heart, for they will see God." This was not his first Barcelona sermon on a text from the Sermon on the Mount; in June he had preached on Matthew 7:1.[27] But Matthew 5:8 prompted him to confess to his friend Rößler, who was also a pastor and theologian: "I have never approached a sermon with such trepidation."[28] Admittedly, the text was a lofty one. But what was it about purity of heart that both challenged and troubled Bonhoeffer? We know how influential the Sermon on the Mount was to become for him personally,[29] and that it motivated him to write his book *Discipleship,* which is largely devoted to interpreting these three chapters from Matthew's gospel. The sermon points us toward an answer.

After the fall, Bonhoeffer said in the sermon, "God left one thing to humanity, . . . a *yearning for its origin,*[30] for its home, for God."[31] Purity of heart, *Reinheit,* is necessary to see God. But what is purity? The opposite of "lies and deception and hypocrisy and passion," the end of the masquerade

[21.] 3/10, p. 518. See also his comments on the Gospels in the lecture on Jesus, 2/2, p. 344–45, and ed. note 37, p. 9.

[22.] 3/10, p. 519.

[23.] 3/11, p. 523.

[24.] 3/8, p. 509.

[25.] 3/8, pp. 506–8.

[26.] Cf. pp. 481, 505, and 547.

[27.] "Do not judge, so that you may not be judged." Cf. 2/6.

[28.] 1/40, p. 128; cf. *DBWE* 4:126, 276, 286.

[29.] Cf. *DB-ER,* 204–6.

[30.] Bonhoeffer's italics, which recall the repeated quotation from Augustine about the restless heart.

[31.] 3/9, p. 512.

in which people hide behind masks. Jesus's beatitude means: "Become simple [*einfach*], clear, genuine, natural, straightforward, pure."[32] "Simple" here means not simplistic but rather single, undivided, integrated, of one mind, as in Kierkegaard's "purity of heart is to will one thing."[33] The use here of the word "simple," *einfach*, points forward to Bonhoeffer's repeated use in *Discipleship* and *Ethics* of the terms "simple" and "simplicity" (*einfältig* and *Einfalt*).[34] In fact, they become technical terms, characteristic of his mature theological vocabulary and inseparable from his Christology and understanding of Christian faith. Bonhoeffer suggests that he is seeking a "simplicity," a wholeness of identity, a singleness of purpose, the overcoming of some division and conflict. He will lead us back to this theme.

Between November 1928 and February 1929, Bonhoeffer delivered three lectures to the congregation on the subject "Crisis and Hope in the Contemporary Religious Situation."[35] Sounding rather like Tillich, whose book *The Religious Situation* he requested from Berlin, Bonhoeffer proposed that the series might show how Christianity could be an answer to the current crisis of European culture. In the first lecture he argued that the prophets in their time spoke to a culture in crisis and were burdened with being messengers of judgment and doom. God is the holy One, beyond all nationalism. Religion is not possessing God; human beings do not have God at their disposal. Rather it is they who are at God's disposal. Only in that perspective is any redemption possible.

Titling his second lecture "Jesus Christ and the Essence of Christianity," Bonhoeffer could hardly have failed to remember the famous lecture series on the essence of Christianity delivered three decades earlier by his teacher Adolf von Harnack.[36] His own lecture argues that Jesus must be retrieved from the process of post-Enlightenment secularization, which has privatized

---

[32.] 3/9, p. 514. Compare the sentence in the catechism on the Fifth Petition of the Lord's Prayer, 3/21, p. 564: "Yes, the notion that we belong to God is meant just this simply [*einfach*] and literally. There is no avoiding it and there are no exceptions. Everything is completely clear and definite, everything completely or not at all."

[33.] Kierkegaard, *Purity of Heart Is to Will One Thing.*

[34.] Bonhoeffer translates the New Testament ἁπλοῦς with *einfältig*. From the numerous references, in *Discipleship* (*DBWE* 4) for *einfältig* see chap. 3 on "Simple Obedience" and for *Einfalt*, p. 76; in *Ethics* see *DBWE* 6:78, 265, 321, 404 ("single-minded") for *einfältig* and 162, 238, 266, 313, 318–21 for *Einfalt*. See both terms also in 3/21, p. 564, and 3/22, p. 576.

[35.] See 2/1, 2/2, and 2/3. Originally four lectures were planned; cf. 1/60a and 1/68a in which he asks Walter Dreß to send him Tillich's *Religious Situation* to use in preparing the fourth lecture. In 1930 Bonhoeffer paid a return visit to the congregation in Barcelona and on April 8 gave a lecture to the congregation; cf. 1/109. One wonders whether this could be the delayed fourth lecture; we have no evidence.

[36.] *Das Wesen des Christentums*, translated as *What Is Christianity?*

and ghettoized him, thus eliminating him from the ultimate and decisive matters of life. That means beginning with Christ's claim to be *the* revelation of God and accepting his absolute claim on human decision.[37] (This note of Jesus "demanding a direct, uncompromising decision . . . in favor of God's will" anticipates a prominent theme in *Discipleship* that was already adumbrated in the 1932 lecture "Christ and Peace." But, unlike later, in this Barcelona lecture it is not yet focused on Jesus's concrete commands in the Sermon on the Mount.) Religion leads not to God but to an idol created by the human heart. Against this, "the essence of Christianity is found in its message about the sovereign God to whom alone, above the entire world, all honor is due; it is a message about the eternally other, the God removed from the world who from the primal ground of his being has loving compassion for those who render honor to him alone, the God who traverses the path to human beings in order to find there vessels of that honor precisely where human beings are nothing, where they fall silent, where they give space to God alone."[38] This is "the Christian idea," the eternal, transcendent God who comes in loving compassion to human beings, above all to the unworthy, to the sinner. The cross is the visible sign of God's path to humanity, and far from being an invention of Paul, it is "the most severe intensification of Jesus's own idea of God, the historically visible form, as it were, adopted by that idea."[39] "Jesus, who is God's love," takes upon himself the death that everyone must die, proving that "divine love extends even to the death of the criminal"[40] and showing that God's eternal love will accompany human beings through death. Because this eternal love is stronger than death, "the meaning of Good Friday and of Easter Sunday is that God's path to human beings leads back to God."[41] Meditating on the cross leads beyond the crisis of the present age to hope for the time when God makes all things new. The lecture ends like a sermon, personally addressing the listener: "You, human being, no matter who you are, you are God's child, you are included in God's love,

---

[37.] Echoing Albert Schweitzer's thesis that it is impossible to write a life of Jesus, Bonhoeffer argued that the first Christians worshiped him as *kyrios*, lord. To convey this status the Synoptic Gospels presented the actual life of Jesus "overgrown with legendary features," while tradition "draped Jesus in the conventional costume of a saint and miracle worker," and "ancient fairy tale motifs . . . contributed to the myth of Jesus of Nazareth such that today little of the actual humanity of this man can be ascertained with any certainty" (2/2, p. 344–45). Later he was to write that the creation stories of Genesis are scientifically naive and contain "undisguised mythology" and "fairy tales" that belong to a "world of the magical" (see *Creation and Fall*, *DBWE* 3:50, 75, 82).

[38.] 2/2, p. 354.

[39.] 2/2, p. 356.

[40.] 2/2, p. 357.

[41.] Ibid.

out of the pure, incomprehensible grace of God; accept this word, believe in it, trust in his rule rather than in yourself or in your own party, rather than in your own work or your own religion. God does as he wills. Turn your misery into God's blessed presence, and from within your guilt and distress hear the voice of the eternal, living God."[42]

Bonhoeffer's third lecture, "Basic Questions of a Christian Ethic," contains some characteristic ideas that will continue to be important in the *Ethics*, his magnum opus, some views that will change through the next decade, and some that will mercifully disappear forever. One enduring foundation is the conviction that Christian ethics is not an ethic of principles, since principles are a way to secure oneself, to "control my own relationship with God."[43] Ethical action is rather born of "immediate relationship with God."[44] Nor is ethics, any more than religion, a human path to God. So the commandments of Jesus, most famously those in the Sermon on the Mount, are not universal Christian norms—biblically speaking, they are not law. Instead, they place the Christian immediately before the face of God, calling the human will to surrender to the divine will, so that every action is before God and accountable to the will of God. Indeed, the human self is awakened by God's call to responsibility from eternity.[45] Accordingly, another persistent theme is that Christian ethics is particularistic and contextual, rooted in times, cultures, and peoples—here summarized in the phrase "blood and history," a locution that thankfully will not reappear. Another enduring idea, which is equally clear in *Creation and Fall* and in *Ethics*, is that Christian ethics is not about the conflict of good and evil; on the contrary, the duality of good and evil is the consequence of the fall.[46]

Notwithstanding the foregoing, there are divine orders [*Ordnungen*] in the world, and one's people, one's *Volk*, is one of these orders of creation.[47] In this context Bonhoeffer addresses the issue of war, quoting at length pas-

[42.] 2/2, p. 359.

[43.] 2/3, p. 365.

[44.] 2/3, pp. 366, 369.

[45.] This summarizes a key point in the theological anthropology of his doctoral dissertation; cf. *Sanctorum Communio* (*DBWE* 1), 48–54, and Green, *Bonhoeffer*, 30–36.

[46.] 2/3, p. 363.

[47.] Cf. pp. 368–69, 371, and 375. On p. 369 Bonhoeffer speaks of "the internal contradictions of two divine orders [Ordnungen]," his first example being the relationship between historical development ("national expansion, growth, war, and the struggle of economic competition") and "the divine commandment of love." Normally these two would be categorized under the orders of state and church. A second example is love and truth, which both have their "origin in God," and a third is "'nature and spirit,' whose common origin

sages from the Sermon on the Mount but ending up justifying war in the name of a concrete ethic in which love for one's own family and *Volk* reveals in the moment of decision that one should defend them against aggression. Those who argue against this conclusion are making a cardinal ethical error, says Bonhoeffer: "[T]hey make the New Testament commandments into new laws, and in so doing enslave themselves to those laws, whereas they should be making decisions in freedom. They judge according to the letter rather than according to the spirit of Christ."[48]

But this is not all. Having focused thus far on defensive war, Bonhoeffer then argues that Christian ethics may actually justify starting a war if this is done to realize the call of God in each people to make history, to grow in strength, to expand. Strong, growing nations are like individuals: the strong push aside the weak. Indeed, "strength also comes from God, and power, and victory, for God creates youth in the individual as well as in nations, and God loves youth, for God himself is eternally young and strong and victorious."[49] The same line of argument is applied to economic life and individual life. At the end of the lecture, Bonhoeffer retreats into the trite assertion that "the incomprehensible contradictions of the divine orders in the world must become clear if the kingdom of grace is to replace the kingdom of the world."[50]

Those who first read these words knowing Bonhoeffer the "pacifist," the antinationalist ecumenist, and the anti-Nazi resister are rightly shocked and embarrassed by this *völkisch* lebensraum theology. (Theologically this lecture graphically illustrates an aspect of the problem of *power*, which is central to Bonhoeffer's theological anthropology, soteriology, and ethics.)[51] A major change must occur to free him from these slogans of German nationalism, this appeal to the right of the stronger, and what Bethge calls the "conventionally Lutheran" attitude to the Sermon on the Mount "spruced up with the titanic ethics of the immediate moment."[52] Three years later we will hear very different assertions. And "order of creation" will disappear from

---

again is God," and is particularly exemplified in sexuality. If the "idea of the cross" gives priority to love, this would appear to rule war out of court. But in fact in war the order of love coincides with the order of *Volk* because one's own family and one's own *Volk* have not only *as much* claim on me as my neighbor (read enemy), but in the concrete moment of decision they have a *prior* claim.

[48.] 2/3, p. 372.

[49.] 2/3, p. 373. In this passage Bonhoeffer uses *Volk* when speaking about the nation.

[50.] 2/3, p. 378.

[51.] Cf. Green, *Bonhoeffer*, esp. chap. 4.

[52.] See, for example, Bethge, *DB-ER*, 119–20.

Bonhoeffer's theological vocabulary already in 1932[53] but emphatically after 1933, when the conceptuality was flagrantly used by the Deutsche Christen in support of Nazi racial and anti-Semitic doctrine.

As in the sermons, so too in the lectures we observe the ideational character of Bonhoeffer's theological language at this time. Repeatedly we hear of "the Christian *idea*,"[54] "the Christian *idea* of God,"[55] "Jesus's own *idea* of God,"[56] "the *idea* of the cross,"[57] "the *idea* of redemption,"[58] and others.[59] Equally abstract usages are references to "the deity,"[60] "the divine will,"[61] and "eternity."[62] By no means are these usages mainly polemical; on the contrary, they are Bonhoeffer's own expressions, as if life and faith consisted of a Hegelian play of concepts. The significance of this phenomenon will become clear later.

Though occupied with his pastoral ministry, plans for his future academic career were never far from Bonhoeffer's mind during the year in Barcelona. He edited his doctoral dissertation for publication and began to plan for his postdoctoral dissertation. He wrote to his professors back in Berlin about this scholarly work and about securing a university position when he returned. To Harnack he complained about feeling like an "academic hermit," deprived of the scholarly exchanges that he had so enjoyed in his professor's seminars. And while he admitted that practical experience could be "quite fruitful" and taught him the limits of "pure scholarship," he nevertheless wrote to Harnack, and not just out of deference, that "scholarship never releases those it has seized."[63] A week later, in a similar vein, he wrote to his doctoral adviser, Reinhold Seeberg: "Basically there is one thing I must do without here and really do miss quite painfully—shared scholarly

[53.] In *Creation and Fall* Bonhoeffer experimented with the alternative idea of "orders of preservation towards Christ" (*DBWE* 3:139–40) but soon dropped all talk of "orders" as though God's will could be institutionalized in the world and separated from God's living command; in *Ethics* he experimented with the category "mandate," which emphasized God's command and commission.

[54.] 2/2, pp. 354, 356; cf. "the *idea* of Christianity," 2/3, p. 363.

[55.] 2/2, p. 356, 2/3, pp. 365, 367, 369; cf. "the *idea* of God," pp. 336, 356.

[56.] 2/2, pp. 356; cf. 352.

[57.] 2/3, p. 369.

[58.] 2/2, p. 344.

[59.] In 2/3, p. 361, see "the central *idea* . . . of truth"; "the *idea* of ethics" (p. 363); and "the *idea* of freedom" (p. 368).

[60.] 2/2, p. 358.

[61.] 2/3, pp. 372, 375.

[62.] 2/2, p. 354; 2/3, pp. 366, 378; and often.

[63.] 1/33.

work. One doesn't know how truly important a seminar or some other shared scholarly work is if one has never had to rely completely on a reclusive scholarly existence."[64]

On February 3 Bonhoeffer preached his farewell sermon to the congregation. His concluding words looked forward to the university: "A different field of work now beckons me away from you."[65]

Berlin: February 1929–September 1930

Even before he went to Barcelona, Bonhoeffer was uncertain about the future, "whether," as Bethge puts it, "eventually to take up practical church work instead of the respected, privileged, and uncommitted career of a professor."[66] His adolescent decision to study theology had provoked criticism from his brothers and, at that time, silent disapproval from his father. The path he had followed, speedy completion of his doctorate at twenty-one, appeared to confirm the self-evident assumption of his family that in a contest between ministry in the church and an academic career in the university, the latter would obviously win. Writing with the benefit of hindsight, Bethge commented on Bonhoeffer's frame of mind in 1927: "His problem was not how to enter the academic world, it was how to escape it. The pulpit appealed more to him than the professor's lectern."[67] (But Bonhoeffer did not know that at the time.) In Barcelona parish ministry was obviously in the foreground, but it did not exclude Bonhoeffer's academic work and ambitions. Now back in Berlin, the academic world was in the foreground, though he continued to move toward ordination by completing in July 1930 his second theological examination required by the church. Although he applied for early ordination, church authorities required him to wait until he had reached the canonical age of twenty-five.

Beginning in the summer of 1929, Bonhoeffer was assistant for systematic theology to Wilhelm Lütgert, who had just come from Halle to succeed Reinhold Seeberg. Bonhoeffer was not yet qualified to offer courses, so in his free time he worked on a major academic project, his postdoctoral dissertation, *Act and Being*. Since the German edition of the present volume was published in 1991, some new discoveries have clarified the process by which Bonhoeffer qualified to teach at the university [*Habilitation*]. The

[64.] 1/36; cf. also the letter to Seeberg, 1/47.

[65.] 3/18, p. 551.

[66.] *DB-ER*, 94.

[67.] *DB-ER*, 96.

manuscript of *Act and Being* was submitted to the faculty on March 14, 1930. On April 15 Lütgert presented his report.[68] In summarizing the argument he points to Bonhoeffer's interest in phenomenology and dialectical theology and to his leaning toward "the transcendentalism that he draws upon and the idealism that he dismisses."[69] He is particularly impressed by the vigor of Bonhoeffer's argument: "occasionally even Heidegger's position is energetically dismissed"; the work "is in a constant argument with dialectical theology," and "occasionally there is also a very energetic objection to Barth."[70] Bonhoeffer's conclusion is recommended as a reading sample to the other examiners, who will find that it "powerfully expresses the deepest religious and theological interests of the author, and does so in a language that very clearly elevates itself above the abstract way of speaking in the epistemological part."[71] Lütgert concludes: "The combination of Luther's thoughts with the epistemological methods of the most recent philosophy and with problems of dialectical theology is characteristic of this work. One may ask whether a unified whole has emerged from these various ideas, but one cannot fail to recognize that the author understands how to preserve his independence over against all the ideas he has adopted here."[72] The faculty voted to accept the dissertation and to proceed to the final step. (Later Bonhoeffer looked back on the intellectual gymnastics of his tour de force in *Act and Being* and gave his own critical evaluation of it.)[73]

The final step was the candidate's trial lecture [*Probevorlesung*]. Delivering this lecture before the theological faculty was in effect the concluding examination of the qualification process. In distinction from the later inaugural lecture, which was a public event on a subject chosen by the new lecturer [*Privatdozent*], the trial lecture was on a subject chosen by the examining professors from several topics proposed by the candidate. Previously the only information about Bonhoeffer's trial lecture was two references he made in letters.[74] In 2005 research by Holger Roggelin discovered that Bonhoeffer held his trial lecture on July 12, 1930,[75] on "The Concept of Dialectic

[68.] See 1/109a. The original German text will be published the *Dietrich Bonhoeffer Yearbook 3*, 2008.

[69.] 1/109a, p. 211.

[70.] 1/109a, p. 210.

[71.] 1/109a, p. 213.

[72.] 1/109a, p. 213

[73.] See p. 35–36 of this introduction.

[74.] See the letters to Rößler and the Leibholzes in June 1930: 1/119 and 1/120.

[75.] The date in the chronology, p. 640, has been corrected. The biography also gives the wrong date of July 18, 1930; cf. *DB-ER*, 135, 1025.

in the So-Called Dialectical Theology." The other two topics he proposed were "The Significance of the Sociological Category for Dogmatics"[76] and "On the Possibility of a System of Dogmatics." Unfortunately no text of the lecture has been found. Given the impact Barth and his allies had been making in the previous decade and Barth's influence on Bonhoeffer, it is not surprising that the faculty chose dialectical theology as the topic. Examining Bonhoeffer's debate with Barth in *Act and Being* presumably gives good clues to the content of the lecture.

Having completed his qualification as a university teacher, Bonhoeffer was invited to deliver his inaugural lecture on July 31. Not surprisingly, it was based on his postdoctoral dissertation and titled "The Anthropological Question in Contemporary Philosophy and Theology."[77] Those who first meet Bonhoeffer through his later writings, especially through his theology in the exegetical mode of *Discipleship*, find *Act and Being* and the inaugural lecture to be alien and demanding. But this only highlights the fact that the postdoctoral dissertation and *Sanctorum Communio* as well are to a significant degree works in philosophical theology and thus have been more the province of scholars.[78] Significantly, they also represent a particular stage in Bonhoeffer's theological pilgrimage.[79]

Acknowledging Bonhoeffer's philosophical competence, however, should not lead to overlooking the existential issue embedded in these sophisticated works. In both *Act and Being* and the inaugural lecture, Bonhoeffer in fact clearly identifies *the* soteriological problem that is at the heart of his theological anthropology. "This is the problem of the powerful, dominant self who, particularly in his intellectual activity, adopts an autonomous, self-referring, isolated, and self-enclosed attitude to reality."[80] Bethge comments judiciously: "This highly abstract discourse, which the uninitiated are hardly able to follow, concealed a passionate personal involvement. Bonhoeffer's deepest feelings were involved in his insistence on the *extra nos* and *pro nobis* of salvation. His own difficulties sharpened his sensitivity to every loophole

[76.] See *Sanctorum Communio* regarding the "sociological category" (*DBWE* 1:21).

[77.] See 2/7.

[78.] See especially Marsh, *Reclaiming Dietrich Bonhoeffer*; Tietz, *Bonhoeffers Kritik der verkrümmten Vernunft*; and Reuter, editor's afterword to the German edition of *Akt und Sein* (*DBW* 2). For earlier works see Dumas, *Dietrich Bonhoeffer*; Green, *Bonhoeffer*, esp. chap. 3; Floyd, *Theology and the Dialectics of Otherness*, esp. chap. 2. See also the bibliography of *Act and Being* (*DBWE* 2), esp. section 3.

[79.] This is not to suggest that many of the ideas in these books are unimportant for Bonhoeffer's future theology; on the contrary, the opposite is true.

[80.] Green, *Bonhoeffer*, 71.

in the system through which fatal self-reflection might invade his own ego and establish its secret domination."[81] In short, a strong autobiographical dimension is present in the postdoctoral dissertation and the inaugural lecture; the latter contains a particularly clear and striking example.[82] More examples are found in other writings of the 1930s, including *Discipleship*.[83] This insight about the relationship of soteriology and autobiography is an important piece of the puzzle of Bonhoeffer's development "from the phraseological to the real" during these years.

Despite his conspicuous academic success from 1927 to 1930, Bonhoeffer was restless, concerned about his vocation and his future. Remarks in several letters make this clear. Already in Barcelona, after settling into his ministry there, he wrote to his friend Rößler about the contrast between his former academic life as a student and his present life as a pastor: in the latter "work and life genuinely converge—a synthesis that we all sought but rarely found in our student days—when one really lives *one* life rather than two, or better: half a life; it lends dignity to the work and objectivity to the worker, and a recognition of one's own limitations [*Grenzen*] of the sort acquired only within concrete life."[84] After returning to Berlin he wrote, in correspondence with Detlef Albers, the teacher of history and geography at the German Protestant school in Barcelona, about "spirit" and humanism: "Perhaps today . . . 'spirit' [*Geist*] really is to be found in the particular, that is, precisely in the 'material,' in concretely given reality—and precisely not in 'intellectuality' [*Geistigkeit*]."[85] To another Barcelona correspondent, Hermann Thumm, also a teacher and a former neighbor, he wrote on June 19, 1929: "Principles are quite good, but only until one is taught something

[81.] *DB-ER*, 134.

[82.] See 2/7, p. 405–6.

[83.] For additional discussion of this soteriological problem and its autobiographical dimension, see Green, *Bonhoeffer*, chap. 4, including the discussion on pp. 150–79.

[84.] Letter of August 7, 1928, 1/40.

[85.] Letter of June 9, 1929, 1/83. Earlier, in March, he had written to Albers: "I must now make a few professional decisions here, albeit nothing of particular consequence. I will go ahead and do my qualifying work for lecturing; why, more on that perhaps sometime later or in August" (1/76). The following month he wrote to Albers, who had just become engaged: "You now have the present, which includes both past and future precisely because it is a clue to more than the present—δος μοι που στω [give me somewhere to stand]. . . . All of us are searching for this. But wherever we seek it, whether in the tasks of our daily lives, in educational ideals of this or that sort, or wherever—one thing remains clear or at least sensed: doubt and temptation [*Anfechtung*] about the meaningfulness of being cast to and fro, of being at the mercy of things, will not cease as long as we remain focused on ourselves, as long as in one form or another 'the other' does not step into our lives" (1/88). See also the immediately following remarks about friendship and community as a δος μοι που στω.

better by the language of reality."[86] And in his continuing correspondence with Rößler, after resuming his academic work in Berlin, he wrote about a visit he was about to make to "my congregation in Barcelona, of which I am very fond, and I feel in general that academic work will not hold me for long. But I do acknowledge that it is quite important to acquire beforehand the best academic training possible."[87]

With both his formal academic training and his theological exams for ordination completed in July, Bonhoeffer stood at a crossroads. Church or university? "Spirit" in concrete reality or "intellectuality"? Reality or principles? He faced the question: whence simplicity, singleness of heart? How to find unity of work and life? As he anticipated the coming year at Union Seminary in New York, Bonhoeffer had an unusual opportunity. No formal requirements awaited him, no exams and dissertations, no professional hurdles. He could explore the issues and concerns of most importance to him. What did he hope to find in the New World?

He provides a clue in his second theological examination. Writing about choosing texts for preaching, Bonhoeffer suggests that one possible theme for a series of sermons is "God's path through history in the church of Christ."[88] And the very first text he mentions for such a series is Hebrews 12:1, the verse that culminates the saga of faith from creation to the first Christian martyrs in chapter 11: "Therefore, since we are surrounded by so great a cloud of witnesses. . . ." This verse had particular importance for Bonhoeffer, as he demonstrates in a passionate comment to his friend Rößler from New York five months later. As he experienced a new country, a different theological culture, the churches of the New World, a nation on the rise, and a country still riven by race, Bonhoeffer was looking for "a cloud of witnesses."

New York: September 1930–June 1931

Of his time at Union Theological Seminary, New York, Bonhoeffer wrote to Diestel in 1942 with thanks for offering him the stipend for 1930–31: "In August I traveled across the ocean and experienced a year there that has been of the greatest significance for me up to the present day."[89] He

[86.] Letter of June 19, 1929, 1/85. Bonhoeffer was responding to Thumm's news that he had given up his celibate principles and become engaged. Bonhoeffer contrasts "die Sprache der Tatsachen" (language of facts, or reality) and "Grundsätze" (principles).

[87.] Letter of February 23, 1930, 1/106.

[88.] 2/5, p. 385.

[89.] Letter of November 5, 1942, *DBWE* 16, 1/207. Actually it was in September that he sailed for New York.

himself provides a summary of his year at Union in two reports, a lengthy one reviewing the whole year for the Church Federation Office and a shorter one reviewing the second semester for the German Academic Exchange Service.[90] The task of this introduction at this point is to supplement these reports with additional information and to interpret this year in relation to Bonhoeffer's personal and theological development. Since those who are acquainted with Bonhoeffer are familiar with the many critical remarks he made about American theological education and churches that year, we need to discover what led him also to this very strong positive judgment. What made this year, a decade later, "of the greatest significance . . . up to the present"?

New York City was a study in contradictions in 1930–31. The Wall Street crash that initiated a worldwide depression occurred a year before Bonhoeffer arrived; Keynes called it "one of the greatest economic catastrophes of modern history."[91] In an ethics course, for one session Bonhoeffer read Norman Thomas's critical article about the banks of New York with its indictment of dishonesty, injustice, and ruthlessness; for another session, he read about unemployment. In November 1930, 254 banks failed, and in December another 344. The Dow Jones Industrial Average lost half its value during Bonhoeffer's year in New York and continued to fall until 1932, when it was only 10 percent of its 1929 value. But the Chrysler Building, the Manhattan architectural icon of the Art Deco movement, was completed in 1930, and on Fifth Avenue the Empire State Building rose during Bonhoeffer's stay, the steel arriving literally still warm from the Pittsburgh mills. The George Washington Bridge across the Hudson was completed in 1931, twice the span of any bridge built before it. Riverside Church, modeled on Chartres and built with money from John D. Rockefeller, held its first service on October 5, 1930; Harry Emerson Fosdick mounted its pulpit to fulminate against fundamentalists.[92] Bonhoeffer was at home not in this cathedral of modernism but rather in Harlem, as we will shortly see; there the Harlem Renaissance in African American literature and other arts was still active.

Among the international students who came in significant numbers to Union Seminary every year, Bonhoeffer was unusual. Most of them would

[90.] 1/181, 1/182. A presumed report on the first semester for the German Academic Exchange Service (DAAD) has not been found.

[91.] Keynes, "Causes of World Depression," 21.

[92.] For the consecration of Riverside, Fosdick wrote the popular American hymn "God of Grace and God of Glory," sung to the rousing Welsh tune of "Cwm Rhondda." If its enthusiasm, optimism, and anthropocentrism were intended as an antidote to the Depression, it was certainly characteristic of the piety of American liberal Protestantism at that time.

take a master's degree at the end of the year, as did Jean Lasserre from France and Erwin Sutz from Switzerland. But Bonhoeffer had already completed his doctorate three years previously, and in the summer before coming to Union, he had qualified as a university lecturer at Berlin. He could as easily have been a visiting lecturer as a postdoctoral student. So it is not surprising that he made bold and uninhibited judgments about seminary students, American churches, and even seminary faculty and leading American theologians.

Having just completed his postdoctoral dissertation and delivered his inaugural lecture in the summer, Bonhoeffer arrived in America with his head full of Kant and Heidegger, suddenly to find himself in the unfamiliar world of James and Dewey, the strange new world of pragmatism. His first challenge was the encounter with American theology.

We now know more details of Bonhoeffer's studies at Union than previously. The seminary's annual catalog and its announcement of courses for 1930–31 provide course descriptions that were not available to the editors of the German edition;[93] this gives us a better understanding of the context and issues to which Bonhoeffer's writings relate. It has also been possible to identify and consult readings Bonhoeffer did for certain courses, especially the course on ethical interpretations of current events, taught by Harry Ward in the second semester.[94] And it has been possible to decipher a number of words in Bonhoeffer's notes—the handwriting no better in English than in German!—some of which yielded significant new information.[95]

[93.] See appendix 2. Courses with odd numbers were in the first semester; those with even numbers were in the second. There are errors in the list of courses in both the German and the English edition of the biography. It omits three courses Bonhoeffer took: The Philosophy of the Christian Religion (PR 13, Lyman), The Present Expansion of Christianity (Missions 11, Fleming), and Parish Administration (PT 56, Coffin). It also includes two courses Bonhoeffer did not take: The Idea of God in His Relations to the World and Man (Systematic Theology 1, Baillie; this was the introductory course in theology) and Brief Sermons (PT 13, Fosdick); cf. *DB-ER*, 159. However, the correct list is given in *GS* 6:190 and *DBW* 10:643.

[94.] See esp. 2/12.1–9. Details of authors of books and journal articles are given in the editorial notes and the bibliography.

[95.] The Bonhoeffer papers contain four sets of notes from courses that, to my knowledge, have not yet been transcribed or studied. They are Niebuhr, "Religion and Ethics" (*NL-Bibl.* A 24,2) in the first semester; and in the second semester, Lyman, "Religious Aspects of Contemporary Philosophy" (*NL-Bibl.* A 24,4); Ward, "Ethical Issues in the Social Order" (*NL-Bibl.* A 24,5); and Webber, "The Cooperation of the Church with Social and Character-Building Agencies" (*NL-Bibl.* A 24,8).

Bonhoeffer took twelve courses at Union, five in the first semester and seven in the second.[96] Of these, two comprised a year-long graduate seminar taught by John Baillie together with Eugene Lyman and Henry Pitney Van Dusen; although listed in the catalog under systematic theology (ST 91–92), the actual title of the course was Seminar in Philosophical Theology, and the topic of the seminar for 1930–31 was "The Bearing of Recent Cosmological Theories on Theology." It was for this seminar that Bonhoeffer prepared his second-semester paper "The Theology of Crisis and Its Attitude toward Philosophy and Science."[97] Of his other courses, three were in philosophy of religion, two in the first semester and one in the second. With Lyman, Bonhoeffer studied "The Philosophy of the Christian Religion" (PR 13)[98] in the first semester and "Religious Aspects of Contemporary Philosophy" (PR 18)[99] in the second semester. (Bonhoeffer also reports taking "extrawork" with Lyman in the second semester, in effect a reading course. They met every two weeks to discuss a book, chosen in advance, on contemporary American philosophy; he found this concentrated study very valuable.)[100] Reinhold Niebuhr's first-semester course "Religion and Ethics" was also classified as a course in philosophy of religion (PR 19).[101] In the second semester Bonhoeffer studied ethics in three courses with Harry

[96.] But two courses in the second semester were in effect "half courses," as were Coffin's courses in practical theology. So Bonhoeffer spent nine hours per week in class in the first semester and eleven hours in the second semester; also, Lyman's philosophy of religion course in the first semester had weekly conferences, of which Bonhoeffer took full advantage.

[97.] 2/17; see esp. p. 462: "Barth has never prepared himself for an examination in science or in philosophy."

[98.] Subjects covered in this course were the essence of Christianity, the meaning and validity of the leading Christian ideas, and Christianity and the religion of the future. Information about course content in this and the following editorial notes comes from Union's "Announcement" for 1930–31.

[99.] Topics in this advanced course included pragmatism, Bergson, modern realism, the reinterpretation of idealism, the new naturalism, personalist philosophy, and the new cosmology.

[100.] 1/182.

[101.] Niebuhr's course description: "Advanced course. Is ethics autonomous? Is religion more than ethics? What validity have the leading philosophical theories as to the relation between religion and ethics? What do the typical historical connections and divergencies between them teach? What is the most constructive interpretation of their interconnection?" In his *Ethics* Bonhoeffer refers to him as "the American philosopher of religion Reinhold Niebuhr" (*DBWE* 6:51).

Ward and Niebuhr. With Ward, Bonhoeffer engaged "Ethical Issues in the Social Order" (CE 42).[102] Niebuhr taught a one-hour course titled "Ethical Viewpoints in Modern Literature" (CE 52a) and Ward a one-hour course, "Ethical Interpretations" (CE 52b), dealing with current events "in the light of the principles of Christian ethics."[103]

Along with these academic courses, Bonhoeffer took four in the practical field, two each semester: Henry Sloane Coffin, the president, offered one-hour courses titled "The Minister's Work with Individuals" (PT 55) in the first semester and "Parish Administration" (PT 56) in the second semester. Daniel Fleming taught "The Present Expansion of Christianity" (Missions 11) in the first semester; in the second semester Charles C. Webber, the "radical socialist,"[104] taught "The Cooperation of the Church with Social and Character-Building Agencies" (Church and Community 16), which Bonhoeffer found extremely valuable. Thus Bonhoeffer focused heavily on philosophy of religion, theology, and ethics in an educational context and theological climate very different from the scholarship he was accustomed to in Berlin. But it is worth noting that in three different places he stressed the value of Webber's course on the work of the church with social agencies.[105]

One of the papers from a course with Lyman was published in the *Journal of Religion* as "Concerning the Christian Idea of God."[106] Given the more polished English of the published version compared to the handwritten first version, it is safe to assume that Bonhoeffer enlisted the aid of Paul Lehmann to revise it for publication. But compared to Bonhoeffer's first draft, there is no substantial change in the ideas or argument such as might be

[102.] This dealt with basic social issues such as disease, crime, war, sex relations, and "methods and ideals of social organization." See Duke, "Radical Social Gospel." See also Duke, *In the Trenches with Jesus and Marx.*

[103.] Union Theological Seminary, *Announcement of Courses 1930,* 21. The seminary catalog and announcement both list Ward and Niebuhr for both of these courses. David Nelson Duke, author of the biography of Ward, believes that Ward taught the current events course that spring, while Niebuhr taught the literature course; see Duke, *In the Trenches with Jesus and Marx,* 143–44. Duke is correct about the teachers; see Green, "Bonhoeffer's Courses." For the course with Niebuhr, Bonhoeffer wrote a paper on "Negro Literature," a fact that Larry Rasmussen confirmed with the course tutor, James Dombrowski, in the late 1960s, but the paper has not been found. See *DBW* 12, 1/31 (but ed. note 4 is incorrect); Rasmussen, *Dietrich Bonhoeffer,* 219.

[104.] 1/182.

[105.] 1/170; 1/181, p. 318; 1/182.

[106.] 2/16.

attributed to Lehmann. Lyman thought the idea of "revelation in hiddenness" was a "perverse expression,"[107] a judgment that would also have to be applied to Barth, Luther, and no doubt St. Paul. The printed version of this article contains one very interesting addition. The typescript for the publisher contains a sentence not found in the fair copy submitted to Lyman. Speaking of receiving knowledge of God, Bonhoeffer writes, "The pathway to this knowledge is action."[108] This action is "the act of faith."

Through papers for Union Seminary courses, this volume offers unique access to aspects of Bonhoeffer's theology not available in his well-known monographs. In his seminar paper "The Theology of Crisis,"[109] for example, we see his thumbnail introduction of Karl Barth, here positively advocated and omitting the criticisms found elsewhere. The same paper contains suggestive remarks about the structure of Western languages as they present problems for theological doctrines, such as original sin, and as they relate to major Christian traditions, the Orthodox and the Catholic; Luther is also mentioned as an exponent of "dynamic-voluntaristic" language, which Bonhoeffer himself prefers. The same paper, and the one titled "Concerning the Christian Idea of God,"[110] contains discussions of the relation between philosophy and theology. So too, of course, does the inaugural lecture at Berlin, "The Anthropological Question in Contemporary Philosophy and Theology,"[111] a distillation of key ideas from *Act and Being.* Several papers find Bonhoeffer expounding core Reformation teachings on grace, faith, and justification. Earlier, similar comments were made about the Barcelona lectures. In short, there is a substantial collection of theological writing in this volume that needs to be kept in mind and integrated into the study of Bonhoeffer's monographs, and the same goes for the theological writings in other volumes of the collected writings (the B series).

To say that Bonhoeffer was unimpressed with the theology he found among the students at Union is a vast understatement. Pragmatism has expelled dogmatics, Bonhoeffer said, and the question of truth has been supplanted by utility. It has come to this, that the seminary has "forgotten what Christian theology in its very essence stands for," as is seen during a public lecture when students laugh at a passage on sin and forgiveness

---

[107.] See 2/16, p. 457. The biography wrongly attributes this comment to Baillie; cf. *DB-ER*, 160. On the same page a comment from Niebuhr refers to judging "actions purely in terms of notions"; the latter word should be "motives."

[108.] 2/16, p. 459.

[109.] 2/17.

[110.] 2/16.

[111.] 2/7.

from Luther's "Bondage of the Will."[112] In practical theology seminars, students ask "whether one really must preach about Christ."[113] "Modern Americans . . . have absolutely no understanding for Pauline and Lutheran Christianity. They are not only the purest Pelagians but also adherents of Protagoras."[114] "An adherence to the central doctrines of dogmatics," he concludes, "is in utter disarray."[115]

Critical as he was of theological students at Union Seminary, Bonhoeffer was equally unimpressed by a conference of "leading American systematic theologians." At the invitation of John Baillie, he attended this conference, which was held at Union on April 10 and 11, 1931. Although he does not identify the occasion, it was actually the annual spring meeting of the American Theological Society. In the uninhibited candor of a private letter, he wrote to his grandmother that the discussions were less than sophomoric, almost like discussions among first-semester freshmen! "The reigning atmosphere," he complained, "is one of inordinate confusion and lack of clarity."[116]

If theology was in such disarray, Bonhoeffer was equally distressed by most preaching in white churches. Good Friday 1931 was an occasion of particular offense. He attended an Episcopal church to hear one of New York's renowned preachers, perhaps hoping to find a traditional Good Friday service. Instead he was deeply shocked to hear the preacher proclaim, "I deny the reconciliation on the cross; I don't want that kind of Christ."[117] It is quite possible that Bonhoeffer attended St. Mark's in the Bouwerie, where William Norman Guthrie was the rector from 1911 to 1937. Guthrie had taught at the University of the South and Kenyon College, among other places, was a prolific writer, and created novel services. Over many years he had created a Good Friday service, which he published in 1935 as *Seven*

[112.] 1/181, p. 310.

[113.] 1/181, p. 309.

[114.] 1/181, p. 311. The allusion is to Protagoras's saying: "Man is the measure of all things."

[115.] 1/181, p. 308. Roger Shinn reported to the editor the following story told him by Reinhold Niebuhr, when Bonhoeffer was taking a course with him. "One day, after the usual vigorous question period at the close of the class, Dietrich came up to Reinie and said, with indignation: 'Is this a theological school or a school for politicians?'" Shinn said that he is certain of the import of the quotation, though he can't be sure of Bonhoeffer's exact words.

[116.] See 1/169, p. 296. Among those who attended the meetings of the Society in the twenties and thirties were Edgar S. Brightman, William Adams Brown, Morton Scott Enslin, Harry Emerson Fosdick, Walter M. Horton, D. C. Macintosh, H. Richard Niebuhr, Douglas V. Steere, and George Thomas. In addition to John Baillie, the Union faculty members included Eugene W. Lyman, Reinhold Niebuhr, Henry P. Van Dusen, and Harry Ward.

[117.] 1/181, p. 316–17.

Oracles from the Cross. Based on the seven last words of Christ, it incorporated poems from St. Theresa, William Blake, and even Ezra Pound's "Ballad for Gloom." In his introduction Guthrie states that "this interpretation has gradually become innocent of the theory of the passion held for ages. . . . If the dogma of the Vicarious Atonement seem a sufficient motivation for the Cross, then this little book is wrong . . . to be led year by year to a fresh and ever more convincing revelation of the Heroic Son of Man." One of Guthrie's Episcopal colleagues, the Reverend Malcolm Douglas, then rector of Christ Protestant Episcopal Church, Short Hills, New Jersey, commended the book in his foreword even more bluntly and, with marked anti-Jewish sentiments, wrote: "Here is a book emancipated from the savage inheritance of sacrificial superstition."[118]

Guthrie was a famous and controversial priest, frequently in the local and national press, and the bane of his bishop, the Right Reverend William T. Manning. Indeed, so bitter was the conflict between them that the bishop refused episcopal visitations to St. Mark's, and the *New Yorker* profiled both of them in its January and February issues in 1931. Bonhoeffer complained about the ease with which modernist preachers like Guthrie used the pulpit to attack Christian dogma.[119] Little did he know that Guthrie was a syncretist of the first order, believing in a universal religion of which Christianity was but one expression. So he created "A Devotion for Buddha's Birthday," invited a Brahmin priest to conduct Hindu rituals and a Mohawk to chant indigenous songs, installed a special altar so that a Zoroastrian priest could conduct a fire ceremony, and, to the delight of *New York Times* reporters, arranged an Annunciation service featuring bare-footed women, students from Barnard College, in eurythmic dance. We cannot be certain that Bonhoeffer heard Guthrie preach on that Good Friday in 1931, but he was typical of many modernist clergy and he certainly held views about Christ and the cross that so troubled Bonhoeffer.

Bonhoeffer's critique of theology and the church culminated in a moving summation in another candid letter, his Christmas greeting to his friend Rößler. He lamented about "the situation of the church here, which, without suspecting it, is now only smiling in desperation. The almost frivolous attitude here is unprecedented, and my hope of finding Heb. 12:1 fulfilled here has been bitterly disappointed. . . . So thank God Christmas is coming just

[118.] Guthrie, *Seven Oracles from the Cross,* xv.

[119.] Theologically he diagnosed the root of the problem as severing the Spirit of God from the Word (1/181, p. 316).

now in the middle of all this; otherwise I would despair."[120] By December 1930 Bonhoeffer had found no "cloud of witnesses."

To find the sources of the very positive assessment of the "year there that has been of the greatest significance," we need to look beyond the official program of seminary studies and the mainline churches of greater New York that Bonhoeffer visited. Crucial in the year at Union was the group of friends Bonhoeffer made, particularly the well-known quartet of Americans and Europeans, Paul Lehmann, Frank Fisher, Jean Lasserre, and Erwin Sutz. The debates and experiences shared with these friends, particularly Fisher and Lasserre, were decisive. The frequency and intensity of discussions among them was unusual. Bonhoeffer "found the time almost nightly during weekdays to 'spend unending hours in theological discussions' with Paul Lehmann, Erwin Sutz, and Jean Lasserre, sometimes 'till two in the morning.'"[121]

The Reformed theologian Paul Lehmann was in Barth's camp, loved European culture, and spoke German. He was writing a dissertation on Ritschl and Barth. In 1930–31 Lehmann was a Norman Thomas socialist and a pacifist. Bonhoeffer helped him make plans to study with Brunner and Barth in 1932–33; while in Europe Lehmann wrote for Bonhoeffer an initial draft of the paper on the social gospel.[122] In the spring of 1933, the friends met again at the Bonhoeffer home in Berlin, where they compiled information on Hitler's anti-Semitic measures that Lehmann was to bring back to Rabbi Stephen Wise in New York. In 1939 it was Lehmann, with Reinhold Niebuhr, who arranged Bonhoeffer's trip to New York to save him from the war. And in 1941 it was Lehmann whom Bonhoeffer asked, as part of his resistance work, to write him a long assessment of American postwar aims for the social and political order in Europe, especially Germany.[123] The apartment of Marion and Paul Lehmann (the only one of the four friends who was married) was a congenial gathering place for these friends.

Erwin Sutz, a Swiss Reformed pastor and also a German speaker, had studied with Barth and Brunner and was therefore a theological ally of Bonhoeffer; he helped to arrange Bonhoeffer's first meeting with Barth in Bonn on his way home from New York. Sutz was an accomplished pianist, a talent he

---

[120.] 1/148.

[121.] Zerner, quoting a January 2, 1976, interview with Marion and Paul Lehmann, in "Dietrich Bonhoeffer's American Experiences," 266. See below pp. 29–31 on Fisher's influence through his introducing Bonhoeffer to Abyssinian Baptist Church.

[122.] *DBW* 12, 2/4; cf. *DBW* 17, 11/1/93a, 12/1/10a.

[123.] *DBWE* 16, 1/92a, 116a.

shared with Bonhoeffer. He accompanied Bonhoeffer on the Christmas trip to Havana and on part of the trip to Mexico at the end of the second semester. As a Swiss citizen he was a useful contact outside Germany during Bonhoeffer's travels for the conspiracy; indeed, he was the intermediary for the aforementioned conspiratorial communications between Bonhoeffer and Lehmann. It was Sutz who, in a letter of June 6, 1945, conveyed to Lehmann the news of Bonhoeffer's death, which he had just learned from Barth, adding: "He was one of the most capable and brave theologians of the Confessing Church, and was in touch with the best elements of the resistance movement. And for us he was simply 'the big one,' without whom that year at Union Seminary would have been inconceivable."[124] By these words Sutz indicated the special nature of the friendships, experiences, and conversations that the group of friends shared at Union.

Jean Lasserre, with whom Bonhoeffer communicated in English, is widely remembered for the impact of his Christian peace witness on Bonhoeffer; he is "the young French pastor" mentioned in the prison letters who, according to Bonhoeffer, "said he would like to become a saint."[125] But the picture is more complex and more interesting. Initially their natural affinity as Europeans was shadowed by memories of French-German enmity in World War I. But a bond developed between them, and by the end of the academic year it was Bonhoeffer and Lasserre who together made the entire road trip to Mexico and back; for only part of the way they were joined by Lehmann and Sutz. In the meantime, in the early spring they attended the film *All Quiet on the Western Front* in Manhattan.[126] Made from a German perspective, the film elicited from the audience strong anti-French reactions that deeply pained Lasserre and embarrassed Bonhoeffer. But because Bonhoeffer responded very sensitively to his friend, they were able to rise above the hostility in the theater and experience their common Christian kinship in the universal

[124.] *DBWE* 16, 1/239a [trans. altered]; cf. Green, *Bonhoeffer*, 347.

[125.] Letter of July 21, 1944, *LPP*, 369.

[126.] The film was released in August 1930 and won an Academy Award in November for Outstanding Motion Picture; it was based on the book by Erich Maria Remarque, *Im Westen nichts Neues* (German 1928, English 1929), which was assigned for the first class of the second-semester course "Ethical Viewpoints in Modern Literature" on the subject "War Literature"; cf. 2/11.1. See Lasserre's account of the incident in Kelly, "Interview with Jean Lasserre," 151. See also Lasserre's article in the *Newsletter*, International Bonhoeffer Society, English Language Section, no. 31 (1986): 1–4, where he writes: "I think our pacifist convictions were deeply laid down for both of us that day. Faith had clearly and decidedly more weight and authority than patriotism." When Lasserre described the experience over forty years after the event, he was still overcome with emotion; cf. Nelson, "Relationship of Jean Lasserre," 75–76.

body of Christ.[127] This broader shared concern for authentic Christian life in a universal Christian community is the context in which to view Lasserre's peace witness. Bethge comments of Bonhoeffer: "In Jean Lasserre he found a man who shared his longing for the concretion of divine grace," who "confronted him with the question of the relationship between God's word and those who uphold it as individuals and citizens of the contemporary world. This soon led Bonhoeffer to a new understanding of the Sermon on the Mount."[128] In this context the commands of Jesus take on an authority they did not have in traditional Lutheran ethics: "Lasserre confronted him with an acceptance of Jesus' peace commandment that he had never encountered before. . . . After meeting Lasserre the question of the concrete reply to the biblical injunction of peace and of the concrete steps to be taken against warlike impulses never left him again. Jean Lasserre's impact on him was deeper than he suspected at the time. . . . It was also Lasserre who provided the initial impulse for Bonhoeffer's great book *Discipleship*."[129] Later we will return to Bonhoeffer's important recollection in Tegel about the concerns they shared at Union.[130] For now it is important to underline the Sermon on the Mount as the main subject of discussion between Bonhoeffer and Lasserre and the context of their attention to the peace commandment of Jesus. Bethge's reference to *Discipleship* reinforces this point, for that book is essentially a commentary on the Sermon on the Mount coupled with the

---

[127.] Cf. Pfeifer, "Learning Faith and Ethical Commitment."

[128.] *DB-ER*, 154.

[129.] Ibid., 153.

[130.] At this point two important asides related to Bonhoeffer and pacifism are necessary. First, there is a common view that Bonhoeffer abandoned his "pacifism" to participate in the conspiracy. I have vigorously argued a contrary interpretation, namely, that Bonhoeffer's Christian peace ethic was intrinsic to his entire theology and his understanding of discipleship, and that he did not abandon this commitment; see Green, "Pacifism and Tyrannicide." Second, Hans Christoph von Hase in his memoir calls Bonhoeffer a "conscientious objector" (*Kriegdienstverweigerer*; see p. 602), but while true to his spirit, this is a misleading way of describing his position. Bonhoeffer never formally registered as a conscientious objector; had he done so, he would probably have been shot under a 1939 law, as was Hermann Stöhr. That conscientious objection was Bonhoeffer's personal stance, however, is documented by himself and others from 1932 onward. In the 1932 lecture "Christ and Peace," he said: "Every form of war service . . . is forbidden to the Christian" (*DBW* 17 [12/2/6]:118; *TF*, 95; cf. *DBWE* 4:292–93); see also Wolf-Dieter Zimmerman's 1936 Finkenwalde notes referring to "Christian conscientious objection to war" and related phrases very similar to the lecture "Christ and Peace" (*DBWE* 4:293 and ed. note 19). In 1942 Maria von Wedemeyer wrote a diary entry that reports a conversation with Bonhoeffer in which he spoke about when soldiers should be conscientious objectors (Bonhoeffer and Wedemeyer, *Love Letters from Cell 92*, 331–32). In Bonhoeffer's own writing as late as 1943, see his defense of conscientious objectors (*DBWE* 6:407).

thesis—novel for a Lutheran—that "the synoptic Christ is neither more nor less distant from us than the Christ of Paul."[131] In short, they are one and the same. Here Bonhoeffer is radically reworking the traditional Lutheran understanding of the law-gospel relationship.

A. Franklin Fisher was one of the black students at Union whose number significantly increased during the presidency of Henry Sloane Coffin.[132] Fisher and Bonhoeffer became good friends. It is not too much to say that studying the black community and involvement in it was Bonhoeffer's major extracurricular activity in 1930–31; by contrast, he gave the Depression comparatively little attention. As early as October he signed up for a "Trip to Negro Centers of Life and Culture in Harlem"; he secured a large bibliography on "The Negro" compiled by the Harlem Branch of the New York Public Library, and also various orienting articles about the NAACP, the civil rights struggle, and legal aspects of the race issue.[133] And he purchased *What the Negro Thinks,*[134] by Robert Russa Moton, a close associate and ideologi-

---

[131.] *DBWE* 4:206.

[132.] Handy, *History of Union Theological Seminary*, 178.

[133.] See *NL*, A 24,9–10. The articles include Johnson and Seligman, "Legal Aspects of the Negro Problem"; a timeline of the civil rights struggle from 1910 to 1930 published by the NAACP; an article on the origins of the NAACP by Mary White Ovington; and an article on winners of the Springarn Medal awarded by the NAACP "for the Highest Achievement of An American Negro."

[134.] *NL-Bibl.* 6 A 9, p. 211. Bonhoeffer's copy contains an inserted typewritten page quoting Lee C. Phillip. According to a typed, appended note, the text that follows was "written during unemployment days in Washington, in the Summer of 1930."

"How do you laugh, when the flesh of your people is dragged through the streets? How do you have the faith to keep singing, when the door of opportunity is slammed in your face because you are black? How are you able to succor those who brought you low and who are yet trying to keep you down? How do you keep smiling, when you are denied comfortable transportation, equity in the laws of the land, and every other right and privilege that would help you become the greatest personality that you might become?

"I laugh, because in the distance I can see the dawn of a new day that is visible only to those who look through the lens of faith and love. As my forefathers sang, 'Swing Low, Sweet Chariot,' I laugh, because I see dimly this world of hate, prejudice and hell gradually becoming the kingdom of equity and love. I laugh, because those who try to keep it otherwise by lynching, mobbing and exploiting cannot prevent the change. I laugh, because the 'time that makes ancient good uncouth also makes ancient uncouth good.' I laugh, because 'Progress is the law of life' (Browning), and 'Man is not man yet,' and there must be an ultimate decency of things" (Staatsbibliothek zu Berlin—Preussischer Kulturbesitz, Nachlaß 299 [Bonhoeffer, Dietrich], Restbibliothek, 6, A, 9, Beilage). The Robert Browning quotation is from *Paracelsus,* part 5; the previous sentence quotes the 1845 hymn of James Russell Lowell, "One to Every Man and Nation." Bonhoeffer probably met Lee Cato Phillip during his visit to Howard University with Frank Fisher in November 1930. Phillip graduated from Howard with a BD in 1931 and spent the next academic year at Union Seminary, where Fisher was still studying.

cal ally of Booker T. Washington, whom he later succeeded as president of Tuskegee Institute. Bonhoeffer was sensitive to the racial slights suffered by Fisher, and when they were in a restaurant where Fisher was obviously being neglected, "the friends ostentatiously walked out."[135]

But it was Bonhoeffer who was most in debt to Fisher because he introduced him to Abyssinian Baptist Church in Harlem. The first African American Baptist church in New York, it was founded in 1808 when a group of African Americans withdrew from the First Baptist Church of New York City because they refused to accept segregated seating. Its sanctuary was not a hand-me-down building that had been deserted by whites; it was a new edifice dedicated in 1923, and it had been entirely paid for by a remarkable tithing program of the members under the pastoral leadership of Adam Clayton Powell Sr. When Powell retired in 1937, the church had a membership of seven thousand and a salaried staff of over a dozen full-time and part-time workers, including a missionary in Africa.

Fisher, who in November had taken Bonhoeffer to Washington for a meeting of the Federal Council of Churches and to meet young African American leaders at Howard University, from which he had graduated in 1930, introduced him to Abyssinian. There for six months Bonhoeffer taught in the Sunday school, sometimes together with Fisher, often alone; he also led Bible study in a women's group and helped in a weekday church school once a week. He was invited into the homes of these families and said, "This personal acquaintance with Negroes was one of the most important and gratifying events of my stay in America."[136]

During these months Bonhoeffer was studying black literature and social issues in his courses at the seminary.[137] In February 1931, going beyond the assigned literature, he read about "the first lynching in 1931,"[138] a horrible crime on January 12 in Maryville, Missouri. An African American accused of rape was chained to a schoolhouse roof and burned to death by a lynch mob. Anyone who saw the photograph of the burning schoolhouse and the lynch mob would never forget it. Two months later Bonhoeffer learned about the infamous Scottsboro case, in which nine young black men were hastily convicted and condemned to death, after being accused "of raping a white

[135.] *DB-ER*, 154–55. For a comprehensive discussion of Bonhoeffer's theology and its antiracist anthropology and ethic, see Young, *No Difference in the Fare*. See also Duke, "Development of an Ethic of (Racial) Justice."

[136.] 1/181, p. 315. It was possibly for this church context that Bonhoeffer prepared his presentation on Francis Xavier (unpublished; see *NL*, A 24,3), excerpted liberally from Stewart, *Life of Francis Xavier*.

[137.] 2/11.2

[138.] See 2/12.1, ed. note 8.

girl of dubious reputation," as Bonhoeffer described it. This "terrible miscarriage of justice" prompted him to ask a German church leader to join the international protest—he declined. The Scottsboro case was still fresh in Bonhoeffer's mind when he wrote about the ethics of office and vocation over a decade later.[139]

While these events were surely remembered when the racism of Nazi anti-Semitism exploded in 1933, it was the preaching and worship at Abyssinian that made the most profound impact on him. Bonhoeffer was so affected by the music of Abyssinian that he took home a pile of records of spirituals and played them to his students.[140] And for a New Year's gift, Fisher gave him James Weldon Johnson's *Book of American Negro Spirituals*, with some sixty pieces that he could play on his piano.[141] Having made scathing criticisms of lectures pretending to be sermons in white churches, he warmed to the unfamiliar but authentic and moving preaching at Abyssinian. "I heard the gospel preached in the Negro churches. . . . Here one really could still hear someone talk in a Christian sense about sin and grace and the love of God and ultimate hope, albeit in a form different from that to which we are accustomed." Alluding to Countee Cullen's *Black Christ and Other Poems*, Bonhoeffer continued, "The 'black Christ' is preached with captivating passion and vividness."[142] In 1939 he made the same point: in the worship of the black churches "the Gospel of Jesus Christ, the savior of the sinner, is really

---

[139.] See *Ethics* (*DBWE* 6), 295 and ed. note 181, where Bethge speculates that the church leader was Otto Dibelius; cf. also Carter, *Scottsboro.*

[140.] Contrast the Nazi directive for dance bands in the Third Reich: "On no account will Negroid excesses in tempo (so-called hot jazz) or in solo performances (so-called breaks) be tolerated; so-called jazz compositions may contain at most 10 percent syncopation; the remainder must consist of a natural legato movement devoid of the hysterical rhythmic reverses characteristic of the music of the barbarian races and conducive to dark instincts alien to the German people (so-called riffs)." Quoted in Ehrenreich, *Dancing in the Streets*, 200.

[141.] See *NL-Bibl.* 8 C 6, p. 228, inscribed by Fisher "to my friend Dietrich Bonhoeffer. . ."; the book has survived to this day in Bonhoeffer's library. So does the farewell gift the Lehmanns gave Bonhoeffer, Johnson's *God's Trombones* (*NL-Bibl.* 5 C 19, p. 205); the dedication reads: "To refresh you in the years to come with a portion of the genuine soul of America."

[142.] 1/181, pp. 315; cf. 2/11.2. In his Christmas greeting to Diestel he wrote: "As long as I've been here, I have heard only *one* sermon in which you could hear something like a genuine proclamation, and that was delivered by a Negro (indeed, in general I'm increasingly discovering greater religious power and originality in Negroes)" (December 19, 1930; 1/150, p. 266). In relation to Cullen, see Young, "'Is the White Christ, Too, Distraught by These Dark Skins His Father Wrought?'" and the "Response" by Duke.

preached and received with great welcome and visible emotion."[143] A fellow student of Bonhoeffer, Myles Horton (a classmate of James Dombrowski)[144] reported a rare occasion on which Bonhoeffer himself uncharacteristically displayed just such visible emotion.

> Early one Sunday afternoon . . . Bonhoeffer came in from the Abyssinian Baptist Church where he was teaching a Sunday School class. He was excited and talkative, and instead of going to his room he described the preaching with excitement and audience participation and especially the singing of black spirituals. He was very emotional and did not try to hide his feelings, which was extremely rare for him. He said it was the only time he had experienced true religion in the United States, and was convinced that it was only among blacks who were oppressed that there could be any real religion in this country.[145]

"Perhaps that Sunday afternoon," Horton commented, "I witnessed a beginning of his identification with the oppressed which played a role in the decision that led to his death. Certainly I witnessed an insight that too few of my countrymen appreciate." To that we can add: perhaps, too, the Spirit-filled preaching and the passionate worship at Abyssinian helped bring home to Bonhoeffer personally the conversations about the Sermon on the Mount and following Jesus that we know he was having with Jean Lasserre and his other friends at that time. Here Bonhoeffer found his "cloud of witnesses."

Horton's report is reinforced, if not trumped, by the memory of another Union student, Rudolf Schade. One Monday morning Bonhoeffer called him out of the library so that he could describe his own experience of preaching to a black congregation, probably at Abyssinian. "Beaming and enthusiastic, Bonhoeffer invited Schade to walk with him on Riverside Drive, so that he could share the previous day's experience with him. Talking intensely in German to Schade, Bonhoeffer conveyed the thrill and joy of having had members of the black congregation respond to his message. They expressed their support and agreement with his points by punctuating his sermon with

---

[143.] *NRS*, 113; *DBW* 15:454.

[144.] See pp. 33–34.

[145.] Letter to Martin Rumscheidt, December 17, 1986; Bonhoeffer Collection, Union Theological Seminary. First published in the *Newsletter*, International Bonhoeffer Society, English Language Section, no. 39 (October 1988): 3–4. Horton and Dombrowski were founders of the Highlander Folk School in Tennessee.

'Amens' and 'Hallelujahs.'"[146] This is the only report we have of Bonhoeffer himself preaching in a black church. That his sermon was enthusiastically received must have reinforced his conviction that here he had found authentic Christianity.

If this quartet—Fisher, Lasserre, Sutz, Lehmann—constitutes the best-known group of friends at Union, there are others, some of whom we have only recently learned more about. In November 1931, Bonhoeffer wrote from Berlin and asked Lehmann about Professor White and King Gordon.[147]

Gaylord S. White was at first head from 1901 of the Union Settlement in East Harlem, an urban ministry venture of Union graduates concerned with immigrant housing, public health, and later the influx of African Americans and Puerto Ricans, all of them hard hit by the Depression. In 1917 White also became head of Union's "new department of home service, which focused on preparing students for home, industrial, and immigrant missions and for social, institutional, and interdenominational ministry"; by Bonhoeffer's time White's department had become the department of church and community, and he was still active in the Settlement.[148]

John King Gordon was one of several progressives who interested Bonhoeffer at Union. A Canadian and a minister of the United Church of Canada, Gordon had a Rhodes scholarship at Oxford and then studied for his PhD from 1929 to 1931 at Union, where he was an assistant to Reinhold Niebuhr and a leader among student activists. He then taught Christian ethics at United Theological College in Montreal from 1931 to 1935 but, many believed, was forced out because of his socialist views; he had visited the Soviet Union and believed there was much to be learned from the communist experiment. A leader in the socialist movement in Canada, he was a founding member of the Fellowship for a Christian Social Order, of the League for Social Reconstruction, and of the Co-operative Commonwealth Federation. Gordon's career was dedicated to peacemaking, for which he received the 1980 Pearson Peace Medal in Canada. After the United Nations was established in New York, he was assigned to cover it by *The Nation* and then by the Canadian Broadcasting Corporation. In 1950 he joined the United Nations secretariat in the Division of Human Rights, serving with a

[146.] Zerner, "Dietrich Bonhoeffer's American Experiences," 269. This sermon must have been during the weeks of the summer of 1939 because Schade was at Union in 1939, not 1930–31. He came from Buffalo to New York, took his undergraduate degree at Columbia in 1936 and an MA in 1938, and then did a BD at Union 1939–41.

[147.] Letter of November 5, 1931, *DBWE* 17 (11/1/16a), p. 96.

[148.] Handy, *History of Union Theological Seminary*, 151, 172. (Just after Bonhoeffer's letter arrived, Gaylord White died on November 25, 1931.)

UN agency working on reconstruction in Korea after the war there, with the United Nations Emergency Force in the Middle East, and also in the Congo. At the end of his career, he returned to teaching as a professor of international relations at the University of Alberta from 1962 to 1967.

Another sign of the importance of the group of friends and acquaintances from Union is the fact that, seven years after returning to Berlin, Bonhoeffer was still inquiring about them. In 1938 he wrote to Lehmann that he still stayed in contact with Erwin Sutz, and that Jean Lasserre had married. "And what about Joe Moor, Franklin Fisher, Klein, Dombrowski," he asked.[149]

"Klein" was William G. Klein, another of the progressives. He is first mentioned in this volume as knowing about a "southern clergy ticket" in connection with Bonhoeffer's Christmas trip to Cuba.[150] A Presbyterian who had already taught at the American University in Beirut in the midtwenties, he took a BD at Union while Bonhoeffer was there and then an MA at Columbia in 1933; he was ordained in 1936. He directed the rural school improvement project in Kentucky run by Berea College; the project attacked educational inequality in the mountains of eastern Kentucky by training young teachers for service in poor, remote areas. Continuing this trajectory, Klein completed his PhD at Cornell in 1953 with a dissertation on the educational and work aspirations of rural youth in upstate New York. He returned to the South in 1954, where he joined the faculty of Warren Wilson College, a Presbyterian college in North Carolina devoted to the "triad" of study, work, and service. Originally founded to serve underprivileged mountain youth, the college was one of the first in the Old Confederacy to desegregate in 1952 when it invited Alma Shippey, a young black man, to enroll. Klein taught at the college until 1972, giving courses in cultural anthropology, sociology, economics, and psychology.

"Dombrowski" refers to James Dombrowski, a white Methodist minister born in Florida who attended Union and Columbia, earning a PhD in 1933, with a dissertation titled "The Early Days of the Social Gospel."[151] He studied with Harry Ward and Reinhold Niebuhr and was a dedicated Christian Socialist, committed to applying the ethics of Jesus to order society and so realize the kingdom of God on earth. With Myles Horton and others he

[149.] Letter of December 14, 1938; *DBW* 15 (1/40), p. 91. "Joe Moor" has not been identified. John Buchanan Moore, a Canadian, studied at Union in 1928–30 but is unlikely to have been in residence when Bonhoeffer arrived. A Karl Francis Moore took a BD there in 1931, so Bonhoeffer could have met him.

[150.] 1/144.

[151.] See Adams, *James A. Dombrowski.* Dombrowski's dissertation was published as *The Early Days of Christian Socialism in America.*

cofounded the Highlander Folk School in Tennessee, where he worked from 1933 to 1942. Highlander (attacked by segregationists as "communist") was an early leader in the civil rights movement. Both Martin Luther King Jr. and Rosa Parks trained there in the 1950s. Dombrowski founded the Conference of Younger Churchmen of the South in 1934, was executive director of the Southern Conference for Human Welfare (1942–46) and then of the Southern Conference Educational Fund (1946–66), and edited the *Southern Patriot* (1942–66). He founded the Southern Organizing Committee for Economic and Social Justice in 1975 and worked for it until his death.

Finally we must add the name of Charles C. Webber, the "radical socialist" whose course Bonhoeffer commended not once but three times. Webber was a Methodist minister and union organizer. In 1929 he wrote "A History of the Development of Social Education in the United Neighborhood Houses of New York." In the early 1930s he was president of the Upper Mississippi Waterway Association, and in 1938 he wrote a study on industrial conflicts and strikes. In the 1950s and 1960s he was the National AFL-CIO Representative for Religious Relations.

If we are clear about the importance of Fisher and Lasserre for Bonhoeffer's personal and theological development, what about this lesser-known group of faculty and students—White, Webber, Gordon, Klein, Dombrowski? These were probably some of the most radical Christians with whom Bonhoeffer ever associated—and they were radicals not only in theory. Most of them were practicing socialists. They worked on urban and rural poverty, on racial justice and civil rights, on union organizing, on peacemaking, and at the United Nations. Interestingly, some of them had careers analogous to Bonhoeffer himself, being expelled from academic appointments, persecuted by the law, and imprisoned. What did these friends and associates mean to Bonhoeffer that he continued to inquire about them years after he had left New York? It is unlikely that they were close to him theologically. But they were all committed to Christian praxis, to lives and careers that lived out their Christian faith, particularly in its public, communal, and political expression. Are they also to be numbered among the "cloud of witnesses"?

What was Bonhoeffer's personal agenda in New York, and how were these friends and associates involved in it? In a lecture in 1932 Bonhoeffer gives us a very clear sign, and in several letters between 1932 and 1944 he provides his own interpretation.

The lecture late in 1932 was given to the Berlin branch of the Student Christian Movement on "Christ and Peace."[152] This lecture is nothing less

[152.] The lecture survives as a transcript of notes by Jürgen Winterhager, who variously dated it December 1932 (*DBW* 12, 232n1) and November 1932 (Green, *Bonhoeffer,*

than the kernel of the book *Discipleship*, and it documents that a decisive change had taken place in Bonhoeffer's theology since *Act and Being* and the inaugural lecture in 1930. Opening with the commandment of Matthew 22:37–39 of wholehearted love to God and neighbor, Bonhoeffer argues that there is only one absolute authority, Jesus Christ. To the *single-minded* reader the Sermon on the Mount speaks unmistakably.[153] The critical issue is not changing the world but discipleship, following Jesus [*Nachfolge Jesu*]. "This discipleship of Christ comes from and depends entirely on single-minded faith and, conversely, faith is only true in discipleship."[154] Understanding the relationship of law and gospel as if the gospel of the forgiveness of sins had nothing to do with civic life—indeed, earthly life as a whole—in other words, calling people sinners but not calling them away from their sins, that is nothing but cheap grace. The commandments are given to us for simple obedience (*einfältig Gehorsam*), and that includes the command "you shall not kill" and the commandment of Jesus "love your enemy."[155] In this lecture, as in *Discipleship*, central to Bonhoeffer's theology is the integrity of faith and obedience, their mutual co-inherence, especially in response to the commandments of Jesus in the Sermon on the Mount. That is what being a disciple means.

This decisive change of theological orientation had in fact been hinted at over a year earlier than this lecture. On August 23, 1931, only two months after returning from New York, he wrote to Lehmann and told him about the catechism he and Franz Hildebrandt had already written.[156] Significantly it refers to discipleship (*Gefolgschaft Christi*), and to the Sermon on the Mount, how little the church obeys it. Another important hint came on February 28, 1932, eight months after he returned from New York. Bonhoeffer wrote to Sutz to thank him for his comments on *Act and Being*, the first serious response he had received. But he then commented abruptly: "You're still seeing far too much good in the thing. In the meantime this product has become rather disagreeable to me."[157] Instead he promised to send

---

151n101). For the complete version, see *DBW* 17:116–20; three concluding paragraphs are lacking in *DBW* 12, 2/6, and in the translation *TF*, 93–95. Translation will appear in *DBWE* 12.

[153.] *DBW* 12 (2/6), p. 232; cf. *TF*, 94. It is not accidental that Bonhoeffer writes "*einfältig Leser*," here translated "single-minded reader."

[154.] *DBW* 12 (2/6), p. 233, translation mine; cf. *TF*, 94. Note *einfältig Glaube*, "single-minded faith." This sentence is of course a key one in *Discipleship*; cf. "*only the believers obey*, and *only the obedient believe*" (*DBWE* 4:63, Bonhoeffer's italics).

[155.] *DBW* 12 (2/6), pp. 233–34; *TF*, 94–95.

[156.] *DBW* 17, 11/1/8a.

[157.] *DBW* 11, 1/39; *NRS*, 149–50. *Akt und Sein* was published in September 1931, and Bonhoeffer apparently sent it to Sutz as soon as it came out; cf. his letter of October 8,

him the catechism.[158] The intellectual gymnastics of *Act and Being* and its debates with philosophical and theological schools have been replaced by the Sermon on the Mount and the existential commitment of discipleship.

In fact, careful reading of sermons and ecumenical addresses from the autumn of 1931 onward reveals additional signs of this change. In a sermon of October 1931, Bonhoeffer gave a highly autobiographical interpretation of a "psalmist" who had a crucial experience when God entered his life and made it completely different.[159] In February 1932, he preached that a faithful church will proclaim to the raging world, even to the point of martyrdom, "the words of Christ that there should be peace."[160] At the Technical University in April 1932, Bonhoeffer told the students that they can recognize Christian truth "solely through the free experiment in living, in once just basing one's life completely on the word of Christ; just to live totally with it, to live by it, to hear it, to obey it."[161] In May he preached on the oft-quoted text of 2 Chronicles 20:12: "We do not know what to do, but our eyes are on you," nevertheless praying, "Do not hide your commandment eternally from us."[162] In July he told the students that the freedom of God's truth is "becoming free from oneself, from the lie that I am the only one there, that I am the center of the world. . . . God's truth is God's love and God's love makes us free from ourselves for others."[163] And at the Youth Peace Conference in July, he asked what is the significance for our actions of the message of the cross and resurrection and the Sermon on the Mount, and then he asserted: "The order of *international peace* is God's commandment for us

---

1931, to Sutz, *DBW* 11, 1/11. In May 1932, Bonhoeffer wrote in a similar vein to Lehmann about his just-published article "The Christian Idea of God," calling it "common-place theology" about which he was "disgusted" and "ashamed," presumably because it did not reflect the theological orientation of *Discipleship* that he would shortly reveal and summarize in the "Christ and Peace" lecture; cf. *DBW* 17, 11/1/59a.

[158.] *DBW* 11 (2/7), pp. 234, 236. The catechism was not published, however, until the May–June 1932 issue of *Monatsschrift für Pastoraltheologie* 28, 167–72.

[159.] *DBW* 11 (3/1), p. 378. See also the Advent sermon of November 29, 1931 (*DBW* 11, 3/2), particularly its references to "the world of the Bible," "people seen from a completely different perspective" (386), and especially the passage beginning "he only wants to live because he can wait for God" and ending "he wants to serve God" (391–92). Translations by Anne Schmidt-Lange, from forthcoming *DBWE* 11.

[160.] *DBW* 11 (3/5), p. 406; cf. the entire passage, 406–7. Cf. *DBW* 11 (3/5), p. 402.

[161.] *DBW* 11 (3/7), pp. 415–16

[162.] *DBW* 11, 3/8; cf. *DBW* 11 (1/59), p. 89; 2/14, p. 335; and 2/18, p. 360, ed. note 23. See also p. 41–42 below, regarding the 1934 report of Hardy Arnold's meeting with Bonhoeffer in London.

[163.] *DBW* 11 (3/13), p. 461; cf. 459–60.

today."[164] "War today, and therefore the next war, must be utterly *rejected* by the church. . . . Nor should we be afraid of the word 'pacifism' today."[165] In these sermons we hear the following themes: basing one's life completely on the word of Christ and obedience to it, which results in a decisive change in one's life; becoming free from oneself and for others; longing to hear God's commandment; and the assertion that "*international peace* is God's commandment for us today." These all come together under the rubric of discipleship in the lecture "Christ and Peace."[166]

Looking back to the years 1931–32, Bonhoeffer wrote in 1936 to Elisabeth Zinn[167] a very revealing letter that describes the change that underlay "Christ and Peace," the commitment to personal discipleship and the church. He had gone about his theological work ambitiously and proudly, he wrote, and then continued:

> Then a change took place, a change that transformed my life and set its course in a new direction to this very day. For the first time I discovered the Bible. Again, that is a terrible thing to admit. I had already preached quite often, I had seen much of the church, and both talked and written about it. But I had not yet become a Christian. In a wild and untamed way I was still my own master. . . . In all my abandonment I was nevertheless quite pleased with myself. The Bible, especially the Sermon on the Mount, freed me from all this. After that, everything changed. It was a great liberation. It became clear to me that the life of a servant of Jesus Christ must belong to the church, and step by step it became ever more evident how far this had to go. Then came the crisis of 1933. It only confirmed the new direction in which I was heading. And I now also found other people who shared the same vision and goal. The renewal of the church and the ministry became my supreme concern. . . . Christian pacifism, which a brief time before . . . I had still passionately disputed, suddenly came into focus as something utterly self-evident.[168]

[164.] *DBW* 11 (2/14), pp. 329, 338; cf. *NRS*, 159, 170.

[165.] *DBW* 11 (2/14), p. 341; cf. *NRS*, 170.

[166.] Of the change in Bonhoeffer evident after 1931, Bethge writes: "The questions that Bonhoeffer now posed to his church, its theology, its ethics, and its attitude to Luther were new, an obvious departure from the purely academic sphere. They revolved around the critical questions of the ethical and pastoral authorization to make binding statements" (*DB-ER*, 174).

[167.] Elisabeth Zinn was a distant cousin, a theologian with a doctorate, and the woman Bonhoeffer was closest to in the early and mid-1930s; he sent her sermons from his London pastorate.

[168.] *DBW* 14 (1/46), pp. 112–13; cf. *DB-ER*, 204–5. The editors of *DBW* 14, where this letter is published, comment that "the encounter with the Sermon on the Mount mentioned here, whose groundwork was laid during the period at Union Theological

In this very candid letter Bonhoeffer refers to the change in his life and thinking as "a great liberation." He attributes it to the Bible, "especially the Sermon on the Mount." It led to a wholehearted commitment to the church and a dedication to the renewal of the church and the ministry. Christian pacifism suddenly became self-evident. Here we have a narrative account of the change that was evident in the "Christ and Peace" lecture—with the additional statement of his commitment to the renewal of the church and the ministry.

In 1944, from Tegel prison, Bonhoeffer wrote two letters that explicitly reflect back to the period of this book. On April 22 he wrote to Eberhard Bethge: "I don't think I have ever changed very much, except perhaps at the time of my first impressions abroad and under the first conscious influence of Father's personality. Then a turning away from the phraseological to the real ensued."[169] He goes on to say that there was a time when he longed for such a break in his life, but now he felt differently.[170] "Continuity with one's own past is actually a great gift," he says, stating that neither he nor Bethge has really had a break in their lives. He allows, nevertheless, that "self-development is, of course, a different matter." In a special memoir for this volume, Bonhoeffer's cousin Hans Christoph von Hase takes the phrase about "turning away from the phraseological to the real" as the title for his observations on this period of Bonhoeffer's life.[171] Whether a "break" or "self-development" is the more appropriate description, Bonhoeffer is clearly referring to an important change.[172] We have seen that this change had certainly not occurred by 1930, notwithstanding the fact that Bonhoeffer's "first impressions abroad" must have included the months he spent in Rome and the

---

Seminary 1930/31, and Bonhoeffer's friendship with Jean Lasserre (*DB-ER* 153–54), probably took place not long before the winter semester 1932/33" (*DBW* 14 [1/47], p. 113, ed. note 2). With regard to the timing, it was certainly well established by the time of the "Christ and Peace" lecture in November or December 1932.

[169.] *LPP*, 275 (trans. altered). Six days before, in a letter to Maria von Wedemeyer, Bonhoeffer wrote: "[When I was twenty,] I still believed then that life consisted of ideas and books, and wrote my first book, and was, I'm afraid to say, inordinately proud of it. But what did I give anyone at that stage? Whom did I help? Whom did I make glad and happy? What did I really know of the things I wrote about?" *Love Letters from Cell 92*, 220.

[170.] *DBW* 8:397: "When I was younger I sometimes longed for something of the kind," i.e., such a break. Translation by Isabel Best from the forthcoming *DBWE* 8. The language of a "break" (*Bruch*) is prominent in *Discipleship*; see the index to *DBW* 4, and also Green, *Bonhoeffer*, 106, 162, 164–66.

[171.] See pp. 591–604.

[172.] Eberhard Bethge wrote to the editor (January 23, 1971) that in the 1930s Bonhoeffer stressed the break, in the 1940s the continuity; cf. Green, *Bonhoeffer*, 106n4.

trip to North Africa in 1924.[173] From 1928 to 1930 he vacillated about his vocation. He longed for an integrated life, for simplicity, a home for his restless heart. He was skeptical about "intellectuality." He set out for America hoping to find a "cloud of witnesses." In the black church and in a group of friends who were serious about their Christian commitment and practice, who were serious about the Sermon on the Mount, he found them. It was a transforming experience.

What is "phraseological"? And why is it lacking in reality? The "phraseological" is theology that exists in words, that is not integral with life, that is therefore abstract, at home in an academic career, not embodied in personal faith; the "real" is faith and theology that are at one, that are embedded in and formative of life, just as *Discipleship* has it: "Only the one who believes is obedient and only the one who is obedient believes."[174]

Bonhoeffer's letter to Elisabeth Zinn gives an especially clear example of the "phraseological" as contrasted with the "real" in what he says about the church. Note Paul Lehmann's comment that he was not a little surprised at Bonhoeffer's casualness about the church and worship in New York.[175] Then contrast the two references to the church in the letter: "I had already preached quite often, I had seen much of the church, and both talked and written about it. But I had not yet become a Christian." This is the "phraseological" church, the church of an academic dissertation that outsmarted the typologies of the sociologists in the service of a theology of revelation, but a phraseological church nevertheless—as also in *Act and Being*, the church as the resolution to the theological conundrum of "act and being," of transcendentalism and ontology. Contrast this to the "real" church, the church to which one gives one's life wholeheartedly, to which one is committed unreservedly as the very body of Christ in the world: "It became clear to me that the life of a servant of Jesus Christ must belong to the church, and step by step it became ever more evident how far this had to go. Then came the crisis of 1933. It only confirmed the new direction in which I was heading. And I now also found other people who shared the same vision and goal. The renewal of the church and the ministry became my supreme concern." The "phraseological" is theoretical, abstract; it is ideas, words without commitment, theology as something "rather more academic," as he wrote to his

---

[173.] Frequently this remark is related to his time in Rome, as if that settled the question of what the phrase "first impressions abroad" applied to. As a matter of fact, Rome was not his first journey "abroad." That was in July 1922 with his siblings and friends to Lake Constance and the Alps in Switzerland; cf. 1/48, where Bonhoeffer gets the date wrong, saying it was *after* his *Gymnasium* graduation, when it was actually *before* it.

[174.] *DBWE* 4:63.

[175.] *DB-ER*, 204.

brother;[176] the "real" is committed; it is theology embodied in life, belief united with action, "a life of uncompromising discipleship . . . peace and social justice are such things, as is Christ himself."[177]

Bonhoeffer comes to the heart of the matter in the famous letter of July 21, 1944, the day after the failed attempt on Hitler's life. Summing up his life when its end was clearly in view, he wrote to Bethge about a conversation he had had in America in 1931 with "a young French pastor," Jean Lasserre. It must be quoted at length.

> We were asking ourselves quite simply what we wanted to do with our lives. He said he would like to become a saint (and I think that it's quite likely that he did become one). At the time I was very impressed, but I disagreed with him, and said, in effect, that I should like to learn to have faith. For a long time I didn't realize the depth of the contrast. I thought I could acquire faith by trying to live a holy life, or something like it. I suppose I wrote *Discipleship* as the end of that path. Today I can see the dangers of that book, though I still stand by what I wrote.[178]

The personal issue Bonhoeffer was wrestling with in New York was *glauben lernen*, learning to have faith, learning to believe. And he connects this intimately with "trying to live a holy life," an effort, he tells us, that continued for most of the decade, at least until the publication of *Discipleship* in 1937. Lasserre later commented about their conversation in terms that Bonhoeffer could heartily affirm. He, Lasserre, was thinking about sanctification, an "aspect of Christian obedience. . . . what is important is *faith*; it's faith which then leads us towards a certain sanctification. . . . It was my desire to put my faith into practice. I've always had a certain desire to make my life agree with

---

[176.] This comment is from a letter of January 14, 1935, to Karl-Friedrich (*DBWE* 13:284–85; cf. *DB-ER*, 205).

[177.] *DBWE* 13:285; cf. *DB-ER*, 206–7. Robert Steiner takes the issue of "phraseology" and "reality" as central to his 2004 University of Cape Town PhD dissertation, "From Phraseology to Reality: A 'Theological Geography.' Bonhoeffer's Early Travels and the Notion of the Boundary." I prefer to retain Bonhoeffer's adjectival form, "from the phraseological to the real." Clarifying an earlier statement, I concur with Steiner that there is indeed a causal relation between seriousness about the Sermon on the Mount in New York and the ensuing "turning away from the phraseological to the real"; what Bonhoeffer's statement does not clarify is the temporal and causal relation between his travels and the influence of his father's personality (cf. Steiner, 297–98). However, I believe that the phrase applies to the period 1931–32: beginning in 1931 "a turning . . . to the real ensued."

[178.] *LPP*, 369.

my convictions."[179] And in that desire Lasserre and Bonhoeffer were at one, as the famous sentence in *Discipleship* declares.

If a turning to "the real" *ensued after 1930,* we can look to what Bonhoeffer was actually doing in the early to mid-1930s that throws light on what he was describing in 1931. In doing so we find that his focus was the Sermon on the Mount, discipleship, Christian community, and peace and political resistance. We have already noted this in the 1932 lecture "Christ and Peace." The fullest documentation of this focus is of course the two books *Discipleship* and *Life Together,* which grew out of the experiences from 1931 to 1937. Another important and confirming piece of evidence, recently discovered, is Bonhoeffer's interest in the Bruderhof community.[180] In June 1934 he invited to his London vicarage Hardy Arnold, son of the founder of the Bruderhof. Bonhoeffer told Arnold that he intended to start a residential Christian community with his theological students "because he considered brotherly community to be a part of the way of Christ."[181] It was his strong love for Christ that "led to his desire to live a communal life," Arnold wrote. "He said that men do not 'know' the will of God but they can 'recognize' it only through obedience in faith to the commands of Jesus in the New

[179.] Jean Lasserre, quoted in Kelly, "Interview with Jean Lasserre," 160. Pace Bonhoeffer, if Lasserre was concerned with sanctification, that is, the integrity of Christian life and Christian faith, and if Bonhoeffer wanted to learn to believe by living a holy life, by integrating faith and obedience, by following the commandments of Jesus, the "depth of the contrast" begins to look more like a nuance or emphasis. (It is worth recalling that Lasserre and Bonhoeffer communicated in English, not French or German.) Perhaps Bonhoeffer reacted like a Lutheran, stressing faith and justification, rather than sanctification. But in fact, as he wrote to Elisabeth Zinn, the 1930s were actually years of attention to sanctification: "There is still a great deal of disobedience and insincerity in my own relation with my profession. I catch myself at it every day. But I must traverse this path its entire length" (*DBW* 14 [1/47], pp. 113–14; translation by Douglas W. Stott from the forthcoming *DBWE* 14). This is the effort to "live a holy life." Cf. *Ethics,* where Bonhoeffer asks "whether faith, so to speak, can be extended through time, or whether it becomes real in life only as the ultimate, the last moment of a time span, . . . whether one must walk the long way through the penultimate for the sake of the ultimate" (*DBWE* 6, 151–52).

[180.] The Bruderhof movement was founded in Germany in 1920 by Eberhard Arnold, a philosophy student. It was pacifist and later became connected to the Hutterites. By 1933 there were several Bruderhof communities in Germany. Arnold and his family group left Germany when the Nazis came to power in 1933; by 1938 the remaining communities had left Nazi Germany as well.

[181.] See the section "On Developing Discipleship Communities, 1932–1935," in Pfeifer, "Learning Faith and Ethical Commitment." See also Bethge, *DB-ER,* 208. Pfeifer refers to the "settlement" idea in the German Youth Movement; in this context see also Gaylord White and the Union Settlement in New York (Handy, *History of Union Theological Seminary,* 110, 151) and Bonhoeffer's enthusiasm for the course of Charles Webber at Union.

Testament, particularly those in the Sermon on the Mount."[182] Arnold also wrote that "Bonhoeffer's opposition to Hitler was very strong, both as a German citizen and a Christian. At that time he considered the Nazi government to be so fundamentally evil that it had to be eliminated by any means short of violence," and that he planned "to visit Gandhi in India for advice on how to overthrow a hostile government nonviolently."[183]

In this 1934 report we can see the development of the themes in the 1932 "Christ and Peace" lecture and the signs that led up to it in 1931–32. A year after this meeting with Arnold in London, Bonhoeffer was at Finkenwalde and the book *Discipleship* was taking shape.

To conclude this part of the introduction, the inner history that accompanied the outer events of 1928 to 1931 can be summarized briefly as follows.

In Barcelona Bonhoeffer was attracted to parish ministry but still set on an academic career. His sermons and addresses have plenty of abstract and ideational language—phraseological language—that disappears in the sermons of 1931 onward. He is agitated preparing a sermon about the "pure in heart," which he understands as "simplicity," single-mindedness. He keeps quoting Augustine about the heart that is restless until it rests in God.

In Berlin there is a tug of war between university and church. He is looking for work (theology) and life to genuinely converge. "Intellectuality" is a problem. The soteriological problem of "the powerful, dominant self who, particularly in his intellectual activity, adopts an autonomous, self-referring, isolated, and self-enclosed attitude to reality" is clearly articulated. Beneath the intellectual tensions and fireworks of *Act and Being* is an urgent autobiographical struggle. He is looking for his που στω, his place to stand.[184]

[182.] Arnold, "Conversations with Dietrich Bonhoeffer," 4. See also the six letters of "Bruderhof Korrespondenz 1934," first published in the *Dietrich Bonhoeffer Yearbook 2* (75–87), now published in *DBWE* 13: 1/92a, 1/114a, 1/114b, 1/115a, 1/115b, 1/121a.

[183.] Arnold, "Conversations with Dietrich Bonhoeffer," 4. Pfeifer ("Learning Faith and Ethical Commitment") quotes Julius Rieger, Bonhoeffer's pastoral colleague in London: "A long time before coming to England Bonhoeffer had wanted to get to know India personally. . . . A person like Gandhi, who thought more highly of the Sermon on the Mount than most Christians, and was beginning to realize his political aims in confrontation with a leading world power by means of non-violent resistance, attracted him with magnetic power" (Rieger, *Bonhoeffer in England*, 27). Gerhard Jacobi, pastor of the Kaiser Wilhelm Memorial Church and a leader in the Confessing Church, wrote that Bonhoeffer "was haunted by the question about the will of God *hic et nunc*. . . . And he wondered whether Gandhi with his teaching of passive resistance, and with his life which personified passive resistance, did not represent God's will for the nations" (Jacobi, "Drawn towards Suffering," in Zimmermann, *I Knew Dietrich Bonhoeffer*, 73.

[184.] Possibly an allusion to Luther's "here I stand."

Thinking that academic life will not hold him for long, he sets out for New York, hoping to find a "cloud of witnesses."

In New York a "cloud of witnesses" is not found in American theology and white churches. Instead he finds the witnesses at Abyssinian Baptist Church and among a remarkable group of friends at Union Seminary. They are all concerned with living an authentic Christian life, several of them with radical social and political ideas of what this entails. In particular, Bonhoeffer's friendship with Jean Lasserre focuses on "learning to have faith." And this leads to the Sermon on the Mount and following the commands of Jesus, embodied in a community of Christian living. Thus is conceived and articulated *in nuce* by 1932 the theology of *Discipleship* and *Life Together*, with its special concern for peace and, after Hitler, church and political resistance.

New and Revised Material

This volume contains letters and related documents that are not found in the German edition or are revised from their form in that volume. All such documents are identified by the letters a, b, and so on after their numbers. The first group is comprised of those letters that were found after *DBW* 10 was published and were then printed in the German volume *DBW* 17, the index volume that also contains additional texts. In this group are eight letters from Bonhoeffer to Walter Dreß, one to his sister Susanne Bonhoeffer, and one to both Susanne Bonhoeffer and Walter Dreß. There is also one letter from Klaus Bonhoeffer to Julie Bonhoeffer; and one from Klaus Mehnert to August Wilhelm Schreiber about securing a position at Union Seminary for Bonhoeffer.

Letters presented in a slightly revised form are, first, one from Bonhoeffer to Adolf Deißmann that was originally printed in an editorial note because of its late discovery; it is now located in the body of the text.[185] Second, during the editing of this English translation, Richard Ern donated to Union Seminary's archives the postcards and letters he received from Bonhoeffer. This made it possible to date three of them more accurately; accordingly, while the original numbers have been retained to provide easy cross reference to the German edition, the letters also have revised numbers in parentheses to indicate their correct chronological location and date.[186] Third, the dates or places of several other letters to various people have been revised.[187]

[185.] See 1/135a.

[186.] Letters redated to March from January and the beginning of February are 154 (165a), 159 (166a), and 160 (166b).

[187.] See 1/142, 1/147, 1/176, 1/179, and 1/180.

A group of materials related to Bonhoeffer's qualification for university teaching is also new in this volume. Very interesting among these is Wilhelm Lütgert's report on *Act and Being*, the postdoctoral dissertation.[188] In the same group we learn for the first time the title of Bonhoeffer's "trial lecture" (*Probevorlesung*). This was the final step that, when successfully completed, qualified him as a university lecturer. According to custom Bonhoeffer submitted three possible topics and the theological faculty chose the one on which he lectured: "The Concept of Dialectic in the So-Called Dialectical Theology." The lecture was given on July 12, 1930. Even though the text of the lecture has not been found, simply learning its subject, and the other topics Bonhoeffer proposed, is an important detail of Bonhoeffer's theological work between *Sanctorum Communio* in 1927 and the course and seminar papers he wrote at Union in 1930–31.

Also new is a group of letters related to Bonhoeffer's postdoctorate, including Lütgert's report on the postdoctoral dissertation and plans for the trial lecture.[189] One new letter from Lütgert concerns engaging Bonhoeffer as a teaching assistant in the department of systematic theology.[190] Finally, see also the first page of Bonhoeffer's notes for the 1931 Ward course on Christian ethics and current events, published here for the first time (2/12a, pp. 428–29).

There are a number of references in editorial notes to unpublished letters and other documents. Where these are cited according to a Nachlaß number (*NL*), they are documented in the catalog of Bonhoeffer's literary estate.[191] Though some are in private hands and in various archives, most of them are available on the microfiche of the Bonhoeffer papers, a set of which is accessible at Union Theological Seminary.

Also new in this volume, expanding the previously available list of courses, are the actual course descriptions of the lectures and seminars Bonhoeffer attended at Union Seminary.[192] In these the faculty describe their subjects and interests in their own words, unfiltered through Bonhoeffer's editorializing. Together they are windows into the intellectual ethos of Union at that time. With this information it is also possible to state with certainty that Bonhoeffer gave his paper "The Theology of Crisis" in 1931 in the second semester of the year-long seminar on philosophy of religion.[193]

[188.] See 1/109a.

[189.] See 1/106b, 1/106c, 109a, 115a, 115b, 117a.

[190.] See 1/110a.

[191.] See Meyer and Bethge, *Nachlaß Dietrich Bonhoeffer*.

[192.] See appendix 2.

[193.] See 2/17.

All new references to books, individuals, scriptural citations, and so forth in the English edition are included in the bibliography, biograms, and other indexes. In the section of the bibliography pertaining to literature used by Bonhoeffer, books marked *NL-Bibl.* are those he owned that still exist in his surviving library. For the history of Bonhoeffer's library, see the editor's introduction to *Ethics*, which also includes information about German texts of the Bibles used by Bonhoeffer.[194]

Matters of Style

Cross-references: where citations refer to texts of Bonhoeffer and others in other volumes of his works, references are given to the volume in the English translation if available (*DBWE*) or to the German edition (*DBW*); previous publication of Bonhoeffer's collected writings in German is indicated by citing the six volumes of *Gesammelte Schriften* (*GS*), edited by Eberhard Bethge. References in the editorial notes to unpublished material in Bonhoeffer's literary estate are to the volume *Nachlaß Dietrich Bonhoeffer* (*NL*).

Where the title of a book or article is cited in German in the text or in an editorial note, an English translation is found in the bibliography.

At Union Theological Seminary virtually all of Bonhoeffer's notes and papers for courses were written in English, except for one paper written for Reinhold Niebuhr. Bonhoeffer's English texts are reproduced as he wrote them, including spelling errors. In some cases, however, inspection of the manuscripts has led to some corrections of the transcription as printed in the German edition, and some words that previously appeared illegible have been deciphered; these corrections are usually made silently. Finally, in his reading notes for the two second-semester courses in ethics dealing with literature and with current events, the manuscripts contain highly inconsistent underlining. Like our German colleagues, we have not turned this erratic underlining into italics but have simply followed normal current style guidelines for italics.

Matters of Translation

In translating letters we have tried to convey the more formal or polite words of address and conclusion (e.g., "esteemed superintendent" and "your very devoted" and "with most obedient regards"), which sound stilted and excessively deferential in English today but were normal conventions in both German and English when Bonhoeffer wrote. The contrast in style, language,

[194.] *DBWE* 6:39–40.

and address between letters written to friends and family members and official letters written to authorities in the church and the university is very obvious.

Translating Bonhoeffer's inaugural lecture was a particular challenge, and not only because of the density of the argument and technical language, which distills the central ideas of his postdoctoral dissertation, *Act and Being.* On the one hand, Bonhoeffer is writing about theological anthropology, "the question of the human being." Thus *Mensch* is properly translated "human being," and also "person" and sometimes "individual." But it was not possible to avoid gendered pronouns, for example, by using the plural. It is intrinsic to Bonhoeffer's argument that he focuses on the questioning, and lonely, individual; this is lost, and hence the argument is changed, if translated in the plural. Also, there is a powerful autobiographical undercurrent running through the whole argument, as Bethge and other interpreters have pointed out.[195] Staying with the singular, and using masculine pronouns as found in the German, is consistent with this. After much discussion, and more drafts of this piece than any other in the book, we decided to translate the pronouns just as Bonhoeffer wrote them.[196]

German academic terms have been turned into their English counterparts, hence "Doctor" or "doctorate" for *Lizentiat*, "postdoctoral dissertation" for *Habilitationsschrift*, "trial lecture" for *Probevorlesung*, and "lecturer" for *Privatdozent. Habilitation*, which was the qualification for university teaching, has been translated as "postdoctorate" or "postdoctoral degree." It may be helpful for English readers to explain the processes by which one attained a doctorate and became qualified for university teaching in Bonhoeffer's time. To attain a doctorate, one took lecture courses and seminars over several years, often at more than one university, and then wrote the dissertation. This was examined by a faculty reader, in Bonhoeffer's case Reinhold Seeberg. Then followed the *Rigorosum*, an oral exam by a group of faculty representing various disciplines. When that was successfully passed, the candidate presented a series of theses for a public oral defense in debate with "opponents," usually a couple of graduate students or recent graduates. At the successful conclusion of this process, the faculty voted the degree (in Bonhoeffer's case summa cum laude) and the candidate graduated (*Promotion*). If one intended to go on to qualify as a university lecturer and ultimately become a professor, a postdoctoral dissertation (*Habilitationsschrift*)

[195.] *DB-ER*, 134; Green, *Bonhoeffer*, 77–80, 107, 115, 121.

[196.] Victoria Barnett and Christiane Tietz worked particularly closely with the editor on this task.

was written. This was read by a professor who wrote a detailed report and recommended to the faculty whether it should be accepted. Members of the faculty read at least sections of the work and cast their votes. When the postdoctoral dissertation was approved, one final step was required, a trial lecture (*Probevorlesung*). In Bonhoeffer's time the candidate proposed three possible topics for this lecture, and the faculty chose one of them by vote. The trial lecture was not a public event, but was delivered before the faculty. With their approval the process of qualification for university teaching (*Habilitation*) was complete. Then followed the first act of the newly minted lecturer (*Privatdozent*), namely, the public inaugural lecture (*Antrittsvorlesung*).

In cases like Bonhoeffer's where the candidate was also preparing for ordination, the foregoing academic steps were supplemented by a separate set of examinations, required and supervised by church authorities. Courses taken at the university prepared the candidate to sit for a first and then a second theological exam. The *Vikariat* (the practical year of working as a vicar) fell between the first and second theological examinations. In general, this period as vicar was immediately followed by a series of practical courses taken at a *Predigerseminar* (preachers' seminary), where candidates could reflect on their experience as vicars and get additional training in practical components, for example, preaching a sermon and conducting a catechesis with children. The preachers' seminary sessions concluded with the second theological examination. After the successful completion of these steps, the candidate was ordained.

For those planning to enter the parish ministry, this process was followed by the *Hilfsdienstjahr*, the first year of ministry. During this year the new pastors were sent to work as assistant pastors; after the successful completion of this year, they were free to seek a call. At this point, however, Bonhoeffer opted for an additional year of study; he requested and was granted a leave of absence to attend Union Theological Seminary in New York (1/123). He was not ordained until November 1931, and his *Hilfsdienstjahr* officially began on October 1, 1931, when he started his work as a student chaplain at the Technical College in Berlin-Charlottenburg.[197] When the candidate was simultaneously following the academic track, some work satisfying academic requirements could also satisfy requirements of church examinations,

[197.] This period is covered by *DBW* 11, *Ökumene-Universität-Pfarramt: 1931–1932*. See also *DB-ER*, 141 and 173–75. Bonhoeffer remained undecided even then whether to pursue parish ministry or an academic career, and he was now involved in ecumenical activities as well. Thus he "would work in three different fields" (*DB-ER*, 174) even during his *Hilfsdienst* period.

for example, Bonhoeffer's postdoctoral dissertation satisfied systematic theology requirements for the second theological examination.

Other terms have been explained in the footnotes as they occur. Two references, however, might be especially puzzling. The reference to the Protestant community and the congregation in Barcelona as a "diaspora" community was a common description in Germany for religious groups that found themselves in the minority: in this case, Protestants in a predominantly Catholic country. The other term is the title of "privy councilor" (*Geheimrat*), referring in this volume to Bonhoeffer's professor Reinhold Seeberg. *Geheimrat* was a courtesy title in pre-1918 Prussia, given to senior public servants (including professors) with many years of service. In most cases, including Seeberg's, it did not indicate another office. Because of his renown and seniority, Professor Adolf von Harnack was sometimes addressed as "*Wirklicher Geheimrat*" and thus was honored with the title "Excellency." Bonhoeffer, it should be noted, faithfully followed these pre-1918 conventions and addressed Seeberg, von Harnack, and others using their titles.

Acknowledgments

With pleasure I acknowledge the indispensable help given by so many people to this volume.

We salute our colleagues—Reinhard Staats, Hans Christoph von Hase, Holger Roggelin, and Matthias Wünsche—who edited the German edition and provided numerous notes, an introduction, an afterword, a bibliography, and other resources without which this English edition would not have been possible.

Next mention must go to Douglas Stott, the translator. In the course of his careful work, he also located many English translations and quotations from works cited by the German editors and integrated this information into the bibliography; he also made a number of helpful observations that have been incorporated into editorial notes by the editor.

Holger Roggelin, a member of the German editorial team, currently a pastor in Baltimore, patiently and cheerfully answered literally hundreds of questions and supplied information for a number of editorial notes. In response to a query from the editor about the difference between an inaugural lecture (*Antrittsvorlesung*) and a trial lecture (*Probevorlesung*), Roggelin's research discovered letters proving that Bonhoeffer had indeed given a trial lecture on dialectical theology as part of the university teaching qualification process, an important fact that had not previously been known; he edited the material and other correspondence related to Bonhoeffer's postdoctoral university qualification. Ilse Tödt assisted with transcription of these documents and provided the citations to *Act and Being* given in the editorial notes of Lütgert's faculty report.

Hans Pfeifer, in addition to serving as the liaison between the German and the English-language editorial boards, has also been a fount of information about translation questions, historical matters, and editorial notes (e.g., concerning the German Youth Movement). Beyond that he has been a research companion and valued discussion partner in larger matters of Bonhoeffer interpretation. His cited essay highlighting Bonhoeffer's time in New York has been particularly stimulating.

Christiane Tietz, author of a major work on *Akt und Sein,*[198] was especially helpful in thoroughly reviewing the translation of Bonhoeffer's inaugural lecture and making numerous suggestions to clarify his meaning more precisely; she also consulted on Lütgert's report on *Akt und Sein.*

Roger Shinn, for many years a member of the faculty of Union Theological Seminary, provided information about the American Theological Society, facilitated communication with Richard Ern, and reported Bonhoeffer's critical question to Reinhold Niebuhr about theological education at Union Seminary.

Richard Ern, whom Bonhoeffer met as a boy on board the *Columbus* and who is now a neighbor of Roger Shinn, donated to the Burke Library original copies of the postcards Bonhoeffer wrote him during his year in New York.

Many librarians assisted with this volume. At Burke Library, Union Theological Seminary, Seth Kasten, the reference librarian, and Ruth Cameron, archivist, patiently and promptly answered many questions and provided documents. At Hartford Seminary, Andrea Jones arranged innumerable interlibrary loans. The staff of Andover-Harvard Theological Library at Harvard Divinity School provided much competent and friendly assistance. In particular, Russell Pollard alerted the editor to the views of William Norman Guthrie.

Clarke Chapman has generously supported the Bonhoeffer Works project in various ways, and in this volume he assisted with the indexes.

Peter Frick kindly checked the typesetting of all Greek words.

Several people read a draft of the editor's introduction and made helpful comments, in particular Roger Johnson, Paul Santmire, Victoria Barnett, and Hans Pfeifer.

Finally, Victoria Barnett played an indispensable role as general editor. She brought her expertise in German and sense of good, clear style to clarifying translation issues; her historical knowledge of the period provided the

[198.] *Bonhoeffers Kritik der verkrümmten Vernunft.*

editor with information and content for not a few editorial notes; and her friendship, collegiality, and good organization made her a reliable and supportive colleague with whom it was always a pleasure to work.

To all these colleagues the editor extends his cordial thanks.

Clifford J. Green
Boston
May 2007

PART 1
Letters, Diaries, Documents

A. Assignment as Vicar in Barcelona. February 1928–February 1929

1. From Fritz Olbricht[1] 15

Barcelona, January 2, 1928

Dear Candidate:

Only today am I getting around to answering your cordial lines of December 1.[2] As is always the case at this time of year, I have had a great deal of work to do. Also, my daughter's wedding, in which virtually the entire colony participated, took place on December 20.

Today, finally, I have some peace and quiet and can respond to your questions. First, however, let me congratulate you on having passed your doctorate.[3] May the coming year also soon grant a favorable outcome to your first examination!

Well, one only needs tails for special occasions, actually only rarely. More often, indeed quite often, one wears a dinner jacket. If you don't yet have your own clerical robe, you can wear one of mine, which will probably fit you just fine.

At the moment, it's winter here as well, and one needs winter clothing here just as one does in Germany. I wear the same heavy winter overcoat here as I do at home. In Spain, too, it is cold, especially in houses, since the heating is poor.

Although we have beautiful days with brilliant sunshine, and although there is no ice and no snow, it's still cold. So bring warm underwear, heavy suits, and an overcoat.

[1.] *NL*, C 18; handwritten. Concerning Fritz Olbricht, see esp. 1/75.

[2.] Bonhoeffer's letter not extant.

[3.] [Bonhoeffer received it for his dissertation, *Sanctorum Communio* (*DBWE* 1); at that time the degree was called a *Lizentiat* and was conferred by the university; the "first examination" was one of two required by the church for ordination.—CG]

Unfortunately I must report that the possibility of tutoring the young boy has not materialized.[4] Because your arrival was delayed, the family hired another teacher, a woman. In this regard, however, you can probably find something else, that is, if you still want to.

I need to know when you will be finally arriving, at least approximately, since I cannot look for lodging in a boardinghouse long beforehand.

I will be traveling to Valencia on the fifth and returning on the eleventh. Too bad you weren't already here for Christmas. That is when there is the most
16 work. Well, you'll probably arrive by the end of January.

In the hope of hearing from you soon, let me close with warm regards. Your humble servant

F. Olbricht, Pastor

2. From Fritz Olbricht[1]

Barcelona, January 19, 1928

Dear Vicar Bonhoeffer:

Although I'm in a hurry, let me write you a few lines. I am about to leave by ship for Majorca to attend a funeral tomorrow in Palma and will not return until early Tuesday. Too bad that you're not here yet; because of this another service must be canceled. On Sunday I am preaching in Palma, where I would have gone in February in any case. You are doubtless taking your examinations now. Good luck!

You wanted to know whether you might take a few trips with your visitor. Of course—though probably not right after church holidays. Because after Easter and Pentecost I generally travel to the diaspora[2] for two weeks. I will be back for good at the end of April, and then you can travel wherever you like. I'll just be getting back from Germany in October, and you could travel then as well. We can arrange all this, since you certainly should see some of Spain.

Many thanks for your offer to bring something along for me. If the fox fur comes from Freiburg im Breisgau, maybe you could bring that. Then you could

[4.] In an unpublished letter of November 17, 1927 (*NL*, C 18), Olbricht had mentioned to Bonhoeffer the possibility of giving remedial tutorials as a way to earn extra money.

[1.] *NL*, C 18; handwritten.

[2.] [Members of the German Protestant community scattered around Spain for whom the Barcelona clergy provided pastoral services, as in the just-mentioned funeral in Majorca.—CG]

perhaps purchase thirty copies of *Kinderharfe*[3] and bring them along as well; we want to use those in the children's service. I'll reimburse you.

Do you want to live in a Spanish boardinghouse so you can learn Spanish well? Or would you prefer to live with Germans? It would be easier for me if I could know your arrival a few days in advance so I can get a firm lease.

And now I must close! Very cordially, your humble

F. Olbricht, Pastor

3. To Max Diestel[1] 17

January 20, 1928

My esteemed Superintendent Diestel:[2]

I greatly regret that I probably cannot accept your kind invitation for January 27 since I will already be departing on my journey to Barcelona on Tuesday or Wednesday.

With the most obedient regards and greetings—from my parents as well—I am your humble servant,

Dietrich Bonhoeffer

4. Order from the Evangelical High Church Council concerning Assignment as Vicar

4.1. Copy for Dietrich Bonhoeffer[1]

Berlin-Charlottenburg, February 2, 1928

In response to the application approved by the Evangelical Consistory in Berlin on the nineteenth of the previous month, we have decided in accordance with your request to assign you to Pastor Olbricht as a vicar at the German Evangelical congregation in Barcelona from February 15, 1928, to February 14, 1929.

[3.] The *Kinderharfe*, "Children's Harp," was a popular songbook used in children's services at that time.

[1.] EZA 29/G 442,22; handwritten; stamped received on January 21, 1928, journal entry no. 237. See also *NL*, A 30,2 (11); typewritten copy from the files of the superintendent's office, Berlin Kölln-Land I.

[2.] At that time, Max Diestel was superintendent of the Berlin church district Kölln-Land I (Lichterfelde), to which Bonhoeffer was assigned. The invitation was to a "candidates' evening," which was part of church training.

[1.] *NL*, A 30,1 (1); typewritten copy with handwritten signature. In the typewritten copy of the personal file *NL*, D 11 (36), the signature of Duske is followed by the

18 During this period you will be introduced to the duties of the ministry under the guidance of Pastor Olbricht, according to the guidelines applicable at home in Germany, although you will be familiarized especially with the circumstances of the diaspora overseas and will at the same time be supported in your continued theological training whenever possible.

In Barcelona you will receive free accommodation and board at our expense. The latter will be available to you in the Barcelona parsonage; the former will be provided by Pastor Olbricht. Because of the limited space, it is not possible to provide accommodation for you in the parsonage.

For additional expenses we have approved a cash stipend of 40 RM a month, which Pastor Olbricht will pay out to you.

Please arrange to arrive in Barcelona on February 15. Please notify Pastor Olbricht in Barcelona-Gracia, Calle Moyá 2, as soon as possible regarding your time of arrival.

To cover the costs of the trip to Barcelona, we have approved a subsidy of 200 RM, which our central cashier, the General State Cashier in Berlin C2, Hinter dem Gießhause 2, will pay out to you by mail. We are also prepared to provide a subsidy in the same amount to cover the return trip upon receipt of your application to be made at the appropriate time.

We have notified the Evangelical Consistory in Berlin.

Before your departure, please introduce yourself to our department head, Privy Consistory Councilor Dr. Rahlwes, weekdays before noon.

For the President:
Duske[2]

4.2. Cover Letter to Fritz Olbricht[3]

Reverend Sir, for your information, we are sending to you a copy[4] regarding the application of August 6, 1927, to the German Evangelical Church Committee, and the discussion with our department head, Senior Consistory Councilor Besig, on September 7, 1927.

---

addendum: "We are sending a copy to the Evangelical Consistory for their information in response to the circular of the twenty-seventh of the previous month, K. VII no. 217. When it arrives, we will send the report required from Pastor Olbricht concerning the continued training and accomplishments of Vicar Dr. Bonhoeffer to the Evangelical Consistory. For the President: Duske."

[2.] Johannes Duske.

[3.] EZA 5/1891; typewritten copy. Previously published in *Mündige Welt*, 5:23–24.

[4.] A copy of 1/4.1.

We have approved 240 RM per month as support for Vicar Dr. Bonhoeffer 19
for the period from February 15, 1928, to February 14, 1929. The sum of 200 RM per month coming to you is to cover costs for the vicar's lodging and board. The remaining 40 RM are to be paid to the vicar as a cash stipend. Please try to arrange a suitable apartment for the vicar.

Please inform the council of your congregation of the vicar's assignment. Please inform us when candidate Dr. Bonhoeffer takes up his duties as vicar. For the purpose of paying the support subsidy, please indicate to us as soon as possible an account in Germany into which money can be transferred.

By March 1, 1929, we will expect a report[5] from you, Reverend Sir, in *duplicate* concerning the continued training of Vicar Dr. Bonhoeffer, as well as concerning his deportment.

Dr. Bonhoeffer passed the first theological examination on January 17, 1928, before the Evangelical Consistory in Berlin with a grade of "quite good."

For the President:
signed, Duske

5. Spanish Diary, January–March 1928[1]

Barcelona 1928–29

In November 1927, Superintendent Diestel telephoned to offer me a position as vicar in Barcelona. This offer seemed to bring to fruition a wish that had grown stronger and stronger over the past few years and months, namely, to stand on my own feet for a longer period completely outside my previous circle of acquaintances. I believe I was already fairly certain of the matter right after the telephone conversation. Because I still had two examinations[2] ahead of me, however, I did not yet really turn my full
attention to the matter. My parents did not really seemed opposed to the 20
plan, and we spoke about it for long periods on many evenings without ever really addressing the substance of the matter, namely, the extent to which it was simply necessary for me to start from the beginning. So I just let the decision resolve itself over time. That is, I cannot really say when I decided to go. The issue decided itself, things just developed such that I wrote letters to Barcelona—and then ultimately went; despite several serious attempts at

[5.] See 1/27 and 1/74.

[1.] *NL*, A 18,1; handwritten. Previously published in *GS* 6:99–108.

[2.] The first theological examination and attaining the doctorate.

dissuasion—I need think only of Priebe[3]—and without really having any persuasive reasons not to go—I finally just wanted to do it.

I myself find the way such a decision comes about to be problematic. One thing is clear to me, however, that one personally—that is, consciously—has very little control over the ultimate yes or no, but rather that time decides everything. Maybe not with everybody, but in any event with me. Recently I have noticed again and again that all the decisions I had to make were not really my own decisions. Whenever there was a dilemma, I just left it in abeyance and—without really consciously dealing with it intensively—let it grow toward the clarity of a decision. But this clarity is not so much intellectual as it is instinctive. The decision is made; whether one can adequately justify it retrospectively is another question.

"Thus" it happened that I went. One farewell party after another came and went. What affected me most was bidding farewell to church work. On January 18, we assistants from the children's service met with Pastor Meumann[4] for the last time. Meumann spoke cordially and nicely. I responded briefly. During our work together we had, without knowing it, grown closer than we thought. Then came January 22, the last children's service. I spoke about the man with palsy[5] and especially about the assertion that your
21 sins are forgiven, and tried once more to disclose to the children the core of our gospel; they were attentive and perhaps a bit moved, for I spoke, I think, with some emotion. Then came the farewell. Pastor Meumann mentioned me in his general prayer and—the congregational prayer has long sent shivers down my spine, and it did so incomparably more when the group of children, with whom I had spent two years, prayed for me. Where a people prays, there is the church; and where the church is, there is never loneliness.[6]

On January 18, I met at home with my Thursday circle for the last time.[7] A newcomer, Peter Rosenbaum, had come along, a young man of unusual intelligence and sensitivity (he defended Luther's doctrine of the real presence!).[8] The young people had brought along questions that we discussed.

[3.] Hermann Priebe.

[4.] Karl Meumann, who accompanied Bonhoeffer and Klaus Bonhoeffer on their trip through Spain; see 1/23, p. 93, and the postcard from Meumann to Bonhoeffer on May 13, 1929 (*NL*, C 22).

[5.] Matt. 9:1–18 and parallels.

[6.] Concerning the subject of prayer and its ecclesiological importance, see Bethge, *Bekennen und Widerstehen*, 159–77.

[7.] See *DBWE* 9 (3/13), pp. 524–25 and 576.

[8.] The reference is to the corporeal presence of Christ in the Eucharist; see the Augsburg Confession, article 10 (*Book of Concord*, 44–45).

Finally I asked them what they thought of the fact that Christianity had conquered the world over against many other religions; this brought us to the question regarding the essence of Christianity, and we discussed the contrast and connection between revelation and religion. It was a genuinely moving session.

Then came the time during which I awaited news from the Evangelical High Church Council, which arrived on February 2. Now things got serious. Packing, farewell visits, birthday, and so on. From then on we were together every evening. Finally, on the eighth, the time had come. We had a festive farewell evening meal with all my brothers and sisters. Uncle Otto B. was by chance also there. We sat around till 10:00 p.m., then two taxis were called, and things got going. Grandmama[9] stayed at home. Saying farewell to her was difficult. The Schleichers[10] went home. Everyone else went to the train station. At 11:00 p.m. the whistle blew, and the train departed.

I traveled through to Paris with a one-hour layover in Liège, where I got a taxi and drove around in the rain.

In Paris I stayed at the Hotel Beau Séjour, Rue de Ranelagh 99. I stayed 22
there till Tuesday. (Olden[11] had reserved me a room there. The weather was almost always bad. I went to the Louvre several times, twice to the opera, *Rigoletto* at the Opéra and *Carmen* at the Opéra Comique.)[12] On Sunday afternoon I attended an extremely festive high mass in Sacré Coeur. The people in the church were almost exclusively from Montmartre, prostitutes and their men went to mass, submitted to all the ceremonies; it was an enormously impressive picture, and once again one could see quite clearly how close, precisely through their fate and guilt, these most heavily burdened people are to the heart of the gospel. I have long thought that the Tauentzienstraße in Berlin[13] would be an extremely fruitful field for church work. It's much easier for me to imagine a praying murderer, a praying prostitute, than a vain person praying. Nothing is so at odds with prayer as vanity.

At five o'clock on Tuesday afternoon, I departed from the Quai d'Orsay. Just before Narbonne, I woke up; the sun, which I had not seen for fourteen days, was just rising and illuminated a pre-spring landscape that looked as if it came from a fairy tale. The meadows were green; the almond and mimosa trees were blooming. I suddenly felt transported to the area around Naples.

[9.] Julie Bonhoeffer.

[10.] Ursula (née Bonhoeffer) and Rüdiger Schleicher.

[11.] Peter H. Olden; see *DB-ER*, 33.

[12.] *Rigoletto*, opera by Verdi, premiered in Venice in 1851; *Carmen*, opera by Bizet, premiered in Paris in 1875.

[13.] Tauentzienstraße was Berlin's "red light district."

Soon I saw the snowy peaks of the Pyrenees shining in the sun and the blue sea to the left. We came to Port Bou, the border station, and then traveled on to Barcelona in a luxury coach. In the train I got to know a young married couple who wanted to move to Barcelona and stay for some years (Bölke). The hours until Barcelona went by quickly; the whole trip was not a moment too long for me. At 12:55 the train pulled into Barcelona. Pastor Olbricht picked me up at the station. A large, dark-haired, and apparently very cordial man who speaks quickly and indistinctly, looks quite unlike
23 a pastor, but is not elegant. He took me to a boardinghouse, where three ladies between the ages of twenty-seven and thirty-two live who speak only Spanish (Calle San Eusebio 59), close to the parsonage. Here I was greeted quite cordially by two Germans who have already lived here quite a while. One is a businessman named Haack,[14] the other an elementary school teacher named Thumm[15] from Aalen. We immediately had lunch. Then, after making a good introduction with the German cigarettes I had brought along—the tobacco here seems to be horrible—I went to the pastor. We chatted a bit and then took a walk, saw the church, which is quite simple but pretty. At nine o'clock on the morning of February 16, I visited Olbricht again; it was supposed to be the office hours for the relief agency,[16] though no one came. That same afternoon we visited the consulate: Consul General Schrötter, Consul Werkmeister, and whoever else was there down to the secretary Lenz, with whom I will deal quite a bit in connection with the relief agency. I have encountered a consistently friendly and cordial atmosphere among the Germans I have met so far.

That afternoon Mr. Thumm and I went to the harbor and the Old City, which is even dirtier than Naples.[17] The sea was sky blue, and the path on the Mole[18] splendid. The ladies in the boardinghouse tried in vain to pronounce my first name. You see, here one is only called by Señor and one's first name, that is, once they know you. That evening they spoke Spanish with us for one or two hours, which was great practice for me but doubtless not very entertaining for them.

Early on the seventeenth with Pastor Olbricht. Visited the congregational council members; all are people engaged in business who hardly go to church at all but still pay. Rückeberg, Schul, Herberg. On the street, we

---

[14.] In 1/60, p. 156, he is referred to as "Haag."

[15.] Hermann Thumm; see 1/85.

[16.] The welfare office for the German colony. See the extensive description of Bonhoeffer's activity in 1/12 and 1/13, p. 73.

[17.] See the 1924 Italian diary, *DBWE* 9 (1/57), p. 94.

[18.] [The Mole is a breakwater forming Barcelona harbor.—CG]

met the head of the German Club (Herberg), who immediately recruited me and invited me to the masquerade ball on the eighteenth and even paid me a visit that afternoon. I won't go to the ball, since that might prompt some sort of dumb gossip. It has already become clear to me that there is a lot of gossip here and that people stare at you a lot since, as I have heard, 24
the seniors at the school have already admired my round hat and consider it modern and worthy of imitation. The pastor's son also immediately wanted to have such a hat.

That morning we visited the entire school. Rector Seyfang, with whom I tried to speak about my plans for giving instruction in religion, then the faculty, among whom I noticed one in particular, by the name of Schröder. I ran into him that afternoon, when Mr. Thumm and I wanted to go to the Tibidabo[19] by streetcar. He was on his way to go for a walk with three small Spanish children from his class, so they joined us. He is an extremely entertaining and educated man and has traveled quite a bit. I made a date to play tennis with him and will probably get together with him occasionally. He is the director of the choral club, which I intend to join. You have to open all the doors to reach the people. The three children were quite cheerful and jolly. From the Tibidabo one has a truly incredibly beautiful view of the city and the surrounding mountains all the way to the Monserrat,[20] so that the popular etymology from the temptation story "all these tibi dabo . . ." [21] has some justification.

Today, February 18, I have off. I have this slight fear that I will have a hard time getting down to practical work as I would like to. I play the piano, write, and learn Spanish.

A week has gone by without my having either the desire or the leisure for writing. Even though there was not really much work, my time gets filled up.

Today, the twenty-sixth, I conducted the liturgy and then the children's service. After having only a single girl there last Sunday, today there were fifteen. Girls up to the age of fourteen, boys on the average ten to eleven years old; the latter are wonderfully fresh and lively. I showed them the splendid things that the children's service could offer, and that caught fire. Have to see what happens next time. This session has virtually transformed me; the 25
slight anxiety that I couldn't get going with the practical work has vanished.

[19.] [A mountain overlooking the entire city, taking its name from the Latin for "I will give you" in the Gospel story of the temptation of Jesus (Matt. 4:9, Luke 4:6).—CG]

[20.] Actually Montserrat (1,241 meters elevation), north of Barcelona, which popular belief identifies with the "Monsalvat" of the grail legend; the "Montsagrat" (sacred mountain) of the Catalonians.

[21.] See Matt. 4:9; see also 1/11, p. 70.

I have gained a foothold and will continue, and, I believe, already have the children on my side.[22] The next step I must take is religious instruction in the school. First, though, I'll build up the children's service, and maybe a door will open up from that angle.

February 26. In the afternoon I paid a visit to Herberg and Rückeberg (congregational council members). At the home of the latter it was very pleasant, except that conversations take a completely different course than is usually the case at home. Since I have been here, I have not had any conversations in the style of Berlin-Grunewald.[23] During the evening I read in my cold room. Because it's been raining since Thursday, the unheated rooms are extremely uncomfortable, so I either work in the sacristy or I go out. One sees a peculiar picture when one goes to a café during the afternoon, or even during the morning, and sees how many people who are capable of work are just sitting around. Children are brought along as a matter of course. One can then sit for many hours with a cup of coffee, meet acquaintances, chat, watch the activity on the Plaza Cataluña, and kill time. The coffee itself is good, while the cakes and pastries are awful. One extremely popular drink is vermouth with soda water, and six oysters with it; altogether that costs 1.50 pesetas. For the rest, you see prosperous, rich, petit bourgeois, and really poor-looking people sitting all mingled together in such cafés, just as in the larger sense the "social question" in the South (Italy) hardly seems to me to play any role here. The incredible conditions in the old part of the city here testify to this.

February 27. Choral club during the evening. I play the piano. It appears to me that Mr. Schröder (conductor) understands very little about conducting. It's a rather undisciplined bellowing. Incidentally—everywhere the same people. The young people, spoiled, often poorly brought up, don't want to listen to the conductor, organized into cliques, growing up to take
26 over their fathers' businesses. On the whole the older people are the more sympathetic group. The young people give the impression of being not at all serious; they have experienced nothing, or very little, of war, revolution, and the painful aftermath of this period, they live well and comfortably,

[22.] Concerning Bonhoeffer's remarkable pedagogical and catechetical talent, see the afterword to *DBWE* 9:576–77.

[23.] [The suburb of Grunewald was home to many professors from the university. —CG]

enjoy perpetually good weather; how could it be otherwise? The era of the youth movement[24] in Germany passed by without leaving a trace here.

February 28. Klaus is taking his examination, and I'm waiting for the telegram. An unbelievable burden will be lifted from the family on this day. Now, finally, the perpetual commotion over the authorities, etc. will come to an end.[25] During the afternoon I had no desire to work and so went to the movies with Mr. Thumm: *Don Quixote* was being shown. Because I had never read the novel, I couldn't really get a good overview of the content, so the film probably had some errors. Besides, like all Spanish films, endlessly long. The cinema is the cheapest form of entertainment here. For one peseta at the most, one is entertained for four consecutive hours. Two or three, often even four films are shown one after the other; the first are generally incredibly dumb and boring. Nonetheless this film did bring the problem of Don Quixote to my attention, and I will probably soon pick up the novel itself.[26] The telegram arrived during the evening meal, and I really breathed a sigh of relief, thought about how they must be celebrating now at home, and thought especially about my parents.

February 29. Today, as usual, office hours from nine to ten for the relief agency. Then to the consulate with Olbricht. There we were introduced to a sailor from Tondern[27] who had deserted and had no papers at all. While drinking, they had forgotten that the steamer was departing. Hence the mishap. The young sailor made such a decent and upright impression on me that I was able to convince Olbricht and Lenz, neither of whom was kindly disposed, to help him. He will probably be sent to Germany soon.

[24.] [The youth movement (*Jugendbewegung*) was an idealistic countercultural movement widely influential among the post–World War I German youth of Bonhoeffer's generation. Especially strong among the bourgeois, it emphasized nature and values considered authentic as opposed to the upper-middle-class lifestyle. Hundreds of youth groups—religious, political, cultural—participated in the movement in varying degrees. Favorite authors included Nietzsche, Dostoyevsky, Spengler, Kierkegaard, and Tönnies. In this comment Bonhoeffer critically observes that the youth of the German colony in Barcelona were untouched by this important cultural phase. See Hans Pfeifer, "Die Bedeutung der Jugendbewegung für Dietrich Bonhoeffer," in *Dietrich Bonhoeffer Yearbook 1*.—CG]

[25.] See *GS* 6:106, note 11: "The father considered Klaus to be the most intelligent but also the most sensitive of his sons; because Klaus generally reacted strongly to the narrowness, pettiness, and injustices of his teachers and superiors, he was always creating problems for himself."

[26.] Concerning the abiding impression on Bonhoeffer of the character of Don Quixote in Cervantes's novel, see, e.g., the passages in *Ethics* (*DBWE* 6:51, 80) and *LPP*, 125.

[27.] Known as Tønder, it had been part of Denmark since1920.

27 March 10. March 4 was a splendid day. Twice as many children in the children's service. I told a story about the lost paradise. In their stunning naïveté about religious questions, the children are lovely and full of responsibility. From my inquiries to the teachers in the school, I seem to have precisely the most difficult children, lazybones, good-for-nothings, precocious, etc. During the week, I visited some of them. Two boys, Fornoff, who had bad reputations at school, turned out to be nice and well raised at home. Similarly, one who had been expelled—Kläbisch. On Sunday afternoon there was an extremely charming group of people at Olbricht's place. We talked, made music. A young married couple—Baum—made an especially pleasant impression on me. The week passed with visits and a great deal of bad weather. Nonetheless I played tennis three times at the Club Pampaia with Mr. Schröder, an elementary school teacher from the school who surpasses most of the others both socially and intellectually. Monday evening choral club, where I play piano and am getting to know a lot of people.

Thursday March 8. During the evening, dinner with Director von Flecken—because of Uncle Otto's reference, I was treated quite cordially. The only mistake, as is usually the case here, is that dinner continues too late into the night. There I heard from Mr. Schul, an old established resident, that on Ash Wednesday I missed a procession in which ashes, bones, children's skeletons are carried around and the priests wear the old vestments from the time of the Inquisition. During periods of bad weather, one sees little of Spain. I'll have to catch up on that soon. This afternoon at the Olbrichts with Backe for music making.

My theology is beginning to become humanistic; what does that mean? I wonder whether Barth ever lived abroad?[28]

¶Wittig's *Leben Jesu*[29] is making a very strong impression on me.

28 ¶Tomorrow I am to preach here for the first time. I decided on Rom. 11:6 as my text, after having begun to work on many other texts.[30]

[28.] By "abroad" Bonhoeffer is referring to non-German-speaking cultures.

[29.] Wittig, *Leben Jesu*, tells the gospel using vivid stories from his Silesian homeland that were more accessible to common people. Not least because of this work, Wittig was excommunicated in 1926, then rehabilitated in 1946. See also 1/13, p. 74.

[30.] See 3/2, p. 480.

6. To His Parents[1]

My dear Parents,

I arrived safely and have found a room in the hotel with Olden. During the journey I had a one-hour layover in Liège, during which I was able to see the city by taxi. The trip was good, hardly any customs formalities. More soon. Affectionately, your

Dietrich

By the way, my freight receipt is probably in my alpaca jacket.

7. To Klaus Bonhoeffer[1]

the 13th

Dear Klaus,

Tomorrow my time in Paris comes to an end. I couldn't decide to leave earlier; now, however, I think I have pretty much seen what I wanted to. I have just returned from Père Lachaise,[2] which really impressed me. The view from the chapel down into the city, which was half-obscured by fog, was incredibly beautiful. Yesterday afternoon I participated in a most peculiar
service at Sacré Coeur. The church was packed full, but exclusively with 29
people from Montmartre. The people I saw immediately after that in the opera today provided an unbelievable contrast. In the larger sense, one acquires such a colorful picture here in such a short period of time that it's difficult to sort through it.

I'm doing quite well, am eating well and sleeping a lot. Papa's letter[3] arrived yesterday. Many thanks! Greetings to everyone! Your

Dietrich

[1.] *NL,* A 19,1 (1); handwritten postcard from Paris; postmarked February 10, 1928. Previously published in *GS* 6:109.

[1.] *NL,* A 19,1 (2); handwritten postcard from Paris, postmarked February 13, 1928. Previously published in *GS* 6:109–10.

[2.] Actually "Cimetière du Père Lachaise," the largest and most famous cemetery in Paris, named after the father confessor of Louis XIV, Père de la Chaise.

[3.] Not extant.

8. To His Parents[1]

the 14th

My dear Parents,

My train leaves for Barcelona in an hour, and in fact is a direct trip, so I will be there tomorrow midday at one o'clock. My time in Paris has been very nice and, I think, with the two extra days it was enough. I never made it to Versailles because of the bad weather, which continued through the last few days; as a result, however, I am now really well acquainted with the city itself.

I was very glad to get the letter from the pastor.[2] Now everything will doubtless go smoothly. More from Barcelona! Your grateful

Dietrich

30 **9. To His Parents**[1]

February 15, 1928

My dear Parents,

I had a good trip. It was about 6:00 a.m. today when I woke up to the most splendid sunrise, in the region of Narbonne. The trip from there on was magically beautiful. I traveled directly into springtime, almond trees, peaches, apricots were in blossom, and the meadows were radiant green; in Paris I never expected such a transformation. There was still a lot of snow on the Pyrenees, but the sky was cloudless, and the sun burned as it often does in Germany in June. The trip was not a minute too long for me, indeed, I almost regretted finally arriving in Barcelona. At customs the Spaniards were the most unpleasant (nonetheless all my suits arrived just fine). Pastor Olbricht received me quite cordially at the train station, took me to my boardinghouse *(Calle San Eusebio 59 pral.).*[2] A so-called presbyter,[3]

[1.] *NL,* A 19,1 (3); handwritten postcard from Paris; postmarked February 14, 1928. Previously published in *GS* 6:110.

[2.] Fritz Olbricht. See the letter to Bonhoeffer from his mother on February 2, 1928 (*NL,* C 1): "The cordial letter from Pastor Olbricht, which Papa forwarded to Paris, also pleased us greatly. We know you will be in a friendly setting." Olbricht's letter is either 1/2 above or has been lost.

[1.] *NL,* A 19,1 (4); handwritten postcard from Barcelona. Previously published in *GS* 6:110–11.

[2.] [In the address *pral.* is a Spanish abbreviation referring to the principal, or main, floor of the boardinghouse.—CG]

[3.] This designation for members of the congregational council was not customary in Berlin-Brandenburg.

who also wanted to come and meet me, sent his greetings instead, since he was suddenly prevented from coming. Two Germans (a businessman and a teacher) live in the boardinghouse;[4] the room is large and clean. I spent the afternoon at Olbricht's place; we discussed several things and took a walk until evening. I think we'll get along well together. I want to go to bed now so I'll be fresh tomorrow. I think I have a splendid time ahead of me here! Many thanks to you, dear Mama, for your dear letter, which made me very happy. Affectionate greetings to you all from your

Dietrich

10. To His Parents, Grandmother, Brothers, and Sisters[1] 31

Barcelona, February 16, 1928

My dear Parents, dear Grandmama, dear Brothers and Sisters,

I want to start at least one sheet of stationery; whether I will fill it up, I don't yet know, for lunch begins soon, and I don't yet know what I'll be doing afterward. At the moment I am sitting in my room, which is fairly large, three-fourths the size of the one at home, but only one bed, one table, two chairs, and a lavatory for washing. Everything else will come later. The floor is made of stone, which is quite pleasant in summer, and on which one immediately notices the dirt. The windows are actually two balconies, so it's as if one were sitting outside. Today it's a bit cooler than yesterday, but still, in Germany one would be quite proud of such weather even in May. The sky is a glorious blue, and I can look out onto two small streets and houses that, except for the roofs, are completely white. Down below, small children are yelling and playing in the street, and people are going by calling out all sorts of things. On the whole, the picture strongly resembles that in southern Italy.

As I already wrote, yesterday at midday I was with Pastor Olbricht; we viewed the church, which is rather pretty but is not allowed to have either bell or tower. Then we talked about the work. The only thing certain thus far is that I will take over the children's service, that is, actually I must first organize it; I am quite happy about this. Everything else must develop in time. This morning we were at the consulate and visited all the people there, from the consul general to the secretary. We were cordially received everywhere; I must use the next few days and weeks to get to know many people from the congregation.

[4.] Haack and Hermann Thumm; see 1/5, p. 60.

[1.] *NL*, A 19,1 (5); handwritten. Previously published in *GS* 6:111–12.

Pastor Olbricht is large, with black hair, in his early fifties, speaks frightfully fast and indistinctly, has a good sense of humor, I think, and is certainly rather energetic; he doesn't look at all like a pastor and is anything but unctuous; I can't imagine yet how he will preach but am anxious to see.
32 He is very friendly and, strangely enough, believes that I might or even must find everything—room, streets, etc.—too primitive, and he is proud when I assure him that all those things are not much different in Berlin. During the summer, I will be living in his house.

Now I want to go to the harbor and beyond, with the German elementary school teacher by the name of Thumm, from Aalen in Swabia.

Mardi Gras is Sunday to Tuesday, and of course I will want to have a look. On Sunday the bullfights also begin again regularly.—That's it, more soon! Affectionate greetings to all of you from your

Dietrich

11. To Paula Bonhoeffer[1]

February 20, 1928

Dear Mama,

I am always very delighted to receive news from you all so often. Many thanks for your letter[2]—which, by the way, was sent at 8–9:00 a.m. on Friday but reached me only Monday—for me, and probably for all of you as well, it's nice to hear that everything is going along normally. Two things right away: hardly anyone gets vaccinated against typhus here; I am very cautious with fruit as well as with water. Second, please send me the certificate from the consistory soon;[3] I would like to have something for amusement.

I have already begun to feel at home here, am already a member of the German club, the tennis club, and the choral club! The first and the last so I can get to know some people, the second for pleasure. I'm finished with my official visits, consulate, congregational council members, and people of particularly high status.

In the club I have come to know such a crowd of people that I haven't
33 been able to remember a great deal. Everywhere people are extremely friendly and accommodating. Almost everyone one meets is a merchant,

[1.] *NL*, A 19,1 (6); handwritten from Barcelona. Partially reproduced in *GS* 6:112–15.

[2.] Letter of February 16, 1928 (*NL*, C 1) from Bonhoeffer's mother, instructing him to get vaccinated against typhus.

[3.] See the certificate for Bonhoeffer's first theological examination in 1928, *DBWE* 9 (1/114), pp. 183–84.

the only exceptions are the few teachers from the school. Naturally the topics of conversation are a bit unfamiliar at first. Today the director of the German Bank here told me that at one ball at ——[4] ten thousand pesetas were spent on decorations alone, how many bottles of champagne were drunk, and that he was surprised that at a different host's party, only eighty-four bottles of champagne were drunk; that at one ball in the club three female dancers from the Moulin Rouge were imported much to the horror of everyone, and that Mr. —— had imported them, who in any case . . . etc.; that is, this is a small town with a lot of money. They are, however, people who have seen a lot of the world and who are, I believe, terribly good-natured. I'll have to see how to approach them.

Incidentally, it just occurred to me—I am getting a total of 240 RM, so I'm sure I'll get along just fine with my own money; only the initial expenses: club, tennis are a bit expensive. Because I have not yet received all my money from the Evangelical High Church Council, I withdrew 100 pesetas from the German Bank today.

Yesterday morning I was introduced in church. The children's service, to which Pastor Olbricht had issued invitations and which is to be established, had to be canceled because only a single girl showed up. That will have to improve. Olbricht seems to me to place far too little value on encouraging church participation, putting much more emphasis on private, informal social contacts. Moreover he has apparently hitherto done nothing in the way of addressing the younger generation in the parish. Religious instruction is given in the school only until the fourth year, but I want to try in some way to include the upper grades as well. I'll try to exploit my relationships with the teachers in this regard; have to see what happens. By the way, Olbricht is a bit like Sellin,[5] whom you do know.

I don't think I've told you anything yet about the city. First of all, the 34
city itself is what one would call a beautiful modern city; broad streets, well landscaped with palms and other trees and, on the whole, with nice houses. It is situated between the sea and the mountains. On the mountain, where we also live, one finds the well-to-do section of the city, while by the sea—St. Pauli.[6] The older part of the city is even dirtier than Naples,[7] which I didn't think was possible, yet supposedly nothing like a social question even

[4.] [Name omitted by the German editors.—CG]

[5.] Ernst Sellin. During the winter semester 1926/27, Bonhoeffer wrote a seminar paper for him on Job; see *DBWE* 9 (2/14), pp. 420–36. Sellin was also one of his doctoral examiners; see *DB-ER*, 85, 96.

[6.] [A reference to the red-light district of Hamburg.—CG]

[7.] See 1/5, ed. note 17.

exists here. I have already been to the harbor a couple of times, which is lovely like all Mediterranean harbors. More often I go to the mountains during the afternoon, where one can walk completely alone in an incredibly beautiful landscape. During one evening up there recently, I watched a sunset whose colors I will never forget. A blue and then ultimately completely violet haze settled around the mountains, and through it one could see shimmering the peculiarly outlined contours of Monserrat, the holy mountain of the grail; in the foreground there were enormous cacti and trees in blossom. The highest mountain near here, that is, an hour from my boardinghouse—is about five hundred plus meters high and is called Tibidabo. People relate that on this mountain—by the way, precisely the one on which I saw the sunset—the devil tempted Jesus and showed him the world and then said: all these tibi dabo (I will give to you) . . . ,[8] whence derives the name, and this etymology has a certain justification.

I could tell all of you much more, for example, about Mardi Gras yesterday afternoon, which we went and saw, about life in the streets here, in the cafés. But I'll tell you about that another time. But now for something funny: By the second day I was here, my hat had already become the topic of conversation and admiration among the seniors at the German school. The pastor's son supposedly came home and said he wanted to have such a hat, too; he thought it modern, and the other students thought so, too. Maybe this is how one introduces oneself here.

And now I really must close. Sabine and Klaus wrote me such nice letters. Please thank them for me for now. A long letter from Grandmama just arrived that made me quite happy. I will write her soon.

I hope things go as well for you as they are going for me. Much love to Papa and to you and to everyone at home from your

Dietrich

I'm just getting by with the language. My three landladies, who, by the way, are not very old, but rather young ladies between the age of twenty-seven and thirty-two, speak only Spanish.

[8.] See Matt. 4:9; see also 1/5, p. 61.

12. To Julie Bonhoeffer[1]

February 23, 1928

Dear Grandmama,

Even though I don't really have all that much to do regularly, my days here are so filled with bits and pieces and all sorts of other things that I just never get around to writing all that often; so only today am I getting around to thanking you for your letter; you can certainly imagine how glad one is to have any news at all from home when, as I am, one is about three thousand kilometers removed from all that is happening.

Yesterday and today I have been performing my duties alone for the first time; Pastor Olbricht is on an outing in the country, so I had to cover his office hours and whatever else. Most of the visitors come to the pastor in his function as information source and as cashier for a relief agency[2] for impoverished and needy Germans in Spain. They come to us from every possible social class, from runaway French legionnaires to impoverished aristocrats, and they want work or, preferably, money. It's extremely difficult for me to determine just by looking at the people how many of the horror
stories they tell are utter lies, exaggerations, or the truth. The pastor is 36
extremely harsh with them, but I have a difficult time being that way and as a result am probably laughed at behind my back by those whose fairy tales I have believed.

For the rest, it seems I have as much work here as I want to make for myself. I think if I wanted to, I could do nothing but laze about here; as far as I can see, though, I will also be able to find all sorts of things to do. I will very soon be preaching and will regularly conduct the children's service. Over Easter Pastor Olbricht will be traveling, so I'll be alone here and will have to preach quite often; after Easter I will take a couple of trips, together with Klaus,[3] I hope; Meumann[4] writes that he, too, would really like to come; that would be great.

I manage to play the piano quite a lot (on very bad pianos) and am even toying with the idea of taking lessons when my Spanish improves a bit. This afternoon I will play tennis again for the first time; I'll be playing with a very nice teacher from the school whom I've come to know, and with a gentleman I don't know yet.

[1.] *NL*, A 19,2 (1); handwritten from Barcelona. Previously published in *GS* 6:115–16.

[2.] See 1/5, p. 60.

[3.] Bonhoeffer's brother Klaus was in Spain from April 6 till June 1, 1928.

[4.] Karl Meumann.

The weather is quite beautiful again today after being a bit somber yesterday. Not a single drop of rain has fallen since I've been here.

¶Would you please send me the receipt for my crate[5] soon; I think it will arrive in the foreseeable future.

I was recently at a ball at the club, where, again, I got to know a lot of people, though their names and faces are all buzzing around in my head. One gets to know people here who have worked their way up from quite simple beginnings and who have acquired such confidence and facility in form and language that in Germany one would not know how to classify them socially. It is simply a certain kind of class, one which, it seems to me, does not exist in Germany at all but is quite common here. The attitude of these people toward the church is just as positive as their attitude toward sports or toward the German National Party,[6] it's just that they are not very active.

37 I may be going to a bullfight on Sunday. More soon. You see, I am doing splendidly; I just hope that you and the others are doing as well. Farewell, dear Grandmama, and I hope you are doing very, very well. Affectionately, your grateful

Dietrich

What are Susi and Walter up to?[7]

13. To His Parents[1]

March 6, 1928

My dear Parents,

Many thanks for both of your letters,[2] which I received on Saturday and Monday. I am now pretty much up to date on the course of the past, eventful[3] weeks. Here things are developing pretty much the way I thought they would. I am getting to know a tremendous number of people, including a

[5.] Bonhoeffer is referring to his freight crate; see 1/6.

[6.] Bonhoeffer is referring to the German National People's Party (Deutsch-Nationale Volkspartei, DNVP), founded in November 1918 by members of various nationalist-conservative circles; its goal was the reestablishment of the monarchy, and it claimed to represent Protestant interests. It was dissolved on June 24, 1933.

[7.] Susanne Bonhoeffer and Walter Dreß; underlined in the original.

[1.] *NL,* A 19,1 (7); handwritten from Barcelona. Previously published in *GS* 6:116–18.

[2.] Letters of February 29 and March 2, 1928 (*NL,* C 1).

[3.] Bonhoeffer is referring to Klaus Bonhoeffer's examinations, among other things.

large number of genuinely nice and educated people, though education here means something quite different than at home. I have already become pretty good friends with some of them so that in the evenings we visit or do things together. Recently—Sunday—at the Olbrichts I met an especially nice young married couple who have invited me over; indeed, I am receiving quite a few invitations now.

Thursday, Friday, and Sunday are already booked, and it will probably continue pretty much the same. I get into some homes through the children from church; I try to visit every child from the children's service and in the
process, of course, the parents as well. My two and a half years of experience 38
in dealing with children are serving me enormously well here; otherwise I think I would find it difficult to create a children's service "out of thin air," and it is precisely through the children that one quickly becomes known in the congregation. After fifteen children came the first time, we already had thirty the second time, so that we already have a certain group of regulars. In their relationships with adults, the children here behave much as they do in Grunewald, that is, with great lack of inhibition and with great matter-of-factness,[4] though also—in my opinion, despite the complaints of almost all the teachers—they are well reared.

One other thing I also find very interesting is the activity at the relief agency, about which I have probably already written you. I quickly became very mistrustful—after two different people defrauded me terribly—and it's really hard to find a balanced position. Here you really do experience just about everything. Yesterday, for example, the pastor kicked out two "ladies" with such rudeness that I was totally shocked, people to whom I assuredly would have given something; later they turned out to be extremely nasty people after all. When the pastor is away I have to take care of these things myself, something that will be an expensive apprenticeship—that is, not my money, but the relief agency's.

I am playing a lot of tennis with a teacher from the school—not the one who lives in my boardinghouse—and two other gentlemen. I've been invited to music making, am playing chess, and only one thing is missing—skat.[5] You really do have to be able to play it well here; maybe I can still learn it.

The only thing I forgot to bring from home is buttons for my dress shirts. Though the general view is that one needs a lot of shoes here. So I'll buy myself a couple of extra pairs soon. Also, at the tennis club of which I'm a

[4.] See 1/5, pp. 62–63.

[5.] [A three-handed card game, popular in Germany.—CG]

member, you have to play completely in white, so I have bought six pairs of white socks. I can use my gray pants only as summer clothing.

39 Papa, do you or Grandmama know the name Eisenmenger from Württemberg? There is a gentleman here[6] who thinks he can establish that he and I are related.

Please go ahead and send me my grade results soon; your hints have made me rather anxious. Klaus needs to write to me soon, especially about his travel plans. I am doing extremely well. The weather here has finally settled down. Incidentally, I drink hardly any water even though many do here, but rather exclusively wine. I would also be really pleased to hear a bit from Suse and Walter. Please thank Sabine for her last letter. I will answer her soon, though there is a lot going on this week.

Sunday I have to preach. I have chosen Rom. 11:6a as my text.[7] I don't get around to much reading. I am finding Wittig[8] really excellent. Walter and Suse should read him together sometime. And now I must close. Greetings to the Czeppans[9] and the Schleichers.[10] I will write to them soon. What's happening with the job?[11] Please especially give Grandmama my love.

Your grateful
Dietrich

14. To His Parents and Grandmother[1]

March 13, 1928

My dear Parents, dear Grandmama,

My time here has already become so filled up that I hardly ever get around to writing anymore. My afternoons this week are totally booked up and
40 some evenings are as well. Tomorrow it will be a month since I arrived, and it's about time to become settled in.

[6.] Eisenmenger was also a congregational council member.

[7.] See 3/2, p. 480.

[8.] See 1/5, p. 64, and ed. note 29.

[9.] Maria (née Horn) and Richard Czeppan; see 1/16, ed. note 2.

[10.] Ursula (née Bonhoeffer) and Rüdiger Schleicher.

[11.] Bonhoeffer is referring to Czeppan's possible change to a different school; see his mother's letter to Bonhoeffer of February 12, 1928 (*NL*, C 1).

[1.] *NL*, A 19,1 (8); handwritten from Barcelona. Previously published in *GS* 6:118–19.

¶On Sunday I delivered my inaugural sermon before a rather full church.[2] Everything went well. New faces appear all the time in the children's service. They are all quite engaged with the material, probably because there is hardly any religious instruction in the school. The news has already spread far and wide in the colony here that I will take a walk with them on St. Joseph's Day.[3] Seems they are not used to that here. Sunday afternoon I wanted to make several visits but was held up by the first family over sandwiches and by the second over supper, so that I had a very nice Sunday indeed. But I did notice one thing again that has bothered me for some time now, namely, that there is a great deal of unpleasant gossip here, and one has to be incredibly cautious because, given the lively and busy social scene, there is no better and more inexhaustible conversation fodder than to run new, unfamiliar people, and others who are not present, through the gossip mill. There seem to be many factions within the colony, and the best tactic seems to be to know nothing about it and take as little interest in it as possible.

Yesterday I spent the whole morning walking around the city again and saw a couple of things with which I was not yet acquainted. Right now during Lent, which is strictly observed here, the Catholic churches have a great many visitors. On Ash Wednesday there was a procession in which ashes, bones, and children's skeletons were carried around by priests in uniforms from the Inquisition period with the black pointed cowls; unfortunately I learned about it too late. Olbricht has little knowledge of or interest in such things; he simply thinks it's all humbug, and that's enough for him. I get my news from a congregational council member who is a long-established resident, so that I won't miss anything in the future. There are some unbelievably beautiful churches here and lovely cloister gardens of the sort found in Italy. We are hoping to have reliable weather now; today it's cloudless again, even though still a bit cool for sitting outside.

Does Klaus want to travel around for four weeks with me? I don't think 41
I'll really be able to. Traveling for fourteen days and eight days here, that would work; then I can preach here and conduct the children's service. Pentecost is the last date for the south; afterward it supposedly gets very hot and unpleasant, and the colors are also not as beautiful. I'm looking forward to Klaus coming.

[2.] See 3/2.

[3.] March 19, 1928.

Why actually haven't you sent me my papers?[4] Is something wrong?—I'll have Olbricht give me the thirty marks and won't withdraw anything.

I hope Ursel is doing well again in the meantime. When is the baby due?[5] Please say hello to her. I don't hear anything from Walter and Suse. Klaus says they are enormously busy. I will write Sabine again soon. Greetings also to the Czeppans.[6]

Your grateful
Dietrich

17:70 **14a. To Walter Dreß**[1]

March 13, [19]28

Dear Walter,

You are probably thinking I have so much time to write, and that if I don't, you don't need to either. But that's not quite right. My days are flying by completely filled with all sorts of new things. Because you have probably heard from me by way of my letters home, I won't recount everything a second time here.

17:71 ¶On Sunday I preached on Romans 11:6[2] and in the process realized that my previous understanding of dogmatics is being severely questioned by all these new impressions in a country that has known neither war nor revolution, neither a youth movement nor Spengler.[3] It's still difficult to articulate these impressions. In any case I now do have serious questions whether Barth could have written in Spain—whether he had any understanding at all for circumstances outside Germany.[4] At the very least, given the circumstances here—both ecclesiastical and political—one really finds oneself forced to reassess one's theology from the ground up. Just as I

[4.] Bonhoeffer is probably referring to the examination results from the consistory. See the certificate of the first theological examination, *DBWE* 9 (1/114), pp. 183–84; see also 1/11, p. 68.

[5.] Ursula Schleicher was expecting her third child, Dorothee, who was born on May 4, 1928.

[6.] Maria (née Horn) and Richard Czeppan; see 1/16, ed. note 2.

[1.] Literary estate of Walter Dreß; handwritten, from Barcelona. Previously published in Staats and Wünsche, "Dietrich Bonhoeffers Abschied," 187–89. Bonhoeffer's letters to his immediate family contain almost identical accounts of Barcelona; see 1/11–17.

[2.] See 3/2.

[3.] Oswald Spengler, whose cultural criticism in his 1923 book, *The Decline of the West,* strongly moved people at the time. See also 2/1, p. 334.

[4.] In this regard see 1/5, p. 64: "I wonder whether Barth ever lived abroad."

already had in Germany a theology of spring, summer, autumn, and winter, so too is the theology of the spring and summer momentarily taking the place of the Berlin winter theology.[5]—Despite all my theological reservations, I read Wittig[6] with a great deal of pleasure. I recommend you and Suse read him together. I'm also planning to get to Barth's *Dogmatics* once more.[7] It's really worth reading. How are your work and prospects? Rückert?[8] Seeberg's successor?[9] I have not had much time to work up to this point. When I do have some free time, I generally write, study Spanish a bit, or play the piano or tennis.

¶The congregational situation here is rather peculiar insofar as a generally supportive disposition toward the church itself is accompanied by extremely poor church attendance. This may be because Pastor Olbricht is not exactly a dynamic pulpit presence. Imagine someone like Sellin, then 17:72
you'll have an approximate idea.[10] I am really enjoying the children's services.[11] The children are so unaware that it is both frightening and beautiful at the same time. They have not yet been tainted in any respect by the church.[12] They are very trusting and quite open in their dealings with adults.

¶Please tell your mother that we already have the book *Das evangelische Deutschland*.[13] Many thanks for the offer.

¶Regards to your family. And warmest greetings to you and Suse.

Your Dietrich

[5.] Concerning this seasonal classification, see also Bonhoeffer's recollections from the summer of 1943: "The sun has always attracted me, and I've often been reminded by it that human beings were taken from the earth and don't just consist of thin air and thoughts" (*Love Letters from Cell 92*, 68); see also the complete citation, 3/24, ed. note 1.

[6.] Concerning the assessment of Wittig's novel, *Leben Jesu in Palästina, Schlesien, und anderswo*, see 1/5, p. 64; 1/13, p. 74; and p. 627.

[7.] Barth, *Die christliche Dogmatik im Entwurf*, published in 1927.

[8.] Hanns Rückert taught church history in Berlin from 1925 to 1928.

[9.] After Reinhold Seeberg retired in 1927, he was succeeded in the field of systematic theology in early 1929 by Wilhelm Lütgert; see 1/49, 1/61, and 1/70.

[10.] Concerning Bonhoeffer's characterization of his senior pastor Fritz Olbricht, see also his diary entry in 1/75 and the letter to his mother, 1/11, which also mentions Sellin.

[11.] Accounts and references to Bonhoeffer's enthusiastic work with the children's services are found in almost all his letters from Barcelona.

[12.] [From various comments, e.g., that they are "unaware," Bonhoeffer seems to mean that the children are like empty vessels who have not been influenced in any bad doctrinal direction.—CG]

[13.] [A manual published annually with addresses of church administrative offices and other information for Protestant pastors.—CG]

41 **15. To Sabine Leibholz**[1]

Barcelona, March 17

Dear Sabine,

Many thanks for your card! You complained a bit because you hear so little from me. Didn't you receive my last letter? I'd be really sorry. To be sure, I am extremely busy here now with social obligations. Every afternoon and every evening during the past weeks I was always paying visits or was myself invited by various people. Mornings I am always in the parsonage working for the relief agency, which has office hours during the mornings; I find
42 this work quite interesting because one meets the most different kinds of people, all of whom have one thing in common: no money.—So you can imagine that I don't get around much to writing. In your last letter, you were surprised that I am in a "choral club," and you can't believe that I spend the whole evening there singing "God greet you."[2] It's not quite like that (and by the way, I play piano for the group); in any event, I do meet all kinds of people in the choral club; most are merchants who over the years have worked their way up and have attained a certain standard of living. That's the prerequisite for participation, so to speak, just as in general people here socialize only with those who are their financial equals, regardless of how much education they may have. Yours truly has the advantage of being admitted everywhere, and even being a rather popular guest, because the relationship with the church also reveals a certain intellectual interest.

I notice more and more that the émigrés, adventurers, and entrepreneurs who leave Germany are damned materialistic and have not received any sort of intellectual lift from their stay abroad; the same applies to the teachers. Over time I am becoming well acquainted with the congregation, especially with the children and through them with the families; until now I have hardly got around to my own work at all. When you receive this letter, I will have been gone from home for six weeks. Time flies. When are you going to Italy? Travel via Corsica to Majorca, where I can then come to visit you. That would be really great.

Enough; I have to go and prepare for tomorrow—Sunday.[3] I hope you are all doing well. I think of all of you often. Your

Dietrich

[1.] *NL*, A 19,2 (15); handwritten. Previously published in *GS* 6:119.

[2.] "Gott grüße dich," a poem by Julius Sturm, set to music by Franz Mücke.

[3.] The sermon has not been preserved.

16. To Maria and Richard Czeppan[1] 43

Barcelona, March 20, 1928

Dear Hörnchen, dear Richard,[2]

From Mr. Meumann I have learned that you want to have the baptism on the twenty-fourth. My thoughts immediately flew to you—faster than it takes me to walk over to you from Wangenheimstraße[3]—to the cradle of your Inge,[4] whose genuine godparent I will now become in a few days. First let me thank you again for entrusting me with certain rights regarding Inge by making me her godparent; now the bond connecting us that was already so close has been strengthened considerably, and that makes me very happy. How wonderful it will be when Inge first sits with us as the fourth member at afternoon coffee, where we have so often sat as a trio, when she begins to tell stories and to ask questions, when she then begins to play the violin—she will, won't she?—and one thing after the other. When I think of the future, I can well imagine that if she inherits a bit of your joie de vivre and your art of living and mastering life, dear Hörnchen, and a bit of your desire and urge to see the world the way it is and was, dear Richard, and, finally, a bit of the love you both share for music and not least some of your energy and tenacity in making things happen—if she inherits a bit of all this, then she will surely master all the things awaiting her in a rich and harmonious life. That other thoughts for your child move me as well, precisely on the day of baptism, you can better imagine than if I try to write you about them. For me baptism is more than a symbolic ceremony, and for that very reason I really wish I could have baptized Inge at that time. Well, since that is not to be, I nonetheless do still have many, many dear wishes—which the church 44
authorities will hardly be able to take away from me.[5]

I have made you wait too long for news from me; many thanks for your kind greetings. (Some sort of reciprocation for the Greek map will still be possible!) But you probably have heard from home that my time is so filled

[1.] *NL*, A 19,2 (18); typewritten copy; original not extant.

[2.] Maria (née Horn) and Richard Czeppan. Maria Horn, the longtime governess of the Bonhoeffer children, had married the secondary school teacher Richard Czeppan, Bonhoeffer's teacher in classical languages, in 1923. [Bonhoeffer addresses his former governess with the affectionate diminutive "Hörnchen."—CG]

[3.] [Where the Bonhoeffer family lived in Berlin at that time.—CG]

[4.] Inge Czeppan, born December 27, 1927.

[5.] See the certification attesting Bonhoeffer's inclusion in the list of candidates in 1928, *DBWE* 9 (1/115), p. 187, which reads: "Permission has been granted . . . to perform official religious duties with the exception of administering the sacraments (including hearing confession), performing marriages and confirmations."

here that I hardly get to even the most necessary things. Although, on the one hand, that is fine, on the other, it's quite unpleasant for those to whom I have promised letters. Well, I know you won't hold it against me.

The weather has changed yet again, and now it's rainy and cool. People here are absolutely indignant about it. Others say that it's always like that—people themselves don't seem to know exactly where they are living. When the weather is good, I often go up into the surrounding mountains. The Montserrat is in any case a one- or two-day journey I have not yet taken, though I can always see it from the ridge of our mountains in its peculiar contours and bluish purple haze in the distance. On the second and third day of Easter, I am planning to go there with the children from the children's service. That will no doubt be very pleasant. I haven't been to the bullfights yet. You're not supposed to go until it's really hot; then the bulls are really wild.

I've already come to the end of this inferior stationery. So I will conclude now. Too bad that I can't be with you on the twenty-fourth; I'll certainly be sending my thoughts to you.

Stay well. All the best for your little one. Affectionately, your

Dietrich

Please excuse this terrible stationery!

45 **17. To Karl Bonhoeffer**[1]

Barcelona, March 24, 1928

Dear Papa,

Many congratulations on your sixtieth birthday. You will now celebrate it peacefully and free of all hustle and bustle. I hope the coming year acquires a bit of the calm with which it has begun; I really would like that for you. I hope that on your birthday Lake Geneva[2] is more springlike, as has been the case for us for quite a while, so that you both can recover from past events and prepare for coming ones.

I am sending you a book, though I don't know how much it will interest someone who is not personally familiar with Barcelona. In any case, maybe

[1.] *NL,* A 19,1 (9); handwritten. Partially reproduced in *GS* 6:120–21.

[2.] Bonhoeffer's parents were planning a vacation near Lake Geneva to begin on March 26, 1928; see the letter to Bonhoeffer from his mother on March 15, 1928 (*NL,* C 1). Bonhoeffer had not yet received his mother's letter of March 20, 1928 (*NL,* C 1) about the change in their travel plans; see also 1/19, p. 83.

it will tempt you even more to come here and will show you the surroundings in which I am living. Something else that I would have liked I have been seeking for fourteen days now on every corner and in every nook in the city, but I can't find what I want. But maybe I'll still get lucky, then I'll send it soon, but I don't want to give it away yet.

This afternoon I wanted to go up into the mountains with a teacher and a few students, but it rained again, so I'm staying home and working on my Easter sermon;[3] at least I'll finally have a quiet afternoon, something I haven't had for a good two weeks. Now that I have started paying visits to people, I have to do them one after the other so there won't be any bad feelings. During these visits, however, the people always tend to keep you there so long—which in a way is also quite nice—that you never get away. Every evening last week was booked up with invitations and other things. One great vice of the people here is that they sit around forever; no nor- 46
mal social gathering in the evenings ever ends before one o'clock in the morning. So getting up at 8:00 a.m. the next day seems a bit early to say the least. It seems the Spaniards have as few needs with regard to sleeping as with regard to eating; maybe the two are related. Our Spanish ladies eat like birds, both in terms of quantity and—in a way—quality. They prepare lunch in ten minutes! From soup to compote. That's not always quite to our taste.

If we have good weather over Easter, from Monday to Wednesday I will travel up to Monserrat[4] and possibly take a couple of the older children along.

Gradually I am really itching to see something of the surrounding area. I will probably also have an opportunity to take additional car trips through the country with the parents of some of the children from church; that could turn out to be very nice indeed.

If the weather cooperates on Sunday, I will finally go to the bullfight; the scheduled corrida[5] is supposed to be especially good, and I probably won't have the chance again soon.

This past Sunday I was invited by some people who have a nice but, it appears, not quite normal son who has trouble concentrating and is intellectually still rather far behind for a twelve-year-old; they want him to develop

---

[3.] See 3/3.

[4.] [Montserrat; see 1/5, ed. note 20.—CG].

[5.] Bullfight.

some interests.[6] I've heard that they want to ask me to help him do that. But I don't yet know. The family is very nice and gets around socially quite a bit, so to that extent it would be advantageous.

By the way, by sending the grades from the consistory, you recently gave me an entertaining afternoon with the teacher who lives with me.[7] They made me burst out laughing.

But now I have to close. I wish both of you beautiful, peaceful, sunny days and a happy birthday. Many greetings from your very grateful

Dietrich

47 **18. To His Parents**[1]

My dear Parents,

Now that Klaus does seem to be coming soon, I'd like to ask you how much I can use for the trip we have planned. Unfortunately it's not cheap here, not even the railway. I've withdrawn 150 of the 1,000 pesetas; today I was shocked to find that I didn't bring any mountain outfit at all, and that [we] have a lot planned for the next few days and weeks. Because Klaus has already left, I bought one for a little over 100 pesetas, one that will also be suitable for the summer. I have absolutely no idea how I could have forgotten the touring outfit. I have no shorts, no socks. So I have now withdrawn 250 pesetas. I also already bought myself some tennis things, socks, ties, and a shirt with the money. Here everything wears out horribly, even shoes. Otherwise the weather is still beautiful. Your grateful

Dietrich

[6.] Probably the first meeting with the Köneren-Köttgen family. During the following period Bonhoeffer closely supervised the son, Karl-Heinz Köttgen, and stayed in contact with him until 1931; see also the letters in *NL*, C 13. Köttgen died on the Russian front in 1944.

[7.] See the results of Bonhoeffer's first theological examination in 1928, *DBWE* 9 (1/114), pp. 183–85.

[1.] *NL*, A 19,1 (10); handwritten postcard from Barcelona, postmarked April 3, 1928.

19. To His Parents[1]

Barcelona, April 11, 1928

My dear Parents,

Many thanks for your letters. From them, and from Klaus's stories, I have
been filled in on how you have been celebrating lately in Berlin and Ham-
burg,[2] and only now have I really felt the pain of not having spent these
lovely days together with you all. It's so nice that you are satisfied with Glot- 48
terbad.[3] I certainly wouldn't mind seeing a beautiful fir forest like that
again myself, even though forests are not nearly as scarce here as in Italy.

Klaus arrived early on Easter Saturday. On Easter Sunday morning I had to preach, then that afternoon a German teacher dragged us to the great Easter corrida.[4] I had already seen one and cannot really say that it shocked me all that much, that is, the way many people think they owe it to their central European civilization to be shocked. It is, after all, a great spectacle to see wild, unrestrained power and blind rage fight against and ultimately succumb to disciplined courage, presence of mind, and skill. The gruesome element plays only a small role, especially since in this last bullfight the horses had stomach protectors for the first time so that the horrible images from my first corrida were absent. What is interesting is that it took a long struggle before they were permitted to start using these stomach protectors for the horses. Probably the majority of spectators do indeed just want to see blood and cruelty. Overall, the people vent all these powerful emotions, and you get drawn into it yourself. I think it's no accident that in the country with the most gloomy and stark Catholicism the bullfight is ineradicably secure. Here is a remnant of unrestrained, passionate life, and perhaps it is the bullfight that, precisely by stirring up the entire soul of the people, indeed by fanning it into a frenzy, renders possible a relatively elevated morality in the other areas of life, since those other passions are killed off through the bullfight—so the Sunday corrida constitutes the necessary counterpart to Sunday mass.

On Monday and Tuesday we were on the Montserrat, and of course Klaus came along as well. I am looking forward to your coming and to showing it

[1.] *NL,* A 19,1 (11); handwritten. Partially reproduced in *GS* 6:121–22; postscript from Klaus Bonhoeffer.

[2.] The celebrations for Bonhoeffer's father's birthday; see 1/17.

[3.] Glotterbad Sanatorium in the Upper Glotter Valley in the southern Black Forest near Freiburg im Breisgau.

[4.] See also 1/20.

49 to you.[5] There is something enchantingly bizarre and fantastic about its whole formation. These two days were very pleasant.

Now we are planning our trip to the south, and Klaus shocked me by telling me he was to withdraw money for the trip and for his stay here in Spain using a letter of credit.[6] Briefly put, this is how things stand. I had 1000 pesetas here = 720 marks. From that, I withdrew 400 pesetas; 120 pesetas of that went for the athletic outfit[7] (which is, however, quite respectable and is considered such a bargain that someone else is having one made as well), ca. 80 pesetas for our Montserrat outing (i.e., 15 marks each day, including travel), also tennis club, racket, socks over 100 pesetas, then I have to pay all sorts of dues, buy all sorts of things like ties, so that over time the 400 pesetas have simply run out, even though on a daily basis I get along on my salary. So there are still 600 pesetas here, i.e., 450 marks. The trip south and back is 3,000 km and costs ca. 225 marks each. If we were to travel third class the whole way, we could save 75 marks, but we would be spending a great deal of time on the frightfully slow railways, would often have to travel for considerable hours at night, etc. Daily expenses will probably be an average of 10 marks, eighteen days = 180 marks, so that the whole thing will cost a bit over 400 marks for each of us. Was that approximately what you imagined, or not? Please write soon concerning this so that we can make arrangements. Klaus still has 500 marks here, so that we can go ahead and depart if that's all right with you, although it would be better if you could raise the limit on the letter of credit (which at the moment would be very advantageous given the low status of the peseta) and Klaus could save his Swiss money for Switzerland. It would be very good if you write soon, considering all the preparations we can begin making only then, and we did want to depart early on the twenty-third. I'm thinking the trip south at this time of year will be incredibly beautiful and I am already really looking forward to seeing a bit more of the country. Gradually one begins to understand it better.

50 I wish you much beautiful weather and a peaceful stay in Glotterbad.

Affectionately, your grateful
Dietrich

[5.] Bonhoeffer's parents visited him in Barcelona from September 19 to October 7, 1928.

[6.] This kind of letter of credit (*Akkreditiv*) was a line of credit restricted to a certain time frame and amount; a German bank had to send it to the Spanish bank.

[7.] Uncertain reading.

All the reasonable people here, including the pastor, have tried to dissuade me from traveling on the third-class train because of the dirt.

It is said to be very unusual here for respectable people to travel third class.

Greetings from me as well. I will write during the next few days Your grateful

Klaus

19a. Klaus Bonhoeffer to Julie Bonhoeffer[1] 17:72

Barcelona, April 16, 1928

Dear Grandmama,

I've already spent a wonderfully full week here in Spain.[2] I have been out and about quite a bit in order to orient myself as quickly as possible. I'm already able to make purchases in Spanish, get a haircut, and have an aperitif in a café so that I can observe at leisure what's happening in the street, as well as for other reasons—reasons having to do with the impossible Spanish cuisine. Because none of the officials at the Spanish border in Port Bou spoke French, I ended up quite at sea with my luggage and was able to set things straight only by enlisting at the last moment the help of a saxophone player from Barcelona, whom I had met on the train itself. Despite that incident, though, I must confess that I have indeed acquired a certain sense of security here after all—though doubtless less because of the modest proficiency in Spanish I have managed to acquire in the meantime than simply because one just quickly grows accustomed to being 17:73
silent. Until yesterday I stayed in a room at Dietrich's pension normally occupied by the German teacher here,[3] who is currently away on a trip to Majorca. Dietrich himself has very good accommodations here, albeit frightfully primitive. The only place to wash up is the toilet room itself, which differs little from the typical toilet room in the third-class car of an express train except that it doesn't shake. The "three ladies,"[4] however, do their best to teach their tenants Spanish and already consider it progress if one can communicate in simple infinitives and hand gestures. I am now living near Dietrich in the house of a French woman, though I do still take my meals in Dietrich's pension.

[1.] Literary estate of Klaus Bonhoeffer; handwritten letter; previously unpublished.

[2.] Klaus Bonhoeffer visited Bonhoeffer in Barcelona, where the two took a sightseeing trip together with Pastor Meumann. See 1/5, p. 58; see also 1/20, p. 90, and Klaus's account from Tétouan, Morocco, 1/23.

[3.] Hermann Thumm; see 1/5, p. 60.

[4.] See 1/5, p. 60.

¶Barcelona itself is as beautiful as it is interesting. Although the old part of the city recalls the picturesque filth in Naples, the poor people here seem in somewhat better shape than in Italy, and one is hardly bothered by beggars at all apart from genuine cripples and Gypsies. The population seems to be quite an ethnic mix. On the one hand, you see small, delicate, sinewy people, and then, on the other, also extremely fat ones. Quite often you especially see children whom you might consider obese. On average, however, and compared to the French and the Italians, the Spanish have strikingly austere, masculine facial features. Indeed, I'm still a bit uneasy about the men here and have not yet dared to photograph anyone in the old part of the city because I just don't know how they will react if I offer them a tip. Another striking feature here is how even the simple people dance with sophistication. Even five-year-olds dance the *sardana* in the street to an orchestrion[5] with quite mature movements. In a tavern yesterday, I saw how Charleston [. . .][6]

17:74 **19b. To Walter Dreß**[1]

Dear Walter:

I was quite pleased when your first letter[2] was followed so quickly by a second. Now I must answer both. First of all let me ask that you write me yet again and tell me what Fendt[3] said about sins against the Spirit. I wasn't quite able to get the whole of it from your brief allusions. To which historical event is he referring? Or is he not referring to any specific one, or does he mean the crucifixion? "Father, forgive them . . ." militates against the latter.[4] So please write about this again. I have the same theological concerns about Wittig as you do. It's really rather peculiar how untheological

[5.] The *sardana* is a Catalonian folk dance during which dancers hold hands and dance in short, bobbing steps, usually in the open air and accompanied by old Catalonian instruments; the children danced to a mechanical musical instrument known since 1850 as an "orchestrion," which was manufactured till about 1920 and can still sometimes be found at fairs today.

[6.] The conclusion to the letter is missing. ["Charleston" probably refers to the jazz dance named for the South Carolina city; it was an international craze in the 1920s.—CG]

[1.] Literary estate of Walter Dreß; handwritten, from Barcelona; postmarked April 20, 1928. Previously published in Staats and Wünsche, "Dietrich Bonhoeffers Abschied," 189–91.

[2.] With a single exception, Walter Dreß's letters to Bonhoeffer have been lost.

[3.] Walter Dreß may have heard the remark to which Bonhoeffer alludes in one of Fendt's sermons; but see also Fendt, *Die religiösen Kräfte des katholischen Dogmas*, 218–21.

[4.] Luke 23:34: "Father, forgive them; for they do not know what they are doing."

the whole of it is; one does not sense much of Luther, but neither does one sense much of Catholic scholastic dogmatism [Schuldogmatismus]. Perhaps the uninhibited theological element here rather recalls the literature of mysticism.[5] What impressed me was the enormous piety that speaks to the reader from this book.[6] Barth somewhat blunted my sense for this for several years.[7] This sense naturally emerges here, where one is constantly 17:75
confronted by distressful situations; and here Barth has become quite dangerous personally for me as well, a fact I sense with increasing clarity here in the life of the congregation when I occasionally—albeit rarely—encounter people characterized by an extremely strong piety or even pietism—and yet initially quite overwhelming for me. Theology constantly runs the risk of standardizing piety, that is, of restricting it by forcing it into specific rules. Of course, that has its advantages but really only bears fruit if there is an excess that must be reined in—otherwise it's dangerous.

I had to break off and am only just now getting back to writing again. Mama[8] has just written that you have been summoned by the president of the Evangelical High Church Council;[9] such scandalous nonsense. How dare these presumptuous consistory bigwigs suggest they can train a person better in a preachers' seminary than when such a person is already preparing for an academic career? That takes gall—and rather obtuse gall at that! I can already see that they will suddenly summon me back to Germany and

[5.] Here Bonhoeffer is making a slightly pointed remark against Dreß and the latter's dissertation, *Die Mystik des Marsilio Ficino.*

[6.] The assessment of piety articulated here and in the following sentences is unique for the Barcelona period. See also Bonhoeffer's letter of September 1, 1928 (1/44a), passim.

[7.] Barth's critical reserve toward such piety is perhaps best described in his own piece published in 1956, where he offers a retrospective on his own theological beginnings. Here he writes: "Evangelical theology almost all along the line, certainly in all its representative forms and tendencies, had become *religionistic, anthropocentric,* and in this sense *humanistic.* What I mean to say is that an external and internal disposition of man, namely, his piety—which might well be Christian *piety*—had become its object of study and its theme. . . . What did it know and say of the *deity* of God?" (*Humanity of God,* 39).

[8.] Paula Bonhoeffer wrote to Bonhoeffer on April 16, 1928: "Walter Dreß was summoned by the president of the Evangelical High Church Council this morning. They just don't want to let up and are intent on getting him into the cathedral seminary [*Domkandidatenstift*]." On February 22, 1928, an implementation decree of the May 5, 1927, church law "regarding the preliminary training and employability of pastors" restructured the legal situation for candidates. See also the consistory application for excusing Bonhoeffer from having to attend the preachers' seminary (1/115) and the subsequent notice excusing him from such attendance (1/116 and ed. note 3).

[9.] The president of the Evangelical High Church Council at the time was Dr. Hermann Kapler.

send me to Kückenmühle![10] But they'll be surprised; what makes them think they can postdate such decrees, these spiritual graybeards. You can
17:76 see that this whole thing really enrages me. Just don't be taken in by them; hide behind the university; surely the dean would have to intervene in this matter.

¶We start our trip on Monday.[11] On Sunday I still have to conduct the children's service, something that gives me great pleasure. While the pastor was away I took his place on two Sundays, preaching at Easter on 1 Cor. 15:17ff.[12] and then on Matt. 28:20.[13] By the way, my first sermon was on Rom. 11:6[14] (not Ps. 11:7).

¶You have probably already heard that I attended several bullfights. I wrote a rather thorough account of this for my parents.[15] And having to write the same thing twice is horribly boring. One more thing: Suse needs to write and tell me what became of the gossip with Bärbel and Anneliese.[16] In the final analysis, that really was just too stupid. Please extend my greetings to your mother and sister. Good luck with the high clerics! Cordial greetings to you and Susi.

Yours,
Dietrich

50 **20. To Sabine Leibholz**[1]

Barcelona, April 22, 1928

Dear Sabine,

Many thanks for your last letter! While all of you were looking peacefully for Easter eggs, I was with Klaus and an acquaintance at the bullfights. Klaus has probably already given an extensive report. I was utterly aston-

---

[10.] Kückenmühle near Stettin was one of the preachers' seminaries (diaspora seminary) serving the Evangelical Church of the Old Prussian Union. Concerning criticism of the preachers' seminary, see also 1/156. In 1935 Bonhoeffer himself became the director of such a seminary.

[11.] A tour of Spain with his brother Klaus; see also 1/20.

[12.] See 3/3.

[13.] See 3/4.

[14.] See 3/2.

[15.] See 1/19.

[16.] Anneliese Schnurmann; "Bärbel" possibly refers to Bärbel Kempner, née Hildebrandt.

[1.] *NL*, A 19,2 (16); handwritten. Previously published in *GS* 6:122–24; see also *NL*, Anh. A 5 (13); typewritten copy.

ished how much more cold-bloodedly I viewed the whole thing the second time than the first, and I must say that I can indeed sense from a distance that there is an allure to the whole thing that allows it to become a passion for some. One looks past the sensational-gruesome aspect more quickly with each bull—even though that may well constitute "brutalization," it does allow one to approach more closely the essence of the thing and to have more understanding for it. Moreover I have never seen the swing from "Hosanna!" to "Crucify!" more graphically evoked than in the virtually insane way the crowd goes berserk when the toreador makes an adroit turn, and they immediately follow this with an equally insane howling and whis- 51
tling when some mishap occurs. The momentary character of this mass mood goes so far that they applaud for the bull and against the toreador if, for example, the latter proves to be cowardly and—quite understandably—his courage fails him for a moment.

You've also already heard about Montserrat, so I'll tell all of you a bit—since you want me to—about daily life.[2] While the pastor was away, I had to hold office hours for the relief agency alone from 9:00 to 11:00 a.m. That usually doesn't make for a very pleasant start to my day—though it is always very instructive and interesting. People continually lie to you—which you learn only later—and there is rarely a case when you really are glad to help and can do so with a good conscience, and that's really too bad.

After these office hours, I am theoretically free for the day, but only "theoretically," since in a practical sense it usually happens that I don't get home until 1:00 a.m., that is, from some invitation or meeting etc., and find, yet again, that I have not managed to get around to writing or reading or learning Spanish or working or whatever else. I spend most of my time visiting members of the congregation, both healthy and sick, where, especially among the latter, one often has some very good experiences. When I have an afternoon or evening free, I like to go into the city to the main café for a change of scene and usually encounter someone I know, with whom I then chat away two or three hours, so that it's either time to eat dinner—that is, 8:30 p.m.—or time to go to bed—here that means 1:00–1:30 a.m.—I get to make music on Monday in the choral club—where I play piano—though not so much at home; otherwise I'm always just playing a piece of music for someone rather than engaging in serious music making—for that, too, people here are just too dull. For the people here really are for the most part dull beyond all measure, both young and old—that is to say, in every-

[2.] The transition in pronoun number (from *du*, the familiar singular, to *Ihr*, the familiar plural, and back) is typical of Bonhoeffer's letters. Letters addressed to individuals were always intended for other family members as well.

52 thing but their businesses. But they are nice, and it's easy to get along with them, and one's academic skills get dulled here very quickly indeed. It's like this: if a boy over the age of fourteen years develops any interests of his own, it's an exception. When they have outgrown *Der gute Kamerad,*[3] they read magazines and—do gymnastics. Otherwise the Basque ball game[4] and tennis take up the rest of the time in which a young boy might do some independent thinking. It was quite in character when recently a boy who had just been confirmed looked at me with a rather puzzled and clueless expression when I asked him whether any difficulties with the Apostles' Creed had arisen during confirmation instruction. What did I mean? And whether he might have any doubts about it?[5] If they're not forced to reflect on something, they push it aside; the worst thing would be one thought too many. So that is what my present life looks like; I am glad to be here and my interest is ever renewed, but whether I could stand it for more than one year—I really don't know!

Now I must close. Tomorrow our trip begins.[6] Say hello to Grandmama and tell her I'll certainly write her very soon. Today it is pouring rain, which it certainly can do here. And you have snow? I hope the weather is better in the south. I was especially pleased to receive Rüdiger's[7] letter. Please give him my warmest thanks. All the best to all three of you![8] With affection, your

Dietrich

[3.] *The Good Comrade.* Bonhoeffer is referring to an illustrated yearbook for boys.

[4.] Pelota, the Basque national sport.

[5.] Here Bonhoeffer is a pupil of Harnack insofar as the Apostles' Creed was insufficient for him as a confession of faith. In this regard see *Sanctorum Communio* (*DBWE* 1:201, ed. note 232), and later the material in the notes from the 1932 lectures on "The Nature of the Church" (*DBW* 11 [2/9], esp. pp. 283–86; see, in part, *TF,* 85–86).

[6.] The trip with his brother Klaus.

[7.] Rüdiger Schleicher.

[8.] Bonhoeffer is referring to Sabine and Gerhard Leibholz and their daughter Marianne, who was born June 30, 1927.

21. To Julie Bonhoeffer[1] 53

Dear Grandmama,

Because I won't be getting around to writing anything longer today after all, let me send you warm greetings from Madrid, where we have been for three days. This evening we will travel on to Toledo. Right now we have just spent two hours in the Prado, where among many especially beautiful paintings I particularly liked the one on the reverse side.[2] Yesterday we spent the day in Escorial,[3] which draws you into the age of the sixteenth century with incredible power.

We were treated with enormously gracious hospitality at the Hubers[4] here. I bought (for 7 marks) a wonderful old southern Spanish portrait of Christ[5] here. Greetings to everyone. Your grateful

Dietrich

22. To His Parents[1]

April 30

My dear Parents,

We have been in Seville since yesterday and also seem to be getting consistently sunny weather now. Quite unexpectedly yesterday afternoon we were able to catch a royal corrida, which was played out with unbelievable courage. The picture shows the cathedral, that is, originally the mosque of Cordoba, which impressed us greatly. Orient and Occident meet here in an extremely peculiar fashion, all the more so the farther south you go. All the 54

[1.] *NL*, A 19,2 (2); handwritten postcard from Madrid, postmarked April 26, 1928.

[2.] *San Benito*, by El Greco.

[3.] The monastery San Lorenzo del Escorial and palace located thirty miles from Madrid; it was built 1563–84 at the initiative of Philip II.

[4.] Uncertain reading.

[5.] Probably the "priceless southern Spanish tapestry with the portrait of Christ that hung above his desk" later in Finkenwalde (*DB-ER*, 104).

[1.] *NL*, A 19,1 (12); handwritten postcard mailed from Seville; postmarked April 30, 1928. Partially reproduced in *GS* 6:125. [The Cordoba "cathedral" pictured on the postcard is a Catholic sanctuary combining Gothic, Renaissance, and Baroque styles carved out of the center of numerous candy-striped arches and pillars of the original eighth–tenth-century mosque, aesthetically an "extremely peculiar" disjunction indeed.—CG] houses here are built in the Arabic style, and I think you would like it here very much as well. Everything is going splendidly for us. Klaus sends his greetings along with mine. More soon! Your grateful

Dietrich

23. Klaus Bonhoeffer to His Parents[1]

Tétouan, May 5, 1928

My dear Parents,

You probably haven't heard anything yet from Dietrich about our stay in Seville, so I'll begin there.

Unfortunately we only stayed a short while in Toledo. The weather was rather raw, so, hoping we would find more sun in the Andalusian plain, we traveled south, to Seville. And indeed, the air was already mild in Córdoba. The fragrance of oranges was intoxicating. Roses, carnations, gillyflowers, and wisteria were blooming in incredible lushness on the squares and balconies. From outside every house, you could look through the finely forged iron fences into inner courtyards colorfully tiled from the ceiling to the floor and landscaped with palms and wonderful flowers. Here, too, however, the weather alternated now and then between sun and warm rain showers, and the Guadalquivir River was yellow with silt. We traveled toward Seville through expansive livestock pastures, huge meadows of wildflowers more charming than any I have ever seen. Then olive trees, cork oaks, and all along the railroad embankment agaves and fig cacti two to three meters high.

In Seville we immediately went to the bullfight. It was completely full, so I found it extremely difficult to take photographs. Nonetheless I had to photograph a group of young people behind us and in the process kicked the person in front of me in the back, which he didn't hold against me, in fact, he even offered me a cigarette afterward. The king and queen,[2] the princes, and Primo de Rivera[3] sat across from us. The presence of the king made the toreadors especially daring. A bull caught one of them between his horns and threw him to the ground. But the red capes of the others, who immediately covered for him, distracted the bull, even though he had already struck once. There were no seri-

[1.] In the possession of Emmi Bonhoeffer at the time *DBW* 10 was published; handwritten.

[2.] Alfonso XIII and Victoria Eugénie von Battenberg.

[3.] Miguel Primo de Rivera y Orbaneja established a military dictatorship in 1923 and was forced to resign in 1930.

ous injuries. The crowd—including those in the royal loge—forgot the incident immediately. The king had only a slightly official air, and he actually seems quite sympathetic. More like an elegant and charming crown prince. On one outing we came across a clubhouse where he and his grandees were hunting dove. Whoever wanted could come up and watch, so Meumann wanted to just sit down and order a "café au lait."

In the streets of Seville, the women and girls wear a comb about twenty centimeters high covered with a black veil, and frequently with fire red carnations or roses in their black hair. It's quite striking how many exceptionally beautiful and well-dressed girls one sees in Seville. The men wear a high, round hat with a broad brim. The street children are an absolutely integral part of the street scenery, pushy but cute as hoards of them surround you and beg for "una perrita," a little bitch, that is, a five-centime coin. As good Catholics, the parents simply bring these children into the world without ever thinking about how they will feed them, so the children just have to get by with begging.

From Seville we traveled to Algeciras and from there to Gibraltar. Because Gibraltar is not actually located directly on the southern tip of Spain, it does not really constitute the straits. Nonetheless the steep cliffs rising up directly from the sea do dominate the entire region all the way to Morocco. The British seem to be quite sure of their position there. We got to Gibraltar itself without any passport controls and were able to climb the cliffs about three-quarters of the way up without being disturbed. There we passed by huge concrete covers—probably for munitions storage—and coastal artillery where exercises were going on. Unfortunately, the monkeys that used to live there as the only European representatives of their species died out a few years ago.

From Algeciras it took us four hours to travel over to Morocco. In Tétouan—my letter was interrupted; we have in the meantime come to Granada—we saw an example of purely oriental life in the Arab and Jewish quarters, something that for us Europeans still has a peculiarly mysterious element. Even in the simple street merchant, one often still senses a bit of the old culture expressed in the measured movements and calm speech. Chills run up your spine when you hear the beggars along the streets loudly reciting suras from the Qur'an. You even believe you can understand the verses, which are articulated with 56
unprecedented expressiveness. We saw the caliph riding to the mosque under a baldachin.[4] He greeted the people from his magnificent, pompously harnessed horses with a strangely cordial, gentle, almost feminine smile in a manner certainly never found in a European prince. I hope I can give you an approximate

[4.] [A canopy, often richly embroidered, carried above a dignitary.—CG]

picture of all these things with my photographs. For the rest, even in Morocco we didn't escape the April weather. I will write later about Granada, where we arrived a few hours ago.

But now something else! At the flea market in Madrid, I was busy as a painting speculator and bought myself an oil painting that seems quite good and interesting—signed Picasso. It is about 60 x 80 cm and depicts a degenerate woman drinking an aperitif (absinthe?). It is done in the French manner—also has a French subject—and to me seems to be genuine and quite valuable. Before selling it, I first want to make precise inquiries. I might send the picture to Berlin.[5] Therefore I got a credit of three hundred francs in Madrid from the Swiss Credit Institution.[6] I don't think there's any risk that I will lose on this investment.

Because of the primitive lodging, one encounters difficulties everywhere here when writing letters. Even though in Tétouan we did indeed have a room about ten meters long with three Arabic archways and Saracene tiles, we had no light. The windows, that is, the window bars, faced the interior courtyard, as in all the other rooms. So at night you could hear all the hotel guests, bitten by fleas, squirming in bed—and the rest snored. From the outside, this scene was interrupted periodically by roosters crowing and by the penetrating songs of pious Muslims. So essentially you don't feel comfortable in your own room either by night or by day. We are now anxious to hear what has been happening with all of you.

I have not received the letter of reference Kastl[7] wanted to send me. I assume he won't send it to me until June.

Affectionate greetings to all, your grateful
Klaus

57 **24. To His Parents and Grandmother**[1]

Barcelona, May 17, 1928

My dear Parents, dear Grandmama,

Let me use the hour remaining today between church and lunch, before I have to get going again for the afternoon and evening, to write quickly

[5.] The authenticity of this "Picasso" remained disputed. The picture hung in the Bonhoeffer house until 1945, when it was destroyed by fire during the air raids over Berlin; see *DB-ER*, 104. A similar picture depicting a "woman drinking absinthe" is reproduced in Daix and Boudaille, *Picasso*, 157.

[6.] [Since 1988, the Credit Suisse.—CG]

[7.] Probably Ludwig Kastl.

[1.] *NL*, A 19,1 (13); handwritten. Partially reproduced in *GS* 6:125–26.

and tell you that we both arrived back safely here from our wonderful trip, and to tell you about the final days of our trip, about which you have not heard anything yet. Without a doubt, the high point of the whole trip was seeing Granada during the beautiful spring weather. The hour in which we sat on one of the towers of the Alhambra and looked at the reddish, radiant Alhambra[2] and, situated further below, the city itself with the Alhambra park (with elms, quite an unusual sight) in which the nightingales were singing like I have never heard, and on the other side a view of the huge snowcapped mountains of the Sierra Nevada rising immediately over Granada—I must count that hour as one of the most beautiful I have ever experienced. I think such a beautiful landscape is actually something quite unique in Spain, for when I consider what I have seen here over time, one really must say that Spain is a desolate country, and that all the talk about "beautiful Spain" is at the least deceptive; just as during the trip everything again was quite different than anticipated. In diametrical contrast to Italy, Spain is a country that ancient culture—in the preliterary period as well as the Renaissance—passed by without leaving a trace, and which instead existed for four hundred years under the rule of Eastern culture.[3] It is a country that, to one who has been educated in the humanities, initially seems totally alien; one lacks all clues, so to speak, for understanding it. This is true not only of the historical but just as much of contemporary 58
Spain. But this alienation is joined by a certain element of sympathy, a feeling of kinship that one does not really sense, at least in this way, toward Italy. Again, I can only explain it by adducing the position regarding ancient and humanistic culture. For Italy humanism and the classical period represented the solution to all problems, whereas in Spain there is an element of resistance, which I think is also evident, to a certain degree, time and again among the Germans. Spaniards and Germans, I think, are similar in that neither culture ever completely opened itself up to humanism; instead, a remnant of something else always persisted.

It almost seems that the Spanish landscape is somehow connected with its history. Almost nowhere here does one find these harmonious landscapes that one does in Italy. I think the area around Barcelona, which I am enjoying more and more, is among the most beautiful in Spain.

¶The hour is up, and I'll close for today. As you see, we are both doing very well. Unfortunately I again have a frightful number of invitations for

[2.] Residence of the Moorish rulers, completed under Muhammad V (1354–91).

[3.] Spain was actually under Islamic influence for over seven hundred years. In this regard see the picture Bonhoeffer draws of the Islamic world in the letter to his parents of April 9, 1924, from Tripoli in 1924: *DBWE* 9 (1/66), pp. 117–18.

the coming week, the last week Klaus will be here; every evening is booked, and I have even hurt some people's feelings slightly by declining.

Many, many thanks again for making this trip possible for me; it has opened my eyes much wider with regard to my entire remaining stay here. Affectionately, your grateful

Dietrich

A quarter of my time has already passed! Time flies!

59 **25. To Julie Bonhoeffer**[1]

June 5, 1928

Dear Grandmama,

Many thanks for your nice letter.[2] It's always a very suspenseful moment in the day when at 3:00 p.m., after lunch, the mail carrier comes with the foreign mail, and we are already calling down from the balcony asking whether he has brought anything along for us. If he has indeed brought something, then in the very next minute each of us sits in the corner of the room and reads and reads—and would like to have something to keep reading until evening.

Klaus has been gone since Friday, and now I must get used to my solitary lifestyle once more; that is, I can't really complain about solitude, and except for a couple of people to whom one is genuinely close, one is after all around strangers day in and day out. Now the heat is coming, and the nights, too, are beginning to get uncomfortable; but I'll probably get used to it soon. School vacation begins in three weeks, and a large part of the colony will be departing, including the Olbrichts—then I'll have the kingdom to myself. I don't completely know yet how I will be spending these three months, since all the teachers with whom I can do things during the week will be away too. But something will work out. I will get to work on my Spanish as well as on the piano and my scholarly work—to the extent this is even possible in 30 degree[3] temperatures. It's really, really a shame that

[1.] *NL*, A 19,2 (3); handwritten from Barcelona. Partially reproduced in *GS* 6:127–28.
[2.] Not extant.
[3.] [Celsius; 86 degrees Fahrenheit.—CG]

the possibility of being with my parents here at the end of this period[4] is dwindling after all; but I think I really ought not try to persuade them, for ultimately it probably would be too strenuous and not a restorative vacation. But I'll keep watching to see if something can be done or happens after all.

There is still a lot going on here before school is out; if only the eve- 60
nings weren't always so long! I am now visiting a young married couple quite often, with whom I make music and through whom I have come into contact with the Spanish clergy. In yet another family, I make music once a week. I recently visited Uncle Otto's[5] colleague Dr. Krebs,[6] a very nice family with whom I had a very conventional breakfast. So over time one really does get to know a large number of people, and even though as a result I rarely get around to my scholarly work, I don't really regret it. I am realizing more and more that here what both adults and young people equally lack is some sort of interest in the larger worldview questions; everything here is so logical and regulated and lacks any real spirit. If you ask ten-year-olds what they want to be when they grow up, quite frequently you get the answer, "I'll take over my father's business." It's just so accepted that absolutely nothing else is even considered. The pleasant counterpart to this, to be sure, is that they find nothing more ridiculous than arrogance, so in social situations people don't try to be something they are not.

Now I must close. It is time for dinner, and even if the food doesn't entice me, the tea I have ordered for myself does.

¶During the evening now I often think, dear Grandmama, about the hours I so often sat with you in your room and which now often come to mind, in all their calm and peacefulness. Just eight more months, and these hours will come again. I'm looking forward to it. Warm greetings to everyone. I will write to my parents very soon. I look forward to any and all news. Farewell, dear Grandmama. Stay well. Affectionately, your grateful

Dietrich

Your letter with the copy[7] arrived—many thanks.

[4.] His father, Karl Bonhoeffer, was being urged to become a candidate for rector of the Berlin university; see the letter from Bonhoeffer's mother on May 19, 1928 (*NL*, C 1).

[5.] Otto Bonhoeffer.

[6.] See also 1/37 and 1/38.

[7.] His grandmother's letter of May 2, 1928 (*NL*, C 2) with the copy of a congratulatory address from Karl Bonhoeffer's students and colleagues on the occasion of his sixtieth birthday.

61 **26. To His Parents**[1]

June 8, 1928

My dear Parents,

Many thanks for the letter from Friedrichsbrunn, dear Mama. Your card just arrived. I'm sorry you're worried, but Klaus is doing as well as I am, that is, I haven't yet heard anything since his departure. The last two weeks together with him here were quite pleasant; as far as possible we did things together. The two months Klaus was here were really nice, and I'd like to thank you for making them possible for him and me; now we have again seen something of the world together and experienced the most interesting things, and that really does create a strong bond. Now that Klaus is gone, things have become quieter again, and for the first time, really, since I've been here, I'm getting around more often to reading. To be sure, the evenings will probably stay consistently booked till vacation begins, though then things will get very quiet indeed, and I hope I'll have stored enough desire for work that I'll be able to take advantage of the time despite the heat.

I am, I must say, *extremely* anxious to see what is developing, that is, whether you will be coming. When will you know for sure?

Summer has now arrived, and although there are no thermometers here, I'm guessing it's about 25 degrees.[2] The weather is like it is in Germany during midsummer. Fortunately the slightly damp air keeps you from getting too thirsty. I don't drink water anymore, and not many cold beverages, usually hot tea, a large glass of which, with lemon, I have before me right now. So until now I have still found the temperature quite pleasant and bearable, whereas most people are groaning, walking on the shady side of the street, and give you a furious look if by accident you cause them to turn and walk in the sun. Thursday, on the feast of Corpus Christi, I swam in the sea for the first time. I traveled by car along the coast with
62 some acquaintances toward Tarragona; then we swam and had a picnic. You can't lie in the sun here for five minutes without getting sunburned, so you move around slowly, cloaked like a pious Arab woman[3]—with a single eye exposed so you can see—in the harsh, scorching sun.

We returned in the evening to a procession[4] where the parade passes by for three full hours. The whole thing has the character of an annual fair. The parade is opened by the so-called giants, huge figures with grotesque

---

[1.] *NL*, A 19,1 (14), handwritten from Barcelona. Partially reproduced in *GS* 6:128–30.

[2.] [Celsius: 77 degrees Fahrenheit.—CG]

[3.] [Bonhoeffer means a pious Muslim woman.—CG]

[4.] [The Corpus Christi procession traditional in Catholic countries.—CG]

flags who dance and beg for alms. The people howl, throw paper serpents and confetti at them; people sell noisemakers for tooting, creaking, and squealing, with which the people greet and accompany the procession. Then for two hours you have all the city dignitaries, the entire military with military music, the clergy, choirboys, recently confirmed children, the civil authorities. By the way, I got another look at the incredibly inferior priestly material here. Alongside monks and clerics who really do recall pictures by Greco, the average nonetheless have shockingly uncultivated, dumb, drunken, and sensual faces—a remarkable contrast to Rome. I think that dumb saying about the stultification of the masses through religion[5] really does find some justification here.

Finally the monstrance[6] comes. The people, the soldiers—everybody goes down on their knees, and at the moment it passes by, flowers, paper serpents, and confetti fly about from all sides toward the vessel with the sacrament—and without betraying the least emotion in his expression, the archbishop strides through the crowd. The final military band follows, and then it's over. From the square where I watched the whole thing, I quickly ran to the cathedral so I could see the parade coming back. It was already twilight. I had a genuinely rare and beautiful view, a sight one imagines from the period five hundred years ago. On the cathedral square to the left, the whole crowd of cathedral choirboys were stationed in their crimson robes, and in the middle the infantry and cavalry joined them in old, colorful uniforms with the large, fantastic, warrior-like knight's helmets, and, from the right, carrying torches, came priests, monks, and pupils from the collegiate school in their white, radiant robes through the mighty main 63
portal of the cathedral, and in the unique illumination of the torches the whole picture came wonderfully to life. Now the monstrance returned, accompanied by people wearing multicolored garments; the wind made the canopy flutter above the bishop, everyone fell down to their knees, and the Host was again in its home church; that moment really made an abiding, solemn impression. Corpus Christi lasts eight days, so I'm hoping to see more as well.[7]

[5.] [Perhaps an allusion to the Marxist statement that religion is the opium of the people.—CG]

[6.] [The monstrance is the vessel that exposes the Eucharistic Host for veneration; it is therefore the highpoint of the Corpus Christi procession. Bonhoeffer uses the term *Allerheiligste*, "holy of holies."—CG]

[7.] Corpus Christi was introduced in the thirteenth century as a liturgical celebration of the dogma of transubstantiation and has since been celebrated on the Thursday after Trinity as the "high festival of the body and blood of Christ"; it was rejected by all Reformation churches. See Very, *Spanish Corpus Christi Procession*.

Tomorrow the choral club is having a big country outing, and I have to go along.

¶Now quickly to money matters. I withdrew 300 of the 800 pesetas when I got home and bought myself a pair of shoes for 40 pesetas. Socks for ca. 20 and ties for a couple. Klaus still had to buy a few things. Klaus used the rest for food, laundry [. . .],[8] shoes, etc., and ca. 50–75 pesetas of the remaining 500. He took along ca. 350 pesetas on the trip. I then used the rest of the ca. 75–100 for Klaus and my own things and for regular expenses, so today there is no more in the bank. However, I will not be needing anything else soon. I'm just now noticing here how all the small expenses add up: having a suit pressed, shoes resoled, etc. I just noticed that it's already 1:30. I finally want to go to bed a bit earlier for once, so I'll close now. Greetings to everyone at home! Affectionately yours, your grateful

Dietrich

64 **27. Excerpt from the Report of Fritz Olbricht to the German Evangelical Church Committee**[1]

[. . .][2] The vicar has been on the job here since February 15 and to the delight of myself and my congregation is a big success. He especially enjoys working with young people. Hence I would already like to request that when he leaves on February 15, 1929, a replacement be sent immediately. Since he has been here, I can travel more easily to the diaspora and spend more time addressing those needs. Moreover the congregation is now not without a German cleric during my own vacations and is not dependent solely on the Spanish Protestant cleric who substitutes for me, who is not so popular at funerals. Now the church services will not all be canceled during the vacation period but can be conducted by the vicar every two weeks.

I will be leaving for vacation at the beginning of July and returning at the end of September, for which I am requesting authorization from the German Evangelical Church Committee.

At the beginning of August, I will tentatively be in Berlin and will be calling on the church committee. Would it be possible to reimburse me in Berlin for the boarding expenses and salary for the vicar that are due in July? I will pay his money out to him here ahead of time during my absence.

[8.] Illegible.

[1.] EZA 5/1891; typewritten. Partially reproduced in *Mündige Welt,* 5:24.

[2.] Excerpted from a longer report Olbricht made on June 10, 1928, in which he sent along the statutes of the congregation and the annual report for 1927 and also applied for support ("Barcelona is the most expensive city in Spain") and leave; see 1/74.

Most respectfully yours,
F. Olbricht, Pastor

27a. To Walter Dreß[1] 17:76

June 14, [19]28

Dear Walter,

Warm greetings and best wishes for your birthday—this year, too, I still don't know whether it falls on the seventeenth or the eighteenth![2] The coming year will doubtless bring you the high honor of an academic teacher (with the good prospects and opportunities of a hopeful young man!);[3]
and this success, too, will probably soon be followed by your entry into the 17:77
dignified status of a husband etc.[4] I feel quite small and ugly looking up to the celestial heights of such honor, dignity, even pride and happiness. Hats off to this man!

¶Here are some wise bits of advice from one who has grown gray in the storms of life: 1. Don't let Seeberg[5] burden you down with too much dumb stuff; you can get someone else to do most of the boring stuff, then take what seems interesting yourself, or it takes care of itself. 2. Attach yourself like a heavy weight to the feet of the powerful. 3. Read Eccles. 12:12, also 2:24–25![6] That's enough for now; embrace these words of wisdom bubbling up from the unfathomable treasure of one who has become experienced and wise in the races of these days and times!

¶I have not yet quite decided about the birthday present, since although Spanish literature does indeed lend a spicy note to one's bookshelf, something more comprehensible is probably better, and since here in the land of the most strictly observed Catholicism there is not much to be had in the way of Latin things that makes any sense, and since German does not really

[1.] Literary estate of Walter Dreß; handwritten, from Barcelona, on stationery with the letterhead "Evangelical Congregation Barcelona, Calle Moyá, 2 (Gracia)." Previously published in Staats and Wünsche, "Dietrich Bonhoeffers Abschied," 191–93. This letter is the birthday letter Bonhoeffer mentions below (1/31). It was found after *DBW* 10 was published, hence the belief that it was lost as reported in *DBW* 10 (1/31), p. 73, ed. note 3.

[2.] Walter Dreß was born on June 18, 1904.

[3.] Dreß attained his postdoctoral certification in 1929; see ed. note 8 to this letter.

[4.] Dreß married Susanne Bonhoeffer on November 14, 1929.

[5.] Erich Seeberg; Dreß was his assistant.

[6.] Eccles. 12:12: "Of anything beyond these, my child, beware. Of making many books there is no end, and much study is a weariness of the flesh"; Eccles. 2:24–25: "There is nothing better for mortals than to eat and drink, and find enjoyment in their toil. This also, I saw, is from the hand of God; for apart from him who can eat or who can have enjoyment?"

appeal to me at the moment, I will risk adding a bit of Spain's elegance to your own—with your and Susi's permission, of course.[7]

¶I'm really quite anxious to hear about your work.[8]—I had to break off at this point and, after returning from the parsonage where I was writing, I found your wonderful letter,[9] which delighted me. Congratulations for having dealt successfully with the consistorial matter.[10] The conditions at the cathedral seminary seem almost medieval. Sometimes one really would like to see heavenly fire descend upon these church administrators—except
17:78 that ultimately they, too, would have to be exonerated on the basis of their excessive ignorance. One hopes that Weber[11] is so fearful that he won't risk the trip to Berlin. How on earth did they think of him? *I* would think that only Koepp[12] and Althaus[13] would be considered; that's what Seeberg told me at the time.[14] Thanks also for the information on Fendt's thoughts;[15] but it still seems rather affected and cheeky, and what is such a statement to mean coming from Jesus? Or is the explanation perhaps based on cultic-historical[16] considerations? I still find the statement extremely puzzling, nor does Seeberg's interpretation satisfy me.

¶Just now the semester is coming to an end. Everyone is making plans for vacation, and the school will be closing soon; the only thing left to weather is the final storm of social life before the dead calm sets in. Every evening is booked for me, and often quite pleasantly. Then—at the beginning of July, when things settle down, I'll digest things and reimmerse myself in theology, which I've only got back to in the past few weeks. I'll practice my Spanish, read a lot, and make music. As far as going swimming is concerned, things are rather awkward insofar as you have to walk a half-hour through the hot city, which is not particularly attractive and is also extremely boring if you are by yourself. But I have a bathtub with a shower head, in which I will spend most of the day. Today it is pleasantly cool and cloudy, something

[7.] The birthday present—as attested by Bonhoeffer's letter to Susanne Bonhoeffer on June 20, 1928—was a piece of "Toledo handwork," a particular kind of embroidery (*à jour* or openwork pattern).

[8.] Bonhoeffer is referring to Dreß's postdoctoral dissertation, *Die Theologie Gersons.*

[9.] Not extant.

[10.] See the letter of April 20, 1928, 1/19b.

[11.] Hans Emil Weber.

[12.] Possibly Wilhelm Koepp.

[13.] Paul Althaus.

[14.] Bonhoeffer is referring in this case to Reinhold Seeberg; these were the people being considered as his successor.

[15.] See Bonhoeffer's query in the letter of April 20, 1928, 1/19b. Dreß's answer has not been preserved.

[16.] Uncertain reading.

one really enjoys, since it can already get quite warm here. When I do manage to think a bit in the summer heat, I think about beginning a longer work—either a complete piece about "consciousness" [Bewußtsein] or a smaller preliminary piece about "the child and theology."[17] At the same time I'm working on my doctoral dissertation[18] and am deleting.[19] What
about your own publication?[20] But now I must close! Say hello to Susi and 17:79
tell her I will write soon. Why is she being so aloof and not writing at all? I'd like to know all sorts of things about her; she can, after all, find out all my news from our parents. But I really will write soon. Warm regards to your family as well! Mama's and Grandmama's letters arrived, as did the panama.[21] Many thanks. Let me also wish you a new year filled with good work and success! Let me hear from you. Every letter is a pleasure for me. Affectionate regards,

Your faithful Dietrich

28. To Max Diestel[1] 64

Barcelona, June 18, 1928

Dear Superintendent Diestel:

I have been here in the south now for four months—a third of my time; the
rather long winter has very quickly turned into summer—by German stan- 65
dards midsummer. Things around me are starting to quiet down now. The heat here allows for no haste or restlessness. You walk silently and slowly about the glaring, hot streets and look for a bit of shade. The well-to-do sector of the German colony is getting ready to travel home, and I will be one of the few here who sees things through. For the first time, the services this

[17.] Concerning this plan, see 1/36, p. 122, and 1/40, p. 128; see also *Act and Being* (*DBWE* 2:157–61) and the comments of Hans-Richard Reuter in *Akt und Sein* (*DBW* 2:8). [See too the numerous references to "consciousness" and "conscience" throughout *Act and Being* listed in the index.—CG]

[18.] Bonhoeffer was preparing his doctoral dissertation, *Sanctorum Communio* (*DBWE* 1), for publication.

[19.] [Bonhoeffer estimated that in preparation for publication he cut 20 or 25 percent; see 1/47, p. 142.—CG]

[20.] Probably the final proofs of the doctoral dissertation by Dreß, *Die Mystik des Marsilio Ficino.*

[21.] Panama hat; see 1/31 and 1/34.

[1.] EZA 29/G 442,27; handwritten; with a handwritten remark by Diestel: "answered July 12, 1928." See also *NL*, A 20,3 (1); later typewritten copy. Partially reproduced in *GS* 6:130–31.

year will continue through the vacation as well, albeit only every two weeks and with no guarantee that anyone will attend. Whoever is able generally goes to the sea on Sunday, which one certainly cannot hold against them. The children who are remaining here have themselves requested that the children's services continue. Together with the relief agency—with its daily office hours—and the ongoing visits in the congregation, I certainly have enough to do. Only one thing is missing: more diversity within the purely church activities. Apart from the services, there is no *church* work. Bible study, young men's association, lecture evenings, religious instruction at the school—there is none of that here. I will try to introduce the latter voluntarily in the higher grades during the coming winter; maybe something can be done with Bible study as well. In general the situation is such that people are positively disposed toward the church—they pay their tithes—but their active involvement and participation is not even closely commensurate. Although individual circumstances may play a role, for the most part it derives from the lifestyle of the colony and from its intellectual level. Lots of business, lots of gossip, moralizing [Moralin], a little literature, and finally a dab of religiosity [Kirchlichkeit]; but on the whole enormous honesty and decency, no dumb posturing or arrogance, and that makes one feel good. I must say that I really like being with most of the people and have an extremely nice social life. (It would be completely wrong to talk about a more extensive religious liveliness prompted by the oppositional stance.)[2] I especially enjoy the children's service here, which I had to reestablish and which has started off well.

You can see that I am glad to be here; and while it is certainly interesting to enter different circles than those to which one is accustomed, one
66 must also add the joy of being in a foreign country and the adjustment to what seems to me to be an extremely alien culture for us, yet one that is certainly stimulating and serious; a three-week trip[3] through the country really helped me in this regard. Let me thank you for thinking of me so graciously on that November morning and thus helping me along into this period, which will certainly be important for my entire life. I still remember how I wavered back and forth at the time, but not for a single moment have I regretted coming; and I owe that to you.[4] So please accept the most

[2.] [That is, a vitality stimulated by a feeling of opposition to the Catholic majority culture.—CG]

[3.] With his brother Klaus from April 23 to May 12, 1928; see 1/20–1/24.

[4.] See 1/5, p. 57.

devoted greetings and regards, which I also request you pass along to your wife, from your always grateful and devoted servant

Dietrich Bonhoeffer

28a. To Susanne Bonhoeffer[1] 17:79

June 20, [19]28

Dear Suse,

Here, finally, is the letter for which you have apparently been waiting so long, as a signal that now you, too, can write to me, the letter that I would gladly have written a long time ago if every time I sat down to do so—I realize this hardly seems credible for four months—some other, more urgent matter had not arisen, which kept me from writing—probably much the same thing you yourself experienced. As you can see, my latest innovation is a typewriter, which I and the two other people here at the pension have rented together for fifteen pesetas a month. Because in any case I must already write a great deal that must be legible to others, I will initially save those others—and then, I hope, myself as well—time and effort.

¶I thought about all of you recently on Walter's birthday. That evening I was invited to enjoy a few bottles of champagne with several nice people here and silently toasted all of you with my first glass. I have a small piece of Toledo handwork here for Walter but am still unsure how best to send
it back to Germany without creating tedious customs problems for you. If 17:80
you do have any problems with customs, you need to declare it as a used item. After a few days of extremely cool weather here, it warmed up again considerably yesterday. I must say, however, that at least till now I have not found the heat all that unpleasant, in contrast to many Spaniards and even more Germans, who are already starting to groan. Because the air is always so humid here, one does not get thirsty at all, which is very good. In the street outside my window, street children have been shooting off pistols and fireworks for days now and have been at it the entire afternoon today as well—all in anticipation of St. John's Eve,[2] when fires and fireworks are set on every corner, all through the night. On that day, the bishop is to go to the sea at night to bless the water, whereupon in the same night the devout Spaniards take their first bath in the sea, inaugurating the season.

[1.] Literary estate of Walter Dreß; typewritten, from Barcelona; the envelope is addressed to Walter Dreß. Previously published in Staats and Wünsche, "Dietrich Bonhoeffers Abschied," 193–94.

[2.] Each year on June 23–24.

¶I recently saw a belated but quite enchanting Corpus Christi procession here in the older part of the city.[3] And, of course, just as everywhere else, the bustle of the annual fair with confetti, paper serpents, wailing instruments, which are engaged especially when the monstrance is carried by—whole baskets of confetti were poured down from balconies onto the "heaven."[4] One particularly unique feature, for example, was an old sword dance performed by young people in the procession with wooden swords, a dance that is doubtless extremely difficult and ancient. I'm not quite sure whether it derives from the period when the power of the sword was associated with the church—something like a heresy deterrent in Inquisition processions [sic!][5]—or even from[6] Arabic traditions.[7] Another quite lovely and interesting feature was the long processions with the children who just had their first communion, all of whom here wear a small bridal gown that sets their dark faces quite apart. A large number of these children were dressed as saints, as mater dolorosa,[8] and an entire holy family arrived,
17:81 and behind them Christ with the cross and crown of thorns; then you saw a whole host of small angels, then St. Anthony, then an ancient hermit, etc. This children's procession alone lasted about half an hour; which is also why occasionally a small, four- or five-year-old saint would begin crying for all he or she was worth and had to be picked up by someone. (In this procession, I also saw how the accompanying men kept their cigarettes in their mouths!)

¶Well, now I've related quite a bit to you, and it is late. I'd also like to hear everything about you as well. What are all of you up to? What about the trousseau work? How is Walter? Also write me about what I had Walter ask you earlier.[9] Best wishes at home and to the Dreßes. And Anneliese,[10] if you see her.

Affectionately yours,
Dietrich

[3.] Cf. the account of a Corpus Christi procession, 1/26, pp. 98–99.

[4.] Canopy over the priest with the monstrance.

[5.] [Bonhoeffer's bracketed insertion.—CG]

[6.] In the German, Bonhoeffer incorrectly wrote "influences Arabic traditions" instead of "derives from."

[7.] Concerning Bonhoeffer's interest in traditions foreign to him, see his letter to Reinhold Seeberg of July 20, 1928, 1/36.

[8.] [Mother of sorrows.—CG]

[9.] See Bonhoeffer's letter of April 20, 1928, 1/19b.

[10.] Anneliese Schnurmann.

29. To Sabine and Gerhard Leibholz[1] 66

Barcelona, July 3, 1928

Dear Sabine, dear Gert,

I wish I could have been more punctual with the letter of congratulations on your Marianne's[2] first birthday, but there's been so much commotion during the past few days that I just never got around to it. Moreover, before the pastor's departure—this evening—I traveled up to the mountains for two and a half days, and in the Spanish mountain villages there's frequently no post office—or even a telegraph office. So I was only just able to get that telegram greeting off to you quickly from the mountains—and at night. Nonetheless, you can well imagine that up there in the solitude of the Spanish mountains I did indeed have time to celebrate this beautiful day with you in thought. And quite instinctively my thoughts then drifted over to you and to the days a year ago, grateful that everything went so well at that time
and that all worry receded before joy and happiness. 67

I wish I could have put a colorful bouquet of summer flowers on your table this year as I did last year, but now others will have done that, and your apartment is probably decorated as it was one year ago. I've been looking here for something pretty for Marianne, but am not yet quite decided; she'll probably have the patience to wait a few more days. May the next year go as well for you as the first so that you have no more worries with your Marianne than you did during the first year of her life, and always just as much joy.

Many thanks to you, Sabine, for your letter. School vacation has started here, and now things will calm down and I can finally get back to real work again—if it just weren't so damned hot. When I walked out of the house this morning it was like stepping into an oven. As long as I don't have to rush, though, I can still bear it pretty well. The people in my boardinghouse urge me to eat, something I otherwise would just skip at times. Only one thing is bad, that you have to do everything in a laid-back, calm fashion, including work. And at first it feels simply terrible that it takes twice as long to read a book here as at home. Everything functions more slowly here.

Mornings I now keep my office hours in the sacristy and work there during the afternoon, and in between play the organ in the church for a while. Lunch is at 1:30. Then the spirit is usually willing, but the flesh is weak, and I sink down onto my bed, initially with a book, but then it's soon all over as

[1.] *NL*, Anh. A 5 (14); typewritten copy. Original in literary estate of Sabine Leibholz.
[2.] Marianne Leibholz was born June 30, 1927.

far as my energy is concerned and I sleep an hour until 3:00 or 3:30. Then I read, write, play the piano, or a young boy[3] from the children's service comes to me; his parents can't handle him, and he must take a makeup exam, for which I am cramming him. Yesterday I found out that he cannot recite the vowels, and he's a third-year student!

68 And so it goes from one day to the next. At coffee time around 5:30, I often go into the city to take care of some errands and then at 6:00 or later meet some acquaintances in a certain coffeehouse here, or I visit some parish members and then return around 8:00. I practically never go swimming. The sea is almost three-quarters of an hour away from us, the road and railway are dusty and hot, the facility full, so I just don't get any great urge to go, even when it's hot. Moreover I'm not all that enthusiastic a swimmer, so I'm not really giving up much.

My evenings are usually booked, with either invitations or regular commitments to friends[4] or, as has been the case for some time now, very often with language practice. A Spaniard replied[5] to my advertisement in the newspaper here, and we meet quite often now.[6] An especially intelligent and incredibly well-read man, twenty-seven years old, employed by a publisher to read foreign works that are worth translating into Spanish. In contrast to many Spaniards, he has very good manners and is really consistently congenial and educated. He has a much larger vocabulary than I, but I speak more fluently, so I profit a great deal. It's only awkward that he then wants to pay for everything, as is the Spanish custom. Yesterday he brought me a nice book about Spanish folk music simply as a gift, so I'll have to see how I can reciprocate. We meet at home or in the café at 9:30 in the evening and then chat away for about two hours. This evening he's coming to me. I really am quite satisfied with this move.

My tour on Peter and Paul[7] was gorgeous. At 10:00 in the evening we arrived in the mountains and immediately started off, the whole night through, till at sunrise we were on the top of the mountain. The Pyrenees
69 lay before us as if dipped in gold by the sun, which we saw rising up from

[3.] Probably Karl-Heinz Köttgen; see 1/17, pp. 81–82.

[4.] Uncertain reading.

[5.] [The original of this word is not legible and the transcription is uncertain, but the meaning of the sentence appears clear.—CG]

[6.] On June 22, 1928, Bonhoeffer placed an ad concerning this in the newspaper *La Vanguardia*, to which Luis Sánchez Sarto, an employee with the publisher Editorial Labor, responded on the same day; see *NL*, C 22.

[7.] On June 29, 1928, the feast day of Peter and Paul, Bonhoeffer climbed Montseny (5,689 feet) with Engler, a musician, and "two others" (see his calendar, *NL*, A 18,2).

the sea down below.[8] We then hiked until midday, when we separated. The others had to go to Geneva; I stayed another day and a half in the peacefulness of what is here a quite rare beech forest. That was gorgeous.

Now I must close. This epistle is long enough. One more thing: I want to thank our parents very much for both of their letters, as well as Susi, whose letter *really* pleased me. Our parents want me to tell about the pastor's family. I'll do that in my next letter, though there really isn't all that much to tell; we get along famously but are so busy when away from work that we usually only see each other during the morning. He will, by the way, be coming to Berlin at the beginning of August and will visit our parents. I'm very sorry to hear that Aunt Helene Schöne has died. An unfinished letter to her is lying on my desk. Today you see only very few women like her, if any! The integrity of her whole manner, the refinement in her house, was something quite rare indeed. And always kind and friendly as well. It is truly too bad that she is no longer with us.—She was the last representative of this manner and refinement that I have always imagined characterized the lives of our maternal ancestors.

And now I really must close. Please tell Mama what is in this letter, since I can't write another one right away. Stay well, both of you. Let me congratulate you, Gerd, on your postdoctoral degree.[9] Warm greetings to you both.
Yours,

Dietrich

30. To Karl-Friedrich Bonhoeffer[1] 70

Barcelona, July 7, 1928

Dear Karl-Friedrich,

You have written me two lengthy letters, and yet I have not personally thanked you; I quickly want to make up for that today. I have always been so glad to hear about you and your work in greater detail,[2] since each person

[8.] [The sentence is garbled in the transcription of the original letter; however, the translation gives its meaning.—CG]

[9.] Gerhard Leibholz attained his *Habilitation*, the postdoctoral qualification for a university lectureship, with a work on constitutional law, *Das Wesen der Repräsentation*.

[1.] *NL*, A 19,2 (9); handwritten. Partially reproduced in *GS* 6:132–34.

[2.] Together with Paul Harteck, Karl-Friedrich Bonhoeffer was working on experiments with hydrogen as an assistant to the chemist Fritz Haber at the Kaiser Wilhelm Institute for Physical Chemistry; see his unpublished letters of March 23, June 17, and October 22, 1928 (*NL*, C 3). [After World War II it was renamed the Fritz Haber Institute as part of the Max Planck Society.—CG]

gets only three lines or so in the general reports from home. You don't seem to be thinking much about vacation and so will probably not extend your Paris trip any further. Since I will still not be able to get away during this period—as Olbricht is taking his vacation till October—probably nothing will come of our meeting. Of course, that's really a shame, but there's probably nothing that can be done. You asked what I have been doing besides going to social events and bullfights, that is, what I have actually been working on. Invitations have decreased measurably since the vacation began, and I haven't been to a bullfight in probably two months now. So I have all kinds of extra time, and if one wanted to work one could get all sorts of things done. But it's simply too hot for the kind of intensive scholarly work one is able to do in Germany; so it's good that all kinds of practical things need to be done. Especially from 9:00 to 10:00, the office hours for the relief organization, which I now keep alone, are extremely interesting and instructive. You get a look at the most varied ways of living and have to deal with the strangest people, people with whom you otherwise would hardly ever have exchanged even a single word: globetrotters, vagrants, escaped criminals, lots of foreign legionnaires, lion trainers and other animal trainers who have run off from the Krone Circus during its Spanish tour, Ger-
71 man dancers from the variety shows here, German contract killers wanted by the police, all of whom tell you their life story to the very last detail. It's often difficult to give and to refuse here according to one's own assessment; but since you can't determine anything of substance, one's personal impression just has to decide. And that impression can often be sufficiently and easily enough deceived, so that many of these people get money who really don't deserve any support at all, something you later learn yourself or from others. So over time you also become ever more sensitive to the plight of those who really are in need and cannot be adequately supported. Since I have been here, it has already happened twice that longtime, well-situated residents have suffered complete financial ruin and could hardly even pay for school tuition and clothes for their children; in such cases there really must be enough money available to help. Dealing with those who are in daily need is not so simple either, since their manner varies considerably. Yesterday, for the first time, one man got so impertinent with me—he maintained that the pastor had forged his signature—that I really had to yell at him and throw him out while threatening to have him arrested; and while he was hurrying to get away, he cursed and yelled out the threat I have already heard so often: "We'll see each other again; just come down to the harbor." Afterward I learned at the consulate that he is an old swindler who has been running around here for a long time now; so I was quite pleased to have been tough with him. On the whole, however, my experience is that

you can best take care of people with kindness and friendliness, which is also the easiest way to get rid of the more unpleasant visitors. Olbricht follows the policy of scolding them and throwing them out if he doesn't like someone, believing that has a greater effect. I guess we'll just have to see. On the whole, this activity, which in itself one would imagine to be so nice and gratifying, is not very pleasant. People lie to you and deceive you whenever possible, and only rarely do you have the pleasure of seeing that you really were able to help, since most of them spend the money as fast as they get it, so nothing has been remedied. The basic problem is that we have no 72
job referrals, and that is because there are far too many businesses here and they are all overstaffed. German businesses are cutting back because they can barely withstand the economic competition from other foreign countries; old established businesses and enterprises are failing, so there is hardly room for the old ones, not to speak of new ones moving in. So there is much unemployment among the Germans here, and hence all the need. We are constantly involved in sending Germans home even though we know things are no better at home.

After these office hours I work peacefully by myself till one o'clock. Right now I am editing my doctoral dissertation for publication[3] and think a lot about the various possibilities for my postdoctoral dissertation.[4] Then I walk home along a sunny, treeless street that ascends slowly to the house, where lunch awaits me. After that I would really like to be more active than I am, for three times a week in any case all my attempts to work or practice fail, and I quickly land in bed under my mosquito net; the other three times I am held up an hour by a particularly bright but infinitely distracted boy[5] who attends my children's services. I pass the afternoon with work, correspondence, practicing, or visiting parishioners in the hospital and at home. Now and then I go into the city to drink coffee, where I generally meet many acquaintances. Many evenings I now get together with my Spanish-language partner, an extremely intelligent, well-read, and industrious Spaniard. He is quite familiar with the most recent German philosophical literature, especially the pedagogical literature, and so we have much to talk about. He knows more words, while I speak better, so we both profit.[6] We also go out

[3.] *Sanctorum Communio*; see 1/36, p. 122.

[4.] The sentence "Right now . . . postdoctoral dissertation" was inserted later. The subject of his subsequent postdoctoral dissertation, *Act and Being: Transcendental Philosophy and Ontology in Systematic Theology*, had not yet been determined; see also 1/36, p. 122, together with *DBW* 2:8 and *DBWE* 2:2–4.

[5.] Probably Karl-Heinz Köttgen; see 1/17, pp. 81–82.

[6.] See 1/29, p. 108.

73 together, so I'm hoping finally to learn Spanish a bit better, since until now my skills in this regard have been quite meager indeed and were limited to a few subjects such as hotel rooms, shopping, railways, etc.

Well, this has unintentionally become a long letter. I must now get to work on my sermon.[7] I am preaching only every two weeks now; the children come each week. That suffices for me, since preaching in this heat is not necessarily very pleasant, especially since the sun shines on the pulpit at this time of year.—Please tell our parents that I will write soon, and that I am anxious to learn of their decisions,[8] that one can travel from Barcelona to Majorca in nine hours overnight. Please say hello to everyone. Wishing you enjoyable work in the summer heat!

Affectionate greetings, Your
Dietrich

31. To His Parents[1]

My dear Parents,

Many thanks for your letters—I just received your last one, dear Mama. First of all, before I forget: The panama[2] arrived; in Walter's[3] birthday letter I asked that you be told, but it was apparently forgotten. About the money for all the supplies for the children's service—including the bill from Grote, some of which will be covered by parish funds: I have already had Olbricht pay me about forty marks of it, apart from the receipt you sent me at that time for ca. forty marks and which is now with the treasurer of the congregation. The other books are in part periodicals, in part things I still needed. So please pay the entire bill, ca. thirty-two marks for me; I have already been reimbursed for the rest.

74 I still have the Picasso,[4] since the postal service didn't want to take it and Klaus hasn't replied to me whether it is all right to send it to him reg-

[7.] See 3/7.

[8.] His parents' travel plans were up in the air due to his father's possible election as rector of the University of Berlin; see 1/25, pp. 96–97.

[1.] *NL*, A 19,1 (15); handwritten from Barcelona; inferred date, July 11, 1928. Partially reproduced in *GS* 6:135.

[2.] A panama hat; see 1/34, p. 117.

[3.] Walter Dreß celebrated his birthday on June 18; see 1/27a.

[4.] See 1/23, p. 94; cf. *DB-ER*, 104.

istered and rolled up. My Spanish-language partner, who understands art and is a painter himself, is very excited about the picture.

You've asked several times about the Olbrichts. They have now left and want to visit you in Berlin at the beginning of August—at least he does. His married daughter, who is expecting and thus can't travel, is still here with her husband. I quite enjoy being around them and meet often with them. The son just did his secondary school final examination and is in Germany. I get along very well with Olbricht himself; if you have perhaps been thinking that something was amiss, that's not accurate. But we each have our different circles of friends, so that we are both engaged and don't socialize much together. If I wanted I could naturally visit them more often, during the afternoon or evening, but when we're together several hours during the morning that's generally enough for both of us. Often during the afternoon when I'm at school or am walking by their house, and they see me, they call me in for a snack, and if they have evening guests, I'm naturally always invited along. Our relationship is really as nice and as reasonable as one could want.

This afternoon, when the city really will be stiflingly hot—it's always ca. 30 degrees in the shade, evenings 25–26 degrees[5] if it's cool—I am taking the children and a book of Andersen's fairy tales[6] up into the somewhat cooler, shady mountains.

It would be wonderful if your trip here did materialize. If you still want to go to Granada, then perhaps Majorca wouldn't be the best choice, since one would have to return by way of Barcelona. But since the train trip to Granada is extremely long (twenty-four hours from Barcelona, you have to go through Madrid!), perhaps flying would be the best and most comfortable option, and you could remain longer in Granada, where the weather is supposed to be splendid at the end of September and beginning of October. I'm anxious to hear all your further decisions. When will you know?—I have to go. Greetings to everyone. Affectionate greetings to you both from your grateful

Dietrich

[5.] [Fahrenheit 86 and 77–79, respectively.—CG]

[6.] [Presumably a volume by Hans Christian Andersen, the popular nineteenth century Danish writer of fairy tales, widely translated into German and other languages. —CG]

75 32. From Max Diestel[1]

Berlin-Lichterfelde, July 12, 1928

Dear Colleague:

Many thanks for your letter,[2] which I was very pleased to receive. I do hope that you won't later reckon this as a lost year. In my view, every person should take advantage of the opportunity once to move in completely different circles than those in which one's education and the formation of one's intellectual identity have taken place. The problem is often, especially among us theologians, that we grow up much too academically and much too unworldly, and then our view of the real world, a world oriented quite differently, ends up being shortsighted. For this reason I also think it quite good that you are dealing with a completely different kind of congregation in Spain than we have here. I am familiar with this type. It is approximately the same as in Italy. In England public church opinion colors the behavior of individuals much more strongly, since Germans abroad do not deny their capacity for adapting even if they don't come from the Kurfürstendamm.[3] I can imagine, however, that it would also be particularly interesting for you if, once you have learned to speak Spanish fluently, you might have some contact with authentic Spanish life itself. As diverse as it may be in the individual provinces, particularly in their various ethnographic peculiarities, on the whole it is still quite alien to me. Light and shadow are as harsh as in Ribera.[4] The uniquely gloomy colors of Goya[5] testify to a wild temperament, which Nietzsche certainly would have traced back to the black-haired beast. To me the Spaniards are a puzzle, despite my aesthetic appreciation for them, and I regard them with Nordic coolness, sensing more the Arab in them than the Goth, and am myself less a friend of Don Quixote than of Franz von Sickingen, who did not unleash such enormous poetic energy. Perhaps one simply has to have lived in the country itself and with its people, eating sheep's milk cheese
76 and drinking brownish wine. I haven't done any of that yet. But I would indeed like to have seen Montserrat.

[1.] *NL,* A 30,2 (2); typewritten. The original of the second page is missing in the Bonhoeffer papers. The letter here has been completed according to the carbon copy in the Evangelische Zentralarchiv in Berlin (EZA 29/G 442,17), Diary no. 2274; see also the later typewritten copy in *NL,* A 30,2 (10).

[2.] See 1/28.

[3.] At that time the Kurfürstendamm in Berlin was known for its fashionable and ostentatious businesses; its residents were looked down upon for their enthusiastic conformity to fashion.

[4.] José de Ribera, Spanish painter.

[5.] Francisco José de Goya y Lucientes, Spanish painter.

That reminds me of something quite pleasant. We always give our elderly a bottle of wine for their birthdays, the milk of the aged.[6] Is there any point, and do you have a good and reliable wine merchant in your congregation who might send a drinkable vintage and, for a decent price, a hundred-liter keg or so to the St. Paul's parish office, Dahlemer Straße 87, Lichterfelde? But only if it's really worth it. Here we pay 1.40 marks for a bottle of Tarragona.[7] But how good the stuff is I dare not try to find out. In matters pertaining to wine, I don't have much confidence in the people of Berlin. Perhaps you can get someone to give us a bid. But I would request such a favor only if it does not present difficulties for you.

With very cordial greetings, your devoted
[Diestel][8]

33. To Adolf von Harnack[1]

Barcelona, July 13, 1928

Your Excellency:

It is no accident that during recent weeks my thoughts have repeatedly been drawn to you and to your seminar as if by a magnet, since it is once again the anniversary of those early days in July, when for years you would take your seminar in the afternoon to Grunewald to give us a few hours, times that are surely as vivid for many others, as for me, as if they were only yesterday.[2] And while during the course of the semester's work I had the chance to express modestly the gratitude I always feel toward you in an
inconspicuous fashion through the actual attempts at collaboration, and 77
because on several occasions over the past few years I was able to take the floor in the name of the seminar and speak to you openly about those unexpressed things that were on our hearts—words that were always as difficult for me—for who can find the right words for such things?—as I would like to have spoken them from my heart—for what is more beautiful than being

[6.] A Ligurian figure of speech [a language spoken in southern France, Monaco, and northern Italy that is closer to French than Italian.—CG]

[7.] [Tarragona, in the southern Catalonia region near Barcelona, produces mostly mediocre wines, both white and red. By his mention of "brownish wines," Diestel perhaps refers to the sweet, fortified Tarragonian dessert wine.—CG]

[8.] Signature supplied, since it was not actually present on the carbon copy.

[1.] *NL*, A 20,2 (1); handwritten. Previously published in *GS* 3:18 (excerpt) and *GS* 6:135–37 (complete).

[2.] Bonhoeffer participated at least six times in Harnack's seminars; see Staats, "Adolf von Harnack im Leben Bonhoeffers," 105 and n. 32.

permitted to speak without reserve about that which moves us? So, too, this year, when I am so distant from all that, such hours of gratitude often come upon me precisely at this time, and such hours should not be left unused. Here amid all my purely practical work, where as a scholar I am completely dependent on myself and my books, where I must live without any exchange of ideas in this regard, I think back to those hours in your house and to those afternoons in Grunewald with a certain sense of longing and melancholy, and often wish I could sit again for but a single hour in your seminar circle or have a conversation with you of the unforgettable kind that I remember from seminar celebrations, outings, and various other occasions. Only here have I come to realize completely what I had and what I have lost, both in a scholarly and in a human sense. But this realization is accompanied by the hope that it will not be much more than six months now, and I will have all that again, and today I am already looking forward to it.[3]

That said, the time I am spending here as an academic hermit, absorbed in so many new impressions from the practical side of life, does seem to have the potential to be quite fruitful in its own way. One gains distance from so many things with which one had become a bit obsessive, one acquires a measure of freedom from didactic doctrines and also learns to recognize much more precisely the limits of the value of pure scholarship; and in turn all that provides the point of departure from which one reexamines every-
78 thing one has worked on. Hence I believe that my time here—precisely this time spent outside Germany—has a significance that I should make the most of. I am glad to be here but will also be glad to return home, for scholarship never releases those it has seized. I have very few others to thank besides you for the fact that it has seized me.

Let me close with the warmest wishes that all is well with you, and allow me to ask that you give my regards to your illustrious wife; I remain with the most respectful regards and greetings to your Excellency, your forever grateful servant,

Dietrich Bonhoeffer

[3.] In the summer semester 1929, Bonhoeffer participated in his last Harnack seminar, which generally met on Thursday evenings. The topic can no longer be determined with certainty (contra Staats, "Adolf von Harnack im Leben Bonhoeffers," 107n32). See also the correspondence with Harnack, 1/93 and 1/95.

34. To Paula Bonhoeffer[1]

July 17

Dear Mama,

Just some brief answers today to your questions. I haven't had a suit made for myself yet because I've still been able to make do till now, but I will perhaps do so soon after all, since one can't just run around here only in a shirt and slacks; that's not considered dressed up.—The panama arrived in good shape, and I only had to wait an hour and a half and told them the hat was used. For anything registered, one has to go to the post office personally, where every package is opened. They are very strict there about chocolate, so that's something you can probably try only as a sample with no value; admittedly a great deal is stolen there. Otherwise you just have to pay duty on it.

If you have to be back on October 15, then Olbricht's travel plans[2] are really *extremely* awkward. He will return about September 25 because he still wants to celebrate his elderly father's birthday on the twenty-second. How would it be if you were to come, if you are coming at all, on about the
fifteenth and then stay ten days in Barcelona or in one of its suburbs by the 79
sea, when I, of course, will always have time, unless something special is going on, and then as soon as I am free, that is, on about the twenty-fifth, we could then travel to Majorca for two weeks. You can find French and German cuisine there, as well as Spanish. Too bad you don't want to travel by air to the south, to Granada. But I keep hearing that Majorca is one of the most beautiful places of all here. So that would be wonderful if it will not be too strenuous for you. I'm anxious to learn what you will decide.

On Sunday I'm leaving to spend four days in the Pyrenees with two married couples, just to breathe some cool air. By the way, I will not be going swimming again very soon; I am sweating today as never before after going swimming again after a long layoff. The Spaniards are by no means wrong when they don't swim very much.

I am hoping to send the Picasso[3] to Berlin with the help of my Spanish friend through one of his acquaintances. That would be the best thing.

Now I must close. I have already written a great deal today and want to go into the city for a cup of coffee and then get a little work done.

Affectionate greetings to all of you. Your

Dietrich

[1.] *NL,* A 19,1 (16); handwritten from Barcelona. Partially reproduced in *GS* 6:137.

[2.] See 1/31, p. 113.

[3.] See 1/31, pp. 112–13.

35. To Julie Bonhoeffer[1]

July 17, 1928

Dear Grandmama,

Many thanks for your lovely letter with the picture of Grandfather.[2] It arrived yesterday, on his one hundredth birthday, and several times on this
80 day I sent my thoughts your way, and I remembered so many things you yourself told me about earlier times and celebrated the day in this way with you. Even though we have already told you often how glad and grateful we are that you now live with us all the time and that we have you completely, let me tell you that again on this day.[3]

In the meantime here everything is going quite normally. I really shouldn't say much more about the heat now that I read that you yourselves have 38 degrees in the shade (though I don't really believe the newspapers here completely!). Compared to that we're polar dwellers, with our 30 degrees.[4] Moreover I must really say that with my present lifestyle the heat hardly bothers me at all; in fact it is rather pleasant even though the Spaniards are about to melt. I recently even managed to catch such a cold—I still don't know how—that I didn't think I would be able to preach the next day; that would have been unpleasant, since it was the first time I was here on my own.[5] So I quickly decided to make a pot of hot lemon tea, took some aspirin, and sweated out the entire afternoon, probably very quickly reaching the boiling point for human flesh. I was completely well the next morning and was able to preach. An unusually large number of people attended, but given the heat I think I can hardly hope that will continue. I am continuing the youth service during the week in a small circle.[6]

Recently I saw something splendid. There was a large group of cars lined up one after the other on the main street here, all pressing to get through two narrow, specially erected gates under which priests were standing and sprinkling the cars with consecrated water as they drove through; there was also a band playing marches and dances, with clowning around and yelling.—What was going on?—It was the day of the saint for cars and tires![7]

[1.] *NL*, A 19,2 (4); handwritten from Barcelona. Partially reproduced in *GS* 6:138–39.

[2.] Friedrich Bonhoeffer, born July 16, 1828, Bonhoeffer's paternal grandfather.

[3.] After 1924, Julie Bonhoeffer lived with the Bonhoeffers in Berlin; see *DB-ER*, 13.

[4.] [Centigrade 38 is 100.4 Fahrenheit; 30 centigrade is 86 Fahrenheit.—CG]

[5.] See 3/9. [Olbricht was away on vacation.—CG]

[6.] Each Wednesday, according to calendar entries (July 11, 18, 25, 1928).

[7.] Probably St. Christopher, whose feast day was actually July 25. [St. Christopher is the patron saint of travelers, and as Bonhoeffer's report illustrates, he had been adopted in modern times by motorists in particular.—CG]

I am really working intensively on my Spanish now and through my Spanish acquaintance have also met together with several others. I've also become friends with a professor here who is extremely anticlerical and theologically 81
well read but is currently a physician; we meet quite often with him and only speak Spanish then. The better I get to know Spaniards, the more sympathetic I find them. But they are completely different from what people in Germany imagine. You can live quite pleasantly with and among them; they don't quarrel, are never restive, are kind and obliging and often very intelligent despite all outward signs of a lack of education. The schooling here is quite miserable. And the nicest thing is that they put on absolutely no airs and possess a social sensitivity[8] of the sort I have never experienced.

Now I must close! Farewell, dear Grandmama. Affectionate greetings from your grateful

Dietrich

36. To Reinhold Seeberg[1]

Barcelona, July 20, 1928

Honorable Privy Councilor:

Finally things have calmed down a bit. School has been out for two weeks and many German families have gone away, so a certain calm has descended after a period of very lively activity lasting from the very first day till now. Now my thoughts turn quite instinctively away somewhat from all the new things I have experienced here and focus back on Germany. And basically there is one thing I must do without here and really do miss quite painfully—shared scholarly work. One doesn't know how truly important a seminar or some other shared scholarly work is if one has never had to rely completely on a reclusive scholarly existence. I don't mean to say that this is a completely fruitless stage, quite the contrary; one soon gets beyond much 82
of one's doctrinaire training. But in my opinion there can be no doubt that only through active contact with other ways of thought is one led to the formation and comprehension of that which is unique to oneself. Hence quite often on Friday evening at the usual, treasured hour, my thoughts wander longingly to your seminar, where I would love to take a seat once again among your audience and reflect with you on the "meaning of history."

[8.] See also 1/36, p. 120.

[1.] *NL*, A 20,1 (1); handwritten. Previously published in *GS* 6:139–43 (complete) and *GS* 3:15 (excerpt).

People have sent me many good, interesting bits of news from your seminar. Such a seminar group can indeed create waves that reach far beyond the homeland borders. I remember with gratitude the hours over the past four years that I spent with you, and often it is some small occasion that suddenly transfers me to one or the other of these seminar sessions and vividly evokes the entire session, even though I may not have thought about it for a long time. All this has become my abiding possession, which will continue to influence me as long as scholarship both delights and torments me. I am happy knowing that it will not be much more than six months before I can once more come to your seminar and doubly enjoy that which I have done without.

Despite everything, I am glad to be here. It is doubtless good to wear down one's horns at the right time, especially with regard to scholarly work, and certainly it is equally good to mix with people who are as far as possible removed from one's own circle of interests and view of life. This congregation is probably typical of parishes dominated by foreign businessmen. In general it is interesting to observe how the war and especially the period of revolution simply passed most of these people by, a fact that does not—as is generally thought today—just have its bad side. There is absolutely no nervousness or tension, no intellectual affectation or mannerism of the sort we enjoy in such abundance in Germany and which is considered so essential to good form. From the human perspective, one encounters quite admirable characteristics here: decency, honesty, simplicity, the inclination not to be anything one is not—the latter probably largely a result of Spanish influence; Spaniards laugh at no one as loudly as they do at the puffed-up
83 and the poseur. Whenever I have spoken with Spaniards about German strengths and weaknesses, they inevitably point out, in that extremely tactful manner common to them all, even down to the common people, that what we call "posing" is alien to them. I fear we have thereby forfeited a great deal abroad.

With regard to the church, the colony here, while certainly positively inclined, is not very active, so that there is little fruitful church work to do; and that's something I really regret. But after all one lives in Spain and there are enough other interesting things to see and to study. Already in April I traveled for three weeks through Spain and now have a better basis for understanding life here in Barcelona. I have made quite a few contacts here that take me into academic circles—I'm also able to practice my Spanish this way—the only problem is that, understandably, most of the people I meet are decidedly anticlerical. It is almost impossible to make contact with the clergy; although I have managed to make the acquaintance of some by chance, after doing so and after seeing the faces of these people, I really don't have any desire to get to know them better. I have never seen the sort of uncultivated clergy[2] I have encountered here. So really nothing at all would ever come of contact with them.

The more I get to know them, the more sympathetic I find the Spaniards themselves; they are completely different, in any event, from what I imagined and from the usual view of them in Germany. They are neither "proud" in our sense nor temperamental, as we imagine. I have never seen the sort of practical democracy in action that I've seen here, where you can see master and servant sitting together at the same café table, where no one yells out after you if you walk through a dark part of the city in nice clothes, where, it seems to me, there is absolutely no social resentment. None are so low that they believe they have to think even less of themselves than of others, and none—least of all the king, whom I have seen several times—think so highly of themselves that they permit themselves to look down on others. The situation manifests itself everywhere in life, in the cafés, in the railway, on the street. Naturally there are closed social circles here as well, nor is 84
that necessarily repugnant to one's social perception, but rather, quite the contrary, is welcomed. The Spaniard is not servile toward foreigners, as the Italian often is, but rather correct and often even cool. Among the Catalans, one does frequently encounter enormous unpleasantness, deriving probably from their political inclination toward France. Barcelona itself is an unusually lively metropolis caught in an economic upsurge in grand style, in which one can live quite pleasantly in every respect. Topographically the immediate surroundings and the city's own location are unusually charming. There are good concerts, good—albeit extremely old-fashioned—theater—and only one thing is missing: the scholarly exchange of ideas, which one also does not find even among Spanish academics, where one seeks it. I think the Spaniards are unusually gifted but are so indolent that they just do not educate themselves. In this calm, patience, and indolence, they doubtless manifest strong oriental characteristics, and in general one never loses the sense—in language, dance, music, often even in the most ordinary movements—of being close to the Orient.

I dare not guess whether Spain as a whole will someday wake up. But much that is unique and much that been passed down from very early times still slumbers in this people, and now and then something does indeed break through and come to life. (I am currently looking for some of the old plays, in which contests between Arabic and Christian theologians are still performed even today in small provincial towns.)

[2.] See also 1/26, p. 99.

As far as my actual theological work is concerned, as much as the ongoing heat allows (which is, by the way, not as bad as one imagines), I am making some deletions and shortening my work,[3] which I then would like to send to you at the beginning of November as agreed. I have to rewrite a great deal and delete entire sections. (By the way, in Brunner's *Mediator*,[4] which by the way rather disappointed me, I found thoughts on original sin
85 and its social meaning similar to those I developed.) At the same time my thoughts are already busy with another project, albeit again not historical but rather systematic. It picks up the question of consciousness and conscience in theology and also several Luther citations from the big Galatians commentary.[5] You also brought up the question of consciousness once in your seminar; but this will be a theological study rather than a psychological one.[6] Perhaps when I am a bit further along you'll permit me to write to you about it in a letter.

I sincerely hope you will be able to relax during the vacation period and find the calm you are seeking, and that you will continue to do as well as you have until now, and that in the spring I may find you as lively and robust at the lectern as always. I send my most devoted greetings as well as my compliments to your esteemed wife, in abiding respect and gratitude

Dietrich Bonhoeffer

37. To Karl Bonhoeffer[1]

Barcelona, July 26, 1928

Dear Papa,

Many thanks for your letter. I really am hoping to get around more to writing during the summer so I can catch up and preserve in letters what I missed in my diary.[2] For I am already beginning to forget some of the things that still interested me a couple of months ago. But even though

[3.] *Sanctorum Communio* (*DBWE* 1).

[4.] Emil Brunner, *The Mediator*.

[5.] [Luther's 1535 *Lectures on Galatians* (*WA* 40/1 and 40/2, *LW* 26 and 27) is cited in *Act and Being*; see esp. *DBWE* 2:150.—CG]

[6.] Preliminary considerations for Bonhoeffer's subsequent postdoctoral dissertation, *Act and Being: Transcendental Philosophy and Ontology in Systematic Theology* (*DBWE* 2); see also 1/40, p. 128, and the foreword to the German edition (*DBW* 2:7).

[1.] *NL*, A 19,1 (17); handwritten. Partially reproduced in *GS* 6:143–44.

[2.] The diary ends on March 10, 1928.

I don't have all that much scheduled work right now at all, my days get so filled up that I just never get around to it.

One evening recently I was with a family that is always particularly pleas- 86
ant and nice to me. The wife told me about her illness and asked whether I could ask you what might be done about it. She is about fifty years old and suffers from very bad headaches; she can hardly read, only a few minutes at a time, before her head and eyes hurt so badly she must stop. She often faints in the street, any kind of work strains her mightily, and on top of it—because she has fallen from extremely well-to-do circumstances into rather simple ones as a result of bad luck in business—she must now take care of a lot of things herself. The physician here says she has neural weakness in her head—the primary pain is at the back of her head on the right side—and is prescribing all sorts of strong medication, including strychnine (is that possible?).[3] She's now looking for some kind of medication to strengthen her nerves again and would like to know if you might be able to suggest something. I promised her I'd write to you, and she was very grateful. If you have a chance, could you write me briefly concerning this matter?

¶I have in the meantime written you about my vacation time here.[4] I really don't think Olbricht can do anything in this regard, since then the congregation here would be without a minister, and that is precisely what they wanted to avoid; nor can one really ask that he return earlier. What do you think about my last suggestion? Would that not fit very well indeed? Olbricht will probably surface at your place there during the next few days. I'm eager to know how you like him. He is also, by the way, one of those people who prefer a good glass of wine and a good cigar to a bad sermon.

I am really looking forward to August 1 and everything associated with it.[5] You'll write me right away then, won't you? People say that October is the most beautiful month here, whereas September is still rather hot; but you're already acclimated. We regularly have temperatures of 32 degrees[6] here now.

[3.] [Strychnine is a strong poison, which nevertheless was available as a pill and was used to treat many ailments in that era.—CG]

[4.] See 1/34.

[5.] His mother, Paula Bonhoeffer, wrote on July 26, 1928: "The election for rector is on August 1. Papa is afraid he won't get away. The head janitor has already told Gert he would probably be the son-in-law of the new rector" (*NL*, C 1).

[6.] [Fahrenheit 89.6 degrees.—CG]

87 I have to go to a meeting with Dr. Krebs (from the I.G.,[7] a contact made through Uncle Otto), with whom I will be traveling by car for two days. Affectionate greetings from your grateful

Dietrich

38. To Paula Bonhoeffer[1]

Barcelona, July 30

Dear Mama,

Many thanks for your letter, which I just found upon arriving back from a two-day car trip. I hope Grandmama is feeling better again now. Please say hello to her for me. The four-day tour I recently planned suddenly fell through, so this trip yesterday provided a nice substitute. I spent two very nice days with Dr. Krebs from the I.G. and a friend who is a teacher at the school. We drove to the foothills of the Pyrenees and then turned down the coast and drove all day today along the rocky coast, which plunges straight down into the water. We returned rather tired, sunburned, and dusty despite swimming in the sea several times. During the trip the other two enthusiastically praised Majorca, saying it was the most beautiful part of all Spain and that one absolutely should go there. Well, we'll soon see if anything comes of it.

It has been unbelievably hot here for four days now; for several nights the temperature has not dropped below 30 degrees,[2] and what wears you out more than anything is when the nights don't cool things off and you sleep so poorly. So I have decided to have a very light summer suit made after all. I made some inquiries; something like that costs 200 pesetas here = 140 marks. There are no linen suits at all, so no one wears them. Now, as
88 you know, during the past two months I have withdrawn 250 pesetas and still have 250 in my account. Also, the money Olbricht advanced me I have already used for all sorts of things—though the boardinghouse has been paid up till February 15. I still needed patent leather shoes, since despite the *best!* care my old ones wore out—my landlady can confirm this!—a couple of ties and socks, athletic socks, ca. 50 pesetas for a three-day mountain tour four weeks ago,—so that, in a word—I will be broke rather soon if I go ahead and have this suit made. One also has more secondary expenses

[7.] The I. G. Farben Company.

[1.] *NL*, A 19,1 (18); handwritten. Partially reproduced in *GS* 6:144.

[2.] [Fahrenheit 86 degrees.—CG]

during the summer now, fruit, drinks, for even the shortest route on the city bus, etc., so that despite holding on to my money it really does just run through my fingers. A couple of birthday presents also did some damage.

So at the moment that is my most pressing concern. Otherwise I am doing extremely well, as always; I'm just very lazy. I am preparing a lecture series for the winter,[3] which I intend to deliver in the church. Attendance at church is still remarkably good—at least that's what people are saying.

Say hello to everyone at home. Affectionate greetings from your

Dietrich

39. To His Parents[1]

Barcelona, August 2, 1928

My dear Parents,

Many thanks for your telegram,[2] which really did bring me very surprising and wonderful news. I had no longer believed that it would come about. But now I am anxious to hear how you nonetheless arranged it, dear Papa, that, as you write, you don't have to toil away.[3]

Now I'm very busy making plans and finding out how I can show you Spain from its best side. The time you will be here—everyone confirms 89
this—is supposed to be quite splendid when the weather is normal. A gentleman acquaintance who has known Majorca for years has written up and described the most beautiful tours for me. But perhaps now that you have more time, you will decide to travel to Granada after all; along the way we could then see Madrid and especially *Toledo,* and you would certainly enjoy that very much. Moreover, I already know my way around there and could do a better job of showing you everything. But Majorca, too, is certainly very beautiful. From here we really should also travel to Montserrat if you like and perhaps also travel a stretch toward the Pyrenees; and then further south. I'm also now considering all the possibilities regarding hotels here. There are the international hotels, Ritz, Majestic, Colon, all of which are supposedly quite good—and the second also *quiet*—but also rather expensive: thirty-five pesetas, that's about twenty-five marks; then there are small

[3.] First reference to the congregational lectures; see 2/1–2/3.

[1.] *NL,* A 19,1 (19); handwritten. Partially reproduced in *GS* 6:144–45.

[2.] Not extant.

[3.] See 1/37, p. 123, ed. note 5. Wilhelm His, professor of internal medicine, was elected rector for 1928/29.

boardinghouses that have good reputations, though I don't know how the beds and food are. Even though it's not customary here and also not very practical because of the effort it takes, one could also eat outside the boardinghouse. One can get along almost everywhere here with French and get a long way with German in the better hotels. But if you do come, it's probably best that I travel to Port Bou and pick you up, since they're so stupid there that not a single customs official speaks French.

I have office hours. So I'll close now. I am really looking forward to your coming and to your next letter, in which you can tell me about your plans. Warm greetings to Grandmama and Sabine, whom I would like to thank very much for her letter.

Affectionate greetings. Your grateful
Dietrich

90 **40. To Helmut Rößler**[1]

Barcelona, August 7, 1928

Dear Rößler,[2]

Well—many thanks for your letter,[3] which gave me genuine joy and calmed me down a bit. Though I was less afraid regarding our closeness than that something might have happened to you—well, thank God that's not the case, and everything is cleared up. Six months—and that's how long it has been since we saw each other!—is a long time to try to cover even marginally the most important things in a letter. From my first letter[4] you know a little bit about my area of work. It certainly is a peculiar experience to see work and life genuinely converge—a synthesis that we all sought but rarely found in our student days—when one really lives *one* life rather than two, or better: half a life; it lends dignity to the work and objectivity to the worker, and a recognition of one's own limitations of the sort acquired only within concrete life.

[1.] *NL*, A 20,4 (1); copy from *Dietrich Bonhoeffer: Einführung in seine Botschaft*, 58–59; with handwritten corrections by Bethge according to the original; the original has disappeared. Previously published in *GS* 1:51–53.

[2.] Helmut Rößler and Bonhoeffer had known each other since 1926; he is mentioned in a March 22, 1927, letter from Bonhoeffer to his parents (*DBWE* 9:169). In the meantime Rößler had become a country pastor in Prignitz; see also the letter from Rößler to Bonhoeffer, 1/164.

[3.] Not extant.

[4.] Not extant.

I'm getting to know new people each day, at least their life stories. Sometimes one can also peer through their portrayals to the person—and in the process one thing is always striking: one encounters people here the way they are, far from the masquerade of the "Christian world"; people with passions, criminal types, small people with small goals, small drives, and small crimes—all in all, people who feel homeless in both senses, people who thaw a bit when you speak to them in a friendly manner—real people. I can only say I have the impression that precisely these people stand more under grace than under wrath, but that it is precisely the Christian world
that stands more under wrath than under grace. "I am sought out by those 91
who did not ask; . . . to those who did not call on my name I said, 'Here I am'" (Isa. 65:1).[5]

During the summer now, when I am here alone for three months, I'm preaching every two weeks. And I'm having the same experience as you. I don't know where to begin with the precious half hour one has. I am preaching much differently from what I would have thought possible of myself. The texts will give you an approximate idea: Rom. 11:6; 1 Cor. 15:14–17; Matt. 28:20; 1 Thess. 5:17; Luke 12:49; Matt. 7:1; Ps. 62:2; 1 Cor. 12:26f.; Matt. 5:8;[6] and I am grateful that I can *see* some success; it is a mixture of personal joy, let's say self-awareness, and objective gratitude—but that, of course, is the judgment of all religion, this mixture of the personal and the objective, which one can perhaps ennoble but cannot fundamentally eliminate, a mixture under which one suffers doubly as a theologian—but on the other hand, who wouldn't be pleased about a full church, or that people are coming who haven't come for years? And on the other hand, who analyzes this joy to determine whether it is completely untainted?

I have long thought that sermons had a center that, if you hit it, would move anyone or confront them with a decision. I no longer believe that. First of all, a sermon can never grasp the center, but can only itself *be grasped* by it, by Christ. And then Christ becomes flesh as much in the word of the pietists as in that of the clerics[7] or of the religious socialists, and these

[5.] [Bonhoeffer's citation varies slightly from the text of his edition of the Luther Bible. NRSV: "I was ready to be sought out by those who did not ask, to be found by those who did not seek me. I said, 'Here I am, here I am,' to a nation that did not call on my name."—CG]

[6.] See the sermons 3/2–3/9; the sermon on 1 Thess. 5:17 has not been preserved.

[7.] [By the distinction of "pietists" and "clerics" (literally, *Kirchlichen*, or "churchly clergy") Bonhoeffer appears to be alluding to Max Weber's church-sect typology.—CG]

empirical connections actually pose difficulties for preaching that are absolute, not merely relative. At the most profound level, people are simply not all one, but are individuals, totally different people, people "united" only by the word in the *church.* I have noticed that the most effective sermons have been those in which I have spoken about the gospel in an enticing manner, the way one tells children a fairy tale about a strange land. The basic, abiding difficulty is that one is supposed to be providing milk and yet does not know what that really means, and whether one is mistakenly providing sugar water instead. It would be very helpful if someone would
92 give me an exegesis of 1 Cor. 3:2,[8] as well as for the "problem of the child in theology"—(on which I intend to work in connection with the problem of consciousness)[9]—and thus for the children's service.

On Sunday I will be preaching on Matt. 5:8,[10] and I have never approached a sermon with such trepidation. But I am looking forward to Sunday. What else should I report to you? You already know that I took a beautiful trip through Spain with my brother Klaus; perhaps I can tell you about it in more detail sometime. In September my parents will be coming to visit, and I'm very much looking forward to that. I'll tell you about the Spaniards as people another time. I'll close for today; this letter is only intended as a small sign of my great pleasure in hearing that everything is fine with you and to close the gap that opened up.

I am looking forward to any further news from you, and with cordial greetings I remain,

Yours truly, Dietrich Bonhoeffer

P.S. I am not a little astonished at Kehnscherper's decision.[11] What prompted the man to leave Germany for so long?

[8.] ["I fed you with milk, not solid food, for you were not yet ready for solid food. Even now you are still not ready."—CG]

[9.] See 1/36, p. 122; see also *Act and Being* (*DBW* 2:8). Concerning the preceding homiletical reflections, see also 2/5.

[10.] On August 12, 1928; see 3/9.

[11.] After attaining his doctorate, Gerhard Kehnscherper was sent to Rio de Janeiro as pastor of the German congregation there, at the personal wish of general superintendent Otto Dibelius.

41. To Ursula and Rüdiger Schleicher[1]

Barcelona, August 10, 1928

Dear Ursel, dear Rüdiger,

Your letter,[2] dear Rüdiger, contains almost as an aside a sentence that seems to me probably to be the main point, namely, that I am to be the godparent to your little Dorothea.[3] In so doing you make me enormously 93
happy, and I thank you both for thinking of me so kindly. What a shame that I can't now be there for the baptism of your third, who is to have such a special connection with me. I look forward to the time when I can actually put into practice my role as godparent, once Dorothea is older; for I must say I have a very pleasant image of what it means to be a godparent and a godchild; and since you know how much I like being around children anyway, you can imagine the twofold joy I will have from my "own" godchild, a child toward whom one has not only certain obligations but also a few modest rights. So, many thanks; rest assured that on the day of baptism I will certainly be with you and with my youngest little goddaughter in my most heartfelt thoughts. You will have a wonderful summer celebration at the baptism, with the Dohnanyis and our parents, a celebration some of whose joy and luster will, I hope, also pass over to your Dorothea forever. And without immediately falling upon your now completely pastoral brother, you must accept it when I tell you that on the day of baptism I will have some very special wishes and hopes for Dorothea, and I also believe we are basically of one mind on that count.

But now you must send me a picture of the little one very soon, so that I have an approximate idea of what awaits me in six months. You'll have to give me a bit of time to think about what I as godparent should give her. This has taken me too much by surprise. I hope you are having beautiful summer days up there in Friedrichsbrunn[4] and are sheltered from all the heat that is gradually starting to plague us; then, dear Ursel, I hope you recover very quickly and that all of you will return to Berlin healthy and

[1.] *NL*, A 19,2 (14); handwritten. Partially reproduced in *GS* 6:145.

[2.] Not extant.

[3.] Dorothee Schleicher, born May 4, 1928.

[4.] See 1/44, p. 134, ed. note 2.

ready to move on to new activities. I hope you are all doing as well as I am. All good wishes to you and to my Dorothea.

Goodbye for now. Affectionate greetings from your grateful

Dietrich

Special thanks to you, dear Rüdiger, for your letter. I will write again soon!

94 **42. To His Parents**[1]

Barcelona, August 14, 1928

My dear Parents,

Many thanks to you both for your letters. And especially to you, dear Papa, for the information for the sick lady I know;[2] she was elated when I told her you might want to visit her when you are here. She says she also often saw Ziehen before the war.[3]

There is a Mr. Alvarez de la Campa[4] at the same place he indicated, as I learned from the telephone book. I have not yet been able to find out anything else about the man because a German acquaintance from the free port is away at the moment, and others I asked didn't know him. Should I telephone him and say you are coming, or do you want to write?

It is wonderful that your trip really is going to happen. I inquired again about lodging; there are, of course, cheaper hotels, but they're all in noisy locations—and in Spain, that's horrible, since the noise goes on the entire night—moreover, I believe you would find only the beds in the European hotels tolerable; also, one has to eat Spanish cuisine in the small hotels, and you would probably find it troublesome to eat both lunch and dinner somewhere else, which also raises the question as to whether one can't travel much more cheaply in general, since the individual meals in the hotels serving European cuisine are disproportionately higher than the entire cost of a boardinghouse. I think you will *on no account*, even at a midrange inn, get away with 25 pesetas per day, and probably need even more (and the Ingleterra costs 35 pesetas), since 8 pesetas at night, 8 at noon, and 10 in the evening is the usual price here in Barcelona. Here it's outrageously more
95 expensive to eat out than in other big cities. I will look around for furnished

[1.] *NL*, A 19,1 (20); handwritten. Partially reproduced in *GS* 6:145–47.

[2.] See 1/37, p. 123.

[3.] Until 1917 Theodor Ziehen was a psychiatrist in Berlin and a colleague of Karl Bonhoeffer.

[4.] Not otherwise identified.

rooms, though I'm not very confident. In my own boardinghouse the other two rooms are occupied, and I wouldn't wish you even a single night in these beds. But perhaps something will turn up by then.

If you come on the eighteenth/nineteenth, I still have to preach on the twenty-second,[5] and we could then probably depart as soon as the twenty-fourth. The sea is still supposed to be calm at this time of year, assuming things are normal, although this year both the rain we had during the spring and the current heat are supposedly completely abnormal. It's possible that the Pyrenees are already rather cool, but there's still time. At the moment I just can't imagine myself in a situation where I would be freezing. After a few days of listlessness when all I did was sleep a lot, I now feel completely healthy again and really think few people are bearing the heat as well as I. Today for lunch I had lentils and roast pork, earlier a pancake, and mastered it all with no ill effects.

You asked what I intend to do after you leave. I think I'll stay here, since, first of all, I don't yet really have any fixed vacation, and second, by then there will again be much to do.

I want to try to introduce religious instruction at the school, am also preparing a series of lectures for the winter that I'd like to deliver in the church and these would begin in October, have to begin the Christmas play with the children,[6] and would like to get a bit done on a new project.[7] So the final four months will fly by. At the end of my time here, though, I would still like to travel a bit.

At the moment I am spending a great deal of time reworking or deleting portions of my doctoral dissertation, an extremely boring and time-consuming but necessary task.

The number of people attending services is still growing, and that pleases
me; last Sunday I had the "fantastic" number of forty people, more than 96
ever before during the summer months. But it's outrageous that one has to be satisfied with so few in a colony of six thousand Germans and a parish of over three hundred. The only advantage is that at least one is acquainted with those few people.

Now I must close! Thank you for increasing the letter of credit.[8] My suit turned out quite nicely indeed. Now my boardinghouse comrade has pumped me for seventy-five pesetas, which I gave him.

[5.] Bonhoeffer is actually referring to September 23, 1928; see 3/12.

[6.] See 1/63, pp. 161–62.

[7.] See 1/36, p. 122, and 1/40, p. 128.

[8.] See 1/19, p. 84, ed. note 6, and 1/38, pp. 124–25.

And something I wanted to mention for a long time now. Dear Papa, could you perhaps send me a copy of your book on vagrancy?[9] Given my current work with such people, I would very much like to read it.

Wishing you all a wonderful baptismal celebration in the Harz Mountains. Affectionate greetings from your grateful

Dietrich

43. To Julie Bonhoeffer[1]

Barcelona, August 17, 1928

Dear Grandmama,

Hearty congratulations on your eighty-seventh birthday. I am sure that you will celebrate it in as lively a fashion as you celebrated it in Berlin during the past few years, and I hope for you and for all of us that it will continue that way throughout the year. Today I reflect gratefully on the time you have been with us. A house in which a grandmother lives has a special bond and a special stability. It is a piece of the earlier, past time that reaches into the present and in its own quiet way provides direction and support, and not
97 only that, but especially connects the old with the young through concern and love. Where there is a grandmother, there is an ear for everyone, a place of true peace, and a word of advice for each individual; there one acquires a living understanding of the meaning of tradition and sees that everything is an ongoing continuum, and that even what seems to be most new derives a large part of its energy from the past. Will Uncle Otto[2] celebrate with you? If so, then please do give him my warmest greetings; I intend to write him again soon. My parents and Klaus have probably also returned from the baptism. Only one person will be absent who truly belongs there, Aunt Helene Schöne.[3] I think we will really miss her at our family gatherings. Over the years a really close bond had developed.

Now half a year has passed, a long time, and yet, when I look back, it has flown by; and the next half year will go even faster, for there is still much to do before Christmas, and afterward I already have to begin thinking about my departure. We can tell that winter is approaching because for

[9.] Karl Bonhoeffer, *Ein Beitrag zur Kenntnis des großstädtischen Bettel- und Vagabundentums.*

[1.] *NL,* A 19,2 (5); handwritten. Partially reproduced in *GS* 6:147.

[2.] Otto Bonhoeffer.

[3.] Helene Schöne had died in June 1928; see 1/29, p. 109.

three days now the heat has fallen from 30 degrees and higher back down to 25 degrees,[4] and many people are already getting out their woolen blankets at night. Everyone is breathing a sigh of relief and feels pleasantly refreshed—at the same temperature that at home means taking the rest of the day off because of the heat! How I will freeze in Berlin.

Otherwise everything is going along normally. I am getting around more to my work, which is also quite necessary, learning more Spanish. I notice again and again how much easier Italian was for me than Spanish. First, I find the Spanish pronunciation difficult, and second, I believe that back then my memory for languages was more receptive. Of course, now I have relatively few opportunities to speak Spanish; rarely do Spaniards come to my office and my language partner[5] doesn't have much time at the moment. In any event, though, my proficiency is still very inadequate; I still make a great many mistakes or suddenly forget even the most common words. Maybe it is the heat. In any event, I don't think it's true that Spanish, 98
as some claim, is an easy language. It takes years to speak it really well. I am reading a lot of Spanish novels—peculiarly, the best are anticlerical; there are some excellent ones. It's time to close again; I have to visit an extremely sick, old, devout woman. One often learns a great deal from the sick.

Be well, dear Grandmama; stay healthy during the coming year and have a wonderful day of celebration.

With all good wishes and affectionate greetings, your grateful
Dietrich

44. To His Parents[1]

the 24th, evening

Dear Mama, dear Papa,

It was just so nice to hear you so directly again. I would have preferred to talk another half hour; for gradually one would have got used to it or it would probably have got better. The dumbest thing was that the Spanish operator constantly broke in to ask whether I was already speaking, whereas I wanted to hear what you were saying. At the beginning it was so soft that

[4.] [Fahrenheit 86 degrees and 77 degrees, respectively.—CG]
[5.] Luis Sánchez Sarto; see 1/29, p. 108, ed. note 6.

[1.] *NL*, A 19,1 (21); handwritten from Barcelona; definitely August 1928. Partially reproduced in *GS* 6:148.

I really thought we would have to break it off. Then gradually I heard your voice, dear Mama, and recognized it again, and that is just incredible to be able to hear you two speaking over a distance of 1,500 km. You asked whether it is still hot here, and I hope you understood me correctly when I said it has become much cooler and better. Then I also understood that you would be in Port Bou on the nineteenth (or on the thirteenth?). That is really wonderful, and I'm already getting advice from the whole German colony about all the things we should do. Then suddenly there was a pause,
99 and I heard nothing at all, then Susi, whom I could understand fairly well because of her high voice. At first I thought I understood that Papa was not there; but then you were suddenly on the line, dear Papa, and I was really very glad. Suddenly the transmission was also better, and I understood quite well; then, surprisingly, Christel and Klaus got on, both of whom I thought were in Friedrichsbrunn.[2] Well, I had made myself a whole list of things I wanted to ask and tell in those six minutes I had; I was hoping to speak with you again, dear Mama, because we had spoken only briefly, but then the French and Spanish operator came on and said I had to conclude soon. I don't know whether I said good-bye to you, dear Papa, or to Klaus. Then this wonderful thing was over, and suddenly I was transported from the home in Grunewald back to the main telegraph office here, where they immediately put a bill in front of me about which I vehemently protested—since they had earlier given me different information—but in the end had to pay after all. (Even so, it isn't really that expensive, 14 marks for the call.) But it was just so nice, a bit too short, and just as over the past few days I have so looked forward to these minutes, now I will savor the subsequent joy for quite a while. It was too bad I didn't speak with Grandmama, but we would hardly have understood each other. The connection only lasted three-quarters of an hour; I began at 9:00, since after that one only pays half price. Perhaps one can understand more clearly during the day. I myself have no telephone and can be reached during the morning for urgent cases only indirectly through the German school (Escuola Alemana),[3] i.e., through a reservation. But it is nonetheless very nice indeed that we can speak with one another during the course of a half hour. Maybe next time it will be clearer.

[2.] The original German is a shorthand reference to Friedrichsbrunn, the Bonhoeffer family's vacation home in the Harz Mountains; see *DBWE* 9 (1/12), p. 30 et passim, and *DB-ER*, 24.

[3.] [The correct spelling is Escuela.—CG]

Well, I still wanted to tell you all kinds of things, but it is already 1:00—I had an appointment in the city. I think I have found very suitable lodgings for you for ca. twenty pesetas, and if it's not quiet enough we can always look further. Would you rather eat in the hotel (the boardinghouse), or would you prefer we went wherever we wanted? Perhaps the latter would be better for the short time you are here—if it's not too much trouble for you. Then something else: Do we want to go to Madrid right at the beginning, stay there, see Toledo, Avila, and Salamanca, and then travel on to San Sebastian? The reason for this suggestion is that I've been told that the place (Palma) with the best hotels on Majorca is relatively boring; I need to find out whether other locales (Soller) have good hotels; but I think they probably do. I will write later in greater detail about that. I am doing extremely well with these cool temperatures, that is, it is still 26 degrees,[4] but on the whole the summer is over; it rained the day before yesterday, and now the ground has cooled off as have the houses. At night I am once again sleeping under woolen blankets.

Professionally things are still going along as usual. Not quite as many vagrants; dear Papa, can you really not send me your book on vagrancy?[5] On Sunday I have church. Gradually many of the people are coming who otherwise never attended but whom I have visited now and then. And the time after next, you will yourselves be in the church! I am looking forward to showing you everything here.

I purchased a fan for Suse that I hope she'll like; my Spanish ladies were carried away, insisting it was really gusto español.[6] All their acquaintances had to see it. I've been advised, though, not to send it by mail, but rather to give it to you to take back, so Suse will have to be patient a bit. Please say hello to her for me. And now I must close. Regards to [. . .].[7] Be well! In a month, you'll be here!

I am really looking forward to it. Your grateful

Dietrich

[4.] [Fahrenheit 78.8 degrees.—CG]

[5.] See 1/42, p. 132.

[6.] [In good Spanish taste.—CG]

[7.] Illegible.

17:81 **44a. To Walter Dreß**[1]

Barcelona, September 1, [19]28

Dear Walter,

Well, another month has gone by. Time flies. Because I am preaching every fourteen days and then working on my own materials for eight days, the rest on the sermon, the time is just moving by at an incredible pace.[2] Thank you for the last postcard. Did I answer your letter about Brunner?[3] I don't really remember. When you wrote you seemed pretty impressed by the book;[4] I read up to about the last sixty pages, where I gave up because I didn't expect much more after finding the entire book extremely disap-
17:82 pointing. Most of what he says is correct; that much is true; but my impression is that he simply "dashed the book off" without any kind of polishing or revising; the whole thing would fit in a volume of fifty to one hundred pages, and in my opinion even then it does not contain much that is new. My impression is that the man is in a rut.[5] What pleased you about it? I keep asking myself that and must confess I still don't understand. (For example, his treatment of faith's connection to history [Historie] lacks all foundation. A lot of words and no results.) Why can't one just concede here that faith depends on historical events and that is all part of the "form of a servant,"[6] the risk? By the way, upon closer examination I do find *Zeit und Ewigkeit*[7] not bad at all. At least it's worth reading. I don't get around to reading much just now, since I'm spending so much time at the moment learning Spanish. Last Monday I had to conduct a baptism in Spanish, of course according to the formula.[8] I am around Spaniards quite a bit and hear a lot of interesting things from them. Today I encountered a completely unique case in my pastoral counseling, which I'd like to recount to you briefly and which despite its simplicity really made me think. At 11:00

[1.] Literary estate of Walter Dreß; handwritten letter, from Barcelona. Previously published in Staats and Wünsche, "Dietrich Bonhoeffers Abschied," 195–96.

[2.] From July to October 1928 Pastor Olbricht was on home leave in Germany.

[3.] Not extant.

[4.] The reference is to Brunner, *Mediator,* first published in German in 1927.

[5.] A similar assessment and critique of Brunner is found in the letter to Reinhold Seeberg of July 20, 1928, 1/36, p. 122. Cf. also the letter to Paul Lehmann of May 30, 1932, *DBW* 17 (11/1/59a), p. 107.

[6.] [See Phil. 2:7 and, in Bonhoeffer's 1933 Christology lectures, the discussion of the humiliation of Christ, e.g., *Christ the Center,* 45.—CG]

[7.] Schmidt, *Zeit und Ewigkeit.*

[8.] This is the only reference to an official pastoral act [i.e., performing a marriage, baptism, or funeral—CG] during this period of Bonhoeffer's work as vicar abroad.

a.m. there was a knock at my door and a ten-year-old boy[9] came into my room with something I had requested from his parents. I noticed that something was amiss with the boy, who is usually cheerfulness personified. And soon it came out: he broke down in tears, completely beside himself, and I could hear only the words: "Mister Wolf is dead," and then he cried and cried. "But who is Mister Wolf?" As it turns out, it is a young German shepherd dog that was sick for eight days and had just died a half-hour ago. So the boy, inconsolable, sat down on my knee and could hardly regain his composure; he told me how the dog died and how everything is lost now.
He played only with the dog, each morning the dog came to the boy's bed 17:83
and awakened him—and now the dog was dead. What could I say? So he talked to me about it for quite a while. Then suddenly his wrenching crying became very quiet and he said: "But I know he's not dead at all." "What do you mean?" "His spirit is now in heaven, where it is happy. Once in class a boy asked the religion teacher what heaven was like, and she said she had not been there yet; but tell me now, will I see 'Mister Wolf' again? He's certainly in heaven." So there I stood and was supposed to answer him yes or no. If I said "no, we don't know" that would have meant "no." So here was someone who wanted to find out, and that is always unfortunate. So I quickly made up my mind and said to him: Look, God created human beings and also animals, and I'm sure he also loves animals. And I believe that with God it is such that all who loved each other on earth—genuinely loved each other—will remain together with God, for to love is part of God. Just how that happens, though, we admittedly don't know.[10] You should have seen the happy face on this boy; he had completely stopped crying. "So then I'll see Mister Wolf again when I am dead; then we can play together again"—in a word, he was ecstatic. I repeated to him a couple of times that we don't really know how this happens. He, however, *knew,* and knew it quite definitely in thought. After a few minutes, he said: Today I really scolded Adam and Eve; if they had not eaten the apple, Mister Wolf would not have died. This whole affair was as important to the young boy as things are for one of us when something really bad happens. But I am almost surprised—moved, by the naïveté of the piety that awakens at such a moment in an otherwise completely wild young boy who is thinking of nothing. And there I stood—I who was supposed to "know the answer"—feeling quite small next to him; and I cannot forget the confident expression he had on his face

[9.] Karl-Heinz Köttgen, who is mentioned several times in the letters of 1928–30.

[10.] Concerning these matters, see the first sentences in the address in the children's service on Remembrance Sunday, November 24, 1929; see 3/20.

when he left. One of those cases of "laughter amid tears," and doubtless a case of the sort that will not recur very frequently.[11]

17:84 ¶Otherwise I'm doing fine. I'm looking forward to my parents' visit.[12] How is your work going? Seeberg's successor? I'm hoping it will drag on a bit so that I can still snap up the assistant's position.[13] But now I must close. Write again soon. Did Suse get [the] birthday letter? Greetings to your family. And to Suse. If you see Stolzenburg,[14] please say hello! Also Mr. Nebe[15] and whoever else you may see. By the way, this letter, too, is specifically for you rather than to be read aloud at home; just pass the news on to the others with the necessary omissions, that is, things I would not have written home. Take care, and my very best regards to you. Yours,

Dietrich

101 **45. To His Parents**[1]

September 6, 1928

My dear Parents,

So, now things are really getting serious—if you already have the ticket to Barcelona in your pocket. Many thanks for your last letter, dear Papa. I leave on the evening of the eighteenth for Port Bou and will be waiting for you on the nineteenth at 9:15 a.m. at the train station—unless there's something unexpected here, which certainly won't happen—then we have to rush to customs, for the other train leaves at 9:40 and won't wait, as I've been told. We would then be at home here at 12:55. For the time being I have reserved a room for you at the *Bristol* Hotel, initially without meals, for ten pesetas per person a day (the bath is included, which is quite pleasant for here). If you don't like it, then we can find something else. They speak German,

---

[11.] [For Bonhoeffer's comment on preaching about eschatological questions, see *DBW* 14 (3/1), p. 325, ed. note 24.—CG]

[12.] Bonhoeffer's parents visited him in Barcelona from September 19 to October 8, 1928.

[13.] On October 10, 1928, Bonhoeffer inquired of Seeberg about this assistantship and asked him to "put in a good word for me" (see 1/47, p. 143); Seeberg agreed to do so (see his letter of October 19, 1928, 1/49, p. 145).

[14.] Arnold Stolzenburg occupied the position that Bonhoeffer was eyeing and then obtained in 1931; see his earlier reference to Stolzenburg in the postcard of October 12, 1926 (*DBWE* 9 [1/99a], p. 166), as well as Seeberg's letter of October 19, 1928 (1/49, p. 145).

[15.] Not otherwise identified.

[1.] *NL*, A 19,1 (22); handwritten from Barcelona. Partially reproduced in *GS* 6:148.

French, English. We can then eat either somewhere else, which will probably often be the case, Montserrat, Tibidabo, Monjuich[2] and [. . .][3] or in the hotel itself, where even the waiters supposedly know German.

Well, I'm anxious to know what kind of plans you have for afterward, whether you still want to see a bit of the country or not. Madrid, Toledo especially would be very nice indeed; or whether you will decide here to go to Granada after all, or would prefer to have complete peace and quiet in Majorca. By the way, there are good hotels in places other than Palma as well, even *very* good ones by local standards, as I am told. But all that will also depend on how the trip down here agreed with you. So, unless I hear something different, let's leave it for the nineteenth at 9:15 in Port Bou.

I am really looking forward to seeing you again,

Your grateful Dietrich

My pen is broken, hence the horrible handwriting!

45a. To Walter Dreß[1] 17:84

Barcelona, September 15 [1928]

Dear Walter,

Just a quick greeting and a question I'd like you to answer as soon as possible. A question I always found theologically unambiguous but which I now find can be quite difficult from the pastoral perspective. Can one refer to sin as God's will with regard to human beings and in this way reassure people about themselves and have them look to Christ alone? Last Sunday I preached on 2 Cor. 12:9[2] and related this element of "being sufficient"

[2.] ["Mountain of the Jews" in Catalan, a hill overlooking Barcelona from the west, site of extensive Jewish properties and a cemetery in the Middle Ages, and an ancient fortress.—CG]

[3.] Illegible.

[1.] Literary estate of Walter Dreß; handwritten letter; postmarked year cannot be deciphered, but certainly from 1928; return address: "Bonhoeffer, Barcelona, S.G., C[alle], S. Eusebio 59"; addressed to "Dr. Walter Dreß, Berlin-Lichterfelde, Zehlendorferstr. 12," forwarded to "Friedrichsbrunn, Ostharz, Post [Office] Suderode, Haus Bonhoeffer." Previously published in Staats and Wünsche, "Dietrich Bonhoeffers Abschied," 197–98.

[2.] See 3/11. [In the sermon of September 9, 1928 (3/11), Bonhoeffer's text differs from the NRSV preferred reading: "And he said to me, '"Let my grace be sufficient for you, for my power is made perfect in weakness.' So, I will boast all the more gladly of my weaknesses, so that the power of Christ may dwell in me."—CG]

17:85 not only to human misfortune, but also especially to sin. "Though I at first feel nothing of your power,"[3] namely, with regard to the remission of sins. I myself found the idea quite reassuring when I came upon it while preparing the sermon; do you think it is too "reassuring"? Is not Luther's *pecca fortiter*[4] saying the same thing? I can well imagine that, without this notion, people could be completely ruined and despair of themselves, which means that they would also despair of God, who does nothing.[5] Is the gospel then only for those outwardly "weak" and not rather for those who are weak in will? Is strength of will a path to sinlessness? "Whoever abides in Christ sins no more,"[6] are we not to take this seriously? Such that one no longer looks at one's sin but only to Christ, that one's conscience is not the voice of God, but of the Tempter, who is only trying to divert our attention to the past, instead of to the present and the future. As un-Barthian as these ideas are, I still find them quite redeeming and liberating. As a student of Holl, your impulse is probably to shatter them soundly as being excessively eudaemonistic. Indeed, but does not God also think "eudaemonistically" in this sense for us? Write me soon what you think about this as a pastoral matter, and its great importance compared to academic theology. How are you? I hope you spent some enjoyable days in the Harz Mountains. My parents are arriving on Wednesday.[7] How is Susi doing? Why does she not write at all? Affectionate greetings to her, and to your family.

Yours,
Dietrich

[3.] Beginning of the third verse of the 1862 hymn by Julie von Hausmann, "So nimm denn meine Hände," *EKG*, no. 376. [See *Lutheran Book of Worship,* no. 333, "Lord, take my hand and lead me," which apparently omits the verse Bonhoeffer cites.—CG] See also the sermon on 1 Thess. 5:16–18, 3/22, p. 578.

[4.] "Esto peccator et pecca fortiter, sed fortius fide et gaude in Christo" (Be a sinner and sin boldly, but believe and rejoice in Christ even more boldly), *WA.Br* 2:372; *LW* 48:252.

[5.] [See the sermon, 3/11, esp. pp. 523–25, where Bonhoeffer preaches that God's word of grace is sufficient in every situation, even though sin and suffering remain in human experience.—CG]

[6.] Cf. 1 John 3:6: "No one who abides in him sins."

[7.] Paula and Karl Bonhoeffer arrived on September 19 and remained until October 8, 1928.

45b. To Walter Dreß[1] 17:86

Dear Walter,

This fortress is still standing today just as the picture shows it. The days here are enchantingly beautiful, and the nights no less so with the full moon, which makes the ancient walls and towers seem even more gigantic and otherworldly.[2]—Many thanks for your letter.[3] Just two requests: Please have sent to me *immediately*—for a lecture I will be giving in the church—my copy of *Duhm: Profeten* as *un*registered printed matter;[4] and then please write in more detail concerning the prerequisites for the second examination so far as they concern me. More about both later. Sorry for the trouble, many thanks and affectionate greetings.

Yours,
Dietrich

46. To His Parents[1] 102

My dear Parents,

The journey went by well; I soon met some acquaintances from Barcelona on the train. I hope things went well for you on the train and that you now have just as good weather in Glotterbad as before

[1.] Literary estate of Walter Dreß; handwritten picture postcard from Carcassonne, with a picture of the fortress; addressed to "Dr. W. Dreß, Berlin-Lichterfelde, Zehlendorferstr. 12, Allemagne"; postmark illegible, dated according to the calendar (*NL*, A 18,2): October 2, 1928. Previously published in Staats and Wünsche, "Dietrich Bonhoeffers Abschied," 198.

[2.] Uncertain reading.

[3.] Not extant.

[4.] For his first congregational lecture in Barcelona on November 13, 1928, "The Tragedy of the Prophetic and Its Lasting Meaning" (2/1), Bonhoeffer drew heavily from the requested book by Bernhard Duhm, *Israels Propheten*. [The title is misspelled in the letter.—CG] On October 11, 1928, Bonhoeffer reminded his parents again of this request (see 1/48).

[1.] *NL*, A 19,1 (43); handwritten from Spain; probable date: October 8, 1928. Previously published in *GS* 6:171. In *NL* and *GS* incorrectly dated April 1930; Bonhoeffer traveled through southern France with his parents October 1–7, 1928 (see *DB-ER*, 103), left them in Avignon on October 7, 1928, and traveled back to Barcelona the next day, while his parents went on to Glotterbad in the Black Forest, where this postcard is addressed.

I am in a tobacco store here, and they want to shut the shop. So I need to close. More soon!

In haste. Your grateful
Dietrich

47. To Reinhold Seeberg[1]

Barcelona, October 10, 1928

Dear Privy Councilor Seeberg:[2]

Before the winter semester begins, allow me to express my best wishes to you for the new half year of work, in the hope that you are able to look back on a restorative and quiet time. This semester will bring me the great joy of being able to participate again at least in the final seminar sessions and thus to celebrate a reunion with the academic realm, which I have done without now for a rather long time.

As far as the revision of my dissertation[3] is concerned, I am basically finished. I was not able to shorten or delete as much as I had hoped, but in any event a fourth or fifth of it has been removed. I recently read an
103 announcement of a book by Althaus that is to appear this coming autumn with the title: *communio sanctorum.*[4] Would you advise me to wait until that book appears, or to go ahead and publish my work independently of that? The answer to this question naturally depends as well on when such publication would be possible; hence I would like to ask that you let me know sometime regarding this matter—perhaps, to save you the trouble, through my father. You once mentioned November; therefore I approach you now with my query. And now pardon me for burdening you with yet another personal question! Shortly before my departure, we spoke briefly about the possibility of my receiving an assistantship after my return, and you gave me some hope at that time. Do you think that something like this might be available to me for the semester after this coming one? Preferably, of

[1.] *NL*, A 20,1 (12); handwritten. Partially reproduced in *GS* 3:16–17.

[2.] See the earlier July 20, 1928, letter to Seeberg 1/36. ["Privy councilor" was a courtesy title in pre-1918 Prussia, given to senior public servants after long service.—CG]

[3.] [Bonhoeffer refers to his first dissertation, *Sanctorum Communio,* for which he received the German *Lizentiat,* equivalent to a doctorate in Anglo-Saxon universities. —CG]

[4.] Regarding the dissertation publication, see *Sanctorum Communio* (*DBW* 1), pp. 3–4. The book by Paul Althaus, *Communio Sanctorum,* was published in 1929.

course, in systematics. Might you be so kind as to put in a good word for me should something become available?[5]

And now enough questions and requests. My time here is flying by; I have announced a series of lectures on theological questions for the winter, and the Christmas preparations for the young people are beginning. And from day to day I become more interested in the idea of a new, larger systematic work, and I should not neglect my Spanish—so the final four months will also fly by, and before I know it I will be sitting in your seminar again and will be able to accompany you on your way home. I am already looking forward to it.

In most grateful appreciation, your ever devoted
Dietrich Bonhoeffer

48. To His Parents[1] 104

October 11

My dear Parents,

I'm very glad to hear you made it through your trip in good shape. Hopefully now the last part has passed pleasantly as well and your memories of the trip are as wonderful as mine. Let me thank you again for undertaking this long journey and giving me these lovely weeks. It was only a pity that here in Barcelona I could not be completely free for you and that as a result we lost many wonderful hours. Three journeys will always hold the most wonderful memories for me: the first with Sabine after our exams,[2] then the one with Klaus to Italy,[3] and now this one with you through southern France. Now I hope only that despite the long trip you have recuperated and have returned to Berlin refreshed from the lengthy vacation; the stay in Glotterbad will doubtless have helped in this regard. The news that you are sitting by a heater has truly horrified me. During my journey it became

[5.] Concerning Bonhoeffer's plans for the future and the situation in Berlin, see *DB-ER*, 120–23. [Cf. also Lütgert's letter, 1/110a.—CG]

[1.] *NL*, A 19,1 (23); handwritten from Barcelona; certainly 1928. Partially reproduced in *GS* 6:149.

[2.] Bonhoeffer is probably referring to the trip to Lake Constance and the Alps during the summer of 1922, that is, *before* his secondary school exams (*Abitur*); see *DB-ER*, 47, and *DBWE* 9, 1/29.

[3.] From April to June 1924; in this regard cf. *DBWE* 9:82–128.

warmer by the hour, and here our average temperatures are again between 20 and 22 degrees.[4] The weather is splendid.

I had to get right back to work, but only for eight days, for then I must travel to Madrid for a week to substitute for the pastor there, which, on the one hand, is quite nice but, on the other, does not really fit into my plans at the moment. In any event, from Wednesday the twenty-first till the twenty-eighth[5] I will be in Madrid (Via Castellana 6, care of Lahusen).[6]

During the last congregational council meeting, I suggested a plan
105 for introducing religious instruction at the school here; the plan was well received but will now involve a lot of work and running around. I also have to work on my lectures now, the first of which I hope to deliver in three weeks.[7] I asked Walter to send a book from my bookcase immediately (Duhm: *Propheten*).[8] The Christmas play is now also coming along. A very large group of new children has also started coming. So there is much to do with all that.

Please say hello to everyone there; I hope you are all doing well. And again, many thanks!

Greetings from your grateful
Dietrich

49. From Reinhold Seeberg[1]

Berlin, October 19, 1928

Dear Mr. Bonhoeffer:

Many thanks for the two letters I received from you. I am sincerely glad to hear that you are doing so well, that you are getting to know the country and people, have settled into the praxis there, have wrapped up your work, and are already looking toward new work.[2] I'm anxious to see what kind of topic you choose.

[4.] [Fahrenheit 68–71.6.—CG]

[5.] According to the calendar, Bonhoeffer departed for Madrid on Wednesday, October 17, 1928.

[6.] Pastor of the German congregation in Madrid; see 1/74, p. 172.

[7.] The congregational lectures; see 2/1–2/3.

[8.] Duhm, *Israels Propheten.*

[1.] *NL*, A 20,1 (3); typewritten with handwritten signature. Previously published in *GS* 3:17–18.

[2.] [Seeberg refers to Bonhoeffer completing the revision of his doctoral dissertation and considering ideas for his postdoctoral dissertation.—CG]

Perhaps it would be advisable to choose something historically or biblically oriented in order to learn to work independently in the approaches and methods of these areas. For example, how about examining the question of why ethical problems receded so strongly in twelfth-century scholasticism, and how the presentation in John of Salisbury's "Metalogicus"[3] is to be evaluated. But this is merely one example, and if you have something that interests you more, so much the better, of course. But the history of ethics and even more so that of morality[4] [Sittlichkeit] is an area on which a young man today might well focus, perhaps with the goal of a systematic and historical treatment of ethics from the Sermon on the Mount to the present.

Now to your questions. I would not wait for the book by Althaus to appear, 106
since a detailed discussion of it is hardly possible now; a few remarks in your preface might suffice. Moreover, I believe that the outcome of your approach will be different. Regarding the publication of your work, I fear that some time must yet pass. The publishing company has a new owner and in addition works frightfully slowly. There are also some other projects there already. Admittedly, if Althaus has been in everyone's hands for a while, then you probably cannot avoid discussing his book, perhaps at the end of your own.[5]

As to the assistantship.[6] Stolzenburg has been reappointed until April 1929, then the position will definitely be free. I will gladly put in a word for you as a member of the seminar for many years; whether that is successful, of course, also depends on who my successor is, who will, I hope, be named by then.[7]

May you continue to do well, and please let me hear from you again.

Cordially yours,
R. Seeberg

[3.] John of Salisbury, *Metalogicon.* [By "presentation" Seeberg refers to the treatment of ethical problems in that work.—CG]

[4.] [Seeberg appears to invoke the distinction between ethics as a scholarly discipline and morality as practical behavior.—CG]

[5.] Bonhoeffer followed this suggestion in *Sanctorum Communio*; see *DBWE* 1:166, ed. note 26; 242, ed. note 111; 257, ed. note 129.

[6.] Cf. 1/47.

[7.] Wilhelm Lütgert; see 1/61.

17:86 **49a. To Walter Dreß**[1]

Dear Walter,

I am already coming to you again with a request. Do you own Zweig: Jeremias?[2] If you do, please be so kind as to send it to me. I'd really like to use
17:87 the book for a lecture I am giving on November 13, on "The Tragedy of the Prophetic [Prophetismus] and Its Lasting Meaning."[3] Otherwise please telephone Grote[4] and have them send it to me immediately. Sorry for the trouble, and many thanks in advance for everything. The year is marching toward its end. I don't know how I will be able to take care of everything I've planned; things are almost going too fast. Apart from my official obligations—once again I have to substitute for Olbricht for a few weeks—I also have Christmas preparations, lectures,[5] etc., have two problem children to take care of, want to keep learning Spanish, and still want to travel quite a bit around the country—in a word, everything is going too fast, the days fly by as if they were nothing at all. I don't know what I will be doing over Christmas vacation. Actually, I'd like to escape all the hustle and bustle; it's just going to be too crazy. More soon. Greetings to all of you at home, to Suse, and to our family.

Cordial greetings,
Dietrich

[1.] Literary estate of Walter Dreß; handwritten postcard, from Barcelona; addressed to "Dr. W. Dreß, Zehlendorferstrasse 12, Berlin-Lichterfelde"; postmark is illegible, in any event *after* October 2, 1928 (cf. postcard of October 2, 1928, 1/45b) and *before* November 13, 1928. Previously published in Staats and Wünsche, "Dietrich Bonhoeffers Abschied," 4), 199.

[2.] Zweig, *Jeremiah*. See also 2/1, p. 333.

[3.] The final title was "The Tragedy of the Prophetic [*Prophetentum*] and Its Lasting Meaning" (cf. 2/1). [In this letter Bonhoeffer uses *Prophetismus*, "prophetism."—CG]

[4.] Berlin bookstore; see also 1/60, p. 156.

[5.] In addition to the lecture on the prophets, he also gave one on December 11, 1928, "Jesus Christ and the Essence of Christianity"; see 2/2. [A third lecture, "Basic Questions of a Christian Ethic" (2/3), was given on February 8, 1929; a planned fourth lecture was not given during Bonhoeffer's time in Barcelona (cf. 1/60a, 1/67, 1/68a, and 1/74).—CG]

50. To Karl Bonhoeffer[1] 106

Dear Papa,

Many thanks for your letter. I immediately inquired of Mrs. Andres.[2] She now wants to know whether it is to be a white or black, a three- or four-cornered lace manton[3] or a mantilla[4] of the sort we saw several times, that is, colorful.

I'm still doing well. Yesterday evening I saw the old Spanish *Don Juan* in 107
the theater, a piece performed here only during the time around All Souls' because of the graveyard scene. I'll tell you about it in detail later.[5] Please let me know soon.

Affectionately, your grateful
Dietrich

51. To Rüdiger Schleicher[1]

The quiet hours in which I cultivated the Arte taurina,[2] have, as you can see, led to tremendous success in the arena. This postcard is available in all the stores in Barcelona.[3] Greetings from the matador.

Dietrich

[1.] *NL*, A 19,1 (24); handwritten postcard from Barcelona; postmarked October 31, 1928. Partially reproduced in *GS* 6:150. A response to Karl Bonhoeffer's letter of October 24, 1928 (*NL*, C 1).

[2.] According to Karl Bonhoeffer, during his visit Mrs. Andres had agreed to find him "a beautiful Spanish head scarf (veil)" as a Christmas present for Paula Bonhoeffer.

[3.] Embroidered Andalusian shawl that covers almost the entire body.

[4.] A lace scarf worn over the head and shoulders.

[5.] See 1/52, p. 148.

[1.] *NL*, A 19,3 (6); handwritten postcard from Barcelona showing Bonhoeffer as a matador; postmarked November 6, 1928. Bonhoeffer sent an almost identical postcard to Hans von Dohnanyi on the same day; see *NL*, A 19,3 (7).

[2.] "Art of the bull[fight]."

[3.] The postcard is reproduced in Bethge and Gremmels, *Life in Pictures*, centenary ed., 43.

52. To Julie Bonhoeffer[1]

November 7

Dear Grandmama,

Let me thank you very much for your two letters; besides a letter from Papa, they are the only news I have received from Berlin for quite a while now. Sabine is cloaking herself in complete silence—I hope not with hurt feelings. There has just been so much going on recently, and on top of that I am only today finally able to get out of bed again after a slight bout of gastric
108 influenza that for eight days kept me from doing anything, but which with the help of a German physician is now completely receding. We have also begun to use the heater again, even though at midday it can still be quite warm. The weather is rather unstable now; we recently had an extremely heavy thunderstorm that lasted from about 6:00 in the late afternoon till the next day at 1:00 p.m. with a nonstop tropical downpour. We had to keep our lights on the entire morning, and then when the sun and blue sky finally appeared again, Barcelona had become a kind of Venice. And yet these are the months in which you really do perceive the advantages of the south, where a rainy day is still something unusual even in November.

A while back I attended a performance of the Spanish classical *Don Juan*,[2] a play performed only around the time of All Souls' because of the graveyard scene. The story is the familiar one. This material has been reworked often over the centuries. The one that is most famous today comes from the year 1840, and it is amusing to see how the Spaniards still become involved with a play with such primitive ideas. The graveyard scene, where revenge and atonement are exacted upon Don Juan, seems quite comical to us because ghosts appear, while the Spaniard takes it rather seriously. You have to recall the times when the Faust plays were making the rounds in Germany.[3] If I had more time, I would go to the theater more often. Next Tuesday I will be giving my first lecture, and I still have much work to

[1.] *NL*, A 19,2 (6); handwritten from Barcelona; certainly 1928. Partially reproduced in *GS* 6:150–51.

[2.] *Don Juan Tenorio*, a verse play by José Zorilla y Moral, first performed in Madrid in March 1844 and performed annually there on All Souls' Day. [On November 3, the day after All Saints' Day; this day commemorates the souls of the faithful departed.—CG]

[3.] Since the seventeenth century the Faust material was part of the repertoire of touring companies.

do on it.[4] Then Olbricht is going away for three weeks again, and I will be remaining here alone with the relief agency, the church, the confirmands.

People are always asking me whether I might not want to stay here after all for a bit longer, or whether I might be inclined to return later. It is certainly true that I have only now really settled in completely and could get all kinds of work done if I were to remain. But when they asked me officially during the congregational council meeting, I declined. There wouldn't be
anything new for me here if I were to stay an extra year or even for some 109
additional time; I have seen what I wanted to see, and ultimately I came here to learn. I have made many good acquaintances here, but I can do that elsewhere as well—and so it shall remain, that I am now entering my last three months here and will be as glad to return to Berlin as I have been to be here. Before that, however, there is still much to see, much work to do, much to learn, much traveling to do. At Christmas, that is, on the twenty-fifth, I would like to get away, perhaps to the Pyrenees or to Majorca.

I hope you are all doing well!

To you, dear Grandmama, affectionate greetings from your grateful
Dietrich

53. To His Parents[1]

My dear Parents,

Today the connection was much better, and I was enormously pleased to be wholly transported into the festive mood there by all your voices.[2] But where were *Sabine*, Suse, and Walter? I did speak with Ursel; but the tone of the voices was extremely distorted, so I still don't know whether Papa was on at the beginning or just who. I was very pleased to hear Grandmama! Please say hello to her for me; and Aunt Ilse[3] was a complete surprise. At the very end, someone wanted to pass on a message to me (from the Czeppans?) that I didn't understand. Today my thoughts are very much with you and your evening celebration; now it will only be another three months, and

[4.] See 2/1.

[1.] *NL*, A 19,1 (26); handwritten postcard from Barcelona; probably November 11, 1928, postmarked November 14, 1928. Partially reproduced in *GS* 6:152.

[2.] The occasion was the double baptism of Dorothee Schleicher and Klaus von Dohnanyi.

[3.] Not otherwise identified.

I will be able to celebrate along with you again. Here there is much to do. I am again quite well. Affectionate greetings to everyone, your grateful
Dietrich

110 **54. To Karl Bonhoeffer**[1]

Dear Papa,

After receiving your letter, for which I thank you very much, I immediately went to Mrs. Andres, who strongly advised me to choose a *white* veil, and we found a *very* lovely antique one with which you will, I hope, be in agreement. On Wednesday I gave it to Mrs. Kuhn,[2] who will be sending it. Perhaps you should send the money to the address of the Señoritas Gallego, my landladies, since I am not at home much. You see, I don't have much money anymore. The price was not yet definite, around three hundred marks. Perhaps you can send a little more just in case (though it will probably cost less!).

Can Suse send me a package, as *samples without commercial value,* of Gelonida stomachica and Leo pills[3] (also for the [. . .][4] of the ladies). Greetings from your grateful
Dietrich

55. To Karl Bonhoeffer[1]

Dear Papa,

We have just finalized the purchase of the white lace veil; it is really fabulous and will doubtless please Mama greatly—it is antique and white. But I didn't have enough money. So Mrs. Andres had to loan me 470 pesetas = 330 marks, which was not so pleasant for me but had to be done because of the Kuhns' departure. Would you please wire the money to me as soon as

[1.] *NL,* A 19,1 (27); handwritten postcard from Barcelona; postmarked November 16, 1928. Partially reproduced in *GS* 6:152.

[2.] The Kuhn family was moving back to Germany from Barcelona, which enabled Bonhoeffer to circumvent customs difficulties.

[3.] [Gelonida stomachica were fast-dissolving pills that stimulated production of gastric juices to improve digestion; Leo pills were a laxative.—CG]

[4.] Illegible.

[1.] *NL,* A 19,1 (28); handwritten postcard from Barcelona; postmarked November 19, 1928. Partially reproduced in *GS* 6:152.

possible, either to the Señoritas Gallego or to the Olbrichts, or possibly to the bank.

I am here in a tobacco shop. Hence the haste.

Affectionately, your
Dietrich

56. To Paula Bonhoeffer[1] 111

Dear Mama,

Many thanks for your letter.[2] I just want to write quickly and let you know that I am completely well again. I lay here in bed, and it was touching how the two gentlemen and the ladies tended to me. Now I've bought myself a huge sausage and butter and cheese, had pork knuckle with sauerkraut for lunch today, so you see that I am really doing *very* well indeed.

Much was going on last week. On Tuesday I delivered my first lecture[3] in a full church; the confirmation classes are a great joy to me even though their ignorance can hardly be believed. The Kuhns are departing on Wednesday but returning in January. I will probably celebrate Christmas at the Forstmanns with Mr. Thumm.

Affectionately, your
Dietrich

57. To Karl Bonhoeffer[1]

Dear Papa,

Tomorrow the mantilla[2] will be sent. Everyone who has seen it is absolutely enthusiastic. Mrs. Andres also added a small piece of pretty damask, which the lady we bought the mantilla from gave to her and which she now would like to give to Mama. I don't quite know whether one should now wait until Christmas, since I think she would appreciate a few lines and really has

[1.] *NL,* A 19,1 (25); handwritten postcard; probably November 19, 1928. Partially reproduced in *GS* 6:151.

[2.] Her letter of November 14, 1928 (*NL*, C 1).

[3.] See 2/1.

[1.] *NL,* A 19,1 (29); handwritten postcard from Barcelona; postmark date not decipherable; probably November 20, 1928.

[2.] See 1/50 and 1/54.

gone to a lot of trouble with this whole matter. In case you want to write her a few words, her address is c. Muntaner 231 (Gracia).[3] I think you will really like the mantilla. In the meantime, Mrs. Andres has loaned me the money (450 pesetas).

Affectionately, your grateful
Dietrich

112 **58. To His Parents**[1]

November 27

My dear Parents,

I would like to have sent a greeting for Sunday or on Sunday itself. But because of my sermon,[2] which was a lot of work this time, I didn't have any free time before Sunday, and since Sunday I have again been completely busy with work. Many thanks for your letter, dear Mama, which I received Sunday. Several times during the service I thought about you.[3] My sermon text was the passage from the Song of Solomon, "For love is strong as death."[4] We had a very celebratory [feierlich] hour. I can preach once again on the first Sunday of Advent, since Olbricht will not return until the next week, and I'm very pleased about that. My text will be Rev. 3:20a.[5] Preparing sermons still demands much of my time. Actually I work on them the entire week, every day. Along with everything else at this time, that is really quite a lot. I am now working on my second lecture, which I am to deliver on December 11, on the "Essence of Christianity."[6] I had to keep the topic extremely general in order to provide any overview at all of the attendant problems.

Moreover, recently the seniors at the school here asked me to form a circle to discuss those kinds of questions with them, which made me enormously happy. We are beginning this evening. It is yet more proof that

[3.] [Gracia was a small town that had been incorporated into Barcelona and made a district of the city by the end of the nineteenth century.—CG]

[1.] *NL*, A 19,1 (30); handwritten from Barcelona, certainly 1928. Partially reproduced in *GS* 6:152–53.

[2.] See 3/15.

[3.] On the Remembrance Sunday, *Totensonntag*, Bonhoeffer's parents used to visit the grave of his brother Walter, who was killed in action in World War I.

[4.] [Song of Solomon 8:6.—CG]

[5.] See 3/17.

[6.] See 2/2.

there is indeed interest, and it is a powerful argument for our venture with respect to religious instruction at the school. I would rather not follow up yet on another suggestion from several parish members to conduct a weekend evening devotion every Saturday, since in the end I want to avoid any possible conflict with Olbricht; for after all I will soon be able to count on 113
my fingers the Sundays I have remaining here.

I'm still completely unclear about what I will be doing at Christmas. As it now stands, I have to preach on December 25 and January 1,[7] so I can't get away then at all; I might have Olbricht give me January 1 off and travel after all; then possibly to Majorca on parish business, where I would also have to preach but would have to travel alone, since the others already know Majorca. Or to the Pyrenees, although I don't really have the winter gear or shoes for such a trip; or to Valencia, Alicante, etc. with Mr. Thumm and possibly someone else; or, finally, one or two day trips from here. I would like to get away to escape the flood of invitations. I also don't know yet where I will be on Christmas Eve. Because I have been invited by many people, I will probably have to spend it with the Olbrichts. I'd be sorry for Thumm in that case, though, since he would then be alone. Perhaps we two can celebrate together, and then no one's feelings will be hurt.

(In a few weeks, a crate will arrive for Christmas; just don't let the others find out anything about it!)

We've had a violent storm here since yesterday, yet the skies are still the same unchanging blue they've been for months. At midday it can still get as high as 21 degrees in the shade.[8] Evenings are cool, and right next to me the water for my afternoon tea is boiling, in a kettle from the Kuhns. 3:00–5:00 I had a session; so it's gradually getting cool, though it's difficult to get into the Christmas mood with this weather!

Now I must close. I hope you are all well. Please say hello to Grandmama. I would like to write more often, but hardly even get around to what is absolutely necessary. Greetings to everyone.

Affectionately, your grateful
Dietrich

[7.] Neither sermon has been preserved.
[8.] [Fahrenheit 69.8 degrees.—CG]

114 **59. To His Parents**[1]

December 10, 1928

My dear Parents,

Today my thoughts are again very much at home. When I see the children looking forward to Christmas in so many homes, it evokes vivid memories of the time when I was that age myself, and sometimes it even seems to me as if the Christmas carols I hear sung had actually been my own.—Otherwise one doesn't get much into the Christmas mood with this blue sky, although it is gradually getting cold, especially at night.

Many thanks for your letter,[2] dear Mama. Today we settled on our Christmas plans. I will celebrate with Mr. Thumm at the Olbrichts and hope that the Forstmanns' feelings won't be hurt; I also had to decline the Köttgens even though the young boy asked me with tears in his eyes to please come, similarly also with several other people. So as not to offend anyone, I'll just have to go to the Olbrichts. On the first day of Christmas I have to preach, as well as when I am here on January 1, 1929; otherwise I have to go to Valencia on parish business and might travel from there to Alicante, but only if Thumm goes along as well, that is, if the vacation period is long enough; otherwise I'll stay here the whole time and maybe just travel to the Pyrenees for three days. None of that has been settled yet.[3]

There is much to do at the moment. Olbricht is back, but now the Christmas play demands my attention;[4] tomorrow I will deliver my second lecture, on the essence of Christianity.[5] Then I must turn my attention totally to the technical preparations for the play, and the fact that I have such little knowledge of technical things is making it quite awkward. But I now have several people helping me. The play itself will end up being quite
115 nice. We will also have the evening for the senior students, which is getting off to a good start. They are very engaged but clueless due to the incredible preparation for school. Right now we are talking about the essence of Christianity and will then discuss individual problems, beginning with the problem of immortality. For this the seniors always have a reading assignment about which there is a report and then a discussion. The young people here of this age and younger are different from those in Germany. A peculiar mix of adulthood in terms of manners and career questions, and

[1.] *NL*, A 19,1 (31); handwritten from Barcelona. Partially reproduced in *GS* 6:155–56.
[2.] Her letter of December 2–4, 1928 (*NL*, C 1).
[3.] See 1/58, p. 153.
[4.] Cf. 1/42, p. 131, et passim.
[5.] See 2/2.

enormous naïveté in other areas. There is not much intellectual arrogance or self-importance. In any event, intelligence is not overrated. One has the impression of greater honesty and clarity, which may derive from the Spanish influence.

Concerning my Christmas wish regarding a trip to Tenerife, my inquiries must actually prompt me to withdraw it immediately or at least postpone it to my birthday. *One* trip alone costs over two hundred pesetas! The stay itself is supposedly no more expensive than in Spain. I was thinking about one or two weeks; but if one adds all that together, you get a dreadful amount. So now my only hope is my Christmas lottery ticket, which I bought for three pesetas.

I really would like to telephone you on Christmas. But I don't know yet when I will have time; I'll write when I know. I withdrew two hundred pesetas of my money; Mr. and Mrs. Olbricht had birthdays, I had to have another pair of shoes, had to have my hat blocked, my watch repaired, all that already cost about one hundred. I still have the rest.

The doorbell just rang. My remedial student is here, so I have to close.

More soon!

All the best to everyone there.

Affectionately, your grateful
Dietrich

My landlady's sister, who is married and lives in Bremen, would like to write to you about medical matters, dear Papa, or even come to see you. I gave her your address.

60. To Karl Bonhoeffer[1] 116

December 17, 1928

Dear Papa,

Today I have another Christmas question. Up until sometime this last summer, my ladies—I only just now learned of this through Mr. Haag,[2] who lives with me—had an independent business within a larger department store here. Things went awry about in May, that is, they had to dissolve their business and pay out money to a number of people. Now, since they are so alone, they have got into a bind with these payments and are suffering

[1.] *NL*, A 19,1 (32); handwritten from Barcelona. Partially reproduced in *GS* 6:156–57.
[2.] Spelled "Haack" in 1/5, p. 60.

mightily under the whole affair. All in all, they still owe about 250 marks; before they can get that together, though, the interest rate keeps going up. Now Mr. Haag mentioned this to me, wondering whether one might be able to help out with an advance that they would pay back in a year at the latest, which Mr. Haag himself would guarantee. So I wanted to ask whether you might be able to give the landladies these 250 marks as an advance; if I could tell them this at Christmas, it would really be wonderful and would help these ladies enormously, all three of whom are under dreadful pressure at the moment. They are not at all unreliable. But I don't know what you think about it. Please write me briefly and tell me what you think; if nothing comes of it, then I need to get them something for Christmas. In any case, I would be very grateful to you if you would agree to do it.[3]

In eight days it will be Christmas Eve. I will spend it with the Olbrichts and would naturally like to telephone you. But the service is at five o'clock, and afterward I have to pay a brief visit to the Forstmanns, and during the evening I fear I will get no phone connection at all or only a very slow one. So I'm thinking maybe of trying between 2:00 and 3:00, while you are eat-
117 ing, for on the first day of Christmas I'll also be spending the whole day with a family. But I'll write you in more detail about this later.

My trip will probably end up as follows: I will remain here till New Year's, when I must preach, then on January 2 till about January 5 I'll spend a few days in the Pyrenees, and then on January 10 or so will travel on parish business to Majorca for about a week, where I will conduct two services. And then it's just about time to start packing my bags. The time has just flown by—almost too quickly.

On Tuesday I delivered my second lecture,[4] which was even better attended than the first, though not as well received, I think. On Saturday and Sunday I had a beautiful tour of the mountains; it's too bad one so rarely gets around to such things.

Much love to Mama and Grandmama.

Affectionately, your grateful
Dietrich

[3.] Bonhoeffer's father acted on this suggestion; see 1/63, p. 162. See also 1/69, p. 167, and 1/94.

[4.] See 2/2.

60a. To Walter Dreß[1] 17:87

Dear Walter,

Cordial Advent greetings from a two-day tour in the mountains.[2] Up here in this solitude, looking at the snow-covered Pyrenees, one finally has at least a sense of our German winter. Many thanks for the parcels. For my third lecture[3] could you send me Barth, "Der Christ in der Gesellschaft"?[4] And 17:88
for the fourth lecture[5] Tillich, religiöse Lage der Gegenwart.[6] Thanks and greetings.

Yours,
Dietrich

61. From Karl Bonhoeffer[1] 117

December 18, 1928

Dear Dietrich,

The paper on which I am writing you is not very festive for a Christmas letter. But I must write; otherwise the letter will be too late. This afternoon I have a meeting, so I want to go ahead and finish the letter here at the clinic and then add the letter from Mama.

It's too bad we have to celebrate without you. We will be a small circle this year in any case, since the Dohnanyis, too, want to stay in Hamburg with their children.

From your letter we see that you have much to do during these days, so even in your thoughts you will be so engaged in the present that the days will go by more quickly for you than you imagine. The photograph you promised is not here yet. This time we didn't have any clear-cut wishes. I hope you will like the 118

[1.] Literary estate of Walter Dreß; handwritten picture postcard of Sant Llorenç del Munt (Cova del Drac), postmarked December 17, 1928; addressed to "Dr. Walter Dreß, Zehlendorferstr[asse] 12, Berlin-Lichterfelde, Alemania." Previously published in Staats and Wünsche, "Dietrich Bonhoeffers Abschied," 199.

[2.] See 1/60, p. 156.

[3.] "Basic Questions of a Christian Ethic," delivered on February 8, 1929; see 2/3.

[4.] Barth, "Christian's Place in Society," the Tambach lecture of 1919.

[5.] A fourth lecture has not been preserved; in this regard see also 1/67, p. 165, and 1/74, p. 173.

[6.] Tillich, *Religious Situation*, originally published in Berlin in 1926.

[1.] *NL*, C 1; handwritten from Berlin; on the reverse side of the envelope: "The Director of the Psychiatric and Neurological Clinic Charité." Excerpt in *DB-ER*, 121.

little picture; it pleased you back then when you saw it.[2] As far as your travel plans are concerned, you need only to write[3] and say how high the anticipated costs will be so that I can see whether it might not still be accomplished with a bit of good will.

Mama probably wrote and told you that we were recently together with Seeberg and Lietzmann at Harnack's. It seems as if the dogmatician from Halle[4] has been asked. Harnack specifically told me to send you his regards and to tell you that you should do your postdoctoral work as soon as possible, that one learns so very much through holding lectures.

I think we will probably speak with you sometime during Christmas. Till then, affectionate greetings and merry Christmas from your devoted

Father

62. To His Parents, Grandmother, Brothers, and Sisters[1]

Barcelona, December 19, 1928

My dear Parents, dear Grandmama, dear Brothers and Sisters,

This letter should reach you on Christmas Eve. You will surely all be together now, and I will be celebrating with you in thought across these two thousand kilometers. Now all your homes have become quiet once again, so that it will be a lovely celebration for everyone. I still cannot believe that an entire year has passed since we decorated our last tree and celebrated Christmas. The time has just flown by; but then when I imagine sitting among you again, we would all certainly know then that a long time has passed because we would all have so much we'd want to know and tell; and that really will be the case in only a few more Sundays. I would, of course, very much like
119 to telephone you on Christmas Eve itself; but that's impossible, so I'll try during the afternoon between 2:00 and 3:00, starting my own Christmas Eve celebration with the phone call, and then your voices will accompany me the entire evening and through the rest of the holidays as a Christmas greeting from Germany. I wish I could have sent you something nicer than this rather prosaic gift for everyone together. But then Spanish customs get

[2.] A Madonna; see the letter from his mother on December 16, 1928 (*NL*, C 1); see also Bonhoeffer's thanks in 1/63, p. 160.

[3.] The next word difficult to decipher; perhaps *mir*, "to me."

[4.] Wilhelm Lütgert; see also Bonhoeffer's reaction in 1/70, p. 169.

[1.] *NL*, A 19,1 (33); handwritten. Partially reproduced in *GS* 6:157–58.

in the way. At any rate, you can assume that at least we will be drinking the same wine on Christmas Eve.

I'm beginning to feel the joy and anticipation of the celebration myself; the children and their performance are taking care of that. I look forward to being able to celebrate in a relaxed fashion with all the people I have come to know better here and am especially looking forward to the nativity play on Sunday afternoon. It's something so new for the children here that they are all participating with real enthusiasm and curiosity. I'll telephone you on Monday afternoon; Olbricht's service is at five o'clock, and after that I'll go with Mr. Thumm to the Olbrichts and celebrate there. I won't stay there long, since I have to preach on Tuesday morning, so I'll return home soon and light a tree in my room and be with you in my thoughts; I do want to put up a small tree in my room for these days even though I won't be there much. On Tuesday I'll be preaching on John 1:14, and the Word became flesh![2] I'm very pleased that I can preach once this Christmas, although it is more difficult than I thought. Then I will spend the entire day with the Köttgens, at the home of my young student. Mr. Thumm departs the next day, and I'll have to see how I can make it through all the invitations without completely losing my time for relaxation. On New Year's I'll be preaching again,[3] and from January 2 to about January 5 I want to go to the snowy Pyrenees, although I'm still unsure with whom, perhaps my Spaniard[4] and one of the other young people; for the teachers are all 120
gone. Then on January 13 I'll go to Majorca on parish business, and in the meantime I'm actually supposed to deliver my third lecture, on "Basic Questions of a Christian Ethic," though I may put that off till February.[5] Those are my plans for my concluding and farewell weeks in Spain.

But it's not even Christmas yet, and there is still a great deal to do before everything has reached that happy point. I must still get an unexpectedly large number of Christmas gifts for the people whom I've visited frequently, or in some cases for their children. The pastor is also quite receptive to nice gifts. I don't know yet what I'll get for myself. I would like to be able to put something nice for myself under the Christmas tree.

I would like to have written each of you individually. Please excuse me; I still have numerous Christmas letters facing me and really don't know

[2.] Not extant.

[3.] Not extant.

[4.] Bonhoeffer is referring to Luis Sánchez Sarto, his "language partner"; see 1/29, p. 108.

[5.] See 2/3, delivered on February 8, 1929.

how I'll get to them all. In addition I'm spending every free moment at the church getting things nicely arranged for our play.

The first Christmas greeting just arrived. Ursel's and Rüdiger's picture with Rüdiger's lovely letter.[6] I really wish I could have written you more often, dear Rüdiger, but, as you say yourself, you can well imagine that things often turn out differently than one would like. I was delighted with your picture. How big the little ones have become, especially little Renate.[7] I think I already thanked you for the picture of Dorothee. Please forgive me if I got it confused. Even the paper in which the picture was wrapped today evoked a whole host of Christmas images that I miss greatly here.

Now I must close. Wishing you all a beautiful, peaceful Christmas together just as it has always been, and I will certainly be celebrating with you from a distance.

Stay well, affectionately, your
Dietrich

121 **63. To His Parents**[1]

December 25, 1928

My dear Parents,

I would have preferred to write you yesterday evening; but when I got back home from the Olbrichts it was almost 12:30 a.m., and then Mr. Thumm and I sat together for a while in front of the lighted Christmas tree—and soon it was 1:30 a.m., and because I had to preach this morning, I had to turn in.

First of all, many thanks for your letters and for the series of photographs, which greatly pleased and surprised me. One particularly big surprise was the picture,[2] which I had repeatedly mourned and that now, quite unexpectedly, appeared on the Christmas table. Even though this rather lonely Christmas gift seemed rather strange to me, I had an enjoyable time and was very near to you all in my thoughts. The whole evening proceeded as follows. At 5:00 I went to the Christmas vespers at church. When I returned at 6:00, the young boy from the children's service whom I am tutoring had set up and lit a wonderful Christmas tree in my room, one he had specially

[6.] Not extant.

[7.] Renate Schleicher.

[1.] *NL*, A 19,1 (34); handwritten from Barcelona. Partially reproduced in *GS* 6:158–59.

[2.] The Madonna; see 1/61, pp. 157–58.

ordered as a greeting from Germany.[3] Beneath it lay your lovely gifts and a number of others. So we three sat before the tree, gazed into the lights, and spoke about Germany and Spain and earlier Christmas celebrations. We sat this way, very quietly, and thus celebrated an extremely lovely Christmas that I will never forget. The Christmas spirit and joy had truly arrived. Then at 7:30, the boy had to go home, and the two of us went to the Olbrichts. Mr. Olbricht gave me a lovely book on ancient Spain, and from the others I received all sorts of cheerful good wishes. The entire celebration had such a warm, friendly atmosphere that the hours passed quickly. We broke up at about midnight; we wanted to light the tree one more time, then sat and 122
chatted for a while until, quite happy with the course of the evening, we went to bed.

My Christmas table is full of greetings from acquaintances here in the congregation, books, and especially with enough German pastries to last me until next Christmas, Swabian Christmas cookies, cinnamon stars, raspberry bread, and who knows what else. The Köttgens gave me a wonderful edition of the collected works of Cervantes, which greatly pleased me.

This morning we had the service at eleven o'clock, then the children's service until one o'clock. Then I spent the whole day until now—it's now twelve o'clock—up at the Köttgens, where we had a quiet, cozy Christmas day. I declined all other invitations so as not to split up the day, since tomorrow and during the next few days until Saturday there will certainly be enough commotion. Today we ate a princely Christmas meal with langoustines and roast goose and ice cream and then celebrated just among ourselves.—As you can see, I cannot really complain about loneliness, perhaps more about the fact that I haven't really had time to enjoy your wonderful gifts and to send my thoughts your way more often.

I will probably be in perpetual motion until next Tuesday, that is, New Year's, when I have to preach; but then I'll make for the Pyrenees and the snow, something I'm really looking forward to; what refreshing days those will be.

The Christmas play on the fourth Sunday of Advent went wonderfully and elicited joy all around. But of course I had a Mary and Joseph of the sort one will probably rarely encounter. Those two identified so much with their roles that through them the play really did acquire a center, something even the other children noticed. Moreover both of them had unusually beautiful singing voices for the many singing parts in the play. After the final song

[3.] See Bethge, Bethge, and Gremmels, *Life in Pictures*, 1986 ed., 69.

everyone was quiet in the church for a while. As everyone was filing out, the congregational council members came to thank us. Then we took the photographs that I am sending along to you. Of course, we worked completely without scenery and backdrops or any lighting effects, so that the whole undertaking really did acquire the character of a service of worship.

I was told that it would perhaps be difficult to get a good telephone connection to Berlin on Christmas day, so I wanted to reach you while you were
123 decorating the tree, and went into the city during the evening. Of course, I forgot that our time zones are different and that I would possibly be disturbing your sleep. But I was so glad to hear your voices on this day that was so lovely for me, and to hear that all is well with you and that you will be celebrating a beautiful Christmas. But now Christmas is already over—for it has already been two days since I began the letter. Yesterday I had a nice but very busy day; during the morning, in May-like weather and with splendid sunshine, I took a walk with the Forstmanns up to the hills behind Barcelona with their view of the Monserrat[4] and the clearly visible, snowcapped Pyrenees before us. Now I am really looking forward to getting out to the mountains. Mr. Thumm went to Madrid yesterday and wants to thank you for the calendar.

When I told my ladies, dear Papa, that you wanted to advance them the money, they were so moved they started to cry, saying that such things just do not happen in Spain and that they would never forget it.[5] I, too, was really glad for them. Since then, it's as if they have changed.

I was very glad to receive Klaus's letter,[6] which just arrived. If I had more free time, I would love to answer each person individually; even with the best of intentions, however, it's just not possible now. So please thank him for me.—Now I must close. By the time you receive this letter, I will probably be celebrating New Year's Eve with the Köttgens or will already be in the snow.

Again many, many thanks for all the love and wonderful joy you contributed to my Christmas celebration. Please say hello to everyone at home.

Affectionately, your grateful
Dietrich

[4.] [Apparently a misspelling for Montserrat, near Barcelona; Monserrat is near Valencia.—CG]

[5.] See 1/60, p. 156.

[6.] Not extant.

64. To Paula Bonhoeffer[1] 124

Dear Mama,

I just now realized that I need to go ahead and write today if you are to receive these greetings by your birthday. After the holidays you will probably celebrate quietly and without many guests. I hope that once more you have a quiet, peaceful year ahead, as you doubtless also wish for yourself, or at least that whatever problems do occur will always end up resolved satisfactorily as in the past year.

There's not much new to report, only that we still have the most splendid springlike weather and a cloudless sky.

As far as my trip to the Canaries is concerned,[2] perhaps I can draw on part of Grandmama's birthday[3] if you can also advance me a bit of money. But I'll write later and find out.

Have a nice celebration and a good beginning to the year.

Affectionately, your grateful
Dietrich

65. To Susanne Bonhoeffer and Walter Dreß[1]

Dear Walter, dear Suse,

It's New Year's Eve afternoon; it's already dark outside, and nothing is lighted in my room but the Christmas tree, before which I am sitting and writing this letter. This sight makes me think of all the love and friendliness I experienced at Christmas, and I'm grateful that I am now able to look back on such wonderful days. I just wanted to thank you again for your 125
lovely letters;[2] the book you sent[3] was one of my nicest presents. I will read it slowly and with the same feelings as you do. Many thanks for it.

Today I have been thinking back on this year here away from home, and beneath this lighted Christmas tree it's as if I am not really so far away or in

---

[1.] *NL*, A 19,1 (35); handwritten card from Barcelona; ca. December 26, 1928. Partially reproduced in *GS* 6:159.

[2.] [Regarding a possible Atlantic voyage to the Canary Islands after his time in Barcelona, see 1/59 (Tenerife), 1/67, and *DB-ER*, 105.—CG]

[3.] Bonhoeffer is referring to Julie Bonhoeffer's gift of money.

[1.] *NL*, A 19,2 (13); handwritten card from Barcelona; December 31, 1928. Partially reproduced in *GS* 6:159.

[2.] See *NL*, C 7.

[3.] Author and title can no longer be determined.

such a foreign country; the reason is that I have experienced nothing but friendliness here, and I must be grateful for this past year. It is a wonderful time that is now coming to a close. And I think that tonight your grateful feelings and thoughts and mine will meet, with all of us able to look back on some wonderful things. I will celebrate the last hours of the year quietly at the home of some acquaintances. Tomorrow morning I must preach.[4] Then tomorrow afternoon I'll head for the snow-covered Pyrenees; what a beautiful start to the New Year! Stay well, and many thanks! And the warmest greetings from your devoted

Dietrich

66. Report from Fritz Olbricht to the German Evangelical Church Committee[1]

Barcelona, January 1, 1929

To the German Evangelical Church Committee in Berlin

Let me humbly report that my vicar, Dr. Bonhoeffer, concluded his year on February 15 and then returned home. He demonstrated competency in every respect and helped me a great deal in my various activities. He was particularly good at engaging the children, who are enormously fond of him. In the end, an average of forty children attended his children's service. He also enjoyed
126 immense popularity throughout the colony itself. I would be extremely grateful if the German Evangelical Church Committee could send me as soon as possible a new, competent vicar who could be active in the same way.[2]

Yours faithfully,
F. Olbricht, Pastor

[4.] Not extant.

[1.] EZA 5/1891; typewritten. Partially reproduced in *Mündige Welt*, 5:24–25. [This is an excerpt from Olbricht's own annual report (it eventually ended up in the files of the Church Foreign Office, which oversaw foreign congregations), whereas 1/74 is his separate report on Bonhoeffer's year as vicar.—CG]

[2.] Following the preceding paragraph is a lengthy report about parish life and Olbricht's travels.

67. To His Parents[1]

the 10th

My dear Parents,

Before my departure for Majorca in two hours, I want to send you a greeting. On Sunday I will conduct two services there and then spend a few days seeing the island; I hope I can find a guide.

I am sending you several pictures from Christmas with Mr. Thumm and young Köttgen,[2] whom I am tutoring and who brought me the tree. These last weeks are just flying by, and yet there is still much to do: two sermons, two lectures.[3]

Today I finally received a brochure for the ships to the Canary Islands. The trip by steamer, departing here on February 15, costs two hundred pesetas second class, three hundred pesetas first class, although I believe it's a large ship so one can travel well even in second class. I'll write more about it when I have some free time in Majorca. Right now all sorts of other things are going through my head.

Warm greetings to everyone. Your grateful

Dietrich

68. To Karl-Friedrich Bonhoeffer[1] 127

Dear Karl-Friedrich,

I am sending you this belated birthday greeting[2] from Majorca, where I arrived this morning after a calm voyage. I am having breakfast outside without a coat! There is still snow on the mountains; below things are already starting to bloom. Tomorrow I will take a trip into the countryside; the day

---

[1.] *NL*, A 19,1 (36); handwritten card from Barcelona; January 10, 1929. Partially reproduced in *GS* 6:160.

[2.] Karl-Heinz Köttgen; see 1/63, pp. 160–61, and Bethge, Bethge, and Gremmels, *Life in Pictures*, 1986 ed., 69.

[3.] The fourth congregational lecture Bonhoeffer alludes to here has not been preserved. Concerning the number of congregational lectures, see also 1/74, p. 173.

[1.] *NL*, Anh. A 14, (2); handwritten postcard from Palma de Majorca; undated, postmarked January 12, 1929. Partially reproduced in *GS* 6:160. See also *NL*, A 19,2 (10); typewritten copy.

[2.] Karl-Friedrich was born on January 13, 1899.

after tomorrow I have to work; then I'll travel around for four more days. I haven't really seen much of the island yet.—What about Prague? When will you hear something definite?[3] Wishing you a good year, yours

Dietrich

17:88 **68a. To Susanne Bonhoeffer and Walter Dreß**[1]

Dear Suse, dear Walter,

Last night, with calm weather, I sailed over here to Majorca to spend eight days of solitude; that is, on Sunday there will be two services here and in a smaller village,[2] then I have the rest of the time to myself. I plan to hike a bit and to sit tight in a small harbor town for a few days of peace and quiet; when I return my final month will begin. It will all be over too quickly.—Please send me *Tillich*: religiöse Lage der Gegenwart![3] Right away!! Affectionately,

Yours,
Dietrich

127 **69. To His Parents**[1]

January 28, 1929

My dear Parents,

Today all the packing begins; my books are returning to the crate largely unread; and I must also finish packing my large suitcase already, since the Kuhns want to take everything I can do without to Berlin in the moving van, which does, of course, make it a lot easier for me. Mr. Thumm and Karl-Heinz Köttgen are nice enough to help me, so that everything is moving forward quickly and merrily. But now as I take down my tent, I do notice

---

[3.] An unpublished letter from Karl-Friedrich Bonhoeffer of October 22, 1928 (*NL*, C 3) mentions a possible professorship in Prague.

[1.] Literary estate of Walter Dreß; handwritten picture postcard from Palma de Majorca, postmarked January 12, 1929. Previously published in Staats and Wünsche, "Dietrich Bonhoeffers Abschied," 200.

[2.] Concerning this trip on parish business to Majorca from January 10 to January 18, 1929, see also 1/67 and 1/68.

[3.] See the postcard to Walter Dreß on December 17, 1928, 1/60a.

[1.] *NL*, A 19,1 (37); handwritten from Barcelona. Partially reproduced in *GS* 6:160–61.

how quickly I came to feel at home here. When I returned from Majorca, it was as if I were returning home, so to speak. And now in less than three weeks I really will be sitting in the train heading back home.

Even though the room will be empty, I still want to have my birthday cel- 128
ebration here at home on the fourth after dinner, a celebration that many people have insisted on. I'll put the bed in Mr. Thumm's room and replace it with a couple of tables. In the meantime, I have already got myself a birthday present ahead of time, I hope with your agreement. I have long been lying in wait here hoping to see a performance of *Carmen*.[2] Then last Saturday there was a special performance in which the idolized Spanish tenor Don José was singing. Although the prices were indeed insane, I wanted to let you give me that for my birthday, so I invited Mr. Thumm to come along, and we sat in the gallery for twenty pesetas each; but the performance was genuinely something quite rare. At the end Mr. Thumm really couldn't get over his enthusiasm, and after the theater we enthused about it so long that we didn't get to bed until 3:30 a.m. So let me thank you for this wonderful evening, an evening you gave me as a gift without even knowing it.

At 4:00 in the afternoon, the Koettgens, the Kuhns, two teachers from the school, and the Spaniard will come over here. I just hope we have enough chairs and glasses to go around. I will—or Mr. Thumm will be taking over the kitchen duties—make rolls and pudding and also go buy a few small things. It will then be my farewell celebration as well. I will probably depart on February 18; I requested the money for the return trip from the consistory and already received it (200 marks). People have generally advised against traveling to S. Sebastian at this time of year, saying it is almost always raining there now. So I'm thinking about visiting Klaus and possibly returning with him. And indeed, I have already seen so many different things in Spain that I don't think S. Sebastian could offer much that is new.

And now quickly to finances. The ladies have received the money and are hoping to have it together by the end of the year, though they would like to pay it back even earlier in installments. Mr. Haag is living here and is providing the guarantee. I withdrew 250 pesetas, had to pay part of it to
the ladies, what I couldn't give them in its entirety because of the trip to 129
the Pyrenees and the Christmas presents, each of which came to ca. 100 pesetas. (The thing with Christmas was especially awkward for me, since I had already received quite a few things two, three, four days before Christmas and hardly had time to reciprocate.) Now I must still pay the physician,

[2.] Cf. 1/5, p. 59.

then Saturday evening, Majorca still cost me a bit despite it being for parish *business.* So I'll still need the remaining 500 pesetas after all. I already have money for the return trip.

Please say hello to Grandmama; thank her for the card, and I wish I had more time to write. On Sunday I deliver my farewell sermon,[3] on the eighth my last lecture.[4] Many thanks, dear Mama, for your letter.

Warmest greetings to you all from your grateful
Dietrich

70. To His Parents[1]

Barcelona, February 6, 1929

My dear Parents,

Many thanks for your birthday letters; as well as for the notebook with its substantive content; this really brings the plans for the Orient[2] significantly closer. Though I now also feel the need to have my days to myself again, for peaceful work from which one thing or the other doesn't always pull me away, and especially to have my evenings at my disposal again. Although I cannot really say that life here gets monotonous—I already have plenty of acquaintances—it always brings a certain disquiet into one's lifestyle. I really do yearn to read again as long and as much as I want—more so than writing, which I've done enough.

130 My birthday was celebrated for the first time at 12:00 midnight at the Koettgens with a few other people. The Koettgens themselves gave me a marvelous piece of Toledo embroidery,[3] but beautiful in a way I've seldom seen. The next morning I was in the city with Mrs. Olbricht to pick up some things, and quite by accident I found, at the last moment, what I wanted to get you for your sixtieth birthday, dear Papa, so I immediately gave it to the Kuhns to put in the moving van. I can't really describe to you what it is, so would rather wait until I can show it to you.[4]

At midday I had a birthday meal with Mr. Thumm and young Koettgen at a restaurant, then that afternoon, when we arrived back home at 3:30,

---

[3.] See 3/18.
[4.] See 2/3.

[1.] *NL*, A 19,1 (38); handwritten. Partially reproduced in *GS* 6:161–63.
[2.] See 1/165, p. 290. Nothing more is known about the notebook, which apparently contained a gift of money.
[3.] A particular kind of embroidery (*à jour* or openwork pattern).
[4.] Cf. 1/17, p. 81.

my room was already half full of children from the children's service who had learned about it and filled my room with flowers; we played all kinds of games with one another, then even more children and other guests came to congratulate me, so the afternoon went by quickly. At 7:30 we threw all the guests out because we had to make preparations for the evening; I had invited my own guests for 9:30, and the conversation and entertainment were so nice and animated that it was 1:30 a.m. before even the first guest thought about going. So the day really was thoroughly and wonderfully celebrated. I received many extremely lovely things that I can show you later; even some things the children made themselves. Because of all the flowers, my room looks quite cozy now again for my farewell.

I delivered my last sermon on February 3 (on "the peace of God, which surpasses all understanding . . .").[5] In the middle of the service, a woman surprised me with a song; I was frequently at her home for music making. Mr. Kuhn, who wanted to play on the violin that short Bach piece I sometimes play with Klaus, was forbidden to play by his wife, to keep him from embarrassing himself. It really was a shame.

Now I still face my last lecture the day after tomorrow;[6] then my work 131
here is over, and I can turn my thoughts completely toward the trip home. I want to depart here on the seventeenth or eighteenth and then, depending on Klaus's time, return so I'll probably be with you again during the last days in February. That's just three more weeks, and I already know how quickly they will fly by. But it's also nice to be going home for good again, and I'm already really looking forward to it.

I'll write the next letter to Grandmama. Please say hello to her for me. Also my brothers and sisters, whom I'd like to thank for their greetings, also Suse and Walter for the instructive book, which aroused everyone's interest here.—I'll withdraw the money before my departure and bring it with me, since the peseta has recovered again.

Again many thanks, affectionately, yours
Dietrich

I know Lütgert only from a lecture in which I didn't like him at all, but I do believe that Seeberg has some influence on him. Lütgert will have even less understanding of my work than does Seeberg.

[5.] See 3/18.
[6.] See 2/3.

71. To Julie Bonhoeffer[1]

Dear Grandmama,

Please pardon me for answering and thanking you for your birthday greeting with a postcard. But you can imagine how my time is just being devoured at the moment. So again, many, many warm thanks for the gift you had already announced at Christmas, which will become reality in the coming year.

132 In all likelihood, I'll be departing Barcelona on Sunday evening, February 17, at 7:00—with one eye weeping and one laughing—and will then visit Klaus in Geneva on Monday and see how much time he has for showing me around the area a bit. From there I'll travel by way of Stuttgart, where I might stop over for a day, home to you, that is, on about February 27–28 or March 1. Until then, looking forward to a happy, healthy reunion with you all! Affectionately, your grateful
Dietrich

72. To His Parents[1]

My dear Parents,

Tomorrow at this time the whistle will sound on the train that will take me home again. So for now just this brief greeting. It was a wonderful time, but I'm looking forward to being with you again soon.

Until our joyful reunion. Your grateful
Dietrich

73. To His Parents[1]

My dear Parents,

Actually I wanted to go ahead and travel on from here tomorrow. When I arrived, Klaus suggested I get some information at the League of Nations

[1.] *NL*, A 19,2 (7); handwritten card from Barcelona; postmark illegible, probably ca. February 10, 1929. Partially reproduced in *GS* 6:163.

[1.] *NL*, A 19,1 (39); handwritten postcard from Barcelona; probable date: February 16, 1929. Partially reproduced in *GS* 6:163.

[1.] *NL*, A 19,1 (40); handwritten from Geneva; probably February 22, 1929; partially reproduced in *GS* 6:164.

concerning the question of the churches and the League; since he has some good connections with the librarian there, he can help me locate materials.[2] Well, I was there for the first time yesterday and tried to get an over- 133
view of things, but have not found anything yet. Today I still have to look through the question of protection of children, minorities, and calendar reform,[3] and if anything catches my attention I'll prepare an article on it; but that would extend my stay here by another week. I am, however, assuming I'll be finished on Tuesday and will arrive in Berlin on Wednesday or Thursday.

The weather is unfortunately nothing special; the mountains are shrouded in haze. And then this barbaric cold; whereas five days ago I had lunch on the Tibidabo without even wearing a coat.

I'm now really looking forward to seeing you again and don't believe I'll stay here very long.

Greetings to everybody. Affectionately, yours
Dietrich

Klaus sends greetings.

74. Report by Fritz Olbricht to the German Evangelical Church Committee[1]

Barcelona, February 26, 1929

Report of Pastor F. Olbricht in Barcelona on Vicar Dr. Dietrich Bonhoeffer

The vicar Dr. Dietrich Bonhoeffer, assigned to me by the kind mediation of the German Evangelical Church Committee, left Barcelona on February 17 of this year after completing his term as vicar with me on February 15.

[2.] With a research grant from the German Research Foundation (Notgemeinschaft der Deutschen Wissenschaft, forerunner of the Deutsche Forschungsgemeinschaft), Klaus Bonhoeffer was doing preliminary work at the League of Nations in Geneva for his book on international law, *Die Meistbegünstigung im modernen Völkerrecht.*

[3.] [The effort to replace the irregular Gregorian calendar, which expires each year, with a perennial calendar that would remain the same from year to year.—CG]

[1.] *NL*, D 11 (38f.); handwritten, from Bonhoeffer's personnel file at the Evangelical Consistory of Mark Brandenburg. Previously published in *GS* 6:165–67. Cf. 1/66. Olbricht apparently sent this report to the German Evangelical Church Committee, but it was filed in Bonhoeffer's personnel file at the Brandenburg consistory.—CG]

Regarding his deportment during this time, I can only say that it was always and in every respect beyond reproach.

Through his sensitive, charming nature and unmistakable character, he was
134 able to gain the sympathy of the entire German colony. He particularly devoted himself energetically and with kindness to the young people, who were enthusiastically devoted to him. This was primarily evident in the well-attended children's services, which took place regularly each Sunday and which were his sole responsibility. In a truly exemplary fashion, he produced a nativity play in the church with the children on the Sunday before Christmas, a project whose endless rehearsals and practice demanded a great deal of hard work. There was enormous participation from the German colony, and the play was performed to great satisfaction.[2]

He also became involved with the older children and recently met with them weekly during the evening to discuss religious questions.

He usually delivered one sermon per month, although he also often represented the pastor by preaching and attending to pastoral matters during the latter's travels to the diaspora.

During my own leave, which I spent in Germany from July to September, a time when services used to be canceled because of the heat, he preached every two weeks and was able to excite his listeners to such an extent that they came regularly. His sermons were well thought through and contained profound and rich ideas; in his presentation he developed a self-confidence remarkable for his young age and gave the impression of a pastor with many years of experience.

He participated with great interest in all the activities of the ministry to this overseas congregation; both with the pastor and independently, he visited families, the sick, hospitals, the English seamen's home, and the Young Men's Christian Association. He also became acquainted with the work in the seamen's mission. During my frequent absences, he took over confirmation classes for me, and I was quite satisfied with his representation and instructional methods.

He familiarized himself with the history and spread of the gospel in Spain, the meaning and breadth of the German foreign diaspora, and the history and meaning of the German congregations in Spain. At one point, he spent a week in Madrid substituting for the pastor there, Lahusen, and had the opportunity to become personally acquainted with the German congregation there as well as the evangelization activity of Fliedner.[3]

[2.] But compare in this regard 1/75, pp. 174–75.

[3.] After 1870, Fritz Fliedner founded numerous churches, schools, and orphanages from his home base in Madrid and in 1899 united the congregations in a Spanish Protestant church, the Iglesia Evangelica Española.

In initial contacts with the congregation and house visitations, he assisted the pastor admirably. 135

Because the pastor functions as the treasurer of the German relief agency, the vicar had the opportunity to become acquainted with and gain actual experience in the difficult work of relief for the poor with regard to transients and residents. For several weeks he was the pastor's sole representative in this work, a task he performed with great competence.

He assisted the pastor in completing office work. He regularly participated as a guest in the congregational council meetings and the meetings of the relief agency. He acquired considerable proficiency in the Spanish language.

With regard to his continued theological training, I can report that he addressed scholarly theological questions as well as practical questions with the pastor and also studied the Bible. He industriously employed his free time for further work and also got to know Spain through traveling. He revised his dissertation for publication and began work on his postdoctoral dissertation. During the winter, he delivered four religious lectures in the church on the following topics:

(1) The Tragedy of Prophecy[4] and Its Lasting Meaning
(2) Jesus Christ and the Essence of Christianity
(3) Foundations of a Christian Ethic
(4) The Contemporary Religious Situation and the Question of Modern Christianity[5]

All four lectures were well attended, even by otherwise indifferent people and those of other confessions. He captivated people and offered them a great deal through his rich knowledge and excellent delivery, so that everyone parted from him with regret.

His activities here justifiably raise the greatest hopes. I wish him God's blessing in his further career.

F. Olbricht
Pastor of the German Congregation Barcelona

[4.] [Olbricht here adds a third term *Prophetie*, "prophecy," to the two terms used above by Bonhoeffer himself.—CG]

[5.] A fourth congregational lecture has not been preserved (though see 1/67, p. 165, where, on January 10, 1929, Bonhoeffer announced *two* further lectures). [Note also Bonhoeffer's requests to Walter Dreß on December 17, 1928, and again on January 12, 1929 (1/60a and 1/68a) for a copy of Tillich's *Religious Situation* in preparation for "the fourth lecture." It has not been confirmed, however, that Bonhoeffer wrote or delivered a fourth lecture.—CG]

136 **75. Diary Entry concerning Fritz Olbricht**[1]

Pastor Olbricht

The first impression at the railway station was quite sympathetic: a man without pathos, without empty phrases, without a blasé manner, without arrogance. He speaks in short sentences, since he often swallows phrases, extremely fragmented, as if he were a bit embarrassed. He comes from Westphalia and is still extremely attached to his home despite his long stay abroad. He is large, with black hair and a broad head on powerful shoulders. It seems he curls his hair sometimes. You never see him without a cigar in his mouth. He gives the impression of being a person who enjoys life, or better: who enjoys pleasure. He likes to smoke and likes to eat and drink. The material side of life is of great importance. He has read little and studied even less. His main reading material is nationalist literature and newspapers. He is intemperate, is quick to rant—though never toward me, but certainly toward women and children. But he's basically quite good natured. He typically first yells at those in need, assuring them they will receive nothing from us, and yet in the end never sends anyone away without something. He roars at the confirmands when they ask something or call it into question, and in the next moment he doesn't even remember it.

His house is furnished quite unconventionally. He's not impressed by bigwigs, and there, too, can quickly start ranting. He is by nature quite honest toward himself; he makes neither himself nor others out to be anything special. Whence his perhaps otherwise uncontrolled worldliness (skatmania!),[2] but hence also his popularity in the congregation—outside the church walls.

He obviously missed his calling. He would have been better suited as a forest ranger or a soldier. His sermons are uninspired and scandalously boring, his pastoral care nonexistent, his instruction hopelessly uncomprehending.

137 I got along well with him; since I was staying only a year, I let many things go that I otherwise would have challenged. He initially did not seem jealous of me. That emerged only after my services were much better attended than his, after which he no longer announced ahead of time who would be

[1.] *NL*, A 18,1; handwritten on pp. 19–21 of the diary; undated, though certainly written toward or after the end of his time as vicar. Previously published in *GS* 6:167–68.

[2.] [A craze for the card game skat.—CG]

preaching. The strong attendance at the lectures was unpleasant for him; the success of the nativity play annoyed him such that we had a clash. Otherwise everything went smoothly. His excitement was almost childish when he received birthday presents, etc.; he knew that I stuck up for him everywhere, so everything ended nicely. The entire year we never once discussed a theological question, let alone a religious one; we basically remained strangers, although we did like each other. He granted me all the freedom I wanted, and for that I was grateful to him.

B. Academic Assistantship, Postdoctoral Dissertation, Second Theological Examination in Berlin. March 1929–September 1930

76. To Detlef Albers[1] 138

Dear Mr. Albers,[2]

The *Sternstunden*[3] on the table here next to me, which I have finished reading, reminds me that I wanted to thank you for the delightful hours I spent with this book and which remind me of the unfortunately rare hours we spent together. In the course of eight days, one world has sunk, and a new, or rather old, gray one, covered with the moss of tradition, stretches out its hand as if it were the most self-evident thing in the world that I should reach out and take it; the air is close in Germany, close and musty enough to suffocate you, and everywhere it smells like sweat.[4] But, then, what else can one do but go ahead and breathe this air and go along with it all? Running away is no way to live. But believe me, it costs me the most resolute energy and self-control. Everything seems so infinitely banal and dull. I never before

[1.] *NL*, Anh. A 37 (1); handwritten, certainly from Berlin; probable date: March 1929.

[2.] Dr. Detlef Albers, teacher at the German school in Barcelona.

[3.] Stefan Zweig's book, translated as *Decisive Moments in History: Twelve Historical Miniatures.*

[4.] See 1/83, p. 182.

noticed what nonsense people speak in the trams, on the street—shocking. Only one thing is important now: never to forget that this kind of life is unworthy, regardless of whether one is able to overcome it or not.

The time in Geneva was quite exciting inasmuch as I made some contacts with people at the League of Nations and was thus able to orient myself a bit with regard to things in the League of Nations that interest me.[5]

I must now make a few professional decisions here, albeit nothing of particular consequence. I will go ahead and do my qualifying work for lecturing [habilitieren]; why, more on that perhaps sometime later or in August.

139 What are you up to? Write and tell me sometime. How is Karl-Heinz doing there with you? Tell me about him sometime, too, and pay a bit of attention to him. Please say hello to Thumm—he needs to write sometime! and Röhrsheim![6] Stay well.

Cordially yours,
Dietrich Bonhoeffer

77. To His Parents[1]

My dear Parents,

April 5 is Seeberg's seventieth birthday. It's supposed to be a rather grand affair. I will have to go as well. Do you want to send something or not? Should I take something? I already made a contribution for the seminar's gift. So it's probably hardly necessary now. If I should get something for you, please do let me know immediately.

Everyone is doing well. Bärbel[2] just has a slight temperature. Rüdiger[3] is back.—Your thanks to Grandmama just arrived. She will see to whatever is necessary. Today I go to Mrs. Schwabach, whom I met yesterday at the St. Matthew Passion.

Otherwise nothing new.

Affectionate greetings from Grandmama and your
Dietrich

[5.] See 1/73, p. 171.

[6.] Ludwig Röhrsheim, classroom teacher of Karl-Heinz Köttgen at the German school in Barcelona.

[1.] *NL*, A 19,1 (41); handwritten postcard from Berlin to Glotterbad; postmarked March 30, 1929.

[2.] Barbara von Dohnanyi, born on June 27, 1926.

[3.] Rüdiger Schleicher.

78. To Helmut Rößler[1] 140

Grunewald, April 5, 1929

My dear Rößler,

That you thought of me on the occasion of your wedding, when I believed that I had long since fallen out of sight and mind, is a truly great pleasure for me. Many, many thanks. I have written your mother-in-law. Your invitation landed on doubly tilled earth: first, only the previous day I had been toying with the idea of visiting you some Sunday morning in your village[2] to pick up the thread that has been severed now long enough; second, and probably as a result of those musings, I dreamed about it the very night before receiving your invitation with the early mail. So I was assured of our mutual wish not to allow the external course of events, or, better, the physical distance, to cause our friendship to lapse, and that made me very glad indeed. Today I can't even write you about all that occurs to me with regard to the two coming events—unfortunately I have neither the time nor the peace and quiet—just rest assured that during the days until I see you again, I will often be with you in my thoughts, as is a friend with a friend and one Christian with another. I'm looking forward to Tuesday, when I'll see you again at this significant moment. Take care and please give my regards to your fiancée;[3] and accept my most faithful good wishes, yours

Dietrich Bonhoeffer

79. To Helmut Rößler[1] 141

April 7, 1929

My dear Rößler,

The news of your father's death,[2] following so quickly on the happy news of a few days ago, has utterly shocked me. And even if one knows that after such a long period of suffering a man has indeed earned peace, one still stands speechless before the language of the facts; and this blow will be particularly hard for you at this time. It must be unspeakably hard to harbor so much pain and so much joy at the same time. But you are not bearing

---

[1.] *NL*, A 20,4 (2); typewritten copy; the original has been lost.

[2.] Probably Beveringen near Pritzwalk; see 1/164, p. 281.

[3.] Alice Jutta Rauth.

[1.] *NL*, A 20,4 (3); typewritten copy; original lost; certainly from Berlin.

[2.] The consul Walter Rößler.

this pain and joy alone; all your loved ones bear it together with you as well, as does the entire congregation and your Lord, who never leaves a person alone; and this will give you assurance and strength and will transform even the harshest blow into a blessing.

I wish I could be with you on Monday afternoon. But I cannot make it possible. And one more thing: if you would prefer to celebrate your wedding on Tuesday with only your immediate families, I beg you, please just let me know.

Rest assured you will be in my thoughts both in difficult and in good times.

Yours,
Dietrich Bonhoeffer

80. From Detlef Albers[1]

Barcelona, April 14, 1929

Dear Mr. Bonhoeffer,

My dilatoriness certainly would have given you as much reason to have Thumm prompt me to write as for having me prompt him to write.

142 Your letter made me feel the same as we so often felt here: whereas you find life in Berlin to be stale and worthless, I can only respond that I feel the same way *here*. I hear people talk only about celebrations and other such events and about themselves, that is, about one another, and if the literary circle or choral club has a well-attended evening, then only because Dr. Seyfang[2] is speaking or Miss Hührling[3] is playing. If, on the other hand, an outsider gives a talk on a substantive topic, then only twenty people are there. People go only for social reasons or out of curiosity concerning their dear neighbors, but not for the sake of the event itself. Especially since my trip, I perceive my own presence here almost as a mere hotel stay during which the others concern me very little. Why did you have a different experience here? It is probably just our respective personal situations that determine what role Barcelona plays in our journeys. Because I know what you had here, I want to be cautious and not let my own feelings turn into a judgment on the German colony here. But I prefer the trouble in Germany to the superficial and egoistic security here, which has a whiff of desertion about it.

[1.] *NL*, C 22; handwritten.
[2.] Rector of the German school.
[3.] Not otherwise identified.

On my trip I saw a great deal of Spanish Catholicism—the Roman variety that tempted you to convert,[4] I think, must have been quite different, for I really cannot possibly imagine such a temptation in my own case.

Hoping to hear again from you, too, occasionally, cordially yours,

D. Albers

81. To Karl-Friedrich Bonhoeffer[1]

Dear Karl-Friedrich,

Would you please ask Mr. Harteck[2] to telephone his marina to see whether by chance a place is available? I'm afraid I don't know its name.[3] And ask if he could give some thought again to whether he might think of something 143
else (perhaps Potsdam?). For I have to decide tomorrow; in any event I can find accommodation in Pichelswerder, though I would prefer something else. Perhaps Mr. Harteck can see about that tomorrow morning, and then could you please call me sometime before midday to let me know whether you have found anything? Many thanks and greetings

Dietrich

82. To Max Diestel[1]

Grunewald, May 14, 1929

Dear Superintendent Diestel:

I only learned just now from my brother-in-law Dreß[2] that he did not have the opportunity yesterday to explain my absence. I was so tied up with work for a seminar session that to my great regret I was unable to accept your

---

[4.] See, e.g., the remarks in Bonhoeffer's 1924 Rome diary, *DBWE* 9 (1/57), pp. 89 and 107.

[1.] *NL*, Anh. A 14 (3); handwritten card from Berlin; postmarked May 13, 1929. See also *NL*, A 19,2 (11); typewritten copy with date and address.

[2.] Paul Harteck; see 1/30, p. 109, ed. note 2. [Bonhoeffer was trying to make a reservation for a boat trip along the Havel River.—CG]

[3.] Referring to the marina.

[1.] EZA 29/G 442, 21; handwritten, date of receipt stamped May 15, 1929, Diary no. 2416; Bonhoeffer incorrectly dated his note April 14, 1929. See also *NL*, A 30,2 (11); typewritten copy.

[2.] Walter Dreß.

kind invitation.[3] Allow me to ask belatedly that you be so kind as to excuse my absence.

With best regards and greetings, from my grandmother and parents as well, I remain respectfully your humble servant

Dietrich Bonhoeffer

83. To Detlef Albers[1]

June 9, 1929

Dear Mr. Albers,

When you opened the envelope just now, you probably thought that such
144 lethargic correspondence probably doesn't make much sense. And yet I would regret it if we didn't hear from each other at least occasionally.

Your last letter was not exactly a paean to Barcelona and its inhabitants. You are probably right that our different impressions derive from different paths of development. But if one believes one understands something of the nature of what spirit really is, can one not somehow welcome a turn away from what has in fact become an all-too-human spirit—including the spirit of humanism (or perhaps *this* very spirit is meant)—and the turn to the "material," which is also bequeathed by the spirit and is less likely to be subject to misunderstanding? Perhaps today as never before, "spirit" really is to be found in the particular, that is, precisely in the "material," in concretely given reality—and precisely not in "intellectuality"; viewed from this perspective, I really do find in Barcelona life something like an unconscious search for truth being expressed. But you say you haven't found that, and I certainly will not ignore this dissenting view.

Do you get to know people more closely? That is, the so-called unintellectual ones? For the impression acquired among the general population is, to be sure, quite different than when one has closer personal contact.—I cannot yet feel comfortable again here in Germany. The intellectual overproduction has something repugnantly nonintellectual about it. To me it smells too strongly of sweat in Germany; that is not an impartial aesthetic judgment of the situation, rather I fear that it is Germany's fateful path from the love of work, the love of science, from the ἔρως of seeking, and from freedom to servitude under all that, and that is the path to the murder

[3.] Probably the invitation to a candidates' evening; see 1/3 and 1/89.

[1.] *NL*, Anh. A 37 (2); handwritten from Berlin.

of the "spirit." I would really like to discuss this with you sometime.[2] Now you will probably triumphantly ascertain that I have become an "academic" again. I hope that's not true, but I really don't care, since one just can't fight what's in one's blood.

Just a few more words about the present turn in my life. I'm currently an 145
assistant to the chair in systematics, am working on my postdoctorate; the work is becoming increasingly broad, and I don't yet know how I will limit it enough to be able to work in depth. I'll write later about it.

By the way, how is Karl-Heinz doing? His regular reports don't tell me much. I'd really appreciate it if you could let me know soon where the problem might be. Since he will be coming to visit me for several weeks this summer, I would like to give him a bit of remedial help should the occasion arise. I would be very interested in the larger sense in hearing what impression you have of him since my departure. Like all boys' letters, his letters are usually quite dry and not very revealing. But he does seem to me on the whole to be a bit calmer and more focused. Please be so kind as to really write me about this! Please say hello to Röhrsheim[3] for me. Don't take revenge on me by also waiting a month to answer, rather requite evil with goodness![4]

Take care. Cordially yours

Dietrich Bonhoeffer

84. From Ludwig Röhrsheim[1]

Barcelona, June 16

Dear Mr. Bonhoeffer,

Please don't hold it against me that you had to wait so long for a response to your letter.[2] But even the best of intentions didn't help; my work was just too pressing. Moreover you have doubtless already learned the essentials regarding the main point of your letter, namely, the welfare of your problem child;[3] now and then I have also asked Albers and Thumm to tell you that, on the whole, everything is just fine. The secondary school examinations ended successfully yesterday—successfully at least for me—and so now you shall finally

[2.] See 1/76, p. 177.

[3.] Ibid.

[4.] [Probably an allusion to Rom. 12:21.—CG]

[1.] *NL*, C 22; typewritten with handwritten signature; certainly 1929.

[2.] Not extant.

[3.] Karl-Heinz Köttgen.

get a response from me. This time the exams did not go quite as smoothly as
146 has traditionally been the case here. We were significantly stricter this time. But it was about time. First of all, we already had to bar both Lydia David, who is otherwise an extremely pleasant and sympathetic girl, and Seither from the written examination. Lydia had been a little too indolent, and Seither was just not mature enough; he was simply one or two years too young and had perhaps only average talent. The student Georg was quite skillful in making it to the oral examination, even though his consistent grades of nothing but fives in mathematics and chemistry certainly would have prevented him from getting further than perhaps the eleventh grade [Obersekunda] at any German secondary school [Oberrealschule]. But here it sufficed. Given the results of his work, there was no doubt here that nothing could balance out his unmistakable gaps, but we went the extra distance and accepted him into the oral examination. Two tries were more than enough to determine his fate once and for all. So of the seven remaining with us, we were able to give the examination and the attendant blessing only to four.

2.

Tuesday

We just said farewell to Stresemann at the train station after he was received this morning with great enthusiasm. It was mostly—including this afternoon—Catalans who filled the railway platform and conducted an enthusiastic rally for the champion of the minorities.[4]

Through others you are doubtless better informed of life and activities in the colony than I am myself. I live rather withdrawn and hear only what is absolutely essential, and even that not always reliably. Our reading evening unfortunately had to be canceled during the weeks preceding the secondary school exams; Miss Richert[5] suddenly had so much to do because of the exhibition that she was chained to her desk for weeks. Now we have vacation, which will take me to England for two months. A week in the Lake District, a week in Scotland (both weeks with four big hikes, each in the company of some English companions), then a fourteen-day vacation course in London (designed for English teachers, with the special feature that in the hotel where we'll be staying and eating lunch, a prominent English citizen, politician, diplomat, writer, etc. will give an address

[4.] The German foreign minister Gustav Stresemann had attended the fifty-fifth conciliar conference of the League of Nations in Madrid, where among other things he delivered a speech on the protection of minorities. On the return trip, he attended the 1929 World's Fair in Barcelona.

[5.] Dr. Richert, art historian.

after lunch in which he will offer insights into his thinking, goals, and work. So I'll 147
get to know at least ten of the most prominent personalities of contemporary England). Then another fourteen days on a trip to Exeter with an additional vacation course with excursions in Cornwall and to the Isles of Scilly at the southwestern tip, and finally the performance in England closes with a week on the Isle of Wight.

Karl Heinz has pretty much held the line to this point. He recently seems to have acquired some sexual enlightenment of the foulest sort from a couple of shady characters (in part older Spaniards) of our own social rank and others, and then (given his predisposition for bragging) immediately passed his newly acquired knowledge on to younger students, whence the whole affair became known. Mothers came to the school and lodged complaints. But he claims he didn't say much. Apparently, though, a foul wave passed over the entire class, for we discovered drawings whose coarseness and nastiness left nothing to the imagination. I did, by the way, immediately notify Mrs. Köttgen at that time of the matter. The direct result apparently of this "period of enlightenment" seems to have emerged in his grades in French this semester: 2/3+; 4. I'll have him write the final paper soon. Otherwise he has on the whole maintained the same level upon which you left him at your departure. To be sure, I have waited thus far in vain for a response that might betray a bit more profound thinking. Mr. Albers claims to have ascertained such recently. It concerned a question of the worship of God, though the more likely explanation was to assume some direct influence from conversations you had with him. By contrast, in a single hour he can indeed offer answers in abundance betraying everything *but* more profound thinking, often for the amusement of the rest of the class. But, of course, that doesn't really mean a lot yet. He'll still be promoted to the eighth grade [Untertertia] with no problems.

That probably tells you enough about how your problem child is doing. If anything special happens here, you will hear about it immediately. I was, by the way, quite surprised to hear your unfavorable judgments about your first impressions in Berlin. How beneficial it is to spend a couple of years here abroad free from all these professional and social ties. I think everyone immediately sees upon returning just how quickly life begins to weigh heavily upon us again. All my colleagues who were abroad write the same thing. Now, of course, you have probably become "acclimated" again and are no longer sensing the pressure
quite so strongly.[6] Similarly, returning to the surface is no longer so easy once 148

[6.] See 1/76, pp. 177–78.

one is submerged in scholarly activity again; the current then just flows over and past a person. I would love occasionally to hear some of your impressions of life in Berlin and Germany.

Take care; cordial greetings, yours

L. Röhrsheim

85. To Hermann Thumm[1]

Grunewald, June 19, 1929

Dear Mr. Thumm,

For two days after your letter[2] reached me, I could not even think straight; only today, then, am I writing. Even now I hardly dare to believe that you so quickly began to waver in all your principles. I can still hear you proclaiming with utter conviction the ideals of the celibate life on one of our last evenings together—and now—I've hardly turned my back and must hear such things from you. It almost seems that my presence was the only thing keeping you from earlier decisions, and I must confess some satisfaction in seeing that my departure has brought about such a total success. Well, first let me tell you how greatly delighted I was by your letter; since the day before yesterday, my thoughts have turned to you repeatedly and I heartily rejoice along with you. Ultimately, of course, principles are quite good, but only until one is taught something better by the language of reality. That which takes a long time[3] . . . and I am certain that you have made the right choice, and you now have the right to begin dating your life anew and after so many instructive experiences to enjoy life to the fullest. Being a bachelor in various rented rooms is, after all, a meager life, even if one has led as
149 pleasant a life with each other as we did; I will always have fine memories of it.

A slightly painful feeling of being the one left behind or abandoned has come over me; you have attained it, you have made the great decision, and now I stand here a bit sheepishly. But who knows how long fate will make me wait. Friendship is certainly something quite pleasant, and it does indeed make me feel wealthy. The most decisive element, though, is still missing—

[1.] *NL,* A 19,3 (1); handwritten. Bonhoeffer's response to the news of Thumm's engagement.

[2.] Thumm's letter has not been preserved.

[3.] [Bonhoeffer quotes the beginning of a German saying, "*Was lange währt, wird endlich gut,*" "That which takes a long time will be worth it in the end."—CG] well, you have, as it were, reached the goal, and I rejoice with you and with Miss Gumprecht. Now I am anxious to learn about your future plans, how everything will go. I'm glad you will be remaining in Barcelona for a while yet; it's surely the right thing to do. Let me wish you all the best for the future from the bottom of my heart! Please say hello to Miss Gumprecht for me and extend to her my warmest congratulations!

Now I am doubly looking forward to your visit in July—on the evening of the twenty-second, right?—We will have so much to talk about.

And now one request: Could you please ask Röhrsheim and Albers soon about Karl-Heinz's[4] possible gaps, and tell him I should like to work on them with him! And please really do take another picture of him before vacation and send it to me!

Now I must close. The Kuhns send their warm regards and are looking forward just as am I; as is my brother Klaus, who unfortunately will be leaving in eight days to spend six months in London and Amsterdam. All good wishes, Yours faithfully,

Dietrich Bonhoeffer

86. From Detlef Albers[1] 150

Hanover, July 18, 1929

Dear Mr. Bonhoeffer,

So, finally I'm getting around to writing you and also to giving you the requested information about Karl-Heinz.[2] There's not much I can say on this point. In general I was pretty satisfied with him and could have given him a grade of "good" in history if at the very end he had not slacked off and given some really dumb answers. For the other subjects, I would have had to get information from Röhrsheim, which, given our differing opinions regarding Karl-Heinz, would not have worked out so well; and I think Röhrsheim himself has written you once.[3] The grades, of course, will tell you something.

One detail will please you. In the IV[4] class, we had come to the persecution of Christians and to the martyrs' principle that one should obey God more

[4.] Karl-Heinz Köttgen.

[1.] *NL*, C 22; handwritten.

[2.] See 1/83, p. 183.

[3.] See 1/84.

[4.] *Quarta*, the seventh grade; third year of the *Gymnasium*.

than human beings.[5] "But," objected Rosemarie Rösicke, "the Christians who were slaves, when they performed their duties at home, then they were serving human beings and not God." To which Karl-Heinz eagerly responded: "Ah, but serving God is something quite different; you can open the door and things like that for people, but you don't serve God with stuff like that (or: God doesn't need us to serve in that way)."

On the trip back here I traveled together with Mrs. Köttgen and the boy as far as Avignon; then my carriage continued by way of Grenoble to Geneva, and then with stops at Lake Geneva, in Basel, Freiburg, and Heidelberg, I traveled on to here. I plan to stop in Paris on the trip back.

As a matter of fact, I now feel at home in Barcelona rather than here, regardless of how much nicer it is in Germany in and for itself. There really is no stronger tie than one's work, or rather only one.

By the way, I will probably be in Berlin August 1–7; perhaps you can let me know whether you will still be there then or will already be in the Harz Mountains. I hope I can then hear something about you and your work. Sincerely, yours

D. Albers

151 **87. To Detlef Albers**[1]

Dear Mr. Albers,

So, you, too, are now in our parts! Many thanks for your letter. What you wrote about Karl-Heinz I find interesting. I was surprised to hear your sober news that Barcelona has recently come to mean more to you than I would have thought after receiving your last letter. I am anxious to hear what impressions you now have of Germany. Nice that you are coming here. Do you have business here? Although it would have gone without saying that you could have stayed with us, the problem is that on August 4 Karl-Heinz Koettgen is coming here with his mother, who is going to visit her acquaintances (the Kuhns![2] you know them already); in addition, there will be a married couple with a child here using and watching over the house during my parents' absence, and they will also be taking care of me and Karl-Heinz

[5.] Acts 5:29.

[1.] *NL*, Anh. A 37 (3); handwritten from Berlin; probable date: July 20, 1929.

[2.] Mutual acquaintances from Barcelona; see 1/54, p. 150, et passim.

during that time. Moreover, I think only one of the girls[3] is still here. So I regret I can invite you to stay with us only from the first to the fourth, though I will be very pleased if you can. Then it would be easier to talk and do things and would be quite pleasant if, that is, you don't find it too burdensome to move for only those few days.

It would have been nice otherwise as well. You would have visited me in the Harz Mountains for a few days at the end of August! We would have had much peace and quiet! But you will write soon and let me know, won't you?

It's murderously hot and humid here now, and yet I'm supposed to be intellectually creative and grade excruciatingly dumb seminar papers! It's good that vacation will soon be here. Thumm is coming the day after tomorrow, so for almost an entire month I will be living in the Barcelona milieu again. Take care, let me hear from you soon, and very cordial greetings from your

Dietrich Bonhoeffer

88. To Detlef Albers[1] 152

August 30, 1929

Dear Mr. Albers,

Our plan in Barcelona was to spend some time together in the Harz Mountains for a few days at the end of my vacation, and it would have been nice had this plan been realized. Now, however, the end of the vacation is bringing me together with you in a completely different, unexpected (i.e., perhaps that's not quite right—it's just what one says), and much more pleasant way not only for you but certainly for me as well as I think of you. I truly rejoice with you, and this joy is tied to thoughts of the future as well as back to the past. But of what use are they to you? You now have the present, which includes both past and future precisely because it is a clue to more than the present—δος μοι που στω[2] . . . All of us are searching for this. But wherever we seek it, whether in the tasks of our daily lives, in educational ideals of this or that sort, or wherever—one thing remains clear or at least

[3.] [This refers to the servants.—CG]

[1.] *NL*, Anh. A 37 (4); handwritten from Berlin.

[2.] According to Pappus, a remark by Archimedes. The complete statement is δός μοι ποῦ στῶ καὶ κινῶ τὴν γῆν (give me a place to stand, and I will move the earth); quoted by Pappus of Alexandria in *Synagoge*, bk. 8; see *Pappus Mathematicus*, ed. Friedrich Hultsch, 1:1060.

sensed: doubt and temptation [Anfechtung] about the meaningfulness of being cast to and fro, of being at the mercy of things, will not cease as long as we remain focused on ourselves, as long as in one form or another "the other" does not step into our lives. Only then, in πάντα ῥεῖ,[3] in the flux of everything, do we find the stability that receives its potential and its strength from elsewhere.

I have always seen something in friendship that transcends the normal course of events; and so probably every form of community is in some way like the request to the other: δος μοι που στω.—And in this sense I am happy you have found what others must perhaps seek for a long time.

153 Of course, I would love to hear something about your plans, but don't think you have to respond immediately to this letter. You have more sensible things to think about. Please give my best wishes to your fiancée[4] and be assured I am heartily rejoicing along with you. Yours,

Dietrich Bonhoeffer

89. To Max Diestel[1]

Berlin-Grunewald, October 6, 1929

Dear Superintendent Diestel:

I humbly thank you for your kind invitation to the candidates' evening on the seventeenth of this month. After going back and forth some in the past few days—which is why I am only now writing—it turns out that I would like to travel to our summer house in the Harz Mountains for a few days of peaceful work and for hiking, and I would like to stay there on the seventeenth to make the trip worthwhile. May I request, esteemed Superintendent, that you be so kind as to excuse me on this particular evening?

With best wishes I remain your obedient servant,
Dietrich Bonhoeffer

[3.] "Everything flows, is in flux," a statement ascribed to Heraclitus; see Diels and Kranz, eds., *Die Fragmente der Vorsokratiker* 1:145, lines 27.

[4.] Albers married the assistant teacher Katharina Rupprich in 1931.

[1.] EZA 29/G 442, 20; handwritten; date of receipt stamped October 8, 1929, Diary no. 4161. See also *NL*, A 30,2 (11); typewritten copy.

90. To His Parents[1]

My dear Parents,

We are now settled here quite nicely.[2] Many thanks for your supplies; the cigars were also most welcome for the long evenings.

The weather is autumnal but beautiful; you can always go outside. Usu- 154
ally we go for a few hours after eating and then get into our warm beds to listen for the deer, though until now it's only been at 3:00 a.m. that we've managed to hear them from our beds. It's usually too rainy in the evening. During the afternoon, we usually gather so many mushrooms that we have enough for an evening meal; today we fetched five or six pounds of champignons from your meadow. We're sending Walter[3] a package of them for his convalescence; the rest we want to dry. With the peace and quiet and the early end of the day, it's easy to get work done. We are both delighted to be here. Please say hello to Grandmama.

Affectionately, yours
Dietrich

Warm regards,
Hans Christoph[4]

91. To Hermann Thumm[1]

October 31, 1929

Dear Mr. Thumm,

Many thanks for your last letter. Although the news about Karl-Heinz[2] was not exactly heartening, it was extremely important for me to hear it; I immediately dispatched a strongly worded letter to him. It probably really hurt his feelings. But that doesn't hurt anything. These stupid things really are scandalous. You expend all your effort on a young rascal like this, and

[1.] *NL*, A 19,1 (42); handwritten postcard from Friedrichsbrunn; after October 6, 1929.

[2.] In the family's summer house; see 1/44, ed. note 2.

[3.] Walter Dreß.

[4.] Hans Christoph von Hase.

[1.] *NL*, A 19,3 (2); handwritten from Berlin.

[2.] Karl-Heinz Köttgen.

in the final analysis he mucks up everything through pure carelessness. That can be really annoying.[3]

It's truly a shame that your plans, that is, those of your fiancée, could not be realized. So Germany will be hosting you again next year. The initial
155 phase is indeed disappointing, but over time you do begin to notice that there are many conveniences here that one does not have in Spain, and that ultimately as a German one does belong in Germany and not in Spain. As far as one's understanding of life is concerned, I think a person very quickly becomes an egoist when abroad. One probably focuses excessively on the conveniences and too little on the ties and obligations life brings you, something you only notice again here. So coming home also has its good side. But that's the way it always is; if you just scrape the wrapping off things, you do ultimately get to some sort of worthwhile core.

You will now really enjoy your last year. Things are already moving toward Christmas again, and we know how fast things start to go then. And yet it's good that the time passes; basically I don't really want to hold fast to any day, I am just glad when each has ended.

What might you be doing down there now? You will not be together much with other people? How are [. . .][4] Wilma's piano lessons? Could you be so good and write me when Olbricht's birthday is? I've forgotten, but it must be sometime soon. Have you spoken to the vicar? I haven't received a single centimo from the ladies yet, but don't say anything.[5]

I'm spending a lot of time writing my postdoctoral dissertation and hope very much to be finished at the end of the semester. It's still completely uncertain whether I will be coming this spring,[6] not for any reasons of betrothal (which would be significantly more pleasant for me), but for domestic reasons. But I can tell you, I guess. One of my sisters, whom the physician insisted should absolutely not have any more children, is expecting her fourth in about March/April.[7] We are all quite worried about this
156 matter, and you will understand that I can hardly bring myself to travel if there really is some danger. But please keep this between us! So it's still

[3.] See 1/84, p. 185, and 1/103, pp. 201–2.

[4.] Illegible; possibly "Doña." The reference is to Karl-Heinz Köttgen's mother.

[5.] An allusion to the loan from his father to the boardinghouse landladies with whom Bonhoeffer lived in Barcelona. See 1/60, pp. 155–56; 1/63, p. 162; and 1/92, p. 194.

[6.] Bonhoeffer finally went to Barcelona from the beginning of April till April 19, 1930.

[7.] Ursula Schleicher, née Bonhoeffer; the fourth child, Christine Schleicher, was born on May 6, 1930.

uncertain when I will be able to come. So it goes when one tries to make plans.

Please write soon, also about Karl-Heinz. Please also ask Albers whether he received a letter from me two months ago. But he needn't write right away just because of that. I just wanted to know whether it arrived.

Cordially, yours
Dietrich Bonhoeffer

92. From Hermann Thumm[1]

November 7, 1929

Dear Mr. Bonhoeffer,

Many thanks for your letter. Unfortunately I didn't get around to responding to you earlier; I am not doing so well at the moment: horrible cold with a catarrh, also a terrible toothache despite weeks of treatment. My work is also regaining the dimensions it had before vacation: three sessions in the evening school (German for Spaniards), woodworking [Werkunterricht], and other lessons. I am also now participating in a language exchange with a pupil from my evening course (student). Things at school are generally going well enough. Karl Heinz wrote a class paper for me today in nature study with a grade of 1–2, recently one in mathematics with a 1; he's supposedly doing somewhat better in the subjects he takes from Röhrsheim.[2] Felix and Doña Wilma are working more firmly with him. I am anxious to see what happens in the grading conference next Thursday. Karl Heinz needs to be taken hold of forcefully, more firmly; then he can do it if he wants.

My plans for the coming year are to stay here (you are probably thinking that I don't know what I want), but it's possible that I can eke out an existence here after all if I can supplement my income a bit with private lessons.

I spoke with the vicar.[3] Right now he is living in the parsonage and gets forty marks in addition to free lodging. He wants to move in with Spaniards now to
learn a bit more Spanish, I believe under the same terms. He asked me to inquire 157
of you how much salary you received.

I contacted Mr. Haag regarding the money, upon which he assured me (and also saw the receipt from the post office) that Mercedes sent you a registered

[1.] *NL*, C 19; handwritten.

[2.] [In the German grading system, 1 is the highest possible mark.—CG]

[3.] Bonhoeffer's successor was Adolf Finndorf; see also *NL*, C 22.

letter with ten marks on October 22. The name and address were correct. Of course, it would be a bitter pill if this letter got lost. Mr. Haag intends to write to you personally about the matter.

Under those circumstances, of course, it's clear you can't take your trip here. Let's hope the matter turns out well despite this.

Mrs. Köttgen is industriously practicing piano, and in two weeks we will already begin with the 𝄢. Felix wanted her to start some music.—The pastor's birthday is on November 12.

That's all for today. Regards to your family and the Kuhn family. Cordially, your

H. Thumm

93. To Adolf von Harnack[1]

Berlin, December 18, 1929

Your Excellency:

As one of those who recently was permitted to become a member of your seminar and to spend unforgettable hours here, allow me, in the name of all those who in the most recent generation of theologians here in Berlin share these sentiments, to thank Your Excellency for the words of farewell
158 with which you addressed us in your recently published book.[2] It remains difficult for us to believe that those are words of farewell; we had all quietly hoped that in the course catalog one day you would invite us to work together with you once more. If, however, it is indeed your intention that this is to happen no more, let us tell you today that there will nonetheless be no farewell for us from this seminar, nor can there be. As long as we are theologians, how can the hours in which we laid our very theological foundations and—even more significantly—in which we sensed the element of Christian self-moderation in theology and life, how can such hours fail to remain vital and incapable of farewell? Nor, Excellency, can we conceal from you that our own joy in your seminar has been powerfully strength-

[1.] *NL,* A 20,2 (2); handwritten. Previously published in *GS* 3:18–19.

[2.] Harnack, *Einführung in die Alte Kirchengeschichte.* The dedication reads: "With the publication of the following pages, I am concluding the seminar in church history I conducted for fifty-four years in Leipzig, Gießen, Marburg, and Berlin (1874–1928) and which has stood at the center of my academic work. A large number of studies and monographs by students on church history has emerged from this seminar; and yet I myself have surely learned more from these sessions than they have. For that I would like to extend to

ened by knowing that what we ourselves hoped is now confirmed by your own words, namely, that these shared hours gave you some joy as well, that you were glad to have been our teacher. That you were our teacher for so many sessions is now past; but that we are permitted to call ourselves your students will remain.

With the most cordial wishes for a merry Christmas and a blessed new year, we now give Your Excellency our own farewell greeting with the deepest gratitude and respect.

On behalf of the old seminar, Your Excellency's most obedient
Dietrich Bonhoeffer

94. To Hermann Thumm[1] 159

December 19, 1929

Dear Mr. Thumm,

Very cordial Christmas greetings from our German winter to your eternal springtime. You are probably thinking more intensively than otherwise about Germany these days, and perhaps some of your thoughts find their way to me as well. For the object of your thoughts is not at all that far away from me.[2] The colony will see to it that you don't have to celebrate Christmas Eve in a fashion too foreign. Where would you like to celebrate? Will you be traveling? Last year it was so pleasant there in our little room, too, from ten to twelve o'clock that night! I recall that time fondly. And it will be even nicer—for you, in any case—next year . . . ! It will probably find me in America. That is, next fall the High Church Council is sending me to North America for a year of study, with my main home base being Chicago and New York—I would prefer the latter. I will probably go and must already decide during the next few days. It will probably be of great use to me, so I really must do it.

---

them my enormous gratitude, especially for the warm trust I always encountered in their midst. These pages are my farewell greeting; they will, I hope, recall for the participants the spirit of the Thursday evening sessions. It was a serious and joyous spirit; may that spirit remain true to them in difficult times—Non potest non laetari qui sperat in domino! Berlin, June 1929, von Harnack." Concerning the concluding Latin statement, see 2/4, p. 381, and ed. note 9. ["Those who hope in the Lord cannot but rejoice."—CG]

[1.] *NL*, A 19,3 (1); handwritten from Berlin.

[2.] [Thumm's fiancée lived near Bonhoeffer.—CG]

I haven't heard anything from you in quite a while! Almost two months now! What's going on? Have you been sick? But someone else would have written me if that were the case. Or have I somehow incurred this silence myself? I really wish I could have had an answer to my question, especially concerning the ladies' money. My parents made the whole matter rather unpleasant for me—so I took on the debt myself. But I must say, I can't just throw 250 marks out the window either.[3]

Where have you been paying visits? At the Köttgens'? Anything new to report from Barcelona? It's already been six months since we last saw each other. How quickly time will pass now till the summer. I'm anxious to hear
160 your plans. Take care, let me hear from you again, and have a merry Christmas Eve celebration. Have a nice vacation and a happy, good, eventful New Year!

With many good wishes, greetings from your
Dietrich Bonhoeffer

95. From Adolf von Harnack[1]

December 22, 1929

Dear Mr. Bonhoeffer,

The cordial echo of your letter to my own "Clement" and preface pleased me greatly, and I would like to thank you.[2] Saying farewell is never easy, and it was a wise providence that often makes it difficult for us to say farewell; but if it must be, then mutual farewell is better than unilateral.

I will continue my theological work and am sorry I cannot allow additional company to participate now in "Possidius, Vita Augustini." Until now this excellent student and biographer of Augustine has not been esteemed highly enough.[3]

Materialism, economics, and sports are threatening our intellectual and spiritual existence, and our theological existence is additionally threatened by con-

---

[3.] See 1/60, pp. 155–56.

[1.] *NL*, A 20,2 (3); handwritten; certainly from Berlin. Previously published in *GS* 3:20. See the reproduction in Bethge, Bethge, and Gremmels, *Life in Pictures*, 1986 ed., 59, though incorrectly dated there.

[2.] See 1/93.

[3.] See Harnack, *Possidius: Augustins Leben.*

tempt for academic theology and by unscholarly theologies.[4] Hence, all those loyal to genuine scholarship must hold its banner high all the more confidently, and they must build as kings, yet at the same time not shy away from the drudgery of cartmen.[5] I am sure that you, dear Mr. Bonhoeffer, will always be mindful of that, and I have the utmost confidence in your work and your progress along 161
the right path. I hope you will come to see me often; let me encourage you to do so.

Greet all the members of the sodality[6] whom you see.

Cordially, yours
v. Harnack

96. To Hermann Thumm[1]

Dear Mr. Thumm,

Could I ask a favor of you? Namely, to pass this letter[2] on (in the school)? It deals with rather unpleasant things that Röhrsheim related to me concerning Karl-Heinz,[3] things his parents best not learn about. You may already have heard about them yourself. The letter is sealed so Karl-Heinz can be assured I didn't first give the letter to you to look over. So, pardon me!

Many thanks for your greetings; I'll write in detail soon. My plans for America are firming up. Many thanks and Happy New Year!

Very cordial greetings, yours
Dietrich Bonhoeffer

[4.] An allusion to the 1923 controversy between Harnack and Barth; see Harnack, "Fifteen questions to those among the theologians who are contemptuous of scientific theology," in Robinson, *Beginnings of Dialectic Theology*, 165–66. [See also Rumscheidt, *Revelation and Theology*.—CG]

[5.] An allusion to Friedrich Schiller's saying in the epigrams of the *Musenalmanach für das Jahr 1797* (212, referring to Kant and his interpreters): "Just look how many beggars a single rich person can feed! When kings build, the cartmen have work."

[6.] [Referring to members of his seminar, Harnack uses the word *Sodalen* (from *sodalis*, "comrade"; English "sodalist"), here an old academic designation for scholarly colleagues.—CG]

[1.] *NL*, A 19,3 (4); handwritten card from Berlin; probable date: New Year's 1929/30.

[2.] The letter to Karl-Heinz Köttgen has not been preserved.

[3.] See 1/84.

97. To Hermann Thumm[1]

Dear Mr. Thumm,

May I once again ask you to pass on the letter[2] as directly as possible? Mine did arrive, didn't it? You see, I haven't received a reply yet. Please pardon me for putting you to this trouble.

In haste, yours
Dietrich Bonhoeffer

162 ### 98. To Max Diestel[1]

January 7, 1930

Dear Superintendent Diestel:

Since I am supposed to send letters of reference to the Academic Exchange Service,[2] I took the liberty of giving them your name.[3] If this causes you some trouble, which I hope it won't, please let me express my humblest gratitude to you already today.

With the most respectful regards, Mr. Superintendent, I remain your humble servant

Dietrich Bonhoeffer

99. Application for a Fellowship from the German Academic Exchange Service[1]

I am herewith applying for an open position for study at an American university. To further my academic efforts, I would like to take advantage of an opportunity to study my own particular scholarly discipline, systematic

---

[1.] *NL*, Anh. A 31; handwritten from Berlin; probable date: beginning of 1930.

[2.] See 1/96.

[1.] EZA 29/G 442, 13; handwritten, date of receipt stamped January 11, 1930, Diary no. 304. See also *NL*, A 30,2 (11); typewritten copy.

[2.] On January 9, 1930, Bonhoeffer applied for a fellowship for a trip to the United States (see 1/99). The German Academic Exchange Service (DAAD) requested a letter of reference from Max Diestel; see Morsbach's letter to Diestel, EZA 29/G 442, 16, date of receipt stamped January 11, 1930, Diary no. 290; see also *NL*, A 30,2 (10); typewritten copy.

[3.] For Diestel's letter of reference, see 1/102.

[1.] *NL*, A 26,3 (1); handwritten; the accompanying application with personal information and curriculum vitae is not reproduced here. The references Bonhoeffer listed

theology, as it has developed under completely different circumstances. Hence I would like to pursue the study of dogmatics and its relationship with its two neighboring fields of sociology and philosophy. The subject of my doctoral dissertation was the systematic foundation of a sociology of the church. Hence I would especially view a solid familiarity with the circum- 163
stances of the church in the United States of America as being of enormous value for my entire further scholarly and ecclesiastical work. From the time of my university studies I have traveled abroad often and with great interest; among other things, I spent a year as a vicar in Spain at the Protestant congregation in Barcelona.

Dr. Dietrich Bonhoeffer, Berlin-Grunewald

January 9, 1930

100. Letter of Recommendation from Adolf Deißmann[1]

January 10, 1930

To your kind inquiry postmarked January 10, 1930, I have the honor to reply that I can wholeheartedly recommend Dr. Dietrich Bonhoeffer. He is the son of our colleague Bonhoeffer in the medical school, was one of the most interesting and industrious students of the past few years, attained his doctorate in our department, and then was a vicar in Barcelona. He combines good manners with a healthy interest in the possibilities offered by study abroad.

Very respectfully yours,
Dr. Adolf Deißmann

---

were Adolf Deißmann, Max Diestel, Wilhelm Lütgert, and Reinhold Seeberg. Seeberg's letter of reference has not been preserved; the others follow (1/100–1/102).

[1.] *NL*, A 26,3 (4); typewritten with handwritten signature; letterhead: "Ecumenical Council for Life and Work—Commission for Ecumenical Cooperation between Professors of Theology—The Chair." On December 20, 1929, Deißmann had already sent a similarly worded letter of reference to Senior Consistory Councilor Schreiber of the German Evangelical Church Federation Office; see *NL*, A 26,3 (3).

101. Letter of Recommendation from Wilhelm Lütgert[1]

Berlin-Dahlem
January 10, 1930

Dr. Dietrich Bonhoeffer is my academic assistant in the seminar for systematic
164 theology. He is preparing for his postdoctoral degree in the department of theology here. In view of the significance that church life and social conditions in the United States are increasingly acquiring for Germany, I consider it urgently desirable for young theologians preparing for academic careers to get to know the American church and American academic life firsthand.

Dr. Bonhoeffer is one of our most gifted younger theologians. He has pursued his work methodically and with particular industriousness, and much can be expected of him. Given his upbringing and personality, he will doubtless represent German scholarship in America in a worthy fashion.

He has already been in Spain. However, a year of study in America would be even more valuable to him.

I can recommend him in the strongest terms and am convinced he will justify the trust placed in him.

Dr. Lütgert
Professor
Consistory Privy Councilor

102. Letter of Recommendation from Max Diestel[1]

Berlin-Lichterfelde, January 11, 1930

Dear Sir:[2]

Dr. Dietrich Bonhoeffer is about to take his second theological examination; he intends to complete his qualification for lecturing later. I have advised him, however, because he is still young—twenty-four years old, I think—to look around the world a bit first. He spent last year as a vicar in Barcelona, and if it can be arranged I would like to send him to England for a few months in the spring, on

[1.] *NL*, A 26,3 (6); handwritten.

[1.] *NL*, A 26,3 (5); typewritten with handwritten signature; letterhead: "Superintendent of Church District Kölln-Land I"; see also EZA 29/G 442, 15: carbon copy; see also *NL*, A 30,2 (10); typewritten copy.

[2.] Dr. Adolf Morsbach, senior government counselor (retired), head of the German Academic Exchange Service. For more on Morsbach and his activities in that organization, see Mehnert, *Ein Deutscher in der Welt*, 175–81.

the one hand, to learn the language and, on the other, so that he might familiarize himself with the ecclesiastical and theological situation on the other side of the channel.[3] Personally he is an extremely well brought up, charming person of 165
good character who grew up in an intellectually active and stimulating environment; his father is a psychiatrist at the university and his mother, née von Hase, a granddaughter of the famous church historian. His academic training to this point has been very good, although his practical skills (sermon, catechesis, etc.) should not be underestimated either. He would doubtless represent our university educational system there in a worthy fashion. I can earnestly recommend him, albeit with the request that he be allowed time to complete his second theological examination and to spend a few months in England for the sake of the language. I also think it important for the young people who go to America to acquire a firsthand view of the different college system in England and of the academic methods customary there so that they can compare those with our own, before getting to know the institutions over there.

Very respectfully yours, your humble servant,
Diestel

103. To Ludwig Röhrsheim[1]

January 25, 1929

Dear Mr. Röhrsheim,[2]

I'm very obliged to you for your last letter. The news about Karl-Heinz was extremely important to me. Shortly after receiving your letter, I also received one from Karl-Heinz with allusions in that direction. After I sent a query to him, he then immediately sent a long, almost embarrassingly open admission of guilt. He almost seems to have been waiting to be prompted to get rid of this thing by talking it out with someone. His letter left the impression of a rather intense feeling of being burdened. Things are coming to the surface in him I had not expected, and his description is so unequivocal that one is almost overcome by a feeling of dread in the face of the issues and intellectual eruptions and the explosive class atmosphere in this begin- 166
ning stage of puberty; I myself have never felt so vividly transported back to

[3.] This plan is not otherwise documented.

[1.] *NL*, A 19,2 (19); handwritten from Berlin; corrected date: January 25, 1930. Previously published in *GS* 6:169–71.

[2.] Cf. 1/84.

eighth and ninth grade [Tertianerzeit] of my own Berlin schooldays, into the mixture of curiosity, anxiety, emergent masculinity, and secrecy of the sort common to school classes in the big city, and at the same time I perceived all this more as pressure, as the assault of a hitherto unknown entity, than as pleasant or attractive.

After the summer vacation, Karl-Heinz was enlightened by the older ones in gymnastics class, pored over the obligatory encyclopedia articles, and was thus pulled into the whirlpool without being able to offer any resistance. He didn't know who he could discuss it with, except for his friends. And by the way, he's not much different from any of them (though the only one who went even further with these things was allegedly [. . .]).[3] As to the rest of it, like his pals after their discussion with you and Seyfang, he allegedly never used bad language again. He seems to have come to dread it in a way, since basically he really is not able to understand any of those things at all, not having yet even reached that developmental stage physically himself. This whole complex of new things seems to have assaulted him with such force that he couldn't offer any resistance. It would be good if one could just let him settle down now as much as possible.

You wrote that Mr. Köttgen did not appear at the school despite being summoned. Of course, that seems foolish of him. But perhaps it's just as well; perhaps he knows himself well enough. He is a man of such sensitive nerves and sensibility, at the same time of an almost senseless rigor regarding his son's upbringing, especially in such matters, that his acquiring any knowledge of details in this case would not help anyone. He would probably undertake such counterproductive pedagogical measures that it seems better to me that you and I and possibly the mother take care of things alone as best we can. This just between you and me.

167 Let me thank you again for your letter, and please be so kind as to keep me informed of the matter as your time allows. After spending so much time with the boy, I really am concerned about his fate.

I was so pleased to hear you were able to take your trip south this Christmas, and I must confess it filled me with not inconsiderable envy, recalling my own trip last year. After completing my postdoctoral degree, I will probably be going to America in the fall to study and to give lectures. Till then, however, I still have much to do, especially with my English, which has really languished. I wish you well for the coming time and must at the same time

[3.] Illegible.

beg your pardon for bothering you with my problem child, who probably does not seem all that important to you.—How are the literary evenings going?

With best wishes, your devoted
Dietrich Bonhoeffer

104. From Reinhard Mumm[1]

Charlottenburg, January 27, 1930

Dear Dr. Bonhoeffer:

Your kind words were doubly welcome to me. First, I learned about your social-ethical work and about your related study trip to North America, and then I also learned about your scholarly work. I spoke personally with Privy Councilor Dr. Seeberg and hope to be of use to you either through the Prussian Minister of Education or in connection with the Seeberg Foundation.[2] It would be a personal pleasure for me if we could discuss this matter in person. Would it be possible for you, for example, to come to the Reichstag tomorrow, Tuesday, January 28, at 3:00 p.m.? Just in case, I have enclosed a card to facilitate your entry into the building; please be so kind as to fill out the date on the card yourself. If this 168
appointment time is not suitable to you, perhaps we could arrange the place and time by phone (Westend 3785) for Wednesday or Thursday morning.

Respectfully and humbly, your
Dr. Mumm

105. To Hermann Thumm[1]

February 8

Dear Mr. Thumm,

Many thanks for your birthday greeting. So, your wedding will be at the beginning of April? In this regard, this spring I will come to Barcelona for about ten days after all. But when? In all likelihood, I can only come after March 20, since my oldest brother is getting married.[2] Now, I would really

[1.] *NL*, C 23; typewritten with handwritten signature from Berlin.
[2.] This matter probably involves publication subsidies for *Sanctorum Communio*; see 1/131, as well as *DB-ER*, 130, and *DBW* 1:4 and *DBWE* 1:10, 22.

[1.] *NL*, A 19,3 (5); handwritten from Berlin; certainly 1930.
[2.] Karl-Friedrich Bonhoeffer married Margarethe von Dohnanyi on March 22, 1930.

like to be down there for two Sundays. So I could leave first on March 26. In this regard, I'd like to know (1) when is school vacation? (2) Does a holiday of any sort fall during this period? Ideally I'd like to come neither completely during the vacation period nor completely when school is still in session, since I'd like to have time for excursions during this period. (3) When is your wedding? I would, of course, be enormously pleased if I could still attend, assuming you would permit it. I have to be back here by April 15 for reasons already mentioned.

Also, where do you think I should stay? I could, of course, stay with the Köttgens. But how would it be if I get back some of my money[3] through free lodging with the ladies so as not to put the Köttgens to any trouble? Could you please see about it, assuming you are still living at Eusebio 59? I'll write to the Köttgens myself. I also want to preach on one of the Sundays and conduct the children's service. So it will hardly be possible for me to come as a surprise. I have resolved to come because otherwise the earliest
169 I could come would be after another two years, and by then I will be long forgotten. Because my parents didn't want me to fly, they have for better or worse had to give me the trip as a birthday present. So now I am unfortunately coming by train, which will take two days.

Please write soon, especially about the vacation period. Many thanks, and greetings till we see each other again soon!

Cordially, yours
D. Bonhoeffer

106. To Helmut Rößler[1]

February 23, 1930

My dear Rößler,

I was delighted by the happy news from your household. How are your wife and the little boy?[2] I hope with all my heart that everything will turn out well and that your wife can come home again soon. Truly, much has been given and entrusted to you. That you, in addition to being a pastor and a

[3.] See 1/94, p. 196.

[1.] *NL*, A 20,4 (4); typewritten copy; certainly from Berlin. Partially reproduced in *GS* 1:54.

[2.] Diethelm Walter Rößler was born on February 18, 1930.

husband, are now also the father of a son—well, it's really a great thing. I join in your happiness from this distance, for our lives did proceed for a short period alongside and with each other, and one doesn't forget that so quickly.

I would certainly like to come visit you on a Sunday or for a day during vacation. But there is just always so much else going on that we will have to make do with occasional mutual greetings. I am just about to hand in my postdoctoral dissertation, will be taking my second examination during the summer, and then in September will be going to North America. There's just so much to do to get ready. I will soon be going for fourteen days to visit my congregation in Barcelona, of which I am very fond, and I feel in general that academic work will not hold me for long. But I do acknowledge that it is quite important to acquire beforehand the best academic training possible.

The book by Fendt[3] seems quite valuable to me, and similarly G. Dehn's 170
interpretation of Mark[4] has really got my attention. I recently heard a sermon by R. Seeberg that was shameful. Shallow religious babble for forty-five minutes; it was painful. Fendt and Dehn are almost the only ones I can really listen to. From most of the others I really do hear consistently—nothing. That's what's so terrible. I'd like to talk with you sometime. My own generation here has basically died out, is already working, or is in the seminar; one really must rely upon oneself here, for the students, sad as it may seem, unfortunately give *very* little reason for hope.

Take care, father Rößler! Please extend my warmest greetings to your wife and many good wishes. I am thinking of both of you and your dear boy.

Faithfully, yours
Dietrich Bonhoeffer

[3.] Fendt, *Der Wille der Reformation.*

[4.] Dehn, *Der Gottessohn.* Concerning Bonhoeffer's later involvement in the "Dehn case" in 1932, see DBW 11, 1/40, as well as *DB-ER,* 177 and 235–36.

17:88 **106a. From Klaus Mehnert to August Wilhelm Schreiber**[1]

March 10, 1930

Dear Senior Consistory Councilor Schreiber:

I am extremely pleased to report that, contrary to expectation, we have suc-
17:89 ceeded in securing Dr. Bonhoeffer a position to study at Union Seminary in New York. We just received the following telegram from Miss Dybwad:

"Bonhoeffer accepted Union."

With respectful best wishes,
Your humble servant,
Dr. Klaus Mehnert[2]

[1.] EZA 5/2865; typewritten with the letterhead "Academic Exchange Service, Berlin C2, Schloss, Board: Prof. Dr. Bruns, Chair, Min[ister]-Dir[ector] Prof. Dr. Richter, Berlin, Vice-Chair, Prelate Prof. D. Dr. Schreiber, Münster, Vice-Chair, Franz von Mendelssohn, Berlin, Treasurer, CHAIR: Senior Government Counselor emeritus, Dr. Morsbach," also telephone number, bank account number, and additional addresses in the margin; addressed to "Senior Consistory Counselor Schreiber, Berlin-Charlottenburg, Hardenbergstraße 12"; previously unpublished. [In an earlier letter of January 10, 1930, Mehnert mentioned a phone call to Bonhoeffer in which he had encouraged him to apply, even though he did not know at the time of positions available in New York and Chicago. See afterword, p. 632.—CG]

[2.] Handwritten signature. This missive is stamped "received" by the Evangelical Church Federation Office (March 12, 1930), with a handwritten remark by Schreiber: "*Note*: I notified Dr. Bonhöffer by telephone, he will receive official word from the Academic Exchange Office." Also handwritten by Schreiber: "Berlin-Ch[arlottenburg], March 14, 1930. Filed. K.B.A."; signature "Gis[evius].," "[illegible] 14.," "Schr[eiber] 3/13"; at the bottom handwritten: "North Am[erica]. 11." See also the German editor's afterword, pp. 632–33.

106b. To Erich Seeberg[1]

Berlin-Grunewald, March 14, 1930

Honorable Sir,[2]

Permit me to submit to you my papers and the enclosed dissertation on the subject "Act and Being: Transcendental Philosophy and Ontology in Systematic Theology." I request that you present my application for the postdoctoral certification to the honorable faculty.

I remain, honorable Sir, your most obedient

Bonhoeffer[3]

106c. Church Letter of Reference[1]

Office of the Protestant Parish
Berlin-Grunewald, March 13, 1930

Letter of Reference

Dr. Dietrich Bonhoeffer, resident of Wangenheimstrasse 14 in this parish, has requested a church letter of reference.

Accordingly, I hereby certify that he, together with his parents, who have lived here since March 3, 1916, has participated diligently in the church life of our congregation and has conducted himself without reproach in every respect.

[Seal][2]
H. Priebe,[3] Pastor

[1.] Humboldt-Universität Berlin, Universitätsarchiv, Bestand Theologische Fakultät 142, Bl. 307; typewritten with handwritten signature.

[2.] This is an English equivalent to the very formal German form of address for the dean, *Euer Spectabilität.*

[3.] A handwritten note follows: "To colleagues Dr. Lütgert and Dr. R. Seeberg with the request that they would agree to do the evaluation and co-evaluation. Afterward return to the signer of this letter. E Seeberg, March 17, 1930."

[1.] Humboldt-Universität Berlin, Universitätsarchiv, Bestand Theologische Fakultät 142, Bl. 308.

[2.] Seal: "Office of the Protestant Parish of Berlin-Grunewald." [Despite the date, this document is number 106c because it was sent as an enclosure with document 106b. —CG]

[3.] Hermann Priebe was pastor of the church in Berlin-Grunewald and had confirmed Bonhoeffer.

170 **107. From Hermann Thumm**[1]

March 28, 1930

Dear Mr. Bonhoeffer,

I have been waiting for weeks for news from you; surely you already received my letter telling you that my wedding will be on April 10. I've received no response. Do you think your letter got lost? Nor can I glean anything from the contents of your postcard.[2] You must be joking! superfluous at my wedding!!! You are the only guest. Things will go as follows.

The ceremony is at 11:00 in the morning of April 10 at the consulate. Let me once more warmly invite you to act as witness with Mr. or Mrs. Teschendorff. The church ceremony is at 4:00 with a meal following at the Teschendorff home. I met with Mrs. Teschendorff yesterday and discussed everything in detail; she, like me, was very excited to hear you might be the extra guest. No one will be there but you, the Teschendorff family, the pastor, and we two. As far as dress is
171 concerned: I don't have tails and can't afford to buy them, so the only alternative is a cutaway or dinner jacket for *me*, so please bring your dinner jacket. (Please don't forget to bring some decent German cigarettes, Attikah for six pfennigs.) Did you receive my telegram? When will you be arriving? On either the fourth or fifth of April, my fiancée will be departing Lyon. So once again: We and the Teschendorff family are very glad you are coming! That's sufficient! When will you be leaving here? We possibly want to go to Majorca, and you? Where to? It's probably still too cool in the Pyrenees. I also thought of going there at first, but everyone says that Easter is still too early.

I hope to be able to welcome you here!

Sincerely yours,
Hermann Thumm

108. To His Parents[1]

April 7, 1930

My dear Parents,

Because I am only today getting around to writing you, you can see how much I have planned to do here and how full my time is. My second impres-

[1.] *NL*, C 19; handwritten from Barcelona.

[2.] Not extant.

[1.] *NL*, A 19,1 (4); handwritten postcard from Barcelona. Partially reproduced in *GS* 6:171.

sion of Barcelona and its surroundings does not in any way fall short of the first. The walk we took last year together[2] on the heights of the Tibidabo was overwhelmingly beautiful in the evening sun this year as well. The lilacs will soon flower; the first strawberries are already there. I have been received graciously everywhere, and it almost seems to me as if I had not been away at all.

Affectionately, your grateful
Dietrich

109. To His Parents[1] 172

Sunday

My dear parents,

I am now here in Tossa resting up from the events in Barcelona. Every day, morning and evening, something different was going on in Barcelona, and I settled into all the events so quickly that it seemed I had hardly been away. On Tuesday evening I gave a lecture[2] at church. Mr. Thumm's wedding was on Thursday.[3] It was a stormy day today here in Tossa; yesterday I went swimming and lay in the sun. This afternoon they danced *sardanas*[4] in the village.

I will be arriving on Saturday the nineteenth at 7:00 a.m. Warm greetings and many thanks for this wonderful time.

Yours
Dietrich

[2.] During his parents' visit to Spain.

[1.] *NL*, A 19,1 (45); handwritten postcard from Tossa; probable date: April 13, 1930. Partially reproduced in *GS* 6:171–72.

[2.] Not extant.

[3.] See 1/107.

[4.] The Catalonian national dance.

109a. Report on *Act and Being*[1]

Report on the manuscript submitted by Dietrich Bonhoeffer with his application for the postdoctoral degree [Habilitation]: "Act and Being: Transcendental Philosophy and Ontology in Systematic Theology." Reported by W. Lütgert.

The theme of the enclosed postdoctoral dissertation by Bonhoeffer seems natural, given the thought he has given to phenomenology. In his opinion, this topic is the deepest theme underlying all the contradictions within the current theological debate (page 1f.).[2] One need not debate with him about the correctness of this opinion; in any case this problem is the starting point for his thought. His interest is in proving the significance of the act-being problem for the whole range of topics in dogmatics; the connection to Husserl, Grisebach, and particularly to Heidegger (with regard to the latter, even in stylistic turns of speech) is easy to recognize. One cannot, however, speak of a dependence on these philosophers, for occasionally even Heidegger's position is energetically dismissed (92f., 163, 1).[3] But the posing of the problem of phenomenology and the connection to its solutions can be recognized throughout.

Likewise, the comment in the curriculum vitae, that the author has followed the progress of dialectical theology with an active interest,[4] is confirmed by this work. Its course is in a constant argument with dialectical theology, and the familiar concepts of this theology are recurring and to some extent adopted. In this respect, the dissertation is a very characteristic document of the interest that the younger generation of theologians takes in dialectical theology. Yet one cannot speak of a dependence here either, for occasionally there is also a very energetic objection to Barth (e.g., 94, 130, 132, 171).[5] But one cannot fail to recognize the sympathy with Barth's religious standpoint, most especially with the eschatological standpoint, when, e.g., faith is described as determination by the future (178).[6] Kohlbrugge is cited with absolute agreement (150, 153, 164).[7] It cannot be denied that the author is a student of Reinhold See-

[1.] Humboldt-Universität Berlin, Universitätsarchiv, Bestand Theologische Fakultät 142, Bl. 301–6 und 312; handwritten.

[2.] *DBWE* 2:25–32. [The page references in Lütgert's text are presumably to the typescript of the postdoctoral dissertation, which has never been found, not to the printed version that was published in 1931 in the Bertelsman series Beiträge zur Förderung christlicher Theologie, of which Lütgert and Schlatter were editors.—CG]

[3.] *DBWE* 2:97 and 148, ed. note 15.

[4.] 1/124.2, p. 235.

[5.] *DBWE* 2: 98, 123, 153–54.

[6.] *DBWE* 2:158.

[7.] *DBWE* 2:137, 139, 149.

berg. Epistemologically he is explicitly tied to him (33, 38).[8] Otherwise, too, the point of departure that the author has taken from Seeberg is expressed explicitly (97ff., 115, 1).[9] But even here, the author intends to proceed beyond Seeberg's position.

Through the detailed projection of the structure of the dissertation,[10] the course of the argument is so clearly delineated that it is not necessary to repeat here the organization of the study. The table of contents alone illustrates that the proper solution to the problem is found in the church. With that the author connects to his doctoral dissertation, a theological study of the sociology of the church.[11] This conclusion illustrates the basic interest of this study. The conclusion has been written with energetic personal engagement and clearly reflects the religious and theological characteristics of the author. The work as a whole is to be understood from this goal, and one might think that the work could also have been arranged from here so that the solution to the problem addressed in this theme could have been illustrated retroactively, in the doctrine of the church. Given the way the dissertation is arranged methodologically, the impression could arise that the metaphysical problem pointed to the solution to the theological problem of the church, whereas the opinion of the author is the opposite. But it is not necessary to debate this methodological question with him. The dissertation's train of thought is justified on page 6.[12] The problem of act and being is an epistemological one. There the author distinguishes between the transcendentalism that he draws upon and the idealism that he dismisses, in such a way that the former states that the world is in "relation to me" and the second states, "the world is through me."[13] This idealism, which attributes a creative power to the ego, is thoroughly dismissed, as is the kind of transcendentalism for which God, as the author himself puts it, remains "behind" [im Rücken][14] the human being. The author's opposition is directed against the objectivity [Gegenständlichkeit] of the concept of God and the corresponding objectification [Versachlichung] of the concept of revelation, which can connect them to the concept of being, whereas conversely, through the concept of act, continuity is jeopardized. Thus the interest here is in dissolving the tension between the concepts of act and being, and, indeed, in the concepts of God, of

[8.] *DBWE* 2:55, 58.

[9.] *DBWE* 2:101–2, 116, ed. note 40.

[10.] [Lütgert refers to Bonhoeffer's own presentation of the structure of the work; cf. *DBWE* 2:30–32.—CG]

[11.] *Sanctorum Communio* (*DBWE* 1).

[12.] *DBWE* 2:30–32.

[13.] *DBWE* 2:44.

[14.] *DBWE* 2:52.

revelation, and of faith. The objective concept of God, which can connect itself to the concept of being, must be dismissed, because God can be conceived never as object but always solely as the subject of knowledge [Erkennen] (82)[15] and of faith (85),[16] and not only as subject but as creator of faith.

Similarly, revelation cannot be conceived as something objective, as a doctrine or institution or psychic experience (100).[17] Finally, the new ego may not be conceived as experience in the sense of a firm substantial asset. For the new ego or being in Christ "is not a datum of experience but is given to faith as revelation,"[18] as is developed in the continuation of the formulation of R. Seeberg, but also in an objection against him (97–99).[19] The act-being problem in its application to these theological concepts should now be expressed with the church as precondition and be resolved based upon the concept of church (109f.).[20] The church is a unity of act and being (109–48),[21] i.e., actuality and continuity of revelation and faith are bound within it, a continuity that is nonetheless not objectivity (117).[22] I hope that I am not misinterpreting the author when I interpret the application of his general epistemological and metaphysical principles to the concept of church in the following manner. The individual always exists as Christian, as believer, and as reborn only within the church-community. Only in the congregation does he hear the word of God, and through this is treated as a person, through this becomes a person, and also treats the others as persons. Personality, however, and community are not objectivity and are nonetheless continuity. In the congregation, revelation is of the moment [aktuell], i.e., it produces living faith, and yet it is continuous, i.e., it produces an interrelatedness that is not only individual. Revelation is only in the faith of the church-community. In this faith there is a being of revelation. Through the connection with it, the faith of the moment becomes continuous. Only in the congregation does the individual become person; only in faith is there a unity of the ego. In faith within the church-community, act and being are united; the person-being in the congregation is a synthesis of act and being. The concept of being as a thing is loosened through the social relationship (114–28).[23]

[15.] *DBWE* 2:91.
[16.] *DBWE* 2:93.
[17.] *DBWE* 2:193–94.
[18.] *DBWE* 2:103.
[19.] *DBWE* 2:101–2.
[20.] *DBWE* 2:108–9.
[21.] *DBWE* 2:108–35.
[22.] *DBWE* 2:113.
[23.] *DBWE* 2:123–35.

A theological anthropology emerges from this basic idea (149–82),[24] under the contrast between "in Adam" and "in Christ." This doctrine articulates that the confession of sin is a confession of faith: we believe God that we are sinners. We believe God that conscience in itself may be understood not as the voice of God, but rather only to the extent that it is awakened through Christ; that in sin the tension between act and being is lifted to the extent that humanity falls in the individual person, so that the fall is neither a historical nor a prehistorical act, but a suprahistorical one. All definitions of being[25] remain bound to the revelation in Christ; even the idea of creation is an idea of faith, achievable only from the contrast between sin and grace. Only valid for the Christian and only applied by him to the human being, therefore no foundation for the doctrine of salvation. Being a creature means being-in-the-world [Dasein] through and for God. Dying with Christ is faith and not asceticism, for example. Faith is characterized as the determination of the present by the future, hence it approaches hope, as in Barth. In this connection, too, infant baptism is justified. This conclusion 149–82, which I would like to recommend as a characteristic reading sample, powerfully expresses the deepest religious and theological interests of the author, and does so in a language that very clearly elevates itself above the abstract way of speaking in the epistemological part. The explanations extend beyond the circle of problems encompassed by the theme. For that very reason, however, they are significant for the evaluation of the author, since they indicate, beyond the formal examinations of the first section, the material theological interest that motivates him. Here, too, one finds his reference to Luther in the view of sin, conscience, predestination, in the definition adopted from Luther, which doesn't suit his train of thought: "Existence is defined as *pati*" (119).[26] This combination of Luther's thoughts with the epistemological methods of the most recent philosophy and with problems of dialectical theology is characteristic of this work. One may ask whether a unified whole has emerged from these various ideas, but one cannot fail to recognize that the author understands how to preserve his independence over against all the ideas he has adopted here.

[24.] *DBWE* 2:136–62.

[25.] [That is, theological concepts that use the idea of being.—CG]

[26.] *DBWE* 2:116.

For this reason I propose, on the basis of this dissertation, to accept him for the postdoctoral degree.

April 15, 1930.

Lütgert

In agreement with the examiner.

R. Seeberg 5/8/30

To the colleagues of the senior faculty, with a response requested

E. Seeberg 5/13

I agree with the vote of the examiner.

E. Seeberg

Since for the moment we only have to vote concerning admission to the trial lecture [Probevorlesung], I vote for admission. Deißmann 5/16/30

Agreed Sellin 5/19/30

Agreed Bertholet 5/19/30

Agreed Lietzmann 5/22/30

Agreed Mahling 5/30

" Richter 6/3

" C. Schmidt 6/3

" Fabr. 6/3

" Doehring 6/4

110. To His Parents[1]

My dear Parents,

I just arrived here after an uninterrupted trip of thirty-eight hours. And I am writing right away because I just heard, much to my annoyance, that the first card I wrote you didn't arrive at all. Of course, I'm sure you wondered what happened, and it really is terrible. I wrote you at that time that there was a lot going on and that I wouldn't be able to write much. And I also wanted to thank you for making the trip possible for me. But now you had
173 to wait until the card to Grandmama and the second card to you arrived. It is really annoying, and I'm so sorry. But I still remember exactly where I put the card into the mailbox.

[1.] *NL*, A 19,1 (46); handwritten postcard from Berlin to Stuttgart; postmarked April 19, 1930. Partially reproduced in *GS* 6:172.

The time down there was again absolutely wonderful, in Barcelona itself and then three days at the seaside. I am, I think, rather brown from the sun and feel that I have a truly relaxing time behind me. Many thanks for this time.

Upon arrival here I immediately found much work to do. Especially correcting proofs,[2] which I hope to get done today if possible. It poured rain yesterday evening while I was traveling through southern Germany. I hope you are having different weather and maybe a little bit of the Spanish sun. Everything is fine here. Wishing you a happy Easter.

Your grateful
Dietrich

110a. Wilhelm Lütgert to Adolf Grimme[1]

May 5, [19]30

The undersigned director of the department of systematic theology requests that Dr. Bonhoeffer be engaged as a teaching assistant in the department of systematic theology with a commensurate compensation of approximately 150 reichsmarks per month.

The official position of assistant in the department of systematic theology is currently occupied by Professor Stolzenburg,[2] and since he is financially dependent on the income from the assistantship, it is not possible to vacate

[2.] The proofs were of *Sanctorum Communio*; see *Sanctorum Communio* (*DBW* 1), p. 4.

[1.] Humboldt-Universität Berlin, Universitätsarchiv, Bestand Theologische Fakultät, Akte 176/1, Bl. 21–22; carbon copy of a letter written on the official stationery of the Faculty of Theology (Friedrich Wilhelm University, Berlin C2, Franz Joseph Platz); two pages. The original was probably destroyed during the war. Grimme was Minister of Public Worship and Education. First publication in *Dietrich Bonhoeffer Yearbook 2 2005/2006*, 58–60. Edited by Hartmut Ludwig. [Letters from Lütgert about Bonhoeffer were discovered after the publication of *DBW* 17, which contains documents found after their respective volumes had already been published; discoveries after *DBW* 17 are published in the *Dietrich Bonhoeffer Yearbook*.—CG]

[2.] Arnold Stolzenburg had been associate professor since 1927 and in 1933 was appointed full professor in Berlin. The department of systematic theology employed two full professors but only one assistant. The position did not open up until 1931; it was bestowed on Bonhoeffer on November 21, 1931, effective retroactively to August 1, 1931 (Humboldt-Universität Berlin, Universitätsarchiv, Bestand Theologische Fakultät, UK B 327, Bd. 1, Bl. 1–7).

the position. On the other hand, given his age and his academic contributions, I cannot expect him to perform the tasks required of a departmental assistant. As long as Professor Seeberg[3] was head of the department, Professor Stolzenburg's position was different insofar as he was originally a student of Professor Seeberg. Since by contrast I do not have authority with Professor Stolzenburg as did Professor Seeberg, I cannot expect him to function in a relationship to me as dependent as that of an assistant. And in fact I have hitherto not required that he perform the work normally associated with the position of an assistant in that sense and have instead had it done by Dr. Bonhoeffer. In the summer semester 1929, when Professor Stolzenburg stood in for me in Halle, Dr. Bonhoeffer was paid the assistant's salary.[4] Since Professor Stolzenburg has been back here in Berlin, however, he has once again been drawing the assistant's salary. Last winter semester, Dr. Bonhoeffer performed the work of the assistant without any pay. I would be quite uncomfortable if in this semester he had to do the same as well, since given the considerable size of the department and the number of papers that have been handed in,[5] and given the effort he expended in transferring the department to its new rooms,[6] it would be quite inappropriate if I were now actually to ask him to perform the duties of the assistant without pay. Dr. Bonhoeffer is about to earn his postdoctoral certificate[7] and is one of the most gifted among our younger scholars; insofar as he has performed the duties of this assistant's position with a considerable investment of time, he has certainly earned a measure of acknowledgment that should not be made dependent on the fact that he cannot be shown to be needy.

[3.] "Stolzenburg" was originally written here but was then written over. Reinhold Seeberg had been professor of systematic theology in Berlin from 1898 to 1927.

[4.] Bonhoeffer occupied the position of assistant from May 1 to July 31, 1929, for which he was paid 900 marks (Geheimes Staatsarchiv Berlin, Bestand Preußischer Kulturbesitz, 1. HA Rep. 76-Va, Sekt. 2 Tit. X Nr. 190, Bl. 392).

[5.] The tasks of the assistant included examining seminar papers.

[6.] The various departments of the faculty of theology had moved to Dorotheenstraße 3. See also Bonhoeffer's notes from this time, *DBW* 17 (11/1/18a), p. 99, and *DBW* 17 (11/1/27a), pp. 99–103.

[7.] The *Habilitation*; Bonhoeffer earned this certification on July 12, 1930.

Hence I urgently request that he be granted the salary of a teaching assistant already for the current semester.[8]

[signed] Lütgert[9]
E. Seeberg
To the Minister of Science, Art, and Public Education
Berlin W 8
Unter den Linden 4

111. To Karl-Friedrich Bonhoeffer[1]

Dear Karl-Friedrich,

Ursel continues to do well. She just must get a lot of rest because she is easily exhausted.[2] Mama is spending a lot of time over there. Klaus went to Amsterdam again yesterday and hopes to get a final answer soon from Shell.[3]

Yesterday in the dining room I found the two volumes of the "1,001 Nights" tales, which you gave me to send on and which before my trip to Spain I asked to send off along with the accompanying letter. Now the letter is gone, and the books are still here, and no one quite knows the details. Be so good and write the address again to which it should be sent so I can get 174
it off soon. During my trip through Frankfurt on Good Friday evening, I learned through Ludloff[4] that you don't have a telephone yet. On the off

[8.] The minister rejected the application on May 21, 1930, because of a "dearth of funds and in view of the high overall number of assistants already at the disposal of the department of theology." Dean Erich Seeberg objected to this reasoning on July 3, 1930, since the faculty of theology had only six assistants, while the law faculty had thirty (Humboldt-Universität Berlin, Universitätsarchiv, Bestand Theologische Fakultät, Akte 176/1, Bl. 20 and 23).

[9.] Dean Erich Seeberg wrote in by hand "signed Lütgert." His own name underneath, also written by hand, might be confirming the addendum or it could mean that he signed off on the letter in the form in which he read it.

[1.] *NL*, Anh. A 14 (4); handwritten from Berlin to Frankfurt; postmarked May 9, 1930. See also *NL*, A 27,4 (1); typewritten copy.

[2.] Ursula Schleicher gave birth to her daughter Christine on May 6; see 1/91, p. 192.

[3.] The allusion is probably to his application for a position as a corporate attorney.

[4.] Hanfried Ludloff, a friend of Karl-Friedrich Bonhoeffer; see *DBWE* 9 (1/23), p. 43.

chance, I didn't want to have my train leave since I didn't know whether I would catch you at home.[5] Just when I wanted to write you a card hastily from the railway post office, the card machine at the steps failed, and the line at the postal window was too long for me to wait. So I quickly had to get to my train and travel on without having seen you. That was truly a shame. Perhaps Papa will visit you in the next few weeks. Affectionate greetings also to Grete.[6]

Yours
Dietrich

112. To Harold H. Tryon[1]

Berlin-Grunewald, 13. V. 30

Dear Sir,[2]

when I returned from a trip to Spain, I received your kind letter. I beg to express you my best thanks for your kindness in conferring to me the appointement at the Union Seminary. I accept that with the greatest pleasure. I am sure, that the year, which I will spend in your Seminary will be of greatest use for me. When starting from here allow me to write you the date of my arrival.

I remain respectfully Yours
Bonhoeffer

[5.] Karl-Friedrich Bonhoeffer had just received a professorial appointment in Frankfurt.

[6.] Margarethe Bonhoeffer.

[1.] *NL*, A 26,3 (11); handwritten; in original English, including errors.

[2.] The receipt stamp identifies the addressee as Harold H. Tryon, registrar of Union Theological Seminary, New York.

113. To Max Diestel[1] 175

Berlin-Grunewald, May 14, 1930

Dear Superintendent Diestel:

I am herewith applying for my second theological examination. With his permission I have written to Consistory Councilor Coulon[2] with regard to setting the date and reminded him that I would like to leave for America in September. I hope everything is in order in that regard.

With sincere respect, I am your devoted
Dietrich Bonhoeffer

114. Application for Admission to the Second Theological Examination

114.1. Application[1]

Re: Application for the Second Theological Examination

Berlin-Grunewald, May 14, 1930

I would like to request of the Evangelical Consistory of Mark Brandenburg in Berlin, Lindenstraße 14, admission to the second theological examination. At the same time I would like to request that a dissertation I have already submitted to the Berlin theological faculty for my postdoctoral degree in systematic theology, "Act and Being: Transcendental Philosophy and Ontology in Systematic Theology," be credited to me in place of the written academic examination. An assessment of this work by Privy Councilor Prof. Dr. Reinhold Seeberg is attached.[2] 176

Dr. Dietrich Bonhoeffer

2 enclosures[3]

[1.] EZA 29/G 442,19; handwritten, date of receipt stamped May 15, 1930, Diary no. 2410. See also *NL*, A 30,2 (11); typewritten copy.

[2.] Albert Coulon.

[1.] *NL*, D 11 (40); typewritten with handwritten signature; from Bonhoeffer's personnel files at the Evangelical Consistory of Mark Brandenburg.

[2.] The assessment reads: "Dr. Bonhoeffer has presented to the theological faculty a theological dissertation on act and being for the purpose of his postdoctoral degree. The dissertation has been *acknowledged* in the judgment of the faculty in systematic theology as a *good accomplishment* demonstrating quite well not only the scholarly capabilities of the author but also his understanding of the religious problems. Prof. R. Seeberg" (*NL*, D 11 [43]).

[3.] For the curriculum vitae, see 1/114.2; see preceding ed. note 2 for Seeberg's assessment.

114.2 Addition to the Curriculum Vitae[4]

Continuation of the Curriculum Vitae since the First Theological Examination

In November 1927,[5] I passed my doctoral examination summa cum laude before the theological faculty in Berlin; on January 17, 1928, I passed the first theological examination in Berlin with the grade of quite good. The Evangelical High Church Council assigned me as a vicar to Pastor Olbricht in Barcelona for one year. Pastor Olbricht introduced me to the manifold practical church duties in a German Protestant congregation abroad. For me this year has been rich in impressions. Since I had already become especially interested and engaged in youth work during my period of study in Berlin,[6] it was a great pleasure for me that in Barcelona I could devote myself particularly to this branch of practical work as well. I was permitted to reestablish a children's service and to assemble for voluntary religious instruction, as individual groups outside the church in private homes, those classes at the local German school currently without religious instruction (from U^{III} on).[7] It was from these German youth abroad that I really first
177 acquired a vivid perspective on the unique character of German life abroad in general. Through many home visits, I quickly made close contact with the colony and almost always encountered genuine interest in church questions, especially concerning the training of young people in the church, and also found that the people were willing to help in all sorts of ways. Whenever necessary, I represented Pastor Olbricht in preaching, confirmation classes, home and hospital visits (German sailors were often treated in the Protestant hospital there). I participated the entire year in the office hours the pastor kept for the German relief agency and was able to gain valuable experience here. During the summer vacation periods and also during his trips to the diaspora, I represented Pastor Olbricht entirely on my own and depended only on special occasions on the help of the Spanish Protestant pastor. The members of the congregational council always

[4.] *NL*, D 11 (41/42); handwritten; from Bonhoeffer's personnel file at the Evangelical Consistory of Mark Brandenburg.

[5.] [Actually December 17, 1927; see *DBW* 9:639 and *DB-ER*, 96.—CG]

[6.] See in this regard *DBWE* 9:576–77.

[7.] *Untertertia*, the equivalent of the eighth grade.

advised and supported me in all questions and in the friendliest fashion. I owe much inner enrichment to these months. During the winter 1928–29 and with the permission of the pastor and congregational council, I gave a series of lectures in the church on questions of Christian life and thought.[8] Here I found that the congregation did indeed take a lively interest in such questions. At Christmas I performed an old Christmas play at the church with the children.[9] Hence at the end of my assignment as vicar, I was fully engaged in my work and only reluctantly left the Protestant congregation in Barcelona. During my free time I read through several works on preaching and catechetical literature and, to the extent possible, continued my studies in dogmatics. But it was precisely the enormous wealth of impressions I gained from my practical work there, work that took up the vast majority of my time, that was, I believe, particularly fruitful for me. After returning to Berlin, I immediately reported back to the Berlin consistory. I then began an extensive scholarly work with the title "Act and Being: Transcendental
Philosophy and Ontology in Systematic Theology," which has now been 178
presented to the theological faculty here as my postdoctoral dissertation. In this work I try to ground Christian epistemology on the concept of the church. During the past year I have as far as possible resumed my youth work again in my own home congregation of Grunewald and have often and gladly represented our pastor in the children's service and in confirmation classes. In January of this year, Senior Consistory Councilor Dr. Schreiber[10] suggested that I spend a year at an American seminary beginning in September. I would like to act on this suggestion. As far as foreign languages are concerned, I speak fluent Spanish, a bit of French, am presently studying English and hope to complete that study in America.

Dr. Dietrich Bonhoeffer[11]

[8.] See 2/1–3.

[9.] See 1/42, p. 131, et passim.

[10.] August Wilhelm Schreiber; see also 1/100, ed. note 1.

[11.] Superintendent Max Diestel wrote the following remark in the margin: "After his return from Barcelona, Dr. D. Bonhoeffer reported to me, took part in my candidates' conferences as much as possible, and established a connection with his home congregation through practical activities in Grunewald. I consider him to be a young man who is enormously gifted both in church praxis and in scholarly activities, a young man who can only broaden his experience through his anticipated activities in the United States. I recommend things be made as easy for him as possible and at the same time that one keep him in mind for future *practical* work. Diestel Lichterfelde, May 15, 1930."

179 **115. Application from the Consistory to Excuse Bonhoeffer from Attending the Preachers' Seminary**[1]

Berlin, May 22,[2] 1930

Re: Excusing the candidate of theology Dr. Dietrich Bonhoeffer from the requirement to attend a preachers' seminary[3]

Uncommissioned[4]

Reporting: Consistory Councilor Coulon

We request that the Evangelical High Church Council excuse the theological candidate Dr. Dietrich Bonhoeffer of Berlin from the requirement of attending a preachers' seminary and declare his practical preparation for the ministry[5] to have been fulfilled with the completion of the vicar assignment in Barcelona.

Dr. Bonhoeffer passed his first theological examination on January 17, 1928, with the grade "quite good." He was thereupon assigned by (title)[6] with the order of February 2, 1928 (E.O.IV.215) as a vicar to Pastor Olbricht in Barcelona for one year. According to the final paragraph of no. K 39 of the implementation instructions for church law regarding training and employability of clerics, as an interim-period candidate, he should have been assigned immediately after February 22, 1928, to a preachers' seminary rather than as a vicar. Since, however, the candidate has already demonstrated that his academic training is good, both through his first theological examination and now again through his postdoctoral dissertation, which the theological faculty has assessed a good accomplishment, it seems to us that his attendance at a preachers' seminary prior to taking his second theological examination, for which he has registered, is no longer necessary, since he has completed his assignment as vicar in Barcelona with great success.[7]

[1.] *NL*, D 11 (44); handwritten; from Bonhoeffer's personnel file at the Evangelical Consistory of Mark Brandenburg, file reference: K VII 1861. Previously published in *GS* 6:173.

[2.] Date added later; the signatures and an additional date in the margin date to May 20, 1930. Presumably the draft was done in the Evangelical Consistory without a date on May 20, 1930, and its final version sent to the Evangelical High Church Council on May 22.

[3.] Aversion toward the recently introduced requirement that candidates attend a preachers' seminary seems to have been widespread; see 1/19b; 1/149, p. 262; 1/156, p. 274; and *DB-ER*, 121.

[4.] Neither is there any extant direct application from Bonhoeffer. ["Uncommissioned" means that the Consistory wrote on their own initiative; they had not been asked to do so by the higher body, the High Church Council.—CG]

[5.] [Literally "pastoral office," *geistliche Amt*.—CG]

[6.] Evangelical High Councilor; see 1/4, p. 55.

[7.] The signatures of Vits, Gensen, and Coulon follow.

115a. From Erich Seeberg[1]

June 7, [193]0

Diary no. 478
Dear Doctor Bonhoeffer:

On the basis of your postdoctoral dissertation it has been decided to permit you to hold a trial lecture.[2]

The trial lecture will take place on July 12 at 5 p.m. I request that you submit your recommended topics. The faculty will select one from among them.

With best wishes,
Your humble servant
Dean of the Theological Faculty
Friedrich Wilhelm University

115b. To Erich Seeberg[1]

June 8, [19]30

Honorable Sir:

I humbly thank you for the notification of the acceptance of my work. I enclose the topics for the trial lecture. Since my second theological exam will take place between July 5 and 8, permit me to request that the date, if possible, be postponed a few days. If that is not possible, then of course I can also be prepared on July 12.

With sincere respect,
I am, Honorable Sir,
your most obedient
Dietrich Bonhoeffer

[1.] Humboldt-Universität Berlin, Universitätsarchiv, Bestand Theologische Fakultät 142, Bl. 313a; typewritten carbon copy, therefore without Seeberg's signature.

[2.] The trial lecture, which concluded the postdoctoral procedure and constituted something like the oral exam for the postdoctorate, was a lecture not open to the public before members of the faculty. The postdoctoral candidate proposed three topics, from which the faculty selected one.

[1.] Humboldt-Universität Berlin, Universitätsarchiv, Bestand Theologische Fakultät 142, Bl. 313b and c; handwritten.

Topics[2] for the trial lecture[3]
1. The significance of the sociological category for dogmatics
2. On the possibility of a dogmatic system
3. The concept of dialectic in the so-called dialectical theology

In the *inaugural lecture* I would like to lecture on "The Anthropological Question in Contemporary Philosophy and Theology."[4]

180 **116. Response to the Application to Excuse Bonhoeffer from Attending the Preachers' Seminary**[1]

Berlin, June 19, 1930

Under the circumstances presented in the report of May 22 of this year—K. VII no. 1861[2]—we hereby excuse the theological candidate Dr. Dietrich Bonhoeffer of Berlin from the requirement to attend a preachers' seminary according to §11, subsection 1 of the Law for Preliminary Training of May 5, 1927.[3]

for the president
Hundt[4]

[2.] Above this is a handwritten note: "No. 483 To the members of the senior faculty committee with the request for a written vote. E. Seeberg 12/6 votes for topic 2."

[3.] Underneath this is the handwritten addition by Seeberg: "of Dr. Bonhöffer"; in the margin are the faculty votes: "[Illegible] 12/6 Ltz [Lietzmann]; 3 12.VI.30. Lütgert; 3 13.5.[*sic*] 30 Mahling; 2 Richter; 3 Bertholet; 3 Schmidt; 3 Doehring; 3 Sellin; 3 Fabricius; Th[eme] 2 Deißmann 17/6.30; 2 R. Seeberg."

[4.] Bonhoeffer then indeed held this inaugural lecture on July 31, 1930; see 2/7.

[1.] *NL*, A 30,1 (4); typewritten copy of the Evangelical High Church Council's reply to Bonhoeffer on May 31, 1930, reproduced here without the procedural information. Previously published in *GS* 6:174.

[2.] See 1/115.

[3.] Section 11, subsection 1 of the church law referenced here reads: "Upon a person's attainment of the academic doctorate or upon demonstration of at least one year of training and practical activity in an important specialized field of church work, the High Church Council can in special cases excuse that person from the prescribed practical training up to one year."

[4.] Under this signature there follows a handwritten note from Superintendent Max Diestel: "Please also submit this at once: a declaration that the sermon and catechesis as well as the academic work were completed without aids other than those included in the bibliography, in addition consultation with Pastor Priebe or Meumann to set up an evaluation of the catechesis in confirmation classes or children's services—*before* the main vacation period. After July 5, it's too late! Let me know by telephone afterward! Greetings, Diestel!" Bonhoeffer submitted the corresponding declaration on June 24, 1930 (see *NL*, D 11 [55]).

117. From Wilhelm Schubring[1]

Berlin N 65, June 19

Dear Dr. Bonhoeffer:

Thank you very much; in a few days you will be receiving the proofs.[2]

In the meantime I received a copy of the *Hanover Courier* 267 of the eleventh of this month with Prof. Piper's[3] long essay on Harnack. I would like to offer a nasty response. But since after a long feud against these kinds of "young" 181
theologians I must now get along with the "young evangelicals"[4] out of church-political necessity, and since I will even attend their conference in Magdeburg[5] on the twenty-fifth of this month as a guest, unfortunately both I and the *Protestantenblatt* must keep silent. But I wish with all my heart that one of the young ones would tell him: "Wrong!"

If you are not familiar with the paper, I can lend it to you for a *brief period*. Perhaps you could telephone me: Wedding 1977; also to consider how and where one might respond to him.

Humbly, your
W. Schubring

117a. From Erich Seeberg[1]

June 19, [193]0

Dear Doctor Bonhoeffer:

The theological faculty has decided upon the topic of your trial lecture: The concept of dialectic in the so-called dialectical theology.[2] The date of the trial

[1.] *NL*, A 27,5 (1); handwritten. Schubring writes in his capacity as editor of the *Protestantenblatt*. [This was a church newspaper read by both laypeople and clergy.—CG]

[2.] The reference is presumably to galley proofs of Bonhoeffer's address at the memorial service for Adolf von Harnack; see 2/4.

[3.] Piper, "Adolf von Harnack gestorben."

[4.] A movement existing from 1927 to the beginning of 1933 whose goal was a "reorientation of the church"; cf. Neumann, *Die Jungreformatorische Bewegung*, 37–39.

[5.] Second church-political conference of the Young Evangelicals on June 24–25, 1930, in Magdeburg; see *Christliche Welt* (1930), col. 517. [Cf. Stier's report, "Kirche und Politik," cols. 749–52.—CG]

[1.] Humboldt-Universität Berlin, Universitätsarchiv, Bestand Theologische Fakultät 142, Bl. 313d; typewritten carbon copy, without Seeberg's signature.

[2.] A manuscript of the trial lecture has not yet been found nor any report or record of it. Regarding the possible content of his remarks, see *DBWE* 2:85, ed. note 10, as well as the lecture in this volume "The Theology of Crisis," 2/17.

lecture cannot be changed. Regarding the topic of the inaugural lecture, I request that you be in touch with me at the appropriate time.

Dean of the Theological Faculty
Friedrich Wilhelm University

118. To the Consistory[1]

Berlin-Grunewald, June 20, 1930

Re: Examination Essays for the Second Theological Examination
In reference to a letter to me from Consistory Councilor Coulon,[2] I have the honor to present herewith to the Evangelical Consistory of Mark Brandenburg, Berlin Section, my essays for the second theological examination.

Dr. Dietrich Bonhoeffer[3]

182 119. To Helmut Rößler[1]

June 24, 1930

My dear Rößler,

I was very pleased to receive your friendly invitation for next Sunday. I have long been wondering how I might keep my promise to visit you. But this time—unfortunately, it won't work again. I have to conduct the catechesis for my examination in the children's service,[2] eight days later is the second

---

[1.] *NL*, D 11 (47); handwritten; from Bonhoeffer's personnel file at the Evangelical Consistory of Mark Brandenburg.

[2.] Coulon wrote to Bonhoeffer on May 20, 1930: "Because the authorization of the Evangelical High Council still needs to be obtained for your admission to the second theological examination, to save time I am going ahead and sending you the questions assigned for you: (1) a sermon on 1 Thess. 5:16–18; (2) a catechesis on the fifth petition of the Lord's Prayer. Sincerely, Coulon, Consistory Councilor." See 3/21 and 3/22.

[3.] After the signature, Superintendent Diestel entered the following handwritten note: "There is no doubt concerning the independent composition of these essays using no aids other than those listed in the bibliography. I have, however, requested a special declaration from the candidate regarding this matter. Diestel."

[1.] *NL*, A 20,4 (5); typewritten copy; certainly from Berlin; the original has been lost. Partially reproduced in *GS* 1:54.

[2.] On June 29, 1930, in the Grunewald congregation.

examination,[3] then another eight days later a trial lecture,[4] and then a week later my inaugural lecture.[5] So I have my hands full.

It would have been a real pleasure to accept your suggestion, but I just can't make it. Many thanks! Will you be at home in July or August? On September 6 I'm leaving to spend three quarters of a year in America. I would really like to see you before I go. Please remember me to your wife and accept my warmest regards as an old friend. Yours,

Dietrich Bonhoeffer

120. To Sabine and Gerhard Leibholz[1]

June 29, 1930

Dear Sabine, dear Gert,

The thought of little Marianne's birthday tomorrow[2] recalls for me the delightful days I was recently able to spend with you. I wish I could have gone along with your father-in-law to see everyone again and to celebrate the day with you. But let me warmly congratulate you and wish you all the best. On first birthdays one actually thinks more of the parents, who better appreciate such good wishes, than of the actual birthday child. But please 183
say hello to little Marianne for me. I wanted to get her something, but just never got around to it, but I don't think she'll hold it against me.

I still have fourteen days of work, and then if all goes well I will be finished with everything, that is, with the second theological examination and with the trial lecture.[3] Even though I had actually planned to do hardly

---

[3.] On July 5, 1930; see the summons, *NL*, A 30,1 (3).

[4.] The trial lecture (*Probevorlesung*) is also mentioned in Bonhoeffer's letter to the Leibholzes a few days later; see 1/120. [Information about this was first discovered in 2005 by Holger Roggelin. The lecture was held on July 12, 1930, on the subject "The Concept of Dialectic in the So-Called Dialectical Theology." A copy of the text has not been found. For more information about the lecture and the other topics Bonhoeffer proposed, see the editor's introduction, pp. 14–15.—CG]

[5.] Actually not until July 31, 1930; see 2/7, ed. note 1.

[1.] *NL*, A 19,2 (17); typewritten copy from Sabine Leibholz; certainly from Berlin. Partially reproduced in *GS* 6:174–75.

[2.] Marianne Leibholz, born June 30, 1927.

[3.] See 1/119. [See also the newly discovered documents regarding this: 106b, 106c, 115a, 115b, and 117a, as well as the commentary on this in the editor's introduction to this volume, pp. 14–15, 46.—CG]

any work for the examination, I just can't decide to do that, and so the whole day is filled and always passes quickly.

Yesterday we had company; Triepel[4] told so many jokes, and Uncle Rudi[5] apparently such inappropriate ones, that it was quite entertaining. Right now through my open window, I am listening to dance music at the Weigerts;[6] solitary couples are walking about in the garden—just as in the old days!—And I long for nothing more than to dance along with them! Mama has been extremely busy with Suse;[7] if only we could have a bit of peace and quiet in the house again. There is probably plenty at your place, and you sense what a wonderful thing it is.

Take care, say hello to little Marianne. I will be thinking of you tomorrow with affection and good wishes, yours

Dietrich

121. Results of the Second Theological Examination[1]

121.1. Cover Letter from the Consistory[2]

Berlin SW 68, September 4, 1930

In the enclosures you will find the certificate prepared for you on the basis of the successfully completed second theological examination. Enclosed also find a
184 copy of the more detailed evaluations of the written essays you turned in and of the presentation of the examination sermon and catechesis.

We welcome you as a future servant of the Word with the cordial wish that the Lord of the church may bless your intentions and successes to the honor of his name.

[4.] Heinrich Triepel.

[5.] Count Rüdiger von der Goltz.

[6.] The family of the state court director Dr. Erich Weigert; their daughter Maria was one of Bonhoeffer's classmates at school; see *DBWE* 9 (1/11), p. 29.

[7.] According to a letter from Emmi Bonhoeffer to her mother (June 11, 1930), Susanne Bonhoeffer was apparently sick.

[1.] *NL*, A 6 (8); handwritten copy for Bonhoeffer (the document is reproduced in Bethge, Bethge, and Gremmels, *Life in Pictures*, 1986 ed., 72); duplicate drafts of the evaluations and judgments are in the personnel files, *NL*, D 11 (50, 51, 54, and 60).

[2.] Handwritten; file reference: K. VII no. 2559.

We anticipate that you will conscientiously comply with the requirements imposed upon candidates by the church law of May 5, 1927, particularly those in §§18 and 19.[3] Until your appointment to a pastorate, please immediately inform your superintendent and us regarding any change of activity or residence.

Dr. Vits[4]

121.2. Certificate[5]

Considering that the candidate of theology

Dr. Bonhoeffer

born in *Breslau*

on *February 4, 1906*, has taken before us the second theological examination with the grade of

"passed with a grade of very good"[6]

he is herewith granted according to §16 section 2 of church law of May 5, 1927, the authorization for appointment to the ministry and is presented with this certificate with our seal.

Berlin, *July 8, 1930*

Evangelical Consistory of Mark Brandenburg
Dr. Vits

121.3. Evaluation of the Catechetical Examination[7] 185

Evaluation of the catechetical examination of the candidate Dr. Dietrich Bonhoeffer for the second theological examination

The catechesis in parts tends to become too broad, and the effect is tiring. Individual questions are not skillfully worded. They go over the heads of the children and will not elicit the anticipated answer. The individual statements from Luther's explanation are brought in as answers from the children without

[3.] The corresponding sections regulate the employability and worthiness of candidates for the ministry.

[4.] Dr. Ernst Vits.

[5.] Form filled out by hand with the seal of the Evangelical Consistory of Mark Brandenburg. Handwritten entries are printed in italics here.

[6.] ["Very good" translates *recht gut* and means B plus.—CG]

[7.] Typewritten; cf. *NL*, D 11 (54); typewritten form with handwritten entries. The evaluation was turned in by Paul Fahland on June 30, 1930.

any discussion of the explanation beforehand. That is, a familiarity with them is apparently being presupposed, a presupposition that will probably prove to be false. According to his meditation, the author is concerned with bringing the children to an understanding of the concept of guilt. It is questionable whether he genuinely will succeed along the path he has taken here. Those are the weak points of this catechesis.

On the other hand, the catechesis is well worked out. The ideas are correct. The structure is appropriate. One can thus view the work as

passed.

Evaluation of the catechesis[8]

1. Bearing of the catechist: serious and dignified.
2. Mastery of material: excellent.
3. Posing of questions: correct.
4. Ability to discuss the children's answers: excellent.
5. Discipline: excellent.
6. Remarks: The catechesis was conducted on June 29, 1930, in the children's service of the Grunewald congregation.

186 121.4. Evaluation of the Sermon[9]

Evaluation of the examination sermon of candidate Dr. Dietrich Bonhoeffer for the second theological examination

---

Despite text-critical problems, the author correctly seeks to discern the internal relationships of the entire text from the perspective of verse 18b and views all three imperatives, to rejoice, to pray, and to give thanks, as arising from God's will for life as revealed to human beings in Christ. Hence the thematic formulation and disposition are justified. The execution is borne by a profound consciousness of the present crisis in Germany, and in a straightforward, penetrating fashion the author is able to make the message of the joyous Christian life relevant for the congregation. The external aspects are without fault.

Overall evaluation: Good.

[8.] Typewritten; see *NL,* D 11 (51); typewritten form with handwritten entries. Max Diestel supplied this evaluation.

[9.] Typewritten; see *NL,* D 11 (50); typewritten form with handwritten entries. Karl Schlabritzky supplied the evaluation on June 27, 1930. [Cf. 1/118, ed. note 2.—CG]

Evaluation of the sermon[10]

1. Bearing: Simple, natural, dignified.
2. Memorization: Excellent.
3. Voice: Powerful, needs strengthening in the lower registers.
4. Emphasis: Appropriate.
5. Gesticulation: Lively.
6. Remarks: The sermon was delivered on July 20, 1930, in the church in Teltow.

121.5. Results of the Second Theological Examination[11]

Results of the Second Theological Examination for the Candidate
Dr. Dietrich Bonhoeffer

born in *Breslau*	on *February 4, 1906*
examined in Berlin	on *July 5–8, 1930*

1. Exegesis of the Old Testament	*very good*	
2. Exegesis of the New Testament	*very good*	187
3. Church History and History of Dogma	*very good*	
4. Dogmatics and Ethics	*excellent*[12]	
5. Practical Theology I (service of worship etc.)	*good*	
6. Practical Theology II (pastoral care etc.)	*good*	
7. Practical Theology III (church law)	*generally good*[13]	
8. Pedagogy	*good*	

[10.] Typewritten; see *NL*, D 11 (51); typewritten form with handwritten entries. Max Diestel supplied the evaluation.

[11.] Typewritten form; cf. *NL*, D 11 (60); typewritten form with handwritten entries. The entries are in italics here.

[12.] ["Excellent" translates *sehr gut* and is equivalent to A, a grade rarely given in German academic exams.—CG]

[13.] [Equivalent to B minus.—CG]

9. Examination essays	biblical theology: *very good*[14] church history and the history of dogma: — systematic theology: — practical theology *good*[15]
10. Scholarly Examination Essay	*Postdoctoral dissertation accepted as examination essay*
11. Examination sermon:	*good*[16]
12. Catechesis:	*passed*[17]
13. Special remarks:	
14. General evaluation:	*very good*

Dr. Dibelius. Coulon.
Fahland. Dr. Bertholet.
Dr. Mahling. Schade.[18]

188 122. Evaluation of Bonhoeffer's Catechesis by Karl Meumann[1]

Evaluation of the catechesis of candidate Dr. Bonhoeffer, Berlin-Grunewald, Wangenheimstraße 14

1. Bearing: serious and dignified but without stiffness
2. Memorization: excellent
3. Voice: clear, understandable, and pleasing
4. Emphasis: appropriate
5. Gesticulation: lively but not exaggerated

[14.] See 2/6.

[15.] See 2/5.

[16.] See 3/22.

[17.] See 3/21.

[18.] Otto Dibelius, Albert Coulon, Paul Fahland, Alfred Bertholet, Friedrich Mahling, Karl August Friedrich Schade.

[1.] *NL*, A 30,2 (12); typewritten copy from the files of the superintendent's office, Berlin Kölln-Land I. This evaluation has been entered on a typewritten form intended for the sermon and appears neither in the personnel files nor in the certificate materials issued to Bonhoeffer himself.

6. Remarks: The candidate was able to rivet the attention of the children and to prompt them to participate on their own. The children's answers were skillfully utilized and the remarks and questions discussed without the catechist being diverted from his train of thought. He has considerable experience in church instruction and understands how to adapt to children.

Berlin-Grunewald, June 30, 1930 H.[2] Meumann, Pastor

123. Application for Leave of Absence from the Probationary Year[1]

Berlin-Grunewald, July 14, 1930

Re: Probationary year

I request that the Evangelical Consistory of Mark Brandenburg, Berlin section, grant me leave of absence for one year and permit me to accept a position offered to me for two semesters at Union Theological Seminary in New York.

Dr. Dietrich Bonhoeffer[2]

[2.] Thus spelled in the copy; correct name: Karl Meumann.

[1.] *NL*, D 11 (62); handwritten; from Bonhoeffer's personnel files at the Evangelical Consistory of Mark Brandenburg. [The "probationary year" (*Hilfsdienstjahr*) was the first year of ministry. During this year new pastors were assigned as assistant or associate pastors; they were free to pursue a call after successful completion of the probationary year.—CG]

[2.] On July 24, 1930, the consistory responded positively to Bonhoeffer and fixed the beginning of the year of assistant ministry for August 1, 1931, with the request for notification on July 1, 1931, "whether you will be applying to take up your year of assistant ministry in the district under our supervision" (*NL*, A 30,1 [5]; draft in *NL*, D 11 [63] with the marginal remark: "Bonhoeffer will probably become a lecturer (*Privatdozent*) in 1931."

189 **124. Communication from the Department of Theology to the Ministry for Science, Art, and Public Education**[1]

124.1. Cover Letter from Erich Seeberg

Berlin C 2, August 1, 1930

I have the honor to report to the Minister that *Dr. Bonhoeffer* qualified [habilitiert] in the Department of Theology as lecturer in systematic theology on July 12, 1930.[2]

I have the honor to enclose:

1. a curriculum vitae,[3]
2. a personal information form,
3. a doctoral diploma,
4. a bibliography.[4]

The doctoral dissertation will be published in a revised form in about eight days and will then be turned in immediately.

The postdoctoral dissertation, which has not yet been published, will be turned in later.

It addresses the topic:

"Act and Being": Transcendental Philosophy and Ontology in Systematic Theology.

The Dean
E. Seeberg[5]

[1.] *NL*, D 4 (1); typewritten form with handwritten signature; reproduced in Bethge, Bethge, and Gremmels, *Life in Pictures*, 1986 ed., 71.

[2.] *DB-ER*, 135 incorrectly dates the postdoctoral certification to July 18, 1930. [July 12 was the date of Bonhoeffer's trial lecture (*Probevorlesung*) that qualified him for university teaching.—CG]

[3.] See 1/124.2.

[4.] Ibid.

[5.] On August 16, 1930, the ministry then sent a memorandum to the *Hochschulkorrespondence*, the university's official gazette, regarding Bonhoeffer's acceptance as a lecturer; see *NL*, D 4 (2).

124.2. Enclosures: Curriculum Vitae and Bibliography[6]

Curriculum vitae

I, Dietrich Bonhoeffer, was born on February 4, 1906, in Breslau, the son of university professor of psychiatry Karl Bonhoeffer and his wife, Paula, née von Hase. In 1918 my father accepted a position in Berlin. Here I attended the Friedrich Werder Gymnasium until the tenth and eleventh grades [Sekunda], then the Grunewald Gymnasium, humanities section. At Easter 190
1923, I passed my secondary school examinations [Abitur] and immediately began studying theology, first with two semesters in Tübingen; then I was able to spend three months in Italy; I began studying in Berlin during the summer semester 1924. With gratitude I would especially mention my teachers Professor Reinhold Seeberg, Professor Adolf von Harnack, Professor Karl Holl, in whose seminars I participated for several years. My main interest from the outset was systematic theology. I have also continued to study the newer and most contemporary philosophy, especially phenomenology. In the field of recent systematic theology, I have continued to follow the progress of dialectical theology with particular interest. With respect to a work on the concept of the church, I studied systematic sociology and the sociology of religion from 1925 on. At the end of the summer semester 1927, I turned in my doctoral dissertation, which grew out of these studies, "Sanctorum Communio: A Theological Study of the Sociology of the Church," here in Berlin and in November 1927 passed the doctoral examination summa cum laude. In January 1928 I passed my first theological examination with the grade of "very good" and was immediately assigned to the Protestant congregation in Barcelona as a vicar. I remained there one year and was engaged during my free time with plans for a study to which I dedicated myself exclusively immediately after my return from Spain, a study titled "Act and Being: Transcendental Philosophy and Ontology in Systematic Theology," which I herewith present to the Department of Theology in Berlin. I have been working since summer semester 1929 as an assistant to Professor Lütgert in the seminar for systematic theology.

Bibliography: 1. Sanctorum Communio: A Theological Study of the Sociology of the Church. 1927, to be published in 1930 by Trowitzsch and Son.

[6.] *NL*, D 4 (1); typewritten with no signature.

191 **125. To His Parents**[1]

August 12, 1930

My dear Parents,

We have settled in very nicely up here together. We are doing most things together without feeling we are disturbing one another. I am running a lot with Hans and Christel,[2] usually twice a day; Karl-Heinz[3] runs along once; the rest of the time he usually stays at home and plays with the children, which is a lot of fun for him. Today is a beautiful summer day, and I want to go into the forest to see some deer. There are an enormous number of mushrooms; you could have a plate at every meal with no problem, and indeed, we do that often. That makes housekeeping a bit easier for Christel.

I'm having a hard time forcing myself to do English. It's incredibly nice being able to be outside day after day. And up here we always resolve to move here permanently, rather than have the house no longer belong to us someday. You really can't imagine a more restorative vacation.

As I see from your letter, dear Mama, for which I also thank you, you are firmly counting on a product for the Polterabend.[4] Until now, though, we have unfortunately all been so inactive and disinclined that we really haven't thought of anything appropriate yet. Sanderhoff[5] is unemployed today for the first time. The boys still have work. Up here, too, things are economically bad, many unemployed people and dissatisfaction.

The Dohnanyis send their greetings. Also Karl-Heinz. Please say hello to Grandmama and Klaus.

Affectionately, your grateful
Dietrich

[1.] *NL*, A 19,1 (47); handwritten from Friedrichsbrunn. Partially reproduced in *GS* 6:175.

[2.] Hans and Christine von Dohnanyi.

[3.] Karl-Heinz Köttgen.

[4.] [A light-hearted party on the eve of a wedding at which crockery is smashed to bring good luck.—CG] The reference is to the wedding of Klaus Bonhoeffer and Emmi Delbrück; cf. also 1/128.

[5.] A neighbor and caretaker of the Bonhoeffers' vacation house.

126. Application from Max Diestel to the German Evangelical Church Committee regarding Bonhoeffer's Ordination[1] 192

Re: Ordination of the ministerial candidate and lecturer Dr. Dietrich *Bonhoeffer*

Berlin-Lichterfelde, August 13, 1930

Pursuant to a personal discussion with Senior Consistory Councilor Dr. Schreiber and Senior Consistory Councilor Besig, I would like to petition the German Evangelical Church Committee to initiate the ordination of ministerial candidate and lecturer at the University of Berlin Dr. Dietrich Bonhoeffer, Berlin-*Grunewald*, Wangenheimstraße 14, and to grant the necessary dispensation, since Bonhoeffer will not have his twenty-fifth birthday until February 1931.[2]

He passed his first theological examination in January 1928, the second in June 1930, both in Berlin and both with a grade of "very good." His postdoctoral certification took place last month at the University of Berlin. According to the recent legal regulation, his work as a vicar is to begin on August 1, 1931.

At the beginning of September this year, he is going to the United States of America and will initially be working at Union Theological Seminary in New York. I understand, however, that he has already been asked to serve the Germans in the diaspora in Cuba during the vacation period.[3] He will presumably also be engaged otherwise with sermons and official duties with other German congregations if, as I hope, he comes into closer contact with the German Protestant congregations there.

It thus seems expedient to me that before his departure he be officially authorized to perform all official ministerial acts. Since both general superintendents 193
of Berlin are currently on leave, I am prepared if instructed to ordain him on August 24 in Lichterfelde.[4]

signed, Diestel[5]

[1.] *NL,* D 11 (65); typewritten copy from Bonhoeffer's personnel file at the Evangelical Consistory of Mark Brandenburg. Previously published in *GS* 6:176–77. The superintendent directed this application to the German Evangelical Church Committee, which was responsible for church work abroad, because Bonhoeffer was to take on some substitute preaching and other help while in New York and thus needed to be ordained.

[2.] The attainment of this age was prescribed by the Church Law concerning Training and Employability of Clergy, §1, section 2, of May 5, 1927.

[3.] Käthe and Elisabeth Horn, who lived in Havana, Cuba, had invited Bonhoeffer. He did indeed travel to Cuba in December 1930. Cf. 1/150, 1/151, and 3/24.

[4.] The application was rejected; see 1/129. The ordination did not take place until November 15, 1931; see *DB-ER,* 231–32.

[5.] Beneath the signature is the following forwarding information: "German Evangelical Church Committee, Church Federation Office. K. A. III 792. Berlin-Charlottenburg, August 16, 1930. Original respectfully forwarded with approval to the Evangelical High Church Council *here.* I would be obliged to be informed of the decision there. On behalf of the committee. Signed Gisevius."

127. To Klaus Bonhoeffer[1]

August 17, 1930

Dear Klaus,

You both naturally want some response regarding the wedding ceremony.[2] I've thought about the following: If, as seems to be the case, I am not to be excused from performances on the Polterabend, it will be almost impossible for me to function as a pastor the next day before the same company.[3] Right now I can't see any solution. I would gladly have performed the ceremony. But when one imagines oneself in the concrete situation, all sorts of difficulties arise.

Maybe you can reconsider. If Emmi just doesn't want Priebe,[4] and if I don't have to perform on the Polterabend, and if the other difficulties can be eliminated, I could still do it. Otherwise you'll probably ask Priebe. If I don't hear any more news from you, I will assume you have asked Priebe. I'll be coming Friday at the latest.

Say hello to Emmi. Affectionately, yours

Dietrich

194 **128. To Julie Bonhoeffer**[1]

Dear Grandmama,

Many thanks for your card.—We are living an unbelievably lazy existence up here. Unfortunately the weather is a bit [. . .],[2] so the children can't get out much. We ourselves are out and about quite a bit.

[1.] *NL*, A 19,2 (12); handwritten from Friedrichsbrunn. Partially reproduced in *GS* 6:175–76.

[2.] The wedding ceremony of Klaus Bonhoeffer and Emmi Delbrück was on September 4, 1930. Concerning the shadow play performed at the *Polterabend*, see *NL*, A 9,5. [For *Polterabend*, see 1/125, ed. note 4.—CG]

[3.] Concerning this sense of professional propriety so typical of Bonhoeffer, a sense prompted by his pastoral ethics, cf., e.g., 1/5, p. 61, and the recollections of Kanitz and Zimmermann, in *Begegnungen mit Dietrich Bonhoeffer*, 114 and 218. [These two pieces are not in the English translation, *I Knew Dietrich Bonhoeffer.* —CG]

[4.] Hermann Priebe, senior pastor in Berlin-Grunewald.

[1.] *NL*, A 19,2 (8); handwritten from Friedrichsbrunn; postmarked August 18, 1930.

[2.] Illegible.

The commotion in the house is making it difficult to get together for the Polterabend play; until now we've had only one idea, and even it has been rendered impossible by the Delbrück plan.[3]

Greetings from everyone! Your grateful

Dietrich

129. Response of the Evangelical High Church Council to the Application for Bonhoeffer's Early Ordination[1]

Berlin-Charlottenburg 2, August 23, 1930

We herewith return the enclosed report[2] (from the office of the superintendent Kölln-Land I from the thirteenth of this month—no. 3402—to the German Evangelical Church Committee) to the Evangelical Consistory for their information with the remark that because of considerations of principle, we are not in the position[3] to approve the ordination of the pastoral candidate and lecturer Dr. Bonhoeffer.

on behalf of the president
signed Karnatz[4]

[3.] The reference is probably to the shadow play for which a series of short sketches had been considered, but this was abandoned; see *NL*, A 9,5.

[1.] *NL*, D 11 (64); typewritten; from Bonhoeffer's personnel file at the Evangelical Consistory of Mark Brandenburg with the letterhead "Evangelical High Council E. O. II 2239."

[2.] See 1/126.

[3.] The "considerations of principle" refer to §1, section 2 of the Church Law regarding Training and Employability of Clergy of May 5, 1927 (see also 1/126, p. 237). §1, section 3 of the same law, however, does indeed expressly authorize the Evangelical High Church Council to waive "the age requirement." Just why this dispensation was not granted in Bonhoeffer's case can no longer be determined.

[4.] Dr. Bernhard Karnatz, consistory councilor and legal advisor on the Evangelical High Church Council.

195 **130. Letter of Recommendation from Adolf Deißmann**[1]

Berlin-Wilmersdorf, September 3, 1930

To the President of Union Theological Seminary New York
My dear President:[2]

By these lines I should like to introduce my dear junior colleague Dr. Dietrich Bonhoeffer, Lecturer in the Theological Faculty of our Berlin University. He is a well trained young scholar and is very anxious to study American Theology and Church life. Perhaps you could give him, so far as it may be possible, some opportunity of travelling in order to see churches and colleges in other States.

With kind regards Yours very sincerely
Adolf Deißmann

196 **131. To Trowitzsch Publishers**[1]

Berlin, September 4, 1930

Dear Doctor Lang:[2]

Many thanks for sending the first copies of my book. Enclosed please find a list of addresses to which I would like to have copies sent.[3] Please send the remainder to my home for distribution later. Financial matters will be handled by my mother, Mrs. Privy Councilor Bonhoeffer, at my address.

The *Seeberg Foundation* and the *Ministry*[4] will presumably be transferring funds directly.

Very respectfully, yours
signed: Bonhoeffer

[1.] *NL*, A 26,3 (9); handwritten; letterhead: "Ecumenical Council for Life and Work—Commission for Ecumenical Cooperation between Professors of Theology—The Chair." [Letter in the original English, including errors.—CG]

[2.] From 1926 till 1945 the president of Union Theological Seminary was Henry Sloane Coffin (see Bethge and Gremmels, *Life in Pictures*, centenary ed., 46); apparently Deißmann was not personally acquainted with him.

[1.] *NL,* A 27,5 (6); typewritten copy, made by Trowitzsch Publishers and enclosed in a missive to Bonhoeffer's father, Karl Bonhoeffer, on January 30, 1931. Partially reproduced in *DBW* 1:4.

[2.] Dr. Walter Lang, authorized signatory of the publisher.

[3.] Not extant.

[4.] Reinhard Mumm had hoped to open these sources up for Bonhoeffer; see 1/104. In the final settlement on the question of financing, differences of opinion arose between the publisher and the father, Karl Bonhoeffer; see *NL*, A 27,5 (4–7) and 1/163, p. 280. Franz Hildebrandt subsequently suggested that the choice of publisher was a "letdown"; see 1/138, p. 247.

C. Fellowship at Union Theological Seminary, New York. September 1930–June 1931

132. To Julie Bonhoeffer[1] 197

September 6, 1930

Dear Grandmama,

Well, this is the first day of my journey. It's 8:30 p.m., and I have finally managed to grab a place in the writing salon. The ship is very quiet. Only the propellers create a bit of ongoing vibration. The day was beautiful. We departed at 10:30 a.m. My parents spent two hours on the ship with me; we had a look at the whole ship. Then we departed amid music and great fanfare and yelling.[2] Until now it's as if we had been on the Wannsee[3] the entire day, totally calm. From our deck you look about twelve meters or more down to the water, through which the ship cuts a deep furrow. My cabin seems not unfavorably located. It lies deep in the belly of the ship. I haven't actually seen my cabin companion yet.[4] I've tried to get a picture of him from the items he has left about. The hat, the walking cane, and a novel

[1.] *NL*, A 27,1 (1); handwritten; letterhead: "North German Lloyd Bremen. On board the steamship *Columbus*." Partially reproduced in *GS* 6:178–79.

[2.] See Bethge, Bethge, and Gremmels, *Life in Pictures*, 1986 ed., 73.

[3.] [A large recreational lake in Berlin.—CG]

[4.] The cabin companion turned out to be a certain Dr. Lucas; see *DB-ER*, 147–48, and *NL*, C 23.

by Seymour suggest an educated young American to me. I hope he doesn't turn out to be an old German prole.[5]

I have eaten two enormous meals with a healthy appetite; in a word, I'm enjoying the ship as long as it can be enjoyed. I've also met several nice people, so the time is going by quickly. I'll soon be going to bed since I'd like to see as much of England as possible early tomorrow morning. Just now we are traveling along the Belgian coast. You can see lights way off in the distance.

198 This letter probably seems a bit confused, but all the impressions flow together so much that you just don't know where to begin writing about it all. Take care, dear Grandmama; say hello to Uncle Otto's family[6] and warmest greetings to you from your grateful

Dietrich

133. To Karl-Friedrich Bonhoeffer[1]

Dear Karl-Friedrich,

The trip has been fabulously beautiful until now, the water completely calm. We are just now traveling along the Belgian coast. And a full moon as well. I'm sitting on deck next to a Dr. von Grosse,[2] who spoke to me because of my resemblance to you; he is also traveling to New York. This first day has raced by. I don't know what I've actually done.[3]

[5.] [Bonhoeffer uses the German cognate, *Prolet*, as in English an abbreviation of "proletarian"; in addition to its class connotation it can also mean "clod" or "lout." —CG]

[6.] The family of Otto Bonhoeffer, where Julie Bonhoeffer was currently staying.

[1.] *NL*, Anh. A 14 (5); handwritten postcard, from the *Columbus*; postmarked September 7, 1930. See also *NL*, A 27,4 (2); typewritten copy.

[2.] In his response of September 1930 (*NL*, C 3), Karl-Friedrich Bonhoeffer was unable to identify him.

[3.] No signature; this companion wrote in the margin: "Best wishes, A. von Grosse." [In all likelihood he was the chemist and atomic scientist Aristid von Grosse, who had worked with Karl-Friedrich Bonhoeffer in Berlin.—CG]

134. To Julie Bonhoeffer[1]

Dear Grandmama,

This card was made on board at departure. You'll find my mother and father on it.[2] Everything continues to go well. We are now on our way to Cherbourg. My next news will be from New York!

Affectionate greetings from your
Dietrich

135. To Karl-Friedrich Bonhoeffer[1] 199

Philadelphia, September 19

The sea journey was perfect. I was picked up in New York, and for the past five days I've been with the Boerickes,[2] where I find it very nice indeed. I do something with the girls every day; we travel around a lot by car. Today I'm supposed to learn how to play golf; in the evenings we're often invited out, or we stay at home and play games. You can hardly believe you're so far away from Europe here, so much is so similar. Mornings I'm often in the clubs. I eat lunch with the Boericke brothers, which is often quite funny. Everyone sends greetings to you. I'm walking here in your footsteps.[3] Please say hello to Grete. Affectionately yours

Dietrich

[1.] *NL,* A 27,1 (2); handwritten postcard from the *Columbus;* postmarked September 7, 1930.

[2.] See Bethge and Gremmels, *Life in Pictures,* centenary ed., 46. [In the published version Bonhoeffer is visible but not his parents.—CG]

[1.] *NL,* Anh. A 14 (6); handwritten postcard. Partially reproduced in *GS* 6:179. See also *NL,* A 27,4 (3); typewritten copy.

[2.] Irma and Harold Boericke with their children Ray, Betty, and Binkie, distant relatives of the Bonhoeffers; cf. *DB-ER,* 11–12.

[3.] Karl-Friedrich Bonhoeffer was in the United States on a lecture trip in 1929; see *DB-ER,* 142.

135a. To Adolf Deißmann[1]

September 23, 1930

My esteemed Privy Councilor Deissmann:

Upon returning from Philadelphia, I found your kind letter of reference to our President Coffin. I would like to express to you, esteemed Privy Councilor, my most humble thanks. Dr. Coffin received me most graciously, and I am to pass on to you his most respectful regards. I hope to have the opportunity to see much of church life here, especially since our seminary is interdenominational and as such offers the chance to make the most varied contacts. Until now I have been working exclusively on my English and am really hoping to get beyond the initial difficulties. I will stay in touch. With best regards and with sincere respect I am, esteemed Privy Councilor,

Your devoted servant
Dietrich Bonhoeffer

136. To Richard Ern[1]

October 14, 1930

Dear Richard,

It's now been over a month since we arrived in New York,[2] and I've already been living here at the seminary for almost three weeks. At the beginning I stayed a while with relatives in Philadelphia. I took lots of excursions there; I really liked it there. How do you like it in New York after spending such a
200 long time in Europe? Are you going to school again? Did you learn English again quickly? Do you still remember Arsenio[3] from the *Columbus*? I've since received a couple of nice letters from him. He told me to send you his greetings as well. Many of the photographs came out quite nicely. Next time we see each other I'll bring you some since you, too, are in a couple of them.

[1.] Bonhoeffer's letter of thanks to Deißmann was only found by Prof. Günter Wirth, Berlin, at the end of the German Democratic Republic. It was located in the Berlin City Library [Stadtbibliothek], Special Collections, Deißmann papers, folder 98, September 1930. The Deißmann Nachlaß is now at the Zentral- und Landesbibliothek Berlin.

[1.] *NL*, Anh. A 33 (1); handwritten from New York.

[2.] On board the *Columbus* Bonhoeffer got to know the young boy Richard Ern and his mother, who were returning to New York after an extended stay in Switzerland. Bonhoeffer became a frequent weekend guest at the family's home; see the letters in this volume to Richard Ern and his parents. [Cf. Bethge and Gremmels, *Life in Pictures*, centenary ed., 46.—CG]

[3.] Yet another acquaintance; there are two letters from him in *NL*, C 23.

You probably thought I had totally forgotten you. But that doesn't happen so quickly with me. I really would be pleased if we could meet again. Would you like to come visit me sometime? Or do you want to go see something in the city? Or should I come out to your family's place sometime? I'd be pleased to do that sometime as well if it suits your parents and if I have the free time.

I hope I'll hear something from you soon. Say hello to your dear mother for me, also to your father, whom I also saw briefly.

Take care. Till we meet again soon! Cordial greetings,

Yours, Dietrich Bonhoeffer

137. From Karl Bonhoeffer[1]

Lugano, October 18, 1930

Dear Dietrich,

Our stay is gradually coming to an end. We're thinking of being back in Berlin on Sunday for Christel's[2] birthday. We hear that you wrote to Claus[3] and that you are doing well. Claus was supposed to send us the letter but has not done so yet. Not much to report about us. Mama's lumbago is better, albeit not yet completely well. We make do with shorter walks and are enjoying the beautiful sun. Yesterday afternoon it was 40° C. in the sun.[4] I'm hoping we might be shortening the long winter evening this way.

We have seen a great many beautiful things, have a beautiful apartment with 201
the entire Monte Rosa chain on the western horizon, lots of charming things in beautiful, nicely situated chapels, villages on the side of the mountain, beautiful vistas of the lake everywhere; one day we were in Bellagio and in the park of the Villa Serbelloni, which was especially nice because we were almost the only people in the broad park between the two arms of Lake Como.

We have not met anyone we know here except the Eichners,[5] whom we met quite by chance—their daughter is here; this evening we will be enjoying a concert at her music school. The guests in the hotel are overwhelmingly Swiss.—The Schleichers may be coming here tomorrow after all.

To help bring you up to date regarding what's happening in the family, I'm enclosing a few letters we received here. Then I won't have to write out all the

---

[1.] *NL*, C 1; handwritten. Partially reproduced in *DB-ER*, 140.

[2.] Christine von Dohnanyi, whose birthday was on October 26.

[3.] Not extant. [Bonhoeffer's brother, normally spelled "Klaus."—CG]

[4.] [Fahrenheit 104.—CG]

[5.] Uncertain reading, not otherwise identified.

details for you. Grandmama probably arrived back in Berlin yesterday evening. On our return trip home, we'll probably stop in at Karl Friedrich's in Frankfurt. I haven't really got around to a vacation here as I originally wanted. We have almost finished *Under Satan's Sun*,[6] which you gave us to read. It interested me very much—I doubt I understood everything; he is probably suggesting that intellectual comprehension is far less important than mystical entry into a kind of different state of consciousness. The dialogue also makes it difficult to discern the trains of thought between the lines. Psychologically the uncertainty whether it is a supernatural experience or a dreamlike creation of illusions, the change in affect with its satanic aspects and its humanly peasantlike, unintellectual simplicity is really extraordinarily vivid. Is that modern or medieval Catholic mysticism?

Mama greets you warmly. She's just writing to Bine;[7] we are sitting on the open veranda. By the way, should we write to the Börickes sometime and thank them for having received you so cordially?

Affectionately
Your Father

202 **138. From Franz Hildebrandt**[1]

Charlottenburg, November 5, 1930

Dear Mr. Bonhoeffer,

Who on earth invented these horrible mornings? In a time when otherwise a call to Pfalzburg 2616[2] used to help one through the worst attacks of yawning, one now sits here helpless before the *Collected Works* of Heussi, Sellin,[3] and Kegel (learn to *kegel* without having to *hegel*!).[4] Your letter is an oasis in the desert—these religio-historical metaphors are unavoidable now, and I then understood the demand so existentially that hardly a half hour after its arrival I ran to the

---

[6.] Bernanos, *Under Satan's Sun*, also translated into English as *The Star of Satan*; see also *DB-ER*, 139–40. [Bonhoeffer was deeply impressed by the novels of Bernanos and recommended *The Diary of a Country Priest* to his students at Finkenwalde.—CG]

[7.] Uncertain reading; probably Sabine Leibholz.

[1.] *NL*, C 10; handwritten. Bonhoeffer had known Franz Hildebrandt since 1927. Concerning the friendship between the two, see *DB-ER*, 138 et passim; see also Hildebrandt, "An Oasis of Freedom," in *I Knew Dietrich Bonhoeffer*, 38–41. [See also Cresswell and Tow, *Dr Franz Hildebrandt*.—CG]

[2.] Bonhoeffer's telephone number.

[3.] Ironic reference to the familiar textbooks on church history by Karl Heussi, *Kompendium der Kirchengeschichte*, as well as Ernst Sellin's *Introduction to the Old Testament*.

[4.] [The German verb *kegeln* literally means "to bowl." Hildebrandt's witticism depends on the similar sound of the two words, *hegeln* being a made-up word. The sense

stationery store so I would now immediately be able to strike all around me with a new sheet of paper, as Eichendorff would say (recalling his violin teacher).

For your own part, you must now reply just as quickly so that you can congratulate me promptly for my examination. After I scheduled the doctoral exam for the twenty-second and Kegel agreed to a date before, I learned yesterday from Sanden that the "first" was not to be until the twenty-second to twenty-fifth, that is, would coincide with the doctoral exam; but because that is not official, I naturally can't do anything about it and must now postpone the exam eight days. The consistory behaves as stupidly as the faculty does things well—and if you were to say anything about it, they would reply: What do we care about your doctorate? But it did give me some consolation when I recently turned in my well-organized essays and read from Luther in his *Papacy at Rome* (1520): "For the sake of authority[5] I have designated this argument with the letters A and B. I want to show that this Romanist (his opponent) knows his alphabet all the way down to B!"[6] Unfortunately, I had to restrain myself from citing this source in a sermon or catechesis. 203

Titius[7] feels that my work can be printed if the publisher wants to and if I receive money. The prospects with the Association[8] and the Seeberg Foundation, of course, are rotten, and yet eighty marks per sheet is considered very little (I was told this by Dress, who by the way also complained that you have already written to me but not to him—this was four weeks ago). If once more I can't pull the money together, then we'll have to publish one together. You'll have to come up with some shameless title—I'm not going to suggest one anymore after you made your views on "advertising" so clear to me. But it serves you right that in return you ended up being let down by Trowitzsch!

There's nothing to report about Berlin theology that's any better than what you are reporting (I'm referring to American theology). Dr. Dr. Dr. Deissmann, Rector Magnificus,[9] spent one and a half hours amid constant applause from

---

of it seems to be: "Learn to think like Kegel without sounding like Hegel!"—CG] The reference is to Martin Kegel; this student quip refers to his book *Away from Wellhausen*, in which Kegel criticizes Wellhausen's alleged Hegelianism.

[5.] [Hildebrandt writes here "for the sake of authority"; the original Luther phrase is "for the sake of clarity." In his letters to Bonhoeffer, Hildebrandt humorously used the Middle German of Luther's era to poke fun at the church authorities. The best example is his 1934 birthday letter to Bonhoeffer in London, which was an extended satirical commentary on the Church Struggle and its leading figures. See *DBWE* 13, 1/66.—CG]

[6.] Luther, "On the Papacy in Rome against the Most Celebrated Romanist in Leipzig," *LW* 39:61. [Hildebrandt's parenthesis.—CG]

[7.] [Dean of the theological faculty at Berlin University at the time.—CG]

[8.] [Association for German Scholarship, which funded research.—CG]

[9.] [The translation of this sentence replicates exactly Hildebrandt's sarcastic reference to Deißmann.—CG]

the students (at the end, the balcony was half empty) describing the fate of the New Testament. He enumerated all the extant and lost manuscripts, codices, and translations and found that the New Testament originated "in the open air and open light, not under the Osram lamps[10] of our academic studies," but that a certain "high mystical temperature" was at work in the Gospel of John. "But he let himself think he be not a bad fellow. . . . What help it, that a poor frog puffs itself up, if he should burst he will never be like an ox. . . . This crude miller's beast still cannot sing his hee haw and yet unsummoned he embarks in such things,"[11] remarks Luther at the end (see above) of his "Contra the famous Romanist in Leipzig."

The Apostles' Creed series with Röhricht[12] is moving along quite satisfactorily. He took care of the virgin birth with John 3:8 (as his text),[13] and did so about as honestly as is possible for an adherent;[14] nonetheless he did clearly delineate what the faith of the congregation does and does not cling to. After "suffered and was crucified," the descent into hell must now come. Figur[15] gave an extremely respectable introduction with 2 Tim. 4:2, and Frederking[16] delivered an excellent Reformation sermon on Rom. 1:16f. (the young Luther and the righteousness of God) with new citations from Staupitz and uncommon "objectivity" and radicalism. By contrast, Schwebel[17] was so markedly inferior with his completely muddled discourse on the prospects and struggle of the church, authorities, school, and the merits of the Hohenzollern[18] and on the spirit of obedience in faith and of discipline that it really must suffice for now.
204 And to conclude my pastor's report: Frederking and Freitag[19] have declared themselves willing to be opponents for me; I haven't been to see Fendt[20] yet.

[10.] [A light bulb invented in 1906 with a filament made of osmium and wolfram, now called tungsten. The Osram fluorescent light was invented in 1936.—CG]

[11.] Luther, "On the Papacy in Rome" (*LW* 39:103). [In the German original Hildebrandt mimics Luther's Middle German.—CG]

[12.] Eberhard Röhricht.

[13.] ["The wind blows where it chooses, and you hear the sound of it, but you do not know where it comes from or where it goes. So it is with everyone who is born of the Spirit."—CG]

[14.] [By "adherent" Hildebrandt makes a somewhat ironic reference to one who subscribes to the dogma of the Virgin Birth.—CG]

[15.] Fritz Figur. [See his memoir of Bonhoeffer in *I Knew Dietrich Bonhoeffer*, 55–56.—CG]

[16.] Alexander Frederking.

[17.] Gerhard Schwebel.

[18.] [The royal family of Prussia, which held the throne until 1918.—CG]

[19.] Probably Dr. Albert Freitag.

[20.] Leonhard Fendt. ["Opponents" were responsible for posing critical questions to the candidate during doctoral oral exams.—CG]

I by no means intend to wait for the work to be published before my degree is conferred, since you would only today be receiving your doctorate had you followed that principle![21]

One more thing: Dehn[22] has had enough of Moabit and wants to go to Schubert's[23] church. I don't blame him—but what if all those with such leanings (Piechowski)[24] end up this way . . . !

Apart from Edgar Wallace,[25] I'm naturally not getting around to much reading. My philosophical friend from Davos[26] is here now—the only partner I have with any *niveau*—and the course of our conversations is making "the problem of mediation" and—from the perspective of the *filioque*—a study of Greek culture, especially of classical Greek culture, ever more urgent.[27] I am, by the way, discovering more and more sympathy and advantages with regard to pietism (we probably talked about this some)—which enables me to see the truth of Frederking's dictum that the philosophy or theology of a person also develops precisely in contrast to that person's natural inclinations (and for me those inclinations are pietistic in one form or another).[28] I hope these rather muddled allusions don't annoy you too much. But I'm just not capable of much more at the moment. Not least because I still want to tell you the latest joke. A Jew on his deathbed is making out his last will and testament. "I want to give my Sabbath cloak to Benjamin."—"Oh," says his wife, "give it to Joseph instead."—"Fine, Joseph shall have it. And Moishe is to have my gold watch."—"Oh, he already has his own," the wife says. "Give it to Samuel instead."—"Fine," he says, a bit annoyed, "then Samuel shall have it. But I want to give my fur to Isaac."—"Oh, but he's getting one for his birthday, give it to Benjamin instead."—The dying man then lifts himself up with his last bit of energy, slams his fist down on the edge of the bed, and says: "Hey, who's dying here anyway!!??"

Cordial greetings and keep having fun!

Yours
Franz Hildebrandt

[21.] [Bonhoeffer's doctoral dissertation, accepted in 1927, had just been published on September 2, 1930.—CG]

[22.] Günther Dehn.

[23.] Not otherwise identified.

[24.] Paul Piechowski.

[25.] [Edgar Wallace was an extremely popular and prolific British writer of detective stories whose books were also translated into German.—CG]

[26.] Not otherwise identified.

[27.] Hildebrandt is referring to the Greek Orthodox tradition that rejects the procession of the Holy Spirit also from the Son (*filioque* in the third article of the Nicene Creed).

[28.] This statement is commensurate with Hildebrandt's lifelong admiration for Paul Gerhardt and John Wesley.

205 **139. From Hans Christoph von Hase**[1]

Dear Dietrich,

The seminar began yesterday.[2] Despite my desperate resistance, Lütgert accepted sixty to sixty-five participants!! Do such numbers flatter him, or is he just not able to defend himself? The topics Lütgert handed out are quite good, and there also seem to be quite a few gifted students among the great masses, which we will organize such that negotiation is still possible and perhaps something of value will emerge after all. I'm looking forward to the sixty seminar essays!—At the bursar's office I learned that the remuneration[3] for October is actually intended for you and that you are asked to indicate where they should send the 150 marks. They want to know soon.

Suse herself is doing well again, as I learned from Walter,[4] whom I met after his lecture.

If Lütgert stays the usual course, it won't be very exciting, and it's absolutely futile trying to take the discussion in a different direction. He can indeed be diverted, but he doesn't keep up substantively.

Very cordially,
Hans Christoph

140. To Richard Ern[1]

November 6, 1930

Dear Richard,

I've certainly made you wait long enough, haven't I? I'm really terribly sorry; but first I misplaced the photographs for a few days, and then I just never got around to writing. I have very, very much to do, and the days go by very
206 quickly. For next week I have to prepare four different presentations,[2] and my English is still anything but exemplary. I fondly recall the wonderful day

[1.] Literary estate of Hans Christoph von Hase; handwritten card; from Frankfurt/Oder; postmarked November 5, 1930.

[2.] Seminar in systematic theology with Lütgert, where Hans Christoph von Hase was representing Bonhoeffer as academic assistant; cf. 1/143, p. 253.

[3.] Assistant's reimbursement.

[4.] Susanne, née Bonhoeffer, and Walter Dreß.

[1.] *NL*, Anh. A 33 (2); handwritten from New York.

[2.] Cf. 2/9, 2/10, and 3/23; a fourth address is otherwise unknown. [Possibly a presentation in a class, perhaps the seminar in philosophical theology.—CG]

I spent out there with all of you; please give your parents my most heartfelt thanks again. I was also very glad to see you again. I only hope we'll get to do it again soon.

Say hello to your dear parents and warmest greetings to you as well from your

Dietrich Bonhoeffer

who definitely has not forgotten you!

141. To Sabine Leibholz[1]

New York, November 7, 1930

Dear Sabine,

Your letter made me very happy. Many thanks for it. It's always nice when I find something from Germany in my mailbox in the morning. Well, you are now already getting ready for the little sibling. You think the beginning of December?[2] In any event, my thoughts wander over to all of you across the water several times each day. [. . .][3] with many good wishes. You'll let me know right away, of course, won't you? Here it's become rather wintry, albeit not 35 degrees below zero Celsius,[4] as your newspaper says, but rather about 35 degrees Fahrenheit, that is, about 0 degrees in Germany. And with a splendid blue sky, but a rather raw wind. So it's not really inviting to go outside, and I wouldn't have time anyway. Right now I am constantly having to prepare speeches and addresses for the most varied occasions; the day after tomorrow I have to preach in English and next week have to speak about Germany before one thousand schoolchildren.[5] I have the rather 207
strong feeling I'm being put on display here, and that's not a completely pleasant feeling.

Life at the seminary is actually quite pleasant and useful. A year will have come and gone before I can get to know all three hundred people here. It's just that most of the time not much comes of one's conversations. I always have the feeling I'm talking with schoolboys [Primaner]. There are, of course, a couple of others; one finds interesting people especially among

[1.] *NL*, A 27,3 (1); typewritten copy by Sabine Leibholz. Partially reproduced in *GS* 6:179–80.

[2.] Bonhoeffer is referring to Christiane Renate Elisabeth Leibholz; see 1/147.

[3.] Lacuna in the copy; original not available for comparison.

[4.] [Fahrenheit 31 below zero.—CG]

[5.] See 3/23, also 2/9 and 2/10.

the Negroes and East Asian students, and there are splendid opportunities here for meeting people from every conceivable country. There are forty foreigners here at the seminary; the "International Student House"[6] is located directly across from us, where we recently had representatives from ninety-seven different nations together.

At the end of November, the seminary has a week vacation.[7] I'll be traveling to Washington with a Negro student.[8] I have to close because I've been invited out; I wish you all the best during the coming weeks. To you, Gerd, and to little Marianne a very warm greeting from your

Dietrich

142. To Julie Bonhoeffer[1]

Dear Grandmama,

I'm back from Washington and am spending the weekend again with the Boerickes. Once again I had a couple of very nice days. Affectionate greetings from us all.

Your grateful
Dietrich[2]

[6.] [International House, on Riverside Drive.—CG]

[7.] [The Thanksgiving holiday.—CG]

[8.] Albert Franklin Fisher, known as Frank; see Bethge and Gremmels, *Life in Pictures*, centenary ed., 48; see also 1/145.

[1.] *NL*, A 27,1 (4); handwritten postcard from Philadelphia; postmark illegible; probable date around November 29, 1930.

[2.] A handwritten addendum follows: "Special greetings, from us to you and the whole family—your Irma, Harold, Ray, Betty, & Binkie"; regarding the Boericke family, see 1/135, p. 243, ed. note 2.

143. From Hans Christoph von Hase[1] 208

Frankfurt,[2] November 30

Dear Dietrich,

I want to give the Cuban Santa Claus a greeting to take along to you.[3] I wanted to send you a small book on Kant by Przywara[4] and ordered it from Uncle Georg,[5] but it's not here yet. So it probably won't reach you until you're back in New York. You are seeing quite a bit of the world these days. I'm really rather envious. Have you also had time to see a bit of the "environs" of middle America?

The seminar meets again tomorrow;[6] I think I'll go out to your folks' place and read through a couple of your letters. Perhaps I can find out from them the extent to which you still belong to domestic theology or have already become an ecumenist.

I'm still chewing a bit hesitantly on my thesis[7] for now (only figuratively, of course!). The leap from a literary historian to a poet is just a bit difficult. I don't have enough genuinely current literature in this regard that I can address, which does, of course, provide a second means of livening things up, even though in the final analysis it is merely "a review of the literature." So I'm coming up with new ideas only every now and then and in the meantime am working on the first part: questions in contemporary theology, where I am currently tempted to place you together with Bultmann behind Ritschl (!!). That is, however, still the best place (where the presence of the Spirit and of history really are one and are viewed from the perspective of the church), if you would not rather be classified with the "image Christology" of Schäder.[8] The whole thing is actually quite brief, however, and I'm classifying types together more in the larger sense and hardly mentioning individual people. How about if I make an exception in your case to the effect: "A noteworthy, promising attempt from one of our young, as yet

[1.] Literary estate of Hans Christoph von Hase; handwritten; date certainly 1930.

[2.] Frankfurt/Oder.

[3.] Bonhoeffer spent Christmas 1930 in Cuba.

[4.] Przywara, *Kant heute*.

[5.] Georg von Hase, a publisher and bookseller.

[6.] See 1/139, ed. note 2.

[7.] His doctoral dissertation, *Die Gegenwart Christi in der Kirche*, which tried to determine the spatial and temporal dimensions of this presence; published in 1934.

[8.] In the final version of his doctoral dissertation, Hase ultimately did not classify Erich Schäder as part of "image Christology" (see Hase, *Die Gegenwart Christi in der Kirche*, 22n1); regarding Hase's "classification" of Bonhoeffer, see *Die Gegenwart*, 35–36 and 74–75.

209 unknown theological hotheads" or something similar? In any case, this typology is not very much fun, but I have to do it to clarify my own point of departure.

In the meantime, I'm trying to get a hold on the main section. *Qua* theology I'm pretty clear in that regard; I just don't quite know yet how to write in a genuinely vivid and readable fashion. The next step is even more difficult, namely, where spatiality is defined as an existential factor in relationship to the person and is to help in dogmatics with regard to the sociological "breadth" of existence.

I went and saw Lütgert on Wednesday; we understood each other quite well. He's able to enter into a foreign train of thought and was effortlessly right on top of everything: the necessity of a presence of the humanity of Christ in the church from the perspective of the Lutheran notion of justification (and correspondingly also in the doctrine of the sacraments) even though in his view that's not really a matter of "Christian experience." Quite astonishingly, he also talked about the nonexperiential character of the effects of the Holy Spirit.

The seminar doesn't have any real momentum yet. Lütgert spends a lot of time discussing biblical passages and individual theological theses but rarely really gets to his own positions, and so the students are not really getting into it. Nonetheless, what he thinks about the Holy Spirit is important to me. Only sixty-five participants in the seminar! Their essays, of course, will be terrific fun.

Hildebrandt made a 2- on his examination, the young Möller a 2; Hildebrandt flew in with Boniface in church history, and Coptic Schmidt[9] didn't ask him about anything further.[10] He's doing his doctoral exams just now. Vandenhoeck is publishing his thesis, eighty-seven marks per sheet.

Klärchen[11] is in art school in Stuttgart; she really likes it there and is learning a great deal. Doerthe[12] is home again and in January will be going to an estate in Mecklenburg to Selschopps, the widow of Ms. Lütgert's brother. She got to know her daughter in Elmau.

On the third Sunday of Advent, I will be preaching on Luke 17, quite apocalyptically. A lot of wonderful church music is being played here just now. Pastor Bahr is conducting very fine liturgical devotionals in which he and the choir sing; then on Christmas we ourselves will be singing along.

[9.] The church historian Carl Schmidt worked mostly with Coptic-gnostic writings, whence his nickname.

[10.] See in this regard 1/149, p. 263.

[11.] Klara von Hase.

[12.] Dorothea von Hase.

Not much to speak of in the way of theological stimulation. It's only with regard to the theological academy professor here that I still have great hopes.[13]
In general, I really would like to start again from the beginning studying at the 210
academy here! It's completely different from the mass operations at the university! The *nova theologia* is also no longer very strongly represented in Berlin. You can't do much theology with Rotermund.[14] By the way, there's a very nice, intelligent American there now, Swithie,[15] who has many acquaintances at Union[16] and wants to get his doctorate in philosophy here, perhaps under Hartmann,[17] who is coming here. (Why only now!?)

That's all I can really say about us. For a "conversation," you'll have to write as well.

Wishing you a happy New Year and a merry Christmas rich with experiences, your

Hans Christoph

Don't forget to have the bursar pay you your money; otherwise it will expire! It will in any event get you a couple of kilometers further around the world. Unfortunately no millionaire with plans to sail around the world has introduced himself to me yet! Perhaps it will still happen!

December 2. I was at your parents' place yesterday. Your mother and Aunt Elisabeth[18] had not yet left for Greifswald.[19] I read the whole package of your letters. Since you write that apparently some letters got lost: I wrote you around mid-October and November 1 (responding to your letter), also a card saying that you should have sent to you *soon* the approximately 150 marks, which Lütgert has apparently earmarked for you, otherwise it will expire.

Also: shouldn't you write to Lütgert? Diestel is discussing your book with his candidates.[20] "But your nephew still needs to learn German," he told my

---

[13.] Helmuth Kittel. The Pedagogical Academy in Frankfurt/Oder, founded in the 1920s, represented Reform pedagogy at that time.

[14.] Perhaps a reference to the inspector of the Johanneum student dormitory in Berlin, Rothermund, who in Hans Lietzmann's view had "completely failed" and supposedly "was neglecting both the seminary and its members" (letter to Emanuel Hirsch, March 28, 1931, in Aland, *Glanz und Niedergang*, no. 729).

[15.] Not otherwise identified.

[16.] Union Theological Seminary.

[17.] Nicolai Hartmann.

[18.] Elisabeth von Hase.

[19.] Sabine Leibholz was expecting the birth of her second daughter; see 1/147.

[20.] See also 1/177, p. 303.

father! Do so few really understand the distinction between "German" and "matter of fact style"?[21]

Today Father negotiated regarding the preachers' seminary here.[22] The Evangelical High Church Council has no money for construction and thus wants to rent a newly constructed home for infants (!) here (for which the city lacks
211 the money for necessary furnishings and operations). The "symbolic significance" certainly is evident in this case. The building is, however, the most beautiful in all of Frankfurt and is quite modern. Unfortunately, the Evangelical High Church Council wants a director no younger than forty-five. Will that happen? Do you know anyone who could do it?

144. To Erwin Sutz[1]

Philadelphia, December 1, 1930

Dear Mr. Sutz,[2]

Too bad you aren't coming! This morning, just at the hour I was expecting you, your letter arrived. We would have been so pleased to have you here. The days here are peaceful, cordial, and full. This evening I'm going to Washington to participate in the Federal Council[3] from the very outset; on Thursday I want to get a bit from the Home Mission Council[4] as well,

---

[21.] [Diestel mildly criticizes Bonhoeffer's German, but Hase comments that the issue is not the German so much as the fact that his style is not easy to comprehend.—CG]

[22.] The increase in number of candidates during this period made it necessary to establish another preachers' seminary in Brandenburg. Superintendent Hans von Hase [Bonhoeffer's uncle and the father of Hans Christoph von Hase—CG] managed to establish Frankfurt/Oder as the location. The seminary was opened in 1931 under the leadership of Pastor Wolfgang Staemmler, but it closed in 1933 due to the Church Struggle. Staemmler was active later as a leader in the Confessing Church in the province of Saxony and as a later provost. He worked closely with Bonhoeffer; see esp. *DBW* 14.

[1.] *NL,* Anh. A 29,4; typewritten copy. Partially reproduced in *GS* 1:17.

[2.] Concerning Erwin Sutz, see *DB-ER,* 152–53 See also Bethge and Gremmels, *Life in Pictures,* centenary ed., 48–49.

[3.] Conference of the Federal Council of the Churches of Christ in America, an alliance of Protestant churches founded in 1908; in 1950 it became the National Council of the Churches of Christ in the USA. Concerning the resolution passed there on the question of war guilt (cf. *DB-ER,* 151), see Besier, *Krieg—Frieden—Abrüstung,* 284–86; concerning Bonhoeffer's impression of the Federal Council, see also 1/150, p. 267.

[4.] [The Home Missions Council of North America, founded in 1908, joined with the Council of Women for Home Missions in 1940 to form the Home Missions Council of North America, which in 1950 became the Division of Home Missions of the National

then I'll come back here; on Friday I'll be hearing Toscanini and will probably return to New York on Saturday evening. If Coffin[5] asks about me, please excuse me. Would you please forward my mail here (till Friday morning) (box 9, key A.6). Many thanks.

Can you in the meantime find out anything regarding Cuba?[6] Klein[7] 212
has information about a southern clergy ticket, and perhaps you can find out more about specific prices. Admittedly I don't know whether you still want to hold to this plan, but I do hope so. I'm looking forward to seeing you again soon. More later.

Cordially, yours
Dietrich Bonhoeffer

145. To His Parents[1]

Philadelphia, December 1, 1930

My dear Parents,

I thought about you yesterday; it was the first Sunday of Advent. I've been at the Boerickes' for two days, and again they have been very friendly to me. I think they would be happy to receive a letter from you sometime. For Christmas I need to come up with something I can give to the little boy.

Last Wednesday I traveled to Washington by car with a white person and two Negro students. The great monuments in Washington, the Capitol, Washington Memorial,[2] and Lincoln Memorial, all lined up and separated only by broad expanses of grass, are very impressive. Especially the Lincoln Memorial is enormously imposing, portraying Lincoln himself ten or twenty times larger than life, brightly illuminated at night, in a mighty hall,—I actually wouldn't have believed the Americans capable of such a thing. By the way, the more I hear about Lincoln the more he interests me.

Council of Churches. The Home Missions Council focused on all those missionary activities falling outside normal congregational life, especially social service work among Native Americans and migrant workers.—CG]

[5.] Henry Sloane Coffin; cf. 1/130.

[6.] See 1/145 and 1/151.

[7.] William G. Klein, a student at Union Theological Seminary from 1928 to 1933.

[1.] *NL*, Anh. A 14 (7); handwritten. Partially reproduced in *GS* 6:180–81. Cf. also *NL*, A 27,2 (1); typewritten copy.

[2.] [Bonhoeffer's English; officially the Washington Monument, which is, of course, a memorial to George Washington.—CG]

He must have been a tremendous person. Are you familiar with Emil Ludwig's book about him?[3]

213 In Washington I lived completely among the Negroes and through the students[4] was able to become acquainted with all the leading figures of the Negro movement, was in their homes, and had extraordinarily interesting discussions with them. It is striking, however, that all the leading figures have a high percentage of white blood and often look like whites. The Negroes insist that's merely an accident, and that on the whole the really black people are much more highly valued. The conditions are really rather unbelievable. Not just separate railway cars, tramways, and buses south of Washington, but also, for example, when I wanted to eat in a small restaurant with a Negro, I was refused service. Their homes, by the way, were often strikingly well furnished.

This evening I'm returning to Washington to the Federal Council of Churches and to the Home Mission Council.[5] On Friday I'll be back here, will hear Toscanini, and then on Sunday will be back in New York. Then it will already soon be time for a Christmas letter. It's already frightfully cold here, and I'm really looking forward to Cuba! I'm wondering whether you are in Greifswald just now.[6] If only the telegram would arrive soon. Please do say hello to Grandmama for me, and to Klaus and Emmi and all my brothers and sisters. Unfortunately I'm not getting around to writing them more frequently. Affectionate greetings to you from your grateful

Dietrich

[3.] Ludwig, *Lincoln.*

[4.] Probably Frank Fisher; see *DB-ER,* 151.

[5.] See 1/144, ed. notes 3 and 4.

[6.] With Sabine and Gerhard Leibholz, who were expecting their second child; see 1/147.

146. To Julie Bonhoeffer[1]

December 10, 1930

Dear Grandmama,

I am just now sitting in this building[2] and sending you many loving Christmas greetings. If after all the turbulent recent months you can at least cel- 214
ebrate these days in peace, and even if a couple of us are not there, the children will certainly manage to keep the celebration from passing by too quietly. I hope you can really enjoy these days when everyone who is otherwise always so busy and has so little time is now at home and can relax for a couple of days. These days are always so wonderful when the family members who are normally scattered in all directions are able to gather together again. At that point I hope everything is in order again with Sabine. I have been waiting anxiously for the telegram.[3]

Thank you very much for your last letter, dear Grandmama. Every time I want to give you special thanks for taking so much time and trouble to write to me. Yesterday your Christmas greeting also arrived, the book by Harnack,[4] which pleased me greatly. It mentions many things that I myself saw emerge and about which he spoke to me. Many thanks for that as well.

A few weeks before I departed in September, we—you and I—spoke one evening about how nice it would be if you could write down a few things you remember from your childhood and early years. I have thought about that often since then and wanted to ask whether you are actually doing it; it really would be so nice, or is it too taxing for you?

Take care, dear Grandmama, please excuse this brief greeting, but I really wanted to send a greeting to everyone, and that's a lot of people, especially since I'm departing next Saturday.[5] Wishing you a very merry and peaceful Christmas together with everyone else. A year from now we'll all celebrate together again.

Greetings from your grateful
Dietrich

[1.] *NL*, A 27,1 (3); handwritten from New York. Partially reproduced in *GS* 6:181–82.

[2.] On the front of the postcard is a drawing of the Brown Memorial Tower at Union Theological Seminary; see the photograph in Bethge and Gremmels, *Life in Pictures*, centenary ed., 47. [The Brown tower is the one in the foreground of the center picture in the left column; behind it is the tower of Riverside Church.—CG]

[3.] See 1/147.

[4.] Harnack, *Aus der Werkstatt des Vollendeten*; Bonhoeffer's own copy (*NL-Bibl.* 10.19) bears the dedication: "Dietrich Bonhoeffer 1930 from Grandmama."

[5.] For his trip to Cuba; see 1/150 and 1/151.

215 **147. To Sabine and Gerhard Leibholz**[1]

December 11, 1930[2]

Dear Sabine, dear Gert,

Well, the telegram I've been waiting for so long is finally here.[3] And because it says that "Sabine is doing *very* well," I can be sure everything went and continues to go well. I'm so happy it all turned out so well and would like to congratulate you again. Too bad I am so far away from you now and cannot just come over for a few hours by train. The days surrounding June 30, 1927,[4] are still as vivid for me as if it were just a few weeks ago. But you probably have enough visitors now, parents, Father, Aunt Elisabeth,[5] and you are probably looking forward to a quiet Christmas. By that time, dear Sabine, you might even be up again. Exactly fourteen days after the little one's birthday, it will be Christmas, and that's about how long it takes for one to get up and about again. It will be a great celebration for little Marianne as well. After all, her first wish has been granted. What will you name the little one? Do you not want to pass your own name on to her, dear Sabine? By the time I get back there, she will already be a little person, and I can already vividly imagine how little Marianne will be taking care of her little sister.

I wanted to wish you happy birthday, dear Gert, and I did indeed think about it on November 25,[6] but I had vaguely hoped that the telegram would perhaps come on that very day, and then I could wish both of you a happy birthday. But when that didn't happen, it was too late. Please pardon me. Thanks so much for your last letter, dear Sabine; you seem to have done
216 quite well during the final weeks, and I was very glad to hear that. You will probably have a white Christmas this year while I sweat beneath the tropical sun.[7] But we, too, will have a Christmas tree, and then my thoughts will be with you, and I will be rejoicing with you and wishing you all the best. And now many loving greetings to all four of you; best wishes for the coming days and weeks, Merry Christmas and Happy New Year.

As always, your Dietrich

[1.] *NL*, A 27,3 (2); handwritten from New York.

[2.] The text incorrectly reads "11.10.12," i.e., October 11, 1912. [The table of contents in the German first edition reads incorrectly December 10, 1930.—CG]

[3.] See *NL*, C 6: telegram of December 10, 1930: "A strong baby girl arrived today Sabine doing quite well"; the birth of Christiane Renate Elisabeth Leibholz.

[4.] The birth of Marianne Leibholz.

[5.] Elisabeth von Hase.

[6.] Correct: November 15.

[7.] Bonhoeffer spent Christmas 1930 in Cuba; see also 1/150 and 1/151.

148. To Helmut Rößler[1]

New York, December 11, 1930

My dear Rößler,

I want to unload my bad conscience in a Christmas greeting that is all the more heartfelt. The final days of August during which I wanted to visit you are now long gone; the wedding of my brother Klaus and Emmi Delbrück[2] made me indispensable at home. I departed on September 5 and since then have had an uninterrupted assault of new experiences, which even today permit me to write only this brief greeting, since I am just about to depart for Cuba, where I'll be preaching during Christmas.[3]

I have rarely had this much trouble getting into the Christmas spirit! One feels like one is standing on an observation tower looking out over the whole world, and no matter where one looks, most of what one sees is infinitely depressing. Then there is also the situation of the church here, which, without suspecting it, is now only smiling in desperation. The almost frivolous attitude here is unprecedented, and my hope of finding Heb. 12:1[4] fulfilled here has been bitterly disappointed. Moreover, theology in Germany seems infinitely provincial to them here; they just don't understand it; they grin when you mention Luther. So thank God Christmas is coming 217
just now in the middle of all this; otherwise I would despair. Sincere greetings from your

Dietrich Bonhoeffer

Have you actually received my book?[5] I was no longer able to send it personally.[6]

[1.] *NL*, A 20,4 (6); typewritten copy. Partially reproduced in *GS* 1:54–55.

[2.] On September 4, 1930; see 1/127.

[3.] See 3/24.

[4.] "Therefore, since we are surrounded by so great a cloud of witnesses, let us also lay aside everything that burdens us" [Bonhoeffer's version differs slightly from the NRSV.—CG]

[5.] *Sanctorum Communio.*

[6.] Regarding this, see Rößler's response, 1/164.

149. From Franz Hildebrandt[1]

Charlottenburg, December 18, 1930

Dear Mr. Bonhoeffer,

I finally have time to answer you. For three weeks now, I have been an "on the whole good"[2] candidate and a "cum laude" Dr.

In the meantime I was in eight cities in eight days, then continually at the bureaucrats, and beginning this week with Siegmund-Schultze.[3] To pursue this topic a bit further: I am officially on leave till Easter to do social work in Berlin-East[4] (heading a youth club of ten- to fourteen-year-olds; courses on world-view with unemployed youth; studying the sects and freethinkers in the eastern section; reading the Gospel of John and something by Kierkegaard with theology students working in the Social Working Group; helping Siegmund-Schultze during office hours). Quite varied work in any event, though it's still questionable whether the consistory will give me credit for it. In the meantime, my application for a vicar's assignment instead of seminary[5] is being reviewed by the Evangelical High Church Council; if it is granted, which Sellin[6] and the overfilled seminaries seem to make likely, after April 1 I will be a vicar in the Mark (possibly with Ungnad in Stausberg or with Schade in Dobrilugk, who examined me on biblical proficiency) and from October 1 in Schöneberg with my *Superus*
218 Raack.[7] During the winter, things will have calmed down enough for me to do the postdoctoral dissertation—I'll still try to do it here, since the prospects in Halle are not particularly promising (new work and the requirement to begin with historical disciplines). For now I'm thinking only of praxis, first the four sermons coming up soon: If you're interested in hearing which texts: Rom. 8:32 on the second day of Christmas, Isa. 38:20 for New Year (both in Teltow), Phil.

[1.] *NL*, C 10; handwritten.

[2.] [Hildebrandt was making a joke, using a standard phrase by which examiners summarized their evaluation of students' work, "im ganzen gut."—CG]

[3.] Friedrich Siegmund-Schultze. Concerning his influence on Bonhoeffer, see, e.g., *DB-ER*, 191, 229, et passim.

[4.] In 1911 Siegmund-Schultze founded the Social Working Group Berlin-East; many students and young academics worked there for brief periods.

[5.] Preachers' seminary; cf. in this regard 1/115.

[6.] Ernst Sellin.

[7.] Paul Raack, after 1904 superintendent and head pastor at the Paul Gerhardt Church in Berlin-Schöneberg. Hildebrandt did become a vicar with Schade in Dobrilugk, and in the fall of 1931 became *Stadtsynodalvikar* (see 1/177, ed. note 4) with Leonhard Fendt at the Heilsbronnen Church in Berlin-Schöneberg. Nothing came of his plans for postdoctoral work, not least because of the political situation; see also *DB-ER,* 186.

1:18 and Luke 2:41–52 for the Sundays thereafter in Berlin.[8] I sit at my desk now only when a letter needs to go off to America. Spare me having to give details of the examinations: How we would have telephoned during that critical final week of November! The examination with Coptic Schmidt[9] on Boniface and the Frankish church was such a catastrophe for me that I spent nine columns fleeing into biblical mission passages and declared the rest to be material for specialists. After that he took me for a crude ride with the same stuff in the oral examination, ruined my grade of "good" as well as the department's mood toward me. On the morning of the last examination day, Sellin declared to me when I reported for the doctoral exams that if I failed before the consistory, the department couldn't examine me! For a moment, I considered canceling the first examination and postponing the doctorate. Erich Seeberg's assurance that the Copt is an ox (!) and Reinhold's[10] that even a "passing" grade was of no consequence for the postdoctoral degree kept me at it. Everything went fine then, even with Sellin and Mahling;[11] in Old Testament, knowledge of the Bible and a couple of specialized things helped out, and in the "practical questions," W's[12] lecture notes (history of catechism); there wasn't much to answer with Reinhold and Deissmann,[13] and Erich[14] began the last subject with the question: What have you ordered, what am I supposed to examine? In the consistory, Mahling was satisfied with a couple of snap questions, was quite friendly in general (I'm wondering whether my organ playing for the seminar may be behind that); Lütgert tested dogmatics in an extremely lively and buoyant fashion; philosophy with Fischer[15] went basically well until I displaced Leibniz biographically to France (!) and Berlin instead of Hanover and couldn't place the "Stagirite."[16] My grade of 2/3 instead of a 1 or 2 in New Testament with Coulon[17] must have been the result of a "mix-up" by the protocol leader (Coptic Schmidt!).[18]

[8.] [Rom. 8:32: "He who did not withhold his own Son, but gave him up for all of us, will he not also with him give us everything else?" Isa. 38:20: "The Lord will save me, and we will sing to stringed instruments all the days of our lives, at the house of the Lord." Phil. 1:18: "What does it matter? Just this, that Christ is proclaimed in every way, whether out of false motives or true; and in that I rejoice. Yes, and I will continue to rejoice." Luke 2:41–52 is the story of the boy Jesus in the temple.—CG]

[9.] Carl Schmidt; see 1/143, ed. note 9.

[10.] Reinhold Seeberg.

[11.] Friedrich Mahling.

[12.] Hermann Werdermann.

[13.] Adolf Deißmann.

[14.] Erich Seeberg.

[15.] Probably Alfred Fischer.

[16.] Aristotle, who came from Stagirus (later Stagira) in Macedonia.

[17.] Albert Coulon.

[18.] See ed. note 9 for this letter.

Things ended up the same way in Old Testament with Kegel,[19] because none of us could count to three or ten in Hebrew! But they were nonetheless quite satisfied with us, even though my own qualification for the doctorate was, of course, doubted—the results in that regard were a nice surprise for the idiots
219 in the consistory. Little Möller (in Old Testament) only got a "good" instead of a well-deserved "very good"; Keil, Miss Knop,[20] and I all got "on the whole good" (what a splendid predicate); one was satisfactory and one failed in Old Testament—fabulous results, since before and afterward 50 percent flunked. Haendler[21] was general[22] but let us say no more (see Nahum 3:16),[23] nor did he examine.

After writing so much here, I still want to wish you Happy New Year (too late for Merry Christmas) and as a consolation for your experiences there to give you the address of my earlier housemate in Tübingen, Rev. Elmer Hoefer, 96 Saranac St., Rochester, New York.[24] I'm writing to him now as well. I hope I'll be hearing some better news from over there. All the best and many greetings,

Yours,
Franz Hildebrandt

P.S. If the money comes through, my thesis will be published with Titius/ Wobbermin (Vandenhoeck und Ruprecht).[25] When I visited Wobbermin in Göttingen, he told me he wanted both you and me to contribute to the *Theologische Literaturzeitung*.[26]

[19.] Martin Kegel.

[20.] Not otherwise identified.

[21.] Gustav Haendler.

[22.] [The general superintendent presiding over the exam.—CG]

[23.] "You increased your merchants more than the stars of the heavens. But now they will spread like locusts and fly away." [Hildebrandt plays on Haendler's name, as the German word *Händler* means "merchant." He quotes the Luther Bible, which the NRSV translates somewhat differently in the second sentence.—CG]

[24.] [At the time Hoefer was pastor of St. Paul's Evangelical and Reformed Church in Rochester, New York.—CG]

[25.] Hildebrandt's dissertation, *EST: Das lutherische Prinzip*, appeared in 1931 as volume 7 of the series Studien zur systematischen Theologie, edited by Arthur Titius and Georg Wobbermin, Göttingen; cf. also *DB-ER*, 138.

[26.] See, e.g., the reviews of Cord Cordes on the concept of community in contemporary German Catholicism and Protestantism (*DBW* 11, 2/20) and of Robert Jelke on reason and revelation (*DBW* 12, 2/3) both published in 1932 in volume 57 of the journal. Previously published in *GS* 3:132–37.

150. To Max Diestel[1]

Havana-Vedado, December 19, 1930

Dear Superintendent Diestel:

Although this letter was actually supposed to be a Christmas greeting, it won't get there in time now or, at best, assuming everything goes well, only in time for New Year's, so let me in any case wish you and yours all the best
for the New Year. During the past few weeks, I have found myself thinking 220
back to the winter evenings when I came to your house as Saint Nicholas.[2] Now, of course, none of the children are still there except for the youngest, who spoke the Christmas poems to Santa with such conviction, as did little Renate in the previous years.

I'll be celebrating Christmas here with a service in the German colony. It's splendidly warm here after the recent icy, cold weeks in New York; today it's 28° Celsius[3] in the shade; the gardens are full of flowers, the trees are as green as in summer. The German school, where I took over the religious instruction during the last days of school, has made an excellent impression on me, and I'm thoroughly enjoying the children.

But a bit about New York. Although I had already started a report about it for you in October, the multitude of events kept me from finishing, and it's probably just as well, since now I have a better overview of things than I did at that time. First of all, life at the seminary is quite stimulating and instructive as far as the personal contacts are concerned, which are also quite cordial with the professors themselves, for the professor, too, must be a "good fellow." One almost has to be cautious lest the mutual visits and chatting take up too much time. For—these conversations almost never yield anything of substance. And that brings me to the sad part of the whole thing. There is no theology here. Although I am basically taking classes and lectures in dogmatics and philosophy of religion, the impression is overwhelmingly negative. They talk a blue streak without the slightest substantive foundation and with no evidence of any criteria. The students—on the average twenty-five to thirty years old—are completely clueless with respect to what dogmatics is really about. They are not familiar with even the most basic questions. They become intoxicated with liberal and humanistic phrases, are amused at the fundamentalists, and yet basically are not even

[1.] EZA 29/G 442,29f; handwritten. See also *NL*, A 20,3 (2); typewritten copy. Previously published in *GS* 1:75–79.

[2.] [*Nikolaus*, that is, Santa Claus.—CG]

[3.] [Fahrenheit 82.4.—CG]

up to their level. They are interested in Barth and now and then also do a bit "in pessimism." That's when it's really bad. In contrast to our own liberalism, which in its better representatives doubtless was a genuinely vigorous
221 phenomenon, here all that has been dreadfully sentimentalized, and with an almost naive know-it-all attitude. It often just burns me up when people here deal with Christ and are then done with him, and laugh insolently if I present a citation from Luther on the consciousness of guilt. The Jamesean notion of the finite God[4] is rooted deep within most of the theologians and pastors here. They find it to be profound and modern and do not sense at all the impertinent frivolousness in all such talk. Despite all this, I am nonetheless grateful to have been so thoroughly introduced to these basic questions again. Indeed, here one once again understands what important questions really are and how much one owes to our own theology.

Things are not much different in the church. The sermon has been reduced to parenthetical church remarks about newspaper events. As long as I've been here, I have heard only *one* sermon in which you could hear something like a genuine proclamation, and that was delivered by a Negro (indeed, in general I'm increasingly discovering greater religious power and originality in Negroes). One big question continually attracting my attention in view of these facts is whether one here really can still speak about Christianity [Christlichkeit],[5] and where the criterion for such might be found. There's no sense to expect the fruits where the Word really is no longer being preached. But then what becomes of Christianity per se? Ultimately it can't really be the responsibility of theology, can it? Well, it's good that Christmas is coming again here as well.

December 26

Well, even though this letter was left unfinished as well, I'll go ahead and send it off, especially since I have been appropriately shamed today by your kind greeting. Please pardon my neglect, my esteemed Superintendent. There were so many new things to see and do here recently that I just never found a quiet moment. In the meantime, our Christmas service[6] is now
222 behind us and on the thirty-first we will be celebrating New Year's Eve.

[4.] See 1/181, p. 311, and 2/13. Concerning this idea, see James, *Varieties of Religious Experience*.

[5.] [A literal translation would be "Christianness."—CG]

[6.] See 3/24.

¶Once again, I enjoy preaching so much. Because the people here have and hear little, it's a special task.

I wanted to tell you before about the Federal Council.[7] I got to know personally all the leading figures here. People talked about everything, except about theology. Only rarely did anyone venture any comments really getting to the point, and if they did, the discussion quickly moved on to the daily agenda. They talk as if all the basic questions have already been answered. But that's not even remotely the case.

I am working regularly at a Negro boys club and like it very much. In a different Sunday school, a little girl recently received—right in front of me—a makeup box as a reward for good attendance! And we're supposed to believe we're sitting in a Christian church.

But enough of that. I am very glad to be here and to see all this, I will be able to follow developments in Germany with a clear eye. I am drawn more and more to the ministry.

The time is going by fast. In four months it will already be over. I'm not sure yet about my route home.

Superintendent, have you heard anything yet from Dr. Dibelius[8] or Dr. Händler[9] about the student chaplain position at the T.C. in Charlottenburg[10] about which Dr. Dibelius once spoke?[11]

(By the way, the fellowship, 1,200 dollars, is very generous, one can easily save 250 dollars, apart from trips. You might pass this information along to my successor.)

Very well, that's enough for now. I have taken up enough of your time. Please give my respects to your wife. With the most respectful greetings and sincere gratitude, Superintendent, I remain your humble servant,

Dietrich Bonhoeffer

[7.] See 1/144.

[8.] Otto Dibelius.

[9.] Gustav Haendler.

[10.] [Anglicized abbreviation for "technical college," translating *Technische Hochschule*, abbreviated "T.H." in the original.—CG]

[11.] Concerning subsequent developments, see 1/161 and *DB-ER*, 222–23.

223 **151. To Karl-Friedrich Bonhoeffer**[1]

January 2, 1931

Dear Karl Friedrich,

We are just now leaving Havana on a ship for Key West. Because it's rolling quite a bit and I'm looking for some distraction where I can concentrate, I'll combine the unpleasant with the useful and use the time to write you a birthday letter.[2] If it's a rather stupid letter, please attribute it to the effect this miserable ship is having on my brain, which has now totally lost its equilibrium.

Many thanks for your Christmas letter. I have been thinking of all of you a lot during these last few days and hope that all is well.[3] By the time this letter arrives, it will all be long over and I will already have received the telegram in New York. Perhaps it will be waiting for me the day after tomorrow when I get home. One would hope you could then celebrate your own birthday in a completely relaxed fashion.

My visit to Cuba was quite interesting and pleasant. I really liked not only the whole school operation, but especially the country as well. The palm tree as the most common tree considerably alters the entire landscape, and especially in the evening, in silhouette, it's incomparably beautiful. Huge pineapple fields, banana cultivation, sugar cane, tobacco plantations are all over the country. The streets are incredibly bad, and there are almost no pedestrian paths at all outside. All the mountain regions still seem to be completely undeveloped. The living conditions are the most primitive I have ever seen. They build windowless huts out of palm leaves and stalks and seem to use them only at night and for shade in the summer. The children often run around completely naked, and usually half naked.

224 January 8, 1931

For reasons I feared at the very outset, I had to interrupt the letter if it were to remain in a condition to be sent at all. The ship was just traveling too unpleasantly. The picture I wanted to give you of Cuba was a bit[4] fragmented. I still want to tell you that I saw the strangest birds. Whole flocks

[1.] *NL*, Anh. A 14 (8); handwritten; on stationery of "The Peninsular & Occidental Steamship Company—Havana—Port Tampa—Key West—S.S. *Governor Cobb*." See also *NL*, A 27,4 (4); typewritten copy. Previously published in *GS* 6:182–84.

[2.] Karl-Friedrich Bonhoeffer's birthday was on January 13.

[3.] On January 10, 1931, Karl Walter Paul Bonhoeffer was born, the first child of Karl-Friedrich and Margarethe Bonhoeffer.

[4.] The rest of the letter is extant only as a typewritten copy.

of pelicans, cranes, herons, flamingos, then some I didn't even recognize, similar to parrots but completely black; we even saw a pair of hummingbirds, which fly almost like butterflies. But you just can't imagine the Cuban landscape without also imagining, no matter where you look, the hordes of vultures hovering very close above the houses. They really are almost as common as sparrows or, better, crows in Germany; I really never imagined such a thing. They live off the numerous decaying animals lying around and for that reason are much beloved by the people. But they really do look repulsive the way they gather en masse around some dead animal, a scene you encounter again and again.

I also found it noteworthy that the Spanish population apparently gets along much better with the Negroes than do the Americans. The separation of whites from blacks in the southern states really does make a rather shameful impression. In railways that separation extends to even the tiniest details. I found that the cars of the Negroes generally look cleaner than the others. It also pleased me when the whites had to crowd into their railway cars while often only a single person was sitting in the entire railway car for Negroes. The way the southerners talk about the Negroes is simply repugnant, and in this regard the pastors are no better than the others. I still believe that the spiritual songs of the southern Negroes represent some of the greatest artistic achievements in America.[5] It is a bit unnerving that in a country with so inordinately many slogans about brotherhood, peace, and 225
so on, such things still continue completely uncorrected.

By the way, I also had great fun in Cuba speaking Spanish again, which to my great horror I found I had almost completely forgotten. And now that I am back here again, I notice how little joy the English language gives me. Maybe it's only here that it sounds so flat and superficial.

Well, I've written a long letter after all even though I actually wanted to get some work done.

By the way, a few weeks ago I made the acquaintance of Professor Angell, about whom you wrote,[6] together with Schacht;[7] I listened to the two

[5.] Bonhoeffer took some records of this music back to Berlin with him and later played them for his students; see *DB-ER*, 208, and Wolf-Dieter Zimmermann, "Years in Berlin," in *I Knew Dietrich Bonhoeffer*, 64.

[6.] On November 30, 1930, Karl-Friedrich had written that he was currently reading "a relatively optimistic book about Germany's reconstruction by an American named Angell, professor of economics at Columbia University. Is he highly regarded by all of 'you'?" (*NL*, C 3). The reference is to Angell, *Recovery of Germany*, which had been translated into German in 1930.

[7.] Probably Hjalmar Schacht.

arguing together, and what Schacht said was incredibly depressing and pessimistic, though Prof. Angell really didn't quite know what to say either. He is still a very young man, but well known. Well, once again best wishes for the next few weeks and for the entire year. Many affectionate greetings to you and Grete from your

Dietrich

152. To Richard Ern[1]

Dear Richard,

I'm so sorry I had to decline your invitation again, but I can't risk going out yet. Today, after having to stay in bed for a couple of days, I got up again for the first time. If it's okay with all of you, I'll try to come on *Saturday*, the twenty-fourth. By that time I'm hoping to be completely healthy again. Cordial greetings to your parents as well, your

Dietrich Bonhoeffer

226 **153. To Sabine Leibholz**[1]

January 21, 1931

Dear Sabine,

Too bad that the ships depart at such inconvenient times; one leaves tomorrow and will already be arriving in Germany on the twenty-eighth, but then not another one till the twenty-eighth. But then you wouldn't get this letter until February 6.[2] So you will be getting a birthday letter at a time when you are perhaps not really thinking of your birthday at all. Unfortunately I have as yet been unable to get the gift I had decided on for your birthday present; because I had the flu, I couldn't go into the city for a very long time, and I hope I can send it along with the next ship, if it can be shipped at all. But don't get too excited, it's nothing special!

It's so unnerving for me that we really are going to be twenty-five now. And it's funny, I can imagine it much less in your case than in my own. I

[1.] *NL*, Anh. A 33 (3); handwritten postcard from New York. [Original postmark January 15, 1931.—CG]

[1.] *NL*, A 27, 3 (3); typewritten copy; certainly from New York. Partially reproduced in *GS* 6:185–87. Original in the literary estate of Sabine Leibholz

[2.] [Bonhoeffer was thinking of the birthday he and his twin sister shared on February 4.—CG]

have gradually just come to terms with it myself, but in my subconscious you are still functioning as a twenty-year-old, probably because we haven't lived together since then. At the same time, I really can't get over the fact that you have in the meantime accomplished completely different things; if I were to imagine I had already been married for over five years, had two children, my own house, well, then I could feel fully justified turning twenty-five.

This next year will again be something very special for all of you since you will have an infant in the house once again.[3] I sincerely hope that you and yours can spend this coming year in the same tranquility and peace as before in your little house, a house I have long wished I could visit again. I will be really curious to see Marianne again in a few months, and certainly little Christiane—is that the correct spelling?—who supposedly looks so much like me. All of you will surely be celebrating a lovely birthday. I don't 227
yet quite know how I will spend the day. Several people have learned of the date and are demanding we have a birthday party, which I would then give at the house of one of the married students.[4] But perhaps I'll also find something nice at the theater. Unfortunately I can't even toast you with a glass of wine at this occasion, since it's forbidden by federal law; how frightfully tedious, this Prohibition in which no one believes.[5]

Just now it is semester break, and I have a lot of time to catch up on things I have been neglecting, especially several visits and many books. I am currently reading a lot of Negro literature, some of which is extremely interesting. I am also systematically studying American philosophy with a professor here.[6] The theater programs here are usually quite dreadful, so I rarely go. Quite by chance, I recently had the opportunity several times to hear the Philharmonic here with Toscanini for free, though till now it hasn't really moved me very much. The programs are often quite shallow; nor do I quite understand why of all people Toscanini had to direct in Bayreuth, as if one of our own people could not have done it as well; that really does give the rather unsympathetic impression of a sham.

Much is said here about the political situation in Germany, and with great sympathy, particularly in academic circles. An economics professor from Columbia University[7] told me he had no doubt that in the foreseeable

---

[3.] See 1/147.

[4.] [In all likelihood, the apartment of Paul and Marion Lehmann, probably with Sutz, Lasserre, and Fisher.—CG]

[5.] Concerning Bonhoeffer's critical position on Prohibition, which was in force from 1919 till 1933, see 2/12; see also his father's letter of November 19, 1930 (*NL*, C 3), mentioned in *DB-ER*, 163.

[6.] Professor Lyman; see 1/151.

[7.] James W. Angell; see 1/151, p. 270.

future America would be initiating a considerable change in the question of reparations. The colossal complaints of the people themselves here don't make a very convincing impression on us Europeans. In reality, the only ones who really have it bad are the unemployed, who have no insurance at all.

My plans for the months after May are still completely up in the air. On the one hand, I really would like to return to Germany and get some work
228 done, though beforehand I'd definitely like to travel around for four to six weeks. Perhaps through the South and West to Mexico, though maybe I'll genuinely go all the way around the world, that is, especially to India if my money holds out and I can find someone to come along and if Germany doesn't pull me back too forcefully. It seems most likely to me that I'll be returning to Germany at the end of June.

Wishing you a wonderful, enjoyable birthday and all the best in the new year. Greetings to you, Gerd, Marianne, and the littlest one from your
Dietrich

Many thanks for your letter, dear Sabine, which arrived this morning.

154. [165a.] To Richard Ern[1]

Wednesday

Dear Richard,

Many thanks for your kind letter! The weather has turned so ugly, though, that if it's still like this on Saturday I think we ought to postpone things for a week. But if the weather is good, I'll certainly be coming. So please count on me only if the weather has improved a bit. Till we see each other again, your

Dietrich Bonhoeffer

[1.] *NL*, Anh. A 33 (5); handwritten from New York. [Written Wednesday, March 4, postmarked Thursday, March 5, 1931. Chronologically this postcard now would follow letter 165.—CG]

155. To Richard Ern[1]

January 22, 1931

Dear Richard,

If it's okay with all of you, I'll be departing on Saturday[2] at 10:00 from 125th Street, will be in Scarsdale at 10:31, and am hoping to be taking a nice walk from there with you. If this doesn't work for you, please call imme- 229
diately and leave a message for me if I'm not home. If I don't hear anything, I'll be looking forward to coming. Cordial greetings to your dear parents and to you from your

Dietrich Bonhoeffer

156. From Franz Hildebrandt[1]

January 23, 1931

Dear Mr. Bonhoeffer,

Although congratulatory letters really shouldn't be typewritten, this activity does have its particular appeal and also gives you a clearer view of my present activities. That's actually a ruse, for in truth I'm just passing time with it because the boss[2] (generally called "Dr." here) is sick and I'm supposed to be covering his office hours—but no one has come. So, first of all my heartiest congratulations for February 4! I thought about it—but now you're also thinking of my birthday![3] And in general: what kind of behavior is that, namely, to have the other one write twice in a row without even budging in the meantime: Is that your understanding of Grisebach?[4] (As long as we're on the subject: Just now an essay on social ethics by H. M. Müller happened to fall into my hands here, one he wants to publish in *Die Eiche*.[5] Unfortunately I was allowed only to correct

[1.] *NL*, Anh. A 33 (4); handwritten card from New York.

[2.] January 24, 1931; see 1/152.

[1.] *NL*, C 10; typewritten with handwritten signature; letterhead: "Social Working Group Berlin-East." [This organization was an *eingetragener Verein*, "registered association."—CG]

[2.] Friedrich Siegmund-Schultze; see 1/149, p. 262, and ed. note 4.

[3.] On February 20.

[4.] Ironic allusion; see in this regard also 2/7, p. 398, where it is said that Grisebach "addresses the concrete You as the boundary of the human being." [See also the references to Grisebach in *Sanctorum Communio* (*DBWE* 1).—CG]

[5.] Hans Michael Müller, "Zur Verständigung über Sozialethik." The journal *Die Eiche* was edited by Hildebrandt's "boss," Siegmund-Schultze.

the typographical errors; otherwise probably nothing would have been left. It will turn out to be the devil's filth!

You recently suggested[6] that my time with Siegmund-Schultze would not pass "without hardship" for me. Perhaps that's right. For now, the effect is different. I am radically returning to the position of my schoolboy days, where praxis seems
230 to be everything to me and scholarship nothing, though without surrendering anything of my theology (it was always ten times more concrete than "existential" wisdom). But the previous problems become secondary before the new tasks, and apart from "official theology"[7] there is basically nothing that could ever tempt me back to my desk. If they don't coerce me by force! Burghart[8] seems on the verge of rejecting my application for lifelong vicar's status, and it is extremely questionable whether Sellin and Lang[9] want to and will force me through in the Evangelical High Council; the negotiations have been postponed a bit because new "guidelines" for candidates are supposed to be appearing again. If they assign me to a preachers' seminary for more than a semester, which in the summer would still be bearable, I would in any event say farewell to the church for the time being and try postdoctoral work—albeit without much enthusiasm, since there are too many doing this in Berlin and those doing it elsewhere are too strange. In Halle, in any case, they would require me to do not only a new thesis but a historical one at that (transition to dogmatics only later?)![10] Be glad you're rid of such worries.

I'm sending you the outline for my doctoral defense theses, which I hope will be accepted and defended by the end of the semester (against Freitag, Frederking, and a certain Dr. Niemeier,[11] a student of Barth associated with the cathedral seminary—unfortunately Fendt couldn't commit for sure). Of course, this depends on whether my thesis will be printed, and that costs money. By the way, do you still remember how much you received from your various aid sources? Because the association[12] and the minister won't be contributing in my case, possibly my only source will be the Seeberg Foundation.

[6.] Bonhoeffer's letter is not extant.

[7.] [A sardonic reference to the consistory examination board that tested all candidates for the ministry. Hildebrandt had taken his theological examinations in December 1930. See 1/149, p. 262.—CG]

[8.] Dr. Georg Burghart. Concerning Hildebrandt's application, see 1/149, p. 262 and ed. note 6.

[9.] Dr. Theodor Lang.

[10.] See 1/149, p. 262.

[11.] Gottfried Niemeier.

[12.] [Association for German Scholarship.—CG]

On the thirty-first Barth will be speaking at the Schleiermacher college on "The Crisis of the Protestant Church."[13] We're all eagerly looking forward to it. I recently heard two excellent sermons by Erich Seeberg (!) on Mark 10:51–52[14] and by Röhricht on Matt. 10:5–6; 16:3; 22:21; 20:26–28 (four texts at once) for January 18.[15]

Write soon again about your church experiences. Did you know that Dehn is 231
going to Heidelberg as a practical theologian,[16] and that Günter Holstein[17] has died quite young? Alfred Fischer is now in the Evangelical High Council and Paul Luther[18] in the consistory; perhaps he will be examining lyric poetry!

Cordial greetings, your
Franz Hildebrandt

[13.] "Die Not der evangelischen Kirche." Barth's 1931 lecture "The Crisis in the Protestant Church" was first published in *Zwischen den Zeiten* and then in Barth, "*Der Götze wackelt*"; this publication contains Barth's afterword in response to a lecture eight days later by Otto Dibelius criticizing Barth, "Die Verantwortung der Kirche: Eine Antwort auf Karl Barth." For the atmosphere surrounding the lecture, see also Scholder, *Churches and the Third Reich*, 1:124–26, esp. 124–25; see also 1/165, p. 288.

[14.] [Mark 10:51–52: "Then Jesus said to him, 'What do you want me to do for you?' The blind man said to him, 'My teacher, let me see again.' Jesus said to him, 'Go; your faith has made you well.' Immediately he regained his sight and followed him on the way."—CG]

[15.] Second Sunday after Epiphany, simultaneously the anniversary of the founding of the "Second Reich," the unification of the German Empire under Otto von Bismarck in 1871. [Matt. 10:5–6: "These twelve Jesus sent out with the following instructions: 'Go nowhere among the Gentiles, and enter no town of the Samaritans, but go rather to the lost sheep of the house of Israel.'" Matt. 16:3: "And in the morning, 'It will be stormy today, for the sky is red and threatening.' You know how to interpret the appearance of the sky, but you cannot interpret the signs of the times." Matt. 22:21: "They answered, 'The emperor's.' Then he said to them, 'Give therefore to the emperor the things that are the emperor's, and to God the things that are God's.'" Matt. 20:26–28: "It will not be so among you; but whoever wishes to be great among you must be your servant, and whoever wishes to be first among you must be your slave; just as the Son of Man came not to be served but to serve, and to give his life a ransom for many."—CG]

[16.] Dehn declined the professorship on January 28, 1931; cf. Bizer, "Der 'Fall Dehn,'" 246–47.

[17.] Günther Holstein; cf. Meier, *Der evangelische Kirchenkampf*, vol. 1, esp. 242–43.

[18.] Dr. Paul Luther, author of a handbook on educational institutions for the people.

157. From Karl-Friedrich Bonhoeffer[1]

January 24, 1931

Dear Dietrich,

Many thanks for your detailed birthday letter,[2] which pleased me greatly. Things are going very well with us. Till yesterday we were still a bit apprehensive because of Grete's fever—the physicians say it was the flu. Today, however, is her first day with a completely normal temperature, so we are all very happy and will be enjoying the coming days. If things remain the same Grete can leave the clinic at the beginning of next week. The boy (*Karl* Walter Paul) is a very good son, already weighs more than at birth, quaffs and shouts like an old man (?), and apart from his behavior at birth has really given us no cause for complaints. They say he looks like me, too. So, even if you are having many experiences, now you can see that I'm experiencing even more here. One doesn't need to go to America for that; one is actually better off just staying at home. Either at home or in any event in the clinic, for we are both quite happy that we went to the clinic.

Would you be so kind as to forward the birth announcement to the Boerickes after having a look at it? I don't have their address here.

I'm glad to hear you have the opportunity for studying the Negro problem
232 so thoroughly. When I was there I had the impression it was really *the* question, at least for people with a conscience, and when I received the offer of the appointment at Harvard it was one of the primary reasons for my disinclination to move there completely, since I wanted neither to come into this inheritance myself nor to pass it on to my hypothetical children. I really can't see how it can be corrected, and I think that in this case as in mathematics there really are some insoluble problems. (A bit stupid! I notice it myself.) In any event, our "Jewish question" is a joke compared to it; only a few would still claim they are repressed here. At least not in Frankfurt.

I almost forgot to congratulate you. I hope things go well for you in this new year of life. If possible, don't fall in love with America, and come home just as you left, just a bit wiser and with more worldly experience, if that's still possible.

[1.] *NL*, C 3; handwritten from Frankfurt/Main.

[2.] See 1/151.

The family has changed considerably in the meantime, so it may well keep your interest again for a while. Many greetings, your

Karl Friedrich

The book *Nachkrieg*[3] is much discussed here. To the extent I'm familiar with it, it's not really to my taste. Perhaps to yours? Try it!

158. To Paul Althaus[1]

New York, January 28, 1931

Dear Professor Althaus:[2]

Let me extend my most cordial thanks to you for your letter.[3] It's painful for me, of course, to hear that the Forschungen[4] series is already filled up for next year, especially since I now see that you would have been willing to accept my work, and since its publication in that series would have been of enormous value to me. Meanwhile, it seems advisable to me, if possible, not to wait till next year. So with this same mail I'm also writing to Bertels- 233
mann[5] at your kind recommendation, and with your permission will add a note to them saying that a few words from you will be arriving a few days later. Many thanks for taking the trouble to write to Bertelsmann in this matter.

Did you consider the possibility of publication in the supplements to *Zwischen den Zeiten*?

With many thanks, again, I remain, Professor, your respectfully devoted

Dietrich Bonhoeffer

[3.] Renn, *After War.* The book was included with the letter as a birthday present; see 1/168, p. 293. Bonhoeffer discussed the same author's previous work, *War* (published in German in 1929), in his Union report on war literature; cf. 2/11.1, p. 420.

[1.] *NL*, Anh. A 10; handwritten.

[2.] It can no longer be determined when and how Bonhoeffer came into contact with Althaus.

[3.] Not extant.

[4.] Forschungen zur Geschichte und Lehre des Protestantismus, a series dealing with Protestant history and teaching, was edited by Paul Althaus, Karl Barth, and Karl Heim and was a possible place for Bonhoeffer to publish his postdoctoral dissertation; see *DBWE* 2:5.

[5.] The publishing house for the theological series Beiträge zur Förderung christlicher Theologie, edited by Lütgert and Schlatter.

159. [166a.] To Richard Ern[1]

Dear Richard,

I hope to see you at my place on Saturday. You are welcome at any time. It would be nice if you could eat lunch with me here; then we could go to the museum. Please let me know soon what time you will be coming and whether I need to pick you up somewhere (125th Street Central Station). Cordial greetings to your parents.

Till we see each other again,
Dietrich Bonhoeffer

160. [166b.] To Richard Ern[1]

Thursday

Dear Richard,

Please ask your dear parents whether it's all right with them if I come out to visit you on Saturday. I would then gladly discuss my final travel plans.
234 Perhaps it might be arranged for me to spend an hour Saturday with the good driving teacher.[2] I'm looking forward to seeing you again. How did you like last Saturday? It's just so nice you were here.[3]

If I don't receive any word to the contrary, I'll come on Saturday with the 10:00 train (10:30 in Scarsdale). Cordial greetings to your parents and to you as well from your

Dietrich Bonhoeffer

[1.] *NL*, Anh. A 33 (5); handwritten. [Postmarked Wednesday, March 18, 1931. Chronologically this and the following postcard would follow letter 166.—CG]

[1.] *NL*, Anh. A 33 (7); handwritten card from New York. [Written and postmarked on Thursday, March 26, 1931.—CG]

[2.] The reference is probably to Richard's mother, from whom Bonhoeffer took driving lessons, as reported by Richard Ern to Eberhard Bethge (letter, December 20, 1976).

[3.] Cf. 1/159.

161. From Otto Dibelius[1]

February 7, 1931

My dear Mr. Bonhoeffer,

Superintendent Diestel gave me the letter to read that you wrote to him in December,[2] whereupon I contacted General Superintendent Dr. Karow.[3] He seems quite disposed to making a position available to you as student chaplain at the technical college. Before he does anything in this regard, however, he must naturally get to know you himself. Hence I would suggest that when you return to Germany you look up General Superintendent Dr. Karow as soon as possible and discuss your future with him.[4]

With cordial greetings, yours very sincerely,
signed Dibelius

162. To Richard Ern[1]

February 11, 1931

Dear Richard,

Let me wish you all the best for your birthday, that things will always go well for you, that school won't be such a worry for you, that you will be able to spend a lot of time outside in the forest with your friends, and that your 235
little sister can also come back to you this year and that you can play with her.[2] I hope I can visit you again soon and bring along a small, belated birthday present for you as well. In the meantime, let me wish you a happy birthday with your parents and friends. Please say hello to your parents. Let me also thank you for sending the book. Take care, stay healthy, and cordial greetings, yours

Dietrich Bonhoeffer

[1.] *NL*, A 30,2 (7); typewritten copy from the files of the Office of Superintendent, Berlin Kölln-Land I. Previously published in *GS* 6:211.

[2.] See 1/150.

[3.] Emil Karow.

[4.] Concerning the further development of this matter, see *DBW* 11 and *DB-ER*, 222–23.

[1.] *NL*, Anh. 33 (6); handwritten from New York.

[2.] Louise Ern became ill with meningitis in 1928 and in February 1931 was being treated in the anthroposophical clinic Arlesheim in Switzerland. [Anthroposophy was the spiritual philosophy developed by Rudolf Steiner after he abandoned theosophy; their clinics emphasized natural and homeopathic treatments.—CG]

163. From Wilhelm Lütgert[1]

Berlin-Dahlem, February 18, 1931

Dear Colleague,

The end of the semester has been particularly burdened by work this time, so unfortunately I was unable to answer you immediately. Let me say right at the outset, however, that I will naturally do everything possible to help you get your postdoctoral dissertation published.[2] So please send it on to Bertelsmann with reference to me; I will write to him, and you will then learn what can be done.

Above all, however, let me thank you for your detailed letter,[3] which interested me greatly. I assumed from the outset that you would not be learning much more in the way of theology over there. It is valuable, however, to get to know America, the university, and the church firsthand. The claim to validity over against us is so great there that criticism made on the basis of your firsthand experience carries much weight for us. And the contrast also helps one appreciate just which advantages we have over America. I have been in a circle of theologians here organized in America by John Mott[4]—do you know
236 him?—that has been discussing the secularization movement in the mission field for several months now. The Americans are naive enough to order a theology and philosophy to suit their purposes the way one orders a car from a factory.

I also feared you would not really be able to learn anything directly from American students about social work. We're working under completely different circumstances.

My semester was full of hard work, the Letters to the Corinthians and Ethics I. I'll probably not be able to maintain the subdivision of ethics because no one is participating here. It's not so easy doing it alone.

For the Letters to the Corinthians, I have an extremely large number of participants who are quite grateful and almost all of whom have stayed the course. Next semester I'll be teaching New Testament theology and social ethics (two hours).

Hase[5] has represented you in the seminar with both great industry and great interest, so I have been glad to have him as your representative. We have been discussing the doctrine of the Holy Spirit, and the question is how to proceed next semester. The crowd wants to discuss the contemporary situation of theology, and I myself would like continue into the present the sketch with which

[1.] *NL*, A 20,5; handwritten. Previously published in *GS* 3:20–21.

[2.] *Act and Being* (*DBWE* 2)

[3.] Not extant.

[4.] John R. Mott.

[5.] Bonhoeffer's cousin Hans Christoph von Hase.

I concluded the fourth volume of my book on German theology.[6] I didn't have much of a vacation this summer. The revisions of my book lasted till the end of August and kept me here. At the end of September, the summer school courses were already beginning; I had to participate in four.

Let me wish you continued stimulating and fruitful work, and send my cordial greetings, yours

W. Lütgert

164. From Helmut Rößler[1] 237

Beveringen,[2] February 22, 1931

My dear Friend,

Your "unloading of conscience" in the form of a Christmas greeting[3] reached me just at Christmas itself and brought great joy to both me and my wife. And now my thanks itself is arriving quite late, something that has almost become a custom between us. Actually the infrequence of our correspondence is remarkable compared to the intensity of our mutual intellectual engagement. In any case, I often think intensely of you—quite involuntarily, wondering what your opinion might be on this or that topic or event. And sometimes Friedrichsbrunn hovers before me like a smiling, melancholy recollection with those few precious spring days in 1927.[4] Your *Sanctorum Communio* doubtless contributes to that feeling, a book I have read halfway through with great engagement and joy in your accomplishment, even though the unfinished character of your thoughts does sometimes seem quite tangible. You'll hear more about this once I have finished the entire book. Even if you have long left this opus "behind" you—I am glad to be reading it for the sake of our own dialogue, and truly without any envy toward *your* systematic superiority, which I have often heard praised among the circle of my colleagues at lectures, etc. But there's truly no art to that.

You are now able to see Germany from the bird's-eye view of the New World and will see many things differently when you return. I was also very moved by what you wrote about the theologically grotesque nature of the American

[6.] *Die Religion des deutschen Idealismus.*

[1.] *NL*, A 20,4 (9); typewritten copy. Partially reproduced in *GS* 1:55–60.

[2.] Near Pritzwalk, East Prignitz.

[3.] See 1/148.

[4.] Cf. *DBWE* 9 (1/100), pp. 169–70. At that time Rößler gave Bonhoeffer the book by Friedrich Zündel, *Jesus in Bildern aus seinem Leben,* with the dedication, "To his dear friend Dietrich Bonhoeffer in grateful recollection of beautiful days in the Harz. Helmut Rössler, April 5, 1927."

church.[5] From that you can probably see what a frightful illusion "world Protestantism" can be as an "ecumenical idea." But are things much different in *our own* church?

Our theology during the past twenty years has doubtless improved, that is, has become more commensurate with the main point (εὐαγγέλιον).[6] Every-
238 thing depends on it having an effect on the *praxis* of proclamation, though little can be seen of that just now. My entire experience till now has been that the "substance" of the church is in horrible shape here as well; in the worst case people just muddle onward on behalf of the lethargy of the old Adam but do not address the break in the ages at all. Or in the most favorable case, people join the currently popular movement of the age (which presently is National Socialism in the rural areas), engage the gospel in the service of one or the other quite respectable human concern, and in so doing violate both its radical nature and its exclusivity. My own heart is hotly engaged in the mighty struggle for national self-assertion and the will for the future, a struggle that, especially in the rural flat country, has grown tremendously (you might compare it to the events of 1806–12,[7] except what at that time was secretly sown and grew *with* the Prussian state must today be fought for precisely *for* that state); and precisely because I am so engaged in that struggle, I often feel sorely challenged lest I betray the gospel to the "most sacred possessions of the nation," especially since by doing so the way of the cross, which the church and thus also the *ministri verbi*[8] *must* travel (when did they not have to?) can be made considerably easier by external success. On the other hand, we are called to a deed of ongoing love in which we must pick up on the questions and distress of today's rural inhabitant. And to the extent these questions do not emerge from naked egoism, they are now of an exclusively nationalistic [vaterländisch] disposition. The quiet work of the *Stahlhelm* over the years[9] and the recent loud and skilled agitation

---

[5.] See 1/148.

[6.] "Gospel."

[7.] Allusion to the reforms in Prussia, both political (through Heinrich Karl von Stein and Karl August von Hardenberg) and military (through Gerhard von Scharnhorst and August von Gneisenau), that paved the way intellectually and materially for the Wars of Liberation from 1813–15. [The widespread reforms introduced by Stein and implemented by Hardenberg included the reform of the military, abolition of serfdom, widespread changes in local governance, and, most radically, the opening of civil service, leading to the emancipation of the Jews. After the French defeat of Prussia in 1807, Gneisenau and Scharnhorst worked to reform the Prussian army.—CG]

[8.] "Minister of the Word."

[9.] The League of Front Soldiers, more generally known as the *Stahlhelm,* founded in 1918, was strongly nationalistic and antirepublican, and quite influential among Protestant nationalist pastors; see also Wright, *"Above Parties,"* 45–47, 76–77.

of the National Socialists have introduced a movement among the younger rural residents—I'm assessing this from the vantage point of Prignitz, so don't smile about it—which previously would have been considered impossible. A war of liberation, the renewal of the Prussian idea of the state (with a monarchical head!), racial purity, war on the Jews and on the Young Plan,[10] death to Marxism, the "third Reich" of German freedom and righteousness (an eschatological-chiliastic remnant!)—those are the ideas moving the German rural population today, who are themselves currently highly agitated. And directly in the midst of all this the preaching of the cross. Especially for me, given my overall background and 239
"genetic makeup"—see Konstantin Rößler![11]—it is truly not easy under such circumstances not to betray the *theologia crucis*[12] and instead to value the kingdom of God higher than the tormented fatherland. You, of course, are "unpolitical" by your very nature, and because you are not involved in the urgency of a struggle for economic existence and of boiling-hot politics, it's easier for you from your high vantage point to examine τὸ πλάτος καὶ μῆκος καὶ ὕψος καὶ βάθος Χριστοῦ.[13] This is not to say I fail to recognize your own temptations. They are perhaps more comprehensive but perhaps not as concrete as among us "frontline soldiers in the filthy trenches."

I think the greatest tragedy of the church and of our people at the moment ἐν καιρῷ[14] is that the powerful *völkisch* movement is combining a purified, red-hot national feeling with a new paganism, which will be more difficult to expose and fight than would be the case—and not merely for emotional reasons—with the religion of freethinkers, since it is clothed in a Christian garb. The basis of this neopagan religion is the assertion of the proven unity between *religion* and *race*, more specifically the Aryan (Nordic) race. The intellectual fathers of this anti-Marxism are Lagarde, H. S. Chamberlain, Günther (the racial research scholar), Albrecht Wirth (*Aufgang der Menschheit*!), the poet Wilhelm Schäfer,

---

[10.] The plan for regulating German reparation payments presented in 1930 by an international commission of experts under Owen D. Young. It was vehemently rejected in church circles; see *DB-ER*, 125, and Meier, *Kirchenkampf*, 1:7. [The Young Plan revised the earlier unworkable Dawes Plan, reducing the amount significantly but requiring Germany to pay $26.35 billion over some fifty-eight years. In 1995, after reunification, the German government resumed interest payments.—CG]

[11.] Konstantin Rößler, one of the most zealous advocates of Bismarckian politics in the press.

[12.] Theology of the cross.

[13.] See Eph. 3:18–19: "that you may have the power to comprehend, with all the saints, what is *the breadth and length and height and depth . . . of Christ*." [The italicized words translate the Greek.—CG]

[14.] "At the moment," a basic concept of New Testament eschatology; see Mark 10:30; Luke 18:30; Rom. 3:26.

and others.[15] *All* the basic critical notions of this religion toward Christianity have been taken from the intellectual arsenal of racial *ressentiment*, whose scholarly integrity is in part highly questionable. Confirmation of the church is based solely on the presupposition of its service to national customs and traditions [Volkstum] and race. Confessional antitheses are negated largely for the sake of a *völkisch* syncretism called "all God-believers of good will."[16] The constitutive
240 elements of this new religious syncretism (always a sign of a descending line!) are humanitarian idealism (the racially pure, i.e., the national person, is good),[17] *rationalismus vulgaris*[18] ("faith in God" in the light of love of the fatherland is the religion of *all* respectable people), and nonhistorical mysticism (union between the divinity and the spirit of the Volk is to be sought and attained *directly*, in an active fashion driven by the will). Nor does this fatherland religion lack the chiliastic element or the notion of the Antichrist. The former resides in the idea of the "Third Reich,"[19] the latter in the hatred toward the "Jews" or toward "capital" [Kapital] as the root of all evil. Only everything is now completely secularized. In an excellent lecture by an authority on India yesterday, I was alarmed to hear her say that the same process of a nationalistically grounded syncretism presently poses the most serious temptation of the Christian mission in India. It's the same everywhere. The world has become smaller. Nations are moving closer to one another. The same ideas and intellectual movements are drawing all the nations under their spell. And the tragedy of our own age is the clash between two fundamentally related fronts: the rigorous secularism of a conscious focus on the here and now, and religiously colored secularism for which only the pragmatic understanding of religion is still accessible. And placed in the middle of it all: the church of Christ, together with *all* religions (though

---

[15.] Paul de Lagarde (early publications under his birth name, P. A. Bötticher); Houston Stewart Chamberlain; Hans Günther; Herman Wirth (not the German-*völkisch* travel writer Albrecht Wirth); Wilhelm Schäfer. Regarding this ideological trend, see esp. Scholder, *Churches and the Third Reich* 1:81–87. [Herman Wirth, not Albrecht, was the author of the book cited by Rößler about the religion, symbolism, and writings of the Teutonic race.—CG]

[16.] Customary designation since the early twentieth century for various nondenominational, Nordic-religious groups; officially introduced in 1936 by a decree from the Reich Ministry of the Interior; see Kurt Hutten, "Deutschgläubige," in *Religion in Geschichte und Gegenwart*, 3rd ed., 2:108–12.

[17.] [In this context "national" meant monarchist and nationalistic attitudes, i.e., people who defined their identities and values purely in terms of the nation and, as Rößler notes, in terms of "racial purity." The National Socialists in 1931 used terms such as "humanitarian" and "idealism" to describe their own agenda to save Germany.—CG]

[18.] "Vulgar rationalism."

[19.] The term first appeared in this context in Arthur Moeller van den Bruck's *Das dritte Reich*, first in 1923 and most effectively in the third edition of 1931; see Nowak, *Evangelische Kirche und Weimarer Republik*, 216–18, and Meier, *Kirchenkampf*, 1:530n51.

as their most dangerous ferment!) consciously assaulted by the former front, and yet wooed by the latter to enter into the battle. And yet the church cannot completely take one side or the other. For it fails to recognize either the consequences of such radical focus on the here and now and the irrelevance of secularized syncretism, or the enormous temptation into which the Antichrist has brought the church through the presentation of these apparent cosmic antitheses, which in truth are ultimately no longer antitheses at all. It sometimes seems to me that the external and internal dimensions of the church's own lost condition in the midst of a hopeless world has never been greater in the course of history. "Come, children, let us go, evening approaches"[20]—I *do*, however, believe in an intensification of the idea of the Antichrist (contra Althaus's eschatology of the vertical!)[21] and that we are standing at the threshold of a *final* stage of world *history* in the sense of Rom. 13:11–12.[22] In any event, for me
all the various spheres of human life, including the completely "profane" and 241
autonomous, are moving ever more strongly under the purview of the eschatological. And the experiences I've had during the past year and a half in the rural Mark Brandenburg have certainly contributed to that feeling.

Tonight in a strange dream I was confronted with the absolutely lost and inscrutable nature of my existence in a world that no one is keeping together. And it became clear to me that faith is not a safeguard against such shock but "only" the staking of great hope in the midst of the hopelessness of contemporary humanity. Hence in his latest lecture about preaching Christ,[23] Fendt is of the opinion that the time has come to proclaim Christ as the great *hope* for startled, distraught humankind. "What counts is not what may be at work with the 'others,' not what is at work with us if we were to assume 'otherness'; what counts is rather what really is at work through God in Christ. Hence the 'others' are not lost in the sense of it-doesn't-matter-to-me and it-doesn't-matter-to-you, since we are saved. But that is what is great about Christ: the certainty [Sicherheit] of being saved. Or put differently: proclaim Christ because this old humanity has used up all hope and expectation, whereas hope does indeed reside and abide in Christ. . . . The proclamation must be turned around! This turn is overdue and is absolutely necessary. The old popular schema . . . will do no longer in this form: First, human beings must fall into fear and distress

[20.] Beginning of a hymn by Gerhard Tersteegen; see *EKG*, no. 393.

[21.] See Althaus, *Die letzten Dinge*.

[22.] ["Besides this, you know what time it is, how it is now the moment for you to wake from sleep. For salvation is nearer to us now than when we became believers; the night is far gone, the day is near. Let us then lay aside the works of darkness and put on the armor of light."—CG]

[23.] Fendt's lecture about preaching Christ, "Christus in der Verkündigung," was published in 1931.

because of their sins; then Christ is proclaimed to them as the savior, and thus faith comes (after penance).[24] No, the new schema must be: The great hope, Jesus Christ, is proclaimed to this hopeless, suffering humanity!"[25] Of course, one should never forget that this Christ of hope is precisely the crucified Christ. But we no longer need to threaten humanity with hell, since reality itself today has completely become a hell. (Dostoyevsky says: "Hell is—when one can no longer love"!)[26] Hence today Christ must be presented and proclaimed as the absolute relief of faith, as the great σεισάχθεια.[27] Everything else is cruelty or a deception of the people.

242 Does all this apply only to the sobered-up Germany that is disappointed to the very root of its being? Or does the famous frenzy of progress of the Americans not also merely disguise "at the level of consciousness" a despair that actually resides "at the level of *essence*"? H. W. Schmidt[28] and recently also Althaus in his fine little book *Der Geist der lutherischen Ethik in der Augustana*[29] fight against a theology focused on sin and teach emphatically that God's deity, his unfathomable will of love, is the *first* thing that asserts itself *despite* sin.[30] The gospel is "older" than the law, the latter having come along only secondarily. Is it not time to replace Barth's call to penance *in this way*? Can we still be prophets who have to bring about hardness of heart through the call to penance? Must we not bring the realism of love to those who are lost?

And now in closing, from these diary-like fragments of thought let me offer a wonderful definition from Macholz in his latest essay, "The distinctly Protestant way of worship,"[31] the worship on which the Thuringian reform of its churchbook is to be based: "The church is there where, *commensurate with the commission*, one spreads the news of the contingent, personal attention shown us by the God who *simultaneously* gives us community and radically calls us to become his (not to penance!),[32] and where this news then manifests itself through God's

[24.] Parenthetical remark inserted by Rößler.

[25.] Fendt, "Christus in der Verkündigung," 84.

[26.] See Dostoyevsky, *Brothers Karamazov*, pt. 1, bk. 1, chap. 2: "What is hell? I maintain that it is the suffering of being unable to love."

[27.] "A shaking off of burdens," "wiping out of debt." The name given to the ordinance of Solon in Athens in favor of debtors, according to which creditors lost the right of lien on the body of the debtor.

[28.] Probably Hans Wilhelm Schmidt, who in 1930 wrote the article, "Die ersten und die letzten Dinge."

[29.] "The spirit of Lutheran ethics in the Augsburg Confession."

[30.] Here Rößler is closely following Fendt, "Christus in der Verkündigung," 83.

[31.] Macholz, "Der Gottesdienst evangelischer Konsequenz"; the essay was published with the title "Grundsätzliches zur Gottesdienstgestaltung."

[32.] Parenthetical remark by Rößler.

own sovereign governance in *those* particular human beings whom God personally gathers together as God's *people*. (Negations follow)[33] . . . The church is found only where there are those who are chosen and gathered by God in Christ, those who have been brought and are brought ever anew out of their own self-glorification and self-determination on God's unpredictable paths into the willing dependence of creatures. This occurs through the unique, historical, accidental, supra-temporal Christ event, through which God speaks in a presence that encompasses both you and me personally."

Perhaps we should be permitted to formulate it thus: distress (= call to penance) is necessary for the self-glorification—*at the level of consciousness*—of the modern human being drunk on progress, but it may not be separated from the hope that is erected above the *essential* hopelessness of the modern generation.

It will probably interest you to learn that I have applied for doctoral work with Schumann[34] with a work in eschatology (Lutheran and early Lutheran 243
[altlutherisch] orthodoxy).[35]

Our health is good. Our little boy, who is already one year old,[36] is thriving splendidly, and as part of a faith that is already there, he remains a daily, visible miracle of God. My wife sends her warmest greetings. May God protect you.

In the warm bonds of friendship, I shake your hand and remain your

Helmut Rößler

165. From Paula Bonhoeffer[1]

February 23, 1931

Dear Dietrich,

I have the feeling I haven't written you in quite a while now. I don't know what happened; I planned so often to do it but just never got around to it. Perhaps part of the reason is that because my sciatica keeps me in bed so much and the nights are always so disrupted, my day is too short for everything I want to do.

[33.] Parenthetical remark by Rößler.

[34.] Friedrich Karl Schumann. This doctoral plan was not carried out.

[35.] [This was the prevalent seventeenth-century Lutheran school of thought, opposed to pietism, that sought to study, apply, and preserve the theological heritage of Luther and the Lutheran confessors. Cf. Schmid, *Doctrinal Theology of the Evangelical Lutheran Church*.—CG]

[36.] See 1/106.

[1.] *NL*, C 1; handwritten from Berlin.

I also recently got Suse everything she needed for her journey[2] and closed up the apartment, brought everything here that was transportable and of value and packed it away, and then I constantly had to jump in and help the Schleichers when their children had a relapse of the flu; in a word, the day is always over before you know it. My mother is also completely dependent on me now, and I can hardly find a quiet half hour at my desk without her talking with me!

Karl-Friedrich was here from Thursday till Friday; he had business with the ministry and the Association for German Scholarship and also attended the masquerade ball given by the Kaiser Wilhelm Institute at the Harnack house. He was asked at the association whether he was the brother of the Bonhoeffer who delivered the excellent address at the memorial service for Harnack.[3] They wanted to know where you were, what you were doing now. A certain
244 privy counselor Schwöner[4] was quite interested in you. At some point, you could probably get something there by being in the good graces of someone like that.

I was recently at the Diestels' home together with Dibelius, who spoke *very nicely* about you and asked when you would be returning; he said he hoped to win you over to the ministry once and for all by engaging you as student chaplain at the technical college.[5]—Senior Consistory Councilor Schreiber[6] also sang your praises.

A certain Excellency Conze[7] from the Protestant church press, who carried on in an extremely ill-mannered and almost obscene way about Barth's lecture,[8] was horrible. Dibelius reproached him a bit and said that Barth couldn't be dismissed quite that easily. Eight days after Barth, Dibelius himself actually delivered an address as a response,[9] which was supposedly quite good as well.

We haven't heard anything else from Trowitzsch, whom you did write, after all. Didn't you write Seeberg about a foundation subsidy in the amount of 200 marks? Did he answer you, or should we give him a ring? Our concern, of course, is what the printing of your book will cost apart from the subsidies.[10] Papa has withdrawn the money from the university for you, so if you need the money for

[2.] She was accompanying her husband, Walter Dreß, to Dorpat.

[3.] See 2/4.

[4.] Not otherwise identified.

[5.] See 1/161.

[6.] August Wilhelm Schreiber.

[7.] Peter Conze.

[8.] See 1/156, p. 275.

[9.] "Die Verantwortung der Kirche: Eine Antwort an Karl Barth" (The responsibility of the church: A response to Karl Barth); see Scholder, *Churches and the Third Reich,* 1:124–26.

[10.] See 1/131, ed. note 4.

your trip, deduct it from the letter of credit. Papa plans to ask Lütgert tomorrow whether he has written to Bertelsmann.[11] Papa has probably already written and told you that Bertelsmann wrote (to Papa) that they received your letter and were waiting only for the recommendations from Lütgert and Althaus. Papa is also planning to write to Bertelsmann and ask whether Althaus has written them, and if not he plans possibly to remind Althaus.[12]

I'm enclosing all sorts of things for you with this letter. A little picture of the "son and heir";[13] a letter from Susi;[14] the address in Manila;[15] a letter from Theodor Dietrich,[16] a letter from Pfizer,[17] Hildebrandt's theses,[18] but I'm putting it in two envelopes. Unfortunately the program for the Rittelmeyer[19] 245
session here has been lost, though I did want to send it to you.

We are always quite glad to get your letters, which interest us greatly. Rüdiger[20] is always so "enthushiashtic"[21] when we read them aloud. What interesting things you are seeing! Write and tell us sometime what they really think about Germany's future. Are you getting any German newspapers at all? It's a miracle that everything has stayed so calm thus far with all the unemployment. Rüdiger's position as second jurist is also threatened by the "savings commissioner," and Hans,[22] too, is worried about where he can make connections; maybe he'll return to Hamburg. He is not yet "in the budget," and with three children, and everything is blocked! For his own part, Gerd[23] fears the Nazis as far as his job is concerned; I think that's exaggerated, but Sabine is also tormenting herself

[11.] [The publishing house in Gütersloh; the director at the time was Heinrich Mohn.—CG]

[12.] On March 4, 1931, Althaus wrote to Karl Bonhoeffer very positively concerning *Act and Being*; see *NL*, A 27,5 (8) and *DBWE* 2:5.

[13.] Karl-Friedrich and Margarethe Bonhoeffer's son Karl; cf. 1/157.

[14.] Susanne Dreß, née Bonhoeffer.

[15.] A sister-in-law of Klaus Bonhoeffer lived there; this was considered as a possible layover for Bonhoeffer should he travel to India; cf. *DB-ER*, 148.

[16.] Should read "Theodor Dieterich."

[17.] Probably Theodor Pfizer.

[18.] The theses for Franz Hildebrandt's doctoral defense.

[19.] Probably Friedrich Rittelmeyer, one of the cofounders of the Christengemeinschaft [a religious society incorporating Christian and anthroposophical elements.—CG]

[20.] Rüdiger Schleicher.

[21.] [A play on the German pronunciation; the German here is *begeischtert* instead of *begeistert*.—CG]

[22.] Hans von Dohnanyi.

[23.] Gerhard Leibholz; concerning the following, see Sabine Leibholz-Bonhoeffer, *Bonhoeffers*, 65–66, 69. [It is striking that Leibholz (whose ancestry was Jewish) was already worried about this possibility in 1931; he subsequently did lose his job, and the Leibholzes had to emigrate to England. See also *DB-ER*, 490, 631–33.—CG]

because of it. They're coming here mid-March. On February 28 we're going to Wiesbaden, "Hotel Schwarzer Bock," and plan to be home on March 22 for little Christiane's[24] baptism on the thirty-first.

We are very concerned what your plans are. I'm thinking that although the price of the trip seems manageable to you, the question of climate during that period is unchanged. I think you could always take a leave of absence for such a trip to India and then be better prepared and go during a more favorable time.[25] But I don't want to interfere with your decisions.

Take care, my dear boy. All the best from your

Mother

Papa sends his warm greetings.

246 **166. To Richard Ern**[1]

Dear Richard,

I'm taking this opportunity to send along greetings to you via a friend who is with Mr. Heusen today. At the same time, I'd like to inquire whether it would suit you all if I were to come visit you next *Saturday* (March 7). I would again depart on the 10:00 train and keep the afternoon free so I could see your father a bit longer. Unfortunately I again can't stay through till Sunday, but I hope to do so later sometime. But, of course, only if it's no trouble for you. Please write and let me know. Say hello to your parents, and cordial greetings, yours

Dietrich Bonhoeffer

[24.] Daughter of Gerhard and Sabine Leibholz; see 1/147.

[25.] Cf. also 1/168, p. 294; Bonhoeffer was unable to realize this travel plan.

[1.] *NL*, Anh. A 33 (8); handwritten from New York; probable date: before March 7, 1931. [See 1/159, ed. note 1; therefore this card was written before March 4.—CG]

167. From Reinhold Seeberg[1]

Berlin, April 7, 1931

Dear Mr. Bonhoeffer,

I still have not yet thanked you for your detailed letter[2] and am all the more pleased to catch up on it because what you had to say does indeed interest me from various perspectives. I did not know that the atmosphere of ever-intensifying economic crisis had been joined intellectually, particularly in theology, by so many new tendencies, albeit tendencies apparently without much content. One can, however, probably hardly talk about a crisis in this field, since such a crisis comes about only when death and recovery are struggling with each other. I sense from your letter that you are more interested in philosophy than in theology there. In any case, it is an important event in your life as a whole that you have seen this western world without all the fog with which we always envelope it, and on the other hand, something that is also important for a German, that 247
you are experiencing firsthand that it is possible for people to live even if they think differently than we do and have different aims in life. Above all, however, given the generally growing tendency toward internationalism in church circles, a complete mastery of the English language will stand you in very good stead in your life. At least for me, in recent years hardly any shortcoming in my own background has been so painful as my lack of proficiency in speaking in the tongues of angels.[3]

You will doubtless also have occasion to give lectures on our own German theology with all its directions and currents. Whenever I am with American theologians, I am shocked at how little they know about intellectual life in German scholarship. A few names from newspapers, and as for the rest, questions and problems we hardly deal with anymore. In such a situation, a young man in whom all this wisdom is still fresh can assuredly be of use and help point the way. In the meantime, while you have been away not much new has happened in our scholarship either, as you yourself probably know—perhaps even better than I—from periodicals. The Luther stocks continue to climb higher.[4] Dissertations and treatises on this subject are appearing in such ever-increasing numbers now that it's hard to find your way through it all. It's all the more important, then, to set certain baselines again and again and to provide examples of them.

[1.] *NL*, A 20,1 (4); typewritten with handwritten signature. Partially reproduced in *GS* 3:22–23.

[2.] Not preserved.

[3.] [The phrase "tongues of angels," *Engelzungen*, may be a German pun on the word *Englisch*, "English." Seeberg is talking of his inadequate proficiency in English.—CG]

[4.] Allusion to the so-called Luther renaissance; see Meier, *Kirchenkampf*, 1:26–27.

I am currently involved in a revision of my own volume on Luther[5] and have thus had to read a great deal of new material. The big question attached to this Lutheranism today is what consequences will emerge from it for systematic theology. It is odd how strongly Holl, too, basically constructed his own Luther theology on certain fundamental features of Ritschlianism[6] and how tenaciously his adherents maintain this direction. But this hardly solves the aforementioned question, especially since various other tendencies are also making their presence known. But you yourself will soon be back here and will be working within that overall movement.

248 I had a lot to do here last winter, since in addition to dogmatics I also had to lecture in New Testament theology. The unrest accompanying the new questions also extends to a remarkable extent to the New Testament, and even those possessing certain unwavering principles are confronted repeatedly with new questions and thus with new discoveries. Even our students are enormously interested in these things. Again and again, I sense that the extraordinarily great difficulty attached to any presentation of this discipline, since detailed exegetical investigation and a broader overview or sweep should constantly merge with and support each other, but then by their very nature will also burden each other. My health is, thank God, still bearable. I can say the same for my wife. You have probably heard in abundance from your family about the other things going on at the university. I am anxious to see how your brother-in-law likes it in Dorpat.[7]

Have you by chance got to know a certain Professor Otto Peterson in New York, a lecturer there in German literature and an enthusiastic advocate of Goethe and Schiller? I've known him since I was a youth. He wanted to establish a Goethe theater in Berlin, but it failed because of the inflation. But enough.

I wish you all the very best for your studies and your life on foreign soil. Soon, of course, you will be home again.

Sincerely yours,
R. Seeberg

[5.] Seeberg was referring to his textbook on the history of dogma, of which the fourth edition of volume 4, part 1, was published in February, 1933; it was titled *Die Entstehung des protestantischen Lehrbegriffs* (a change from the title *Die Lehre Luthers*, used through the third edition); see also the similar foreword there.

[6.] A school of theology named after Albrecht Ritschl, characterized by the linking of practical faith and doctrine as well as by an emphasis on morality over against metaphysics.

[7.] Walter Dreß was working at the Luther Academy in Dorpat—the Estonian town of Tartu.

168. To Karl-Friedrich and Margarethe Bonhoeffer[1]

April 12, 1931

Dear Karl Friedrich, dear Grete,

It's really bad form that I've waited two months before thanking you for your birthday greeting.[2] The book[3] did indeed greatly interest me; and 249 since by chance I received two copies of it, I passed one along to a professor here. I have in the meantime read so much other stuff, even novels, that I can no longer really write you about your book. In any case, many thanks for it.

The closer I get to the end of things here, the more filled up my time becomes. In three weeks I will already be on my way to the South and Mexico. I want to have a look at church conditions in the South, which allegedly can still be quite peculiar, and get to know the situation of the Negroes in a bit more detail. I don't quite know whether I have not perhaps spent too much time on this question here, especially since we don't really have an analogous situation in Germany, but I've just found it enormously interesting, and I've never for a moment found it boring. And it really does seem to me that there is a great movement forming, and I do believe that the Negroes will still give the whites here considerably more than merely their folksongs.

On June 20, I will depart New York for home and will be in Berlin at the beginning of July. If you really want to wait that long, then I'll be glad to baptize your little one,[4] even though I would need special permission since I am not ordained and don't know what the story is in the Frankfurt church. Otherwise it might not be possible till the autumn, and that would probably be too long for you to wait. Perhaps Mama could speak with Diestel about it sometime. It would be a shame if it didn't work out.[5] Many thanks also for your last letter[6] and for the nice picture of the little one. By the way, I think this is the first child this small that I really do like.

I am reading and trying to see what I still can here. I have come to know American philosophy quite thoroughly and have in the process often

[1.] *NL*, Anh. A 14 (9); handwritten from New York. Previously published in *GS* 6:187–88. See also *NL*, A 27,4 (5); typewritten copy.

[2.] See 1/157.

[3.] Renn, *After War.* [See 1/157 and ed. note 3.—CG]

[4.] Karl Walter Paul Bonhoeffer, born January 10, 1931.

[5.] The baptism was performed on September 13, 1931, in the Berlin Grunewald Church by Pastor Priebe.

[6.] March 27, 1931 (*NL*, C 3).

thought of you, Karl-Friedrich. Even though I haven't gained much more faith in the whole business than I had before, I have, however, learned a
250 great deal from it. James[7] especially is extremely interesting to read.

Will I be hearing from you again before I leave here? In any case, I think of you often and am looking forward to seeing you this summer. It's sad that nothing came of the trip to India; it was unfortunately just too far after all. That still remains for me. But I don't want it to take too long![8] All three of you take care. Greetings from your

Dietrich

169. To Julie Bonhoeffer[1]

April 12, 1931

Dear Grandmama,

I still need to thank you for a letter and a card[2] and probably already did so a couple of times in letters to my parents. I'm always so sorry when I can't answer you immediately. During the past few weeks I still had a lot to do on my postdoctoral dissertation,[3] which I hope has in the meantime arrived there. In the three weeks that still remain here, I naturally really have to use my time. I want to read a great deal, something I'm sure I'll never get to once I am home; I am not even close to being finished with everything I planned; one just blabs away so frightfully much time here. Ultimately, though, one does learn from it, if nothing else then certainly English, and in any case, one can no longer have such discussions later. Even though I am myself not at all satisfied with my English yet, it is some comfort that people repeatedly tell me I speak it well. And that certainly must be counted as a considerable gain that this year has brought.

I stayed in New York over Easter. Good Friday is not a holiday here at all;
251 most people work. By contrast, Easter is the day on which everyone goes to church, even those who only go once. They are generally in agreement here that Easter is celebrated more than the beginning of the spring season. Everyone shows off their new spring clothes in church. You have to get entry

[7.] Cf. 1/150, ed. note 2, and 2/13.

[8.] Cf. 1/165, p. 290.

[1.] *NL*, A 27,1 (5); handwritten from New York. Partially reproduced in *GS* 1:79–81.

[2.] See *NL*, C 2.

[3.] *Act and Being* (*DBWE* 2). [Bonhoeffer was presumably reading proof; it was published in September 1931.—CG]

tickets for the larger churches far ahead of time. Because I didn't know that, nothing remained but to go hear a famous rabbi here[4] who preaches every Sunday morning in the largest concert hall before a full audience; he delivered an enormously effective sermon on corruption in New York and challenged the Jews, who make up a third of the city, to build from this city the City of God, to which the Messiah would then truly be able to come.

That afternoon a friend and I then drove out to the ocean, where ships from Europe sail by. Easter morning I took an excursion with a group of Negro boys. Several of them are already in the upper classes in the secondary school, some at an astonishingly young age—for example, one at fifteen, another who did his *Abitur*[5] (actually they don't have that here) at sixteen—and then others who are intellectually very slow and hardly make it through a couple of grades in elementary school. The strange thing is that all of them absolutely seem to belong together to the extent they are the same age. That does, of course, have considerable advantages, but on the other hand, it does very clearly demonstrate the situation here, namely, that the intelligent young Negroes simply cannot have social contact with intelligent whites, but are simply dependent on members of their own race who are their own age. That, of course, necessarily slows down any advancement; but it probably also intensifies their energy. I just finished another quite excellent novel by a very young Negro.[6] Here, in contrast to the either cynical or sentimental American literature, I find an extremely productive energy and warmth that always make one want to get to know the man 252
himself.

On Friday and Saturday there was a conference here of the leading American systematic theologians to which Professor Baillie,[7] a professor here who presided, invited me. The discussions, however, were so unsatisfying, really almost like discussions among students in their first semesters, that I

[4.] Probably Rabbi Stephen Wise; see 1/181, p. 313.

[5.] [The final secondary school examinations necessary for university study.—CG]

[6.] Concerning the literature of African Americans, see 2/11.2. [Langston Hughes's 1930 novel, *Not Without Laughter*, won the Harmon Gold Medal for Literature and may be the book to which Bonhoeffer refers in this letter. Another possibility is Wallace Thurman's 1929 novel, *The Blacker the Berry: A Novel of Negro Life*, dealing with intraracial prejudice. In a message to the editor, Henry Louis Gates suggested Jean Toomer's *Cane* as a strong candidate for the book that so impressed Bonhoeffer.—CG]

[7.] John Baillie; concerning his influence on Bonhoeffer, see 1/181, p. 308, and *DB-ER*, 159–60. [The meeting referred to was most likely the annual spring meeting of the American Theological Society, which met at Union; Baillie was the president in 1930–31. For more information see the editor's introduction to this volume, p. 23.—CG]

am still quite depressed. The reigning atmosphere is one of inordinate confusion and lack of clarity. Those are the most recent events here.

I will presumably depart on May 2. My address will remain this one here. I'm asking a student here to have a look at the letters and forward them, as well as any telegrams. My exact itinerary is not yet fixed. In any case, Mexico is the goal.

Spring has been in full bloom here since yesterday. The crocuses are up, and one yearns to get out of the city. How quickly all that has come around again. Please say hello to my parents and my brothers and sisters; all good wishes to you, dear Grandmama, and warmest greetings from your grateful

Dietrich

170. To Max Diestel[1]

April 25, 1931

Dear Superintendent Diestel:

The semester is now coming to an end, and I cannot deny that after the long winter in New York, which has been completely filled with new experiences, I am almost yearning to get out again. If you really try to experience New York completely, it almost does you in. As frequently as one hears people insist that New York is not America, this is true only to the extent that it is
253 in a way the center of all of America's problems and of many others as well. Since it is the seat of almost all the headquarters of the larger organizations in which I am interested, the so-called character-building agencies, you can get almost all the materials here that are available. During the last few months, I have visited a large number of these agencies with a professor here[2] who knows a great many people, and I have learned a great deal. I have also kept up my contacts in the Federal Council[3] and learned many interesting things. The brochure issued a few weeks ago on the position of the Protestant church on birth control stirred up a lot of dust.[4]

My course of studies here at the seminary, apart from some regular sessions on American philosophy with an extremely competent professor,[5] did not yield very much. Only the social gospel people really address con-

[1.] EZA 29/G 442, 31–32; handwritten; date of receipt: May 11, 1931; Diary no. 2066. See also *NL*, A 20,2 (3); typewritten copy. Previously published in *GS* 1:81–83.

[2.] Charles C. Webber; see 1/182, p. 320.

[3.] See 1/144 and 1/150, p. 267.

[4.] See also 2/12.8.

[5.] Eugene W. Lyman; see 1/182, p. 320.

temporary issues, and they are completely untheological.[6] Interest in Karl Barth is quite lively here, though they are completely without understanding;[7] yet another sect![8] That's what they think!

After all that, I'm really looking forward to Germany again. Before I come home in July, I still want to go to Mexico and then spend a few days in England.[9] I have one more question: In August and if possible also in September and October, I would like to summarize and complete for myself some thoughts about America that I never got to here and would like to write a piece that is very close to my heart[10] (not in connection with America), and finally would like to have time to prepare my course of lectures for the winter, since with my twofold job, a great deal will presumably be happening all at once. My leave of absence, however, ends on August 1. Would it be possible to request a one- to three-month extension of my leave?[11] I
myself fear that if I take up my full load of church work on August 1, all the 254
other plans will never get done, and the year over here will thus not be fully and adequately assessed. I have also written home about these plans and asked my father whether he might call you sometime, esteemed Superintendent, and ask your opinion. Because I will in the meantime be on a trip to Mexico, could my father possibly write the consistory or telephone one of the members? Or can that wait till the beginning of July, when I'll be back in Berlin myself? General Superintendent Dibelius wrote me[12] to suggest I introduce myself to General Superintendent Karow when I return. Before doing that, however, I would like to discuss the entire matter once more with you, esteemed Superintendent. Will be you be in Berlin in July?

Please extend my greetings to your esteemed wife.

With respectful greetings I am, esteemed Superintendent,
your grateful servant
Dietrich Bonhoeffer

[6.] [See Bonhoeffer's survey based on a draft by Paul Lehmann, *DBW* 12, 2/4. This American Protestant movement in the early twentieth century addressed the social ills of industrial capitalism and urbanization, emphasized social salvation, and challenged the churches to work for the kingdom of God on earth ("the fatherhood of God and the brotherhood of man") through social reform.—CG]

[7.] See also 2/17 and *DB-ER*, 157–58.

[8.] [Bonhoeffer means that Barth and his followers are regarded as just one more option in the multiplicity of American denominations, or "sects."—CG]

[9.] Apparently nothing came of the latter plans.

[10.] Possibly the "short piece about contemporary theology's demarcation from Catholicism"; see *DBW* 11 (1/6), p. 20, including ed. note 6, which contains references to 2/17 and 3/14 in *DBWE* 9.

[11.] The extension of leave was rejected; see 1/177 and 1/178.

[12.] See 1/161.

171. To Karl Bonhoeffer[1]

May 3, 1931

Dear Papa,

I'm enclosing the announcements.[2] I had some doubts regarding the times. Could you perhaps phone Dean Bertholet[3] about this and ask him which hours he might consider most appropriate, or the elder Seeberg?[4] I didn't enter any hour at all for the lecture. It is to be *two hours.* The sem-
255 inar hour is also only a suggestion. Should the same lecture already be announced by someone else, and if I *absolutely* had to change the topic, then I would announce the current seminar topic as the two-hour lecture topic and change the seminar topic to "The Nature of the Church."[5]

Our departure has been delayed a bit by someone who wants to travel along part of the way. We'll probably leave on Tuesday. Aunt Elisabeth wrote me the address of Ms. Hystock;[6] that might be important for me. My Frenchman, Jean Lasserre,[7] has a very good friend who is a Mexican and with whom we will be spending a few days. I already had to pack my bags, because the seminary is closing. In eight weeks, I'll already be home again. I'm really looking forward to it.

Greetings to everyone from your
Dietrich

[1.] *NL*, A 27,2 (2); handwritten from New York; correct date according to the postmark is May 3, 1931. Previously published in *GS* 6:188–89.

[2.] For Bonhoeffer's university offerings during the winter semester 1931/32.

[3.] Alfred Bertholet.

[4.] Reinhold Seeberg.

[5.] This then became the main lecture course during the summer semester 1932; see *DBWE* 11, 2/9. During the winter semester Bonhoeffer gave a lecture course, The History of Twentieth-Century Systematic Theology, and a seminar, The Concept of Philosophy and Protestant Theology; see *DB-ER*, 212.

[6.] Elisabeth von Hase; for her letter of April 19, 1931, see *NL*, C 8: "Perhaps you'd like the address of Dr. Will née Hystock, an acquaintance both of mine and Mama's who was long a guest at the Neissers. (I'm enclosing a note.) She lives in the Legacione alemagna, Marsella 44, Mexico D.F."

[7.] Concerning the friendship between Jean Lasserre and Bonhoeffer, see *DB-ER*, 153–54.

172. To His Parents[1]

May 4

My dear Parents,

Tomorrow we'll finally be leaving by car; four of us as far as Chicago, the American Lehmann,[2] with whom I have spent a great deal of time here, the Frenchman,[3] the Swiss fellow,[4] and I; then as far as New Orleans without the American, then only the Frenchman and I. All of us except the Swiss 256
man can drive. My driving teacher, from whom I took extra lessons, told me I drive like a chauffeur. So you don't need to worry. In any event, the old car itself will keep any of us from driving too fast. Of course, I took my driver's license test here. I didn't withdraw any more money. I have enough with what I have saved here. We're having splendid spring weather.

Greetings to you all from your grateful
Dietrich

173. To the Ern Family[1]

Dear Ern Family,

After traveling the first one hundred miles in three hours (with very little traffic), we have arrived in the mountains of Pennsylvania, are eating lunch and enjoying the beautiful surroundings and the beautiful, warm weather![2] Many thanks again! More soon![3]

your Dietrich Bonhoeffer[4]

[1.] *NL*, A 27,2 (3); handwritten from New York; certainly 1931. Previously published in *GS* 6:189.

[2.] Paul Louis Lehmann; concerning his friendship with Bonhoeffer, see *DB-ER*, 155–56.

[3.] Jean Lasserre.

[4.] Erwin Sutz.

[1.] *NL*, Anh. A 33 (9); handwritten card from Portland, Pennsylvania (postmark); probable date: May 5, 1931. [Postmark indistinct; cf. 1/172.—CG]

[2.] For photographs from the trip, see Bethge and Gremmels, *Life in Pictures*, centenary ed., 49. [More pictures can be found in the 1986 ed., p. 78.—CG]

[3.] See 1/174.

[4.] [Under Bonhoeffer's signature appears in their handwriting "Jean Lasserre" and "The car is running fine. Paul L. Lehmann."—CG]

174. To the Ern Family[1]

Fort Worth, May 14, 1931

Dear Ern Family,

I'm using a brief stop at a gas and service station to tell you that I am doing well and that we have really enjoyed our trip thanks to your car. We are seeing a great deal of the country and have summer weather. The car is still
257 alive, though every now and then it does show its age. We had to replace the part from the shaft to the fan,[2] since it finally broke off. We are just now stopping to repair the carburator.[3] With our two new tires,[4] the car is now driving excellently. We hope to bring the car back to you in good shape and are grateful to you every day. Many thanks for the insurance policy. More again soon. Cordial greetings and thanks from your grateful

Dietrich Bonhoeffer

175. To Julie Bonhoeffer[1]

Dear Grandmama,

Many greetings from our splendid auto tour, the first half of which is almost over. We have traveled through what is in part beautiful country; everything seems so fresh and untouched. For two days we drove though a mountain range that repeatedly made me think of the Harz Mountains. Today we came through the great areas where entire cities quickly emerged and people made their money overnight. The day after tomorrow, we will travel to Mexico by train. We are doing wonderfully.

Affectionately, yours
Dietrich[2]

[1.] *NL,* Anh. A 33 (10); handwritten. [Postmarked May 16, 1931.—CG]

[2.] "Shaft" and "fan" in English in the original.

[3.] [Bonhoeffer's misspelled English in the German text; deciphered from the original donated by Richard Ern to the Bonhoeffer Collection at Union Theological Seminary in 2003. The German edition used copies given by Ern to Bethge in 1977.—CG]

[4.] "Tires" in English in the original.

[1.] *NL,* A 27,1 (6); handwritten postcard; the reverse side depicts a "Texas Long Horn" bull; date according to the postmark: May 16, 1931.

[2.] A handwritten addendum in French from Jean Lasserre follows: "We are really enjoying our trip through an extremely interesting country. Both Dietrich and I are looking forward to getting to Mexico soon. Best wishes—Jean Lasserre."

176. To the Ern Family[1] 258

Laredo, May 17, 1931

Dear Ern Family,

We just arrived at the Mexican border and are eating our last dinner in America.[2] The trip was splendid, the roads good to this point. We are doing well despite the rather severe heat, and the car fulfilled its term of service admirably well. Many thanks and greetings, your

Dietrich Bonhoeffer[3]

177. From Max Diestel[1]

Berlin-Lichterfelde, May 29, 1931

Dear Colleague,

Many thanks for your cordial letter of April 25.[2] It was of great interest to me.

I immediately requested leave for you till October 1. The situation is as fol- 259
lows: your primary service obligation begins on August 1. You are being assigned to General Superintendent *Dr. Karow*[3] as a Stadtvikar.[4] He is prepared to grant you further leave with special consideration for your participation in the

[1.] *NL*, Anh. A 33 (11); handwritten postcard. [Dated May 17 by Bonhoeffer; postmarked May 18.—CG]

[2.] At the continuation of the journey (rather than on the return trip, contra *DB-ER*, 152), there were unexpected problems at the Mexican border; see the telegram draft (*NL*, A 27,6 [1], reverse side, in original English) from Lasserre and Bonhoeffer: "Cannot enter Mexico—we need authorisation to reenter States—can we be registered for Summer Course at Union—or can Tryon telephone. Are [in] Laredo Texas St. Paul Hotel. Thanks [deleted: Jean] Dietrich"; and the response from Paul Lehmann (*NL*, A 27,6 [2], May 19, 1931): "Proceed to Mexico City When Returning Apply American Consul For Transit Visa Commissioner General Assures No Trouble—Paul." See also the written confirmation of Union Theological Seminary dated April 29, 1931 (though surely backdated) and of the German Embassy in Mexico dated May 30, 1931, both in *NL*, C 23.

[3.] [Jean Lasserre added a postscript that is legible in the original: "Après un voyage merveilleux, je pense aussi à vous avec reconnaisance—L'auto a très bien marché et nous a fait jouir beaucoup [du] voyage—Avec mes meillieurs sentiments Jean Lasserre" (After a marvelous trip I too think of you with gratitude. The car has run very well, and we have enjoyed the trip very much. Best wishes Jean Lasserre).—CG]

[1.] EZA 29/G 442, 4–5; carbon copy; letterhead: Office of the Superintendent Kölln-Land I TgG 2333. Dr. Bonhoeffer, 600 West 122nd Street, New York; author certainly Max Diestel. See also *NL* A 30,2 (5); typewritten transcript.

[2.] See 1/170.

[3.] Emil Karow.

[4.] [*Stadtvikar* (literally, "municipal vicar") was a misnomer for Bonhoeffer's actual position, which was *Stadtsynodalvikar*, or vicar for the municipal synod. He was assigned

international conference of the World Alliance for Promoting International Friendship through the Churches in Cambridge on September 1–3.[5] I have had you listed there as a representative of the "youth." Pastor Lilje[6] and others are also traveling under this flag. The World Alliance will cover the costs. You might be expected to say a few words during the discussion on "national" and international obligations; length: ten to fifteen minutes, and to say something of fundamental and practical interest in the sense of the World Alliance from the youth perspective regarding this two-sided obligation. I have not yet heard directly from *Dr. Karow*, but Consistory Councilor Coulon[7] told me there were no problems from that quarter with granting you leave, especially with respect to the conference in Cambridge. You will in any case still have sufficient time to work through your American experiences on the side.

Your brother-in-law Dress returned from Dorpat with rounded cheeks and quite cheery. His time there was extremely valuable and revealing for him.[8] He is now hard at work here.

I keep wanting to pay your grandmother a visit. But it's terrible; one just cannot get around to anything. Your parents once pleased us by spending an evening with us. But that was already some months ago. The time just flies by.

Tomorrow morning I'm going to a conference of the World Alliance in Hamburg that has caused considerable trouble for me.[9] Quite against my will, they made me the deputy chair of the German Union, and I must now represent Dr. Burghart,[10] who now feels totally relieved.

Last week we had our district synod, and things were very lively indeed. The
260 *Deutschkirchler* and *Stahlhelm* members[11] are making grand gestures, but there's not much behind it. We needed an hour longer than usual and then went to lunch exhausted at 5:00.

---

not directly to a parish, but to the municipal synod on special assignment, supervised by the superintendent.—CG]

[5.] Concerning Bonhoeffer's participation at this conference, see *DB-ER*, 189–202.

[6.] Hanns Lilje.

[7.] Albert Coulon.

[8.] See 1/167, p. 292, ed. note 7.

[9.] Concerning this conference and the associated radical critiques from Althaus and Hirsch of all church ecumenical efforts, critiques that prompted "an ecumenical scandal," see *DB-ER*, 194–97, and Scholder, *Churches and the Third Reich*, 1:168–70.

[10.] Georg Burghart.

[11.] The *Deutschkirchler* were adherents of the Alliance for the German Church and precursors of the "German Christians." Cf. Nowak, *Evangelische Kirche und Weimarer Republik*, 247–50; concerning the *Stahlhelm*, see 1/164, p. 282. Concerning the "trouble," cf. EZA 29/G 264/I, which also contains the minutes of the synod. [As this indicates, in 1931 there were already debates within the Protestant church about nationalism and the growing demands for a *völkisch* church, predating the Church Struggle that broke out in early 1933.—CG]

We're having sweltering midsummer heat here now. I hope you are not suffering too much in your southern latitudes. When you are here again, you'll have to give a report on your American experiences in our candidates' circles.[12] Did you know we had a report on "the *communio sanctorum*"? Our young colleague entered into a hearty debate with you.

And now may God be with you. Return healthy and intellectually enriched to your forest green homeland.

Faithfully,
your Ephorus[13]

178. Order from the Berlin Consistory regarding an Extension of Bonhoeffer's Leave of Absence[1]

Berlin SW 68, May 30, 1931

In response to the report of May 11, 1931—Diary no. 2069—.[2]

Commensurate with §1 (2) of Church Law concerning assistantships of March 4, 1930, we regret we are not in a position to extend beyond July 31, 1931, the leave of absence granted to Dr. Bonhoeffer on July 24, 1930[3]—K. VII 2919—. 261

[12.] See 1/3.

[13.] [From the Latin *ephor* (to oversee); the term Ephorus sometimes refers to magistrates, teachers, or others with authority; it is used in some churches for a leader such as a bishop.—CG]

[1.] EZA 29/G 442, 3; typewritten with handwritten signature, date of receipt: June 4, 1931, file K VII Nr. 1907. See also *NL*, A 30,2 (4); typewritten copy. Previously published in *GS* 6:235. See also the draft in *NL*, D 11 (68) with Coulon's signature.

[2.] Diestel's report read as follows: "In August there will be meetings in England having to do with Stockholm and Lausanne. Following these, in September there will be an international conference of the World Alliance for Promoting International Friendship through the Churches in Cambridge. We do not have many younger theologians who are so proficient in English that they are able to function with sufficient freedom within the intellectual context of scholarly presentations. A young German theologian is supposed to speak in connection with one of the topics being discussed there, and I have suggested Bonhoeffer as someone who would be particularly well suited to such a task. I also believe that his participation in these negotiations would be of great significance for his later work (e.g., if he were to become a student chaplain). In order to facilitate his further preparations in this matter, I am requesting now that the leave of absence of Dr. Bonhoeffer be extended till October 1. I would be extremely grateful to be informed as soon as possible. Diestel" (EZA 29/G 442, 6; carbon copy, Diary no. 2069; publication: *GS* 6:234).

[3.] See 1/123, ed. note 2.

Bonhoeffer is being considered for a position as Berlin Stadtvikar, beginning August 1, 1931. General Superintendent Dr. Karow will then determine his subsequent assignments.
On behalf of the Consistory,
[...][4]

179. To Richard Ern[1]

Dear Richard,

I just spent a long time sitting on this pyramid[2] and talking with an Indian shepherd boy who could neither read nor write but had a great deal to tell. It's beautiful here and not very hot at all, since the elevation is over two thousand meters.[3] Everything is completely different from the States. There are apparently a great many poor people here. They often live in tiny huts, and the children often wear only shirts or nothing at all. The people look nice and are quite friendly. I'm looking forward to getting back into your car and to seeing you again. Take care, dear boy. Cordial greetings to you and your parents.
Dietrich Bonhoeffer

180. To the Ern Family[1]

Dear Ern Family,

Each day I am getting closer to you by great leaps and in a few days hope
262 to find you all healthy again and to drive the car back into your garage
intact.[2] I can only reiterate what marvelous service this car has given us

[4.] Illegible handwritten signature.

[1.] *NL*, Anh. A 33 (12); handwritten postcard from Mexico. [The postmark date is June 5, 1931.—CG]

[2.] [The picture on the postcard is of the Aztec pyramid Teopanzolco, built ca. 1350 and situated in the north of Cuernavaca.—CG]

[3.] [More than 6,500 feet. —CG]

[1.] *NL*, Anh. A 33 (13); handwritten postcard from the United States. [Postmark probably June 12, 1931, at Wytheville, Virginia.—CG]

[2.] Bonhoeffer was back in New York on June 17, 1931; see the telegram announcing their New York arrival and plans to come to Scarsdale the following morning (*NL*, Anh. A 33 [14]). Bonhoeffer departed for Europe by ship on June 20, 1931. For an additional letter to Richard Ern on December 13, 1931, see *DBWE* 11, 1/25.

and how it has made our trip easier. Tomorrow we will have a splendid trip through the mountains. See you soon! Cordial greetings, your

Dietrich Bonhoeffer[3]

181. Report on His Year of Study Prepared for the Church Federation Office[1]

**Report on My Year of Study
at Union Theological Seminary in New York, 1930/31.
Presented to the Church Federation Office by
Lecturer Dr. Dietrich Bonhoeffer**

Being introduced to the ecclesiastical and theological circumstances of the United States as a fellowship recipient at Union Theological Seminary in New York has all the advantages and disadvantages that emerge for foreigners insofar as they get to know a foreign country from the location of the 263
most incisive critique. The critique from the bulwark of Union Theological Seminary is as notorious as it is venerated and is directed as much at political, social, and economic circumstances as toward theological and ecclesiastical conservatism. It is in part radically and passionately open, and in part a slow but steady process of decline, which leads to the seeping of pragmatic philosophy into Christian theology. The seminary is a place of free expression between all members, which is made possible by the civil

[3.] [A postscript from Jean Lasserre follows: "Le pays est très beau, et c'est merveille de le parcourir. Avec mes meilleurs messages Jean Lasserre" (The countryside is very beautiful, and it is a marvel to travel through it. With my best wishes Jean Lasserre). —CG]

[1.] EZA 5/196; typewritten; undated. See also *NL*, A 26,1; handwritten draft and fragments (pp. 1–4, 8, 15) of the typewritten final version. Previously published in *GS* 1:84–103. Bonhoeffer sent this report to the Church Federation Office on August 25, 1931, with the following cover letter: "Berlin-Grunewald, August 25, 1931. I am herewith presenting according to the missive of the president of August 29, 1930, K.A.I.853, a report on my theological and ecclesiastical experiences in the United States of America. Your humble servant Lecturer Dr. Dietrich Bonhoeffer." Concerning the order of the president to all fellowship recipients to hand in an "extensive report . . . giving insight into the ecclesiastical and theological gains from your stay," see EZA 5/2865. Adolf Deißmann wrote to Bonhoeffer on May 12, 1932: "I just read your Stockholm [*sic*] report and found it very interesting. Even though my own acquaintance with the individual churches is only fragmentary, I would generally agree with you, especially in regard to the Negro churches. I have a more favorable opinion of the current situation of the Episcopal Church and of the major Lutheran churches. Perhaps you had less contact with these churches" (Zentral- und Landesbibliothek Berlin, Nachlaß Adolf Deißmann).

courage unique to Americans[2] and by the lack of professional constraint in personal contacts.

A year of fruitful study can be built on such a foundation. I was personally allowed to follow my own interests entirely, that is, not to be bound temporally by having to finish a thesis to attain an academic degree.[3] From the multitude of experiences each new day brought, I can only touch on a few here that seem essential to me.

The Students

The process by which American students are brought up and educated differs significantly from ours in several respects. From a very young age—often even upon entering high school (13–14 years old), and almost universally at the college level—Americans become accustomed to community living. Being acquainted with dormitory[4] life is important for understanding American students. Daily life together generates a strong spirit of camaraderie, of mutual readiness to help. The thousandfold "hello" resonating through the halls of the dormitory during the course of the day and which one doesn't neglect even when hurrying past another person is not as empty as one might think. No one stands alone in the dormitory. The unreserved nature of living together prompts one person to be open to another; and in
264 the conflict between a resolve for truth with all its consequences and the will to community, the latter wins. This characterizes all American thinking, something I observed especially with regard to theology and the church; they do not see the radical claim of truth on the way one structures one's life. Community is thus based less on truth than on the spirit of fairness. One does not say anything unfavorable about a fellow dormitory resident as long as he is still a good fellow.[5] This characteristic and pedagogical spirit—and anyone who has sensed it can say a great deal about this—leads to a certain leveling of intellectual standards and accomplishments. This situation lacks not only the peace and quiet but also the peculiar impetus for developing one's own thoughts that is fostered at German universities by the more reclusive life of individuals. Hence there is little intellectual competition and little intellectual ambition, as a result of which seminars, lectures, and discussions tend to assume a rather harmless character. It is

[2.] [A decade later, in "After Ten Years," Bonhoeffer laments the lack of such civil courage among Germans; see *LPP*, 5–6.—CG]

[3.] Bonhoeffer could have earned a Master of Sacred Theology (STM) degree as did Sutz and Lasserre; see *DB-ER*, 157. [At Union Seminary this would be highly unusual for someone already holding a doctorate.—CG]

[4.] "Dormitory" in English in the original.

[5.] "Good fellow" in English.

more a cordial exchange of opinions than an undertaking on behalf of knowledge. The average American theological student does not feel in his element in seminars on dogmatics.

Of course, many other circumstances contribute to this situation. Although high school and college preparation for seminary study does indeed teach students a great deal, there is one thing it does not teach them, namely, to work independently. The textbook[6] method and the professors' treatment of students as utter children have disastrous results. It is not until seminary itself that theological students become acquainted with theology in the narrower sense, and even here they become acquainted with it such that, e.g., at Union Theological Seminary it is possible to enter the ministry without having taken any courses in dogmatics. They preach from the first semester on. Hence the academic preparation for the ministry is extraordinarily poor. American students do have one enormous advantage over German students: they know much more about the things of daily life. During the vacations they work in a practical field and get to know people and relationships. This gives their academic thinking a certain 265
practical orientation alien to our own seminarians; but for that reason it cannot necessarily be judged positively, since the concept of praxis itself is subject to extremely varied interpretations. For example, one prominent group at Union Theological Seminary concentrates exclusively on social problems. Because American students view the question of truth largely in the light of the practical community, their sermons become edifying narrations of examples, willing proclamations of their own religious experiences to which, of course, they assign no substantively binding character. The conference of the student body each semester—a kind of retreat—always brings to clear expression precisely this viewpoint, one ultimately based on fundamental individualism. Whereas German students' first sermons serve to transmit their own dogmatic positions as quickly as possible, the initial sermons of American students serve to unfold their entire previous religious experience before the congregation.

The Theological Spirit of Union Theological Seminary

The faculty at Union Theological Seminary represents what the enlightened American demands of theology and the church, from the most radical socialization—Professors Ward[7] and Niebuhr[8]—and philosophical and

[6.] "Textbook" in English.

[7.] Harry F. Ward.

[8.] Reinhold Niebuhr; concerning his acquaintance with Bonhoeffer, see *DB-ER*, 160 and 655.

organizational secularization—Professor Lyman,[9] Professor Elliot[10]—of Christianity, to a liberal theology that takes its orientation from Ritschl—Professor Baillie.[11] The students can be classified accordingly into three or four groups. Doubtless the most lively if not the most profound among them belong to the first group. Here they have turned their backs on any sort of proper theology, study many economic and political problems, are actively engaged in all sorts of corresponding organizations, conduct one of the endless "surveys" of the sort commonly conducted by the more progres-
266 sive elements in America, and all this within a so-called ethical interpretation. Here one senses the renewal of the gospel for our age and develops a strong self-consciousness in which one believes it possible to pass over various "theological" objections rather hastily. At the initiative of this group, the student body of Union Theological Seminary provided ongoing board and lodging to thirty unemployed persons during the winter, including three Germans, and advised them as much as possible. This undertaking involved great personal sacrifice both in terms of time and money. I must add that the theological training of this group is practically zero, and the self-confidence with which they gently smile at every specifically theological query is both unjustified and naive.

Another group, which includes a certain type of student in addition to numerous missionaries, is looking for a congregational theology. Here hardly anyone has a firm position; they waver between liberalism and "Buchmanism" (Oxford perfectionism).[12] One theology, represented by Professor Baillie and standing somewhere between Ritschl, Herrmann, and the Scottish tradition, has generated a response. The whole critique comes from a certain Enlightenment rationalism that one believes one owes to the sense of truthfulness. The notion of an internal theological criticism is completely unknown and not understood. An adherence to the central doctrines of dogmatics is in utter disarray. Although those in this circle are indeed interested in K. Barth, the presuppositions are so insufficiently realized as to preclude any real understanding.

The third group with which I had very close contact is interested in philosophy of religion and studies especially with Professor Lyman, in whom one has a genuine representative of pure American philosophy. In regular

---

[9.] Eugene William Lyman.

[10.] Harrison Sacket Elliott.

[11.] See 1/169, p. 295, ed. note 7.

[12.] The Oxford Group Movement, founded by Frank Buchman, later renamed Moral Rearmament; concerning Buchman's position during the Church Struggle, see also *DB-ER*, 333 et passim.

personal meetings with him, I discussed various problems of American philosophy and its relationship to theology as manifested in recent literature; I learned a great deal from these sessions. In his courses, students have the opportunity to discuss the crudest forms of heresy and intellectual difficul- 267
ties. The "philosophical approach" is very attractive to students because of its reputation as "scientific."[13] The carefree manner with which students speak about God and world here is for us at the very least quite surprising.

The subjects of practical theology play a major role here. Here, too, one sees what the students have really learned by the end of their three years of study and similarly also what Union Theological Seminary has to say in the service of the church-community. The question of the message of the church is hardly raised at all—one exception is Professor Fosdick,[14] one of the most influential preachers in America (and one who had a picture of Einstein mounted at the door of his church!), who answers this question in an extremely humanistic sense; and probably because of the inchoate feeling that one is presupposing something here that cannot really be presupposed. This lack is compensated for by an enormous emphasis on organizational questions. The perspective from which one urges the enlargement of membership and religious education is basically caught up in organizational matters. Here, too, the almost anxious propagation of modern methods betrays the disappearance of the content, from which these questions should be clearly distinguished as secondary. The undignified servility with which American pastors often engage in organizational and missionary activities completely lacks the sovereignty of a person who knows what content is at stake here. It's difficult for someone here to imagine the innocence with which people who are about to enter or are already in the ministry ask questions in the practical-theological seminars—for example, whether one really must preach about Christ. Ultimately one can take care of this matter with a bit of idealism and a bit of cleverness—that's approximately the attitude here.

The theological spirit at Union Theological Seminary is accelerating the process of the secularization of Christianity in America. Its criticism is directed essentially at fundamentalism and to a certain extent also at the radical humanists in Chicago; such criticism is healthy and necessary. But the foundation on which one might rebuild after tearing down is not able 268
to support the weight. The collapse destroys it as well. A seminary in which numerous students openly laugh during a public lecture because they find

[13.] ["Philosophical approach" and "scientific": Bonhoeffer's English.—CG]

[14.] Harry Emerson Fosdick. [Fosdick was senior minister at Riverside Church. —CG]

it amusing when a passage on sin and forgiveness from Luther's *de servo arbitrio*[15] is cited has obviously, despite its many advantages, forgotten what Christian theology in its very essence stands for.

Pragmatism

Soon after attending my first classes in the philosophy of religion and the seminar in systematic theology,[16] I sensed that certain presuppositions must lie behind this thinking that were so self-evident to students and professors but so alien to me, and that one must discover those presuppositions before really being able to comprehend this foreign style of thinking. The theological literature of the liberal and humanistic direction exhibited the same peculiar forms of thought, which I was unable to account for. I observed an inclination to hasten past difficult problems and to linger inordinately with things that are either self-evident or that without additional preparation cannot possibly be adequately addressed. The fact that the linguistic and conceptual forms of our own German theology are essentially determined by preliminary philosophical concepts convinced me of the necessity of studying American philosophy as a prerequisite for any fair assessment of this theology. Professor Lyman was very willing to accommodate this wish, and for one afternoon every two weeks I was able to discuss with him the salient philosophical literature I had prepared beforehand. We began with pragmatism. I read almost the entire philosophical works of William James, which really captivated me, then Dewey, Perry, Russell, and finally also J. B. Watson and the behaviorist literature.[17] My study of White-
269 head, Knudson, and Santayana[18] was not nearly as informative for me as these radically empirical thinkers. In them, and especially in James, I also found the key to the modern theological language and conceptual forms of liberal enlightened Americans. The destruction of philosophy as the question of truth, and its recasting as a positive individual discipline with practical goals—as most radically carried through by Dewey—alters the heart of the concept of scholarship, and truth as the absolute norm of all thinking

[15.] ["On the Bondage of the Will"; *LW* 33:3–295.—CG]

[16.] [In the first semester Bonhoeffer took "The Philosophy of the Christian Religion" with Lyman and the "Seminar in Philosophical Theology" taught by Baillie and Lyman (assisted by Van Dusen); he is probably also alluding to the course "Religion and Ethics" taught by Niebuhr, since it too was announced as a course in Philosophy of Religion. —CG]

[17.] Concerning William James, cf. esp. 2/13; John Dewey; Ralph Barton Perry; Bertrand Russell; John Broadus Watson.

[18.] Alfred North Whitehead; Albert Cornelius Knudson; George Santayana y Borras.

is restricted by what proves to be "useful in the long run."[19] Thinking is essentially teleological, aimed at serving life. We would not contest this; we would merely question the demonstrability of this intentionality. Questions such as the Kantian question of epistemology are "nonsense"; they are not problems at all because they do not advance life. Truth is not "valid," but rather "works," and that is its criterion. Thinking and living take place visibly here in very close proximity. This has various consequences for theology. It no longer runs the risk of speaking in an unengaged manner about God. God, too, is not valid truth, but rather "effective" truth, that is, he is either active in the processes of human life or he "is" not at all. Although this turn of phrase almost recalls Luther's notion of transcendentalism, it differs essentially insofar as the active God must first be confirmed by the "usefulness" of his activity with regard to human beings in order to be true, and second, insofar as God enters to such an extent into his own activity that it is only within that very activity that he actually grows. Union Theological Seminary and the realm of enlightened Americans [Amerikanertum] have greeted and parroted with extraordinary liveliness James's thesis of the "growing God."[20] This thesis combines religion and faith in progress in a virtuoso manner, so that the one finds its support and justification through the other. It cannot be concealed that religion here in its embryonic form is what it already exclusively was in Dewey, namely, "social ethics." The wealth of Jamesean observations in the field of religion was later confined by his
own theme. Whereas James himself still wants to leave space outside human 270
beings for the real existence of God, especially in Chicago the pragmatism of James and the instrumentalism of Dewey have been developed further into radical immanent ethical humanism.

Given this situation, the German is now able to understand why modern Americans have absolutely no understanding for Pauline and Lutheran Christianity. They are not only the purest Pelagians[21] but also adherents of Protagoras.[22] In a discussion before numerous students, one of the leading professors at Union Theological Seminary confessed to me amid the applause of the students that justification by faith[23] was not only unimportant but also a matter of indifference to him. And surprised students

[19.] In English in the original as "in the long run as useful."

[20.] "Growing God" in English; see 1/150, p. 266, and esp. 2/13.

[21.] [Pelagianism is the heresy that holds that human effort, in addition to God's grace, contributes essentially to human salvation.—CG]

[22.] Fifth-century BCE Greek philosopher who said, "The human being is the measure of all things" (the so-called *homo mensura* statement). See Sprague, *Older Sophists*, 18.

[23.] "Justification by faith" in English in the original.

themselves repeatedly asked me how I could really still invoke Paul, insisting that doing so was simply no longer appropriate.

The pragmatic concept of truth helped me understand not only the theological situation but also the lifestyle of wider circles in America. I think one social consequence of pragmatism is that truth no longer possesses the inner strength to sunder community and precisely by doing so to build it up and render it fruitful, that is, to be genuinely close to life through its apparent distance from life. People trust in "facts" and in their "own development," and view truth only immanently rather than in its transcendent claim. It is clear that this view basically conceals a purely individualistic understanding of life that would grant happiness to each individual and yet contains very little beyond this. That it is precisely in America that this view was able to gain such a strong foothold derives from the political and intellectual history of America as recently portrayed by Thomas Hall in a completely new way in *The Religious Background of American Civilization.*[24]
271 His thesis that American Protestantism is older than Reformation Protestantism and thus bears a definitively churchless individualistic character accords very well with the overwhelming influence of pragmatism. As a philosophy of life, pragmatism and instrumentalism have doubtless freed up energy for recasting the previous forms of life in education, politics, and social work in the sense of the great idea of social progress, and this has fallen upon fertile soil.

Church and Preaching

Apart from daily morning devotions in chapel, I often had the opportunity every Sunday to hear two sermons in the most varied denominations and independent churches. With its brief reviews of the previous day's outstanding sermons, the Monday morning *New York Times* offers an extremely valuable complement to any study of contemporary preaching. Every better sermon has its specific topic, and these topics are posted ahead of time in the churches; from this information it already becomes surprisingly clear where the contemporary sermon sees its real task, and how all the denominations push in the same direction. Let me quote at random from the *Times* of October 13, 1930:[25] "Science found void compared to faith," "Virtues stressed," "New freedom," "Holmes denounces Curry and Walker," "Stockdale scores wet candidacies," "Call praises theatres," "H. urges spiritual values," ". . . puts needs above creeds." From October 27: ". . . wants liquor sold

[24.] Thomas Cuming Hall; the correct title is *The Religious Background of American Culture.*

[25.] See the newspaper clippings, *NL*, A 24,10 (2).

only in churches," "prohibition betrayed," ". . . asks church to act in social problems," "Dr. Fosdick holds creeds hide Jesus," "Dr. Coffin decries naturalism."[26] These sermons were delivered in very different denominations. 272
In America one wants to preach to the present and identifies a sermon to the present as a political-social and apologetic sermon. The external dangers of such sermons are not as severe as in Germany because of the leveling of public political opinion in America. This situation allows a more abiding illusion that such uniformity of preaching also implies a unity of the Spirit of Christ. One is also initially astonished to find that such sermons can be heard in almost the same form in a community church—which is not a "Christian" church—as well as in a synagogue—for example, from the excellent preacher Rabbi Wise[27]—as well as in a Methodist or Baptist church. (In the Episcopal and Presbyterian churches, churches of the upper classes, one hears more apologetics than political discussion.) The enlightened American, rather than viewing all this with skepticism, instead welcomes it as an example of progress. The fundamentalist sermon that occupies such a prominent place in the southern states has only one prominent Baptist representative in New York, one who preaches the resurrection of the flesh and the virgin birth before believers and the curious alike. In New York, they preach about virtually everything; only one thing is not addressed, or is addressed so rarely that I have as yet been unable to hear it, namely, the gospel of Jesus Christ, the cross, sin and forgiveness, death and life. In Dr. Fosdick's homiletics seminar, at the end of the distribution of sermon topics some "traditional themes" were to be assigned as well, including a sermon on the forgiveness of sins and on the cross! This is quite characteristic of most of the churches I saw. So what stands in place of the Christian message? An ethical and social idealism borne by a faith in progress that—who knows how—claims the right to call itself "Christian." And in the place of the church as the congregation of believers in Christ there stands the church as a social corporation. Anyone who has seen the weekly program of one of the large New York churches, with their daily, indeed 273
almost hourly events, teas, lectures, concerts, charity events, opportunities for sports, games, bowling, dancing for every age group, anyone who has heard how they try to persuade a new resident to join the church, insisting that you'll get into society quite differently by doing so, anyone who has become acquainted with the embarrassing nervousness with which the pastor lobbies for membership—that person can well assess the character of

[26.] Sermon topics listed in English in original.
[27.] Stephen Samuel Wise; see also 1/169, p. 295.

such a church. All these things, of course, take place with varying degrees of tactfulness, taste, and seriousness; some churches are basically "charitable" churches; others have primarily a social identity. One cannot avoid the impression, however, that in both cases they have forgotten what the real point is.[28]

The situation in the Sunday schools is really not much different. The progressive ones resolutely employ the new methods of religious education; in the majority of the others the external organization of liturgy and instruction is already so defective and boring that the lameness of the inner life must be replaced by all sorts of small attractions. When, as I saw, a twelve-year-old girl in a Methodist Sunday school receives a makeup and powder kit as a reward for regular attendance, and the pastor takes pride in this sign of being up-to-date, that is a foul symptom of radically poor health. In order to balance out the feeling of inner emptiness that arises now and then (and partly also to refill the church's treasury), some congregations will if possible engage an evangelist for a "revival" once a year. The primitive means with which these people are then able to play with the emotions of the congregation, since there is absolutely no healthy criterion, is shameful.

The same psychological devices are also used to attract audiences to the enthusiastic-eschatological-radical sects. For the German observer the question becomes ever more urgent about just how this peculiar form of the church and its distortion could have arisen.

274 When we attempt to assess this situation, we must draw attention to one church group to which most of what has been said applies only to a small extent; the church of the outcasts of America stands fairly untouched, indeed, avoided by the white church: the Negro church. During my overall stay in America, I spent a great deal of time getting to know the Negro problem from every angle and also observing white America from this rather hidden perspective. Through my friendship with a Negro student at the seminary,[29] I was introduced not only to the leaders of the young Negro movement at Howard College[30] in Washington, but also in Harlem, the Negro quarter of New York. For more than six months, I was in one of the large Baptist churches in Harlem every Sunday at 2:30 in the afternoon, and together with my friend, and often as his substitute, had a group of young Negroes in the Sunday school; I conducted Bible study for some Negro women and once a week helped out in a weekday church school. Hence

[28.] See the similar criticism in *Ethics* (cf. esp. *DBWE* 6:127 and ed. note 108).

[29.] Frank Fisher; cf., e.g., 1/145.

[30.] [Howard University.—CG]

not only did I become well acquainted with several young Negroes; I also visited their homes several times. This personal acquaintance with Negroes was one of the most important and gratifying events of my stay in America. I completed my experiences during my trip to the southern states. Here I can only briefly describe the peculiarities of these churches. First, I heard the gospel preached in the Negro churches. In a Negro church it is not difficult to observe where the interest of the congregation awakens and where it does not, since the enormous intensity of feeling among the Negroes repeatedly finds expression in their outcries and interrupting shouts. But it is clear that whenever the gospel itself really is mentioned, their participation peaks. Here one really could still hear someone talk in a Christian sense about sin and grace and the love of God and ultimate hope, albeit in a form different from that to which we are accustomed. In contrast to the often lecturelike character of the "white" sermon, the "black Christ" is 275
preached with captivating passion and vividness.[31] Anyone who has heard and understood the Negro spirituals knows about the strange mixture of reserved melancholy and eruptive joy in the soul of the Negro. The Negro churches are proletarian churches, perhaps the only ones in all America. Admittedly, however, among the youth who see how Christian preaching made their fathers so meek in the face of their incomparably harsh fate, an element of opposition against such forms of religion is emerging, that is, against Christianity, and if this opposition ever spreads its might, then white America will have to take the blame that these black masses became godless. Here we are standing at a powerful crossroads.

A word too about the German churches. There is no longer any purely German church in New York nor, as far as I know, in America. People still preach in German in the Lutheran Church and the Evangelical Synod.[32] My experiences with this preaching in New York as well as in Florida and in the southwest were rather dismal. The pastors generally are not well trained; to the extent they come from Concordia Seminary (which I saw in St. Louis), that is, from the Missouri Synod, their exclusive orthodoxy is unbearable, and despite enormous financial sacrifice they are doubtless

---

[31.] See also 1/150, p. 266. *The Black Christ and Other Poems* is the title of a volume of poetry by the black poet Countee Cullen; cf. also 2/11.2.

[32.] The Lutheran Church and Evangelical Synod were both Protestant churches of German heritage in America. [Bonhoeffer appears to use "Lutheran Church" generically to include the Lutheran Church–Missouri Synod and others, possibly the United Lutheran Church in America that was formed in 1918 from three German synods. The Evangelical Synod was a Reformed denomination dating from 1849; in 1934 it became part of the Evangelical and Reformed Church, which eventually became part of the United Church of Christ in 1957.—CG]

heading toward collapse. I also often observed that only a few older people came to the German services, but hardly any young people at all. One reason for this is the language; another is that one cannot claim to reach young Americans with a sermon that is read aloud in the manner, for example, of Ahlfeld.[33] I sensed nothing of any special understanding of the Reformation legacy in the German churches.

276 Last year the book appeared that I mentioned above, *The Religious Background of American Civilization*,[34] by Thomas Hall. Even though I cannot check its historical accuracy, the thesis developed there, that American Protestantism developed essentially untouched by Reformation Protestantism as a continuation of Wycliffean[35] ideas and of radical dissent, was very informative for my understanding of the American church situation. The lack of a creed—the denominations differ not in creed but in rituals or sometimes only in their social positions—a dogma and a system of dogmatics, is grounded in universal religious individualism of the sort most pristinely preserved among the Quakers and the Congregationalists, a kind that corresponds to the individualism of the pioneer days and that still exerts an influence today. Among the Quakers there is accordingly no real sermon, no pastor, no "church." The spirit manifests itself directly in feeling and action. The Quaker assemblies, too, have admittedly also lost their original element of enthusiasm,[36] and there predominates a soft, almost lyrical atmosphere in everything presented there. Here the basic form of the American church is preserved under whose sign the large churches of America still stand today. The churches of English and German heritage are still furthest removed from this basic form, though even they are already certainly under its spell. Because the Spirit of God is in a profound sense not conceived as being tied to the Word, they do not understand what sermon, confession, dogma, church, community are. Whence the lack of restraint with which Christian dogma is attacked from American pulpits—on Good Friday I heard one of New York's great preachers[37] in an Episcopal church (!) say, "I deny the reconciliation on the cross; I don't

[33.] Friedrich Ahlfeld; an American translation of a volume of his *Sermons on the Catechism* appeared in 1924.

[34.] See ed. note 24 above.

[35.] The English theologian John Wycliffe.

[36.] [In this context, by "enthusiasm," *Enthusiasmus*, Bonhoeffer refers to the spiritual trembling that had been sometimes experienced at meetings of the Society of Friends and that gave rise to the name Quaker.—CG]

[37.] [In all likelihood William Norman Guthrie, rector of the Manhattan Episcopal church St. Mark's in the Bouwerie, 1911–37. See the editor's introduction, pp. 23–24. —CG]

want that kind of Christ" (note the use of "I"!)—and with which one then immediately acts. The church is really no longer the place where the congregation hears and preaches God's word, but rather the place where one acquires secondary significance as a social entity for this or that purpose. 277
Hence it is not even important to study dogmatics; this is self-evident for the personally serious Christian and would only put the contradictions into unnecessary relief. Any who in whatever fashion say they confess Christ in whatever fashion are Christians and can become members of the church society [Gesellschaft].

The usual designation of the American church as a voluntary church is in a formal sense not universally accurate. A person is baptized as a child into the majority of American churches. The decisive thing is the other factor, namely, that the original voluntary character of the church has been preserved in a distorted form, through the way people confuse the role of the church with that of a religious association, a mix-up especially obvious here. Instead of the priesthood of all believers, you have the right of association membership, and instead of the *rite vocatus*,[38] the pastor functions as the association chair who is still basically dependent on the will of the members. In America one can study in an unadulterated form the harmful consequences and caricatures of a misunderstood voluntary church.

This whole manner of thinking is radically opposed by fundamentalism and its primary leader, Professor Machen in Philadelphia.[39] Although Reformation views are doubtless preserved here, they are distorted by the crassest orthodoxy, especially in the Southern Baptist Church. Here a different side of the American character manifests itself, namely, an unrelenting harshness in holding on to one's possessions, possessions either of this or of the other world. I acquired this possession with trust in God, God made my success happen, so whoever infringes upon this possession is infringing upon God. It's obvious that no understanding for the vitality of the church can emerge on such a basis, for this thinking, too, is basically individualistic. And although this position is decisively waning in the religious context, it persists with almost unaltered strength in the social and ethical thinking of enlightened Americans.

Social Work 278

The sundering of the traditional American ethos at this juncture can be observed particularly well in New York and particularly at the present time. With the horrific unemployment in New York during the past winter, it

[38.] "Properly called"; see the Augsburg Confession, article XIV (*Book of Concord*, 47).
[39.] John Gresham Machen.

dawned on many Americans for the first time that the presupposition of their social thinking is antiquated. People no longer really have the status in the world they have earned through their own work and competence. This situation, however, now makes the principle of voluntary charity as a means of social aid immoral. That principle was based on a false valuation of other life. Such notions predominate in the so-called social gospel, which has been overcome in name but is still powerfully present in substance. The other person's right to exist is to be respected. *The Prayer for the Social Gospel*, by W. Rauschenbusch,[40] is one of the most passionate and beautiful witnesses of this thinking. In connection with a course taught by Mr. Webber, former pastor at the Church of All Nations who is thereby acquainted with almost all the social institutions in New York, I visited one of these character-building agencies almost every week:[41] Settlements, YMCA, home missions, cooperative houses, playgrounds, children court, night schools, socialist schools, homeless shelters, youth organizations, Association for advance of coloured people.[42] Here I got a look at attempts to provide social relief through voluntary social welfare. The state still subscribes to the old theory.[43] It is a powerful experience to see here how much is done and attained through personal sacrifice and with how much commitment, energy, and sense of responsibility people work here. They are doubtless working under easier
279 conditions than in Europe; there is little proletarian class consciousness in America. But the stronger it becomes, all the more urgent does the cry become for state intervention.

In a lecture course by Dr. Niebuhr,[44] the social and Christian problem was discussed in the context of modern American literature. That was extremely informative. I learned much from my own experiences in Harlem. The impressions I got of contemporary representatives of the social gospel will remain determinative for me for a long time to come. The sobriety

---

[40.] Walter Rauschenbusch; his work *For God and the People: Prayers of the Social Awakening* appeared in 1910; concerning the "social gospel," see also Bonhoeffer's 1932 essay on the subject, *DBWE* 12, 2/3. [See also *DBW* 17 (11/1/93a), pp. 112–13, for Bonhoeffer's letter of October 30, 1932, requesting Paul Lehmann to draft a paper for him on the social gospel as quickly as possible, as well as Bonhoeffer's 1939 reflections in "Protestantism without Reformation," *DBWE* 15, 2/6.—CG]

[41.] See also 1/170, p. 296.

[42.] [All these agencies are listed in English and with the original orthography, except for "homeless shelters," which translates *asyls*.—CG]

[43.] That is, to the old American Puritan ethos, "Every one should help himself." [Bonhoeffer refers to the situation prior to the reforms of Roosevelt and the New Deal, especially in its second phase, 1935–41.—CG]

[44.] See Bonhoeffer's lecture notes on "Religion and Ethics" in *NL*, A 24,2, and the short reports in 2/12.

and seriousness of a book such as that of H. Ward, *Which Way Religion?*[45] is irrefutable; and yet the entire protest must repeatedly be raised if that is preached as *real* Christianity while abbreviating all the crucial Christian ideas. In many discussions and lectures I tried to show that Reformation Christianity does indeed include rather than exclude all these things, but that their assessment is different. But people basically just didn't want to believe that.

Personal

My days were usually dedicated half to my studies and half to seeing things.
Each week I had about twelve course hours. Frequently I had to give talks
and even occasionally preach (Methodist and Baptist churches) and speak
in Sunday schools and normal schools, something I initially gladly accepted
but later did less often because of too many other commitments. The semi-
nary students used to ask me to come to their Sunday schools and to speak
there. I frequently had to speak on war and peace and always had under- 280
standing audiences. Over Christmas I was invited to preach twice in Havana, Cuba,[46] in the small German congregation, which is held together by the director of the German school there but has no pastor. Both services were well attended and gratefully welcomed. In Florida I offered to preach at several German congregations, but the pastors told me that was not necessary, that it was just as good if one simply read Ahlfeld aloud.[47] So I did not get to preach there. In November I attended the conference of the Federal Council in Washington, where, among other things, they discussed the question of war guilt; I was introduced by the president of the assembly and was able to make many interesting contacts.[48]

On a long auto trip through the Midwest and the South to Mexico City after the conclusion of the school year, I sought out several theological seminaries and German congregations but never got to preach.

Looking back on the wealth of experiences, it would be foolish to say that the most important thing was the details that I learned "for our situation." As a matter of fact, I am of the opinion that one can learn very little over there "for our situation" if one is thinking of some direct application.

[45.] Bonhoeffer received this book as a gift with the dedication: "To 'the Big One' in appreciation for fellowship with a really kindred spirit. From two in whose lives you have a place unique and secure through the years. Marion and Paul Lehmann. N.Y. June 19th, 1931."

[46.] Only one of these sermons has been preserved; see 3/24.

[47.] See note 32 above.

[48.] Cf. 1/144.

It does seem to me, however, that basically even where one views the threat that America does represent for us, one comes away with tranquil insights "for our situation." It is simply no more and no less than that one has begun to become acquainted with a different part of the world.

281 **182. Report on His Second Semester**[1]

Second Report by Lecturer Dr. Dietrich Bonhoeffer[2]

A student is able to study more intensively during the second semester than during the first, not least because the linguistic difficulties have passed. One knows more people and also knows better the direction in which one's special interests lie and where those might be addressed. The most valuable experience I had at the seminary was a practical course on Church and Community with Mr. Webber, former pastor at the Church of All Nations and a radical socialist.[3] We made weekly visitation to the various socio-pedagogical or so-called character-building agencies in New York. We saw settlements, night schools, YMCAs, church organizations, the Association for the advancement of coloured people,[4] among many others. Each had its specialized area of work. I had to become acquainted with several American youth organizations. This ongoing personal contact with Americans in the context of social work was of enormous value to me. I would advise everyone to take this course during the second semester. Another large part of my work was my study of American philosophy as extrawork[5] with Professor Lyman. The advantage of such extrawork is that one can become truly familiar with specific material, something likely impossible in normal courses—and that a person earns a number of credits for the work. Every two weeks I would meet with Professor Lyman, and we would discuss a book I had read in the interim that we had determined beforehand. Professor Lyman is an excellent authority on contemporary American philosophy, so

[1.] *NL*, A 26,2; handwritten, undated. Previously published in *GS* 6:191–93.

[2.] This report is not a direct continuation of 1/181. Since it confines itself to the second semester and almost wholly ignores church experiences, one can assume it was written not for a church office but rather for the German Academic Exchange Service. No corresponding report on the first semester has been preserved.

[3.] Cf. 1/181, p. 318. ["Church" and "Community" in English in the original. —CG]

[4.] See 1/181, ed. note 42.

[5.] [Bonhoeffer's English.—CG]

I learned a great deal from these sessions.[6] Among the other courses during the second semester, I was particularly interested in the ethical interpretation of recent events and of modern literature[7] and the social ethics of Professor Ward, which was especially valuable in connection with the course with Mr. Webber.[8] 282

One's personal contacts during the second semester are naturally more extensive than during the first. Numerous personal contacts acquired outside the seminary are added to those already made inside it. I found that certain restrictions were quite appropriate. One often hears interesting things at the open evenings held by the professors. I completely stayed away from the German club life. Besides, the second semester goes by so quickly that one really is not able to make that many plans at all, so one simply goes for whatever seems interesting at the moment. Through my friendship with a Negro student[9] at the seminary, I came together with a group of Negro boys each week and also visited them at home. This opportunity was one of my most important experiences in America. Here I had the opportunity to get to know America quite intensively at one of its delicate points without being in a position where someone might dazzle me. And the results of such an experience are, I must say, deeply distressing. Here one gets to see something of the real face of America, something that is hidden behind the veil of words in the American constitution saying that "all men are created free and equal."[10]

On Sundays I attended the most varied churches and denominations, often during the afternoon as well. Here, too, America reveals itself, albeit not as crassly but certainly no less clearly. I did not spend much time in the German churches. It seems to be a hopeless task with not very hopeful workers. In the seminary one hears quite enough about those to whom "one" goes to hear preach. At the end of the year I took a six-week auto tour

[6.] [For Bonhoeffer's unpublished notes on his course with Lyman, see *NL*, A 24, 4. —CG]

[7.] Cf. 1/181, p. 318. [These courses were taught by Ward and Niebuhr, respectively.—CG]

[8.] [See 2/12, 2/11, and Ward's course "Ethical Issues in the Social Order"; notes from Ward's course, and from Webber's about the church and social agencies, are not published but are available on microfiche (see *NL*, A 24, 5 and A 24, 8).—CG]

[9.] Frank Fisher; cf. 1/181, p. 314.

[10.] [The proposition that "all men are created equal" comes from the American Declaration of Independence. In an interpretation of that document, the phrase "that all men are created free and equal" was made famous by Abraham Lincoln in a speech against slavery in Chicago on July 10, 1858; see Lincoln, *Collected Works*, 2:502.—CG]

to Mexico with the French fellow,[11] with a tent and little money. Then, accompanied by a couple of good friends, I was glad to catch my ship back to Germany again. One certainly cannot speak so glibly about the "promise of America" or even about the "threat." In the larger sense, it is less important what it is for us than what it is in and for itself. And in that sense one thing is certain, namely, that it is certainly worth the effort to spend ten months there.

[11.] Jean Lasserre; cf. 1/171. [Bonhoeffer uses the English word "fellow" meaning a person appointed to a program of advanced study or research supported by a stipend. —CG]

PART 2
Essays and Lectures

A. Lectures to the Congregation in Barcelona. Crisis and Hope in the Contemporary Religious Situation. November 1928–February 1929

1. The Tragedy of the Prophetic and Its Lasting Meaning[1] 285

The Tragedy of the Prophetic and Its Lasting Meaning

Two simple considerations have prompted me to invite you to this series of lectures, and the same two considerations have probably also prompted you cordially to accept that invitation. First, the subject matter itself is incomparably serious. Second, all of us feel obliged to take a position ourselves, to evaluate, to enter into, and to participate in the struggle and crisis of contemporary intellectual movements. The questions that we shall address are profoundly contemporary, even though their outer dress may seem not modern but archaic. Every word is to be spoken out of the present for the

[1.] *NL*, A 22,1 a; handwritten, with a handwritten note by Bethge: "lecture in Barcelona." See also *NL*, A 22,1 b; a later typewritten copy. Previously published and annotated in *GS* 5:116–34. Bonhoeffer delivered this lecture on Tuesday, November 13, 1928. In it he draws extensively from Duhm, *Israels Propheten*; cf. also 1/48, p. 144. [Cf. also his January 1934 London sermon on the prophets, *DBWE* 13, 2/7. "The Prophetic" in the title translates *Prophetentum*, meaning the office or phenomenon of prophethood; see also the postcard to Walter Dreß (1/49a, p. 146) where Bonhoeffer uses *Prophetismus*, "prophetism."—CG]

present and, though not always specifically articulated, it will be obvious enough to anyone observing the contemporary scene. We are twentieth-century people and, like it or not, must come to terms with that fact; indeed, even more, we should have so much love for this contemporary world of ours, for our fellow human beings, that we should declare our solidarity with it in its crisis as well as in its hope.

Events of recent decades have plunged us into an unprecedented crisis characterized by unclear political ideology as well as by complete helplessness in the face of pedagogical, ethical, and religious questions. The
286 rug—or let us say the bourgeois parquet floor—has been ruthlessly pulled out from under our feet, and we must now search for a bit of *earth* on which to stand. We have been utterly and completely shipwrecked and are now horrified to see just how utterly at sea many of us are. Some still cling desperately to the timbers of the sinking ship; others have abandoned all hope and simply throw themselves on the mercy of the waves—and go under; still others—indeed, most—who just a short while ago were able to save themselves in lifeboats, now cry out in triumph as if the danger had been overcome. Only a few have struggled onto a sliver of solid land on which they can gain a foothold and from which they are now able to conduct rescue operations.[2] But before any of us is too hasty to identify with any one of these groups, let us all admit that we are still, even today, in enormous, serious crisis, and we have absolutely no justification for looking down, as those who have been rescued, on those who are yet at sea. All of us who still feel bound to the church in one way or another, and still feel responsible for addressing questions of morality[3]—we are ourselves still in crisis, still searching, still perplexed. Who among us dares to answer unequivocally the question about the meaning of Europe's contemporary fate? Or who

[2.] Cf. Harnack, who once suggested in a manner characterizing his own Christian understanding of the world and of politics that "whatever my private opinions regarding the best constitution may be, they should not constitute the actual *foundation* of whatever edifice I ultimately build, not as long as a sliver of respectable land is still left from what has gone before. It is on this sliver of land that I must stand and build and attempt to acquire new land" (Harnack in a letter to Wilhelm Stapel, September 24, 1925, in Zahn-Harnack, *Adolf von Harnack*, 377). The political ethics of German liberalism used the metaphor of "gaining a firm foothold" on a sliver of remaining land as an expression to warn against taking a position "*outside* the world" (ibid., 376). Beginning in Barcelona, Bonhoeffer used this as a fundamentally ethical metaphor that drew to some extent on the legend of the giant Antaeus, who lost his powers if he lost contact with the earth. This is documented in Feil, *Theology of Dietrich Bonhoeffer*, 112n22. [More information may be found in the German edition of Feil, *Theologie Dietrich Bonhoeffers*, 247n39.—CG]

[3.] The typewritten version of the manuscript reads *Ethik*, "ethics," instead of *Sittlichkeit*, "morality."

can claim to have found *the* right path, the one and only appropriate path? Who dares to make blanket judgments about the burning problems of ethics, the question of the right to wage war, the problem of economic competition, concerning the new social order, the education of the new generation, or the mysteries of sexuality?

No one person can find the answer—such an answer will come only 287
through a broad, universal, human process in which Asia, Europe, and America take part—and yet, at the same time, individuals will still try to find an answer both for themselves and for others. So let me say right here at the beginning: we will indeed try to find an answer and will try to find it precisely where we believe we can perceive traces of God's presence on earth, either in ancient or in modern times, since God's traces are eternal, supra-temporal, timeless, even amid the transitory nature of history; in other words, we hope to find an answer by taking seriously the seemingly obsolete cause of Christianity, by confronting it with serious questions born of crisis itself. The God who has forged our fate will not fail to respond; from within Christianity, God will provide a full response to those burning to know and will do so in an almighty voice and with full clarity.

We are not saying that *we* ourselves are able to point out *the* way, the *one* path to take, for only God can do that. What we are saying is that perhaps we can suggest the direction one might take, even though ultimately one must forge and clear one's own path through one's own effort and labor. The object here is merely to erect signposts here and there that can at least point us in the right direction, and it is in this sense that we shall begin our work.

¶Two considerations prompt me to take us so far back during this first hour. The first is personal. Over the course of time I have become so attached to the history of the prophets, and it has become such a favorite subject of study for me[4] that I cannot help trying to address the widespread lack of familiarity with this material; by presenting individual vignettes, I hope to provide an introduction to its overall mood and to make it both enjoyable and interesting. But this consideration already brings me to the second. Around the turn from the eighth to the sixth pre-Christian centuries, a world went under amid the stormy events of emerging world history—a
world woven in the passionate colors of the Orient, a world in which passion 288
and zeal for God held sway, a world in which a thousand pulses hammered and pounded—a world similar to ours and yet not similar at all, and yet a

[4.] During the summer semester 1926, Bonhoeffer had attended a course on Isaiah given by Kurt Galling, and during the winter semester 1926–27 a seminar on Job given by Ernst Sellin; cf. *DBWE* 9:586.

world in which everything came alive that should also come alive today, a world from which in any case each voice speaks even more clearly to us today than ever before: the world of Israel's prophets.

I will not enumerate all the possible parallels a portrayal of that age might offer, since someone might take offense. And yet everyone will implicitly see and hear where things also become critical for us today.

These were men who wrestled with God and with their own age, an age in which everything was out of joint, an age in which national and *völkisch*[5] arrogance was paired with godlessness and immorality, men who felt called by their God and stepped out among their people, men for whom the covenant with God became their undoing—and today we will try to understand these men as a prelude, as it were, to what was to come, and will try to reexperience and understand their tragedy.

What is a prophet? Let us first completely reject any understanding of a prophet as something like an augur or a soothsayer. Even though this view is widespread, it is fundamentally false. A prophet is a man who in a specific, convulsive moment of his life feels seized and called by God, and now cannot help but go out among the people and proclaim God's will. This calling becomes the turning point of his life, and now there is no other course for him but to follow it, even if it leads to his own undoing or ultimately to his own death. As Amos says:

> Does a lion roar in the forest,
> when it has no prey?
> Does a young lion cry out from its den,
> if it has caught nothing?
> Does a bird fall into a snare on the earth,
> when there is no trap for it? . . .
> Is a trumpet blown in a city,
> and the people are not afraid? . . .
> The lion has roared;
> who will not fear?
> The LORD GOD has spoken;
> who can but prophesy?[6]

[5.] [Bonhoeffer's usage in this lecture, although it is prior to the Nazi era, suggests that *völkisch* already had a nationalistic connotation.—CG]

[6.] Amos 3:4–8. Here and in all the following citations from the prophets, Bonhoeffer follows Duhm, for the most part using his quotes, sometimes citing Duhm's German translations of the Hebrew exactly and other times varying to a greater or lesser degree; cf. ed. note 1 above). [For this reason, the translations of several biblical passages in this lecture vary slightly from the NRSV.—CG]

This entire passage resonates with the terror, the experience: I have heard Yahweh speak; I *must* prophesy; I *must* go out among the people; a fearful, coercive power is upon me, incomprehensible to anyone who has never experienced what it means to have Yahweh speak to you. This claim upon me: I must respond to it; I must accept responsibility for it. The young Amos lay out in the distant steppe; he had heard of the wickedness and injustice of life in the city. Then one day, as he looked out across the infinite steppe in the searing midday sun, God Yahweh frightened him in a vision. He saw a terrifying, threatening cloud coming, and when it was close to him he saw that it was a cloud of locusts descending upon the fields and decimating them. Amos fell to the ground and cried out, "O Lord God, forgive, I beg you! How can Israel stand? He is so small!"[7] Twice more Amos is startled by visions. In one, he sees a man striding with a shower of fire amid lush grain fields, and again Amos falls down with the cry, "O Lord God . . ." In the next vision, he sees a man with a plumb line standing on a fallen wall and measuring the uneven places; Amos hears Yahweh say that just as he has destroyed this fallen wall, so also will he destroy the people of Israel. This is Amos's calling. He rushes away toward the city, where he emerges as a prophet of Yahweh; and he proves himself to be a genuine prophet—this is an important point—by delivering a message of disaster, misfortune, and judgment. As Jeremiah says,[8] it is not those who always cry out peace, peace and victory, who are genuine prophets, but rather those who have the courage to prophesy disaster. This appears in its most terrifying form in the call vision of Isaiah. He sees the thrice-holy One on the throne in the temple and is quick to offer his services in delivering the message; yet then he hears the terrifying words 289

> Go and say to this people:
> "Keep listening, but do not comprehend;
> keep looking, but do not understand."[9]

To the anxious question, "How long, O Lord?" God answers, 290

> Until cities lie waste
> without inhabitant,
> and houses without people,
> and the land is utterly desolate.[10]

[7.] See Amos 7:1–9. [NRSV reads "Jacob" instead of "Israel."—CG]
[8.] See Jer. 23:9–15. [Cf. also Jer. 6:14 and 8:11.—CG]
[9.] Isa. 6:9.
[10.] Isa. 6:11.

Isaiah has been saddled here with an almost unbearable burden. He must prophesy to his beloved people—the prophets were the most ardent patriots imaginable—and yet know that he is speaking to deaf ears; indeed, even worse, his own prophecy will increasingly provoke the evil itself, make it even more evident, and in so doing bring the day of judgment ever closer. Hence the prophetic calling itself already spins the thread of a man's life to its end and clearly determines his path beforehand. These were men in whose gloomy gaze and sorrowful brow words of suffering were deeply etched; yet they were also men to whom the words of Tasso applied in the highest sense, namely, that

> When in their anguish other men fall silent
> A god gave me the power to tell my pain.[11]

¶The only thing we have left from them is, as it were, one great lament on the prophets' own suffering, on the suffering of those who were faithful to God. They suffered in the alleyways, at the magnificent festivals, at the celebrations of the gods, when their own zeal overwhelmed them and in wild passion and unprecedented ruthlessness they intervened against that which could threaten them as well. They suffered when they saw the crowds flee with cries of fear, or when timid, fearful eyes avoided them wherever they looked. They suffered at home when they lay before God in tears of sorrow, in prayer for their beloved people. They suffered, for they hated their people precisely because they loved them.

Their own people often considered them to be sick and ridiculed and avoided them. Many of the prophets suffered under strange psychological, obsessive behavior. They felt suddenly seized by some power forcing them to speak out, sometimes in the middle of a crowd and in utterly incompre-
291 hensible riddles; or in the very midst of joyous celebration they would begin to weep.

> Look away from me,
> let me weep bitter tears;
> do not try to comfort me
> for the destruction of my beloved people,[12]

[11.] Goethe, *Torquato Tasso,* act 5, scene 5, vv. 3424–25 (Goethe, *Collected Works,* 8:138).

[12.] Isa. 22:4.

Isaiah once lamented; and when the curious crowd starts gathering, the prophet announces with insane rage the message of disaster concerning Yahweh's judgment on the startled festival celebrants. Such scenes often end with the prophet being stoned. When the prophet speaks, he falls into a rapturous ecstasy, and his language often assumes the form of ancient Hebrew poetry. Here one always senses an uncanny, unnerving excitement smoldering in the prophet, an element possessing something of the demonic, an element that for the oriental sensibility of every age thus evokes a sense of the sacred, the terrible, the taboo. No one dares touch him; one can sense the *mysterium tremendum*[13] of the deity—and yet one wants nothing more than to get rid of these strange spirits. At home these men suffer the most frightful torments. For days they lie in cataleptic stupors, that is, utterly still, until God's word comes over them, startles them with some vision, drives them out of bed, and sends them out into the marketplace to prophesy.

Or they sense a burning, singeing feeling in their limbs, prompted by their thirst for an encounter with God. Once God's word drives them out into the streets, one can often recognize them by their peculiar clothing. Isaiah walked around in Jerusalem for six months wearing nothing on his upper body, a sign that it was time to do penance.[14] Jeremiah was seen walking across the marketplace with a wooden yoke over his shoulders, a sign that Israel should bow to Yahweh's will, that is, to the power of the Assyrians.[15]

Hence even in those days people often thought the prophets were insane, and today scholars still subscribe to such superficial views. The implication is that these people were abnormal, psychopaths, and nothing more. Such 292
views, however, utterly block any prospect for understanding the unprecedented seriousness of the prophets' tragedy.

The central consideration enabling us to understand the prophetic soul is that the prophet knows himself to be allied with God. This alliance or bond turns his life into a tragedy, and precisely because it is an alliance with God, that tragedy acquires unprecedented seriousness. The prophet's alliance with God is what prompts him to speak such strange words, what makes him so unrelenting, so frightening. It elevates him above anything

[13.] An expression coined by Rudolf Otto in *The Idea of the Holy*; see esp. chap. 4. [Otto used the phrase *mysterium tremendum et fascinans* to speak of the numinous experienced as the "wholly other" that was an awe-inspiring, overpowering energy beyond rational comprehension, evoking simultaneously terror and attraction.—CG]

[14.] See Isa. 20.

[15.] See Jer. 27–28.

that can be explained through recourse to human psychology and makes him inaccessible to the understanding of the psychiatrist and the psychologist. To alter slightly one of the familiar sayings about Luther: "His spirit is the battlefield of two worlds; I'm not surprised he sees demons!"[16] God has chosen a vessel of his will, but he breaks that human vessel to pieces because he is too powerful; God rips apart, breaks to pieces, destroys the spiritually harmonious human figure through whom he makes himself known. He permits the prophet to collapse under the weight laid upon him that no mortal can bear, namely, to be the bearer of the living God. God causes the tragedy of the prophetic life so that in this human defeat the power, claim, and burden of the divine demands can be seen in the full light of day. The alliance with God is terrible—that is the new realization gained from the prophetic phenomenon. Even though the prophets themselves knew that this alliance was their unavoidable undoing, they nonetheless often groaned under the burden, often cried out to God. They who by nature were often such anxious, timid individuals were, after all, cast into the whirl of events, into the turmoil of national and world history, where they were supposed to decide, act, condemn, and pronounce judgment.

It was with just such a feeling of being pressed beyond his own powers that Jeremiah, in the most profound, distressing despair, once fell down
293 before God and uttered the following indescribably moving words, words to be reckoned among the most beautiful in world literature:

> You have enticed me,
>   and I was enticed;
> you have overpowered me,
>   and you have prevailed.
> I have become a laughingstock all day long;
>   everyone mocks me.
> For whenever I speak, I must cry out,
>   I must shout, "Violence and destruction!" . . .
> If I say, "I will not mention him,
>   or speak any more in his name,"
> then within me there is something like a burning fire
>   shut up in my bones;

[16.] Meyer, *Huttens letzte Tage*, 67.

I am weary with holding it in,
and I cannot.
For I hear many whispering.
Terror is all around![17]

In his drama, Stefan Zweig has Jeremiah say the following: "Oh, but you do not know the terrible one, he who has torments and tortures no mortal can imagine. The living soul subjected to God's tortures no longer fears the pains suffered by the body. . . . I have known the divine torment, and the torture of death is blessedness itself compared to the torture of life, and human torment pleasure compared to divine torment."[18]

Here Jeremiah's soul lies open before us. He made one slip in his life, namely, when he began to hold to God. Something enticed him, blinded him, seduced him; he could not help himself, let himself be drawn in, rushed in blindly—into divine ruin. Now the crisis is there. He can no longer come free from God; yet neither can he bear the torment any longer of continually having to confront his beloved people as an accuser, something that tears his soul asunder. But God is too strong; God has won. God's path leads over the broken souls of the faithful.

Once more, however, the enormous, maddening pain of this man of superhuman strength overflows in the cry

Cursed be the day
on which I was born!
The day when my mother bore me,
let it not be blessed!
Cursed be the man who brought the news to my father, saying, 294
"A child is born to you, a son,"
making him very glad. . . .
Why did I come forth from the womb
to see toil and sorrow
and spend my days in shame?[19]

And the great son falls at the feet of his mother with the words,

---

[17.] Jer. 20:7–10. [NRSV: "For I hear many whispering: 'Terror is all around.' "Bonhoeffer preached on this passage in London in 1934, incorporating many of the same observations from this early lecture. See *DBWE* 13, 2/7.—CG]

[18.] See Zweig, *Jeremias*, 180. [This passage was omitted from the English translation that the author condensed somewhat; cf. Zweig, *Jeremiah*, viii.—CG]

[19.] Jer. 20:14–15, 18.

> Woe is me, my mother, that I am alive, berated by all,
> I am neither a believer nor a debtor,
> Yet all of them curse me.[20]

These are moving, distressing witnesses from the lonely chambers of the great advocates of the divine cause, witnesses still attesting eternal truth and eternal seriousness because they show how God's burden overwhelms every human being in every age, and because they show that God triumphs precisely where human beings collapse. Those who even once let themselves be enticed by God will no longer be quite as cheerful with the course their lives take, will no longer be quite as carefree, or quite as free. The proximity of the divine is the antagonist of harmony, of happiness—both internal and external. God's claims destroy contentment, destroy the peace of the soul. For the prophet, religion and happiness no longer coincide,[21] but religion and human power, strength and feeling, will and understanding, all challenge one another.

Two imposing groups of ideas make it impossible even for critical observers to remain entirely with the psychological abnormality of the prophets and rather force us to acknowledge the presence of something that quite transcends all that is familiar to us. These ideas are the inheritance that world history and the philosophy of all Europe, down to Kant and Hegel and even to Spengler,[22] acquired from the prophets and which provided the foundation on which Jesus Christ built.

The first idea is associated with the enormous political upheaval that
295 took place during the eighth century before Christ. This eighth century is the hour of the birth of world history. Whereas the peoples had previously lived side by side without really taking notice of one another, now, suddenly, the dreadful notion of shaping world history arises in one particularly powerful nation, that is, the idea of conquering the world through murder and conflagration and war. Seething unrest arises for the first time; the Assyrians set out to rule Asia, and the world begins to quake.

This was in the era when the Solomonic kingdom had collapsed into two parts. These two kingdoms, however, were nonetheless living with a sense of robust security and in the belief that, because God loved them above all

[20.] Jer. 15:10. [The translation here follows Bonhoeffer's wording, which differs considerably from the NRSV translation.—CG]

[21.] Cf. in this regard also the sermon on 2 Cor. 12:9 from September 9, 1928, 3/11, pp. 522–23.

[22.] Cf. Spengler, *Decline of the West.*

others and preferred them above all others, God would also continue to protect, coddle, and spoil them. They were the only people in the entire world who possessed the law, God's will. No wonder they developed the impudent belief that they had God at their disposal or even possessed God. No wonder also that wickedness and arrogance increased amid this naive, unabashed sense of religious security. Or that social and moral circumstances assumed scandalous forms amid the belief that God will not hold it against us, for we are our God's favorite child. And no wonder, finally, that even if war should come, they believed it self-evident that victory would be theirs, for it would, they insisted, be a holy war against the godless world. God was a God with purely nationalistic interests; in other words, religion itself was conceived in purely nationalistic terms.

The powerful emergence of other peoples, however, now made this problem acute. Will Yahweh always protect and spoil his people? And what about these other peoples in the world? Though the mere idea was almost heretical, what if not all of them are devils? What is God's position then toward those peoples? Does God really know and love only Israel, even the Israel that has become impudent and self-confident? The world began to stir; was Israel to be the center around which it moved? What does this change in world affairs mean? The Assyrians were moving ever closer. It was time to take a position. The prophet Amos was the first who dared assert that those
very Assyrians would win the day, overrun Israel, turn Israel's land to rubble 296
and ashes, and all of this—the Jews hear Amos only as a cursed apostate!—all of this is brought about by none other than God. It is God, the Lord of the nations, who has summoned the Assyrians against Israel as punishment, as judgment. Everything has been reversed. Israel had indeed had a special covenant with God, had had special gifts and enjoyed special graces. But it had abused and ignored them by becoming religiously overconfident.

> You only have I known
> of all the families of the earth;
> therefore (!) I will punish you
> for all your iniquities. (Amos)[23]

[23.] Amos 3:2.

Religion turns against those who abuse it, against those who believe they have it at their disposal like a fixed personal or national possession, and who then think they can rest on that possession. Religion conceals in itself a deadly thorn for those who betray and violate it, and this thorn struck Israel's heart such that Israel bled to death from the wound. To violate religion means to believe that one possesses it. It is not we who possess God, but rather God who possesses us. It is not human beings who have God at their disposal, but God who has human beings at his disposal. To be religious means to recognize that one can never be religious; to have God means to realize that human beings can never have God.

Hence the people of Israel must now experience that religion can lead either to redemption or to disaster, and that there can be no neutrality in religion. In other words, where God has granted recognition of the truth, he also makes the greatest demands. Where there is much, or where God's people believes it has much, God also demands much—indeed, very much. And when these demands are not met, judgment is all the more severe and unrelenting.

God guides the nations and is the Lord of history. God bestows grace on whomever he will. Religion is not bound by national boundaries; national boundaries disappear before God. Here neither status nor nation is privileged. "Are you not like the Ethiopians to me, O people of Israel?"
297 (Amos).[24] God created the world; he is a distant God who brings about world and historical change, who weaves the colorful fabric of world history and causes peoples to prosper and then to die; in the words of the psalm, the nations are smashed like pottery.[25]

Such considerations free the idea of God from the ceremonial garment of nation once and for all. God stands above the nations, though he does indeed have a specific plan for every people, and whatever takes place in world history does so at God's own initiative. If Assyria is to destroy Israel, God will have a specific reason and a specific goal in mind. We must accept, understand, and assess the events of world history as events taking place at God's initiative. Here there are no longer any accidents, but also no excuses.

This deepening of the understanding of God by the prophets can be understood only in connection with the other powerful notion, namely, that God is the holy one, the unrelenting righteous one, the God of con-

[24.] Amos 9:7.
[25.] See Ps. 2:9.

science. Thus did Isaiah experience God in his own call vision,[26] as did the other prophets. God's people are all over the world, among Gentiles no less than among the Jews, wherever his will is done and he is obeyed. God demands nothing, absolutely nothing more from human beings than this: You shall be holy, for I am holy.[27] "He has told you, O mortal, what is good: and what does the LORD require of you but to do justice, and to love kindness, and to walk humbly with your God."[28]

The prophets embraced this demand with radical seriousness. No more cult, no more sacrifices—what sense does it make to bring God sacrifices, since the whole world already belongs to God in any case (Ps. 50)? Instead: "Let justice roll down like waters, and righteousness like an ever-flowing stream" (Amos).[29] Disaster is at the door. And as surely as Yahweh is the holy and moral one, just as surely is there only one path to take, namely, to do penance and bring about righteousness. The portrayals of the social and moral degeneration in the land are dreadful.

Amos writes:

> Disaster is near:
> because they sell the righteous for silver,
> and the needy for a pair of sandals— 298
> they who trample the head of the poor into the dust of the earth,
> and push the afflicted out of the way;
> father and son go in to the same girl,
> so that my holy name is profaned;
> they lay themselves down beside every altar
> on garments taken in pledge;
> and in the house of the God they drink
> wine bought with fines they imposed.[30]
> . . .
> Alas for those who lie on beds of ivory,
> and lounge on their couches, . . .
> who sing idle songs to the sound of the harp,
> and like David improvise on instruments of music;

[26.] See Isa. 6.
[27.] Lev. 19:2; cf. 1 Pet. 1:15.
[28.] Mic. 6:8.
[29.] Amos 5:24.
[30.] Amos 2:6–8.

who drink wine from bowls,
 and anoint themselves with the finest oils.[31]

Or Isaiah:

In that day the Lord GOD of hosts
 called to weeping and mourning,
 to baldness and putting on sackcloth;
but instead there was joy and festivity,
 killing oxen and slaughtering sheep,
 eating meat and drinking wine.
"Let us eat and drink,
 for tomorrow we die."[32]

At some point, however, the day will come when Yahweh gets serious, the terrible day of Yahweh.

For the LORD of hosts has a day
 against all that is proud and lofty,
 against all that is lifted up and high; . . .
against all the high mountains,
 and against all the lofty hills;
against every high tower,
 and against every fortified wall;
against all the ships of Tarshish,
 and against all the beautiful craft.
The haughtiness of people shall be humbled,
 and the pride of everyone shall be brought low;
 and the LORD alone will be exalted on that day.[33]

An unforgettably powerful poem for anyone who reflects a bit with open eyes on the history of the world up to the present.

299 With such speeches the prophets stood in the marketplace before the temple in the face of the impending disaster. Down in the dust before Yahweh, down on your knees! But no one listened. Then the news came that the Assyrians had overrun the northern kingdom of Israel and destroyed it.[34]

[31.] Amos 6:4–6.

[32.] Isa. 22:12–14.

[33.] Isa. 2:12, 14–17.

[34.] 722 BCE; cf. 2 Kings 17.

The question now became whether Judah, i.e., Jerusalem, should join the powers opposing Assyria or should wait until the Assyrians attacked. Now the prophets' most difficult period of suffering began. They were always opposed to those who advocated war, advising instead to wait and trust completely in Yahweh's guidance and not to depend on human strength or even on the most powerful allies. "The Egyptians are human, and not spirit," Isaiah says with great insight.[35] "One who has faith will not panic; if you do not stand firm in faith, you shall not stand at all."[36] Here, quietly, the word emerges for the first time that for two thousand years would become the guiding word of world history: the word "faith."

Israel did not listen. It entered the struggle, was overrun by Assyria, and only Jerusalem itself was miraculously saved one more time.[37] As a result, national arrogance increased even more. The year was 701 BCE. After these events, Isaiah probably withdrew into solitude, certain that his people were lost but hopeful in God's eternal goodness and eternal reign. A hundred years passed before the tragedy of the most patient sufferer of all, Jeremiah, came to its despairing end with the fall of Jerusalem. Assyria had in the meantime been conquered by the Babylonians, to whom Jerusalem was now paying tribute. But things were the same as before in Jerusalem itself. A few examples from Jeremiah's poetry suffice to evoke the mood at that time.

> Can Ethiopians change their skin
> or leopards their spots?
> As little can you do good
> who are accustomed to do evil.
> I will scatter you like chaff
> driven by the wind from the desert.
> This is your lot,
> the portion I have measured out to you,
> says the LORD.[38]

And when he sees that Israel is revolting against Babylon for the second 300
time on its own initiative, he goes to the marketplace with a yoke on his shoulders:

[35.] Cf. Isa. 31:3.

[36.] Cf. Isa. 7:9; 28:16.

[37.] Cf. 2 Kings 19; Isa. 36–37.

[38.] Jer. 13:23–25. [Translation altered from the NRSV. The NRSV meaning is the same, though stated sarcastically: "Then also you can do good who are accustomed to do evil."—CG]

> I will take up weeping and wailing for the mountains,
> and a lamentation for the pastures of the wilderness,
> because they are laid waste so that no one passes through
> and the lowing of cattle is not heard;
> both the birds of the air and the animals
> have fled and are gone.[39]

And elsewhere:

> Hear, O women, the word of the LORD,
> and let your ears receive the word of his mouth;
> teach to your daughters a dirge,
> and each to her neighbor a lament.
> "Death has come up into our windows,
> it has entered our palaces,
> to cut off the children from the streets
> and the young men from the squares." . . .
> "Human corpses shall fall
> like dung upon the open field
> like sheaves behind the reaper,
> and no one shall gather them."[40]

These last two poems are among the most beautiful but also most profoundly sad pieces of prophetic literature. He who loved his people with such ardent fervor then had to experience being imprisoned as a coward and defector—ultimately, so that he might be completely eliminated by being thrown into a deep cistern[41]—until his prophecy was fulfilled. Jerusalem deserted the faith, was taken in no time at all, the temple destroyed, the royal family executed, and the people led off into captivity, away from the promised land, far from the temple, far from the home Yahweh had given them. The last words the aged Jeremiah receives from Yahweh are devoid of hope: Behold, I have broken down what I have built, and plucked up what I have planted, and you, Jeremiah, wanted to desire great things for yourself.[42] "God himself is suffering; how dare a human being complain about suffering? A moving eulogy for all the hopes the prophet had kept

---

[39.] Jer. 9:9–10 [NRSV: v. 10.—CG].

[40.] Jer. 9:20–22.

[41.] Cf. Jer. 38.

[42.] Jer. 45:4–5 [NRSV translation altered to conform to Bonhoeffer's German. —CG]

alive."[43] God's own heart has been broken; should not the hearts of God's faithful also be broken? It was over, the prophets had lost, the tragedy of their lives had played itself out, the curtain came down, the fifth act was over. 301

¶And yet in the ensuing night, a dawning day was already discernible in the distance, and it was as if the shadows[44] of the great prophets were invisibly surrounding their people. They had sacrificed everything for their people, but surely what they sacrificed would not be lost forever. No, indeed; this bleeding seed had to sprout, and sprout it did. The prophets' tragedy had a threefold cause. First, they had a covenant with God in which they were given two overwhelming experiences of God, namely, as the world ruler who guides history according to his will, and as the holy One. Whoever would be part of God's people should fall down into the dust before him. Although proclaiming this message cost the prophets their lives, the message itself became a permanent possession of humanity. We ourselves, through German philosophy, partake even now of the inheritance of the bloody seed of the prophets.

Our own age is getting out of joint. The vital force of our people, of Europe, seems broken. The hideous face of decadence, of immorality, of cynicism, of depravity grins at us from every corner and every crevice. In the face of such developments, one must embrace simplicity again, and for that reason we have listened once more to the words of the ancient prophets. They said it then and could not have said it better: a people who would rise up must be serious about God's will and must be serious about a life of morality. All the blows of fate that come upon a people are both justified and merited, for it is God who has sent them. The point now is to draw the appropriate conclusions from such blows and to bear them as a burden that God lays upon us.[45] Any people can go astray, can lapse. But they can then also find their way again by following God's path. God recognizes no
distinctions between peoples except that one people does God's will while 302
another does not. God remains the holy One, the relentlessly righteous One before whom even the highest human summit must fall to the ground. Walking with God, however, means walking a hard path, a path on which the heart's blood of the best people flows and has flowed, as the example of the prophets has amply taught us. Need we apply it further to our own age?

[43.] Duhm, *Israels Propheten*, 282.

[44.] The word "shadows" was written originally and then "figures" was added below it, either as a replacement or as an alternative.

[45.] Cf. also the concrete examples Bonhoeffer offers in his lecture on war, 2/9, pp. 415–16, and in the sermon on 1 John 4:16, 3/23, p. 582–83.

Whoever has ears to hear, has heard, and for that person, a look at our own age will invariably also evoke the vanished world of Israel's prophets.

2. Jesus Christ and the Essence of Christianity[1]

Jesus Christ and the Essence of Christianity

The question before us today is whether in our own day Christ still stands in the place where decisions are made concerning the most profound matters we are facing, namely, concerning our own lives and the life of our people [Volk]. We want to examine whether the spirit of Christ can still speak to us concerning the ultimate, final, decisive matters. We all know that, for all practical purposes, Christ has been eliminated from our lives. Although we still build his temple, we live in our own houses. Christ, instead of being the center of our lives, has become a thing of the church, or of the religiosity of a group of people. To the nineteenth- and twentieth-century mind, religion plays the part of the so-called parlor into which one doesn't mind withdrawing for a couple of hours, but from which one then immediately returns to one's place of work. However, one thing is clear, namely, that we understand Christ only if we commit to him in an abrupt either-or. He was not nailed to the cross as an ornamentation or decoration for our lives. If we want to have
303 *him*, we must recognize that he makes crucial claims on our entire lives. We understand him not if we make room for him in merely one province of our spiritual life, but only if our life takes its orientation from him alone or, otherwise, if we speak a straightforward no. Of course, there are those who are not concerned with taking seriously the claims Christ makes on us in his question, Do you want to commit completely, or not? They should rather not get mixed up with Christianity at all; this is better for Christianity, since such people no longer have anything in common with Christ. The religion of Christ is not the tidbit after the bread; it is the bread itself, or it is nothing. Those who would call themselves Christians should understand and acknowledge at least that much.

[1.] *NL*, A 22,2 a; handwritten with a note by Bethge: "Tuesday Barcelona." See also *NL*, A 22,2 b; later typewritten transcript. Previously published in *GS* 5:134–56. This lecture was delivered on Tuesday, December 11, 1928. Concerning the general level of the topic, see Bonhoeffer's letter to his parents on November 27, 1928, 1/58. [Bonhoeffer could hardly have used this title without thinking of Harnack's famous Berlin lectures and book *Das Wesen des Christentums* (translated as *What Is Christianity?*) and perhaps also Feuerbach's book of the same title (translated more precisely as *The Essence of Christianity*).—CG]

Various attempts have been made to eliminate Christ from the contemporary life of the human spirit [Geistesleben].[2] And indeed, what is seductive about these attempts is that they seem finally to put Christ into the appropriate and worthy position. Those undertaking such attempts explain Christ according to aesthetic categories as a religious genius. They declare him to be a great ethicist or admire his path to the cross as a heroic sacrifice for the sake of his idea. The only thing these attempts do not do is take him seriously. That is, they do not draw the center of their own lives into contact with Christ's claim to speak and indeed to be *the* revelation of God. They preserve a certain distance between themselves and Christ's words, thereby thwarting any serious encounter. I can live with or without Jesus as a religious genius, as an ethicist, as master[3]—just as I can certainly also live without Plato or Kant; all this has merely relative significance. But if there is something in Christ that makes claims upon my entire life, from top to bottom, and does so with the full seriousness of the realization that it is God who is speaking here, and if it is only in Christ that God's word once became a present reality, then Christ possesses for me not only merely relative but also absolutely urgent significance. Although I am still free to say yes or no, it can no longer be an ultimately indifferent matter to me. To understand Christ means to understand this claim; taking Christ seriously means taking seriously his absolute claim on human decision.

Our concern now is to make the seriousness of this matter clear and to remove Christ from the process of secularization into which he has been
drawn since the Enlightenment. Finally, we will also show that in our own 304
age the questions to which Christ provides the answers are as acutely relevant as ever, and that the spirit of Christ is quite justified in raising its claims.

Hence our first, and main, question concerns the essence of the Christian message, the essence of Christianity.

People are utterly at sea not only in lay circles but in professional theological circles as well. From the pulpits and the lecterns, we hear things described and preached as "essentially Christian" that could just as easily find their spiritual author in Plato, Buddha, or Goethe. Moreover, the

[2.] [*Geistesleben* might also be translated "life of the mind" or even "contemporary culture."—CG]

[3.] [Translating *Herr* in this sentence as "master" does not at all mean—as in some Christian discourse—an equivalence with "Lord" in the sense of "*the* revelation of God" who makes an "absolute claim on human decision." As the context shows, the meaning in this sentence has the sense of guide, teacher, leader, etc.—CG]

far-reaching history-of-religions research[4] of the past few decades has pushed Christianity so completely into the culture of Hellenistic religious syncretism that we have gradually lost sight of what is unique in Christianity to begin with, a uniqueness to which Christianity does, after all, owe its victory over the Mithras cult and the mystery religions.[5]

The central idea of the Hellenistic cult during the period when Christianity emerged is the idea of redemption. We hear, for example, about a world redeemer who will be born of a virgin, about a primal being who descends into the world, whose scattered parts are the souls of people who will one day come together again, whereupon the primal human being will once more be resurrected with all its members. We hear about the god Osiris, who dies and whose bones the women seek and bring together and the god once again is resurrected, analogous to what is still the contemporary custom in the Greek church, where, during the night before Easter, women seek Jesus until they break out in cries of joy at morning: He is risen! Similar elements are found in the cults of Antaeus, Attis, and Dionysus. The myths of the dying and resurrected gods are nature myths symbolizing the sleep of winter and the reawakening of spring. We also hear about sacramental meals similar to the Christian Eucharist where, through physical connection with the god, adherents seek to deify themselves. Such similari-
305 ties extend even into details. Just as today the bishop still blesses the people with three raised and two folded fingers, so also in distant antiquity did the priest of the god Sabazios bless the adherents of that god.[6]

We see that Christianity is embedded in the religious forms of its age. This also applies to the portrayal of the life of Jesus of Nazareth. As portrayed by the first three Gospels of our New Testament, his life has become so overgrown with legendary features that scholarship is able to peer though the foliage in only a few passages. Tradition all too hastily clothed and draped Jesus in the conventional costume of a saint and miracle worker. Ancient fairy-tale motifs, in part from India and the Orient, and miracle stories of the sort also told about the more popular Roman emperors, all contributed

[4.] [The History of Religions School (*Religionsgeschichtlicheschule*), a group of German biblical scholars who flourished in the late nineteenth and early twentieth centuries, used data from the comparative study of ancient Near Eastern and Hellenistic religions to interpret the Bible and Christian origins.—CG]

[5.] Concerning this problem, see Drews, *Christ Myth*, esp. 37–45.

[6.] Sabazios was worshiped as a Thracian-Phrygian god of agriculture and life and as a physician associated especially with birth. The Jewish diaspora in Asia Minor associated him by syncretism with Yahweh as God of the Sabbath. Concerning the blessing gesture, cf. Cancik and Schneider, *Der Neue Pauly*, 10:1180–81.

to the myth of Jesus of Nazareth such that today little of the actual humanity of this man can be ascertained with any certainty.

The most concrete result yielded by one and a half centuries of New Testament source criticism is the familiar assertion: Vita Jesu scribi non potest.[7]

The main reason for this situation is that our New Testament originated in a church-community that worshiped Jesus not as a historical personality but as the *kyrios*, the Lord (the Greek translates the Hebrew "Yahweh"), and thus as God himself. Any psychologizing or historicizing interest is thus quite naturally absent. Its interest is rather purely to the point, immediate, and aims at the center of the phenomenon of Jesus of Nazareth, over against which all historical elements become unimportant. Even in the Synoptics, that is, the first three Gospels, which seem to express some historical
interest, the main focus is invariably on portraying Jesus as the Son of God 306
and doing so through Jesus's deeds and words. The historical arrangement is wholly unreliable.

This whole situation has prompted one group of scholars to draw a false historical conclusion, namely, that the entire figure of Jesus is to be understood as a mythological character, as a product of the church-community analogous, for example, to Mithras. This suggestion has proven to be utterly erroneous.[8] Nonetheless, we have reason enough to view our sources quite critically in terms of their historical assertions. At the same time, however, we must get beyond this shortcoming if we are to discover the essence of Christianity and grasp the undeniable uniqueness of the Christian message despite Christianity's seemingly utter congruency with the religions of its own time. A brief general observation can help us get under way.

Two possible modes of historical observation are possible, and here I am understanding specifically "historical" investigation to involve an understanding and interpretation of history. The first mode was influenced by idealist philosophy. Here one interprets history according to a system. One possesses the method through which one can interpret history and has access to the idea and thus apparently also to history. For such observation, history itself can offer nothing essentially new; everything fits into the system one already possesses. That is, history can now no longer possess

---

[7.] "It is not possible to write the life of Jesus"; see the beginning of Albert Schweitzer's concluding observations in his *Quest of the Historical Jesus*, 478: "Those who are fond of talking about negative theology can find their account here. There is nothing more negative than the result of the critical study of the Life of Jesus."

[8.] See Schweitzer, *Quest of the Historical Jesus*, 355–424, regarding the contested historicity of Jesus.

absolute significance for me; history itself is relativized through the idea. Put concretely, this means that in understanding historical circumstances one cannot transcend the standards of evaluation already at one's disposal from the very outset, even if those standards cannot hope to do justice to a particular set of historical circumstances. One does not want to learn anything new from history; history is not allowed to make any urgent claims on human beings.

307 The other mode of historical observation is completely different. It is interested in history only to the extent that the latter possesses absolute significance. That is, one approaches history with no preconceived ideas, categories, or tables of values according to which one will judge; one allows history itself to speak, and one listens as it does so. One does not have access beforehand to what history can say to us, but rather allows history to present its claims to us. One even allows one's own preconceived notions to be shattered if necessary, since history is more than the idea. The only thing that concerns us is what in history still has the power to speak to us down through the millennia, to make claims on us to which we must respond responsibly and with our entire existence rather than just with our ideology. Only here does time become transparent. We experience contemporaneity with historical events only where we perceive the claims of history, that is, where we accept or reject those claims and allow ourselves to be touched by them in our most profound existence. Here, however, the path is clear.

Either we already have access to what a Jesus of Nazareth might have to say, that is, we are already familiar in principle with the psychological laws and probabilities and can speak confidently, as those who basically already know everything in advance, about Jesus's psychology; then we can give free rein to our imagination in the way that Jesus novels have naively done even up to the present. Moreover, because we already know from our own philosophy about the best possible morality, and the highest, most appropriate idea of God, we can simply insinuate this information into Jesus's own words.

Or we allow the New Testament truly to speak, and for once we are only listeners, hearing the claim this book presents in its entire power, and thus at the center of the matter we genuinely try to come to terms with history. That is the path we will take. There is absolutely no value in reading the New Testament according to twentieth-century concepts; one must read it rather as it was intended. In so doing, however, we do indeed encounter a great deal that runs contrary to modern psychology and philosophy.

The first thing we encounter throughout the entire New Testament is a surprising lack of interest in anything concerning the psychology of
308 Jesus; the same goes for chronological considerations. The primary focus

is on the unsettling experience the church-community had in the figure of Jesus of Nazareth, who called himself the Christ, that is, the Messiah, God's anointed, that is, God's revelation in the world. It is about these concerns that we want to hear, since even Jesus himself is only important as the essence of Christianity.

About midway through the three Synoptic Gospels, we read that Jesus asked his disciples what the people thought of him. They responded that some were saying he was the resurrected Elijah, or John the Baptist, others that he was one of the prophets. "He said to them, 'But who do you say that I am?' Simon Peter answered, 'You are the Christ, the Son of the living God.' And Jesus answered him, 'Blessed are you, Simon son of Jonah! For flesh and blood has not revealed this to you, but my Father in heaven.' . . . Then he sternly ordered the disciples not to tell anyone that he was the Christ."[9]

This is the great, overwhelming, decisive moment in Jesus's life. He, the son of a carpenter, hears others call him the Son of God, the Christ, and he conceals this secret in the most profound silence. He knows God has sent him into the world with enormous authority. He is the bringer of God's kingdom into the world. "But if it is by the Spirit of God that I cast out demons, then the kingdom of God has come to you."[10] Or as he says in the one rather strange image, "I watched Satan fall from heaven like a flash of lightning" (Luke 10:18), that is, the kingdom of God is here. To the question "when is the kingdom coming?" he answers, "the kingdom of God is not coming with things that can be observed; nor will they say, 'Look, here it is!' or 'There it is!' For, in fact, the kingdom of God is among you" (the translation "within you" is wrong), "the blind receive their sight, the lame walk, the lepers are cleansed, the deaf hear, the dead are raised, and the poor have good news brought to them."[11] Such is Jesus's cry of joy regarding the new age. He acts with the full authority of God's Spirit. His coming confronts the world with a decision: either with him and for 309
God, or against him and against God. "Whoever is not with me is against me, and whoever does not gather with me scatters" (Matt. 12:30). Because he bears God's revelation, because he is the Christ, it is with regard to him and his word that a person's life is decided. "Do not think that I have come to bring peace to the earth; I have not come to bring peace, but a sword. For I have come to set a man against his father, and a daughter against her mother. . . . Whoever loves father or mother more than me is not worthy of

[9.] Matt. 16:15–20 [NRSV has "Messiah" instead of "Christ."—CG]
[10.] Matt. 12:28.
[11.] Luke 17:20–21; Matt. 11:5.

me; and whoever loves son or daughter more than me is not worthy of me" (Matt. 10:34ff.). Or even more harshly in another passage: "Whoever comes to me and does not hate father and mother, wife and children, brothers and sisters, yes, and even life itself, cannot be my disciple" (Luke 14:26). Jesus is demanding a direct, uncompromising decision, a decision in favor of God's will, leading to participation in God's kingdom. To a man grieving at the death of his father, Jesus says, "Let the dead bury their own dead; but as for you, go and proclaim the kingdom of God."[12] Or, "No one who puts a hand to the plow and looks back is fit for the kingdom of God."[13] God's lordship requires everything or nothing: "The kingdom of heaven is like treasure hidden in a field, which someone found and hid; then in his joy he goes and sells all that he has and buys that field. Again, the kingdom of heaven is like a merchant in search of fine pearls; on finding one pearl of great value, he went and sold all that he had and bought it."[14] Before God's will, there is no consideration of human matters: "If your right eye causes you to sin, tear it out and throw it away; it is better for you to lose one of your members than for your whole body to be thrown into hell. And if your right hand causes you to sin, cut it off and throw it away; it is better for you to lose one of your members than for your whole body to go into hell" (Matt. 5:29–30.). "Enter through the narrow gate; for the gate is wide and
310 the road is easy that leads to destruction, and there are many who take it. For the gate is narrow and the road is hard that leads to life, and there are few who find it" (Matt. 7:13).

Jesus is able to confront human beings with this alternative of "all or nothing" only because he knows he is acting with God's authority; "and blessed is anyone who takes no offense at me."[15] At the same time, however, anything involving his own person as an individual personality, for example, with whatever fascinating or repulsive characteristics may attach to that personality, is infinitely insignificant to Jesus compared to the main issue, which is the decision for God's will. Luke recounts how, "while he was saying this, a woman in the crowd raised her voice and said to him, 'Blessed is the womb that bore you and the breasts that nursed you!' But he said, 'Blessed rather are those who hear the word of God and obey it!'"[16] This statement constitutes an unequivocal renunciation of any cult attaching to Jesus's individual, personal human appearance. Those who venerate Jesus

[12.] Luke 9:60.

[13.] Luke 9:62.

[14.] Matt. 13:44–46.

[15.] Matt. 11:6.

[16.] Luke 11:27–28.

as a genius or as a fascinating personality do not understand him; they only understand him who hear his message and accept him as the one sent by God.

Jesus's consciousness of his messianic authority prompts his family to think him crazy. They go to bring him home: "Then his mother and his brothers came; and standing outside, they sent to him and called him. A crowd was sitting around him; and they said to him 'Your mother and your brothers and sisters are outside, asking for you.' And he replied, 'Who are my mother and my brothers?' And looking at those who sat around him, he said, 'Here are my mother and my brothers! Whoever does the will of God is my brother and sister and mother'" (Mark 3:31–35). Jesus consistently turns attention away from his own person and back to the only important and urgent issue, the decision for God's dominion. "I came to bring fire to the earth, and how I wish it were already kindled!"[17]

In all these episodes, we thus see Jesus up on the icy heights of that unrelenting demand on human beings. Who will dare to follow him? Who will enter his discipleship? It is no accident that Ibsen's *Brand*, in which the 311
demand for all or nothing tears a family apart, takes place high up in the icy Nordic regions. This either-or is unrelentingly cold. Nor is it inappropriate that Dostoyevsky has the Grand Inquisitor ask Jesus:

> But is it only to the elect and for their sake that you descended straight down from heaven?[18] Let me assert that human beings are weaker and baser than you thought. Can they really successfully do all the things you have directed them to do? By thinking so highly of them, you in fact acted like someone who felt no compassion for them at all and as a result constantly demanded too much of them; and it was you who did this, you who loved them more than you loved yourself. If you had thought less of them, you would have demanded less of them.[19] . . . Your great prophet says that in his visions he has seen all those who took part in the resurrection, and that there were twelve thousand from each tribe[20]—but if there were no more than that, then they were not human beings at all, but already gods. They bore your cross, lived ten years in the hungry, barren wilderness, living on locusts and roots—certainly, you can now point to them with pride, these children of freedom, of free love, of free and noble

[17.] Luke 12:49.

[18.] [The sentence Bonhoeffer placed at the beginning actually comes from the end of the citation.—CG]

[19.] [Bonhoeffer omits several following sentences at this point.—CG]

[20.] [An allusion to the visions of John; cf. Rev. 7:1–8 and 14:1–3.—CG]

> sacrifice in your name. But do not forget that their number was only a few thousand, and that they were gods. But what happens to the others? What did the remaining ones, the weak ones, do to you by not enduring what the strong were able to endure? Is it the fault of the weak soul that it is not strong enough to endure such terrible gifts?[21]

Everywhere we encounter the same trembling apprehension before the terrible severity of Jesus's demand. He turns to the moral heroes and pays no attention to the weak; he leads the way to the Overman [Übermensch].[22]
312 Closer examination, however, reveals a surprising picture. He who was seemingly so unapproachable, who came with his razor-sharp either-or, now appears not among the ascetics or moral heroes or Pharisees, but rather among two groups of people hitherto living completely unnoticed beneath the surface, people who seemed least to fulfill his severe demands. Jesus turns his attention to children[23] and to the morally and socially least of these, those viewed as less worthy. This turn is something totally unprecedented and new in world history, and in the person of Jesus it seems to constitute a break. Plato opened his school for those who love wisdom, for the philosophers, for those who strive to live an ethical life. Buddha sought his following among the ascetics, among those who had turned their backs on the world. Jesus goes to the children and holds them up as examples to those who are already decidedly moral. When Jesus enters Jerusalem, apparently so many children already know him that they surge toward him

---

[21.] [The translation follows Bonhoeffer's wording. His text does not correspond to the German translation Bonhoeffer owned (*Nachlaß Dietrich Bonhoeffer,* 228), nor to several other German editions that were available in December 1928; since 1890 there were numerous Spanish translations of European works, including Dostoyevsky, and Bonhoeffer may have worked from a Spanish version of the text. Cf. below, p. 366, and Dostoyevsky, *Die Brüder Karamasoff,* 1:513–14; see also *The Brothers Karamazov,* 334–35 (pt. 2, bk. 5, chap. 5, "The Grand Inquisitor").—CG]

[22.] With this phrase, "the way to the Overman," and later "the transvaluation of all values" (see pp. 366–67), Bonhoeffer uses key concepts of Nietzsche's anti-Christian later writings, especially from *The Antichrist* and *The Will to Power;* see, for example, "Not 'mankind' [*Menschheit*] but *Overman* [*Übermensch*] is the goal!" (Nietzsche, *Will to Power,* 519, no. 1001; cf. also *Übermensch,* in Oehler, *Nietzsche-Register,* 460–62. Nonetheless, "Jesus's unprecedented new understanding of God," which Bonhoeffer develops in the following discussion, contains a thorough critique of Nietzsche's concept. [The phrase, "transvaluation of all values," is the subtitle of Nietzsche's *Will to Power.*—CG]

[23.] In both Barcelona and America, Bonhoeffer applied himself with special intensity to youth work. The "discovery of the child" and the projected piece on the "theology of the child" (see 1/40, p. 128) are to be viewed in this biographical context. Cf. also the passage in *Act and Being, DBWE* 2:159–61.

and sing hosanna to him in the temple[24]—quite to the consternation of the moral party, the Pharisees. The apocryphal, or extrabiblical, Gospels recount many fantastic stories about how Jesus played with the children in the streets.[25] When mothers bring their children to have Jesus bless them, those who consider themselves to be the real, genuine disciples of Jesus run in and want to drive the women out. It was then that Jesus said, "Let the little children come to me."[26]

Once when Jesus is out with his disciples and they are arguing over the rewards they will receive for living in his discipleship, Jesus "called a child, whom he put among them, and said, 'Truly I tell you, unless you change and become like children, you will never enter the kingdom of heaven'" (Matt.
18:2–3), or "if any of you put a stumbling block before one of these little 313
ones who believe in me, it would be better for you if a great millstone were hung around your neck and you were thrown into the sea" (Mark 9:42). For Jesus the child is not merely a transitional stage on the way to adulthood, something to be overcome; quite the contrary, he or she is something utterly unique before which the adult should have the utmost respect. For indeed, God is closer to children than to adults. In this sense, Jesus becomes the discoverer of the child. He sees the children and wants to belong to them; who would block his path? God belongs to children, the good news belongs to children, and joy in the kingdom of heaven belongs to children. "Woe to anyone who puts a stumbling block before one of these little ones."[27] This notion is so utterly alien to the sensibility of antiquity that only one other might seem even more alien, namely, that Jesus, this man of the ruthless either-or, goes not only to children but also to sinners. He traffics with the socially despised, the outcasts,[28] the tax collectors, the deceivers, and the prostitutes. People see this preacher of purity and holiness eating at midday among these people—a horrible sight for a Jewish rabbi—going into their homes, talking with them on the street, defending adulterers before the entire community. They are horrified when they hear him speak out against

---

[24.] Cf. Matt. 21:1–9 and parallels. Matt. 21:15 mentions children in connection with Jesus's entry into Jerusalem.

[25.] Cf. *The Infancy Story of Thomas*, chap. 2 (Hennecke and Schneemelcher, *New Testament Apocrypha*, 1:392–93). In 1925 Bonhoeffer attended a lecture course given by Harnack on the "History of the Origin of the New Testament and of the Apocryphal Gospels" (cf. *DBWE* 9:585).

[26.] See Matt. 19:14.

[27.] Matt. 18:6. Luther translates "least ones," *Geringste*, instead of "little ones," *Kleine*. [Bonhoeffer summarizes, rather than quotes.—CG]

[28.] [Literally "the fifth estate," the class below the proletariat. In Germany the term *Der 5. Stand* was made famous by the 1925 film of Gunter Lamprecht, *Die Verrufenen*, released in the United States as *The Slums of Berlin*.—CG]

those who are in fact moral: "Truly I tell you, the tax collectors and the prostitutes are going into the kingdom of God ahead of you" (Matt. 21:31).

In one scene, a prostitute comes to Jesus while he is eating, anoints him with ointment, and, overcome by his presence, sinks down on her knees and breaks out in tears. The tears wet his feet, and the woman, in her distress, dries his feet with her hair. To the Pharisees, who take offense at this display, Jesus says: Leave her alone; she has been forgiven much, for she has loved much.[29]

Jesus tells a parable about two brothers. One takes his father's inheritance and squanders it on dissolute living and prostitutes; the other stays at home with the father. When the first remorsefully returns home, his
314 father greets him, the sinner, the lost son, with more love than the son who remained at home ever experienced.[30] Jesus also tells about a Pharisee who prays in the temple and offers all his earnings to God, and about a tax collector who has nothing to bring to God but a broken heart and the words, "God, be merciful to me, a sinner." Jesus concludes with the words: "This man went down to his home justified rather than the other."[31] All traditional values seem to topple, to be revalued.[32] The equation "ethics is religion" seems to teeter when God's emissary really does commit himself to the villains instead of to the righteous. Jesus's own behavior appears profoundly contradictory.

The answer, or rather the paradox, is found in Jesus's unprecedented idea of God. God is utterly superior to the world, utterly transcends it, that is, is removed from the world, is totally different;[33] God is wholly unlike human beings and human nature and is eternally inaccessible to human thought and will. This God wants only one thing from people, namely, that they be nothing before him, and demands nothing from people but that they make absolutely no claims. God wants human beings to be inwardly completely poor, completely unknowing, God wants an empty space in them into which he can move. God wants only the outstretched hand of the beggar so that he can fill it, God wants those who have nothing; God does not want the

[29.] See Luke 7:37–47. [Bonhoeffer summarizes.—CG]

[30.] See Luke 15:11–32.

[31.] See Luke 18:10–14.

[32.] See ed. note 18 above. An allusion and a Christian response to a key concept of Nietzsche's ethics, the "revaluation of all values," found esp. in his work *The Antichrist* (*Portable Nietzsche*, 656): "And time is reckoned from the *dies nefastus* [abominable day] with which this calamity began—after the *first* day of Christianity! W*hy not rather after its last day? After today?* Revaluation of all values!" For additional examples, see Oehler, *Nietzsche-Register*, 463.

[33.] [An echo of the "*ganz andere*" of Barth's *Epistle to the Romans*.—CG]

righteous or those who already know, the saints, but rather the unrighteous, the foolish, the sinners. Every knowledge, every moral claim before God, violates his claim for exclusive honor, encroaches upon his honor and majesty. God is the absolute sovereign and is utterly superior to human beings even with regard to any ultimate human holiness. And from the perspective of human initiative, this chasm remains unbridgeable. Human knowledge of God remains precisely that: human, limited, relative, anthropomorphic knowledge. The human desire to believe remains precisely that: human 315
desire accompanied by ultimately human goals and motives. The human religious path to God leads to the idol of our own hearts, which we have created in our own image. It is not knowledge or morality or religion that leads us to God—even religion is merely a piece of our own bodily nature, as Luther once put it—there is absolutely no path leading from human beings to God, for such a path is ultimately based on human capabilities. The tower of Babel is the arrogance that infringes upon God's honor.[34] If human beings and God are to come together, there is but one way, namely, the way from God to human beings. Here all human claims are at an end; God alone has the honor. As the sovereign, God bestows his grace on whom he will. Who dares grumble if that grace be denied to him? God is the potter, we are the clay, as Paul puts it.[35]

God comes to those who make no claims. In Paul's words, "God chose what is foolish in the world to shame the wise; God chose what is weak in the world to shame the strong; God chose what is low and despised in the world, things that are not, to reduce to nothing things that are, so that no flesh might boast in the presence of God."[36] When people merely listen, merely receive, that is, when they seem to be farthest from God in irreligion and immorality, then God is closest to them. Religion and morality contain the germ of hubris, the quintessential Greek concept of hostility toward the divine, the germ of pride, of arrogance. People think they have discovered deep within themselves something that does after all resemble the divine, or even is divine, something elevating us to the level of the divine, something giving us the right to make claims. In this sense, religion and morality can become the most dangerous enemy of God's coming to human beings, the most dangerous enemy of the Christian message of good news. Thus

[34.] Cf. among others Luther, *Sermons on the Gospel of St. John: Chapters 14–16*, in *LW* 24:39–40 (*WA* 45:495, 36–38; 496, 23–26), and *Hauspostille* 1544 (*WA*, 52:641, 10–12).

[35.] See Rom. 9:21.

[36.] 1 Cor. 1:27–29. [NRSV has "one," not "flesh."—CG]

316 the Christian message is basically amoral and irreligious, paradoxical as that may sound.

With that we have articulated a basic criticism of the most grandiose of all human attempts to advance toward the divine—by way of the church. Christianity conceals within itself a germ hostile to the church. It is far too easy for us to base our claims to God on our own Christian religiosity and our church commitment, and in so doing utterly to misunderstand and distort the Christian idea. And yet Christianity needs the church; that is the paradox we will be able to elucidate and understand only in the next session. Here we encounter the enormous responsibility placed upon the church.

Ethics and religion and church all go in this direction: from the human to God. Christ, however, speaks only and exclusively of the line from God to human beings, not of some human path to God, but only of God's own path to humans. Hence it is also fundamentally wrong to seek a new morality in Christianity. In actual practice, Christ offered hardly any ethical prescriptions not already attested among his contemporary Jewish rabbis or even in pagan literature. The essence of Christianity is found in its message about the sovereign God to whom alone, above the entire world, all honor is due; it is a message about the eternally other, the God removed from the world who from the primal ground of his being has loving compassion for those who render honor to him alone, the God who traverses the path to human beings in order to find there vessels of that honor precisely where human beings are nothing, where they fall silent, where they give space to God alone.

Here the light of eternity falls upon that which is eternally disregarded, the eternally insignificant, the weak, ignoble, unknown, the least of these, the oppressed and despised; here that light radiates out over the houses of the prostitutes and tax collectors—one need only recall Dostoyevsky's Raskolnikov[37]—here that light pours out from eternity upon the working, toiling, sinning masses. The message of grace travels over the dull sultriness of the big cities but remains standing before the houses of those who spiritually speaking are satisfied, knowing, and possessing. It pronounces
317 upon the death of people and nations its eternal: I have loved you from eternity; stay with me, and you will live. Christianity preaches the infinite worth of that which is seemingly worthless and the infinite worthlessness

[37.] Dostoyevsky, *Crime and Punishment*; which also appeared under the title *Raskolnikov*.

of that which is seemingly so valued. What is weak shall become strong through God, and what dies shall live.

Against this understanding of Christianity, something in us rises up in protest, what I would call the Greek spirit, the most severe enemy of Christianity ever: humanism. It is the spirit that we as children of the nineteenth and twentieth centuries have absorbed, as it were, along with our mother's milk. After the Renaissance and the Enlightenment, it reached its high point during the classical period of German literature and philosophy. Born of cultural confidence, it believes in the divine in every human being, in the unlimited potential of the human spirit in the general sense, and in a progressive history moving toward God. The crown of human culture, however, is morality and religion. The moral-religious person (a characteristic combination) is godlike. A divine soul dwells within each human being, and the presence of sin in the world results merely from the subjugation of the soul to the body, a body in which it is trapped as if in a prison.

Such notions are diametrically opposed to Christianity.[38] In the first place, the concept of human beings here is a completely different one. It is not the body that is bad but the will, the spirit; that is, precisely the human soul is bad and is the seat of evil. The assertion of the infinite value of the soul is un-Christian. The New Testament passages that speak of the soul can usually be translated with the term "life." The concept of the soul is Greek; the Jew understands human beings to be a unity of body and spirit that was created by and has fallen away from God. All else derives from this
understanding. Nothing in human beings makes them similar to God; but 318
this assertion again levels criticism at the idea of culture, an idea that is, by the way, specifically Greek and not at all oriental or Semitic. Christianity is neither congenial to culture nor does it have faith in progress. It has peered too deeply into the two deepest realities of life. The trembling fear of death and guilt has seized Christianity too powerfully. The seriousness of having to die and of having to bear guilt—this universal human fate is too frightening to allow any hope in solutions deriving from human initiative. Christians see a terrible rift running through the world, a rift that is utterly irreparable through recourse to any human initiative; and they see this rift—thus the tragedy of their lives—still or even for the first time in its full scope precisely at the heights of human initiative, that is, in culture itself. Greek sensibility understands nothing of such things; from its very

[38.] In this statement Bonhoeffer is clearly distancing himself from Harnack's understanding of the "infinite value of the human soul" (cf. Harnack, *What Is Christianity*, 63–70).

inception, gentle fate blessed it with an undivided joy of life. The naive Greek faith in immortality can be seen in this connection. The divine soul must be eternal. By contrast, Christianity knows nothing of such faith in immortality; in its place, however, it does indeed entertain hope in a resurrection of the dead. Although human beings die in body and soul, the command of the sovereign God calls the dead back to life, to a genuinely new, genuinely pure, holy life. We are led again and again back into the depths of the Christian understanding of God. Wherever the Greek spirit is regnant, the Christian idea of God is not understood.

The religious consequences of the Greek spirit ultimately lead to mysticism. Mysticism and the good news, however, mutually and radically exclude each other. Mysticism is the religious attempt to attain, in various forms, unity with the deity on one's own initiative and based on one's own divine potential. Such unity can be intellectual, voluntaristic, or emotional, but it is in any case un-Christian because it overlooks the humanly unbridgeable gulf between God and human beings, a gulf that remains as that between the creator and the creature even when God does indeed incline toward human beings. Humanism and mysticism, the seemingly most beautiful blossoms put forth by the Christian religion, extolled today as the highest ideals of the human spirit, indeed often as the crown itself of the Christian idea—it is precisely the Christian idea itself that must reject them as an
319 apotheosis of the creature and as such as a challenge to the honor belonging to God alone. The deity of humanism, of the idea of humanity, and of mysticism is the idol of human wishes; only the idea of God presented by Christianity orients those human wishes to itself rather than the reverse.

By turning against ethics and religion and church as human knowledge of God, against humanism and mysticism with their cultural confidence and idolization of creatures, we seem to have robbed humanity of its highest possession. Only in the next session will we be able to show how Christianity gives all this its perfectly limited, relative due once more. The first thing we must do, however, is radically to turn away from all this. What is Christianity's counteroffer? Merely another religion? A new cultural idea? Has it merely pointed out a path to God not yet taken? No, the Christian idea is the path of God to human beings, and its visible manifestation is the cross. At this point, we generally shake our heads and turn away from Christianity. It was Paul, we point out, who first placed the cross into the center of the Christian message; Jesus said nothing of such things. And yet the correct understanding of Christ's cross is nothing more than the most severe intensification of Jesus's own idea of God, the historically visible form, as it were, adopted by that idea. God comes to people who have nothing but space for God, and the language of Christianity calls this void, this

emptiness in human beings "faith."[39] In Jesus of Nazareth, the bearer of God's revelation, God inclines toward the sinner. Jesus seeks the company of sinners, follows them with limitless love; Jesus wants to be where human beings are no longer anything. The meaning of Jesus's life is the documentation of this divine will toward the sinner, toward the unworthy. God's love is wherever Jesus is. This documentation, however, acquires its true seriousness only when Jesus or God's love not only is present where human beings are mired in sin and misery, but when Jesus also takes upon himself that
which stands above every person's life, namely, death; that is, when Jesus, 320
who is God's love, genuinely dies. Only thus can human beings be assured that God's love will accompany and lead them through death. Jesus's death on the cross of the criminal, however, shows that divine love extends even to the death of the criminal, and when Jesus dies on the cross with the cry, "My God, my God, why have you forsaken me?"[40] it shows once more that God's eternal love does not abandon us even when we despair and feel forsaken by God. Jesus genuinely dies despairing in his own work and in God, and yet precisely that situation constitutes the crown of his message; God loves us so much that with us, for us, and as a documentation of that love, God accepts and experiences death itself. And only because Jesus in the humiliation of the cross proves both his own love and God's love does resurrection follow death. Death cannot keep back love; love is stronger than death.[41] The meaning of Good Friday and of Easter Sunday is that God's path to human beings leads back to God. Thus Jesus's idea of God is summed up in Paul's interpretation of the cross; thus the cross becomes the center and the paradoxical emblem of the Christian message. A king who dies on the cross must be the king of a rather strange kingdom. Only those who understand the profound paradox of the cross can also understand the whole meaning of Jesus's assertion: my kingdom is not from this world.[42] Remaining faithful to the idea of God that led him to the cross meant declining the royal crown offered to him and renouncing the idea of the "Imperium Romanum" that tempted him on that path.[43]

This understanding of Christ's cross also answers another urgent question. What are we to make of other religions? Are they nothing compared to Christianity? The answer is that it is not the Christian religion itself that,

[39.] Concerning faith as proceeding from a void, see Barth, *Epistle to the Romans*, 57. [Here Bonhoeffer's critique of religion, in particular of Christianity, echoes Barth's treatment in *Romans* that was further expounded in *Church Dogmatics* 1/2:280–361.—CG]

[40.] Matt. 27:46 par. Mark 15:34; see Ps. 22:1.

[41.] Song of Sol. 8:6.

[42.] John 18:36.

[43.] [Cf. Matt. 4:8–10.—CG]

as a religion, is something divine. It is itself merely one human path toward God, just as is the Buddhist and the other religions, albeit, of course, of a different sort.

321 Christ is not the bringer of a new religion, but the bringer of God. Hence as the impossible path from human beings to God, the Christian religion stands alongside other religions. Christians can never boast of their own Christian religiosity, for it, too, remains humanly all-too-human. Christians do, however, live from God's grace, grace that comes to us and to every person who opens up to it and comes to understand it in Christ's cross. Thus Christ's gift is not the Christian religion but God's grace and love, which culminate in the cross.

And now we must address the question: What does the cross say to *us, today*? Can it replace the ideals of humanism? The cross and the twentieth century is the problem. Here we shift from scholarly concerns to personal concerns. Like the Roman imperial age, our own age thirsts for something ultimate, for substance that transcends all that is customary and banal; it thirsts for redemption. This situation is attested by the youth movement[44] and by phenomena such as sectarianism, mysticism, anthroposophy, the so-called occult sciences, as well as—we hope—by the unquenchable desire of our age for sensation and entertainment. It is a thirst that only becomes more burning with every drink. And now we ask: Is not the expression concerning the transitoriness of all human wishes and concerning the enormous dying in the world written on the brow of our wrecked[45] age. Do not all of us who have a world war behind us, who live in an age of horrific economic competition, an age in which all values and ideals are in decline—do not all of us bear an enormous guilt whose weight threatens to burden us down to the ground? And does the cross have nothing to say to us in this situation, the cross that speaks about the compassionate, revivifying love of God toward those who die and those burdened by guilt? Does looking at the cross of Jesus Christ not open up our gaze far beyond our own age to that time when God will make everything new again? And one more thing: Anthroposophy and mysticism and sectarianism all make claims on people before they get to God that not everyone can fulfill (humanism did this as
322 well). Christianity is completely different in this sense. It requires neither training nor any specialized aptitude for a person to understand the depths of life and of the deity. It requires merely that we acknowledge the exclusive honor due the eternal God and acknowledge our own nothingness before

[44.] [Regarding the youth movement, see 1/5, ed. note 24.—CG]
[45.] Uncertain reading.

God. It speaks of God's grace toward the sins of the big cities, about God's love where misery and guilt accumulate in frightening proportions, where calloused hands perhaps are clenched fists, in defiance of fate. You, human being, no matter who you are, you are God's child, you are included in God's love, out of the pure, incomprehensible grace of God; accept this word, believe in it, trust in his rule rather than in yourself or in your own party, rather than in your own work or your own religion. God does as he wills. Turn your misery into God's blessed presence, and from within your guilt and distress hear the voice of the eternal, living God.

It is said that before the battle that ultimately brought him victory and established his rule, the Emperor Constantine saw the sign of the cross emblazoned across the heavens with the words ἐν τούτῳ νικᾷς . . .[46] Spiritual battles of unusual proportions are taking place among our people [Volk]; the birth of modernity is accompanied by severe labor pains; our age senses this, but the moment of decision is nearing. Will we conquer what is oppressing us, our fate, or will we be defeated? Will the twentieth century be the hour of death for Europe and Germany? Let us point to one thing here, to the sign of the cross. The God of the world will incline toward us, we who are dust before God, if we but accord honor to God alone, if we but entrust ourselves to God alone. God will cause grace and compassion to radiate over the dark guilt of our century and the human race; God will enter into our time, live with us, for us, even unto death, taking the path to human beings all the way to the cross.

German people [Volk], that is your God, the God who formed you and will abide with you. In your struggles with fate, keep your eyes on the cross, the most wonderful emblem of your God, and be assured that only in this sign will you be victorious!

3. Basic Questions of a Christian Ethic[1] 323

Basic Questions of a Christian Ethic

In speaking today about basic questions of a Christian ethic, we do not intend to embark on the essentially hopeless attempt to present universally valid Christian norms and commandments applicable to contemporary

---

[46.] "In this sign you will be victorious"; see Eusebius, *Life of Constantine*, 1.28, *Nicene and Post-Nicene Fathers*, 2nd ser., 1:490.

[1.] *NL*, A 22,3 a; handwritten with a handwritten remark by Bethge: "postponed till February 8, 1929" and "Friday, Barcelona." See also *NL*, A 22,3 b; later typewritten copy.

ethical questions. We intend instead merely to examine and to participate in the peculiar movement of ethical problems in today's world from the perspective of basic Christian ideas. The deepest reason why we confine ourselves in this manner is that, as we will see in greater depth later, there are not and cannot be Christian norms and principles of a moral nature. Only in the actual execution of a given action do the concepts of "good" and "bad" apply, that is, only in the given present moment; hence any attempt to explicate principles is like trying to draw a bird in flight.[2] But more on that later.

Ethics is a matter of blood and a matter of history. It did not simply descend to earth from heaven. Rather, it is a child of the earth, and for that reason its face changes with history as well as with the renewal of blood, with the transition between generations. There is a German ethic as well as a French ethic and an American ethic. None is more or less ethical than the other, for all remain bound to history and all are [. . .][3] decisively influenced today by the terrible experience of the world war and by how that war
324 is viewed from various perspectives. The only common feature is that this experience has stirred up the depths of the people's [Volk] soul and that now things are everywhere emerging that have hitherto gone unnoticed and have remained concealed in the depths of the sea. In Germany the experience of war was joined by the experience of revolution, and the one absolutely unmistakable result seems to be that these historical events have prompted a hitherto unprecedented revolution in morals. If I see it correctly, we can distinguish four groups of people in working Germany today, each of which has arrived at a different ethical ideology through recent historical developments. The first are those whose years of development and maturation lie before the beginning of the war; then those whom sooner or later the war itself brought to maturity; then the generation of youth associated with the revolution, those whose awakening and development took place between 1918 and, say, 1923; and finally, let us not forget those to whom the future belongs, those who know war and revolution only from

---

Previously published in *GS* 5:156–80; excerpt in *GS* 3:48–55. The attendees E. and H. von Wild recalled a "solid, riveting presentation . . . carried by the warmth of personal conviction" (*NL*, C 22, February 9, 1929). See also the letters to his parents of January 28 and February 6, 1929, 1/69 and 1/70. Regarding the ideas addressed by the lecture, see also the ed. notes in 3/19; see *DB-ER*, 118–20, and Heinz Eduard Tödt, "Discrimination against Jews in 1933," in Tödt, *Authentic Faith*, 73–112, esp. 79–82.

[2.] Concerning the metaphor of a "bird in flight," see Barth's Tambach lecture of 1919, "The Christian's Place in Society," 282.

[3.] Illegible.

hearsay and who are now eighteen to twenty years old. Hence the rapid sequence of events spanning fewer than twenty years has produced four spiritual or intellectual [geistige] generations, and if we are to understand the unprecedented confusion with regard to the ethical problems in their broadest scope within contemporary Germany, we must constantly keep in mind that not two, but four different generations are now struggling with one another.[4]

The significance of the revolutionary year 1918 only marginally derives from the political turn in Germany's history. The enormous intellectual revolution that erupted and in which we still find ourselves has had incomparably greater consequences. It would be difficult to find a period in history that has experienced as radical a change in, say, literature as has the period between 1910 and approximately 1925. All that seemed solid has become soft, all that seemed certain has become uncertain, all that seemed self-evident has become questionable—politically, literarily, philosophically, ethically. This onslaught began and was carried and enthusiastically 325
received by young people. Despite the unmistakable fact that unprincipled circles exploited and debased the excitement and lack of clarity of these spirits, one can reasonably say that the deepest foundation of this intellectual movement was a genuine and sincere idealism. The central idea emerging again and again from all this literature is that of truth. The intent is to mount an assault on a culture that in the broader sense has become inwardly untrue, and in so doing to break the bonds that fetter truth. This is what one hears everywhere. Unless one insists on remaining utterly skeptical, this intent does guarantee the profoundly ethical character of the movement.

Consider the so-called belles lettres as but one example. Without a shadow of a doubt, never before in all of world history have so many and such crudely obscene things been written or been brought to the stage as they have today. Equally certain is that a great many authors as well as readers and spectators seek nothing more in such material than to satisfy their own derailed imagination. And yet it would be unfair for us to present this as our final judgment. Rather, it is a matter of the aforementioned need to confront the various aspects of life honestly, truthfully, even if such things offend public morals. An almost naive idealism permeates this literary

[4.] The generational problem as a specifically German problem following World War I still informs the presentation "The Leader and the Individual in the Young Generation" in March 1933 (*DBW* 12, 2/9; *NRS*, 190–204).

genre; at the same time, though, we cannot deny the presence of an ethical concern within the overall undertaking, even if we believe it to be moving in the wrong direction.[5]

The same seems to apply to the youth problem. The freedom of youth in so many aspects of life, a freedom the prewar generation naturally finds almost incomprehensible, is based on the desire of youth to avoid imposing unsuitable fetters on its life merely because the previous generation may
326 have borne such fetters. And what seems to overstep the mark can often be attributed simply to the previously mentioned naive idealism. I am not even remotely suggesting, however, that everything in Germany today looks wonderful and full of hope. Quite the contrary. This movement has stirred up so much filth along the way that we can now hardly see through the murky waters.

That the contemporary ethical will also assumes such forms today is profoundly disturbing, and this should be taken seriously, since, truth be told, we are indeed still far from finding solutions to the problems that confront us. But the situation is this, that there is a will toward new ethical formation and fullness of life, and the only thing lacking is the correct point of departure. Our task, no more and no less, should be the attempt to show this point of departure.

We said earlier that there is a German, an American, and a French ethic, since ethics is a matter of blood and history. But what about the idea of a so-called Christian ethic? Are these two words not perhaps intrinsically utterly incompatible, "Christian" and "ethic"? Does such a combination not secularize the idea of what is Christian? Does the so-called Christian ethic not thereby become merely one alongside others, one of many, perhaps a bit better or even a bit worse, but in any case now drawn wholly into historical relativity? If so, then alongside the German ethic there is also a Christian ethic, without either being in a position to claim superiority.

Hence talking about a Christian ethic while at the same time maintaining the exclusive claim of such an ethic will apparently be an extremely awkward undertaking.

During the previous lecture, we encountered an assertion that was perhaps not yet entirely clear, namely, that Christianity is basically amoral, that Christianity and ethics represent two entities that at first are not entirely compatible and in fact are quite disparate.[6] And why? Because Christianity

[5.] The period Bonhoeffer is criticizing here (1910–25) coincides with the period known as "expressionism" in German literature, which included authors such as Trakl, Lasker-Schüler, Benn, and others, whom Bonhoeffer avoided reading his entire life.

[6.] See p. 354.

speaks of the exclusive path from God to human beings from within God's own compassionate love toward the unholy, the sinful, while ethics speaks
of the path from human beings to God, about the encounter between the 327
holy God and the holy human being; in other words, because the Christian message speaks of grace while ethics speaks of righteousness.

Because there are innumerable human paths to God, there are also innumerable ethics. But there is but one path from God to human beings, and that is the path of love in Christ, the path of the cross, as we saw during the last session.[7]

The question of Christianity is not the question of good and evil among people but the question whether God wishes to be gracious or not. The Christian message stands beyond good and evil,[8] and this is how it must be; for if God's grace is made dependent on human beings according to the categories of good and evil, this would constitute a human claim on God. This, however, would challenge the power and honor due exclusively to God.

One particularly profound feature of the old story of the fall is that it was caused by eating from the tree of the knowledge of good and evil.[9] The primal—let us say, childlike—community between human beings and God stands beyond this knowledge of good and evil; it knows only one thing: God's limitless love for human beings.

Hence the discovery of the world beyond good and evil is by no means to be attributed to the enemy of Christianity Friedrich Nietzsche, whose polemic against the self-righteousness of Christianity derived from this perspective. It belongs rather to the original, albeit concealed material of the Christian message.

If our line of argument is correct to this point, then the conclusion seems quite clear. Christianity and ethics have absolutely nothing to do with each other. There is no Christian ethic. From the idea of Christianity, there is absolutely no transition to the idea of ethics. And yet this line of reasoning clearly leads us off track. We simply must raise the question: Why, then, are all the Gospels and the entire New Testament nonetheless full of obviously ethical regulations? What is the Sermon on the Mount doing in the New Testament?

The question is as obvious as it is serious. What is the meaning of the so- 328
called New Testament ethic?

[7.] See p. 356 above.

[8.] Cf. Nietzsche, *Beyond Good and Evil.*

[9.] Gen. 3.

Since the third and fourth centuries, numerous movements have arisen presenting the proclamation of a new ethic as the center of Christianity; the new commandment, of course, was the commandment of love.[10] Such a view, though doubtless extremely shallow, was possible and even tenable into the nineteenth century. Since then, however, history-of-religions research and literary scholarship have thoroughly examined the rabbinic literature both contemporary with and prior to the time of Jesus as well as the contemporaneous philosophical-ethical tractates of the philosophical schools in the West. The results clearly show that such statements about the New Testament are demonstrably false. Rather than being something specifically or uniquely Christian, the commandment of love was already widely acknowledged and familiar at the time of Jesus.

The first thing we should notice is that the Synoptic Gospels very rarely mention it. We are all familiar with the passage in which Jesus is asked about the highest commandment and offers the twofold response, "'You shall love the Lord your God with all your heart, and with all your soul, and with all your mind.' . . . And a second is like it: 'You shall love your neighbor as yourself.'"[11] We also recall Jesus's words concerning love of one's enemies: "Love your enemies, bless those who curse you, do good to those who hate you and pray for those who persecute you, so that you may be children of your Father in heaven; for he makes his sun rise on the evil and on the good, and sends rain on the righteous and on the unrighteous. For if you love those who love you, what reward do you have? Do not even the tax collectors do the same?"[12] If the proclamation of this particular commandment really had been the focal point of Jesus's whole ministry, he would have commenced at precisely this point ever anew. But he did not. This same conclusion emerges with unequivocal clarity from a comparison
329 of the words of Jesus with those of Jewish rabbis and pagan philosophers, which often resemble one another even in their wording. When asked what the highest commandment is, Rabbi Hillel responded: "Love your neighbor as yourself. That is the highest commandment." Another advised: "What you would not want to happen to yourself, do not to others." The Roman philosopher Seneca urged us "not to tire of working for the common good,

[10.] Bonhoeffer is probably referring to the Novatians (third century) and the Donatists (fourth century) in the ancient church. The commandment of love as a new commandment, however, better fits the Marcionites (second century), the subject of the last great work of Bonhoeffer's teacher Adolf von Harnack; see Harnack, *Marcion*, esp. "The Redeemer God as the Good God," pp. 81–92.

[11.] Matt. 22:37–39.

[12.] Matt. 5:44–46 [The translation here of Bonhoeffer's text varies from the NRSV.—CG]

of helping individuals, and of providing help even to our enemies." To the objection, "But anger gives us a release! Requiting pain refreshes us!" he responds, "No; it is honorable in the case of good deeds to repay good with good, but not injustice with injustice. It is despicable to allow oneself to be conquered in the first instance and despicable to conquer in the second."[13]

But what is now left of a Christian ethic? Does the Sermon on the Mount really have nothing new to say to us? It has nothing "new" in the sense of new demands, but it does have something completely different to offer. The significance of all of Jesus's ethical commandments is rather to say to people: You stand before the face of God, God's grace rules over you; but you are at the disposal of someone else in the world. You must act and behave such that in each of your actions you are mindful of also acting before God, mindful that God has a certain will and wants to see that will done. Each particular moment will reveal the nature of that will. You must merely be perfectly clear that your own will must in every instance be accommodated to the divine will; your will must be surrendered if the divine will is to be realized. Hence to the extent that acting before God requires utter renunciation of personal demands and claims from us, Christian ethical acts can be characterized as love. This assertion is not a new principle, however, but derives rather from the status of human beings before God. There are no ethical principles enabling Christians, as it were, to make themselves moral. Instead, one has only the decisive moment at hand, that is, every moment 330
that is of potential ethical value.[14] Never, however, can yesterday decisively influence my moral actions today. I must rather always establish anew my immediate relationship with God's will. I will do something again today not because it seemed the right thing to do yesterday, but because today, too, God's will has pointed me in that direction.

This ongoing relationship to God's will is the great moral renewal Jesus brought about, the dismissal of principles, of fundamental rules—in biblical terms, the law. And precisely this dismissal is a consequence of the Christian idea of God. For if there were indeed a universally valid moral law, following it would involve taking the path from human beings to God. If I have principles, I feel I am secured *sub specie aeternitatis.*[15] In that case, I would control my own relationship with God, as it were, and there could

[13.] Here Bonhoeffer is drawing on work he did during his university years, esp. his seminar paper on *1 Clement*, concerning Hillel, see *DBWE* 9 (2/4), p. 245, ed. note 207; Seneca, *Dialogues* 8: *De Otio* 1.4 (*Moral Essays*, 2:180–201); *Dialogues* 4: *De Ira* 2.32.1 (*Moral Essays*, 1:106–355).

[14.] [Cf. this idea in *Sanctorum Communio*, *DBWE* 1:48–49.—CG]

[15.] ["Under the aspect of eternity."—CG]

be ethical action without any immediate relationship with God. But the most important aspect is that I would then become a slave to my principles and would be surrendering the most precious human possession, my freedom. When Jesus places people immediately under God, new and afresh at each moment, he restores to humanity the immense gift that it had lost, freedom.

Christian ethical action is action out of freedom, out of the freedom of those who have nothing in themselves and everything in their God, those who ever anew have their actions confirmed and reinforced by eternity. The New Testament speaks of this freedom in great words. "Now the Lord is the Spirit, and where the Spirit of the Lord is, there is freedom."[16] John says that "if you continue in my word, you are truly my disciples; and you will know the truth, and the truth will make you free. . . . So if the Son makes you free, you will be free indeed."[17] Or, "The creation itself will be set free from its bondage to decay and will obtain the freedom of the glory of the children of God."[18] Or, "For freedom Christ has set us free. Stand firm,
331 therefore, and do not submit again to a yoke of slavery."[19] We could cite many more examples. Christ is the bringer of the freedom to become free from the world, free for eternity. There is now no other law for Christians except the law of freedom, as the New Testament puts it paradoxically,[20] not a universally valid law imposed by others or even by themselves. Those who surrender their freedom also surrender their status as Christians. Christians stand in freedom, without any backing, before both God and the world; they alone bear the entire responsibility for how they will deal with this gift of freedom. Through precisely this freedom, however, Christians become creative in their ethical actions. Acting according to principles is unproductive and merely reflects or copies the law. Acting in freedom is creative. Christians draw the forms of their ethical activity out of eternity itself, as it were, put these forms with sovereignty in the world, as deed, as their own creations born of the freedom of God's children. Christians create their own standards for good and evil; only Christians themselves provide the justification for their acts, just as they alone bear responsibility for them. Christians create new tables, new decalogues, as Nietzsche said of the Overman. Indeed, Nietzsche's Overman is not, as he imagined, the opposite of the Christian; without realizing it, Nietzsche imbued the Over-

---

[16.] 2 Cor. 3:17.

[17.] John 8:31b–32, 36.

[18.] Rom. 8:20–21.

[19.] Gal. 5:1.

[20.] Cf. James 1:25, 2:12.

man with many of the features of the free Christian as described and conceived by both Paul and Luther. Traditional morals—even if propagated for Christians—or public opinion can never provide the standards for the action of Christians.[21]

Christians act according to how God's will seems to direct them, without looking sideways at others, that is, without considering what is usually called morals. No one but Christians and God, however, can know whether they are indeed acting rightly or wrongly. Ethical decisions lead us into the most profound solitude, the solitude in which a person stands before the living 332
God. Here no one can help us, no one can bear part of the responsibility; here God imposes a burden on us that we must bear alone. Only in the realization that we have been addressed by God, that God is making a claim on us, does our self [Ich] awaken. Only through God's call do I become this "self," isolated from all other people, called to account by God, confronted, alone, by eternity. And precisely because I am face to face with God in this solitude, I alone can know what is right or wrong for me personally.

There are no acts that are bad in and of themselves; even murder can be sanctified. There is only faithfulness to or deviation from God's will. There is no law with a specific content, but only the law of freedom, that is, bearing responsibility alone before God and oneself.

The law has been overcome once and for all. It follows from the Christian idea of God that there can be no more law. It is from this same perspective that we must thus understand the ethical commandments and apparent laws we find in the New Testament itself.

It is the most serious misunderstanding to turn the commandments of the Sermon on the Mount once again into a law by applying them literally to the present. Not only is such transference meaningless because impracticable, it also goes against the spirit of Christ, who brought freedom from the law. The whole life of someone like Count Tolstoy, and many others beside him, was based on this misunderstanding.[22] The New Testament

---

[21.] See Nietzsche, *Thus Spoke Zarathustra*, "On Old and New Tablets" of the law, esp. 3–4 (Kaufmann, *Portable Nietzsche*, 310–11). With regard to Luther, Bonhoeffer is drawing on what he learned from Karl Holl; see *DBWE* 9 (2/10), p. 346, ed. notes 115–16, and Holl, *Reconstruction of Morality*, 85. The Holl school, which Bonhoeffer is following here, overinterpreted Luther's unusual discussion of the "new decalogues" (*LW* 34:112); cf. Martin Brecht, *Martin Luther*, 2:165–66 and 2:285.

[22.] Cf. Holl, "Tolstoi nach seinen Tagebüchern": "no leader for us, no one who might show us the way out of the confusion of the present into the open, into the future" (449). Concerning the discussion of Tolstoy, see Max Weber's 1919 lecture "Politics as a Vocation"; concerning the shift in Bonhoeffer's criticism in *Discipleship*, see the editors' afterword to *DBWE* 4:289–94.

contains no ethical prescription that we are supposed to adopt literally or even that we could so adopt. The letter kills, but the Spirit gives life, as Paul put it in a familiar passage,[23] meaning that the Spirit is found only in the
333 execution of actions, in the present; a fixed Spirit is no Spirit at all. Hence ethics is found only in the execution of a deed, not in the letter, that is, in the law. The Spirit that is indeed at work in our own ethical actions, however, is to be the Holy Spirit. The Holy Spirit is found only in the present, in ethical decision, not in fixed moral regulations or in an ethical principle. Hence Jesus's new commandments can never be taken as new ethical principles; they are to be understood in their spirit, not in their letter. Nor is this view merely an excuse to avoid an otherwise uncomfortable situation; the idea of freedom and the concept of God that Jesus articulated demand it. The familiar radical edge that Jesus's demands have acquired derives from the radical renunciation of one's own person and one's own will that is required of Christians in ethical decision before God. But not every one of Jesus's behavioral rules is valid for us; merely imitating them would be slavish and unfree.

From all these considerations it follows that one absolutely cannot speak about specific ethical problems from the Christian perspective. There is absolutely no possibility for establishing universally valid principles, since each individual moment lived before God can confront us with completely unexpected decisions. Hence for our own age, too, we can only repeat that we must put ourselves under God's will when making ethical decisions and consider our actions *sub specie aeternitatis*;[24] then regardless of how things go, they will go correctly.

From day to day and from hour to hour, however, we are confronted by utterly new situations in which we are supposed to make decisions and in which we repeatedly have the surprising and terrifying experience that God's will as a matter of fact does not reveal itself to us as clearly as we might have hoped. Because God's will seems to contradict itself, because two of God's orders [Ordnungen] seem to conflict, we find ourselves in a position of having to choose not between good and evil but between evil and evil.[25]
334 It is here that we encounter the real, most difficult problems of ethics. And

[23.] 2 Cor. 3:6.

[24.] ["Under the aspect of eternity."—CG]

[25.] Unclear. Bonhoeffer is presumably referring to the "order of creation" and the "order of preservation." See this related passage in *Creation and Fall* (*DBWE* 3:139–40): "The Creator is now the preserver; the created world is now the fallen but *preserved* world. . . . Humankind remains between tob and ra, remains split." ["tob and ra": Hebrew for "good and evil."—CG] After 1932, when the concept of the "order of creation" moved one-sidedly toward a nationalistic discussion of the separateness and differences between

in the following discussion what we have just said should make it clear that we will not be able to present any universally valid decisions that might be designated as uniquely Christian; to do so would merely be to present new principles, bringing us into conflict with the law of freedom. All we can do is examine the concrete situation of decision and point out one of the possibilities for decision that emerges there. The decision demanded in reality, however, must be made in freedom in the concrete situation by the individual involved.

There is one set of problems that is never settled, since it suffers from the internal contradictions of two divine orders [Ordnungen]. The first general question involves the relationship between historical development[26] and the divine commandment of love. Here the problem of national expansion, growth, war, and the struggle of economic competition unfolds before us. The second question involves the relation between love and truth, love and righteousness, both of whose origin we seek in God; this question in its own turn involves the questions of social forms and of the administration of justice. And finally the question that is more burning than any other today: the problem "nature and spirit," whose common origin again is God; or, more precisely, the problem of sexuality.[27]

The difficulty in solving these problems is that of finding a hierarchy in the divine orders [Ordnungen]. With what right do I put the commandment of love above that of truth, or vice versa? We again find a point of 335
departure in the Christian idea of God, that is, by making our decision in immediate relationship with God's will, rather than isolated from God. In every instance the idea of the cross, as the example of God's love actualized even unto death, determines our actions, since it places divine love above all other characteristics of God. Now, the possibility always exists that the

---

peoples, Bonhoeffer moved away from the concept. See *DBW* 11:323–25, partial translation in *NRS* 179–80; see also Martin Rüter and Ilse Tödt in the editors' afterword to *Creation and Fall* (*DBWE* 3:148–49). [Another reading of "two of God's orders seem to conflict" would be to understand the orders as church and state or people (*Volk*, see p. 371 below) the one preaching peace and love of enemy, the other legitimating war and destructive economic competition, as discussed by Bonhoeffer below; see below on "two divine orders," and also p. 375, conflict between divine orders in the world. "Order of creation" and "order of preservation" are alternate conceptualities and do not entail an ethical choice "between evil and evil."—CG]

[26.] [By "historical development" Bonhoeffer means political-social changes, especially as seen in social, economic, political, and national conflicts mentioned in the following sentence.—CG]

[27.] Concerning this topic, see Althaus, *Religiöser Sozialismus*, esp. chap. 4, "Die Idee der Gerechtigkeit und das Leben." [On "nature and spirit," see Green, *Bonhoeffer*, 197–99, 325–26, and note 98.—CG]

commandment of love itself might seem self-contradictory; here we encounter that particular problem that has been discussed again and again, the problem of war. During the war and after the war, we heard, and we are still hearing, that the entire weakness and wretchedness of Christianity, its churches and followers, was revealed in the inability to prevent the war; even more, it is said that if Christians really wanted to be true Christians, they would resolutely have refused to serve in the war. Just as various Christian sects indeed paid for their Christian position by going to prison, so also would it be the duty of those who seriously call themselves Christians to accept the most horrible punishments rather than go to war. For it is clearly written: You shall not kill; you shall not requite evil with evil; rather if anyone strikes you on the right cheek, turn the other also; and if anyone wants to sue you and take your coat, give your cloak as well; and if anyone forces you to go one mile, go also the second mile.[28] You have heard that it was said to those of ancient times, You shall not murder; and whoever murders shall be liable to judgment. But I say to you that if you are angry with a brother, you will be liable to judgment.[29] You have heard that it was said that you should love your neighbor and hate your enemy. But I say to you, Love your enemies and pray for those who persecute you, so that you may be children of your Father in heaven.[30] For what will it profit them if they gain the whole world but forfeit their souls?[31] Thus do we find it clearly and unequivocally stated in the New Testament, and no amount of
336 quibbling will help: You shall not resist against evil; you shall not kill.

And now one dares to justify war somehow from the Christian perspective? Now millions of Christian men go to war, and not just because they are compelled, but presenting it as God's will? They hold services of worship in the field and dare drag God and the holy name of Jesus Christ into this horrific murder? War is nothing but murder. War is a crime. No Christian can go to war. This case for this seems entirely clear and convincing, yet it suffers at the central issue: it is not concrete and as a result does not look into the depths of Christian decision. It invokes the commandment not to kill and believes that commandment to be the solution.

Here, however, we are overlooking the decisive dilemma that precisely when my own people [Volk] are attacked, the commandment of love does extend at least as far as defending them as it does to the commandment not to kill one's enemy. It would be an utter perversion of one's ethical sensibil-

---

[28.] Matt. 5:39–41.

[29.] Matt. 5:21–22.

[30.] Matt. 5:43–45.

[31.] Matt. 16:26. [NRSV translation altered here.—CG]

ity to believe that my first duty is to love my enemy and precisely in so doing to surrender my neighbor to destruction, in the most concrete sense. It is simply not possible to love or, as the case may be, to protect both my enemy and my people. I am confronted by the concrete situation of surrendering to destruction either my brother or my enemy. I am put in this dilemma at the very moment when war is declared against me, that is, when I either go to war or do not go to war. If out of conviction I do not go, then I am leaving my people in the lurch in their hour of distress, and am doing so by citing Christ, who said to me love your neighbor as yourself, which doubtless means love your neighbor more than your fearful conscience, love your neighbor first and foremost; what then follows is a secondary question.

Indeed, is not my enemy just as much my neighbor as is my biological brother? Is not the great deed of Christianity precisely that it leveled these distinctions, through the powerful notion of universal brotherhood? Although this is doubtless the case, these questions derive from a consid- 337
eration of principles rather than from the concrete situation. If ever I find myself in the distressing situation of having to decide whether to expose my biological brother, my biological mother, to the hand of the attacker, or to raise my own hand against the enemy, then the moment itself will doubtless tell me which of these two is and must be my neighbor, including before the eyes of God. God gave me my mother, my people [Volk]. For what I have, I thank my people; what I am, I am through my people, and so what I have should also belong to my people; that is in the divine order [Ordnung] of things, for God created the peoples. If for a single dangerous moment I do not act, then I am doing nothing other than surrendering my neighbors.[32]

And now one more thing. Christians who go to war will not hate their enemy, since they cannot hate in any case. In battle they will still pray for their enemies and for their souls when they deliver their bodies to death

[32.] Discussing the situation of Christians in times of war, before a German congregation in a foreign county, Bonhoeffer comes closer than anywhere else to the views of the nationalist Protestantism of his era, and in so doing becomes entangled in a contradiction. Allegedly only the moment itself, the concrete situation, can determine which decision a person should make. Nonetheless Bonhoeffer relates the decision to a criterion that transcends the situation, namely, ties to one's own people (*Volk*), as a divine order. In times of war, when one's own blood relatives are threatened, these ties cause the Christian notion of love of one's neighbor, and the extension of that commandment to include all people, to recede: "Love for my people will sanctify murder, will sanctify war" (see p. 372). This development corresponded to the prevalent thinking of Protestant theology and proclamation between the world wars and was susceptible to *völkisch* thinking and thereby National Socialist thinking. At the Königsberg church meeting (*Kirchentag*) in the summer of 1927, Paul Althaus, for example, presented a widely accepted argument

and will still bless those enemies when they themselves, the Christians, are mortally wounded by them. For those enemies are in the same distress as are the Christians themselves; the enemies, too, are defending their mothers, their children, their people.

338 The situation seems clear to me. In such cases, I no longer have the choice between good and evil; regardless of which decision I make, that decision will soil me with the world and its laws. I will take up arms with the terrible knowledge of doing something horrible, and yet knowing I can do no other. I will defend my brother, my mother, my people, and yet I know that I can do so only by spilling blood; but love for my people will sanctify murder, will sanctify war.[33] As a Christian, I will suffer from the entire dreadfulness of war. My soul will bear the entire burden of responsibility in its full gravity. I will try to love my enemies against whom I am sworn to the death, as only Christians can love their brothers. And yet I will have to do to those enemies what my love and gratitude toward my own people commands me to do, the people into whom God bore me. And finally I will recognize that Christian decisions are made only within the ongoing relationship with God, within a constantly renewed surrender of oneself to the divine will. I can rest assured that even if the world does violence to my conscience, I can make only one decision, namely, the one to which God leads me in the sacred hour of encounter between my will and God's will, in the hour in which God conquers my will.

If we examine once more the argumentation of the other party, we find the decisive point is that they make the New Testament commandments into new laws and in so doing enslave themselves to those laws, whereas they should be making decisions in freedom. They judge according to the letter rather than according to the spirit of Christ. They act according to principles rather than from the concrete situation of crisis with which God confronts me. Sparks, however, are not created in empty space; sparks are created when hard stones strike against each other. The sparks of the Holy Spirit flash not in ideas and principles but in the necessary decision of the moment.

---

in favor of such "nationalist-popular [*Volkstum*] theology" in his lecture "Kirche und Volkstum" (see Althaus, *Evangelium und Leben*, 113–43). As documented during his stay in America beginning in September 1930, Bonhoeffer soon abandoned this nationalist-popular theology as well as its ethics of war and instead was inspired by the Sermon on the Mount to develop a Christian, ecumenical peace ethic. [By the early 1930s, Bonhoeffer was openly critiquing theologians like Althaus and Emanuel Hirsch and the influence of *völkisch* ideology on their theology; see Jørgen Glenthøj, "Bonhoeffer und die Ökumene," in *Mündige Welt*, 2:129 and 140–41.—CG]

[33.] See ed. note 32; concerning the problem of war, see *DBWE* 1:118–19.

Admittedly, this discussion does not yet exhaust the problem of war. One 339
might also ask whether war can be justified from the Christian ethical perspective when one starts the war oneself. This question, however, leads back to a broader problem, to the question of the relation between history and God, people and God, growth and God. Peoples [Völker] are like individuals. At first they are immature and need guidance. Then they grow into the blossom of youth, mature into adults, and die. This situation is neither good nor bad in and of itself, yet profound questions are concealed here. For growth involves expansion; an increase in strength involves pushing aside other individuals. In that respect the life of an individual person is no different than that of a people. Every people, however, has within itself a call from God to create its history, to enter into the struggle that is the life of nations.[34] This call must be heeded amid the growth and development so that it takes place before the face of God. God calls a people to diversity, to struggle, to victory. Strength also comes from God, and power, and victory, for God creates youth in the individual as well as in nations, and God loves youth, for God himself is eternally young and strong and victorious. And fear and weakness will be conquered by courage and strength. Now, should a people experiencing God's call in its own life, in its own youth, and in its own strength, should not such a people also be allowed to follow that call even if it disregards the lives of other peoples? God is the Lord of history; and if a people bends in humility to this holy will guiding history, then with God in its youth and strength it can overcome the weak and disheartened.
Then God will be with it. The determination as to when this moment has 340
arrived for a people can and may only be made by human beings who are conscious of the grave responsibility for what they do, surrendering their own selfish will to the divine will that guides world history.

The same applies to the individual. If our own intellectual growth, our own intellectual youth, our own power leads us beyond others, that is, if through God's actions with us we find ourselves inwardly prompted to

[34.] See *Sanctorum Communio* (*DBWE* 1:119): "*Where peoples are called, God's will for their purpose in history is at work.*" See also *DB-ER*, 119–20, and Feil, *Die Theologie Dietrich Bonhoeffers*, 248–50 [the English translation, *Theology of Dietrich Bonhoeffer*, 113, abbreviates—CG]. The notion that God "calls" peoples, a notion variously expressed in the Old Testament, was a means of countering the humiliation and distressing situation of the German people after their loss in World War I. The peace terms were perceived with deep indignation as a means for the victorious powers to "push aside" the German people. The distress of one's own people became a predominant theme, as shown, e.g., in literature by the thoroughly popular 1926 novel by Hans Grimm, *Volk ohne Raum*. With this statement, Bonhoeffer, too, tries to counter this depressing mood and in so doing adopts categories widespread especially among Germans living in foreign countries.

separate from a friend, there is no room for sentimentality. God wants us courageously to resolve to go beyond the other even if by moving beyond the other person we hurt that person. For God wills strength of life, not anxiety. And it is God who will find a way of amply healing the wounds he inflicts through us, that we inflict for his sake. This is the Christian criticism of the assertion—an assertion so often understood in the manner of the petit bourgeois—concerning faithfulness and gratitude and love. Live from God and you will live strongly, and even if you do not notice it, you will live from love.

History and love, two entities born of God and yet apparently not always reconcilable in this world, only reach their synthesis in eternity.[35] The history of our life—and our life ought to have a history if it is to be something other than a divine life—often takes us down paths seemingly at odds with love; but if we remain on this path with God, we will also always remain on the path of love.

The problem of history, however, conceals yet another question of great importance today, namely, how one is to judge contemporary economic life ethically. Perhaps some of us are already familiar with Friedrich Naumann's *Briefe über Religion*[36] in which he speaks almost despairingly about this problem, suggesting that Christian ethics leaves us completely in the lurch here.[37] Such might be the case, however, only if one understands Chris-
341 tian ethics as individual commandments and laws, something inapplicable in this case. If by contrast we understand Christian ethics to be rooted in responsibility before God, such an ethic will never fail us. Put briefly, the situation is the following. We find ourselves today in an economic and business climate in which smaller parties must be ruined by the larger ones, and in which we ourselves, if we are to participate in economic life, are compelled to be part of all this. Can a Christian responsibly be a businessperson in this sense? We often hear of a double morality, one for personal life and one for business. But this assertion is obviously impossible because we have but *one* conscience, which we must obey in all situations. The question is merely whether with this *one* conscience we can also be business people. The first consideration is that the way things are, our economic and business life is indispensable to our people; moreover, Christians are obliged to do what they can for the welfare of their neighbors, that is, to

[35.] See ed. note 25.

[36.] ["Letters on Religion."—CG]

[37.] Naumann, *Briefe über Religion*, 61–63 and 75: "[A]s soon as we say we have only the principle of love, we can never be free before God and the world to do something that seems harsh. Doing things that are harsh, however, is sometimes necessary for the sake of life itself." Cf. *DB-ER*, 119–20.

become engaged wherever there is something to be done. The question is merely whether they are serving some broader purpose with their business lives. If so, then here, too, one is choosing not between *good* and *evil*; rather, what is recognized as the good, right decision also leads us to engage in harsh actions strongly resembling evil ones. Precisely here, too, we end up in distressing situations that require the ever-renewed relationship with the divine will. In such cases Christians will find ways to help, if such help is possible, even when ruining someone else in business. And if they can no longer help, they will go silent in reverential, humble astonishment before God's strange ways with humanity and pray: Give us all this day our daily bread.[38]

We are living in a strange world, and yet we do want to be Christians. Fleeing that world does not help; the only thing that helps is entering this complicated reality fully conscious and fully trusting that, as long as we abide with God, he will also guide us through this world. And the more 342
deeply we look into this odd life of the world, the more deeply we understand that it is apparently only through evil that good is realized, the more we are astonished at how the divine orders [Ordnungen] of the world permeate and contradict one another—then all the more deeply will our souls sigh: rescue us from evil, do not bring us into temptation, your kingdom come.[39]

It is easier to address the problem of truth and love. It confronts us with the questions of life in society, the questions of conventional lies and white lies. I believe too much moral indignation has arisen and still arises about the so-called conventional lies. In direct address and other forms of social intercourse, the so-called conventional lie does not really constitute a lie as long as the person uses the socially established form, a form that will not cause misunderstanding among those to whom it is directed about the actual opinion of the person using it. No one will assume that the familiar forms of address mean something different, and thus there are, it seems to me, really no ethical objections for Christians in normal social intercourse. The case of the white lie has also been amply discussed, and it does indeed offer an extraordinarily peculiar example of how love and truth can come into conflict. As long as the white lie serves purely personal interests, it is, as a lie, simply unethical. But if a serious conflict with the commandment of love arises—something that does, however, happen more rarely than one might believe—then truth must genuinely be violated by love. This situation is indeed wholly peculiar and directs us again to a time to come, when

[38.] See Matt. 6:11.

[39.] See Matt. 6:13, 10.

all these interrelationships may be clearer to us. In any case, the apparent conflict seems to obtain more in our own incapacity to articulate truth in a loving fashion and thus does not seem to be an absolute conflict.

By far the most turbulent and difficult problem today is the sexual question. The generally increasing value given to the physical—for example, in
343 sports—has also prompted us to concede new rights to the body. Nature originates in God no less than does spirit, perhaps even more immediately.[40] This realization, doubtless a genuinely Christian one, begins to sink in, and leads to the charge to grant to nature what it demands, if indeed it is divine. The seriousness of this question cannot be overestimated, for here perhaps we find Germany's entire future at stake. Our first duty is to examine things without prudery. Those unable to do so will never attain a healthy understanding of the question. God created us as man and woman[41] and wants us to be completely man and woman. God sanctified our maleness and femaleness, sanctified those emerging as men and women; our body is the temple of God the Holy Spirit.[42] God calls the genders each to its own specific role in God's service; we live our lives as men and women before God, who is the God of purity and of holiness. Each of us, however, must decide alone with God, who made us, what it means to be pure. Being pure means allowing God to radiate through us, through our physical and spiritual lives, in eternal purity. But this radiance emerges only where I conduct my life as a man or as a woman before God's eyes. There nature and spirit will mate in the beauty and harmony of a well-created being, neither against nature nor against spirit, rather both being ordered and permeated by God's spirit.

It is in this sense that we should present these problems to our youth. Real enlightenment comes about when, through the mysteries of nature and spirit, a child begins to sense something of God's eternal mysteries and revelations, when it senses that these questions touch on questions of eternity and that its own body, in all its strange and wonderful qualities, points to the eternal miracle and eternal holiness and purity of the Creator. Then each individual will be able to attain and find his or her own answer to the question, "Are we permitted to do this or that?" and, "What should we do now?"

Let us break off here and summarize. Ethics is a matter of earth and
344 blood, but also of God, who made them both; it is from this duality that the

[40.] ["Nature," *Natur,* and "spirit," *Geist,* are two central and consistent categories in Bonhoeffer's theological anthropology; cf. ed. note 27.—CG.]

[41.] See Gen. 1:27.

[42.] See 1 Cor. 3:16.

crisis arises. The ethical can be found only within the bonds of history, in concrete situations, in the moment of the divine call, of being addressed, of the demands made by concrete crisis and the concrete circumstances of decision, of a demand I must answer, to which I am accountable. The ethical does not exist as a principle in a vacuum; good and evil exist not as universal ideas but as qualities of a will that makes decisions. Good and evil exist only as something effected in freedom, while a principle binds us to the law. Bound to the concrete situation by God and with God, Christians act with the authority of those who have become free. They are subject to no other court than their own and God's. Precisely through this freedom from the law, from principles, however, Christians must enter into the complicated reality of the world. They cannot decide a priori what to do but rather will know only when they have actually entered into the situation of crisis itself and are conscious of being addressed by God. They remain bound to the earth if they are intent on attaining a relationship with God; they must partake of the entire anxiety before the world's laws, must experience paradoxically that the world offers them the choice not between good and evil, but between evil and evil, and that nonetheless even evil can provide a path to God. They must experience the crass contradiction between how they want to act and how they must act; they must mature through this crisis, must mature better, by not turning loose of God's hand, in the words: Your will be done.[43] It is only through the depths of the earth, only through the storms of a human conscience, that the window to eternity opens itself up to us.

An ancient and profound legend tells us about the giant Antaeus,[44]
who was stronger than all the men of the world. No one could defeat him 345
until during one battle his adversary lifted him up off the ground, whereupon the giant lost the power that had flowed into him only from his contact with the earth.[45] Those who would abandon the earth, who would flee the crisis of the present, will lose all the power still sustaining them by

[43.] Matt. 6:10.

[44.] Son of Poseidon and of Gaia. One of Bonhoeffer's favorite motifs; see p. 531 of this volume, and a passage in his prison fiction (*DBWE* 7:68). Ernst Wendel (*Studien zur Homiletik,* 45) suspects that "Bonhoeffer adopted this motif from the broad current of ideas deriving from the philosophy of life (*Lebensphilosophie*) after 1900, though especially from Hans Freyer"; cf. his *Antäus.* The Antaeus metaphor also represents a popularized philosophical modification of Nietzsche, *Thus Spoke Zarathustra* (prologue, pt. 3): "Let your will say: the Overman *shall be* the meaning of the earth! I beseech you my brothers, *remain faithful to the earth,* and do not believe those who speak to you of otherworldly hopes!" (Kaufmann, *Portable Nietzsche,* 125).

[45.] "Mother" deleted before "earth."

means of eternal, mysterious powers. The earth remains our mother just as God remains our father, and only those who remain true to the mother are placed by her into the father's arms. Earth and its distress—that is the Christian's Song of Songs.[46]

All the examples that we have examined show that we must place ourselves in the concrete situation and from there direct our gaze toward eternity. Within the contradictory nature of each situation, we must then struggle ever anew to reach our decision from within God's will and let that decision be whatever it may be. In the final analysis, however, ethics will not become merely one more path from human beings to God. Like everything else done by human beings whom Christ has liberated from the world, ethics remains merely a sacrifice, a demonstration of our weak will, that emerges from our own gratitude for what God has done through us, a sacrifice, an offering, a demonstration that God can accept as easily as reject. Human deeds originate in the recognition of God's grace toward humanity and toward each person; those deeds hope in God's grace, which releases us from the crisis of our age.[47] In this way the kingdom of grace establishes itself above the kingdom of the ethical. The crisis and anxiety of conscience must come to an end, the incomprehensible contradictions of the divine orders in the world must become clear if the kingdom of grace is to replace the kingdom of the world, if the kingdom of God is to replace the kingdom of human beings. Only those who have tasted the entire seriousness and the entire depth and crisis of the kingdom of the world, the kingdom of the ethical, yearn beyond this, and have but one wish: May our world pass away and your kingdom come.[48]

[46.] [Bonhoeffer's use of *Hohelied* is an allusion to the biblical Song of Songs; see his comments in *LPP*, 303. See also the chapter "Song of Songs," in Rasmussen, *Earth Community, Earth Ethics*, esp. p. 297.—CG]

[47.] [In this concluding paragraph of the third lecture, Bonhoeffer refers back to the title of the whole series, "Crisis and Hope in the Contemporary Religious Situation."—CG]

[48.] Usually freely translated: "May this world pass away and your kingdom come," *Didache* 10:6.

B. Essays from the Berlin Period. 1930

4. Eulogy for Adolf von Harnack[1] 346

Thousands of young theologians look back with me in this hour at their great teacher. Today his legacy is passed down to us, and we accept this legacy proudly and with a strong consciousness of the responsibility it brings. In so doing, however, we look to the future, to what Adolf von Harnack will continue to mean to the present generation of theologians.

[1.] *NL*, A 23,1 a; typewritten; five pages with handwritten corrections and underlines, apparently the copy used for the oral address. Cf. also *NL*, A 23,1 b; carbon copy of the former with virtually identical handwritten corrections, apparently the copy to be used for publication (handwritten additions by a second hand on p. 1: "9-point type, expedite, proofs to the author," as well as the title and "5 pages," on p. 5: "Berlin-Grunewald" and "Dr. Dietrich Bonhoeffer." Cf. also *NL*, A 23,1 c; a later typewritten copy with editorial changes. Previously published in Harnack, *Ausgewählte Reden und Aufsätze*, 210–11, and in *GS* 3:59–61, and in *Protestantenblatt* 63 (1930): 402–3; a copy of that in *NL*, A 23,1 d; the basis of the present version is *NL*, A 23,1 b, the carbon copy mentioned above.

Adolf von Harnack had died on June 10, 1930, in Heidelberg. "At the simple memorial ceremony in Heidelberg, his student, Professor Martin Dibelius, spoke; at the cremation ceremony in Berlin, the address was given by Professor Heinrich Weinel. The Kaiser-Wilhelm Society, which grieved for Harnack as 'its founder and great leader,' assembled its members and a large number of guests on June 15 for a memorial service in the Goethe Hall of the Harnack Haus. Addresses were given by Minister Schmidt-Ott on behalf of the society, Prof. [Hans] Lietzmann on behalf of the university, Ministers Wirth and Grimme on behalf of the Reich and Prussia, General Director Krüß on behalf of the Prussian State Library, Dr. Dietrich Bonhoeffer on behalf of the deceased's final circle of students. His ashes were interred in the Old Matthäi-Cemetery, where a simple stone marks the spot; its inscription is the one great petition under which Harnack lived his entire life: 'Veni creator spiritus'" (Zahn-Harnack, *Adolf von Harnack*, 442). Cf. also the program for the service in *NL*, A 23,1 (2); reproduction of the program in Bethge and

Almost two generations separate us from him, whose original students have become our own teachers.[2] We know him only as the aged master whose opinion the entire cultural world listened to attentively; who
347 prompted everyone who met him to have reverence for a life led in the spirit and in the struggle for the truth; who, regardless of where he was, always brought an entire world along with him, a world that inevitably made an enduringly profound impression on whoever came into contact with it.[3]

We young theologians who were fortunate enough to sense something of this world[4] acknowledge it as something great, something that distinguishes us from all those for whom this world must remain something past.

He became our teacher; he became close to us the way true teachers become close to their students. He stood beside us with questions and across from us with superior judgment. The sessions of intensely serious work in ancient church history, for which he assembled us in his house during his latter years, allowed us to get to know his unerring striving for truth and clarity. Empty ways of speaking were alien to the spirit of his seminar. Clarity had to reign at all costs, though that did not exclude the possibility that questions of the most inward and personal nature also had a place and might expect to find in him an ever-ready listener and adviser who was always concerned with one thing: the authenticity of his response. But it became clear to us through him that truth is born only of freedom. We saw in him the champion of the free expression of truth once it was recognized, who formed his own free judgment each and every time, and expressed it clearly whatever the anxious inhibitions of the crowd. This made him the foe of all inauthentic academic loyalty, of all rigid pettiness; he was beyond all obsequiousness, so that he respected deeds and human beings, and this made him—something about which we are especially qualified to speak—the friend of all young people who spoke their opinions freely, as he asked of them. And if he sometimes expressed concern or warned about recent developments in our scholarship, that concern was motivated exclu-
348 sively by his fear that the opinion of others might be in danger of confusing irrelevant issues with the pure search for truth.

Because we knew that with him we were in good and solicitous hands, we saw him as the bulwark against all trivialization and stagnation, against all fossilization of intellectual life.

Gremmels, *Life in Pictures*, centenary ed., 44; concerning the acceptance of Bonhoeffer's eulogy in the *Protestantenblatt* and the interpretation of Wilhelm Schubring, see 1/117.

[2.] Esp. Karl Holl.

[3.] Bonhoeffer maintained this high regard for Harnack throughout his life; see, e.g., *LPP*, 200, 219, and 227; see also, as already in 1927, *DBWE* 9 (2/16), p. 439.

[4.] Deleted: "that surrounded this personality."

But Adolf von Harnack—and this was the greatest thing for us—was a theologian, a committed theologian,[5] and we believed we could understand him only from this perspective, and that is why this should be stated clearly once more in this circle. Theologian—that means first of all not only that he wrote a history of dogma.[6] Theology means speaking about God. The work of the theologian is concerned with nothing less. In Harnack the theologian we saw the unity of the world of his intellect; here truth and freedom found the true unifying bonds, without which they become arbitrary. It was consistent with his personality to speak few words here; better many words too few than one word too many in such things. Here everything must be completely truthful and completely simple. But what little he said sufficed for us, whether he said it in the seminar or, better yet, outside, in the open air, in Grunewald, where summer after summer[7] he gathered his earlier and later students. He believed that the zeitgeist was always determined through the Holy Spirit of Christianity,[8] and that the message of the Father God and the Son of Man held eternal rights and thus also rights to us. It is here that we find Harnack's legacy to us. True freedom of research, of work, of life, and the most profound support by, and commitment to, the eternal ground of all thought and all life.

I think it fitting that I should close with a statement that was one of his 349
own favorite sayings, one he passed along to us a year ago on a summer outing of his old seminar: Non potest non laetari, qui sperat in Dominum.[9]

[5.] Otto Dibelius's judgment of his teacher was quite the opposite: "We yearned for a teacher whose heart was so filled by theology that he could not and did not want to be anything other than a theologian. But that wasn't Harnack. . . . I learned a great deal from Harnack—just not theology" (handwritten vita 1933; see Stupperich, *Otto Dibelius*, 36–37.

[6.] See Harnack, *History of Dogma*.

[7.] Deleted: "in some quiet corner."

[8.] The determination of the zeitgeist through the Holy Spirit was a familiar theological motif within liberal Protestantism since Ernst-Moritz Arndt. Cf. esp. the motto of the church history of Bonhoeffer's great-grandfather Karl August von Hase; see 3/12, p. 531.

[9.] "Who hopes in the Lord cannot but rejoice." This citation may derive from an excursus of Martin Luther on the words in Ps. 5:11, "Laetabuntur omnes, qui sperant in te" ("All who hope in you will rejoice" [NRSV: "But let all who take refuge in you rejoice"—CG]) in the *Operationes in Psalmos* (1519/21), where he writes: "Contra impossibile est, ut non laetetur, qui sperat in Domino" (On the contrary, it is impossible that those who hope in the Lord do not rejoice) (*WA* 5:158–77, 181, and *Archiv zur Weimarer Ausgabe*, 2:329, 3; this is also the opinion of Gerhard Ebeling in a letter to Reinhart Staats). To our knowledge, Harnack first used this citation in the words of congratulation for Martin Rade in 1927 (now in Harnack, *Aus der Werkstatt des Vollendeten*, 260), then as the concluding statement in his dedication in *Einführung in die Alte Kirchengeschichte* (see 1/93, ed. note 2). [Cf. Harnack, *History of Dogma*, vols. 6–7:186 n1, where Harnack quotes this sentence, citing *Operationes in Psalmos* (1519/21).—CG]

5. Examination Paper: The Meaning and Choice of a Biblical Text for the Sermon in the Worship of the Congregation[1]

The Meaning and Choice of a Biblical Text for the Sermon in the Worship of the Congregation[2]

1.) There has been a return to preaching on the biblical text from the attempts to preach on nonbiblical texts. It was believed that this[3] satisfied a need within the "cultured world" by presenting a Christian interpretation of intellectuals they admired. Hence there were sermons on Goethe and Nietzsche.[4] That has proven to be the wrong path. One came too close to
350 the temptation of placing the wisdom of the world above the foolishness of the cross.[5] What right does the exclusive use of biblical texts have in sermons to the congregation? Orthodoxy has spoken about the *sufficientia scripturae*.[6] Here indeed we find the heart of the matter. The Bible can claim *sufficientia* because it contains God's revelation in Christ. As such the Bible is given to the Christian congregation as the word, which becomes God's revelation ever anew and in a living fashion within the *sanctorum communio*. Thus it constitutes the foundation of the word the congregation itself speaks—the sermon. Because the sermon carries God's revelation in Christ further, it is necessarily a sermon on a biblical text. But this tells us something else, namely, that the preaching of God's revelation in Christ is God's word to the present—precisely because God remains God, yesterday as today. The sermon draws this divine word to the present out of the historical word of God in the Bible; as a sermon on the biblical text, it is thus the locus at which past and present come together in God, but only because the God of Christ is our God, the God whom the Bible reveals, which in its own turn is given to the church-community *qua sanctorum communio*. That precisely the Bible is God's word, however, and a religious poem by Nietzsche is

---

[1.] *NL*, D 11 (58); handwritten; undated, probable date July 5, 1930; on page 1, upper left, the signature "Dietrich Bonhoeffer," and under it "'Good' (though in places the handwriting is virtually indecipherable). Fahland July 8, 1930."

[2.] The phrase "for the Sermon" was added to the title at a later time.

[3.] [That is, preaching from texts other than the Bible. The phrase "cultured world" recalls Schleiermacher's *On Religion: Speeches to Its Cultured Despisers*.—CG]

[4.] Referred to as the "Bremen fashion" by Friedrich Niebergall (*Die moderne Predigt*, 212), whose primary representative was Julius Burggraf; cf. his 1913 *Goethepredigten*; cf. also Traub, *Aus suchender Seele*, with words "as a motto from the entire world, from Emerson, Ibsen, Fichte, Lessing, and other spirits of all sorts" (Niebergall, *Die moderne Predigt*, 118).

[5.] Cf. 1 Cor. 1:18–19; this sentence was marked by the examiner.

[6.] "The sufficiency of scripture." Cf. already the Formula of Concord, "Concerning the Binding Summary, Rule, and Guiding Principle. . ." (*Book of Concord*, 486–87, 526).

not, is the irresolvable mystery of God's revelation in hiddenness. The biblical text as such, however, unites the entire Christian church-community. It assures us of our bonds of kinship, not only with the church-community of Christ in all the past and all the future (*quod ecclesia perpetuo mansura sit*!),[7] but also with the entire church-community of the present. As such, the biblical text is of enormous unifying, ecumenical significance. This is understood not only objectively but also psychologically (unity/concord). The awareness of our brotherly concord, however, increases so markedly in those who hear the biblical text that everything they encounter in such a
text in the way of profound knowledge and experience they also experience 351
and gratefully and reverently hear and learn as the ancient possession of Christian thought and life.

And yet, these latter reasons supporting the exclusive use of the biblical text for the sermon are all ultimately anchored in the first reason mentioned, namely, that here God is speaking to us from within his historical revelation and thus overcomes the ages. This consideration reveals the two poles of a sermon on a biblical text, namely, its accordance with revelation (perhaps more accurately described as "accordance with scripture") and its accordance with the church-community (based on the unity of the church-community and the concord concerning the historically revealed God. Accordance with the church-community thus also includes "in accordance with the times").

2.) What follows such a definition and significance given to a sermon based on a biblical text, and the related formal definition of a sermon, for choosing a biblical text for the worship of the congregation? According to the definition given above, the text must contain two things: (1) reference to God's revelation in Christ; (2) relation to the concrete situation of the congregation. Which texts do I choose to correspond with these things? How do I bring God's revelation in the past together with my own present hic et nunc[8] such that an arc leaps from the one to the other? That is the problem. Here one is as important as the other: How today can I become a Jew to the Jews,[9] [a Gentile] to the Gentiles, a German to the Germans, a liberal to the liberals, a merchant to the merchants, and a worker [to the] workers—and yet at the same time remain ἔννομος Χριστοῦ[10] (1 Cor. 9:18–21)?

[7.] It is also taught "that there must be and remain [one holy] Christian church" (Augsburg Confession 7; *Book of Concord*, 42).

[8.] "Here and now."

[9.] Cf. 1 Cor. 9:20.

[10.] "Under Christ's law." [Cf. 1 Cor. 9:21.—CG]

a. For young pastors, the *lectionary* is the first aid that suggests itself in choosing a text. Anyone's attention will be aroused if he considers Luther's sharp comments regarding the pericopes in the *formula missae*[11] (whereby one does, however, have to consider that the lectionary of Paul the Deacon[12] omits passages such as that on the prodigal son and the Beatitudes!)
352 and then hears him nonetheless recommend using these pericopes in the "German mass,"[13] and who considers that Luther himself preached a great many pericopes.[14] The lectionary relieves young theologians of the great task of choosing a text by tying them to a κανών.[15] But it also prevents pastors from repeatedly drawing their own favorite ideas from the Bible or reading those ideas into it and consequently offering increasingly monotonous sermons to the congregation. The lectionary—particularly of course the Eisenach Series[16]—does guarantee a certain variety and at the same time a certain cohesion among the sermons. So it seems to me that the lectionary is virtually indispensable for young pastors. Even if they believe they do not need it, such discipline deepens and expands a person. Of course, the lectionary, especially when it has already been preached all the way through several times, does run the risk of failing to relate to the concrete situation of the congregation. What should I preach if special circumstances arise in the congregation, if perhaps the congregation has become tired of the lectionary?

This consideration raises the question of b. free choice of texts.[17]

Of course, the church year itself provides a certain structure, and this must remain. But what internal organization can I impose on the church year in order to guide both the congregation and ourselves to a deeper

[11.] *LW* 53:23–24 (*WA* 12:209–10).

[12.] At the behest of Charlemagne, Paul the Deacon compiled a collection of homilies with 244 sermons on the Gospels whose selection and organization were the basis for Luther's own *Kirchenpostille,* though the exact influence is unclear; cf. Kunze, *Die gottesdienstliche Schriftlesung,* 156. [Luther's *Kirchenpostille* are volumes of sermons based on Gospel and epistle readings; see Luther, *Sermons of Martin Luther: The Church Postils.*—CG]

[13.] Cf. *LW* 53:68 (*WA* 19:78).

[14.] Remarkably similar argumentation is found in the 1935 Finkenwalde lectures on homiletics; cf. *DBW* 14 (2/10), p. 491, and Fant, *Bonhoeffer,* 158–61.

[15.] "Canon," that is, a rule.

[16.] The 1896 Eisenach church conference decreed a revision of the "ancient church" pericopes and introduced a second new series on the Epistles and the Gospels.

[17.] The views presented in this examination, especially concerning the freedom of choice of texts and the pastor's responsibility, remained decisive for Bonhoeffer throughout his life; see esp. the previously mentioned 1935 Finkenwalde homiletics lectures, *DBW* 14 (2/10), pp. 489–92, and Fant, *Bonhoeffer,* 156–61, translating the version in *GS* 4:267–71. See also Wendel, *Studien zur Homiletik Dietrich Bonhoeffers,* 20–33.

understanding? Here pastors must develop a plan for the entire church year. I could imagine such overall themes including:

1.) "God's path through the old covenant to Christ," with the Old Testament representing the primary source of sermon texts, especially the Prophets and the Psalms, though also historical material (Abraham Gen.
15:6![18] Joseph, exodus, Moses, David, exile), albeit only to the extent such 353
material can be understood as pointing in some way toward Christ.

2.) Our path to Christ. Here we would address questions affecting our present life, perhaps touching on topics such as contemporary religiosity, morality, our understanding of vocation, of marriage, and we might especially consider the Sermon on the Mount, though also topics from the letters, such as catalogs of virtues and vices, 1 Cor. 13, passages dealing with the foundation of morality. At church festivals, such a sermon series would especially have to articulate the contrasting nature between our own understanding today and the original Christian understanding.

A third overall theme might perhaps be

3.) God's path through history in the church of Christ. Here one might begin with Heb. 12:1, the "cloud of witnesses,"[19] and move on through *Acts* to a further development of church history. In such a series, the festivals would variously provide references to the ground of all Christian discourse.

Alongside such broader themes, one can at the proper time also find smaller thematic groups appropriate for special occasions, groups particularly applicable during Trinity.[20] Such might include "the church and national customs and traditions [Volkstum]," for example, in connection with the prophets or Paul (Rom. 9:1f.), "church and government" [Obrigkeit] (Rom. 13:1ff.; 1 Tim. 2:2ff.; Mark 12). Church and marriage (Eph. 5; Heb. 13), church and morality in general. Individual ethics and social ethics (Gal. 5:25f.; Eph. 4; though also the Sermon on the Mount).

If fate deals the congregation a harsh blow, pastors will doubtless reach for 1 Peter or Hebrews or will base a sermon series on Romans 8. In times like ours, when individual piety is prominent, pastors will probably want to put together a sermon series on the church itself (Rom. 12:5f.; 1 Cor. 12; Eph. 2:4).

[18.] ["And he believed the Lord; and the Lord reckoned it to him as righteousness." —CG]

[19.] [Five months later Bonhoeffer wrote from New York to his friend Helmut Rößler (December 11, 1930; 1/148) that he had hoped to find a "cloud of witnesses" in America but instead was bitterly disappointed.—CG]

[20.] [That is, the Sundays after Pentecost.—CG]

And now, when the congregation sees that contemporary questions are also questions of the church of Christ, the pastor and the congregation will come together on the foundation of an ancient and yet ever new and inexhaustibly rich word.

354 **6. Examination Paper: What Is Paul's View on Earthly Suffering?**[1]

What Is Paul's View on Earthly Suffering?

One the one hand, Jesus said that the heavenly Father makes the sun rise and sends rain on both the righteous and the unrighteous (Matt. 5:45); on the other, he told his disciples that those who would be real disciples must take up their cross (Matt. 16:24; cf. Luke 9:57ff.). These statements articulate the two basic ideas with which the disciples can come to terms with the problem of suffering in the world and their own suffering in the community of Jesus. That the disciples had to struggle mightily to understand such statements made by Jesus is attested by the questions they asked Jesus and by the harsh answers he sometimes gave.

Jesus's words to his disciples and Paul's letters are separated by Jesus's death on the cross. Here the problem of suffering had come to a head. The Messiah, the Son of God, had died as a criminal, had surrendered himself to the world, had taken upon himself the most terrible suffering. This crucified Jesus revealed himself to Paul as the living Lord, thus turning Paul's earlier world upside down. Job's friends (chaps. 3ff.) and the wisdom of Elihu (chaps. 28ff.)[2] offer no help in solving this riddle. Here a completely new start had to be made; here all thinking had to start completely anew with the cross of Christ. And thus Paul views the present "terrible" world (cf. Gal. 1:4) only from the perspective of Christ's death.

Paul sees suffering spread out over the *entire world,* for he sees that all human beings must die. Death is suffering κατ' ἐξοχήν[3] (Rom. 1:18ff.; Rom. 5:12ff.). He understands the suffering of the world to be based on God's anger at sin.

355 But how do things look where sin has been overcome, where Christ is risen? That is, what meaning can suffering then have within the church-

[1.] *NL,* D 11 (59); handwritten; undated, probable date July 5, 1930; on p. 1, upper left, the signature "Dietrich Bonhoeffer," under that: "Good grasp of the problems, resolved within a good systematic structure. Quite good. [*Recht gut;* this was the second highest mark Bonhoeffer could have received.—CG] Coulon July 6, 1930."

[2.] Should read Job 32–37.

[3.] "Preeminently."

community of Christ? Why must they, the apostles, suffer? Why are the disciples persecuted?

The answer: because Christ died, Christians must die with Christ. This applies not only to sin, but just as much to suffering. Paul carries Christ's dying around with him in his own body (2 Cor. 4:20; cf. Gal. 6:17). The Christian must enter the κοινωνία τῶν παθημάτων αὐτοῦ[4] (Gal. 3:10).[5] Is this God's punishment? No, it is grace. "*For he has graciously granted you* τὸ ὑπὲρ Χριστοῦ[6] the privilege not only of believing, but of suffering for him as well" (Phil. 1:29) Those who would engage themselves with the gospel must accept suffering συγκακοπάθησον τῷ εὐαγγελίῳ[7] (2 Tim. 1:8). Christ himself suffered, and you would avoid suffering?

Paul looks at his own life and probably wonders, for he, the messenger of Christ, sees nothing but suffering all around. We carry our treasure in clay jars (2 Cor. 4:7ff.). He finds himself slandered, reviled, abandoned, and miserable (2 Cor. 4:7ff.; 2 Cor. 11:26ff.; 2 Tim. 2:9), he bears Jesus's own death on his body so that Jesus's life might be revealed.

Suffering is grace. To what extent? "If we suffer with him, we will also live with him" (1 Tim. 2:11).[8] "But even if I am sacrificed, I am glad and rejoice" (Phil. 2:17).[9] How does this work? Rom. 5:2ff. answers. I boast in my sufferings because they lead to hope, and hope has its place in the love God has poured into our hearts (5:5). This passage expresses incomparable joy. Not just "endure" sufferings, but boast in them. That is because they come from God (Phil. 1:29) and lead to God and are grounded in the cross of Christ. With hope, however, Paul looks at the last things, whose paradoxical premonitory signs are the cross and sufferings. "All things work together for good for those who love God" (Rom. 8:28). Those whom God calls, God also ultimately glorifies.

The crucified Christ lives. Hence we, too, will live with him (Rom. 8:17; 356
1 Tim. 2:11).[10] For we are united with him in the cross (Gal. 5:24 et passim). Christ lives in glory, and the sufferings of this age disappear before such glory. Indeed, if one experiences them to the fullest, they themselves create that glory (2 Cor. 4:17) precisely because they mean community with Christ.

[4.] "Community of his suffering."
[5.] Should be Phil. 3:10.
[6.] "For Christ, on his behalf."
[7.] "Suffer for the gospel."
[8.] [NRSV translation altered. Correct: 2 Tim. 2:11.—CG]
[9.] [NRSV translation altered.—CG]
[10.] [Correct: 2 Tim. 2:11.—CG]

Suffering is grace? Should I then seek suffering? The path leading to martyrdom is more broadly trod in 1 Pet. 3. Paul did not tread this path. He wanted to spare his brethren suffering (1 Cor. 7:28). He himself asks to be freed from suffering (2 Cor. 12); three times he calls to God, asks for the intercession of his brethren that he might be freed from his fetters (Col. 4:2–4; Phlm. 22). But he knows how far such requests may go. He himself gets the answer from God: let my grace be enough; and he ceases to plead precisely because God has answered and has spoken his word. Paul repeatedly sees himself as the earthly vessel with the infinitely precious treasure; he boasts in his weakness so that God's power and glory might be revealed all the more through him.

Finally, Paul sees suffering as taking place within the community of Christ. No one suffers alone. The church-community is Christ's body, hence "if one member suffers, all suffer together with it" (1 Cor. 12:26); none have anything by themselves; their sufferings all contribute to the consolation of their fellow Christians (2 Cor. 1:5). He sees "Christ's suffering growing strong" over him and rejoices because in this way the consolation for his fellow Christians also increases. His own suffering completes what is lacking in Christ's afflictions for the sake of his body (Col. 1:24). But this is rooted exclusively in the fact that Christ himself is the unity of the church-community and all of us are his body (cf. Gal. 3:28). From this perspective Paul is also able to console those who suffer, indeed to admonish them to share the suffering of others (Phil. 4:14). The basis of his consolation, however, is found in the life of Christ. We are his body, his chosen church-community (Eph. 1:5, 26),[11] "who will separate us from his love?" (cf. Rom. 8:35). God did not spare his Son, neither does God spare us;
357 God's children must suffer, but eternal community [Gemeinschaft] with God and Christ awaits them, glory compared to which all the sufferings of this age are as nothing (Rom. 8:17), glory that is bestowed upon the church-community. So here, from the perspective of Christ's death, Paul is able to come to terms with the riddle that has tormented and stirred up all peoples and all ages, and can do so precisely because he sees the turning point of world history and the interpretation of all reality in the cross and the resurrection. Time does not permit me to take this discussion beyond the Pauline understanding of suffering nor to discuss martyrdom.

[11.] [In this exam Bonhoeffer is quoting from memory; see Eph. 1:4, 23; and 5:30. —CG]

7. Inaugural Lecture: The Anthropological Question in Contemporary Philosophy and Theology[1]

The Anthropological Question in Contemporary Philosophy and Theology

The question[2] as to what it means to be a human being is kept current by two factors. First, by human works themselves; and second, by the experience of limits [Grenze]—physical limits, intellectual limits, and the limits of the human will. Wherever the human being[3] begins to be astonished at his own capabilities and his own works, and wherever reality ruthlessly demonstrates human limits, the ancient biblical questions emerge: "What are human beings, Lord, that you are mindful of them? . . . You have made them a little lower than God" (Ps. 8),[4] and the other, "What are human beings, that you . . . haunt them every morning, test them every moment?" (Job 7:17).[5] Stated historically, this means that the question about the human being is necessarily raised anew and more urgently, on the one hand, by a century of engineers who built a new world on the foundations of the old and, on the other hand, by a lost war. Two great possibilities pres- 358
ent themselves. The human being tries to understand himself either from the perspective of his *works*[6] or from that of his *limits*.[7] Understanding emerges only from a still *point of unity*. A person tries to find such a point either in his works or in his limits, that is, where his essence seems to be suspended from temporal change, where it seems graspable in the condi-

[1.] *NL*, A 23,2; typewritten with handwritten corrections and additions; inaugural lecture in the great hall [Aula] of the Berlin University, delivered on July 31, 1930; a facsimile of the first page is reproduced in Bethge and Gremmels, *Life in Pictures*, centenary ed., 44. Previously published in *GS* 3:62–84. [First English translation in *NRS*, 50–69.—CG] This lecture is closely related to the conclusions Bonhoeffer reached in *Act and Being* (*DBWE* 2), his postdoctoral dissertation. The brackets in the text are from Bonhoeffer's hand and probably refer to possible ways to shorten the piece.

[2.] [In the lecture Bonhoeffer stresses the questioning subject and the act of questioning.—CG]

[3.] [The German text always speaks of the human being (*Mensch*) in the singular, and this should be remembered while reading the text because this usage suggests the loneliness of the one who is asking, a theme Bonhoeffer develops in the lecture; see also the editor's introduction, pp. 45, 46.—CG]

[4.] "Ps. 8" added to the text later by hand.

[5.] [NRSV translation altered.—CG]

[6.] [Bonhoeffer uses "works" not only in the everyday sense but above all with the theological overtone of "works righteousness" (*Werkgerechtigkeit*) as rejected in Reformation theology by the teaching of justification by grace through faith.—CG]

[7.] [*Grenze* is a technical term in Bonhoeffer's theological anthropology and includes both the English senses of "limit" and "boundary."—CG]

tion of rest, of objectification. The unity of a human being means first that the person's existence is genuinely addressed, and second that his existence can be conceived in continuity. [These are the formal definitions within which the question of the human being must be posed and answered.] Human works and limits are the places from which self-understanding is sought; they are deeply grounded in the idea of the human quest for self-understanding. This question differs fundamentally from all other questions since the one who poses the question is himself a human being; that is, one cannot simply ask about the human being in such a way that he appears as an object [Ding]. Rather, the person who is thereby made into an object is already no longer the same as the person who himself is now engaged in the act of posing the question. The questioning person does not simply enter into the person about which the question is asked. The I is unable to capture itself. It views itself as something transcendent to itself. In the question about himself, the individual encounters the boundary [Grenze] of transcendence. Here he finds himself transcended within himself. In this situation, the person who questions must decide between two possibilities, a decision that logic cannot compel. Either the person acknowledges that here he encounters an insuperable boundary [Grenze], namely, that the I being searched for can never become an object of reflection but rather has its essence [Wesen] in relation to the questioning self, that is, to transcendence; the essence of the human being then rests no longer in itself, but rather in the ever-renewed act of relating to transcendence. The other possibility is to draw the transcendent, questioning I itself into the question, to gain control of one's own I such that one then views the act of the I coming-to-itself as the central occurrence of all intellectual processes.

359 The characteristic feature of the first decision about the question is that the person can be understood only from his boundaries or limits; the characteristic feature of the second is that the person is fundamentally accessible and transparent to himself and understands himself through himself; he finds within himself the point of unity from which his own essence reveals itself. The I becomes an object to itself by thinking its I.[8] Here conceptualization of one's own I, as the process of conceptualization out of unity, becomes the primal position of all philosophy. Hence philosophy means posing the question about the human being and providing the answer in one and the same act. The person understands himself because he philoso-

[8.] Deleted: "But because on this view thinking can proceed from the perspective of unity only where I think my own I, hence . . . is."

phizes. Philosophy is the human work κατ' ἐξοχήν[9] The individual understands himself out of his most characteristic activity [Werk].

Work or activity, however, is the concretization of a possibility. If the person understands himself on the basis of his work, then he understands himself out of his possibilities. Even a way of thinking that endeavors to distinguish fundamentally between the actualized and the nonactualized possibility, as for example Judaic thought, does not thereby move out of the category of possibility. The essence of the person is his possibilities, which means that the person remains within himself, [grasping his essence immanently]. A human being is a self-subsisting world, needing no others (only itself) in order to come into his own essence. By contrast, the self-understanding that emerges from the first decision is always reaching beyond itself. The essence of the human being resides not in immanent quiescent[10] possibilities but in the ever-active relating to his own boundaries or limits. The person is in his essence act-movement [Aktbewegung][11] [precisely because he comes to his essence at any given time only through limitation]. In the first instance, we have the person of the infinite, inalienable wealth of possibilities; in the second, the person who loses himself at his limits in order to find himself, who protests against every insistence on something inalienable.

We see how the idea of this question about the human being directly generates two differing understandings of the essence of the human, depending on whether the question concerning the person becomes the point of 360
limitation or the systematic point of departure of all philosophy. [We saw further that the question about the human being touches directly on the problem of transcendence; everything depends on whether the I misappropriates transcendence and draws it into itself or instead acknowledges this limit. Hence whenever we inquire about how the human being is understood in any philosophy or theology, the question of transcendence must be raised as the decisive question.]

[9.] "Preeminently, par excellence," in the sense of "quintessential, *the* supreme human activity."

[10.] "At rest within itself." [Bonhoeffer writes "*quieszierenden*."—CG]

[11.] [As he wrote in *Act and Being*, for Bonhoeffer "act" is a technical term encompassing both "pure intentionality" (*DBWE* 2:28) or relationality [*Beziehung*] and also "occurrence" from time to time (*DBWE* 2:29 and 113). In short, "act" has dimensions of intentionality-relationality and eventful temporality. *Aktbewegung*, which highlights movement (*Bewegung*), thus emphasizes the ongoing event of act, which always begins anew.—CG]

If as theologians we turn to hear what contemporary philosophy has to say about the human, we find first of all that the question[12] about the human being is one of the most passionately posed questions in contemporary philosophy. Today one sees old ideologies collapse and must fear that the human being is being buried along with them. One sees a new intellectual and cultural reality emerging in which the human being is assaulted by powers and demons and yet is intent on not surrendering. One finds oneself imprisoned and yet wants to be free. One feels the ground pulled out from under one's feet and yet does not want to fall. Here the person must preserve himself in the most passionate search for himself, in positing himself anew, in finding himself in the question about himself, the question about what could ground his existence anew. We can only outline these attempts here.[13]

First attempt: the person reaches for himself into the deepest unrevealed strata of his being, strata that are untouched by change and persist in eternal rest and order. Beyond himself and beyond the reality of the world, he grasps for the cosmos of pure values, which are captured and reflected by the beholding soul. This is Scheler's[14] initial point of departure. His phenomenological epistemological theory, [the legitimacy of which I will not
361 discuss here,] enables him, on the basis of a material a priori, [juxtaposed to Kant's formal a priori,] to construct a world of the being [Sein] of values transcending consciousness.[15] God is in this world. The human being is able to behold God not in the intellectual process but in his feeling of values, a feeling whose purest form is love. [Only in love is there true recognition of values.] In love the person swings aloft to a vision of the eternal and highest value of the Holy One, of God. Here the person grasps the All within himself and can even grasp God in passionate beholding. This is the "totality of life," namely, that it discloses and encloses within itself the totality of values. With riveting pathos, Scheler unfolds the motionless, unchangeable, shining heaven of values above the world of subjectivity and relativity that has been constructed and distorted by thinking, a world restricted to consciousness; and into that world he places the human being as the spirit

---

[12.] In the manuscript, the phrase "we find first of all that the question" replaces "a rich field of fertile ideas does indeed seem to open up. The question."

[13.] Literally, "We can only provide a picture of this in outline here," whereby the manuscript deletes the expression "of this" [*davon*] and also deletes the phrase above it reading "of these attempts by contemporary philosophy."

[14.] Max Scheler; cf. *DBWE* 2:64–67. [Scheler is also prominent in *Sanctorum Communio* (*DBWE* 1).—CG]

[15.] See Scheler's section on "The A Priori and the Formal in General," in *Formalism in Ethics and Non-formal Ethics of Values*, 48–81.

who seizes control of God in the reflection of love. The human being is understood from his possibilities. He bears within himself the possibility of drawing the transcendent into himself, through his beholding. And that is his essence. Here everything is conceived statically, the world of values as well as the possibility of beholding them. [The manner of being of both is that of something existing (Seiendes), that is, of something given, objective.] This is why Catholicism has been able to celebrate triumphs here;[16] the person is secured as a human being because he holds within himself the possibility of coming to God, because he bears within himself from creation onward potential points of contact with God. [Hence *the question about* the human cannot as such be a real problem here. One inquires about the human as concerning a thing, some existing entity (Seiendes). In Scheler's early literary period, we find not even the slightest trace of the notion that the person, as the one who must first inquire about himself and who in and for himself obviously does not yet possess the answer, finds himself in a truly questionable situation, one characterized essentially by precisely this question concerning himself.] But something else has already begun to emerge. Over against the realm of values is juxtaposed a realm of being 362
[Sein] of the world, of evil. Scheler still believes that the latter is unable to harm the former. But an enormous upheaval is coming. It is shocking to see how Scheler's system collapses under the overwhelming impression of the demonic world of human desires. The rigidity of Scheler's conceptual edifice proved to be too brittle to offer resistance to this suddenly erupting reality. It collapses completely. And Scheler's understanding of the person ends in his final literary period[17] with the resigned recognition that the human being is the being [Wesen] in whom the world of the desires gains control of the world of values. Here the human has helplessly fallen prey to demonic powers. The divine human being becomes the plaything of a world emptied of all meaning.

How did this happen? Scheler tried to understand the human being as an entity [Wesen] whose sphere of being [Sein] was conceived beyond its existence [Existenz] as *ens creatum*[18] in a created world, that is, as an entity basically untouched by the fact that it must first inquire regarding itself, an entity that "is" in the form of a timelessly existing being [Seiendes]. As such an entity [Wesen], however, the human being could no longer recognize himself the moment he found himself violated in the very ground of his

[16.] Bonhoeffer is presumably referring to Scheler's reception by Przywara, "Drei Richtungen der Phänomenologie," 252–64.

[17.] Cf. *DBWE* 2:66–67.

[18.] ["Created entity."—CG]

essence [Wesen] by the powers of his own creatureliness, by the powers of society running diametrically opposite to that presumed original being [Sein]. Scheler separated the *essentia* from the *existentia.*[19] He was well able to conceive the continuity, but not the existentiality, of human being [Sein]. Hence the magnificent edifice of Schelerian metaphysics had to collapse at the first storm. The human being misunderstood himself. If one wanted to get beyond this misunderstanding, the path had been indicated. The concept of existence [Existenz] had to become constitutive for understanding the human. The person exists, that is, he is in time and in the world as the one who must inquire about himself at any given time. The person
363 thus does not know in general who he is, but rather it is part of his essence [Wesen] to inquire about himself. The being [Sein] of human beings—that is, their Dasein[20]—does not have the same manner of being as an extant being or thing [Seiendes], of something present-at-hand [Vorhandenes], something accessible; being is found instead only in self-understanding, that is, in the intellectual act of reflection.[21]

¶Such was the point of departure of Martin Heidegger.[22] Dasein, however, can understand itself not floating freely in space but rather only in being bound to a historical situation of existing in the world. [For Dasein, too, it is decisive not that the *understanding of being* is, but that the understanding of being *is.*] Dasein thus always finds itself already determined in some way; [hence it obviously does not posit itself. Rather] it always already *is* as that which it understands itself. This being [Sein] in the concrete situation, however, is the decision, one always already made, of a potentiality-for-being [Seinkönnen], that is, the concept of possibility comes into sight. The being of existence is construed as being in possibility and dissipates. In Heidegger's words: "Dasein is primarily being-possible. Dasein is in every case what it can be, and in the way in which it is its possibility."[23] Dasein finds itself in the world in "being with others [Mitsein mit

---

[19.] "Essence from existence"

[20.] [A key term in Heidegger, the German word *Dasein* has been adopted into philosophical English; for Bonhoeffer's understanding of the term, including his critique of Heidegger, see his usage in the following sentences and the numerous references in *Act and Being* (*DBWE* 2).—CG]

[21.] "Of reflection" was added subsequently to the manuscript by hand.

[22.] Cf. the extensive discussion in *Act and Being* (*DBWE* 2), pp. 67–73.

[23.] Literally and in full: "Dasein is not something objectively present which then has as an addition the ability to do something, but it is rather primarily being-possible. Dasein is always" (Heidegger, *Being and Time*, 134).

Anderen],"[24] in "being fallen into captivity to the anonymous [Verfallensein an das Man],"[25] in day-in, day-out sameness [Alltäglichkeit], to use Heidegger's own expressions. Dasein is in a world it cares for [besorgen]. Dasein is care [Sorge].[26] It recognizes itself as having been thrown into this world of care, as "something having been thrown [Geworfenheit]" into the world, that is, it cannot dispose over itself; it always finds itself only in the situation for which it has already decided. In its captivity to the world, to the anonymous, to talk, however, Dasein disintegrates; it does not come to its own wholeness, something that is, after all, essential for it. Because it is historical, Dasein is subject to death. The totality of Dasein is oriented toward death; it is "being toward death." If Dasein wants to come to its wholeness, then precisely because self-understanding is part of its essence it must understand itself from the perspective of death, that is, it may not accept death as an existing [seiend] event when it comes, but rather must 364
in every instance go to it ahead of time, incorporate it into its own self-understanding, and thus in the "decision unto death" bring itself to wholeness. Instead of grasping Dasein in its authenticity as being [Sein] toward death, Dasein falls captive to its own inauthenticity in the world. This being [Sein] in inauthenticity and nonwholeness is revealed as guilt where Dasein is summoned to its authenticity and out of that captivity—in the call of conscience. But it is Dasein itself that summons in conscience, "anxious in its thrown state" [. . .][27] about its potentiality-for-being.[28] Dasein summons itself back to itself; it has lost itself to the world, it is in a foreign country, the world's uncanniness [Unheimlichkeit] makes it anxious, that is its guilt [or its nullity (Nichtigkeit), as Heidegger conceives[29] the concept of guilt]. In the summons of conscience Dasein takes its guilt upon itself and comes to wholeness by entering into resoluteness to death and in that way finding itself. Dasein seizes its most authentic possibility, its most authentic existence, by coming to itself and in this way understanding itself.

Hence for Heidegger, the wholeness of Dasein means Dasein's being-for-itself [für sich Sein]. Dasein bears its unity within itself. This is the necessary consequence of understanding Dasein as being-possible and nothing else. The possibilities of Dasein include the possibility of coming to unity. Hence

[24.] Cf. Heidegger, *Being and Time*, 107–18.

[25.] Cf. Heidegger, *Being and Time*, 118–22.

[26.] Cf. Heidegger, *Being and Time*, 168; this whole section closely follows a passage in *Act and Being* (*DBWE* 2:68–69).

[27.] Bonhoeffer's own omission.

[28.] Cf. Heidegger, *Being and Time*, 256.

[29.] "Conceives" was added by hand to replace a deleted "explains."

the person understands himself from the perspective of his possibilities. Nonetheless an essential distinction obtains compared with Scheler's construction. Scheler conceives the possibilities of the human being statically, hence in continuity but not in existentiality. Heidegger succeeds in combining the two. The human being exists within time, and only within time are the possibilities actualized; indeed, whenever the human being reflects on them, he already finds himself in a chosen possibility. Every moment is a
365 decision for the possibility of authenticity or inauthenticity. This protects Heidegger's understanding of the human being against the eruption of the world powers that destroyed Scheler's construction. Ultimately Heidegger's human being does not bear any divine features, [and is not, as spirit, lord of the world,] but instead is to be the human being existing in the world [who is threatened precisely by that world], who is exposed to the forces of death, exposed to day-in, day-out sameness, exposed to the anonymous, who falls captive to the world [through his own existential possibilities], who ever anew must ask about and seek himself. This is why Heidegger's human being lacks the otherworldly pathos and the luster of Scheler's human being. This person is introduced as the worried [besorgt], anxious human being of resignation, of daily life; [this person has been accused of being petit-bourgeois,] but that is not all; the element of pathos resides only a bit deeper in Heidegger's understanding of the human than in Scheler's and is colored differently. Where the person is summoned by conscience, he is able to extract himself from his captivity to the world, albeit not in such a way that he might escape the forces of temporality without responsibility, but such that he takes his guilt, [the nullity of his life] upon himself and orients himself toward the most unconquerable of all forces—death. He draws death into his life and lives a being [Sein] toward death. [Up to this point, Heidegger seems to remain faithful to his will genuinely to grasp existence, but] By knowingly taking upon himself these realities even unto the reality of death, he overcomes them in their character as boundaries [Grenze] and so attains not the end but rather the completion, the wholeness of Dasein. The person gains command of the world by elevating himself into a tragically isolated individual. [The person remains alone, understanding himself from himself; being in the world has no meaning for one's authentic self-understanding. Ultimately the person himself answers the question about the human being.] The world of demonic forces has been overcome and dominated in the spirit [Geist]. Captivity in this world is merely the transition to the spirit's finding itself. [And precisely by grasping his own existence completely in this world, the human being ultimately is able to do violence to the world. We sense that we are getting extremely close to Hegel, and yet, on the other hand, it comes as no surprise that Heidegger refers

to the Kant of the first edition of the *Critique of Pure Reason*.][30] Although 366
Heidegger does indeed acknowledge the human being's self-questioning as the fundamental problem, ultimately here, too, the question becomes the answer; the human being basically knows about himself; the question has no ultimate seriousness.

Only one step remains, and the whole picture seems to change completely. It is part of human nature that the human being must inquire about himself, that he remains absolutely questionable to himself, albeit not such that he might entice an answer to this question from even deeper strata of his own being; instead, he remains in the questionableness of his existence. Paul Tillich,[31] whose thought begins at this point, views the human being as a finite being [Wesen] characterized by not coming to his own essence [Wesen] through himself, since there is absolutely no secure, unified point from which self-understanding might be possible. The human being is not able to elevate himself to lord over the world because all that is human is basically called into question [by the ground of all being,] [all that is finite by the infinite]. Hence the person comes to his essence only where, standing at his boundary [Grenze],[32] he experiences the inbreaking of the infinite. Here he understands himself in "living through the boundary situation," in "being threatened in the unconditional sense," that is, in acknowledging the responsibility attaching to every moment, the irresponsibility of[33] daily life.[34] He understands himself because[35] the preeminent characteristic of the boundary situation is that, where the human being stands radically under the No, the Yes to the human being is perceived. Not in the form of
a Christian proclamation—here all religious content also falls under the 367

[30.] Cf., e.g., Heidegger, *Being and Time*, 294 and 411n15. [Bonhoeffer does not write out the actual title of Kant's critique.—CG]

[31.] Cf. also *DBWE* 2:77 and 88, ed. note 15, where Bonhoeffer refers to Tillich, *Die Religiöse Verwirklichung*.

[32.] [Tillich's English writings (such as the autobiographical *On the Boundary*) and writings about him normally used the word "boundary" for *Grenze*.—CG]

[33.] The clause "that is . . . of daily life" was inserted subsequently by hand. At this point the words "one's own" were deleted from the inserted clause.

[34.] Deleted: "The threat, however, is that human beings are free and must decide in each and every moment for their authentic being, and further that such decision is responsible insofar as being and nonbeing depend on it. In other words, the threat to being means that human beings are free and yet cannot seize their own most authentic possibilities, apparently because they are unsure of themselves, since they do not dispose over themselves, because they remain questionable to themselves."

[35.] The handwritten phrase "They understand themselves because" replaces "Now admittedly . . . is."

No, "even Christ or God"[36]—but rather the Yes in its absoluteness. The absolute *boundary* is the inbreaking of the absolute itself; the absolute No *is* the absolute Yes. The human being understands himself on the basis of his boundary. This is apparently a fundamental contrast to the person who understands himself on the basis of his possibilities: the person who completes himself from within himself is juxtaposed to the one who at the boundary protests against all human self-positing and securing. The human being at the boundary is the human being of fundamental protest.

Before we examine this contrast more closely, however, we must follow the most recent philosophy one step further. Starting from the recognition that as long as the person encounters the world as a thinking being he will interpret the world according to himself and do violence to it, Eberhard Grisebach[37] manages to [fix the boundary of the human being in a fashion other than by thinking, namely,] address the concrete You as the boundary of the human being. In reality existence is only in an encounter with a You. Here is the real boundary, not the boundary that is thought nor the boundary that enters into reflection, [here is "presence"]. Human existence is only [in the present,] where it bears the claim of the other person, does not do violence to the other person, but rather enters into a διαλέγεσθαι[38] with that person. Hence the person genuinely understands himself only in concretely bearing the claim at the concrete boundary that [is erected before him and that allows the person being encountered always to be himself][39] disrupts a person in every act of self-absolutization. Here we seem to have the most incisive articulation of the recognition that the person can understand himself only on the basis of his boundaries [that is, in relation to transcendence], in contrast to all human self-understanding from the perspective of immanent possibilities. What is really new in Grisebach's position is that he cannot conceive the human being apart from the concrete other person. This position clearly expresses the will to overcome every sort of individualism, that is, any restricting of the I only within itself.
368 Grisebach manages to do this, however, only by absolutizing the You in the

[36.] Cf. Tillich, *Religiöse Verwirklichung*, 38; see also Bonhoeffer's footnote 15 in *Act and Being* (*DBWE* 2:88)

[37.] The reference is to Grisebach, *Gegenwart*; cf. also *DBWE* 2:87.

[38.] "Discuss, speak with one another." [The Greek is the root of the English "dialogue."—CG]

[39.] [This terse and seemingly opaque statement that was omitted from the actual lecture recapitulates fundamental ideas about persons, encounter, boundary, and reality that Bonhoeffer had worked out in his theological anthropology in *Sanctorum Communio*; cf. *DBWE* 1:44–57, esp. 45–46, 49–52.—CG]

place of the I and attributing to it a status belonging only to God.[40] Hence the I posits the other as absolute, acknowledges that other as its concrete, absolute boundary only to have its own absolute essence ultimately returned to it through that absolute You. [After all, since I myself posit the claim of the You as absolute, I could just as easily relativize it,] and thus with my own possibilities I remain the master of the other person as well. Although Grisebach's intentions are certainly worthy of serious attention, he cannot carry them out by these means. Here, however, we find ourselves in the very midst of the critique of what philosophy can even call the boundary of the human being

We must raise one significant objection against the attempt to understand the human being on the basis of his limits [rather than from that of his possibilities]. The boundary by which the human being limits himself remains a self-drawn boundary, that is, a boundary the human person essentially has already crossed, a boundary that person must already have stood beyond in the first place in order to draw it. The boundary is thus the absolute possibility that turns against itself. By limiting my own possibilities in thought—and I really cannot limit them in any other way in philosophy—I demonstrate through the very possibility of limitation the infinity of my possibilities, from which I can no longer go back. Here, however, these attempts to understand the person on the basis of his boundaries or limits joins the ranks of those they objected to in the first place, namely, the attempts to understand the human being on the basis of his possibilities. The human being essentially has no boundaries within himself; he is infinite within himself. To that extent, idealism is correct. The question is merely how this fact is to be understood. In philosophy, the question about the human being is ultimately always posed such that the human being himself finds the answer, because that answer is already contained in the question. The human being remains within himself, either as the one with eyes that behold the eternal values, or as the tragically isolated individual, 369
or as the individual at the boundary with the rigid gesture of protest. The human being understands himself on the basis of his possibilities in self-reflection, meaning further that he understands himself only in connection with his works.

Although theology accepts these results of philosophical inquiry, it interprets them in its own fashion as the thinking of the *cor curvum in se.*[41] The I

[40.] Cf. also *DBWE* 2:88.

[41.] "The heart curved in upon itself"; one of Luther's favorite expressions, here taken from his lectures on Romans (*LW* 25:291); cf. *Act and Being* (*DBWE* 2:41, Bonhoeffer's footnote 11 and ed. note 20 et passim).

does indeed remain self-enclosed; this, however, is not to its credit but is its guilt. This self-imprisoned thought is the true expression of self-questioning human beings in *status corruptionis.*[42] In a clearly related fashion and yet with an essential difference, as we will yet see, theology is unable to conceive the human being except in relation to his boundary, which here is called God. If the question about the human being is to be posed seriously, it can be so only where the human being is before God. [Whenever this question is posed elsewhere, it is never really posed seriously.] That is, the human being is torn completely out of himself, drawn as a whole person before God, and here the question about the human being becomes serious precisely because it no longer includes its own answer. Instead, God gives the human being the answer completely freely and completely anew, since it is now God who has placed the human before God himself and instructs the human being to question in this way. That is, the human being experiences his foundation not through himself, but through God. Whomever God summons is in essence a human being. The point of unity from which the human being understands himself thus resides with God. To this extent, contemporary theology is agreed since its latest reorientation toward Luther.[43] The great points of contention reside only in the interpretation of these statements. The two approaches we encountered in philosophy now recur in theology.

First, the human being understands himself from his self-reflection on his possibilities. If the human being is to understand himself only in connec-
370 tion with the transcendent, in this case God, then God somehow must attest himself in that human being; otherwise there is no relation to God. The place where God attests himself must be the place from which the human being understands himself and at the same time the place where his unity is founded. This place, however, is obviously conscience. Here the human being knows himself to be summoned, called to accountability, judged, and justified. Here is God's gateway into the person; here we find the immediate connection with God. The human being is a person of conscience who understands himself out of the reflection on his own conscience in which God encounters him. We mention the name of Karl Holl[44] here merely as one particularly impressive representative of the overwhelming majority of contemporary theologians. [Holl characterized Luther's religion as

[42.] Literally "state of corruption," the status of human beings after the fall.

[43.] The phrase "toward Luther" was added subsequently by hand. [The meaning of this sentence is clarified in the following paragraphs referring to Holl but also to Barth and dialectical theology.—CG]

[44.] Cf. *DBWE* 2:141–43.

"religion of conscience."[45] For now I will merely point out that this position included a peculiarly meager estimation of Christology in Luther. The human being finds God within himself in some fashion; he has God in self-reflection. Because the human being is able to hear and have God within his conscience, he is able to understand himself from within his conscience as his most authentic possibility of being human.]

At precisely this point, however, Holl encountered the most spirited opposition from the so-called dialectical theology. The question in which the human being reflects on himself always remains a question; he cannot find answers from within himself since there is no point within him at which God might gain space. Indeed, the essence of human being is to be *incapax infiniti*,[46] that is, it is impossible for the finite human essence to unite directly with the infinite, and this precludes the possibility that the human being might absolutize himself at even a single point within his essence. He remains totally unsecured because he remains completely within himself. Even thought, ethical consciousness of responsibility, and religiosity remain hopeless attempts to anchor the I within the absolute. All these belong to the φρόνημα σαρκός[47] [in all this the human being is 371
misappropriating God's honor insofar as he does not want to remain unsecured or want to secure himself at least through his own self-understanding. He declares himself good, he declares himself bad, but whether good or bad, both declarations are merely attempts at least to be secured; but he does not recognize one thing, namely, his own guilt before God in his good and his evil, guilt consisting precisely in wanting to self-posit and self-secure himself once and for all. That is, he does not want to be broken apart and healed, judged, and pardoned ever anew by God alone; he does not want to be justified by grace. The human being wants to justify himself; that is his guilt, since he could do so only if he had God in his power. But God remains eternally beyond, eternally distant, even and precisely where God comes close to human beings, in revelation. Barth says that "those to whom God is revealed are the very ones to whom God cannot become revealed" (*Dogmatik*, 1:287).][48] If the human being is to get an answer to the question

[45.] See Holl, *What Did Luther Understand by Religion?* 54–57.

[46.] This is an allusion to a formulation that had caused controversy within Protestantism. Lutherans had described the phrase "*finitum non est capax infiniti*" (the finite is not capable of bearing the infinite) as the *extra calvinisticum*; for further discussion, see *DBWE* 2:84, ed. note 7.

[47.] "Way of thinking of the flesh"; see Rom. 8:6.

[48.] Bonhoeffer means Barth, *Die christliche Dogmatik im Entwurf*, and quotes the 1927 edition that he owned; cf. Barth, *Gesamtausgabe*, 2:383). [Cf. also *Act and Being*, where Bonhoeffer cites the same passage (*DBWE* 2:99).—CG]

about the human, to the question he not only raises but is himself, then he must be torn completely out of his inversion into himself[49] and be directed to that which is absolutely exterior to his own existence. Only from beyond himself[50] can he perceive the answer as God's answer. The human being is established by God's constantly renewed deed, which God can either do or not do *quia sic vult.*[51] [Never, however, does God's word of justification enter into the person such that the latter now merely has to adduce it; rather, God must in every case speak it ever anew, it must come to the person from the outside.] The human being understands himself ever anew out of the word of God that comes from without, out of his absolute boundary that is called God. [Whereas Barth amplifies these ideas from the perspective of the Kantian idea of the person who exists (ist) only in relation to transcendence, Bultmann tries to make Heidegger fruitful for theology.[52] The human being does not dispose over himself, for he exists within his-
372 tory, not in the manner of objective things (Dinghaftes), but rather his being (Sein) is potentiality-for-being, that is, being-determined (Bestimmtsein) by sin or by God. Here the idea of the human being at the boundary seems to be united with that of the human being of infinite possibilities.] Friedrich Gogarten went beyond these ideas of Barth [and Bultmann].[53] Gogarten maintains that Barth's point of departure is speculative, that Barth ultimately views the human being not in the existential situation but somehow in the absolute sphere. Human existence is not grasped until it is conceived as being addressed by the historical You posited by God. The neighbor takes God's place. Just as with Grisebach, with whom Gogarten initially concurred, the neighbor is posited absolutely here in order to set historical reality against all speculative flight. [History is the encounter between I and You; there is no I without You.] Gogarten's corrective to Barth here reveals that Barth's thinking, too, is individualistic, that is, the human being remains alone with himself. Gogarten sees, however, that the theology of revelation excludes individualistic thinking. By granting God's absolute claim to the neighbor, however, Gogarten slides from the theology of revelation into an inner-worldly ethic; this, in turn, means that the I and the You can bring each other mutually to their essence. Thus they understand themselves in such a way that one is there for the other, in order to

[49.] "His inversion into himself" replaces "himself."

[50.] Deleted: "there, where the human being stands before God."

[51.] "Because [God] wants it thus"

[52.] Particularly in "The Historicity of Man and Faith," 104–10. For further discussion, see *Act and Being* (*DBWE* 2:97–98, as well as the afterword there, 170–72).

[53.] Cf. Gogarten, "Das Problem einer theologischen Anthropologie," 439–511, and *DBWE* 2:88.

enable the other to understand himself; this however excludes revelation. [The human being perceives the claim of the neighbor as the absolute only if God's absolute claim in Christ has encountered him and given him the answer to the question about himself. Thus, according to Gogarten, human self-understanding is still possible quite independently of revelation; that is, the question about the human being can be answered immanently.] Hence Gogarten's boundary, too, is not the real boundary of revelation.

As long as the human being can posit a self-imposed boundary by thinking, that boundary is characterized by the possibility of being transcended;
that is, even the person who intends to understand himself on the basis of 373
his boundaries ultimately understands himself on the basis of his own possibilities. By contrast, we maintain that *the concept of possibility has no place in theology and thus no place in theological anthropology.*[54] The following arguments support this.

I. The person who understands himself from the perspective of his possibilities understands himself from within his own self-reflection. In revelation, however, the human being is torn out of this reflection and receives the answer to his question only from and before God. The question about the human being is derived from the question about God. Here we find the fundamental difference between philosophical and theological anthropology.

II. The concept of possibility rationalizes reality. It determines every reality according to the manner of a logically existing thing [Seiendes]. That is, it fixes it, makes it universally accessible. [In this way, it is possible to place the point of unity of self-understanding into one's own ego through rationalization.] For theological anthropology, this means that the human being is conceived with certain possibilities in relation to God, to which he can withdraw at any given time. That human being is *capax* or *incapax infiniti*, that the being [Sein] of the human is potentiality-for-being, these are conditions that fix a person's being a priori and independently of the reality of revelation, and thereby yield revelation itself to human interpretation.

III. The concept of possibility is inadequate because [the human being is either understood from revelation or not, because] one cannot speak at all about a possibility of, or capacity for, revelation independent of the reality of revelation, since otherwise it would not be absolutely external. Hence it is precisely because of the emphasis on revelation coming from beyond existence that one has to reject every fixed *finitum incapax.*[55]

[54.] Cf. *Sanctorum Communio* (*DBWE* 1:126–30). [Cf. graduation thesis 4, criticizing the use of the concept of "potentiality" (*Potentialität*) in theology; *DBWE* 9 (2/16), p. 440.—CG]

[55.] See ed. note 46; cf. also *DBWE* 2:177–78.

IV. The concept of possibility includes semi-Pelagianism.[56] If sin and faith are among the possibilities of human beings, then the complete incomprehensibility, inexcusability, and infinity of the fall is rationalized into a
374 comprehensible actualization of immanent possibilities. Here sin loses the weight of infinity, the result being that the forgiveness and the wiping out of sins can be understood only as the actualization—albeit from God—of human possibilities that are no more infinitely significant than sin itself. That is, from this perspective one cannot comprehensibly explain how sin and grace mean eternal judgment and eternal life.

V. The concept of possibility does indeed allow an understanding of the human being in continuity. The human being is perpetually his own possibility. If, however, this possibility is fixed in the form-of-being [Seinsform] of some extant thing [Seiendes], then it does not affect the human being's existence, which cannot be conceived in the form-of-being of an extant thing but transcends such a form. The true continuity of the human being must be grounded at the center of that person's existence.[57]

VI. The critique of the concept of the boundary [Grenze] occurs simultaneously with the concept of possibility. We have already shown that this concept itself falls prey to the concept of possibility. Clearly, however, theology must also speak of a boundary between God and human. Three things, however, should be kept in mind. *First,* that this boundary constitutes not a formal boundary between two manners-of-being [Seinsweisen] in the form of some extant thing [Seiendes] but rather a boundary between persons. *Second,* that the content of this boundary is determined by the concepts of sin and holiness. *Third,* that the theme of theology is the crossing of this
375 boundary by God, namely, forgiveness of sins and sanctification. What follows, however, is that the theological concept of boundary is determined not

[56.] For further discussion, see *DBWE* 2:136–37.

[57.] Bonhoeffer left behind a note (*NL*, A 23,3; handwritten, on the back of a letter from the German Academic Exchange Service [DAAD] from May 15, 1930) that probably fits best here at the end of his discussion of the concept of "possibility." Bethge takes a different position (*GS* 3:83), viewing it instead as belonging to notes for the lost next-to-last page of the manuscript (see ed. note 65 below). The note reads: "Despite all that has been said about the concept [uncertain reading] of possibility, however, one ultimately cannot affirm the question about the human posed by human beings themselves as a possibility of the human being. If it is posed in its real meaning [uncertain reading], then it is posed under the reality of God, that is, in that case it is the question concerning the gracious God, concerning eternal righteousness; the question of salvation, which God induces the human being himself to pose in order to give him the answer. Wherever and however else it is posed otherwise, it is not the question about the human being himself, but rather about his possibilities."

through the rational stasis of the concept of possibility but rather through the dynamic reality of God.

Even though this position excludes the concept of possibility from theology, we can add positively that it is not in self-reflection that the human being understands himself but in the act-of-relating [Aktbezug][58] to God, that is, only where the person genuinely stands before God. Not where the person finds the possibilities within himself by virtue of which he can then stand before God. Here we must distinguish between *actus directus* and *actus reflexus*.[59] True self-understanding is found only in the *actus directus*; in the *actus reflexus* immediacy has already been disrupted, and thus there can no longer be any self-understanding. Since theology takes place only within the *actus reflexus*, it cannot itself constitute the true self-understanding of the human being—as philosophy claims for itself—but can only trace it. In such tracing, all depends on not rationalizing reality again through the category of possibility.

The human being understands himself only by his act-of-relating [Aktbezug] to God, which only God can establish. The human being sees his own unity grounded in God's word directed toward him, a word whose content is judgment and grace. Here the human being recognizes that his own essence is neither to be *capax* nor *incapax infiniti*, that his essence is not his own possibilities but rather is determined by the statements, "You are under sin," or "You are under grace."

Now, how does the essence of the human appear in sin and in grace? In recognizing sin, a recognition that occurs within God's revelation, the human being knows himself to be under God's judgment and finds himself as part of a humanity that has fallen away from God, fallen away because he wanted to be like God; now he stands under God's judgment. He finds himself condemned both as an individual and as a human being per se. Every person represents fallen humanity, and when each person fell from his common vocation as a human being, humanity fell as well. Each and every person is Adam, who brought sin into the world, and the entirety of humanity stands under the aeon of Adam. The human being is no longer 376
alone, because he stands in the humanity of Adam in which each person is Adam. Within this humanity, however, that person remains lonely. The spirit of sin has torn him away from the spirit of God and from his neighbor.

[58.] [See ed. note 11 regarding "act"; here "act-of-relating" stresses the active moment.—CG]

[59.] Bonhoeffer adopted this distinction from Franz Delitzsch and already employed it as the "central idea," according to Hans-Richard Reuter, in *Act and Being*; see *DBWE* 2:28, ed. note 17, and 158–61.

Now the human spirit circles perpetually around itself. Now this spirit is master of the world, but only of the world its ego interprets and thinks up, master in its own, self-restricted, violated world. He sees his fellow human beings as things and sees God as the one who satisfies his religious needs; and now he seeks to posit himself eternally in this world; he does not want to die; he wants to justify himself and live eternally. But during this search, which leads him through philosophy and through religion, the human being begins to sense his enormous solitude. He becomes anxious in the face of this dominion[60] over a dead world; in his anxiety he breaks the terrible silence of his solitude and breaks away from himself, stands over against himself in order to replace the missing other, and accuses himself. That is conscience. But since he is simultaneously accuser, accused, and judge, this summons of conscience proves to be merely the last grasp of the ego for itself, for its own possibilities. And its summons dies away in the silent, dominated world of the ego.[61]

This is the world in which the human being finds himself and into which God enters, brings him before his judgment, and condemns him. This takes place in the cross of Christ. In his death, however, the old, violated, interpreted world of the ego dies along with the ego, and the new aeon, the aeon of Christ, dawns in his resurrection and his life. The humanity of Adam is overcome by the humanity of Christ, albeit not such that the former is completely extirpated, but such that it is fundamentally robbed of its power. Just as the world of Adam violated Christ, so too does it violate the new humanity of Christ. But just as Christ deprived it of its power in his own death, so too is it deprived of power over human beings in the new
377 humanity of Christ, over human beings in Christ. The human being who has been initiated into the death and resurrection of Christ through God's word, that is, the Christian,[62] now understands his present being [Sein] as determined from two sides. First and decisively through his future, which is Christ alone, but then also through his past, which is Adam and which must ever and again be given over to the death of Christ. The person in Christ is one who is tempted,[63] to the extent that Adam's humanity remains in effect. The law, the flesh, and the world all stand against that person, grasping, creating fear, obscuring the view of Christ, and driving conscience so

[60.] Deleted: "of itself over the world," and handwritten: "in solitude."

[61.] For additional documentation of this motif, which Bonhoeffer frequently employs, see *DBWE* 2:161.

[62.] "That is, the Christian" was added later by hand

[63.] [Cf. *DBWE* 2:155–56.—CG]

that the devil himself speaks in it.[64] The person in Christ has not been removed from the world. That person is the person of normal daily work, of labor, of vocation [. . .][65]

mystery of the church-community that Christ is in it and only through it seizes the human being; Christ exists among us as church-community, as church in the hiddenness of historicity. The church is the hidden Christ among us. Hence the human being is never alone; instead he exists only through the church-community that brings Christ, a community incorporating the human being, drawing that person into its life. The person in Christ is the person in the church-community; wherever that person is, there is the church-community. But because that person as an individual is simultaneously wholly a member of the church-community, only here is the continuity of that person's existence in Christ guaranteed.

Hence the human being can understand himself no longer from within himself but rather from within the Christ who exists as church-community, from within his word that supports the church-community and without which that church-community does not exist. But because this word affects his existence and as the word of the church-community simultaneously founds the continuity of that person's being [Sein], the human being can understand himself only in direct relation to that word. People of the children of God, "children of mercy" (Luther): that is the self-understanding of the person in Christ, tempted here and repeatedly brought down, torn 378
out of the *actus directus*, ultimately completely surrendered in the relaxed disposition of a child toward its father.

I have been able to examine only briefly the distinctiveness of the question about the human being; my attempt to provide guidelines for a genuine theological anthropology had to limit itself to an outline. To the extent that this attempt represents a piece of genuine theological thought, it escapes the charge that it too derives from reflection and does not offer any genuine self-understanding, if this is acknowledged without qualification, and only if this theological undertaking is itself incorporated into the reality of the church in which Christ is present. Ultimately, only as the thinking of the church does theological thought remain the only form of thought that

[64.] "That . . . speaks in it" was added later by hand

[65.] Page 20 of the typescript has been lost. After the discussion of the human being in sin, "in Adam" (cf. *DBWE* 2:136–48), and now in grace, "in Christ" (ibid., 150–61), the lost page probably discussed how this "being in Christ" takes place in a continuing and contingent fashion within the church and finds its locus of recognition in the church (ibid., 108–9).

does not rationalize reality through the category of possibility. Therefore, every individual theological problem not only points back to the reality of the church of Christ, but theological thought in its entirety also recognizes itself as something that belongs solely to the church.[66]

8. Review: Friedrich Parpert, *Das Mönchtum und die evangelische Kirche*[1]

379 The author describes the lines leading from early monasticism to the heretical sect of Valdes,[2] the order of St. Francis, the latter distinguished from the former less by its substantive intentions than by its authoritative ecclesiastical power claims, then further to the time of Luther's own monasticism, thence to the Anabaptists, and finally to the emergence of Protestant sectarian movements. Parpert convincingly shows that, and in what sense, Protestant sects represent a phenomenon paralleling Roman monasticism. Both personally and in principle, Luther had a difficult time separating himself from the monastery, and when he saw his own new church becoming alienated from all monastic ideas, he himself reached back for the genuine wealth he believed was still hidden beneath the ruins of the monasteries. He picked up the living motifs that had once led to monasticism and, in his preface to the German Mass, wrote about establishing communities [Gemeinden] within the church itself composed of "those who want to be Christians in earnest."[3] Luther corrected himself; his struggle against the monastery was ultimately not of a fundamental sort. But Luther did not succeed in incorporating monastic communities into the community structure of the Protestant church, and thus sects developed alongside the church. The author might well wonder whether the development of sects might not effectively be countered by establishing a Protestant monasticism.

[66.] See the editor's afterword in *Act and Being* (*DBWE* 2:175–77).

[1.] Parpert's book treated the exclusion of monasticism from Protestant sociology; see bibliography for publication details. There is no handwritten manuscript of Bonhoeffer's review. It appeared in *Deutsche Literaturzeitung* 51, no. 50 (December 13, 1930): 2356–58. See also a copy: *NL*, A 35,2. Bonhoeffer doubtless finished this piece in Berlin before leaving for America. Previously published in *GS* 3:130–32.

[2.] [Valdensis, later known as Peter Valdes, was a twelfth-century leader of a group of Waldenses who were eventually condemned as heretics along with the Cathars and others at the Council of Verona in 1184. Some Waldenses in the Piedmont valleys aligned themselves with Calvinism in the sixteenth century, giving rise to the Waldensian Protestant Church.—CG]

[3.] Cf. Luther, "The German Mass and Order of Service" (*LW* 53:63).

The author does not really answer *the question* regarding what such Protestant monasticism might mean theologically and sociologically, for the concept of monasticism itself ultimately remains undefined. The reason is that it is not at all clear just what is meant here by "Protestant sociology." The book's subtitle[4] suggests the concept of sociology is to be understood in the sense of "social structure" or community (cf. in this regard also pp. 56, 65, 70), whereas sociology is obviously something like the science—a systematic and independent discipline, rather than an appendix to history—of the nature of social structures.[5] In that case, "Protestant sociology" would be the theological and systematic examination of the nature of the Protestant community. Once this is recognized, genuine theological concepts can 380
be applied to the understanding of social phenomena within the Christian church. An understanding of the phenomenon of monasticism and sects, however, would first have to provide a thorough sociological assessment of the theological concept of the law. This category would include everything the author says along with E. Tröltsch and others about the voluntary character, asceticism, and so on within monasticism and sects.[6] A sociology of the law, to be conducted with regard to all these phenomena, would have to be juxtaposed with a sociology of the gospel or of faith; here, in my opinion, one could systematically demonstrate the impossibility of a concept such as that of Protestant monasticism. The fruitfulness of solitude mentioned by the author has nothing to do with the essential sociological definition of monasticism. "Protestant monasticism" would essentially no longer be monasticism at all. Asceticism of faith, which repeatedly allows the whole person to die, and asceticism of the law, which seeks to justify a person before God, not extra-worldly and inner-worldly asceticism,[7] freedom of faith and the law's lack of freedom, not the voluntary character of a religious association etc., the solitude of faith in the church-community and the individualism of the law—those would be the genuinely theological-sociological concepts needed to address this problem in the sense of "Protestant sociology." The author addresses his topic in an essentially historical

[4.] ["A Contribution to the Exclusion of Monasticism from Protestant Sociology." —CG]

[5.] [For Bonhoeffer's understanding of sociology, and particularly systematic sociology as an independent discipline and not a branch of history, see *Sanctorum Communio*, esp. chap. 1.—CG]

[6.] See, e.g., Troeltsch, *Social Teaching of the Christian Churches*, 2:815–18 et passim.

[7.] Concerning the notion of "inner-worldly asceticism," see Weber, *Protestant Ethic and the Spirit of Capitalism*, chap. 4. [See also translator's note 1 on pp. 193–94 concerning his rendering of *innerweltliche Askese* as "worldly asceticism."—CG] Concerning criticism of Weber, cf. also *Sanctorum Communio* (*DBWE* 1:31–32, ed. note 4).

fashion and guides the reader up to the real questions of the present, questions, it seems to me, that can no longer be answered with the concepts of a historical-genetic sociology, e.g., in the sense of Tröltsch.

Berlin (currently New York) Dietrich Bonhoeffer

C. Papers and Essays at Union Theological Seminary, New York. September 1930–June 1931

9. Lecture on "War"[1] 381

It is indeed a strange feeling for me just coming over here from Germany now to stand for an american christian young people group trying to talk about this event of the recent history, which had seperated our peoples for many years. But I think, that only an open and franc discussion just of these questions, can help us for the deeper understanding of each other and for a more successful common work in the future. For I stand before you here in the church not only as a Christian, but as a German, who loves his home the

[1.] *NL*, A 25,6; in original English, including errors. The notebook that Bonhoeffer prepared for his trip to the United States and in which he made notes on English vocabulary and practice sentences (pp. 1, 49, 50) also contains two versions of this address: a) pp. 4–25; b) pp. 26–34; there is also a handwritten final version of b) on thirteen loose pages, which because of its sermonlike character is included in this volume under 3/23. Parts of b) were used again for an edited version Bonhoeffer did of a) as pp. 15–18, 23, and 22. The version that emerged through this process is the basis of the one used here. For another combination of these texts, see *GS* 1:66–74. Bonhoeffer probably delivered this address several times to different congregations, cf. 1/141, p. 251: "Right now I am constantly having to prepare speeches and addresses for the most varied occasions; the day after tomorrow I have to preach in English [cf. 3/23] and next week have to speak about Germany before one thousand schoolchildren." The International Fellowship of Reconciliation also had member groups in many congregations among the various churches of the New York region, which regularly invited foreign students to deliver addresses, particularly to their youth. [Written in English. All Bonhoeffer's texts in English from Union Seminary are reproduced exactly as he wrote them.—CG]

best of all, who rejoices with his people and who suffers, when he sees his people suffering, who confesses gratefully, that he received from his people all that he has and is. So I bring you today a double message; the message of Germany and of the Christianity in Germany. I hope you will hear this message with a christian heart, with the readiness of the christian soul to understand and to love, whereever and whomever it might be. The 11. of
382 November 1918[2] brought to Germany the end of a frightful unparalleled time, a time, which we pray if God wills, will never return. For four years german men and lads stood for their home with an unheard of tenacity and intrepidity with the imperturbable consciousness of their duty, with an inexorable selfdiscipline and with a glowing love for their fatherland and with the believe in its future. For weeks and months these people suffered privations of every kind, they persevered in hunger and thirst in pain and affliction, in craving after the home, after mothers and wifes and brothers and children. In the country did not cease the stream of tears, of old and young people. Every day the message came to more than 1000 familys, that the husband, the father, the brother had died in a foreign country. Hardly any family was spared. I tell you from my personal experience, two brothers of mine stood on the front. The older one 18 years old was wounded,[3] the younger one 17 years old was killed.[4] 3 first cousins of mine were also killed, boys of 18 to 20 years old.[5] Although I was then a small boy, I never can forget those most gloomy days of the war. Death stood for the door of almost every house and called for entrance. Once came the message about the death of many thousands seventeen and eighteen years old boys killed in a few hours.[6] Germany was made a house of mourning. The break down could not be delayed longer. Famine and enervation were to powerful and destructive. In the treaty of Versailles Germany was compelled to sign that she and her allies bore the sole guilt of the war and that she was responsible

[2.] The decisive historical date in Germany was November 9, 1918, the symbolic date of Kaiser Wilhelm II's abdication and the end of the *Kaiserreich* (cf. Erdmann, *Die Zeit der Weltkriege*, 141–43 and 181; see also *DB-ER*, 30). Here Bonhoeffer prefers the date November 11, 1918, because this day was celebrated as Armistice Day, a holiday in the United States.

[3.] Karl-Friedrich Bonhoeffer.

[4.] Walter Bonhoeffer.

[5.] Fritz Bonhoeffer and Werner Bonhoeffer (sons of Otto and Hedwig Bonhoeffer) along with Hans Count von der Goltz.

[6.] Bonhoeffer is referring to the Battle of Langemarck in September 1914 in which "young regimental soldiers," including many high school and university students, poorly trained, poorly equipped, and poorly led, were senselessly slaughtered in an assault through the mud on regular British troops in fixed positions. Propaganda turned this tragedy into a heroic deed.

for all reparations.[7] I think you release me from talking about our feeling in Germany in the first days after this end. The recollection of this time is 383
gloomy and sad. Very seldom you will hear today in Germany anybody talking about those days. We will not reopen an old and painful wound. But however we felt, the war and its dreadful killing and dying and suffering was finished. Our minds were still too confused and bewildered, we could not yet conceive and quietly consider the meaning of all these events of the last years and months. As a matter of fact, we had neither time nor rest for a quiet and objectiv consideration. While Germany still was trembling and quailing under the last shots of the canons a fatal revolution was prepared in the country, which threatened to overthrow the last foundations of our external and internal life. Germany was broken down economically and inwardly. The same 11. November 1918 which brought to us the end of the war, was the beginning of a new epoch of suffering and grief.[8] The first years after the war showed to us the corruption in our public life, in our social and economic order. Very hardly you can imagine the poverty of our people and its consequences in those days. England had cut off Germany from any import of food. This hunger blockade[9] was against all international law, since only ships carrying arms could be attached and sunk. The consequences of the blockade were frightful.[10] I myself was in these years a schoolboy and I can assure you, that not only I had in those days to learn, what hunger means. I should wish, that you would have to eate this 384
food for only one day, that we had for 3 or 4 years and I think, you would get a glimpse of the privations, which Germany had to endure. Put yourself

[7.] Bonhoeffer wrote down article 231 of the Versailles Treaty (of June 28, 1919) in English on p. 3 of his notebook: "The Allied and Associated Governments affirm and Germany accepts the responsibility of Germany and her allies for causing all the loss and the damage to which the Allied and Associated Governments and their nations have been subjected as a consequence of the war imposed upon them by the aggression of Germany and her allies." This article became one of the important psychological arguments used by opponents of the Weimar Republic, including and especially in National Socialist propaganda. Cf. Erdmann, *Die Zeit der Weltkriege*, 208–10, 328, and 337. For Bonhoeffer's immediate impressions of the effects of the Versailles Treaty, see his letter of May 20, 1919 (*DBWE* 9 [1/11], p. 29).

[8.] Bonhoeffer's negative assessment of the effects of the 1918 November revolution here derives especially from his experience of the economic crisis that developed during the postwar years. It is worth noting that Bonhoeffer avoided the widespread legend of the "stab in the back," which alleged that the military defeat was brought about only by the revolution (cf. Erdmann, *Die Zeit der Weltkriege*, 219).

[9.] Deleted: "began during the war and lasted."

[10.] Cf. in this regard also the 1919 polemical pamphlet by Siegmund-Schultze, *Die Wirkungen der englischen Hungerblockade auf die deutschen Kinder* (The effects of the English hunger blockade on Germany's children), which prompted a wave of relief activity.

in the situation of the german mothers, whose husbands were standing or were killed in the war and who had to provide for growing hungry children. Countless tears are flowen in these last years of the war and the first years of the[11] peace by desperated mothers and hungry children. As a matter of fact, instead of good meal were many percent saw dust in our bread, and the fixed portion for every day[12] was 5 or 6 slices of that kind of bread. You could not get butter at all. Instead of sugar we had sacharin tabletts. The substitute for meat, fish, vegetables, even for coffee, jam and toast—were turnips for breakfast, lunch and supper. Germany really was starved out. Thousand and thousand of old and young people, of little children died simply, because there was not enough to eate. Fatale epidemics ran through the country. The "Grippe" of 1918 demanded more than hundred thousand victimes. People were physically to enervated and could not resist. When the wintertime came, we had not enough coal for heating our rooms. We had not cloth for our clothes, it is not exeggerated, that many people had to buy in these days suits made more by paper than by real cloth. On the street you could see the undernourished and poorly dressed people, the pale and sickly children. The number of the suicides increased in a terrifying way. I remember very well, I had on the way to my school to pass by a bridge[13] and in the winters from 1917–1919 almost every morning when I came to this bridge I saw a group of people standing on the river and everybody, who passed by, knew, what had happened. These impressions were hard for young boys.

I will stopp picturing these frightful months and years; but before I go on, I will not forget to tell you, that the Quaker congregations of the States
385 were the first, who after the war in an admirable work supported the german children. Many thousand children were saved from starvation. Germany remembers in deep thankfullness this work of love of the Quaker society. Hearing all that, you can get no more than a glimpse of the reality. Such were the conditions in Germany in the end of the war, really unparelled months and years. But there was one wound, which was much more painfull than all these privations and needs, that was the art. 231 of the treaty of Versailles.[14] I will tell you francly, that this is the wound, which still is

[11.] Deleted: "socalled."

[12.] Replaces: "wood meal."

[13.] Although the Bonhoeffers moved to Wangenheimstraße in 1916, Bonhoeffer still attended Friedrich Werder Gymnasium until Easter 1919; on his way to school he had to go through the Brückenallee. The bridge had been a source of great fear to him as far back as the beginning of his school years; see *DB-ER*, 24, and Sabine Leibholz-Bonhoeffer, *Bonhoeffers*, 33.

[14.] See ed. note 7.

open and bleeds in Germany. I will try to explain to you briefly, what our attitude toward this question was and is. When the war broke out, the German people did not consider very much the question of guilt. We thought it to be our duty to stand for our country and we believed of course in our essential guiltlessness. You cannot expect in such a moment of excitement an objective and detached valuation of the present conditions. The war has its own psychology. The german soldiers stood in the war in the confident faith in the righteousness of their country. But already during the war you could hear in Germany some skeptical voices: who can tell, who is wrong and who is right? We all fight for our country and believe in it, Germans no less than French. Now 12 years after the war the whole question has been thoroughly searched historically. I personally see many faults in our policy before the war, I am not going to defend my country in every point. But a study of the diplomatic documents of Belgium of the years before the war for instance shows irrefutably, that other countrys had committed the same or greater faults than Germany, I mean especially Russia and France. In 1914 everybody in Europe expected more a war caused by Russia and France, than by Germany. It can be proved historically, that the art. 231 of the treaty of Versailles is an injustice against our country and we have a right to protest.[15] That fact is recognised by the largest parts of educated 386
people in Europe and in America. When I think of the guilt of Germany, I mean something deeper, than some political faults. But now I am going to speak from a Christian point of view. Christian people in Germany, who took the course and the end of the war seriously, could not help seeing here a judgment of God upon this fallen world and especially upon our people. Before the war we lived too far from God, we believed too much in our own power, in our allmightiness and righteousness. We attempted to be a strong and good people, but we were to proud of our endeavours, we felt too much satisfaction with our scientific economic and social progress and we identified this progress with the coming of the Kingdom of God; we felt too happy and complacent in this world, our souls were too much at home in this world.

[15.] On page 2 of his notebook, Bonhoeffer enumerated examples of Allied "atrocity propaganda," and both here and on page 25 listed the opinions of persons who had come out against the "sole guilt" thesis. The question of guilt [for the outbreak of World War I—CG] was discussed from the first day of World War I onward and is occasionally debated even today. Influential historical works in German that have argued the question included Fischer, *Germany's Aims in the First World War.* Cf. Erdmann, *Die Zeit der Weltkriege*, 52–54, and Wehler, *German Empire, 1871–1918*, 192–201. Concerning the ecclesiastical discussion, see Besier, *Krieg—Frieden—Abrüstung.*

Then the great disillusionment came. We saw the impotence and weakness of humanity, we were suddenly awaked from our dream, we felt the wrath of God upon us, and we recognised our guiltiness before God. But let me go on to a further point.

Everyone who knows the conditions in Germany today, 12 years after the war, knows, that inspite of some changes in their external aspect social conditions are almost as unhappy as 10 or 12 years ago. The debts of the war press us not only in regard to our financial standard but likewise in regard to our whole behaviour, we see the hopelessness of our work; it is impossible for us to provide social and economic conditions for our children in the future, in which we can trust for security. I must know, that my grandchildren still will have to pay reparations and war debts.[16]

The Germans are a suffering people today, but thei will not despair. Thei will work for building up a new and better home, thei will work for peace in their country, thei will work for peace in the world. When I came over here, I was astonished on beeing asked again and again, what German people think about a future war. I tell you the truth, German people do not speak
387 at all about that, they dont even think of it. You almost never would hear in Germany talk about war and much less about a future war. We know, what a war means for a people. I have been accustomed once in every year since my boyhood to wander on foot through our country, and so I happen to know many classes of German people rather well. Many evening I have sat with the familys of paysants[17] around the big stove talking about the next generation and their chances. But always when the talk happened to touch the war, I observed, how deep the wound was, which the past war had caused in every one. The german paysants like the paysants of every country want above all peace. They want to work peacefully in their fields, they fear any disturbance. But it is not different among other classes in Germany. In the workers class for instance started the german peace movement, and the interest for an international trade makes those people naturally pacifistic. It was in Germany, that the thought arose, that the worker in France and in Germany are closer to one another, then the various classes within each country separatly belong to one another. You will find large worker organisations with a particularly pacifistic programme, especially also the christian organisations of workers work in this very direction. The bourgeois in Germany had to bear the hardest burden after the war, but nevertheless I

[16.] According to the stipulations of the Young Plan (see 1/164, ed. note 10), Germany would have had to pay reparations until 1966.

[17.] Bonhoeffer means "peasants."

can assure you, that by far the most of them would abominate a war more then anything else. You might be interested in hearing something about the attitude of the youth toward war and peace. The youthmovement,[18] which started immediately after the war, was in its tendencies entirely pacifistic. In deep religious feeling we recognised every people as brothers, as children of God. We wanted to forget all hard and bitter feeling after the war. We had anew discovered an genuine and true love for our homecountry and that helped us to get a great and deep love for other people, for the whole mankind. You see, there are many various motives working for peace, but whatever motive it might be, there is one great aim and one great work; the peacemovement in Germany is an enormous power.[19]

Returning to the Christian point of view, it seems to me one of the great- 388
est tasks for our church, to strengthen the work of peace in every country and in the whole world. It must never more happen, that a christian people fights against a christian people, brother against brother, since both have one Father. Our churches have already begun this international work.[20] But more important than that is, it seems to me, that every christian man and woman, takes seriously the great idea of the unity of Christianity, above all personal and national desires, of the one christian people in the whole world, of the brotherhood of mankind, of the charity, about which Paul says: 1 Kor 13,4.[21] Let us consider, that the last judgement comes for everyone, in America and Germany; and God will judge us according to our faith and love. How can the man, who hates his brother, expect grace by God.[22]

This is my message for you: hear the voice of your german brothers and sisters, take their stretched out hand. We know, it is not enough only to talk and to feel the necessity of peace, we must work seriously. There is so much

---

[18.] [This is a reference to the *Jugendbewegung* in Germany; see Pfeifer, "Die Bedeutung der Jugendbewegung für Dietrich Bonhoeffer."—CG]

[19.] This positive description does not, however, correspond to the actual situation of the peace movement in the Weimar Republic; see Holl and Wette, *Pazifismus in der Weimarer Republik,* as well as the excursus in Röhm, *Sterben für den Frieden,* 41–72, esp. 68.

[20.] Bonhoeffer is presumably thinking in particular of the World Alliance for Promoting International Friendship through the Churches, founded in 1914, whose youth secretary he would become a year later, and of the International Fellowship of Reconciliation, also founded in 1914 by Friedrich Siegmund-Schultze and the British Quaker Henry Hodgkin.

[21.] Bonhoeffer is probably thinking here of the phrasing of Luther's German translation: "Love is patient and kind, love is not envious, love is not boastful, love is not arrogant."

[22.] Cf. 1 John 4:20.

meanness, selfishness, slander, hatred, prejudice among the nations. But we must overcome it. Today as never before nations of Europe—except Germany—are preparing for war. This makes our work very urgent. We must no longer waste time. Let us work together for an everlasting peace. And the peace of God, which passeth all understanding shall keep your hearts and minds through Christ Jesus.[23]

389 **10. Greetings to American Students**[1]

I bring you greetings from the youth of Germany. At this time there comes to my mind just an evening, which I spent no long time ago with a group of young people from our German youthmovement.[2] It was a glorious summer night. We were outdoors far away from the noise and bustle of the city[3] on the top of a mountain, above us the sky with its millions of stars the quietness of the evening, below us the lights of the villages the misty fields and the black woods, no one of us spoke a word. We heard nothing but the peaceful rustling of the brooks and the trees. On that evening a great and deep love came anew in our hearts, a love for our home and for the starry sky. The boys hat carried branches of trees and lit a big fire on the top of the mountain and while we were standing around the blazing fire in silence, a boy began to speak about his love for his own country and for the starry sky, which at that very time was shining upon people of all nations, upon all mankind and he said: how wonderful it would be if people of all nations lived in peace and quiet as the stars in the heaven above, if only nations could live together like brothers as they do in their own country.[4] When he finished all the boys and girls raised their hands as a sign that they were willing to work for this peace in the country and in the world. Then we

[23.] Cf. Phil. 4:7.

[1.] *NL*, A 25,6; handwritten on pp. 35–37 of the notebook; repeatedly corrected and revised draft; in original English, including errors. Partially reproduced in *GS* 1:74–75, ed. notes 2 and 1. These greetings were probably delivered several times; no specific occasion is verifiable. Cf. also 1/141.

[2.] This piece attests to Bonhoeffer's participation in the German Youth Movement and his assessment of it. The excursion to which he is referring must have taken place in the summer of 1929. Hardly any biographical sources are available for the entire Berlin period between February and August 1929.

[3.] Uncertain reading.

[4.] Written to the side, with no indication of its relationship to the rest: "about the brotherhood."

sat down and while the fire was burning out we sang our most beautiful folk songs about the love of our country and the peace of all mankind. With the deep understanding of our great task before us we went home. More than a year has passed since that time and I wish to bring you this message from students of Germany to the students of this great country:

Students of U. St. A.,[5] hear this voice of your German friends: brothers 390
and sisters, take the stretched out hand of german boys and girls. We know, that the hard work for peace is difficult, it is not enough merely to talk and to feel the necessity for peace, we must work seriously. There is so much meanness, selfishness and hatred among the nations of the world but we must overcome it.[6] Against that we know only one mean:[7] keep your eyes open and your hearts.[8]

And I think there are two great premises for our work: at first: love your home better than all, better also than all political and economic ideas, then you will be a true watchman of the peace in the whole world. Secondly: keep your eyes open and most important keep open—your hearts. Today as never before nations are preparing for war. This has made this task of those working for peace very urgent and therefore we need every will and force, and I think this work is urgent, we must no longer waste more time. Let us work together, but also [. . .][9] for an everlasting peace.[10]

[5.] [United States of America.—CG]

[6.] Deleted: "and I think you will allow me to tell you, what the german youth think about the ways to overcome it."

[7.] [Presumably read "means."—CG]

[8.] Considering its partial duplication, what follows may have been an alternative conclusion.

[9.] Illegible; deleted: "support."

[10.] Without any indication of its relationship to the rest: "Before we begin"; "Be on your guard against."

11. Reading Notes for the Course "Ethical Viewpoints in Modern Literature"[1]

11.1. War Literature

Christian Ethics
Ethical values in modern literature
War literature.

E. M. Remarque:	*Im Westen nichts Neues.*[2]
Sheriff:	*Journey's end*
Graves:	*Good bye to all that* (some chapters.)
Renn:	*Krieg*[3]
	Kriegsbriefe gefallener Studenten[4]

391 The most impressive of all war books I read, has been for me *Journey's end.*[5] Here is no tendency neither in a pacifistic nor in an idealistic-patriotic way, nor is it only a description of events. It is written out of the concrete situation in its immense earnestness.[6] It does not belittle great idealistic feeling nor does it veil the naked reality. In the dialogue between the old school teacher and the young Raleigh before both leave the trenches for their last journey two entirely different view of war come to their sharpest issue and it is amazing to see how by virtue of the simple but deep human understanding of the older comrade these differences are overcome. Both go into the same war and both gave their lives.

[1.] *NL,* A 24,7; handwritten with a remark by Eberhard Bethge: "Union S."; in original English, including errors. Partially reproduced in *GS* 6:198–202. Concerning these notes, cf. in general *DB-ER,* 160–66. [This second semester course, "Christian Ethics" 52a, was taught in 1931 by Reinhold Niebuhr. Bonhoeffer notes 2/11.1–2/11.8 all written in English. The text here reproduces Bonhoeffer's text, including errors of spelling and grammar. However, Bonhoeffer's inconsistent and idiosyncratic underlining of names and titles has not been duplicated. Italics in the notes represent Bonhoeffer's emphases.—CG]

[2.] [*All Quiet on the Western Front.*—CG]

[3.] [Renn's book *War* appeared in English the same year that it was published in Germany, 1929.—CG]

[4.] [Philipp Witkop's book, first published in 1918 and again in a much expanded edition in 1928, was translated into English in a selected edition in 1929 as *German Students' War Letters.*—CG]

[5.] [First performed in London in 1928 with Laurence Olivier in the leading role, the play about World War I was an enormous success in Europe and America. The author was Robert C. Sherriff.—CG]

[6.] ["Earnestness" was not deciphered in the German edition.—CG]

It has always been difficult to me, to explain psychologically the sudden rise of such an enormous flood of war literature 10–12 years after the war. It is very questionable of the task to picture war in *literature*, which means in the last analysis, in an *aesthetic* shape, leads rather to a pacifistic mood than to a kind of dangerous excitement. Is not perhaps even the most radical presentation of the horribilities and the terror of war in literature an attempt to idealize or romantisize war? My experience at least in Berlin of talking with people, who were not in the war and saw warshows and pictures made this question very serious.

11.2. Negro Literature[7]

18. Febr. Negro Literature.

Johnson: *Autobiography of an excoloured man*
B. T. Washington: *Up from slavery*
Dubois: *Soul*[8] *of black folks*
A. Locke: *The new Negro* 129–149
C. Cullen: *Copper sun*

Johnson in his autobiography, (which is half reality and half fiction), says 392
that the american negro sees everything in the light of the race question. This question is always with him. This applies to the negro literature as well as to the everyday life of the average negro. Although there are large parts of negro literature which are not concerned with the race question in particular, one gets the impression that also in these parts the consciousness of a suppressed and offended race is the driving power. The attitude of the various authors to an overcoming of this question is very different. B. T. Washington preaches the gospel of working, with regard to the white people separate like the fingers and one like the hand.

Dubois criticizes Washington sharply, accuses W. to agree with the statement of the inferiority of the black race. More race-proud! Johnson p. 56 says: the salvation of the american negro is the laughter, which prevent them from the fate of american Indian.[9]

[7.] Dated by Bonhoeffer February 18, 1931, with a remark by Bethge: "Wednesday."

[8.] [Correct: *The Souls of Black Folks.*—CG]

[9.] [For another quotation about laughter and oppression written by an African American that Bonhoeffer acquired and kept, see the editor's introduction, p. 28. —CG]

The poetry of Langston Hughes[10] and Cullen is often very passionate and satiric in its accusation against the suppression of their race. In Hughes a strong socialistic interpretation of the situation is very obvious.

In reading the autobiographies it struck me to see how naively the respectiv author praises his own work, his gifts, his recognition he found.

According to the whole mood in present negro literature it seems to me, that the race question is arriving a turning point. The attempt to overcome the conflict religiously or ethically will turn in a violent political objection.[11]

Quotations: Johnson p. 56. 22. 72. 75ff.! 87[12]

393 **11.3. Ibsen**[13]

Ibsen. 4. III. 31

Readings: all dramas[14]
Especially for today: *Brand*

For everybody who knows Ibsens dramatic work it is always anew astonishing to see Brand among all the other characters of his dramas. The main theme of Ibsens whole writing namely the daimoniac power of society over the individual and the tragedy which society bring into the life of the individual, is seen in *Brand* from quite the opposite side. Ibsen is enclined to the pessimistic view, society is right because society has the power. But he sees clearly the decline of society and sees how the individual person is pull into the decline of society. Now *Brand* is the tremendous and powerfull protest of the individual against society. Society weakens and blunts ethical decision,

---

[10.] Because Bonhoeffer does not list Hughes in his bibliography, he is probably not referring here to any specific work. [Hughes, who was very influential in the Harlem Renaissance of the 1920s, published his first book of poetry, *The Weary Blues*, in 1926, followed by *Fine Clothes for the Jew* in 1927. See also Bonhoeffer's comment to his grandmother, 1/169, and ed. note 6, on his 1930 novel *Not Without Laughter*.—CG].

[11.] ["Objection" here apparently means "resistance."—CG]

[12.] [First published in 1912, Johnson's book was reissued in 1927, the reprint edition Bonhoeffer probably read. Pagination is identical in the 1912, 1927, and 1979 Knopf editions.—CG]

[13.] Dated by Bonhoeffer March 4, 1931, with a remark by Bethge: "Wed[nesday]"; concerning Ibsen's *Brand*, see also 2/2, p. 349.

[14.] [At the top of the opposite page, which is otherwise blank, level with the heading and reading list, Bonhoeffer wrote:

Particular passages: II act
III act discussion with the doctor
IV act Brands woman, Agnes
V act end—CG]

it makes compromises. Brand, a norwegian priest (Ibsen once said, he could as well be an artist, a sculptor or a politician) recognises the will of God as demanding the whole life and the full surrender of man to this will. There is no compromise possible. The whole drama is one great struggle of Brand against the spirit of compromise. Very important for Brand's own development of his idea is the figure of Agnes. She is willing to give up all halfness and to live with Brand, but the moment comes where she herself becomes weak (occasioned by an apparently unimportant event) and here for the first time the call for a Deus caritatis[15] becomes aloud. Brand becomes more and more alone, he lives in the icy mountains alone with his hard and severe God. Only the insane Gerd is with him sometime. But at the end of a life of permanent misgivings and failure he sees that his ideal made him proud and separated him from the love of his fellowmen. In this acknowledgement he breaks down; the last word is again the word of the "Deus caritatis." The individual's attempt to protest against society fails. All men need the love of God, Brand no less than all the other ones.

11.4 Bernard Shaw[16] 394

Bernard Shaw.

St. Joan. Androcles and the Lion. Candida. Major Barbara. I never can tell. Man of destiny. Kaiser von Amerika. and others.

Bernard Shaw has as far as I see never taken up any problem of serious ethical or religious importance. The story of the old Christianity in *Androcles and the lion* is a completely shallow and sometimes almost blasphemic presentation of christian ethical ideals. Not so crude is *S. Joan*, although there is not very much difference in the last analysis. B. Shaw is not a paedagogue and does not claim to be. His educational principle, if he has any at all, is to tell people truth, to desillusion people. So especially the religious problem attracts him, to show how human man always has been even in this highest [. . .][17] of his life. He approaches this truth which he considers *the* Truth by means of psychology and the fact is, that his presentation of psychological facts are highly incredible particularly in relig. and ethical matters. At least they are very one sided, and a man, who intends to say the truth, does not fulfil his own proposition if he gives only one side, which even is not very deeply explored. So I cannot avoid the impression of great shallowness in

[15.] [God of love.—CG]
[16.] Not previously published.
[17.] Illegible.

reading Shaw; there is a certain desire to make himself popular which is not artistic. Even a play like *Candida,* which has been praised in highest terms, [. . .][18] neither a very interesting subject nor a deep psychology except of course some single features. Shaw is complete relativist and that makes his work, not only little interesting, but much more ethically irrelevant. He is a brilliant writer, the dramatic form of his plays is convincing, but I cannot but miss any great earnestness.

395 **11.5. Sinclair Lewis**

Sinclair Lewis

Readings: *Babbit.*
Elmer Gantry

Elmer Gantry usually—at least here in America—is not considered a work of art, neither as far as the content nor as far as form is concerned.[19] I like to oppose this judgement very strongly. We have to do only with the content. S. Lewis succeeded fully in picturing the atmosphere of unsound spiess-bürgerlichen[20] pietism. It might have been directed especially against the conditions in the United States, the fact is however that this picture is of so general adequacy (not less for the conditions in Europe) that anybody will find in it features of his own. It is admirable how Sinclair Lewis has understood all difficulties of the pastorat, how in some single features the terrible temptation to abuse one's position is perfectly well seen. I believe that exactly this book should be read by as many ministers as possible, and it is very bad tactic to tell the minister before, that this book has not to be taken seriously at all. This book could do for the church a great service. But the church has always been too proud to recognise this kind of service. The church as such should have taken the chance to say ex officio a word about *Elmer Gantry* instead of a simple and shortsighted refusal of the whole question. *Elmer Gantry* could serve to many a pastor as the counterpart of the catholic "mirror of confession."[21] There is without doubt often exag-

[18.] Illegible. [Perhaps "reveals" or "contains."—CG]

[19.] Bonhoeffer does not seem to have been aware that Sinclair Lewis received the Nobel Prize for literature in 1930.

[20.] [This term, literally "conventional bourgeois," connotes a narrow-minded focus on conformity and convention.—CG]

[21.] Bonhoeffer is referring to the genre "mirror of confession" rather than to a specific work.

geration and brutal taktlesness in this book, but it is foolish and consists of great selfrighteousness if one takes only these parts of the book and turns them back against the author.

The book is perhaps too long, and toward the end a little monotonous. Very good are the following scenes: conversion of E. Gantry and his thought on his way home. The prayer-meeting in the presidents house. Evening after 396
the ordination. The characteristics of the girl of the dean. E. Gantry in the house of his student friend from the Y.M.C.A.

11.6. Theodore Dreiser[22]

Theodor Dreiser.

Free and other stories.[23]

In the first story called "free" Th. Dreiser pictures an New Yorker well off business man, who at the end of his own life sees how his life was completely formed by tradition and convention as he thinks mostly by guilt of his wife. He always had had certain more independent ideas, he had a feeling for beauty and art, he was not mentally indolent; now his wife lies in her agony and he recollects his own lifestory, how he never was happy, never was free, how he believed in the right and the power of convention because his wife believed in it, how he never had loved his wife. Even his marriage was more or less a matter of convention. He always has been faithful to his wife, but his life had been empty. Now he almost hopes that his wife is going to die, he wants to be free for his last years. When finally his wife really is dead, he sees that he himself has no more power to live, that nothing had remained with him, that he is free—to die, convention has murdered his life.

The art of Dreiser is great in this story. The permanent emotional struggle against convention and yet the complete weakness to oppose to it only once has been worked out with a fine psychology.

The form of the story is highly original.

[22.] *NL*, A 24,7. Previously unpublished.

[23.] [Dreiser's book *Free, and Other Stories*, first published in 1918, was reissued in several editions in the 1920s.—CG]

The main ethical issue, the struggle against [. . .][24] convention, and
397 yet the insight, that most men are not worth and able to be free, has been worked out with high psychological art and is very powerfully pronounced.

"I am a poetic melanchic crossed with material lust."[25]

11.7. Ludwig Lewisohn[26]

Ludwig Lewisohn.

Stephen Escott (partly)
Midchannel (partly)

These are two problems in the center of Ludwig Lewisohn's writings: the question of the Jews and the question of sex. In *Midchannel* a very strange attitude toward the question of the Jews comes. He wants to be as untraditional and free as possible and yet he sees that a Jew can fulfill this essential task only by submerging entirely in the tradition of his own people, otherwise a Jew becomes weak and looses his character. Only the connection with his people can give him the strength he needs for love. Lewisohn propagates the idea of a Jewish culture of their own, he does not want the Jews to assimilate them entirely to American culture. It is a similar aspect as in the negro question.

With regard to a new sex morality Lewisohn goes the same way. He intends to be free from tradition and sees in the old idea of marriage and sex relations the only possibility for a sound and strong living. So not because it is tradition, but because it is healthfull and sound and good, Lewisohn becomes an advocate of tradition.

[24.] Uncertain reading [perhaps "prevailing"—CG].

[25.] Uncertain reading. [For the fifth word the German editors had read "melancolistic"; perhaps "melancholic" is meant. The sixth word may be "cursed." This quotation appears to have been added at a later time, but its source has not been identified.—CG]

[26.] *NL*, A 24,8. Not previously published.

11.8. Ernst Toller; Karel Čapek 398

Ernst Toller: *Masse Mensch*
Maschinenmenschen[27]
Capek: *R.U.R.*[28]

E. Toller, student and communist, who was in prison because of political actions, had an enormous success when he first brought out his agitative dramas. Although not particularly well written and full of common places and argumentations taken from the street, the strong passion of his writing and its ethical implication made an impression. The decay of bourgeois society and ideals and the growth of a proletarian society is his theme. In *Masse Mensch* he bring this struggle out in the different position of the "Frau" and the "Mann," she being representative and agitator of the new age, he being bound to tradition and bourgeoisie. The presentation again is more passionate than profound. The literary value certainly is not high although Toller will hold his place as a poet of the proletariat. *R.U.R.* by Capek is perhaps more of a worked out drama than Toller's dramas are. The story of the invention of the machine man, of the robot, his development in its different stages from just crude workers to man with soul and love is dramatized with many good ideas. The implication of the machine age seem to me to been seen more deeply here than in Toller's work. The question of war in its connection with the industrial system is treated in a great satire. This perhaps is the best passage in the play. The end seems to me a little sentimental and perhaps not very well connected with the previous scenes. It has something of the "happy end."

[27.] [The latter was translated into English in 1923 as *The Machine-wreckers: A Drama of the English Luddites in a Prologue and Five Acts,* and the former in 1934 as *Man and the Masses: A Play of the Social Revolution in Seven Scenes.*—CG]

[28.] Abbreviation for Rossum's Universal Robots.

399 **12. Reading Notes for the Course "Ethical Interpretations"**[1]

12.a First Page of Notes for the Course "Ethical Interpretations" of Current Events[2]

Ethical interpretation[3]

Notebook. Estimation. Passages.[4]
World Tomorrow[5] Febr. 1931 p. 47f.[6] the suppressed "sensational story"[7]

[1.] *NL*, A 24,6; handwritten, with a remark by Bethge: "Harry Ward." Partially reproduced in *GS* 6:193–97 (12.2, 12.3, 12.5, 12.7, 12.8). Bonhoeffer summarizes the contents in an academic and catalog-like manner, almost without any personal assessment. The reports were homework assignments for the course; cf. *DB-ER*, 163–64. Only with this qualification can these texts be adduced here and there as reflections of Bonhoeffer's own positions. [These notes for 2/12.1–2/12.9 were all written in English. This second semester course, "Christian Ethics" 52b, was taught by Harry Ward; it met for one session per week. Bonhoeffer had not participated in the first semester of this course. The text here reproduces Bonhoeffer's text, including errors of spelling and grammar, but it does not reproduce his inconsistent underlining. Italics in Bonhoeffer's text are his emphasis.—CG]

[2.] This page is found in Bonhoeffer's notebook with notes for courses and other occasions that he kept at Union Seminary. It is the first page of notes for the course taught by Harry Ward in the spring semester 1931, and it immediately precedes the page of notes on the Wickersham Report, *DBWE* 10, 2/12.1. Handwritten in English. In the upper right corner Bethge has written in German script "Kollegheft New York." This page has not previously been published and will simultaneously appear in the *Dietrich Bonhoeffer Yearbook 3* in 2008.

[3.] The official title of the course in the Union Seminary catalog is "Ethical Interpretations."

[4.] Notes from the professor's remarks about how the course will proceed. They suggest that the course will have a lot of discussion. Students should read the assigned journal and newspaper passages about current events and bring a notebook to class with a summary and evaluation of the issues.

[5.] *The World Tomorrow* was a journal; see 2/12.1, ed. note 16. In 2/12.1 Bonhoeffer lists *The World Tomorrow* as containing one of the "other articles read"; however, this journal does not contain the article on "the first lynching in 1931"; see 2/12.1, ed. note 16. It was listed because the professor had referred to it in the first meeting of the class.

[6.] Pickens, "Suppressed 'Sensational Story.'" The story told of a black woman who was caring for a white girl, who had just given birth, and her little sister. The police burst in with reporters, hoping to publish a sensational story of a white girl in "colored" hands. Instead they learned that the black woman had cared for the two girls at her own expense for months, after they had been abandoned, homeless, and abused by their parents. She had done so because a white woman had cared for her as a girl when she was in similar circumstances. This story, painting a black woman in a very favorable light, had not been reported by the press, which would have been all too ready to publish a story of a white girl who had been made pregnant by a black man. In fact her own mother had prostituted the girl with a criminal white man.

[7.] Two words are inserted between this and the following line: under the journal title "Zeitschrift" in German script, possibly written by Bethge; it is followed by a four-

Rope and faggot.[8] on negro lynching
2 x as many negro girl at college than boys
tendencies toward war. moral equivalent of war
creativ development of human society
America will be responsible for the next war, because the only nation which is in the position to prevent it.
Nationalism militant and[9] economic. What is the flag to God?

12.1 The Wickersham Report on Prohibition[10]

Christian Ethics
Ethical interpretation of current events.

Febr. 11.31 **The Wickersham report on prohibition**
Christian century Febr. 31, p. 159f.[11]

There are made four important points in the agreement of 9 members of the commission. 1.) opposition to the return of the saloon 2.) opposition to the nullification of the law by light wines and beers 3.) opposition to the governments going into the liquor business 4.) no relegation of the prohibition question to the single states. So the 18th amendment seems to be secured, prohibition has a firm foundation. There is in the Wickersham report mentioned an eventual revision of this 18th amendment but not a repeal. *Christian Century* agrees with the results of the Wickersham report and considers them important for conservation of prohibition.

---

letter word in Roman script, which looks most like "dead" (?). Thanks to Ilse Tödt and Hans Pfeifer for assistance in deciphering several words.

[8.] White, *Rope and Faggot*. This is a study of lynching by an author who had made many investigations for the NAACP. It also appears in "The Negro—A Selected Bibliography," compiled by the Harlem branch of the New York Public Library and acquired by Bonhoeffer (cf. *NL*, A 24,9).

[9.] Written as "+" sign.

[10.] Prohibition (the prohibition of the production, transport, and sale of alcoholic beverages) was regulated by federal law in the United States beginning in 1920. During Bonhoeffer's stay in America, the disadvantages of Prohibition, such as organized crime and tax losses, became increasingly clear. Public discussion led to Prohibition's repeal in 1933. Concerning Bonhoeffer's own negative assessment, cf., e.g., the letter to his sister Sabine Leibholz, 1/153, p. 271.

[11.] [Editorial article, February 4, 1931, 159–61; Bonhoeffer's four points are almost a verbatim quotation from p. 161.—CG]

Forum p. 4–10. Zechariah Chaffee[12]

He proposes repeal of the 18th amendment this repeal should contain new provision about the control of liquor. This should not embody specific
400 scheme, but give to the Congress the power over liquor business. Chaffee points out, that prohibition is one experiment among countless others for the solution of the intoxication problem. It is against the essence of an experiment to be made constitutional.

America. catholic magazine. A picture of prohibition 432–34

Quotations of Wickersham report and comments.[13]

Survey. Arthur Kelly S. 539.[14]

Other Articles read: The first lynching[15] in 1931. *World tomorrow.*[16]

Conditions are getting worse and worse but still better than 1919. How emprove the enforcement. The Commité is wet, the report is dry. Hoover is dry. It is impossible for 60 percent drys to coerce 40 percent wets. So one will have to recognize, that the ideal of prohibition cannot be put through.

12.2. Bank Situation and the Court Corruption

Bank situation and the court corruption.

The Nation Febr.11.31 Norman Thomas: The Banks of New York.[17]

The crash of the bank of the United States with a deficit of $75 million[18] which did damage to more than 400 000 depositors, among them 350 thou-

[12.] [Chafee, "After Prohibition—What?" The article by Chafee (correct spelling) refers to a poll on Prohibition conducted by the magazine *Literary Digest* that may have been assigned for this course session; see ed. note 16 below.—CG]

[13.] [Blakely, "Picture of Prohibition."—CG]

[14.] [*The Survey* was a twice-monthly magazine for social work professionals; the correct name of the author of the article, "The Eleven Wickersham Reports," is Arthur Kellogg.—CG]

[15.] [This word had not been deciphered in the German edition.—CG]

[16.] [*The World Tomorrow* was the title in 1931 of the monthly magazine of the Fellowship of Reconciliation, Norman Thomas and Reinhold Niebuhr being among its editors at that time; the circulation in 1934 was forty thousand (see also 12/6). However, the lynching article, unrelated to the assignment for the day but which Bonhoeffer made a point of noting, is not found in this journal, nor does it have an article on the Wickersham Report. The horrible crime on January 12 in Maryville, Missouri, was widely reported, and the article Bonhoeffer recorded was in the *Literary Digest* of January 31, under the title "Missouri Heads 1931 Lynching Parade." The third paragraph begins, "It was the first lynching of 1931." The same issue also opened with an article on the Wickersham Report.—CG]

[17.] [Thomas, "Banks of New York."—CG]

[18.] The New York stock market crash on "Black Thursday," October 24, 1929, led to a world economic crisis, with thirty million unemployed. It represents a decisive date in

sand people with a small deposit of $400 or less, is an exceedingly fatale event in a winter of large unemployment. It has a sharp social and ethical issue. The causes of this failure are to be sought firstly in the roothless operations of the directors of the Bank of the United States, secondly in an insufficient control of the bank by the State of New York, thirdly in the atti-
tude of the strong banks toward the bank of the United States. It is doubt- 401
less that it would have been possible for them to go a little farther in the attempt to save the bank of U. St. The whole story shed a bright light upon a very dark situation of personal unhonesty, unfairness, ruthlessness, lack of the consciousness of social responsibility. "The strong banks[19] are the principle masters of America." It is frightful to see that the "principle masters" do not know their responsibility for the majority.

Other articles: *Foreign affairs* Jan 1931. The permanence bases[20] of German foreign policy. R. v. Kühlmann.

12.3. Situation in India[21]

Situation in India

After the London Round Table Conference the Viceroy of India has numerous discussions with Gandhi. In the beginning all these discussions are strictly confidential. Nobody knows what is going to happen. By and by it becomes known that the Viceroy and Gandhi are working at an agreement.[22] The result of this provisional settlement is of enormous importance, and leaves hope for a new peaceful regulation of the whole problem. The result are, that the London conference shall be pursued by another conference, in which the Indian Nationalists participate. The British are supposed to make much wider concessions than before. Gandhi's aim is not so much self-rule, but, constitutional government. Gandhi stops for a while the disobedience campaign, the boycott. The political prisoners become free. The Situation seems to be, that Gandhi sees possibilities for a fulfill-
ment of at least the greater part of his claims and so he leaves the minor 402

the emergence of radical mass movements and of National Socialism in Germany. [The Bank of the United States was a private bank with 450,000 depositors, the fourth largest bank in New York; its collapse was the largest bank failure in U.S. history and spread fear across the land.—CG]

[19.] [Bonhoeffer misquoted. The article reads "the stronger bankers."—CG]

[20.] [Von Kühlmann, "Permanent Bases of German Foreign Policy."—CG]

[21.] An Indian commission was formed in 1929 that demanded dominion status from the British government. After London rejected this demand, Gandhi organized his protest with the famous "salt march," which led to the ultimately futile Round Table Conferences of 1930–33 discussed here.

[22.] The viceroy of India from 1926 to 1931 was Lord Irwin (E. F. L. Wood).

part for a later time. Gandhi already is rebuked as a traitor of his ideas, although these in the present moment only can be seen an act of political wisdom.

New York Times:[23] Reports from February 17. 18. 19. 20. 26. 27. II. 2. 6. 8. III.

Nation (London) 18. February.[24]

Other Articles read:	Our School burns down[25]	} *New Republic*
	National Planning[26]	March 4.

12.4. The Power Utility Issue: Muscle Shoals

11.IV.31 The power utility issue. Muscle Shoals[27]

Readings: *Forum* Febr. 1930. The real power problem[28]
The New Republic Apr. 1930 The Muscle Shoals Lobby.[29]
The Nation Dez. 1930 The Power fight goes on.[30]

The main issue of the power utility problem is the question, whether the government should operate or at least regulate the power works. It is a fact, that the competitive system in The United States makes the price for the consumer considerably higher. The consumer in New York pays five times as much as the consumer in Canada, where the government runs the powerworks. Roosevelt demands regulation by the government, the[31] big companies oppose. The question became acute in connection with the Muscle-Shoals plan. Norris[32] succeeded in fighting through the idea of

[23.] Titles of the newspaper articles and some commentary are given in Green, "Bonhoeffer's Courses."

[24.] [This refers to the article "India and the Round Table Conference," by George Slocombe, a reporter on the Paris staff of the London *Daily Herald*; the conference was held in London, which may explain Bonhoeffer's parenthesis.—CG]

[25.] [Chase, "Our School Burns Down." The article about the Hessian Hills School, a progressive school at Croton-on-Hudson, reported the impressive cooperative effort to rebuild after the fire.—CG]

[26.] [Soule, "National Planning."—CG]

[27.] [Muscle Shoals was an area of the Tennessee River in northwest Alabama hazardous to navigation until the Wilson Dam, with its power generation and nitrate plants, was completed in 1925. A major debate over public versus private ownership ensued until 1933, when the Tennessee Valley Authority was established and took over the facilities.—CG]

[28.] [Insull, "Real Power Problem."—CG]

[29.] [Gilfond, "Muscle Shoals Lobby."—CG]

[30.] [Finney, "Power Fight Goes On."—CG]

[31.] Deleted: "Norris fights."

[32.] [Senator George William Norris.—CG]

operation by the government, Senate and House agree. Mr. Hoover refused this decision by vetoing it. His argument was based on the opinion, that the project would lose money. One principle purpose of governmental operation of Muscle Shoals is to limit the rates charged ultimate consumers. Mr. 403
Hoovers statement is not very probable. "The prices, which the generating plant could charge distributing companies and industries, based on what these purchasers of current now pay in the region, would be so low as to prevent a profit beering made in generating." The spread is far too wide between costs of generation and the consumers rate.

12.5. Forced Exports in Russia

Forced Exports in Russia

Articles read: Russia and the World Crisis by Chamberlain
New Republic, February 18. 1931.[33]
The 5 Year Plan
New Republic Dec. 3. 1930.[34]
An American Loan to Russia?
New Republic December 17. 30.[35]

The economic world crisis has a strange aspect in Russia. Russia alone has escaped the evils of unemployment and of slackened production. On the contrary there is a shortage of labor and of workers. Russia of course sees here one of the convincing effect, which the 5 year plan already has had as opposed to all capitalistic countries. But the fall of prices in the whole world affected Russia's own production and trade very much. Russia received much less for the export of oil, lumber, fur, grain. And she could not pay the machinery for the agricultural organisation. The only way out of this situation for Russia was to increase her export and this has led to the question of "dumping" of Soviet Union. The fact of Russian "dumping" is so complicated because the ruble has no buy-worth abroad and so it [is] impossible to compare the market prices in Russia with the prices in foreign markets. The trade relation between Russia and France are pretty bad. France has introduced discrimination in the tariffs against Soviet goods. This hostile relation find an expression in Italy's extraordinary approachment[36] to Russia. 404

[33.] [William Chamberlain, "Russia and the World Crisis." Bonhoeffer draws heavily on this article.—CG]

[34.] [Soule, "Will the Five Year Plan Succeed?"—CG]

[35.] [Sherover, "American Loan to Russia?"—CG]

[36.] [Probably "rapprochement" is meant.—CG]

Russia takes the part of Italy in the Franco-Italian conflict. This of course influences again Russia's attitude to Germany and its growing anti-franco nationalism, which is related with italian fascism.

Russia's dumping is an act of economic necessity and it seems that in the United States itself the same procedure is not rarely done without receiving the reproach of dumping.

Survey. March 15. 1931. How big shall the Big Brother be?[37]

12.6. Germany—Poland—Russia

Germany—Poland—Russia[38]

Treaty of Versailles gave the corridor to Poland, in order to give Poland access to the sea. 1910 1 1/2 millions, 1930 1/2 millions Germans.[39] Danzig was completely German. So they made it a free City-State. Polish trade does not go through Danzig; extra polish harbour Gedinca.[40] Problem of Eastprussia is the complete separation from the Reich. One of the gravest problems is the problem of settlement in the corridor and in Eastprussia. The corridor becomes more and more polish, the Germans go out because very badly treated. In Eastprussia likewise more and more polish people settle down and many Eastprussian come back to the Reich. This is particularly in the present pressure of unemployment in the Reich highly disagreable. Poland in her situation between Russia and Germany, her hostile attitude toward both and her friendly relations to France, sympathizes with Tchechoslovakia and Yugoslavia, while Russia with Italy and Germany is in very good relations. The second announcement of the German Austrian customsunion gives to the situation a sharp issue.

[37.] [Rubinow, "How Big Shall the Big Brother Be?" The article does not use "Big Brother" metaphorically as in George Orwell's personification of state power in his *1984*; rather, quite unrelated to the summary to which it is appended, this article discusses complexity and ambivalences in sibling relationships with reference to the Big Brother movement.—CG]

[38.] No bibliographical sources are given.

[39.] [The drop in German population refers to the corridor, not to Danzig.—CG]

[40.] [Gdynia.—CG]

Other Articles: *The World Tomorrow*[41]
Socialism by Norman Thomas[42]
New Republic: John Dewey. The need for a new political party[43]

12.7. The German-Austrian Customs Union 405

The German-Austrian Customs Union

Articles in the *New York Times*, 21.III–1.IV[44]

Facing an impossible economic situation (Germany with 5 million willing workers without the possibility of competition on the world market (: english coals in Cologne are cheaper than Ruhrcoals!))[45] Germany and Austria are planning a customs union. Herewith the first step in the direction, which had been proposed by Mr. Briand in his plan of Pan-europe, has been taken. Germany has invited all other nations to join the customs union. Now this action has excited the french press highly. It is supposed to be directed against the treaty of Versailles and the settlement in Geneva 1922, which forbids Austria any trade union and which state the complete independence of Austria. Dr. Curtius denies that and is willing to bring the whole issue before the session of the League of Nations next May in Geneva. The real issue of course is that France sees a new alliance emerging between Germany, Austria, Russia, Italy and so she sees in this customs union not only an event of mere economic importance, but a political action with great consequences. As yet Germany has denied this aspect of the action seriously.

[41.] [Regarding this magazine, see ed. note 16. This layout of Bonhoeffer's notes accurately reproduces the manuscript.—CG]

[42.] [Thomas, "Socialism."—CG]

[43.] [Dewey, "Need for a New Party. I: The Present Crisis." See ed. note 46 indicating that Bonhoeffer read the second article in this series, but he does not mention the third article promised for April 1.—CG]

[44.] [March 21–April 1. Titles of the numerous newspaper articles and some commentary are given in Green, "Bonhoeffer's Courses."—CG]

[45.] The information concerning coal prices came from Bonhoeffer's father, Karl; cf. the latter's letter of March 10, 1931 (*NL*, C 1). [This letter is unpublished.—CG]

It is interesting to see in the light of this situation, what the original meaning of Mr. Briand's plan for Pan-europe was. There is no doubt that the whole incident is based upon the untolerable financial situation, into which Germany has been brought by the payment of war reparations. And this aspect of the situation brings the whole issue home to the United States.

New Republic: John Dewey.[46]

406 **12.8. The Report of the Federal Council of Churches on Birth Control**

The Report of the Federal Council of Churches on Birth Control

Information Service of the Federal Council[47]
Outlook Apr. 1.st 1931[48]
Commonweal Apr. 1.st 1931[49]

The committee for family and house of the Federal Council has published a report on birth control with the main idea that birthcontrol by means of "contraception by married people is valid and moral." "It is important to provide for the proper spacing of children, the control of the size of the family." The committee agrees that "sex union between husbands and wifes as an expression of mutual affection, without relation to procreation, is right." These are the main reasons for the justification of birth control. It is to be added the fact that a very large part of the population already uses contraceptives, and that so the decision of the Church was made urgent. "The public therefore has a right to expect guidance from the Church on the moral aspect." Characteristic is the following formulation "guidance should be sought from the Holy Spirit, the Lord and Giver of Life. It should be expected that guidance will find expression through the researches and experiences of physicians and men of science as well as through the corpo-

[46.] [Dewey, "Need for a New Party. II: The Breakdown of the Old Order."—CG]

[47.] [On March 20, 1931, the Information Service of the Federal Council of Churches issued a report of the council's Committee on Marriage and the Home, and the following month the council published the text in its bulletin, the source of Bonhoeffer's quotes; see "Churches and Birth Control."—CG]

[48.] ["Federal Council on Birth Control," editorial in *The Outlook and Independent*. —CG]

[49.] ["Birth Control Revolution," editorial in *Commonweal*. Note that the papal encyclical "Casti Connubii" (Concerning Chaste Marriage) had been published on December 31, 1930.—CG]

rate conscience of the church." Already the Lambeth conference[50] last August had gone a step in this direction. The main opposition comes from Rome. *Commonweal* claims this document be the death of the Reformation and keeps up the position of the Lutherans. It is interesting to see, that the issue of fight between Protestants and Catholics turns to be an ethical one, since the dogmatical is no longer understood by Protestants.

12.9. Unemployment[51] 407

Unemployment

Unemployment as an international problem. Geneva special studies March 1931[52]
Unemployment insurance.[53] (Series on social insurance) and current articles.

The paradoxical situation of today is this, that general poverty goes hand in hand with an overproduction, with abundance, low prices and unemployment. For the second time after the war the world is faced with the unemployment situation. The reason being a maladjustment in production and distribution. Most countries have met this situation with some kind of unemployment insurance. The question here arises as to who would be obliged to pay the costs. The usual practice in Europa is that three factors work together: state, employer, employee, except in Russia where the employee and Italy where the state is exempt. The german regulation is as follows (after several variations): employer and employee have to pay together 6 1/2% of the wages. The government contributes only to the extended benefits. The Nation pays 4/5 of these, localties 1/5. A waiting period of 7 days, then standard benefits payed for a maximum of 26 weeks.[54] In the U.S.A. there is no official governmental regulation at all. Some attempts have been made, but only by private societys. Remarkable is the attempt of

[50.] [The conference of bishops of the Anglican communion throughout the world held about every decade.—CG]

[51.] Previously unpublished.

[52.] [Spates, *Unemployment as an International Problem*.—CG]

[53.] [*Unemployment Insurance: A Summary of Some Existing Governmental and Private Plans* was a twenty-six-page booklet published by the Metropolitan Life Insurance Company of New York; it was the first monograph in a series on social insurance published by the company between 1931 and 1935.—CG]

[54.] The workers' insurance legally regulated by Bismarck's social policies (1881–89) did not provide unemployment insurance, which was not legally implemented until 1927.

the "General Electric Company." But it is obvious also here that a sufficient support for the unemployed can be garenteed only by state insurance. The state as well as the average employer refuses the payment of support, so the situation in the U.S.A. is particularly bad, although there is no doubt that for instance Germany must break financially if the period lasts for a longer time. A way out of the whole situation can be seen, it seems to me, only in a new regulation of the question of war debt, and in a cancellation of those by the U.S.A.

408 **13. Short Report on William James, *The Varieties of Religious Experience*[1]**

James: *Varieties of relig. exper.* chapter XX.

In the last chapter of his great and extensiv study on the varieties of religious experience William James gives a short summary and draws his systematic conclusions. Having seen the enormous richness, manifoldness and efficiency of religious experience James cannot but try to fit that in into his own world view. It is for his whole way of thinking impossible, that a complex of exper. with so farreaching importance should not have any definit right and meaning. In order to find out the right interpretation of this fact James abstracts the most general religious ideas from their accidental content and sums them up as follows 1.) First idea: that the visible world is a part of a more spiritual universe 2.) That union with that higher universe is true 3.) that prayer is a process, wherein work is really done. These believes are accompanied by the following psychological characteristics: 1.) a new zest which adds itself like a gift to life, 2.) an assurance of safety and a temper of peace. After a short statement about the necessity of many religious types James takes up the question as to whether religion be only a survival of primitive thought and whether now science takes its place. James denies that, explaining that science deals only with general ideas and abstractions leaving out the concrete individual experience. Sci-

[1.] *NL*, A 35,1; handwritten, with a remark by Bethge: "Union Sem."; in original English, including errors. Previously published in *GS* 3:127–29. The report was presumably delivered in 1931 in Professor Lyman's second-semester course, "Religious Aspects of Contemporary Philosophy." Cf. Bonhoeffer's own report on his year abroad, 1/181, p. 310: "I read almost the entire philosophical works of William James, which really captivated me." [This manuscript, written in English, has numerous deletions, insertions, and abbreviations, such as "relig.," "exper.," and "psycholog." which are not consistently reproduced here; they confirm that it was for an oral presentation, since Bonhoeffer wrote fair copies of papers that he handed in.—CG]

ence is impersonal, religion personal. Here religion holds its place, and goes deeper than science does, because it is based in the feeling of man; and (Quotation 1) "the recesses of feeling are the only places in the world in which we catch real fact in the making."[2] Therefore Religion must play an eternal part in human history. Now James goes on and distinguishes a subjective right of religion and an objective right of religion. He states, 409
that subjectively the religious man has enough if he can use his God, if God works for him so that he does not question more the real existence. But only this question exactly would answer the problem of the objective right of religion. James undertakes the answering of this most important question in two steps: First: is there a common nucleus of all religions? Second: is the unanimous testimony of religion true? In the first place James reduces religion to two most general experiences 1. a feeling of uneasiness 2. and its solution, its deliverance. The second experience James describes as follows: man becomes conscious that his higher part is continuous with a *more* of the same quality, which is operative in the universe outside of him. Now the question arises: what is the objective Truth of this feeling of something "more" . . . Here James introduces the subconscious self as a mediating term between science and religion. Herewith the contact with science is preserved as well as is given an explanation and a justification of the religious experience of a reality outside of one's self. It is a fact that the conscious person is continuous with a wider self through which saving experiences come. After the statement of this minimum of relig. truth, James gives what he calls his own overbelief, that is a belief, which is not scientifically justifiable. He holds, the most interesting and valuable thing about a man are usually his overbeliefs, though he is afraid that most of the readers will consider his overbelief a sorry underbelief. Then he gives his idea of a great consciousness in which we all have our ground, from which our ideal impulses come and calls this being which proves himself real by his action God. Quotation "We and God have business with each other"[3] "where God is, tragedy is only provisional and partial."[4] His God is not omnipotent, but neither is he a mere idea, he is an effective power in the world and only this justifies religion.

The last proof for God's objective existence lies in his activity, a world with God is indeed another world than a world without God.

[2.] [James, *Varieties of Religious Experience* (1928), 501. After "recesses of feeling," Bonhoeffer omits the words "the darker, blinder strata of character."—CG]

[3.] [Ibid., 516–17.—CG]

[4.] [Ibid., 517.—CG]

In the very strange postscript James confesses his belief in a certain kind of polytheism and in what he calls a piecemeal supranaturalism. This is understandable only as a religious consequence of his philosophical pluralism.

410 Critical objections: 1. it is not true to say, that the religious individual does not care so much for the reality as for the efficiency of God. The reality of God is of course for most religious people no philosophical question but a basic conviction.

2. Concerning the term "subconsciousness" is to be asked: if subconsciousness shall be satisfactory for the religious experience of the outside, then it must be considered really outside of the individual person. But if it is not really outside, then the religious experience of the outside is an illusion, if it is really outside, then the term subconsciousness seems to be misleading and it is to be asked, why we do not say: God, which would of course show, that the appearent contact with science is illusory. So it seems to me not be possible to find a mediating term between relig. and science.

14. Course Paper: The Character and Ethical Consequences of Religious Determinism[1]

The Character and Ethical Consequences of Religious Determinism

All primitive religious and theological thinking stands between determinism and indeterminism. God and human beings act together. Ethics would be threatened if human beings were not able to contribute to their own situation before the world and before God. On the other hand, if human beings were able to do everything needed to determine their situation at
411 any given time, religion would lose its point. The only solution is for human beings and God to act together according to their respective abilities. This compromise is as old as religion itself, and although not consciously carried out initially, in any given moment it is actualized in religious activity and

[1.] *NL*, A 25,1; handwritten manuscript, with a note by Bethge: "USA 1930/31 for what?" Previously published in *GS* 3:85–90. On the first page a handwritten evaluation, doubtless from Niebuhr: "The question concerning God's guidance in the world has been handled a bit too cursorily. Calvin emphasizes this side of the idea of God so strongly that one [can] hardly [speak] of any sharp distinction between general religious determinism and the Christian belief in God's exclusive activity." [This is the only paper that Bonhoeffer wrote in German for Union Seminary courses. Since it is concerned with ethics and has a response from Niebuhr, it was most likely written in the first semester for the philosophy of religion course "Religion and Ethics" taught by Niebuhr.—CG]

thought. In the history of the Christian church, this compromise is associated with names such as Pelagius, the later Scotists, Erasmus, the philosophers and theologians of the Enlightenment, and all of liberal theology in its different variations. All concur in their objection to any sort of one-sided determinism that might destroy in essence all ethical values.[2]

We can clarify the discussion by distinguishing between (1) philosophical determinism, (2) general religious determinism, and (3) Christian belief in the sole efficacy of God or belief in justification by faith.

Utter confusion invariably results whenever these three, essentially different, forms of determinism are confused, which is generally the case.

(1) Philosophical determinism is based on the idea of causality. The ultimate ground conceals within itself the realization of all consequences. No event bears its origin within itself. This idea aids in interpreting what takes place in the world. In itself it is both ethically and religiously irrelevant; indeed, it inherently excludes any ethical or religious assessment, unless one reinterprets the two categories of evaluation by explaining them solely with regard to categories inherently alien to them ("usefulness," "happiness," etc.). Because philosophical determinism is essentially "explanatory," no amount of creativity will ever derive any *genuine* categories of "value" from it. The impossibility of doing so, however, prompts us to characterize this first form of determinism as ethically and religiously irrelevant, albeit without drawing any conclusions regarding its objective philosophical validity.

(2) Rather than explain the world, general religious determinism wants 412
instead to "justify" it in some way. It engages in a value judgment of the world. The world as it is comes from God's hand as the ultimate "world cause," that is, God can be found everywhere, that is, ultimately the world is essentially good. The relation between God and the world is conceived dynamically. Because God is at work even in what is bad or evil, these things, too, contribute in some way to the glorification of God. Because the world is the world of God, however, the good always stands behind the bad. I always know that evil has already been overcome; it follows from my concept of God, which I always have at my disposal in order to explain "rightly" all misfortune in the world or to justify God in the world.

[2.] Regarding the typical "Pelagian" cooperation (synergism) between God and human beings since Pelagius (died after 418), Duns Scotus (died 1308), and Erasmus (1469–1536), see the brief presentation in Müller, *Die Rechtfertigungslehre*, 19–21, 48–50, and 59–60. Bonhoeffer's charge of Pelagianism against the Enlightenment and the whole of liberal theology adopts objections from dialectical theology under Karl Barth's leadership. [Bonhoeffer explicitly refers to the "later Scotists" but does not identify members of the school, which remained influential into the eighteenth century, esp. among Franciscans.—CG]

¶Inquiries concerning the ethical consequences of this form of determinism cannot become involved in a psychological discussion, for example, in the sense of the question: what influence must such a view have on ethical actions? In psychology we never get beyond the category of possibility, since we are again moving within the schema of causality. The question is rather whether the idea of good and evil can be conceived on the basis of such premises. The answer is no. In the idea of God used (and thus misused) as "interpretation," the contrast between good and evil is always conceived as an antithesis that has already been suspended [aufgehoben] in the synthesis of nondifference [Indifferenz].[3] There is no radical evil; evil is merely a paradoxical means of actualizing the good. Here I always have the possibility of interpreting away evil as such, of justifying the world from the perspective of my own understanding of God, instead of leaving the justification of the world to *God's* pronouncements. It is difficult to demonstrate historically that this form of determinism leads psychologically to quietism, but this makes no *substantive* difference here. Even the highest "ethical" activism does not yet constitute proof of a genuine understanding of ethical categories, just as little as utter quietism demonstrates the opposite. The ultimate reason for the weakness of general religious determinism
413 is its concept of God. God is conceived as the world cause, rather than as Creator. The two are completely distinct so that the one excludes the other, something rarely taken into account even though everything follows from this premise. General religious determinism is not "Christian determinism," to which we now turn our attention.

(3) Christian belief in the sole efficacy of God or belief in justification by faith alone.

Here we are dealing not with an interpretation of the world but with the question concerning human beings and their situation before God; that is, the question is raised whether the human being can stand before God, whether human beings are "just"-"ified" ["recht"-"fertig"] by God. Rather than engaging a certain idea of God in interpreting what happens in the world, here we expect an answer to our question from the real God. Rather than already knowing the answer beforehand, the human being expects it from outside, from God. This changes the whole picture. God and human being stand facing each other, as person and person.[4] Human beings

[3.] [In this context "Indifferenz" is used in a Hegelian sense; differences between the two contrasted concepts end up in a "nondifference."—CG]

[4.] [The concept of person in ethical encounter is central to Bonhoeffer's doctrine of God and his theological anthropology; cf. *Sanctorum Communio* (*DBWE* 1), esp. chap. 2, and Green, *Bonhoeffer: A Theology of Sociality*, esp. 28–45.—CG]

believe themselves to be placed by God before the question of existence and must hear the answer from God. And this answer is initially the radical "no" pronounced over the human being. These human beings cannot stand before God; they are judged because they have departed from community [Gemeinschaft] with God, they are no longer in truth and in love, and are evil. If the miracle nonetheless is to occur that the human being is just-ified before God, it can only occur on God's own initiative. Human beings themselves are caught in sin; they cannot get back to God, that is, cannot step out of sin. They are no longer free. But now God comes despite everything, pronounces the "yes" over human beings, tears them out of sin, and is merciful toward them. This is God's free and sole act; human beings remain completely in God's omnipotence.

That, briefly, is the Protestant doctrine of justification by faith alone and is essentially "Christian determinism." It is a question of human freedom and lack of freedom with reference to the ultimate, to salvation. This was also the main point of Luther's *De servo arbitrio*,[5] though one cannot deny that Luther did not always clearly distinguish this idea from others 414
of a more speculative or cosmically interpretive nature. Nonetheless, he is ultimately concerned with only one thing, namely, with God's exclusive freedom with regard to just-ifying [Recht-fertigmachung] the world. We repeatedly encounter Luther's self-evident presupposition that although human beings are indeed able to act ethically with regard to the *iustitia civilis*,[6] that is, with regard to relative questions involving good and evil apart from the real question of salvation, they cannot be "good" or "justified" before God.

If we now also inquire here concerning the ethical consequences, our substantive concern focuses not on the psychological aspect but on the question whether the idea of good and evil has genuinely been taken completely seriously. The answer is yes. Evil is evil against God. Every culpable human fault is a fault against God. Good does not always stand behind every evil; the human being as a personal evil will stands radically over against and separated from God as the personal Creator. God does not want evil; God wants the good. The question is now whether the idea of the good has been taken seriously in this sense. Good is good before God. Human beings know

[5.] Luther's 1525 book *De servo arbitrio* (*The Bondage of the Will*, *LW* 33:3–295) was newly revived for Protestant theology only during the "Luther Renaissance" and the emergence of dialectical theology, although Harnack had already assessed this work as, from a certain perspective, Luther's "greatest writing" (*History of Dogma*, 3:202).

[6.] Concerning Luther's understanding of "civil righteousness," cf. Althaus, *Theology of Martin Luther*, 143–44.

they are incapable of accomplishing this good. They recognize their own sin and struggle against it, yet it is as if they were in a moving train running in the opposite direction from the train itself. Yet precisely by recognizing their own lack of freedom before God and their exclusive determination by God, they begin to perceive God's sole power; their faith in this determinism through God, rather than becoming a means of interpreting the world, reveals itself as power within them. This recognition of faith, recognition bestowed by God, is creative power that makes human beings free—free from the world and for God. Where human beings see they are weak, God is strong, bringing about the good, but God alone does this. There is no proof
415 of whether this power for good [manifests] itself psychologically as quietism or activism, and this is no longer part of theology.

Two questions remain open. If human beings are completely determined by God, then the evil they do must also be determined by God; but in that case we are back at general religious determinism. Here we encounter the final antinomy of Christian thought. Luther dared to assert that God brings about both evil and good, though this view represents an ultimate speculative insight[7] that should not itself be used to interpret other circumstances. That God as the Creator hates evil and that nonetheless nothing can occur in the world that God does not want is an insoluble antinomy; it is no longer understood as an antinomy, however, as soon as one believes oneself able to draw conclusions from it for a Christian devaluation of evil.

The second question (emerging from the first) concerns God's guidance in the world. The notion that everything happens in the world according to God's plan is biblically well grounded. The assertion is that ultimately we are unfree even with regard to the *iustitia civilis*.[8] We must always remember, however, that the God of guidance can be recognized only from the God of justification; the reverse is not true. This consideration puts the problem on the right track.

[7.] Harnack also recognizes risky "speculations" on Luther's part: "For when Luther here reflects on what the hidden God (*deus absconditus*) is, as distinct from the God who is preached (*deus praedicatus*), when he admits a double will in God, and so on, this is only a proof that he has not yet rid himself of the bad practice of the scholastic understanding of treating theological perceptions as philosophical doctrines. . . . In the main, however, with his doctrines of predestination and the enslaved will he has very clearly discarded metaphysics and psychology as the foundation for Christian knowledge" (*History of Dogma,* 3:203.) [Translation revised.—CG]

[8.] See ed. note 6.

15. Course Paper: The Religious Experience of Grace and the Ethical Life[1] 416

This formulation of the topic includes two important premises

1.) that there is something like an "experience" of "grace"

2.) that such an experience of grace can be defined sufficiently as "religious" experience.

In the following we will have to treat the relation of those three notions—"religious," "experience," "grace"—to each other. Two of them can be conceived in terms of psychological categories. The third one belongs in its essence to an absolutely different realm of notions, nevertheless it is impossible to prevent psychology from transgressing its own limits and from attempting its own interpretation of the notion of grace. That takes place in this very moment, when grace is conceived as a psychological reality, that means as one fact among others, as psychologically "vergegenständlicht,"[2] as accessible for all desinterested research. According as we start this enquiry with the interpretation of psychological notion or with the interpretation of the theological notion of grace, the whole research will run in a different way. I will try to give a systematic outline of both these ways of interpretation and their consequences.

I. Psychological interpretation.

Here "grace" might be defined as a superhuman power which is in its essence dynamic, and which is as far as it is experienced, entering the realm of human feeling, willing, thinking and so giving to the finiteness an eternal worth and character. The acknowledgment of one's own finiteness and of an infinite grace, which nevertheless enters this finiteness, is general and essential, no matter with what concrete contents grace is considered to be endowed. In any case grace is conceived as a fact which can be considered objectively, "gegenständlich."

The ethical life might be defined as the personal active attitude toward 417
the human world, including the ego. Questionable is the relationship

[1.] *NL*, A 25,2 b; handwritten final version; with a remark by Bethge: "Winter 1930/1" and the handwritten assessment by Niebuhr; in original English, including errors. Previously published in *GS* 3:91–99. Cf. also *NL*, A 25,2 a; handwritten draft. [The draft, a twenty-one-page document in Bonhoeffer's literary estate, was also written in English. Possibly this was a second paper for the first semester course with Niebuhr, "Religion and Ethics," for which 2/14 was probably written. For the second-semester ethics course he took with Niebuhr (CE 52a), Bonhoeffer wrote a paper on "Negro Literature" as noted in the editor's introduction, p. 21, note 103. Note that this course was "Philosophy of Religion 13" and see Bonhoeffer's reference, p. 448, to "Philosophy of Religion."—CG]

[2.] ["Objectified"—CG]

between this kind of grace and the ethical life. I make the contention that "grace" always is used to give to man the possibility for forming and justifying his ethical life. That is to be proved. Man receives and possesses grace (according to the psychological interpretation); that means he possesses to a certain extent God, he knows God, he knows his will, but not only that: in the experience of grace he receives God himself or at least godlike power. His human existence has got union with God; his finiteness is justified and endowed with infinite value.

Here religion is directly identified with experience of grace, religion becomes the highest value, because it is an experience of the holy transcendence. Yet this idea of transcendence is not taken seriously, since transcendence is found only in human immanent experiences. This idea of transcendence is used only to give value to human endeavour. The main interest is not an adequate idea of grace, but the highest possible valuation of humanity.

When grace is considered to be working in the midst of human experience, when grace can be experienced quite directly, it follows, that this experience must work in any way into the actual life. There are only two ways in which this experience can work out.[3]

A. The first one is the *nomistic* way.

Here the religious experience of grace involves the acknowledgement
418 of a fixed moral commandment. This commandment is considered to have authority from God. The mere fact of having gotten this commandment includes not only the possibility of fulfillment of it, but also it grants me the presence of God and my union with him. After the experience of grace I am really put in the fortunate position of the man, who knows exactly, what he has to do, and whose life is in security when he strictly follows this commandment. The presence of God is conceived as the presence of any object, which I have at my disposition. The experience of grace gives to man

[3.] Bonhoeffer's following critique of a psychological understanding of the concept of grace derives a bit one-sidedly from a specific Lutheran position (e.g., like that found in Luther's "The Bondage of the Will") and is also dependent on Barth in its understanding of essentially future-oriented, that is, forensic justification. Bonhoeffer does not consider here the "effective" understanding of grace and justification that is also present in Lutheranism and is especially pronounced in Andreas Osiander; cf. in this regard Ernst Bizer's article on "Osiander" (in *Die Religion in Geschichte und Gegenwart*, 3rd ed., 4:1730). Nor does he consider the relationship between grace and spirit. Cf. Luther's own interpretation of Rom. 5:5 in his preface to the Epistle of St. Paul to the Romans (1522; *LW* 35:365–80; *WA.DB* 7:3–27): "This pleasure and love for the law is put into the heart by the Holy Spirit, as St. Paul says in chapter 5[:5]" (*LW* 35:368; *WA.DB* 7:7), which became the programmatic text of pietism as in Johann Arndt, Philipp Jacob Spener, and John Wesley, the latter in connection with his conversion experience of May 24, 1738.

a trust in this security because he has the moral law and because he is put in the situation of being able to live an ethical life. Man puts his trust in this knowledge of the moral law and its fulfillment.

We can distinguish historically between two types of this nomistic conception of the relationship of grace and ethical life.

1.) The experience of grace *creates* a new moral law. This law is the "gegenständliche"[4] presence of God and of his grace. It can be a social or an individual law.

a) Two great examples from history of "Verhärtung"[5] of the grace-experience to a social law with its own historic organisation are the Jewish Theocracy and the Catholic Church. (The calvinistic idea of a theocracy is in its essence different, since there underlies a different conception of grace.) The experience of grace causes the building up of a fixed institution of divine law, only in which grace-experience is possible. In the midst of history there is a separate realm, which is holy and which is entirely excluded from all relativities of historical development. Men who belong to this realm, must submit themselves to the laws of the institution and they are thereby excluded from all human insecurity. Their lives are secure, because this objective grace in the shape of the Theocracy or the church bears them up. Grace gives to man the possibility of gaining security through the observation of some divine laws.

b) The experience of grace can be creativ for the individual life. In this case the individuum receives some special illuminations for sanctifieing himself. Here is the root of asceticism of every kind, of monachism u.s.f.[6] Grace is "verhärtet" to an individual law. Asceticism not only arises from grace-experience, but also leads back to a new experience of this kind.

2. The experience of grace is not necessarily creative. There is another 419
way of experiencing grace, in which the given conditions are taken as they are. In this case grace does not reserve a certain holy realm of life for itself, but man has to live in the human world according to the task or work, which he has to do. He has to be a good citizen, father, husband, and being all that he fulfills the will of God. Experience of grace is in that case not so much reception of creativ power, as the experience of being cleansed through forgiveness. This is the type of misunderstood protestantism, which is very common in protestant countries nowadays.[7] It underlies in the last analy-

[4.] ["Objective"—CG]

[5.] [Literally "hardening," that is, solidifying, turning into an objective principle, institutionalizing.—CG]

[6.] ["Monasticism, and so on."—CG]

[7.] [Here Bonhoeffer anticipates his critique of "cheap grace" in *Discipleship*.—CG]

sis the ethics of Kant. Kants notion of duty is the strongest secularisation of the protestant "experience" of grace. Grace becomes law.

B. The other extreme of the "experience of grace" involves antinomianism. Grace is interpreted here as the strict contradiction of "law," law is abolished because we have experienced grace. Antinomianism exists in two forms as quietism and as libertinism. The former knows, that he "has" grace and he does not need anything more, he possesses grace, forgiveness, peace, release from all tension, he recognises the insufficiency of his own work and so he stops striving and working and enjoies his possession. Libertinism takes its justification from the same experience of grace. The libertinist feels, that the Holy Spirit itself dwells in him, and that now, after having received grace—that means: the Holy Spirit—he can do, what he wants to do. He is sanctified, therefore his deeds also are sanctified. It was the great discovery of Martin Luther, that he was able to show in struggling against the enthusiast ("Schwärmer"), that libertinism is in itself a kind of nomism, a relapse into the slavery of the law instead of the pure interpretation of the idea of grace.[8] The reason is, that here grace is conceived of as fully received in my experience, that grace becomes identified with my *consciousness* of grace, so that I have to look only at myself in order to know that I have to do; in other words, grace was again "vergegenständlicht" and grace as a static substanciality[9]—living in me—is as such no more merely grace, but law.

420 Psychology cannot think in these extremes (of grace and "law"), it knows differences of degree not of kind. The reason is that the psychologically interpreted notion of grace is in the last analysis essentially immanent. For this interpretation all experience of grace in regard to ethical life runs the danger either of making man "nomistic" or "antinomian" (that means here: unethical). Between both these extremes there is a long scale in the midst of which is the "ideal and sound religion,"[10] in which the extremes are balanced. Nobody can be hindered from undertaking this interpretation in a general Philosophy of Religion. But it is certain, that here the specific christian idea of grace and its counterpart the idea [of] law is not touched, and that means for christian *theological* thinking, that the psychological interpretation is unable to conceive of the reality of grace at all. Christian theologi-

[8.] Clearly illustrated in Luther's struggle against Karlstadt and the Wittenberger "enthusiasts" [*Schwärmer*]. Cf. Brecht, *Martin Luther,* 2:59–61.

[9.] [Grace "objectified" and made into a "substance," a fixed, perduring entity. As such it is a "law" because it is not God's love and mercy freely given but a human possession.—CG]

[10.] [This sounds like a reference to a term of art found in a course reading or the professor's discourse.—CG]

cal thinking claims to give the only adequate interpretation of the problem of the relations between grace and the "ethical life" which means "law." There is of course a further possibility, to consider also christian thinking psychologically, but therewith we loose again the only way to solve the problem of grace and law. Christian thinking makes the statement, that if there anybody is, who claims to have experienced grace and then becomes nomistic or antinomian—that he has not really experienced "grace"! Since psychological interpretation of the relationship between grace and ethical life can only think in both these extremes, theological thinking contests the competence of psychological interpretation for treating this question. Christian thinking admits, that it thinks in a circle, because it thinks with the premise, that God really has revealed himself in Christ and that this revelation is the only truth; but it insists, that all thinking of truth must think in a circle, because it presumes, what it is going to prove. It is obvious that a thinking which does not reside in truth cannot think truth. That is the general philosophical form of the christian claim. Christian theological thinking alone can interpret grace and only upon this basis a true foundation of ethics is possible.

II. Theological Interpretation. 421

"Grace" here cannot be defined by the experience of Grace; on the contrary, the psychological category of experience must be criticised, modified and interpreted anew by the theological category of grace. It is essential for grace not to unite with human beeing, to be conceivable only in the any happy experience of union with God; but grace is in its essence directly opposed to every human beeing, to human experience of value and of God. It condemns all human effort to reach God as the attempt of man to be like God, as justification by works, by ethics, by religion. Man feels himself secure, he has got some possibilities to stand before God in security, because he is religious and ethical, he experiences grace. The basis of religion and of ethics is here the selfjustification before God. Grace destroys all these attempts, destroys religion and ethics and experiences of grace and it declares the man in all his ways as a sinner, who offends the sole glory of God. Grace is the absolute opposite to all human endeavour, otherwise it would not be entirely grace. Grace condemns utterly and forgives utterly. For psychological understanding the former is as inconceivable as the latter; it sees only something condemnable and something, that must be forgiven, but it is unable to conceive of man as absolute sinner and as absolutely justified by grace. Because the essence of grace in this way transcends our rational understanding, grace cannot be experienced, conceived, thought, but only believed *in spite of* all experiences of a "grace," which is not grace.

To grace corresponds faith. That means that grace always remains transcendent to our thinking, feeling etc., further that grace never can be possessed by or in human experiences in a way, that I could say: I am secure, because I have grace. Grace every moment must be believed anew, because it is never static, objective, "gegenständlich," but ever acting, judging and forgiving, "persönlich"[11] and only in these acts actual; it is always in opposition to man, therefore it always must be believed anew.

One might ask; is not the act of faith a certain kind of "religious experience" too? The answer is: certainly, the act of faith is imbedded in religious experience, especially "christian experience." But we must interpret this
422 experience theologically; that means, not the experience of faith is important, but the actuality of grace, experience is only a dim and inevitable reflection of the absolutely different reality of grace. Not because we have "christian experience" but because we have grace "in" and at the same time "beyond" this experience, christian faith is absolutely different from every other religion.

One often hears it said: if grace is *all* and man is nothing, then the natural consequence is that all ethical life is obviated. But this argument is a relapse into the psychological interpretation. Grace is not in this sense "all" that I can possess it once for all, that I can be secure once for all. Grace is essentially "coming Grace" not "being and remaining Grace."[12] That makes impossible every kind of human security, that destroys all security—as we discovered it in nomism and antinomianism, but it is the only basis for a genuine ethical life. Grace makes man free from himself (from his trust in his religion, in his ethical life etc.) und free for God, for hearing his word. It points every moment to God himself and gives to the man the only possible basis for being ethical—namely God himself. Man is free as long as he refers to God. If in the reference the *whole existence* of man is actually touched, then his behaviour in the world must be ethical, he can not do otherwise then conduct himself according to the reality of grace. Every single ethical decision might be wrong and sinfull—like every single "experience" of grace is wrong and sinfull; but nevertheless man lives in faith of his justification and sanctification; he never can say: I am good, he always must say: "forgive my debts" and he must believe in his justification. In this faith grace is made the only and new foundation of human life, not as "gegenständliche" grace—with its consequences of nomism and antinomianism—but always "coming grace"—with its consequences of making man free and

[11.] ["Personal" in the sense of an encountering word, not a static object.—CG]

[12.] Here Bonhoeffer is emphasizing a "forensic" understanding of grace and justification that is not entirely Lutheran; see ed. note 3.

at the same time responsible before God. Only when man is solely bound to God the ethical life has got its genuine foundation. All glory is here taken away from man and given back to God, man stands in the obedience and the service of God and that is his only and greatest glory. Every other ethics 423
makes man secure and break down therefore, because the glory of man as the last motiv of ethics is no more an ethical motiv, man becomes a slave of himself. Only the christian conception of grace makes man before God free and gives so the only possible basis for ethical life.[13]

16. Essay: Concerning the Christian Idea of God[1]

Concerning the Christian Idea of God

In the present article I do not pretend to present the Christian idea of God in its entirety. I am trying to give no more than the framework within which this idea should be thought. The fact that I am concerned only with the Christian idea of God and not some general speculation, that is to say, the fact that the theme is essentially dogmatical,[2] has led me to select the following topics for discussion: First, the reality of God with regard to the problem of the theory of knowledge;[3] second, God and history; third, the paradoxical God in the doctrine of justification. The connection between

[13.] In the margin of the last page, Niebuhr remarked: "In making grace as transcendent as you do I don't see how you can ascribe any ethical significance to it. Obedience to God's will may be a religious experience, but it is not an ethical one until it issues in actions which can be socially valued. Any other interpretation of 'ethical' than one which measures an action in terms of consequences and judges actions purely in terms of motives empties the ethical life of content and makes it purely formal."

[1.] This text (*NL*, A 25,3 b) is version B, from an offprint of *The Journal of Religion* 12 (1932): 177–85, with a remark by Bethge: "Lyman"; in original English. Previously published in *GS* 3:100–109. Cf. the related handwritten course paper, "The Christian Idea of God" (*NL*, A 25,3 a) with comments by Professor Lyman, referred to here in subsequent notes as version A. [Bonhoeffer took two courses with Lyman, "The Philosophy of the Christian Religion" in the first semester, and "Religious Aspects of Contemporary Philosophy" in the second semester. This paper was probably written for the course in the first semester, which included in its description "the meaning and validity of the leading Christian ideas." Another typescript of this essay, presumably a carbon of the copy sent to the journal for publication, was found in the papers of Herbert Jehle, to whom Bonhoeffer had apparently sent it; it is referred to as version C. The English of the published version is more polished than the handwritten draft and most likely reflects Paul Lehmann's assistance in revising. Only more significant variations will be mentioned in the notes.—CG]

[2.] [Lyman comment: "Meaning?"—CG]

[3.] [Version A reads: "the problem of a theological theory of knowledge."—CG]

these three parts and the progress from the first to the last one will be seen in the course of the treatment.

I. God and the Problem of Knowledge

If this inquiry were purely philosophical we should never be permitted to start with the reality of God; and as long as theology does not see its essen-
424 tial difference from all philosophical thinking, it does not begin with a statement concerning God's reality but tries rather to build a support for such a statement. Indeed, this is the main fault with theology, which in our day no longer knows its particular province and its limits.[4] It is not only a methodological fault but, likewise, a misunderstanding of the Christian idea of God from the very beginning. Philosophical thinking attempts to be free from premises (if that is possible at all); Christian thinking has to be conscious of its particular premise, that is, of the premise of the reality of God, before and beyond all thinking. In the protection of this presupposition, theological thinking convicts[5] philosophical thinking of being bound also to a presupposition, namely, that thinking in itself can give truth. But philosophical truth always remains truth which is given only within the category of possibility. Philosophical thinking never can extend beyond this category—it can never be a thinking in reality. It can form a conception of reality, but conceived reality is not reality any longer.[6] The reason for this is that thinking is in itself a closed circle, with the ego as the center.[7] The last "reality" for all consequent[8] philosophical reflection must be an ego, which is removed from all conceivability, a "nicht-gegenständliches Ich." Thinking does violence to reality, pulling it into the circle of the ego, taking away from it its original "objectivity." Thinking always means system and the

---

[4.] Version A: "Supposed this inquiry would be purely philosophical we never would be allowed to start with the reality of God and as long as theology did not see its essential difference from all philosophical thinking [cf. Lyman comment 1] it did not with the statement of the reality of God either, but it tryed to give some substructure [cf. Lyman comment 2] for this statement. This is the main fault of theology, which no longer knows its particular right and its limits." Lyman comment 1: "Theology starts with the *conviction* of the reality of God. Why can it not take this conviction into the open forum of philosophy?" Lyman comment 2: "Why this figure?"

[5.] [In version A Bonhoeffer wrote "vindicates," which Lyman corrected to "convicts," which is then found in version C and the published version.—CG]

[6.] [Lyman comment: "May it not be an aspect of reality?"—CG]

[7.] [Lyman comment: "Experience breaks into the circle, and experience is of reality."—CG]

[8.] [That is, consistent, systematic, thoroughgoing, as in the German *konsequent*. —CG]

system excludes[9] the reality. Therefore, it has to call itself[10] the ultimate reality, and in this system the thinking ego rules.[11]

It follows that not only the other man but also God is subordinated to the ego. That is the strict consequence of the idealistic[12] and, as far as I see, of all exact philosophical thought[13] which tries to be autonomous. 425
This fact of the captivity of human thinking in itself, that is to say, of its inevitable autocracy and self-glorification[14] as it is found in philosophy, can be interpreted theologically as the corruption of the mind, which is caused by the first fall. Man "before" the fall[15] must be thought of as being able to think of "reality," that means to think of God and of the other man as realities. Man "in" and "after" the fall refers everything to himself, puts himself in the center of the world, does violence to reality, makes himself God, and God and the other man his creatures. He never can get reality back because his thinking is no longer "in reality"; it remains in the category of possibility. But there is no bridge between possibility and reality. Possibility might be conceived of and even proved, reality must be given before and beyond all thinking.[16] Reality is consequently beyond my own self, transcendent—but, again, not logically transcendent, but really transcendent.[17] Reality limits my boundlessness from outside, and this outside is no more intellectually conceivable but only believable. This remains to be explained below.[18]

[9.] [Lyman comment: "Rather, it does not give a complete account of reality." In version A Bonhoeffer underlined "excludes."—CG]

[10.] [Underlined in version C to be printed in italic.—CG]

[11.] Lyman comment: "In a physical experiment, do not the processes of nature *rule*?" [In version A Bonhoeffer underlined "rule" and so did Lyman in his comment. —CG]

[12.] Lyman comment: "Suppose one's philosophy were more realistic?" [Bonhoeffer had underlined "idealistic."—CG]

[13.] [Version A reads "of all exact philosophical thinking in the whole," meaning philosophical thinking in general.—CG]

[14.] Lyman comment: "Is there not real humility in science? And may not philosophy aim at disinterestedness?" [Bonhoeffer had underlined "self-glorification."—CG]

[15.] Version A: "interpreted theologically as the cor curvum in se, as corruptio mentis, which is caused by the first fall. Man in the status integritatis."

[16.] Lyman comment: "Rather, without thinking little or no reality can be given."

[17.] [Version A: "'really' transcendent." Version C: the next two sentences are a separate paragraph.—CG]

[18.] Version A: "Reality limits my boundlessness from outside, and this 'outside' is no more conceivable intellectually but only experiencable practically, that is to say: believable. This term of experience remains to be explained a little later one. We said before, theology." Lyman comment: "The two must interact."

Theology, then, starts with the statement of the reality of God and that is its particular right. But that at once gives rise to the question, how can theology state the reality of God without thinking it? And, if it thinks it, how can it be avoided that God should again be pulled into the circle of thought? That is the central and most difficult problem of a genuine theological epistemology,[19] which springs from the Christian idea of God.

The basis of all theology is the fact of faith. Only in the act of faith as a
426 direct act[20] God is recognized as the reality which is beyond and outside of our thinking, of our whole existence. Theology, then, is the attempt to set forth what is already possessed[21] in the act of faith. Theological thinking is not a construction a priori, but a posteriori as Karl Barth has maintained.[22] Therefore, it has to be conscious of its limitations. As thinking per se,[23] it is not excepted from the pretension and boundlessness of all thinking. But the property of theological thinking is that it knows of its own insufficiency and its limitations. So it must be its highest concern to guard these limitations and to leave room for the reality of God, which can never be conceived by theological thinking. That means that there is no one theological sentence which could presume to speak "truth" unless it refers to the reality of God and the impossibility of embracing[24] this reality in theological sentences. Every theoretical sentence generalizes. But God does not permit of generalization. Because he is reality, he is absolutely free of all theoretical generalization. Even a sentence like "God is love"[25] is, in the last analysis, not the truth about God, because it is not a matter of course that by such a sentence I could calculate that God is love. On the contrary, God is wrath as well as love and this we also should know.[26] Therefore,

---

[19.] Version A: "theory of knowledge."

[20.] [Version A: "actus directus, not necessarily as actus reflexus, God is . . ."—CG] The concept of *actus directus* (in contrast to the *actus reflexus*) derives from early Protestant thinking and was suggested to Bonhoeffer by Delitzsch, *System of Biblical Psychology*; cf. esp.: "The processes named and promised by the word (such as rebirth) themselves happen to us in the depth of the unconscious, and only now and then do reflexes thereof enter into our consciousness" (403, trans. altered). Bonhoeffer responds: "Here, of course, a theological interpretation has to take the place of the psychological one" (*DBWE* 2:158, ed. note 29).

[21.] Version A: "draw after what is drawn before."

[22.] Cf. the adoption of this notion from Barth, *Epistle to the Romans*, p. 206, in *DBWE* 2:45, 81, et passim.

[23.] Version A: "in itself."

[24.] Version A: "to catch."

[25.] Cf. 1 John 4:8.

[26.] Version A: "God is as well wrath as he is love and I have to know that."

every statement concerning God's essence must contain both of these contradictory aspects in order to give room to the reality of God.[27]

This reality, which is said to be transcendent to all thinking, is now to be defined more exactly as "personality."[28] The transcendence of God does not mean anything else than that God is personality, provided there is an adequate understanding of the concept[29] of personality. Idealism 427
defines personality as the subjective realization of objective spirit—that is, of absolute spirit. Each personality is constituted by the same spirit, which is, in the last analysis, reason.[30] Each personality is personality as far as it participates in reason.[31] Thus each one knows the other. Personality is no secret and, therefore, another personality is no real limit for me because, in the last analysis, I have at my disposal the spirit of reason, as does also the other person.[32]

For Christian[33] thought, personality is the last limit of thinking and the ultimate reality. Only personality can limit me, because the other personality has its own demands and claims, its own law and will, which are different from me and which I cannot overcome as such. Personality is free and does not enter the general laws of my thinking. God as the absolutely free personality is, therefore, absolutely transcendent.[34] Consequently, I cannot talk about him in general terms; he is always free and beyond these terms. The only task of my theological thinking must be to make room for the transcendent personality of God in every sentence. Only when he himself avows a human word, whenever and wherever he pleases, is my word "about" God to be accepted as truth—that means, only then is my word God's own word.[35] But the question is, Where does God speak? Where can I find his inaccessible reality which is so entirely hidden from my thinking? How do

[27.] Lyman comment: "But are love and wrath contradictory? Were they so in Jesus? Good and bad are contradictory."

[28.] God as "personality" corresponds to the "God as unconditional personality" from Brunstäd, *Die Idee der Religion*, 99–100. Cf. *DBWE* 2:40–41 et passim. [By using "personality" instead of his normal "person," Bonhoeffer adapts to the early twentieth-century usage of American English. For Bonhoeffer's use in *Sanctorum Communio* of "person" in theological anthropology and also for God, see *DBWE* 1:44–57, 79.—CG]

[29.] [In version A Bonhoeffer wrote "notion" and then wrote "concept" above it.—CG] Lyman comment: "Notion—is not this a concept?"

[30.] Version A: "Vernunft" [reason].

[31.] Version A: "Vernunft" [reason].

[32.] Version A: "I dispose of the spirit, of 'Vernunft' and likewise of the other person."

[33.] [Underlined in version A.—CG]

[34.] Lyman comment: "It is impossible not to regard personality as a general term."

[35.] Version A: "my word 'about' God is truth, that means it is Gods own word."

I know about his being the absolutely transcendent personality?[36] The answer is given and must be given by God himself, in his own word in Jesus Christ, for no one can answer this question except God himself, in his self-revelation in history, since none can speak the truth except God.

428 **II. God and History**

The problem that thus sets itself to us is complicated. We see[37] that there is no other way to talk about God than that God himself speaks his word in his self-revelation. This self-revelation is executed in history.[38]

No man can reveal God because God is absolutely free personality. Every human attempt to discover God, to unveil his secret reality, is hopeless because of God's being personality. All such attempts remain in the sphere of the idea.[39] Personality as reality is beyond idea. So that even the self-revelation of personality cannot be executed in the sphere of idea.[40] The idea is in the realm[41] of generality. Personality exists in "once-ness" because of its freedom. The only place where "once-ness" might occur is history. Therefore, revelation of personality—that is to say, the self-revelation of God—must take place[42] in history if at all. That happened according to the testimony[43] of the Bible and the present Christian church in the revelation of God in Christ. God spoke his word in history, yet not only as a doctrine but as the personal revelation of himself. Thus, Christ becomes not the teacher of mankind, the example of religious and moral life for all time, but the personal revelation, the personal presence of God in the world. It is important to point out emphatically[44] that it is not Jesus who reveals God to us (that view is the consequence of all theology which is not in the strict sense theology of revelation, and leads to a very confused Christology),[45] but it is God who reveals himself in absolute self-revelation to man. Since God is accessible only in his self-revelation, man can find God

[36.] [In version A this sentence is written in the margin.—CG]

[37.] Version A: "The problem is getting rather involved. We saw."

[38.] [Version A then reads: "This is to be explained."—CG]

[39.] Version A: "idea (thinking, conception etc.)."

[40.] Lyman comment: "But personality applies in some sense to man."

[41.] Version A: "sphere."

[42.] Version A: "must be executed."

[43.] Lyman comment: "What does this appeal to 'testimony' mean?" [Above "testimony" Bonhoeffer has written "witness."—CG]

[44.] Version A: "strictly."

[45.] Instead of the parenthetical statement, version A reads: "—this is the consequence of all theology which is not 'Offenbarungstheologie' in the strict sence and lead to a very modern Christology—." [Alternate reading: "very unclear Christology."—CG]

only in Christ. That does not exclude God's being elsewhere too,[46] but he cannot and should not be grasped and understood except in Christ. God entered history and no human attempt can grasp him beyond this history. 429
This is the great stumbling-block[47] for all general religious thinking. God revealed himself in "once-ness" from the years from one to thirty in Palestine in Jesus.

The main difference between a so-called revelation in the sphere of idea and a revelation in "once-ness"[48] is that man always will be able to learn a new idea and to fit it into his system of ideas; but a revelation in "once-ness" in a historical fact, in a historical personality, is always anew a challenge to man. He cannot overcome it by pulling it into the system which he already had before. That is the reason why God reveals himself in history: only so is the freedom of his personality guarded. The revelation in history means revelation in hiddenness;[49] revelation in ideas (principles, values, etc.) means revelation in openness.

We are going to speak below concerning the content of this revelation. Christianity gives us a new conception of history. The idealistic philosophy conceives of history as of the realization of ideas, values, etc. History becomes "symbol," transparent to the eternal spirit. The essence of single historical facts is that they mean something general,[50] but not that they really are something.[51] The earnestness of ontological consideration is weakened through reinterpretation in axiological judgments. Jesus becomes here the symbol of God's love, his cross means forgiveness, and in the very moment that we know what all that means we could, theoretically, forget the facts forever.[52] The fact being only the transient bearer of eternal values and ideas—that is to say, Jesus being only the transient bearer of the general new truth taught by him according to the will of God. In short, idealistic philosophy does not take seriously the ontological category in

[46.] Lyman comment: "How can he be elsewhere? How can he be in a prophet?"

[47.] Version A: "σκανδαλον."

[48.] Lyman comment: "Is not the 'Thus saith the Lord' of Jeremiah a 'revelation in onceness'?"

[49.] Lyman comment: "Is not this a perverse expression?"

[50.] [Version A lacks the word "general" and adds quotation marks to the word "mean" to read: "The essence of single historical facts is that they 'mean' something, but not that they really are something." Version C contains the word "general."—CG]

[51.] Lyman comment: "Is it legitimate to make this antithesis?"

[52.] Lyman comment: "Perhaps the idealistic philosophy could, but more empirical and realistic philosophy could not." [In version A the words "symbol" and "means" in this sentence are in quotation marks.—CG]

history. Which means that it does not take history seriously.[53] This is true, not only as far as an interpretation of the Christian revelation is concerned,
430 but likewise everywhere; and it becomes very conspicuous in the interpretation of the other man, of the neighbor, that is, of present history.[54]

We cannot pursue this point further here. The fact is that Christianity brings a new interpretation of history. History in its essence does not enter our system of ideas and values. On the contrary, it sets for us our limitations. History in its essence is to be interpreted ontologically. The true attitude of man toward history is not interpretative, but that of refusing or acknowledging, that is to say, deciding.[55] History is the place of decision, nothing else. Decision in its most inward sense is possible only as a decision for or against God. This decision[56] is executed in facing Christ.[57] Within the world of ideas there is no such thing as decision[58] because I always bear already within myself the possibilities of understanding these ideas. They fit into my system but they do not touch and challenge my whole existence. Thus, they cannot lead me into the situation of personal decision.[59]

III. The Paradoxical God of the Doctrine of Justification

Here the Christian "idea" of God comes to its sharpest issue. The question becomes one of applying[60] this most objective "idea" of God to man—which is absolutely necessary if the whole treatment is not to remain merely in the metaphysical realm. If God alone[61] can speak truth and I with all my thinking remain within my own limitations, not being able to reach
431 God, how can I know anything at all about God? Moreover,[62] there must

[53.] Lyman comment: "I feel a real force in this argument." Version A reads: "seriously at all."

[54.] Despite all proximity to Barth, including in this section on God's self-revelation in history, Bonhoeffer does differ from Barth precisely in his interpretation of love of one's neighbor. This is already the case in *Sanctorum Communio* (cf. *DBWE* 1:168–70); cf. also Feil, *Die Theologie Dietrich Bonhoeffers*, 45, esp. ed. note 63.

[55.] Lyman comment: "But decision without interpretation is not important. Consider Jesus' attitude toward sinners."

[56.] Version A: "decision—as only possible in history—."

[57.] Version A: "Jesus Christ. (How far such a position can be considered as free or not, cannot be treated here)."

[58.] Lyman comment: "Without ideas there is no such thing as decision."

[59.] Lyman comment: "The[y] cannot *fully replace* decision."

[60.] Version A: "The question is how to apply."

[61.] Version A: "the whole treatement shall not remain in the merely metaphysical realm. If only God."

[62.] Version A: "how finally can I know anything about God at all? On the other hand."

be some knowledge of God, if Christianity has a message to bring to the world.

The pathway to this knowledge is action.[63] I can[64] know God only if I can effect an act—an act which makes me transcend the limits of myself, which carries[65] me out of the circle of my self-hood in order to acknowledge the transcendent God. While it is obvious that I myself cannot effect such an act, there is, nevertheless, such an act, which is executed by God himself,[66] and which is called "faith." In my faith God reveals himself through Christ in me. In his self-revelation in Jesus Christ he gives himself to be known. In my faith no one speaks other than God, because, if so,[67] it would not be the truth. The word of God spoken to me in the act of my faith in Christ is God in his revelation as the Holy Spirit. Faith is nothing but the act of receiving this word of God. God remains always and entirely subject,[68] and even the answer of man can never be more than "I believe, help thou mine unbelief."[69]

It is just here that the personalities of God and of man come in contact with each other. Here God himself transcends his transcendence, giving himself to man as Holy Spirit. Yet, being personality, he remains in absolute transcendence; the immanence of God means that man hears God's own word, which is spoken in absolute self-revelation, always anew.

It[70] is not unessential to note that we have been able to conceive of the idea of faith only from the rigorous conception[71] of the self-revelation of God, and this without having touched the matter of the content of this revelation. The formal idea of self-revelation has as its counterpart[72] the idea of faith, whatever content the self-revelation may possess.[73] Faith is primarily directed toward the authority of God, not to the content of his word,[74] whether it be understandable or ununderstandable.[75] It is the

[63.] This sentence is absent in version A. [It is found in version C.—CG]

[64.] Version A: "I could."

[65.] Version A: "tears."

[66.] Lyman comment: "The old question arises: why does God deny faith to some—to so many?"

[67.] Version A: "Here in my faith nobody else speaks then God, because otherwise."

[68.] Version A: "subject (Karl Barth)."

[69.] Mark 9:24.

[70.] [Versions A, B, and C all begin a new paragraph here.—CG]

[71.] In version A also: "strictly conceived."

[72.] Version A: "correspondent idea."

[73.] Version A: "might contain."

[74.] Lyman comment: "What does authority mean without content?"

[75.] Lyman comment: "'Ununderstandable authority' sound Romish."

432 authority that gives weight to the content, not the reverse. In the Christian message, the particular proportion between authority and content is expressed by saying[76] that the latter is not only an appendix of the former, but that the content itself is the message of the sole authority of God. Therefore, when we come to interpret the content of the self-revelation of God, we will see that this content is only the explication of the fact of the absolute self-revelation and authority of God.[77]

God entered history in Jesus, and so entirely that he can be recognized in his hiddenness only by faith.[78] God gives an amazing proof of his sole authority in the cross of Christ. In the very same moment when Christ dies upon the cross, the whole world dies in its sinfulness and is condemned. That is the extreme judgment of God upon the world. God himself dies and reveals himself in the death of a man, who is condemned as a sinner.[79] It is precisely this, which is the foolishness of the Christian idea of God, which has been witnessed to by all genuine Christian thinking from Paul, Augustine, Luther, to Kierkegaard and Barth. God is where death and sin are, not where righteousness is. Further, it is to be said that the absolute knowledge of the sinfulness of the world or of the single individual person is a judgment of faith. Without faith no one can know what sin is. He will inevitably confuse sin with moral imperfection, which constitutes a grave misunderstanding.[80]

But the cross would not be the revelation of God were it not followed by the resurrection of Christ. With Christ's death and resurrection[81] the old world of righteousness is dead. He who is in Christ is a new creature. The resurrection of Christ as well as the resurrection of man was and is conceivable only by faith. God remains in His hiddenness. In Christ all men are
433 respectively condemned or resuscitated and it is the work of God, the Holy Spirit, to apply this general condition in which all men are, to the single person.[82] The act of application is the act of faith—that is to say, of this faith, which believes that God's word in Christ is valid for itself; or, in other words, the act of justification.

[76.] Version A: "The particular proportion between authority and content in the christian message is," [This sentence begins a new paragraph in version A.—CG]

[77.] Lyman comment: "Then the form does have a content *implicit* in it."

[78.] Lyman comment: "That is, He can be recognized only by an act of recognition."

[79.] Lyman comment: "Condemned by men, God knew that he was not a sinner."

[80.] Version A: "which is a great misunderstanding and not at all the same."

[81.] Version A: "With Christ the world of death and sin is resuscitated and."

[82.] Version A: "work to the single person."

Here the paradoxical essence of God becomes visible to the faith of the Christian believer. Justification is pure self-revelation, pure way of God to man. No religion, no ethics, no metaphysical knowledge may serve man to approach God. They are all under the judgment of God, they are works of man. Only the acknowledgment that God's word alone helps and that every other attempt is and remains sinful,[83] only this acknowledgment receives God. And this acknowledgment must be given by God, as the Holy Spirit, as faith. That is the foolishness of the revelation of God and its paradoxical character—that just there, where the power of man has lapsed entirely, where man knows his own weakness, sinfulness, and consequently the judgment of God upon him, that just there God is already working in grace, that just and exactly there and only there is forgiveness, justification, resuscitation. There, where man himself no longer sees, God sees, and God alone works, in judgment and in grace. There, at the very limits of man, stands God, and when man can do nothing more, then God does all.[84] The justification of the sinner—this is the self-proof of the sole authority of God. And in this justification man becomes a new personality by faith, and he recognizes here—what he never before could understand or believe—God as his creator. In the act of justification God reveals himself as Holy Trinity.[85]

[83.] Lyman comment: "Men remain sinful, but it is *ir*religious *un*ethical conduct, and failure to seek truth which is sin. 'Why call ye me, Lord, Lord and do not the things that I say?' '*First* be reconciled to thy brother and then offer thy gift.'" [Cf. Luke 6:46, Matt. 5:24. Lyman drew a vertical line in the margin between his comment and Bonhoeffer's sentences "No religion, no ethics . . . remains sinful. . . ." Lyman interprets sin as "unethical conduct" compared to Bonhoeffer's more radical Reformation understanding.—CG]

[84.] [Lyman comment: "But man cannot bring himself to this point, can he?"—CG]

[85.] Version A (from "There, where man . . ." on): "God is working in judgement and grace, where the man does not see longer himself at all, but only God. On the limits of man stands God, and when man cannot do anything more, than God does all. This is the selfproof of the sole authority of God in the justification of the sinner—iustus = peccator. It is to be added that in the justification man becomes a new personality by faith and he recognises here—what he never before could understand and believe,—God as his creator. So in the act of justification God reveals himself as holy Trinity."

434 **17. Seminar Paper: The Theology of Crisis and Its Attitude toward Philosophy and Science**[1]

It is a difference of method, whether at the occasion of examining a man one asks him for things, which he probably will know or whether one tries to find the limits of his knowledge by asking him questions, which he very likely cannot answer quite as well; the more modern and for the examined man by far more pleasant education principle at least is the first way of asking. However Barth today is supposed to be the victim of the other type of examination, and [. . .][2] it is not merely his fault if the result of this examination is not going to be as satisfactory as it could have been. Barth has never prepared himself for an examination in science or in philosophy,[3] but he always has prepared himself for a quite different and distinct field, namely for christian theology; that is to say, Barth has been thinking all the time exclusively and intensively of the λογος θεου[4] and he found—perhaps strangely enough for our allinclusive and extensive kind of thinking—in this object manifold and most important problems, that he felt not very much attracted by the variety of countless other problems, before he would have thought through the richness of his proper field, of theology in its strict sense. Now theology does not answer every question in the whole world; but since it tries to answer at least one question, namely that question about God, it contains a certain attitude toward all other questions. That is to be admitted, although it will have to be shown that the essential[5] possibility of this attitude as well as its concrete character is a problem of exceeding difficulty.

In order not to confuse your impressions, I will give you in this paper
435 mainly the position of the founder and most original thinker of the theol-

[1.] *NL*, A 25,4; handwritten, with a remark by Bethge: "Baillie. Union Sem: 1930/1"; in original English, including errors. Previously published in *GS* 3:110–26. This version contains numerous deletions. These are noted only if they offer substantive variations from the later text. [Written in English for an oral seminar presentation as seen in various remarks to seminar members and the reference to "the following discussion" (476; cf. p. 463). Bethge smoothed out the English of the version he published in *GS*.—CG]

[2.] Illegible. [Possibly "thus."—CG]

[3.] [Bonhoeffer refers to the topic of the seminar in philosophical theology and especially the problem addressed in the paper of the relationship of theology to philosophy and natural science; cf. also ed. note 7.—CG]

[4.] "Word of God."

[5.] Written above: "(prinzipielle)." [The alternative formulation would then read: "the possibility of this attitude as well as its concrete character is in principle."—CG]

ogy of crisis, of Karl Barth.[6] The differences between him and Fr. Gogarten and Emil Brunner will be better explained in whatever brief ways the discussion will point.

Since Barth never has published any comprehensive treatment of our problem, we will have to use some single utterances of his and try to show the lines of connection with his whole thought, which sometimes Barth himself did not draw. Coming after half a year of consideration of the problem of the relation between cosmology, philosophy and theology,[7] to a man like K. Barth I confess that I do not see any other possible way for you to get into real contact with his thought than by forgetting at least for this one hour everything you have learned before concerning this problem. We have in Barth's theology not one of the countless variations of the solution of this problem from the Scholastics over[8] Kant to Bergson or Dewey,[9] but here we stand at an entirely different and new point of departure of the whole problem. We stand in the tradition of Paul, Luther, Kierkegaard, in the tradition of genuine christian thinking. We do injustice to Karl Barth if we take him as a philosopher, he is not and does not claim to be, he is just a christian theologian. This at least has to be clear, what we intend to be, christian theologians or philosophers. To be unclear in this point means, that we in any case are not christian theologians. For the christian theologian must know the proper and steadfast premise of his whole thinking, which the philosopher does not recognize: the premise of the revelation of God in Christ or on the objective side: the faith in this revelation.[10] Two

---

[6.] The expression "theology of crisis" more accurately describes the theological situation in the German-speaking realm evoked by Barth's commentary on Romans than the otherwise frequently used expression—one Bonhoeffer also adopts—"dialectical theology."

[7.] [This phrase indicates that the paper was written in the second semester for the seminar Philosophy of Religion 92, taught by Lyman and Baillie, which had as its topic for the year "the bearing of recent cosmological theories on theology."—CG]

[8.] [A literal translation of the German *über.*—CG]

[9.] The philosophy of life and nature of Henri Bergson exerted virtually no influence at all on German Protestant theology, apart from Albert Schweitzer (see his *Civilization and Ethics*, 198–99 and 203). The same applies even more so to John Dewey, the most significant representative of American pragmatism, who enlisted philosophy primarily for the sake of improving social conditions. [Bergson was listed for study in the course Bonhoeffer was taking with Lyman in the second semester ("Religious Aspects of Contemporary Philosophy") at the same time as he was taking the second half of the year-long systematic theology seminar; "pragmatism" in the course description probably includes Dewey.—CG]

[10.] [By "objective side" Bonhoeffer means that "the revelation of God in Christ" is the "object" of the "whole thinking" of the Christian theologian.—CG]

436 questions arise: 1.) What is the meaning of this premise according to Karl Barth? 2.) What makes such a premise necessary? *Firstly*. The meaning of the proper presupposition of christian theology is, that God entered history in Jesus Christ, made himself known to the world in this revelation. The word or the will of God, God himself was made flesh. But the revelation of God in Christ was a revelation of his judgement as well as of his grace. Christ's cross is the judgement of God upon the world. Christ's resurrection is his grace. That is to say, the revelation of God in Christ is not a revelation of a new morality, of new ethical values, a revelation of a new imperativ, but a revelation of real reacting of God for mankind in history, a revelation of a new indicativ; It is not a new "you ought," but "you are."[11] In other words the revelation of God is executed not in the area of ideas, but in the area of reality.[12] The importance of this difference is to be explained later. The *fact* that God himself comes into the world convicts the world of impossibility to come to God by itself; the fact, that God's way in the world leads to the cross, that Christ must die condemned as a sinner on the cross, convicts the world that this impossibility to come to God is its condemnation, its sin and its guilt. The fact of Christ's resurrection proves to the world that only God is right and powerfull, that the last word is his, that by an act of his will alone the world can be renewed. Finally the fact that the holy Spirit still comes to man and moves man's hearts with the message of Christ's death and resurrection convicts the world that God is still God and the world still the world, that God's word in Christ is God's word for ever. In short, the fact of God's coming into the world in Christ makes the world see, that here in the life of Jesus of Nazareth God is acting with mankind in an eternal way, that in this life the decision upon the world fells, and that in this decision God does everything, man nothing.

Yet it is exactly the fact, that God really entered history, which makes him
437 invisible for human eyes. If the revelation was a revelation of new ideas, new moral imperatives, then it would be a revelation, which everybody could recognize as such by virtue of his own ideal or ethical presuppositions; for then it would have its place in the world of general truth, which is selfevident to the human mind by its generality. This is the conception of revelation in other religions and in our modern liberal thought. The objects of revelation are ideas, which are supposed to be congenial to our deepest

[11.] Deleted: "God has done for you this and this."

[12.] Barth's essay "Fate and Idea in Theology" (in Rumscheidt, *Way of Theology in Karl Barth*, 25–61) shows, as Bethge points out, "that this absolute antithesis between idea and reality is not what Barth means" (*DB-ER*, 159 and ed. note 37, p. 959).

essence, to the good in man. The christian idea of revelation is the strict opposite of this view; it is revelation [. . .][13] not in ideas, but in historical facts, not in imperatives but in indicatives, not in generality, but in onceness; it is revelation because it is not congenial to our own deepest essence, but entirely beyond our whole existence. For would it otherwise have had to be revealed, if it has been before potentially in us? The fact of God's encarnation in Christ, the fact of Christ's suffering and death, the fact of his resurrection[14] are the revelation of God. But of course who would be willing to see in these facts God's word? Who would[15] not be offended by the foolishness of such a claim? God revealed in the poor life of a suffering man, God revealed on the cross, God revealed in the[16] depth of history, in sin and death, is this a message worth hearing by a wise man, who really would be able to invent a nobler and prouder God. Karl Barth finds the Bible full of the testimony of the awkwardness and foolishness of God's revelation. "Blessed is he, whosoever shall not be offended in me,"[17] Jesus says; and Paul: "the cross to them is foolishness; . . . it pleased God by the foolishness of preaching to save them that believe . . . we preach Christ crucified, unto the Jews a stumbling block and unto the Greeks foolishness . . . the foolishness of God is wiser than men; and the weakness of God is stronger than men. God hast chosen the foolish things of the world . . . that no flesh should glory in his presence."[18] All that means that God's revelation in Christ is revelation in concealment, secrecy, all other socalled revelation is revelation in openness. But who then, can see the revelation in conceal- 438
ment? Nobody but to whom God himself reveals this most secret mystery of his revelation in weekness, nobody but to whom God gives the faith, which is not offended, but which sees God's judgment and grace in the midst of human weakness, sin and death, where otherwise man can see only godlessness, faith which sees God coming most closely to man, where a man hanging on the cross dies in despair with the loud cry: my God, my God, why hast thou forsaken me?[19] And the centurion, which stood over against him saw that he so cried out and gave up the ghost, said: truly this man was the Son

[13.] Illegible. [Though not written here, elsewhere Bonhoeffer uses the formulation "in hiddenness"; see below on "concealment" and "secrecy."—CG]

[14.] Replaces: "revelation."

[15.] Replaces: "could."

[16.] Deleted: "midst and the."

[17.] Matt. 11:6.

[18.] 1 Cor. 1:18, 21, 23, 25, 27, 29.

[19.] Mark 15:34 (Ps. 22:2). [Here and in the following lines Bonhoeffer quotes the Authorized (or King James) Version.—CG]

of God.[20] This is the real world of biblical faith, which sees God's work not on the top but in the depth of mankind;[21] and because faith sees God in Christ it sees God, the same God of Christ, in man's own life, in man's own sin, weakness and death as judgment and as grace. It is God's own work to let men see into these secrets of his revelation; as Christ says to Peter after his confession: flesh and blood hath not revealed it unto thee, but my Father which is in heaven.[22] So everything points back to God's own decree, to his free predestination. He comes where he wants to come, and he renounces whoever he pleases. For he is unconditioned and free.

This is the way Barth tries to make living the world of biblical thinking. He sees everything in the Bible referring to God's sole truth, right, freedom, judgment, grace. This precisely is the logic of the Bible, God's coming which destroys all human attempts to come, which condemns all morality and religion, by means of which man tries to make superfluous God's revelation. God's sole truth and word, which has to be spoken anew again and again, God coming not to the most seriously moral and pious group of Pharisees and Scribes but to those who were entangled in public sin. "Verily I say unto you, that the publicans and the harlots go into the kingdom of God before you."[23] Here all human order and ranking is subverted, for God's new order has been established, which is contrary and beyond all
439 human understanding. It convicts man of his godlessness in his bad and his good deeds. God's coming in Christ is the proof of God[24] himself, that man cannot come to God; that is to say: God's coming in Christ must be the judgment upon mankind, in other words it shows to man his limitations, which are lieing exactly there, where God's work begins. Therefore God's work with man does not begin as a continuation and perfection of his highest, although as every decent man will admit imperfect enterprises, as religion and morality, but on the contrary it begins as the[25] irrefragable limitation of man, it begins at man's limits that is to say in sin and death. This act of limiting man is God's judgement and grace *in one*; for the limited man is the judged man and at the same time the limited man giving all righteousness and glory to God is so justified by God's work and grace

[20.] Mark 15:39; concerning the status of Mark 15:34 and 39, cf. 2/2, p. 357, and *LPP*, 360; *DBWE* 7:165.

[21.] Deleted: "God himself suffers in Christ."

[22.] Matt 16:17.

[23.] Matt 21:31.

[24.] Replaces "judgement before."

[25.] The word "transgressible" was inserted but does not fit. [Bonhoeffer was looking for a word like "inviolable."—CG]

alone. The acknowledgment of one's limits before God is faith, not as a possible act of man, but only as an act of God, who sets and shows these limits to man. This is the message of justification by grace or by faith alone.

But the revelation of God in the justification by faith and grace implies that man's continuity always is continuity in sin, that he by himself can never get outside of the circle of sin, for otherwise grace would not be grace, and justification would not be necessary. Revelation in Christ, justification, means breaking through the circle of sin.[26] Thus God's first word is the radical breaking of all continuity with man in his radical judgement upon man as sinner, and his act of grace is the creation of a new man, with whom God remains in continuity. Since only the revelation in Christ claims to constitute the real outside of man it implies that it is the only criterion of any revelation. Since this claim puts itself essentially beyond all proof, it demands to be taken as a presupposition of thinking or to be refused at all. It is perhaps too obvious to mention, that as a consequence of this notion of revelation the question of grounds for belief in God is superfluous because it involves a contradiction. For what better ground does one need and is possible than God's word itself. Any theology that is ashamed of this petitio 440
principii cannot escape being ashamed of Him who gives it whatever meaning it posesses.

Herewith I think we have the chief presuppositions, which are indispensible for an understanding of Barth's attitude toward all other problems. The category which Barth tries to introduce into theology in its strict sense and which is so refractory to all general thinking and especially religious thinking is the category of the word of God, of the revelation straight from above,[27] from *outside* of man, according to the justification of the sinner by grace. Theology is the scientific[28] consideration of this category. But exactly here the difficulty comes in. Scientific consideration is based upon general formal presuppositions of thinking. Since these presuppositions cannot be taken from the object of theological thinking—just because it

[26.] Deleted: "this is strictly to be distinguished from the epistemological circle of consciousness."

[27.] Concerning this familiar formulation of revelation "vertically, from above," cf. Barth, *Epistle to the Romans*, 30, 102, et passim.

[28.] [Here Bonhoeffer is almost certainly thinking of the German *wissenschaftlich*, which could also be translated as "academic" or "scholarly." Bonhoeffer is aware that Barth defines dogmatics as the theological discipline concerned with the "scientific self-examination" of the church concerning its language about God (*Church Dogmatics* 1/1:3), and he points out that theology defines "science" according to its own distinctive subject matter, while sharing certain "general forms of thinking" with other disciplines and "sciences."—CG]

never becomes actually object but always remains subject—and since on the other hand they must be taken from this subject—object, if they should be at all adequate, the deepest contradiction in the task of theology becomes obvious. It is in the last analysis the great antithesis of the word of God and the word of man, of grace and religion, of a pure christian category and general religious category, of reality and interpretation.[29] In every theological statement we cannot but use certain general forms of thinking. Theology has those forms in common with philosophy. Thus our next problem will be to consider the relation between theology and philosophy with regard to the use of forms of general philosophical thinking in theology. Let us take the following example: Theological thinking, which is based upon the general notion of substance and accidence (and it seems to me that our western thinking[30] at least will never be able to overcome completely this basic presupposition for the one reason if for no other namely the grammatical constructions of our languages)—this type of thinking,
441 I say, will conceive for instance of sin as substance in man or as accidens. Both in their pure form seemed inadequate for the notion of sin to orthodox dogmatics. The consequence is either to express the real fact of sin in rather contradictory terms of the type of substantial thinking as it was done after the famous struggle with Flacius Illyricus by orthodox protestants,[31] or to look for different presuppositional forms of thinking for example for a dynamic-voluntaristic thinking, if that can be considered a genuine form of thinking at all. The history of theology was to a large extent a permanent seeking for more adequate forms of thinking in order to express the facts of the revelation. Two great christian churches have settled in a long history of exceedingly keen and serious thinking their forms of thinking definitely; both of them are based upon the scheme of substance and accidence, the greek church more in the platonic, the roman church more in the aristotelian interpretation. (Quite recently it seems that a movement in Benedictine order tries to modify this old form of thinking; specially in the modern catholic theories of the sacrifice in the Holy Communion this becomes obvious.)[32]

Luther recognized the insufficiency of the scholastic form of thinking for an interpretation of the facts of revelation. He sees in the notion of

[29.] Deleted: "of beeing and thinking, of [illegible]."

[30.] Replaces "philosophy."

[31.] Concerning the differentiation from Matthias Flacius, cf. the Formula of Concord, Epitome I (*Die Bekenntnisschriften der evangelisch-lutherischen Kirche,* 774 and 884), *Book of Concord,* 488n5 and 490n11.

[32.] Bonhoeffer is probably referring to the liturgical reform movement that began in the Benedictine monastery Maria Laach, south of Cologne, in 1914. The leading

substance a great danger of making revelation static and depriving it of its actual liveliness. Luther sees this static character attributed to grace in the catholic Church which gives grace into the disposal of man. Thus the whole misinterpretation of the doctrine of justification in the catholic church is deeply connected with the basic presuppositional form of thinking.

Luther himself has not developed his own philosophical terminology. Without doubt his forms of thought are essentially dynamical voluntaris- 442
tic[33] herewith accepting a tradition which came from Paul over[34] Augustine and the Mystics to him. But very often he himself falls back into the substantial form of thinking (for instance in the Christology) and it has to be confessed that Protestantism as yet lacks its proper philosophical terminology. Orthodox Protestantism took up the old substantial form of thinking and it was Kant, who showed its impossibility[35] and substituted for it a transcendental philosophy.[36] The theological language of 19th century until our present day has been based not so much upon Kants as upon the idealistic philosophy, even where the respective theologie was not conscious of the fact.[37] Ritschl, in whose theology I was brought up in Berlin, could not succeed in his attempt to free theology from wrong metaphysical premises, because he had not thought through the christian category of revelation, as it becomes obvious in his christology, doctrine of sin and of justification.[38]

---

figures included the Benedictine abbot Ildefons Herwegen and Odo Casel, the editor of the *Jahrbuch für Liturgiewissenschaft*. One of the most significant notions was the actual-presence interpretation of the Eucharist, which overcame the scholastic substance-oriented thinking by drawing on the New Testament and patristic concept of anamnesis (remembrance). It was, however, disputed as being "theology of mysteries"; cf. Casel, *Das christliche Kultmysterium*.

[33.] [By "voluntaristic" Bonhoeffer means an emphasis on the will; cf. *DBWE* 1:19, 35, 48, 296.—CG]

[34.] [See ed. note 8 regarding *über*.—CG]

[35.] Deleted: "in his critic of the pure reason."

[36.] Cf. in this regard the section in *Act and Being* on the transcendental approach in *DBWE* 2:33–59.

[37.] Deleted: "for instance." [In the manuscript an entire page and four lines are crossed out at this point, and a new page contains the following sentences from "Ritschl" to "a whole philosophy."—CG]

[38.] Cf. Ritschl, *Christian Doctrine of Justification and Reconciliation*. The reference to the Berlin Ritschlian school includes especially Holl and Harnack, who in 1899 could say, "[W]ith all the energy God has given me, I will engage myself on behalf of the nexus I have learned from Paul, Luther, and Ritschl—and I think they have it from someone even greater—faith in Christ, trust in God, peace in God, humility, patience, and working in one's vocation and position in life" (to Martin Rade, in Zahn-Harnack, *Adolf von Harnack*, 228). [In 1931 Paul Lehmann was beginning work on his dissertation, which dealt with

There is finally a realistic philosophy, which could offer its service to theology.[39] Now Karl Barth is faced with this situation, when he looks for a philosophical terminology for his theology. He is well aware of the fact though, that in accepting a certain philosophical terminology theology is insolubly connected with a whole philosophy. In his Römerbrief and his later writings Barth uses the philosophical terminology of Kant and the Neokantians in Marburg[40] and he is conscious of this fact. Like everything in Barth's thought this also is in closest connection with the doctrine of justification by faith and by grace alone and we will have to explain that. Three
443 questions are to be answered: 1.) what is for Barth the task of philosophy in general? 2.) what kind of philosophy is adequate to the christian idea of justification by faith. 3.) what is true philosophy[41] from a theological point of view.

1.) The task of philosophy has always been an interpretation of the general principles of the universe according to some principles which have been considered as true. Philosophical interpretation claims to be true, even if it is skeptical. More accurately: the predicate "true" can essentially be referred only to the *interpretation*, and *all* philosophy *is* interpretation, whether it be idealistic or realistic. The statement: there is a table is by no means selfinterpretiv for philosophical thinking: What does "there," what does "is," what does "table" mean? All that is matter of interpretation.[42] Idealism recognizes that, as well as critical Realism and even Behaviorism,[43] as I understand it, only "naiv Realism" tries[44] to ignore the complexity of the problem and can hardly be considered a philosophical position. But even critical realism still has to prove its logical consistency over against the superior logical right of idealism. As long as philosophy has to do with the sheer question of truth and not with some arbitrary statements, logical consistency is an essential predication of every relevant philosophy. Barth's theology was from the very beginning connected with

Ritschl and justification; with Bonhoeffer's help, he went to Europe to study with Brunner and Barth in 1932; cf. his doctoral dissertation, "A Critical Comparison on the Doctrine of Justification in the Theologies of Albrecht Ritschl and Karl Barth."—CG]

[39.] Bonhoeffer is presumably referring to a precursor of Marburg neo-Kantianism such as Alois Riehl. Cf. *DBWE* 2:55.

[40.] Concerning neo-Kantianism, cf. *DBWE* 2:47–48. [Here Bonhoeffer refers to Hermann Cohen and Paul Natorp.—CG]

[41.] Deleted: "as autonomous science."

[42.] [This sentence is missing from Bethge's publication in *GS* 3:119.—CG]

[43.] The kind of behaviorism founded by J. B. Watson in 1913 recognizes psychology as a science only to the extent that it focuses on the objectively measurable behavior of living beings.

[44.] Deleted: "through pseudo-simplicity."

an energetic attack against Idealism. Here the ego is found as not only the interpreting but even a creative ego; it creates its world itself. The ego stands in the centre of the world, which is created, ruled, overpowered by the ego. The identification of the ego with the ground of everything which has been called God is inevitable. There are no limits for the ego, its power and its claim is boundless, it is its own standard. Here all transcendence is pulled into the circle of the creative ego (which of course must not be confused with the empirical ego). Man knows himself immediately by the
act of the coming of the ego to itself and knows through himself essen- 444
tially everything, even God. God is in man, God is man himself. Barth and his friends discovered in this philosophy the most radical, most honest and most consistent expression of the philosophical enterprise as such. Although realism claims to leave room for transcendent reality, it still owes us the proof, which of course it never will be able to bring, that its definition of reality is not its own interpretation of it; As long as realism fail here, it must admit that reality has to be referred to the interpreting ego, which constitutes reality and which, even although it denies it remains the center of reality. The ego knows reality, it knows itself, it is essentially autonomous. At the basis of all thinking lies the necessity of a system. Thinking is essentially systematic thinking, because it rests upon itself, it is the last ground and criterion of itself. System means interpretation of the whole through the one, which is its ground and its center, the thinking ego. Idealism saw and affirmed that as the proof for the freedom, autonomy, the deity of man. Realism tries to escape this consequence and fails. There is only one philosophy, which recognizes this fact and states it as the definite and essential limit of man; this is according to Barth and his friends the essence of Kantian philosophy. (It be shortly noted, that Barth and his friends here do not care so much for a complete presentation of the manifold sides of Kant's philosophy, but that they trie to point out, what seems to them the most important trend in Kant's thought) Kant did not want to be called an idealist nor a dogmatist, he considers both of them[45] as equally untenable, his philosophy is critical philosophy or transcendental philosophy; "transcendental" means for Kant (as it has been shown clearly by Knittermeyer and others)[46] not involving transcendence, but referring to transcendence. Thinking is an act which never involves transcendence, but refers to it. The transcendence itself does not enter thinking. The ego never knows itself

[45.] Deleted: "to be in the same boat."

[46.] Hinrich Knittermeyer's essay on the bicentenary of Kant's birth, "Die Transzendentalphilosophie und die Theologie," profoundly influenced Bonhoeffer's understanding of Kant in *Act and Being*. See *DBWE* 2:33–34 et passim.

445 in coming to itself, but it always remains transcendent to itself, because it never is static-objective, but always acting. Likewise thinking does not reach the transcendence of the object, but it always is directed to it, because transcendence never can be "object." This is the deep meaning of the "Ding an sich"[47] and the transcendental apperception for Kant. Thinking is limited and put into the midst between two transcendences, to which it refers, but which always remain transcendent. In the very moment when the Idealists pushed away the "Ding an sich" Kant's critical philosophy was destroyed. The philosophy of the pure act turned to be a new ontology; a fact, which Hegel clearly recognized. Kant had tried to limit human thinking, in order to establish it anew. But Hegel saw that limits only can be set from beyond these limits. That means applied to Kant, that his attempt to limit reason by reason presupposes that reason must have already passed beyond the limits before it sets them. So Kant's critical philosophy presents itself as the attempt of man to set himself the limits in order to avoid the boundlessness of his claim, but the fact is that thinking never can limit itself; in limiting itself[48] it establishes itself. Thinking as such is boundless, it pulls transcendent all reality into its circle. The last consequence of this knowledge has been drawn by E. Grisebach (and from another side by M. Heidegger.) Grisebachs question is the question of reality.[49] He sees that thinking as essentially systematic thinking does violence to reality in pulling it into the circle of the egocentricity. Systematic thinking remains far from reality. Reality only is given in the concrete situation of the ethical meeting of man with man; Thus thinking has to remove itself in order to give room to reality. Grisebach's philosophy is the ultimate possible critic[50] of thinking toward itself, but even here thinking remains dominant and constitutive of the world of reality. For the limits of thinking is[51] thought limit. This is the inevitable circle of all philosophy. Here at the limits, where philosophy tries to remove itself and cannot but establish itself where philosophy comes to its own crisis we are ready for our second question, namely what
446 philosophical terminology could be adequate for a theology of revelation, of the justification by faith, for the theology of Barth.

Barth sees in the essential boundlessness of thinking, in its claim a closed system, in its egocentricity a philosophical affirmation of the theological

[47.] ["Thing in itself."—CG]

[48.] Deleted: "it pulls transcendence into itself and so."

[49.] Here, too, Bonhoeffer is able to draw on the research for his postdoctoral dissertation. Cf. also *DBWE* 2:26–28.

[50.] [Bonhoeffer uses the English "critic" like the German *Kritik*, which means "critique."—CG]

[51.] [Bethge adds "a," to mean "a limit that has been thought."—CG]

insight[52] of the Reformers, which they expressed in terms of cor curvum in se, corruptio mentis. Man in statu corruptionis[53] is indeed alone, he is his own creator and Lord, he is indeed the center of his world of sin. He made himself God, and God his creature. The fact that the basic question of philosophy necessarily leads into this situation proves the deepest godlessness of man, even in his profoundest philosophical ideas of God. Man remains with himself, in his thinking not less than in his ethical and religious attempt. The world of man is the world of egocentricity, of godlessness. The fact that philosophy essentially gives its sanction to this situation in making man inevitably the God of his world, even if it denies it, shows the impossibility for philosophy to interpret the situation right as well as it shows philosophy as the most dangerous grasp after God, in order to be like God is and thus to justify man by his own power—in godlessness. We ask: Can then man do anything in order to overcome this fatale situation? Kant still believed, critical philosophy could make room for faith by means of limiting reason by reason. But he failed. Barth sees there is no way out. Man must die in his sin inspite of philosophy, must remain alone in his overpowered and misinterpreted world. But now the christian message comes: entirely from outside of the world of sin God himself came in Jesus Christ, he breaks as the holy Ghost into the circle of man, not as a new idea, a new value by virtue of which man could save himself, but in concreteness as judgment and forgiveness of sin, as the promise of eschatological salvation. God makes himself known to man who is sinner in his whole existence. The whole existence of man in his egocentric world has to be shaken (erschüttert) before man can see God as really outside of himself.

Therefore there is no spectator-knowledge of God, but only man in the 447
act of despair of himself[54] can know God by faith. Idealistic and realistic philosophy fail to give the term for describing these facts. And yet Barth discovers in both of them elements which could be used by theology. Idealism sees God as eternal subject, realism sees reality as transcendent object. Barth can express his idea of the transcendent God in terms of God's essential subjectivity, and his idea of God's coming to man in history in terms of God's most objective reality. But he knows that both these terms are essentially inadequate since they derive from a godless philosophy. Barth's own

[52.] Replaces: "doctrin."

[53.] "The heart turned in on itself"; "corruption of the mind"; "in the state of corruption," that is, the condition of human beings after the fall. Bonhoeffer cites these expressions extensively in *Act and Being* according to Luther's commentary on Romans (*DBWE* 2:40–41).

[54.] Replaces "justification."

writings are based upon a Kantian terminology. Here he finds expressed the critic of thinking upon thinking, here he sees man considered not in his full possession of transcendence but in the eternal act of referring to transcendence, man not in boundlessness, but in limitation. Although Barth knows that even this philosophy remains in boundlessness he sees here the attempt of philosophy to criticize itself basically and takes from here the terminology in order to express the eternal crisis of man, which is brought upon him by God in Christ and which is beyond all philosophical grasp. Barth sees that there is no christian philosophy[55] nor philosophical terminology at all. So he can say, it does not make very much difference what philosophy a theologian has, but everything depends upon how strongly he keeps his eyes on the category of the word of God, on the fact of revelation, of justification by faith.

Now our third question can be answered: what ought to be according to Barth and his friends the task of philosophy. Barth himself has not answered this question sufficiently, but his friends have thought a great deal about this problem: philosophy remains profane science, there *is* no christian philosophy. But philosophy has to be critical philosophy, not systematic. But since even critical philosophy is bound to be systematic (as we have seen before), philosophy must work in sight of this fate, it must try to think truth with regard to the real existence of man and it must see that it is itself an expression of the real existence of man and that it by its own power not only
448 cannot save man, but that it cannot even be the crisis of man. By doing so it gives as far as it can room to God's revelation, which indeed makes room for itself by itself. The deepest antinomy seems to me to be the antinomy between pure act and reflection as the old dogmaticians said: actus directus and reflexus.[56] God is known only in pure act of referring to God, theology and philosophy are executed in reflection, which God does not enter. Philosophy essentially remains in reflection, man knows himself and God only in reflection, theology at least knows of an act of God, which tears man out of this reflection into an actus directus toward God. Here man knows himself and God not by looking into himself, but by looking to the word of God, which tells him that he is sinner and justified, which he never before could understand. So as Luther said pecca fortiter sed crede fortius Barth could say reflecte fortiter, sed crede fortius.[57]

[55.] Deleted: "and likewise theology."

[56.] Cf. *DBWE* 2:158–59.

[57.] See Luther's letter to Melanchthon of August 1, 1521: "Esto peccator et pecca fortiter, sed fortius fide et gaude in Christo" ("Be a sinner and sin boldly, but believe and rejoice in Christ more boldly still" [*LW* 48:281]). Bonhoeffer's interpretation of

Concerning science not very much has to be added. As far as science is a discovery of happening facts, theology is not touched (because theology is concerned only with an certain interpretation of facts.) If science itself gives its own interpretation of the world, than it belongs to philosophy and is subjected to the critic of theology. The attempt of cosmology,[58] that is of a genetical interpretation of the world on the basis of natural science, can never reach beyond the limits of human thinking. Cosmology may come to the assumption of a last ground of the world and may call that "God," all we can say in the name of christian theology is that this God is not the God of revelation and not the creator. Two reasons are to be given: firstly I know
God as creator not without the revelation in Christ. For God's being the 449
creator means being the judge and the saviour too; and I know all that only in Christ. Secondly: creation means creation by absolute freedom, creation out of nothing. So the relationship of God to the world is completely free, it has been set and is always set anew "creatio continua"[59] by God. Thus God is not the first cause, the ultimate ground of the world, but its free Lord and creator as such he is not to be discovered by any cosmology, but he reveals himself in sovereign freedom wherever and whenever he wants. The world is fallen away from God; therefore it is the world of sin and evil and death. No human attempt can unify "what has been broken asunder, no thinking, no moral acting, no religion."[60] Only an act of God himself can do, what no man can do. God has unified the broken and contradictory world. In Christ death and evil and sin are overcome by an act of God visible for faith; and at the end of everything God will show his power over death and sin to everybody. He will solve this problem of death and evil and sin by an act of his power.[61]

Our thinking in terms of a Theodicee tries to justify God in the world. But for christian thinking God justifies the world and that has been done in Christ. Thus only through Christ we see the creator and the preserver and

---

Barth implies hypothetically that Barth, too, could have said what Bonhoeffer himself had already formulated as his own thesis in *Act and Being* at the end of section B. 3. (*DBWE* 2:135). Concerning the adaptation of the Luther citation ("Think boldly, but believe and rejoice in Christ more boldly still"), see also *DB-ER*, 159 and 959n37).

[58.] [The year-long seminar in systematic theology and philosophy of religion dealt with "the bearing of recent cosmological theories on theology."—CG]

[59.] The concept of "continuing creation" derives only from more recent theology, esp. that of Brunstäd and Barth (*Church Dogmatics* 1/2:688–89), and then through a neo-Lutheran doctrine of creation (cf., e.g., Gerstenmaier, *Die Kirche und die Schöpfung*, 70–72) became untenable for Barth (see *Church Dogmatics* 3/3:6 and 68–70).

[60.] Citation not verifiable.

[61.] Deleted: "which we never can solve."

the Lord *of* the world *and in* the world; and only through Christ we see the world in God's hands. Far from Christ we live in our own overpowered and egocentric world, which is not the world of God.

Here at the end we stand again where we stood in the beginning; and that cannot be otherwise; for *everything* is included in God's revelation in Christ, in the justification of the sinner by faith and grace alone. And must not the solution of *everything* be there, where *God himself* is?

In the following discussion we shall not be able to do justice to Barth, if we do not refer every thought to its theological premise of the justification by faith.

PART 3
Sermons, Catechetical Lessons, and Addresses

1. Draft for a Liturgy, Barcelona, Reminiscere (Second Sunday in Lent, Memorial Day), March 4, 1928 453

1.1. Opening liturgy[1]

Pastor: In the name of the Father . . .

Our help is in the name of the Lord who made heaven and earth. Blessed are those who suffer, for they will be comforted. Blessed are the dead, those who die in the Lord from now on. Yes, the Spirit says that they will rest from their labors, for their deeds will follow them. Jesus speaks through the apostles: Be faithful unto death, and I will give you the crown of life.[2]

Come, let us pray.

Congregation: Glory be to the Father . . .

Pastor: In the midst of life we are surrounded by death. Whom can we seek who might help, that we might attain grace? You, Lord, alone. We are sorry for our misdeeds that have angered you, Lord. Holy Lord God, holy mighty God, holy merciful Savior, Thou eternal God. Let us not sink into the distress of bitter death. *Kyrie eleison.*[3]

Congregation: Lord have mercy.

1.2 Prayer[4]

Holy God, from the melancholy remembrance of great days of our people
we return to the present, to daily life. Bestow some of the radiance of the 454
greatness that happened years ago for us out there upon our present lives. May our steps be strong and sure; may the seeds you have sown bear fruit for us.[5] Give us strength from your strength, give us life from your life; be and remain our Lord over death and life and make us strong in your ser-

[1.] *NL,* A 21,1; handwritten, with a note by Bethge: "Liturgy given in Barcelona Memorial Day? February 26, 1928" (according to the calendar, however, Memorial Day fell on March 4, 1928). Memorial Day [*Volkstrauertag*] was introduced in 1922 at the behest of the People's Association for the Care of German War Graves; in 1934 it was renamed Heroes' Memorial Day as a state holiday. Since 1950, it has again been known as Memorial Day, though it is now celebrated not in Lent but on the next-to-last Sunday in the church year.

[2.] Cf. Matt. 5:4; Rev. 14:13; 2:10.

[3.] A chorale reworked by Luther; *EKG,* no. 309, verse 1.

[4.] *NL,* A 21,2; handwritten. Previously published in *GS* 5:416–17.

[5.] In Bonhoeffer's prayer here, his personal pain at the loss of those killed in action is clearly discernible. The latter included his brother Walter. The "great things . . . that happened years ago for us out there" apparently refers to the sacrifice of so many lives,

vice, for your service is holy service. Give strength to those who are lost in the pain of remembering their dead. Graciously ignore the weakness and half-heartedness of our days and may your holy kingdom grow powerful among [us]. We pray for your kingdom and for your church. We pray for our homeland and for all its leaders, for the government of Switzerland and for the king of this country. We pray that you strengthen the religious and moral energy of our people; we pray for our youth, for the confirmands and the children of our people and of our congregation, that their will may be moved by your holy will, that their life will be a piece of your life. But we all bow beneath your mighty hand and plead: Lord, may we behold your salvation: Lord's prayer.

455 **2. Sermon on Romans 11:6, Barcelona, Oculi, March 11, 1928**[1]

Rom. 11:6: But if it is by grace, it is no longer on the basis of works, otherwise grace would no longer be grace.[2]

Paul is naturally talking—for what else is important enough for him to talk about in this world after the cross of Christ?—he is talking about God's will to grant us salvation, that is, about justification. "But if it is by grace, it is no longer on the basis of works, otherwise grace would no longer be grace." An unpretentious text one might easily overlook, and perhaps some of you might wonder why I have chosen such a text today, the first day I stand before you in the pulpit. Why should we be concerned with talk about justification by grace alone when there are so many other more important and more serious things to talk about? One hears such remarks everywhere today. Are they really right? Should we have gone beyond that which was

---

which should be understood as a fruitful seed for the living. Memorial Day, when one remembers the dead with love and tries to find meaning in their deaths, seems unsuitable to Bonhoeffer—as it did to the great majority of Protestants at that time—for recalling the senseless brutality of war. As early as 1934, Bonhoeffer was fighting a passionate ecumenical battle against the new danger of war, and already here he expands the liturgy internationally by including intercessions for the Swiss—Swiss merchants were among the founders of the German congregation in Barcelona—and for the Spanish king Alfonso XIII. [Contrast the attitude to war in the congregational lecture of this time (see 2/3) and that in the 1932 address "Christ and Peace" (*DBW* 17:116–20; incomplete trans. in *TF*, 93–95), which contained the key ideas of his book *Discipleship*.—CG]

[1.] *NL*, A 21,3 a; handwritten, on stationery with the letterhead "Evangelical Congregation Barcelona," with a note by Bethge: "March 11, 1928, Oculi," the third Sunday in Lent. Previously published in Bonhoeffer, *PAM* 1:137–44. See also *NL*, A 21,3 b; typewritten copy by Bethge with editorial changes previously published in *GS* 5:417–23.

[2.] See the editor's afterword, p. 628.

so serious and important to Paul and to early Christianity, by virtue of the two thousand years separating us from that era? Certainly not; in fact quite the opposite is the case. We have sunk, sunk far below the sublime thoughts that stirred early Christianity. And our first concern should be to take seriously, in fact, to take extremely seriously, what was once so important to Paul; and we will see that if there is anything at all on this earth that is not ultimately trivial or even comical, however seriously it may present itself, it is the fact of justification. This is so precisely to the extent it reveals God's honor and glory, God's seriousness and goodness. In it our gaze is opened to the entire world, to that which is vain and to that which is serious in that world; in it we understand both ourselves and—what does "understand" mean here?—our God.

Our text outlines two strong lines here, two possibilities that belong to 456
each other and yet oppose each other, the only possibilities available if one is to conceive of God and the human being together. Works are one possibility, grace the other. In other words, one line leads from human beings up to God, the other from God down to human beings, and both exclude each other—and yet belong together. That is the miracle of the Christian faith we want to fathom. Let us speak first about the first possibility, which Paul calls works and which we will call the human path to God. The great church father Augustine began his *Confessions* with the statement, "You have made us for yourself, and our heart is *restless* until it rests in you."[3] "Restless": this is the word that concerns us. Restlessness is the characteristic feature distinguishing human beings from animals. Restlessness is the power that creates history and culture. Restlessness is the root of every spirit that elevates itself to morality; restlessness is—let us go ahead and say it—the most profound meaning and the bloodlike power in all religion. Restlessness—not in any transitory human sense, where all we find is nervousness and impatience—no, restlessness in the direction of the eternal. Instead of restlessness we could also say dread, anxiety, yearning, love.

There is in the soul of human beings, as truly as they are human beings, something that makes them restless, something that points them toward the infinite, eternal. [. . .][4]

This notion of something eternal, something infinite, makes the soul anxious in its own transitoriness. It wants to transcend itself, into permanence and stability; it wants to be unchangeable and immortal itself and yet does not know how to begin. It wants to draw the eternal into itself,

[3.] Augustine, *Confessions* (1.1), 3; a favorite quote during the Barcelona period (see below, 3/7, pp. 505 and 547. Cf. Staats, "Das patristische Erbe," 183–97, esp. 193n51.

[4.] Illegible.

wants to acquire power over the eternal so that it can rid itself of anxiety and restlessness. It wants to take the path itself to the eternal, bring the eternal under its control. From this restlessness of the soul the colossal
457 works of philosophy and of art emerged, the systems of Plato and Hegel, the Adam of Michelangelo, the quartets and symphonies of Beethoven, the cathedrals of the Gothic period, the paintings of Rembrandt, or the Faust and Prometheus of Goethe. All were overwhelmed by the idea of something eternal and unchangeable. They relieved the anxiety and restlessness of their hearts by painting, building, sculpting, and writing, that they might perhaps gain control of the infinite. The same applies to the great preachers of morality, a Plato, a Kant, those who stand perhaps at the pinnacle of humanity as regards rigorous morality, the Pharisees. They felt called in their hearts in an eternal fashion, and by directing their spirit toward morality, they themselves entered into a relationship with the eternal; they themselves found the path to the eternal; indeed, they made themselves eternal. At the same time, the most grandiose and most gentle of all human attempts to attain the eternal from out of the anxiety[5] and restlessness of the heart—is religion. The eternally puzzling, unsettling element is sought and found, and placed into an abiding relationship and the most secret contact with the soul, until the soul itself has become eternal. Here the human spirituality emerging from restlessness attains its most splendid blossom. Here, if anywhere, one must find the path to the eternal, here where the human being utterly subjects himself to the eternal. Here the path to the eternal must be found, be *earned.* From the darkness, from anxiety, from enigmatic mysteriousness,[6] from the transitoriness of the temporal, the human being has found the path to light, to joy, to eternity. The human race might well point proudly to this blossom of its own spirit except for one thing, namely, that God is God, and grace is grace.[7] Here is the source of the great disturbance[8] of our illusions and of our confidence in culture, the great disruption, which God brings about and which the ancient myth[9] of the Tower of Babel illustrates. "But if it is by grace, it is no longer
458 on the basis of works, otherwise grace would no longer be grace." Our path toward the eternal is interrupted; we plunge back into the depths from which we came, with our philosophy and art, our morality and religion.

[5.] Replaces "distress."

[6.] Replaces "distress."

[7.] The following discussion strongly recalls Barth's sermon "The Righteousness of God," particularly its references to the Tower of Babel; cf. *Word of God and the Word of Man,* 14–15, 17, 20, 22, 25, 27.

[8.] Cf. Barth, *Epistle to the Romans,* 424.

[9.] Uncertain reading.

For another path emerges, the path of God to human beings, the path of revelation and of grace, the path of Christ, the path of justification by grace alone. "My ways are not your ways"[10] is what we now hear; it is not we who go to God, but God who comes to us. It is not religion that makes us good before God, but God alone who makes us good. It is God's deed that is important here, God's deed before which all our claims sink. Culture and religion both stand under divine judgment.[11] The motives of our morality and our religion have been unmasked; we wanted to be masters of the eternal and now we are its slaves. Only one means of rescue remains, namely, God's path, and that means grace. But if it is by grace, it is no longer on the basis of works; otherwise grace would no longer be grace. But this means that the path to God is forever a hopeless one, if God does not come to us; it means that our religion, too, is nothing if God does not say yes to it. Not religion, but rather revelation, grace, love; not the path to God, but rather God's path to human beings, that is the sum total of Christianity. Here we find the great disappointment and yet also the much greater hope. Our works, our pride—our honor—all this is over. But God's grace, God's glory, God's honor all begin now. Not our religion—not even the Christian religion!—but rather God's grace, that is the message of our text as well as of all Christianity. Not our outstretched beggars' hands, but rather that with which God fills them is what matters; and that means precisely not us and our actions, but rather first of all God and God's actions. It is a matter of our actions only insofar as they create space for God's actions, only insofar as they allow God's grace to be grace.[12] Our hope rests not in ourselves, but in God. Where could that hope rest more securely than in God? 459

One question forces itself upon us now. Is it all over for our religion and our morality, if none of that can lead us to God and if God's paths are indeed different from our paths? Certainly not, for we are called to serve the God who gives us grace. Our religious and moral life, which is now placed under God's judgment and which has become transparent as human, all too human, is our attempt to present an offering to God. But it remains merely an attempt and nothing more, and whoever would make more of it is choosing the path toward God anew, the Tower of Babel. Religion and morality pose the most serious threat to knowledge of divine grace, for they bear the

[10.] Cf. Isa. 55:8.

[11.] Deleted: "But this robs us of our weapons; we stand naked before God's eyes; it is dark around us, and there is but a single flickering light: the hill of Golgotha with the dying Lord on whom the light of heaven falls."

[12.] Deleted: "But is there any greater assurance in the world than when God himself acts?"

germ of wanting to find one's own way to God, to make oneself master over God even though such attempts are merely human works and as such are subject to the judgment of eternity. And yet as long as there is grace, they remain necessary as a weak attempt, as a representation, as an offering to which God can say yes or no as he pleases.[13] We have gradually come to understand that we cannot attain it with our morality; but our text today, if we understand it correctly, emphatically states that our religion, too, as Luther says, is part of human flesh. Woe to us if we do not understand![14]

In years past, people argued a great deal about why it was Christianity that was victorious over the world rather than one of the many other competing religions; several different answers have been suggested.[15] Basically, though, only one answer accurately addresses the matter. The idea of God in Christianity is absolutely different from that of all other religions.
460 To what extent? Wherever we look, we see that religions have always shown human beings a path that leads to God, a path of holiness, righteousness, truth. Christianity alone reveals the impossibility of this undertaking. Even in their most spiritual spirituality—in religion—human beings remain human beings, and that means sinners; their religion is part of their flesh, and that means part of their desire for happiness, for blessedness, for pleasure, and that means for their own ego. Human beings, just as they are, stand in their entirety under God's judgment. Only one thing remains, namely, that God comes to human beings and bestows grace; the path from eternity into time, the path of Jesus Christ, that is the paradoxical message that moved with such power through the ancient world—a world that had become skeptical of that which came from human beings themselves. Not religion, but revelation and grace: this was the word of redemption, revealed to the world.

We stand before Good Friday [and] Easter, the days of God's almighty deeds in history, deeds in which God's judgment and grace became visible for all the world, judgment in those hours in which Jesus Christ the Lord hung on the cross, grace in that hour when death was devoured in victory. It was not human beings who did anything here, but God alone. God took

---

[13.] Strong resonance with Barth, *Epistle to the Romans,* 431–32.

[14.] In the margin, without any exact relationship to a specific part of the text, Bonhoeffer wrote: "'walk before me, and be pious,' that is God's radical, irrevocable demand to us. 'When you have done all that you were ordered to do, say "We are worthless slaves: we have done only what we ought to have done!"' Jesus's word eternally sets a boundary for all our actions and classifies it under the world of transitoriness that is subject to God's judgment." Cf. Gen. 17:1; Luke 17:10.

[15.] Cf. esp. Troeltsch, *Absoluteness of Christianity and the History of Religions.*

the path to human beings in infinite love. God judged what is human and bestowed grace beyond works.

After the aged Luther died, a note was found on his writing table on which during his last hours he had written the words: "We are beggars in spirit."[16] And so it will remain as long as there are human beings. But he who is king in the Spirit, the Lord of all life and of all grace, may he teach us to understand that our hope and our life stand and fall with God's grace. The deed is God's, the path is God's, the grace is God's, the Spirit is God's, our service and our life are God's, and the glory over all creatures is God's.

3. Sermon on 1 Corinthians 15:17, Barcelona, 461
Easter Sunday, April 8, 1928

3.1. Sermon[1]

1 Cor. 15:17: If Christ has not been raised, your faith is futile and you are still in your sins.

Easter 1 Cor. 15:17
A dangerous Easter text. For if we look at it more closely, allow ourselves to be impressed by it, it could possibly rob us of all our Easter joy; so it seems inappropriate to speak about such serious, dangerous things on Easter. And yet—there is not a single one of our Christian festivals that doesn't seem threatening, if we take it very seriously, bringing fear and woe to our hearts. Our entire existence and our whole spiritual being is assaulted and dragged before judgment and placed before a decision. In this, the Christmas message is no different than the Easter story. Yet only if we allow this assault to come over us ever anew in all its profundity can we master it and sense something of the real joy of Easter, which is anything but sentimentality.

If Christ has not been raised, our faith is futile, and this means that we are still living in guilt before God, meaning ultimately that we of all people on earth are most to be pitied.[2] In other words, if Christ has not been

---

[16.] Correct: "We are beggars, that is true" (*WA* 48:241); see Brecht, *Martin Luther,* 3:367–68.

[1.] *NL,* A 21,4 a; handwritten, on stationery with the letterhead "Evangelical Congregation Barcelona," with a note by Bethge: "Easter April 8, 1928." Previously published in Bonhoeffer, *PAM* 1:144-50. See also *NL,* A 21,4 b; typewritten copy by Bethge with editorial changes; published in *GS* 5:423–28.

[2.] [Cf. 1 Cor. 15:19.—CG]

raised, that which supports our life is pulled away, and everything collapses; our life disintegrates into meaninglessness. All talk about divine things is illusory, all hope imaginary. Our life depends on Easter, as Paul tells us. What can we say about this?

462 Easter, with the joy at the coming of spring, with all the happiness with which the sun warms our hearts, has become for each of us since childhood a festival dear to our hearts, a festival filled with warm memories from which we do not want to part. Who among us would want to lose even a single spring from our lives? But to say that our entire life depends on Easter, that our existence would be threatened if there were no Easter—who among us would want or even could bear such a thing? But Paul did indeed say it. And because he reflected a bit more thoroughly on this question than we tend to do, we may assume that such a statement does indeed harbor a certain meaning about which one might perhaps reflect further. "If Christ has not been raised, your faith is futile."

Hence, all apparently depends upon our understanding of exactly what Paul meant by the word "raised." What does resurrection mean and what can it mean for us? These are the old Easter questions that we cannot avoid unless we are thoughtless. The overwhelming phenomenon of perpetually self-renewing spring enables humanity throughout the world to sense something of the primal struggle between darkness and light in which, after intense fighting, light emerges victorious—spring emerges from the dark winter. Each year renews this colossal spectacle of nature, awakening in humankind an intimation of hope in resurrection. All that is dark must ultimately become light. This is a law of nature; indeed, darkness is not really an entity in and for itself; it exists only as the absence of light. A single ray of sunlight destroys it. And the sun comes, comes most assuredly, and with it the resurrection of nature. The seeds of life are already contained in the death of nature. Indeed, death is not really death at all, but a stage of life that abides in embryonic form within the seemingly rigid bodies. Life and light must emerge victorious, and death and darkness are merely their manifestations. These ideas are the common property and primal possessions of humankind, even back to its most primitive spiritual and
463 intellectual life, and it is from such ideas that our own modernized Easter faith draws without noticing that Christianity has far different things to say about Easter.[3]

[3.] Not only in modernity, as Bonhoeffer insinuates, but in the early church, too, the Easter faith oriented itself toward the natural examples of night and day, winter and spring (cf. *1 Clement* 20–26). Bonhoeffer already covered this in his 1925 seminar paper on *1 Clement* (*DBWE* 9, 2/4).

Easter is concerned not with a struggle between darkness and light, which ultimately light will win in any case since darkness is, after all, actually nothing, because death is already life; nor with a struggle between winter and spring, between ice and sun, but with the struggle of guilty humanity against divine love, or better: of divine love against guilty humanity, a struggle in which God appears to be vanquished on Good Friday and in which God, precisely by losing—wins—on Easter. Is God victorious—or is Prometheus[4] victorious? That is the question that is answered on Easter by God's mighty deed. Good Friday is not the darkness that must necessarily yield to light. It is not the winter sleep that contains and nourishes the seed of life within. It is the day on which human beings—human beings who wanted to be like gods—kill the God who became human, the love that became person; the day on which the Holy One of God, that is, God himself, dies, truly dies—voluntarily and yet because of human guilt—without any seed of life remaining in him in such a way that God's death might resemble sleep. Good Friday is not, like winter, a transitional stage—no, it is genuinely the end, the end of guilty humanity and the final judgment that humanity has pronounced upon itself. And here only one thing can help, namely, God's own mighty deed in the midst of humanity from within God's eternity. Easter is not an immanent or inner-worldly [innerweltlich] event, but a transcendent, world-transcending [überweltlich][5] event,
God's intervention from eternity through which God professes loyalty to 464
God's Holy One and raises that Holy One from the dead. Easter speaks not about immortality but about resurrection, resurrection from the dead through God's mighty deed, from death that is genuinely death with all its horrors and terrors, death of the body and of the soul, of the entire person. That is the Easter message. Easter speaks not about some divine seed in human beings that might celebrate repeated resurrection as in nature, but about human guilt and about death, but also about God's love and about

[4.] Prometheus, the titan of Greek mythology who represents human culture before the highest god Zeus and who, for the sake of that culture, deceives Zeus. Beginning with early dialectical theology during the 1920s, Prometheus represented the quintessence of un-Christian cultural piety [*Kulturfrömmigkeit*]. Cf. the chapter on Prometheus as myth in Ernst Bloch, *Atheism in Christianity*, 27–83. ["Cultural piety," *Kulturfrömmigkeit*, in distinction from "cultural Protestantism," *Kulturprotestantismus*, is a purely secular and sometimes anti-Christian attitude that worships progress, human achievement, and so on—whether in capitalist or Marxist forms.—CG]

[5.] [Literally "otherworldly," though Bonhoeffer means not an event happening beyond the world and not affecting the world, but an event coming from "beyond" the world, from God's eternity, into the midst of humanity in the world.—CG] the death of death itself, about God's eternal and mighty act, not about immanent laws of nature.

If God's history among human beings had ended on Good Friday, then the final pronouncement over humankind would be guilt, rebellion, the unfettering of all titanic human forces, a storming of heaven by human beings, godlessness, godforsakenness, but then ultimately meaninglessness and despair. Then your faith is futile. Then you are still in your guilt. Then we are of all people most to be pitied. That is, the final word would be the human being. On the cross of Jesus Christ, not only does our moral and religious life come to nothing by being convicted in all its culpability, but our entire culture is judged as well; if the cross had been the end, then it would have been over for scholarship and for art. All our cultural activity represents a striving for something ultimate, for meaning, for a logos, for God. What is the point of searching for truth if there is no truth, if human beings rather than God represent the ultimate standard for what is true and false? Eliminating this orientation toward something ultimate, something meaningful, something divine, means severing the vital nerve of our art. If God is dead—we of all people are most to be pitied. We now understand this, together with the apostle.

A strange story from antiquity tells how a small ship of Greek mariners sailed along the coast of southern Italy and suddenly heard a powerful, mournful voice calling out the name of the helmsman. When the helmsman answered, the sailors heard the same voice cry out: The great Pan is dead,
465 the great Pan is dead! A great panic and confusion seized the ship, and wherever this news spread, one saw people fleeing in terror and fright. This puzzling story has been variously interpreted.[6] One thing seems certain to me: it represents a pagan counterpart to the message of Good Friday. God is dead; the world is godless, godforsaken. And the people's confused consternation expresses the terrified, horrified question: What do we do now? It seems the world must collapse and disintegrate into meaninglessness if God is dead. The ancient world had no answer for the great lament, "The great Pan is dead!" The Christian Easter message provided the answer. The meaning of the *Easter* message is that God is the death of death; God lives and so Christ lives also; death could not hold Christ against the superior power of God. God pronounced a decree against death, destroyed it, and resurrected Jesus Christ.

[6.] As early as 1924, Bonhoeffer recalled this passage in Plutarch (*Moralia* 419 B–E), one of the most widely read authors in European cultural history: "Antiquity is not dead at all, the saying Πᾶν ὅ μέγας τέθηκεν [the great Pan is dead] is false" (*DBWE* 9:84).

What does this mean? How are we to understand this? A multitude of questions emerge. What does physical resurrection mean? What about the empty grave? The appearances? A multitude of questions—prompted by curiosity, by our inquisitiveness regarding superstitious things, by mystery-mongering, questions in which we can have no pleasure, questions that go from A to Z and are never satisfied. Certainly the grave will have been empty. But only one thing is important: God professed loyalty to Christ and touched Christ with God's eternal life. Now Christ lives because God lives and because God's love lives. That suffices. Though we may ponder the "how," nothing changes regarding the "that."[7]

But if God lives—well, then love lives despite the cross, and we no longer live in guilt; God has forgiven us. God professed loyalty to Jesus, and Jesus professed loyalty to us. If Jesus lives, then our faith acquires new meaning. Then we are the most blessed of all people. God's yes to guilty humankind,
a new meaning for all our actions—that is Easter. Not "the great Pan is 466
dead," but rather God lives and we with God. That is Easter. Not godforsakenness—but the fullness of God; not human beings and their titanic victory over the Godhead, but God and God's mighty victory over humankind, over death and guilt and rebellion, that is Easter.

But one more thing. One particular hope grows gently and secretly in our hearts on Easter. "If for this life only we have hoped . . . ," Paul remarks.[8] Easter is God's intervention from eternity, we said. Easter is a prologue of ultimate, ineffable things, things that will one day happen when the consummation is near, things about which we can speak only in images and parables. It is not only today that Easter concerns us—no, it reveals to us the entire glory and power of God. God is the Lord not only of Jesus Christ's death, but of my death and your death as well. And just as God raised Jesus in inexpressible power, so too will he lead his holy people from death to life. This is where we look in hope today.

3.2 Pulpit Notes[9]

A dangerous Easter text—For if we look at it more closely . . it could possibly rob us of all our Easter *joy*. Seems inappropriate . . . Christian festival . . threatening . . allow this assault *to affect us*, then joy of Easter.—*Text* . .

[7.] [See Bonhoeffer's rejection of the "how" question in favor of the "who" question in his Christology lectures (*Christ the Center*, 28–31).—CG]

[8.] 1 Cor. 15:19 reads in full: "If for this life only we have hoped in Christ, we are of all people most to be pitied."

[9.] *NL*, A 21,4; handwritten. These notes document that the vicar delivered his sermon almost extemporaneously.

supports pulled away, meaninglessness . . illusory . . *Our life depends on Easter.* We? Easter dear to our hearts . . . *Paul. Text.* "Resurrection"?—Easter question.—Spring enables to sense primal struggle between darkness and light . . . spring emerges from winter; *each year*; hope in resurrection . . . all that is dark must become light . . . law of nature . . darkness and noth-
467 ing. Death of nature—stage of life. Primitive and modernized. Easter faith. Struggle: divine love and guilt. Humanity. *Prometheus. Good Friday. not dark . . .* God who became human crucified; *God's Holy One dies. End* of humanity. *Transcendent event.* Not *immortality* . . not divine seed . . If God's history ends on *Good Friday, final pronouncement: guilt . . .* godlessness. "Most to be pitied." Culture. for God dead. "Great Pan is dead." Pagan Good Friday. "What do we do now without God?" Easter message: God lives, Jesus *raised.* Questions? Curiosity. Jesus lives . . . *Love despite the cross.* Professed to us.[10] The "most blessed." New faith, new meaning of our culture.[11] "Pan is dead"—God lives.—fullness of God—God's victory

4. Sermon on Matthew 28:20, Barcelona, Quasimodogeniti (First Sunday after Easter), April 15, 1928[1]

Matt. 28:20: Remember, I am with you always, to the end of the world.[2]

Fairy tales and legends from the oldest times tell of the days when God walked among human beings. Those were splendid times when one met a wanderer on the road who asked for lodging, then at home one recognized in this simple man the Lord God and was richly rewarded.[3] Those were wonderful times when God and human beings were still so close that people could walk and talk with God. Indeed, those were the days recounted only

[10.] [See the full text of the sermon, p. 489: "God professed loyalty to Jesus, and Jesus professed loyalty to us."—CG]

[11.] This statement is clearer here than in the manuscript (cf. p. 489: "new meaning for all our actions").

[1.] *NL,* A 21,5 a; handwritten, on stationery with the letterhead "Evangelical Congregation Barcelona," with a note by Bethge: "Low Sunday." Previously published in *PAM* 1:150–57. See also *NL,* A 21,5 b; typewritten copy by Bethge with editorial changes published in *GS* 5:428–34. Cf. also the calendar *NL,* A 18,2. This sermon is closely related conceptually to the fragment "The Wanderer on the Country Road" (see 3/19, p. 551. [The phrase *Quasi modo geniti,* "Like newborn infants" (1 Pet. 2:2), which begins the Introit of the Mass on Low Sunday, is a traditional name in the Western church for that day.—CG]

[2.] [NRSV reads: "to the end of the age."—CG]

[3.] Allusion to the legend of Philemon and Baucis and similar stories.

by fairy tales and legends that spoke of all the slumbering, secret human 468
hopes as if they had already become reality. The beginning of our own Bible also relates how the Lord God walked about in the garden of paradise in the evening and lived and conversed with human beings. Probably very few peoples do not have similar stories. Blessed were those people permitted to experience those times when God and human beings were still close.

How quickly things changed. Our Bible recounts the story of the fall as the turning point in history.[4] Human beings were driven from the garden in which they lived with God; now they lived separated from God in guilt and unhappiness that increased from generation to generation. The rift between God and human beings deepened. Humanity sank into the night. And as long as human beings can remember, they know only the night, the time when God no longer moves freely among human beings, and many look longingly back to the primal age of the fairy tale, to paradise, as if to a lost home they themselves never even knew. Or people of powerful hope speak and spoke about coming days, when God would once more dwell among human beings,[5] when the kingdom of God would be established on earth. God and human beings somehow belong together, and God will return and be their guest.

There was one day in human history when this hope had to be radically demolished, a day on which people had to become aware of the eternal distance between human beings and God—the day humanity raised its hand against the God dwelling among them and nailed Jesus Christ to the cross—Good Friday. But there was also a day of divine response to human action, a day when God took up dwelling among human beings anew and for all eternity, the day when the outstretched but unholy [hand] of human
beings was filled against all hope with divine grace, the day when Jesus 469
Christ was raised, Easter. Remember, I am with you[6] . . . that is the Easter message, not the distant, but the near God, that is Easter.

A searching, an anxious groping and questioning for divine things permeates our own age. A great loneliness has come upon our age, the kind of loneliness found only in a godforsaken age. The enormous distress of isolation and homelessness has come upon the colossal, wild activity of countless masses of people in the midst of our big cities. Yet the yearning for the time grows when once again God might abide among human beings, when God might be found. A thirst for contact with divine things has come upon

[4.] Cf. Gen. 3.
[5.] [Cf. Rev. 21:3.—CG]
[6.] [Cf. Matt. 28:20.—CG]

people, a burning thirst demanding to be quenched. Currently a great many remedies are being offered for sale[7] that promise to quench this thirst in a radical fashion and for which hundreds of thousands of hands greedily reach[8]—in the midst of this wild activity and marketing frenzy with new means and ways we find the One Word of Jesus Christ: Remember, I am here. . . . You don't need to search very far at all, nor to question or engage in all sorts of mysterious activity, I *am* here; that is, Jesus does not promise his coming, does not prescribe paths that might take a person to him, but simply says: I am here; whether we see Jesus or not, feel him or not, want him or not—none of this makes any difference over against the fact that Jesus is here with us, that he is simply wherever we are, and that we can do absolutely nothing. I am with you always . . . But if all this is indeed true, if Jesus really is with us, then God is also with us wherever we are, and we are no longer abandoned, homeless, lonely—then—let us follow this line of thinking to its conclusion—then the age of the legends[9] has become reality again, and God is living among us. The only important thing now is to keep our eyes open to see where we find God—as was true for those people in the legend who had to recognize the Lord God in the foreign wanderer.
470 God wants to be among us—do we want to make a liar of God by not believing? God is still with human beings despite Good Friday—Remember, I am with you always. . . .

But before we all start rejoicing too quickly, one serious reflection. What does it really mean to say that Jesus or God is with us? That God is in the world? Where and how are we aware of that? God lives, lives for the world, the world is filled with God, is transfigured, meaningful *sub specie aeternitatis*[10]—that was the Easter message. But now we ask further: Where can I sense something of this divine fullness in the world and in my own life?[11] And we answer that today, too, God is still walking among us; today, too, we can speak with God; we are together with God, walk down the street with God, encounter God in the foreigner on the road, the beggar at the door.[12] The world is God's world; wherever we go, we encounter God, and Jesus, the Resurrected, is with us. Remember, I am with you. . . .

[7.] Deleted: "and held up for sale."

[8.] Deleted: "and yet it's just lies and deception, for instead of quenching that thirst."

[9.] [See the opening line of the sermon.—CG]

[10.] "Under the aspect of eternity."

[11.] Deleted: "Where does meaning come from now?"

[12.] Deleted: "The incomparably profound meaning of our fairy tales is that they"; cf. further below.

But isn't all this merely metaphorical language? What can we possibly mean by saying that Jesus is with us? Isn't that merely an approximate, undefined feeling?

Not at all. It is completely clear. Jesus is with us in his words, and that means clearly and unequivocally that he is in that which he wants and in that which he thinks about us. He is with us with his will, in his words, and only in our dealings with Jesus's words do we sense his presence. The word, however, is the clearest and most unequivocal means of expression by which intellectual [geistig] beings connect. If we have a person's word, then we know that person's will; indeed, we know the whole person. If we have Jesus's word, then [we] know his will and his entire person. Jesus's word is always one and the same and yet is also always different. It tells us: You are standing under God's love, God is holy, and you should also be holy; God wants to give you the Holy Spirit that you might also be holy. And it says this in other ways to every person in every moment. God's word is one 471
thing to a child and [. . .][13] different to a man, one thing to a boy and a girl, something different to a man and a woman, and yet there is no age, no moment in life when Jesus's word does not have something to say to us. Our entire life stands under that word and is sanctified by that word. From baptism to the grave, the word of the church accompanies us, places us under the assurance of the word: Remember, I am with you. As a symbol of this situation, the church places the decisive stages of a person's life under the church's own proclamation. To the child, not yet of age, Jesus's word is already proclaiming how God's grace comes before all human actions; it then speaks to the child of the sanctity of a mother's love. To the boy at play it speaks about God's truthfulness, about his seriousness and his goodness, about service in Christ's host, about heroic deeds and knightly deeds. To the young man it speaks about the sanctity of the divine commission and about eternal goals, opening that person's eyes to the glory of the world and allowing his yearning to roam beyond the temporal; and the word tells of the purity of God and of the heart. To the young girl it speaks about much joy and cheerfulness, though also about what the girl owes to the prospect of becoming a wife and mother. To the mature man the word speaks about the seriousness of work, about fate and guilt, about responsibility and loyalty and [. . .][14] about God's will that the person himself takes his life in his hands and shapes it. To the mature woman, the word tells how God has sanctified motherhood. To the elderly it speaks about that world from which

[13.] Illegible, perhaps "something."

[14.] Illegible.

death separates us and about the last things. And yet it speaks one and the same thing to both the young and the elderly, namely, that God loves you and is with you, depend on it. And the other thing: God is holy, and you should also be holy; the word about God's ineffable compassion is spoken to people of all ages, as is the word about God's seriousness and beneficence in every moment of human life.

Remember, I am with you . . . . This applies *whether we want it to or not.* Are
472 there any moments when we might not want it? Moments when God's presence [Dasein] is irksome to us? We all know there are such moments; these are the moments of God's judgment upon us. God is with us—suddenly the consequences of this word become transparent. If God is with us, and yet we are not with God—what happens then? Let us once more follow this notion in all seriousness all the way to its conclusion. No respected man of the world, no prophet, no prince of the earth comes to us and abides perpetually with us; but the prince of life and of the whole world is with us with his judgment and his claim on us. Can we do justice to this claim? And even if we wanted to revolt or resist, God is there always, to the end of the world. The blissful notion that God once again dwells among human beings, that God once again lends meaning to human life, that the world is full of God, this notion becomes threatening and frightening precisely because it demands responsibility. Our life and action are not to be meaningless; but what if we live our lives in apathy and thoughtlessness? Every age in life has its divine destiny. What if we ignore that destiny? Every moment of our life is related to God. What if we wish to sense nothing of that relationship? Thus a heavy burden is suddenly placed upon us, once we take seriously the statement "Remember, I am with you. . . ." But where God assigns [aufgeben], he also gives [geben] and forgives [vergeben]. Where God's judgment is, there also is his grace. Did God come into the world and live life in the world in order to ruin that world? No. God wants to give to the life of the world as much of the divine life as the world wants; God wants to draw into himself, into his blessed partnership, those who are lonely and all who seek his life. "I am with you always. . . ." God lives, lives in the world, lives for the world, lends it meaning and life, makes it our home, gives our own life a relationship to eternity and a closeness to God—that is the grace we take with us from this passage.

But one more thing. One profound element in the fairy tale we mentioned earlier is that it has God move about among human beings as a human being. This promise, too, has become a reality. Jesus Christ is not
473 only with us in lonely hours; Jesus Christ also encounters us in every step we take, in every person we meet. Remember, I am with you . . . Jesus Christ, God himself, speaks to us from every human being; the other person, this

enigmatic, impenetrable You, is God's claim on us; indeed, it is the holy God in person whom we encounter.[15] God's claim is made on us in the wanderer on the street, the beggar at the door, the sick person at the door of the church, though certainly no less in every person near to us, in every person with whom we are together daily. "Just as you did it to one of the least of these, you did it to me," Jesus says.[16] I am for you, and you are for me God's claim, God himself; in this recognition, our gaze opens to the fullness of divine life in the world. Now life in the human community acquires its divine meaning. This community itself is one of the forms of God's revelation.[17] God is with us as long as there is community. The most profound meaning of our ties to social life is that through it we are tied all the more securely to God. Remember, I am with you always, to the *end of the world.* Again we hear about the last things. "I am the first and the last," "Jesus Christ is the same yesterday and today and forever"; such are the words we hear.[18] Jesus is the Lord of ages and is always with his own, even when things are difficult, and will abide with us; that is our comfort. If tribulation and anxiety come upon us, Jesus is with us and leads us over into God's eternal kingdom. Jesus Christ is the breadth of our life, Jesus Christ is the [. . .][19] of our community, Jesus Christ is with us to the end of the world. This we owe to Easter.

5. Sermon (fragment) on Luke 12:49, Barcelona, Trinity Sunday, June 3, 1928[1] 474

Luke 12:49: I came to ignite a fire upon the earth, and how I wish it were already burning![2]

[. . .] who with one hand reaching up to heaven swings a torch of heavenly fire over the earth lying at his feet, and already the sparks are flying to and

[15.] [Cf. *DBWE* 1:54–56.—CG]

[16.] Matt. 25:40.

[17.] A major theme since *Sanctorum Communio.* Cf. *DBWE* 1:126–27.

[18.] Isa. 41:4; Rev. 1:17; Heb. 13:8. [The German edition also cites Rev. 1:11, since the Luther Bible Bonhoeffer used included the phrase "alpha and omega, first and last" before the statement about writing in a book; cf. also Rev. 1:8.—CG]

[19.] Illegible.

[1.] *NL,* A 21,6 a; handwritten, with a note by Bethge: "Luke 12:49, June 3, 1928, Barcelona." See also *NL,* A 21,6 b; later typewritten copy by Bethge. The beginning of the sermon has been lost.

[2.] [NRSV: "I came to bring fire to the earth, and how I wish it were already kindled!" The translation has been revised here and elsewhere in the sermon to make it closer to Bonhoeffer's German.—CG]

fro and catching fire and glowing and smoking and blazing; and above this image stand the words "I came to . . . . how I wish it were already burning!"—this image belongs in our picture book from now on. What does the picture mean, so harsh, so gruesome, so terrible? Everyone is familiar with fire and how relentlessly it seeks and greedily devours victim upon victim and everything people have created and made. Everyone is familiar with this majestic, horrific power, and now Jesus supposedly enlists its service. Indeed, Jesus impatiently yearns for the fire *to go ahead* and burn, that the world go up in flames—"and how I wish it were already burning!"

What shall we say about this fire? We all know Jesus is not talking about natural fire, and we also know that the fire is not yet burning. Jesus tell us this much. Some suggest the reference is [. . .][3] to the fire of the great world revolution and the great world war. Jesus the revolutionary is summoning his multitudes.[4] Such talk is nonsense, for Jesus subjected himself to the authority of the state. "Give therefore to the emperor. . . ."[5] Is it perhaps the fire of religious fanaticism? For more than a millennium, this fire has burned and consumed human victims, has often destroyed what was sacred to people, has blown as a storm of annihilation over the world and wrought murder and destruction in the name of Jesus Christ. Is that
475 the fire Jesus yearns for? This fire looks all too earthly to be the fire of Jesus Christ. Not as much impure heat, not as much wild passion burns in [. . .].[6] But what then?

Now is the time of *Pentecost*. The mysterious prophecy of John the Baptist has been fulfilled concerning the one who would come after him and baptize with fire and with the Spirit. It came like fire from heaven on Pentecost, and fast as a burning fire the excitement spread, storming over Jerusalem and the surrounding countryside. Now we clearly see what Jesus means by fire. Heavenly fire, divine fire is what Jesus wants to hurl over the earth, and how—ah, how full of yearning until he sees the bright flames blazing up from within the dense smoke, until flame upon flame shoots up and a sea of fire blazes up to heaven. From time immemorial the spirit of the divine has been compared to fire. The great mystery of divine life seemed almost too similar to the mystery of fire. And this comparison has profound meaning. The divine spirit comes into the world like a fire, and with the power of fire it seizes control of people. With a passionate rush it seizes us and chases us

---

[3.] Illegible.

[4.] Cf., e.g., Kautsky, *Foundations of Christianity*, 331–36 ("Communism") and 363–71 ("Jesus as a Rebel").

[5.] Matt. 22:21 par.

[6.] Two illegible words.

out of our lethargy. "Fire! Fire everywhere!" we cry out, perhaps in fright. Save what you can! But it quickly begins to burn and scorch everything around us, to destroy it, to melt it. Whatever we try to use against the fire is annihilated. We fetch our most precious, dependable treasures: our morality and our religion. But behold, the divine fire scorches and burns till nothing is left of our glory. We want to resist and defend ourselves, but it doesn't help, and even before we lament what we have lost, we find that now the fire remains in us and that we ourselves—let those who can understand, understand—have become part of the eternal divine fire that burns and blazes and glows in us. Indeed—glows! "I want people who glow like torches," a great poet once said.[7] Torches of divine fire, divine clarity, divine light in the midst of a world that has sunk into night, torches pointing toward the light, torches on which others can light their own torches, torches ignited 476
by the magnificence of the divine glory—this is what Jesus wants to make out of us. To purify and glow and warm. Indeed—to warm! Here the hymn to Christ's love commences. If the spirit of God, the divine fire is in us, then the power is also in us to master the world, the power that renews the world from within—love. Then the divine fire is not captive within us. It radiates out into the world, warms the hearts that have grown cold, melts away the layer of ice covering so many souls, draws our neighbor into its glory and blessedness. It can no longer be cold in the world if Christ's love is urging us on. It becomes warm and bright and clear wherever God's spirit appears, wherever Jesus hurls fire upon the earth. Here we have once more talked about wonderful things and perhaps even warmed ourselves with such thoughts. If only things could be the way we have described them. But we cannot get there without bitter penitence. Have we forgotten that our text actually represents a great lament of Jesus: "How I wish it were already burning!" But that obviously means it is not yet burning, things have not progressed that far yet, at least not when Jesus spoke these words. But what about today?

I once spoke about this text in a children's service and then asked the children: Tell me, what about today? Is the fire burning in our hearts? A small boy responded with a longing, radiant look I will never forget—"If we only knew!" It is not difficult to see inside the boy's heart. He really was waiting for the fire to begin burning and yet was repeatedly disappointed to find that some obstacle, something frightfully powerful prevented it from blazing up, and instead the fire always threatened to go out. This "If we only knew!" contains Jesus's entire longing. "How I wish it were already

[7.] The source of the citation is unknown.

burning" and at the same time the painful realization that we are not yet that far along, a completely different fire lives in our world, the fire of diabolical human passions and desires, and this fire is devouring human beings and will not stop until the world itself ceases to be. An ancient Teutonic legend tells of a world conflagration that will inaugurate the end of
477 the world.[8] Our words, too, are directed today, full of yearning, forward into the future. When will we have reached the point that the divine fire alone illuminates the world? When will all the world finally be ablaze with the holy fire? We must be patient. It will only happen when the new world comes. But in the world of darkness and godlessness, we cry out with the old prayer of Pentecost: Come, Holy Spirit, into the hearts of your believers and ignite within us the fire of your divine love.[9]

6. Sermon (fragment) on Matthew 7:1, Barcelona, Third Sunday after Trinity, June 24, 1928[1]

Matt. 7:1: "Judge not, that you be not judged."[2]

If we would only genuinely take this passage to heart, the command not to judge would no longer seem so harsh. Rather, we would accept it as God's gift that we no longer need to judge amid so much misery and guilt, that we may love, that we need not separate ourselves like the Pharisees and could rather step out into all that misery and distress, that we may help and love and be compassionate among sinners, that our heart may break beneath the distress of our big cities and their immorality, that we may embrace the disinherited and those gone astray. Thanks be to God and to God's love for this gift. Jesus himself said, I came not to judge the world;[3] Jesus loved throughout his entire life, this was his happiness and blessedness. If we want our own happiness and blessedness, let us leave judging alone.

[8.] Concerning the old Germanic understanding of the world conflagration, see Vries, *Altgermanische Religionsgeschichte*, 392–405.

[9.] The ancient church antiphon: "Veni sancte spiritus"; cf. *EKG*, no. 98.

[1.] *NL*, A 21,7 a; handwritten, with a note by Bethge: "probably June 24, 1928; 3rd Sunday after Trinity; Barcelona." See also *NL*, A 21,7 b; later typewritten copy with editorial changes by Bethge. [The German editors followed Bethge, who cataloged this as a "fragment," but it may be a short sermon or a meditation for an evening devotion, with the final words being supplied by a Trinitarian formula, for example; cf. *Nachlaß Dietrich Bonhoeffer*, 18–19, *NL*, A 21,7 a and b.—CG]

[2.] [This RSV corresponds closely to Bonhoeffer's German text.—CG]

[3.] [John 12:47.—CG]

So let us give thanks that we may love, that we may be like Jesus, that we 478
may believe in human beings because they are God's children, that we may support them in love; love is patient, it believes everything, hopes for everything, bears everything.[4]

God loved human beings in Jesus Christ, made them into children of God while they were yet sinners. Let us love the child of God in our neighbor, even if that person makes a mistake, even if that person falls. In our neighbor, we love God; that is the great gift of Christianity. This also brings us back to what we said earlier. Judging destroys every community. Loving, pardoning, interceding, that alone builds it up. No marriage, no friendship endures without this most profound, forgiving, nonjudgmental love. No rearing of youth can succeed unless we make ourselves equals in love; not arrogance and self-righteousness of [. . .],[5] but love, forgiving, interceding love of those who draw their energy from God alone and who stand before God with their pupil or child. Neither can there be any national community [Volksgemeinschaft] as long as people seek to judge. Class hatred will never end if we do not finally do away with judging the other class. Judging creates arrogance and self-righteousness; arrogance creates separation, alienation, hostility. Love creates humility and trust in God's compassion; humility creates unity and friendship, for it comes from God.

A new week is beginning,[6] and each day we will find occasion for judging, for speaking hardheartedly and mercilessly about people. God grant that we might find our way to his love, that we might recognize our own misery, our own wretchedness before God's holiness, that we might become small before God so that the power of God's own love might grow within us into a blessing for our community. May God tear out our hearts of stone and replace them with hearts of flesh that beat in love for the miserable and
guilty.[7] May God let his love shine over the guilt and distress of our big 479
cities and radiate over the lost and fallen that they might all return to God, the Father, and grant all love. May God grant that this be so. . .

[4.] [Cf. 1 Cor. 13:4, 7.—CG]

[5.] Illegible.

[6.] [Bonhoeffer follows the tradition of Sunday as the first day of the week, as still observed in England, Canada, the United States, and parts of Africa. Since the later twentieth century, most countries in Europe, along with Asia, Australia, and South America, have counted Monday as the first day.—CG]

[7.] Cf. Ezek. 11:19.

7. Sermon on Psalm 62:2, Barcelona, Sixth Sunday after Trinity, July 15, 1928[1]

Ps. 62:2:[2] My soul is silent before God, who helps me.

Thousands of years ago, at a distant place far to the east, a pious man, standing amid the storms of life, knelt down before God in the solitude and silence of the holy Jewish temple, deeply partaking of that holy silence, drinking it into the depth of his soul, and spoke these words: "My soul is silent before God, who helps me." Oh, you ancient singer of our psalm, you sensed the bliss and sweetness of God's peace on this earth; you are like the image of a gentle dream to us, so longed for and yet so distant, ah, so distant. We love your image, but we no longer understand it, no longer want to understand it. Ah, come close to us, very close in this sacred hour and tell us about the silence of the soul, about silence before God. Imprint your image deep into our hearts and show us something of your bliss, for we know you have much to say to us.[3]

My soul is silent before God. Like a song from ancient times, like a medieval picture, painted on a gilt background, like a childhood memory, this strange, alien statement about the soul drifts down to us in the twentieth century. Is there still something like the soul in an age such as ours, an age
480 of machines, of economic competition, of the dominance of fashion and sports;[4] is this nothing more than a cherished childhood memory, like so much else? It just sounds so strange and peculiar amid the confusion and loud voices extolling themselves, this little word "soul." It speaks such a gentle, quiet language that we hardly hear it anymore amid the tumult and chaos inside us. Yet it speaks a language full of the greatest responsibility and of profound seriousness: you, human being, have a soul; beware, lest you lose it, lest you awaken one day amid the frenzy of life—in both work and private life—and find that inwardly you have become empty, a plaything of events, a leaf before the wind, driven to and fro and blown away—that you have lost your soul. Watch out for your soul. What should

[1.] *NL*, A 21,8 a; handwritten, with a note by Bethge: "July 15, 1928, Barcelona 6th Sunday after Trinity Summer 1928." Previously published in *PAM* 1:157–65. See also *NL*, A 21,8 b; typewritten copy. Previously published with abbreviations and editorial changes in *GS* 5:434–39.

[2.] [Verse 62:1 in the English enumeration. The NRSV here is, "For God alone my soul waits in silence; from him comes my salvation"; translation here is altered to conform to Bonhoeffer's German.—CG]

[3.] Cf. the childhood recollection of Bonhoeffer's sister Sabine in Hase's memoir, p. 594.

[4.] Harnack makes similar reproaches; see 1/95 as well as 3/18, p. 551, ed. note 21.

we say about this soul? It is the life God gave us; it is what God loves in us, what God has touched from eternity. It is the love within us and the longing and the sacred restlessness and the responsibility and joy and pain. It is the divine breath breathed into a transitory being. Human being, you have a soul. This is no sweet childhood memory, no dream, but accurate[5] reality; and thus a weighty, serious responsibility has been laid upon us and for which we will one day have to give account in eternity.

Now, however, perhaps this person or that realizes indeed that he has a soul. But, ah, look at what has become of it down through the years! A restless, distracted, tormented, despondent thing, shaken to and fro by daily events, a thing that knows not whether it's coming or going. And now it encounters the statement: my soul is *silent* before God. It is primarily about this silence of the soul that we want to speak today.[6]

We can probably say that not many people have even an inkling what this silence of the soul means, fewer still are those who know something 481
of the silence of the soul waiting for God. Yoked to the day's work, people hardly have time to catch their breath before society—so-called entertainment—seizes them and sucks what energy is left over from work. No wonder that, left alone, people are only able to attend to their physical needs. And yet our entire being thirsts for solitude, for silence, since ultimately we have all, at one time or another, experienced such silence and have not forgotten the benefits of such hours. Today, however, we are not talking about being silent while reading a book or listening to a song or something like that, but about being silent before God.

[. . .][7] silence of the soul before God. But what does this mean? Ah, it is something so great and so sacred that one can speak of it only in human metaphors. My soul is silent before God. Like the infant who is nursed and becomes calmed at its mother's breast and finds all its wishes fulfilled here, like the young boy who is speechless gazing upon his hero and leader, like the crying child that yearns for its mother to lay her gentle hand upon its brow and dispel and silence all its cares, like the young girl who quietly reflects on the prospect of one day becoming a mother, like the man who finds all his passion and restlessness calmed by the gaze of his beloved woman, like the person who becomes quiet before the eyes of a loyal friend, like a sick person who is calmed by the physician, like the old person who becomes calm before the face of death, like all of us who are silenced in

---

[5.] Uncertain reading.

[6.] Deleted: "Anxiety and lethargy are the two forces in the life of the human soul that prevent people today from attaining this silence."

[7.] Two illegible words.

reverence and awe at the heart of nature, under the starry heavens—just so should the soul be calmed from all the restlessness and chaos and haste, before the eyes of God; here it should quench its thirst, here its desire should become bliss, here its longing should be fulfilled, here it should find rest from the heat of the day in the protective shadow of God's hand, here it should cast off its burdens and troubles and become free and calm beholding God, here fall silent and quiet in worship and reverence. My soul is silent before God. Becoming silent means genuinely not being able to
482 say anything, means feeling as if an alien but beneficent hand is laid upon our lips, telling us to be silent. Being silent means blissfully beholding the one who is yearned for, the beloved, means surrendering oneself entirely, capitulating before the superior power of the other, the wholly other; it means not being ourselves for a moment but rather merely beholding the other, but it also means waiting, specifically for what the other has to say to us. Being silent before God means yielding to God the right to have the first and last word concerning us, and means accepting that word whatever it may be, for all eternity. It means not trying to justify oneself but rather listening to what God might have to say about our justification. Being silent does not mean doing nothing but means breathing in God's will, means tensely listening and being prepared to obey. The hour of silence is an hour of serious responsibility, of being genuinely serious with God and with ourselves, and yet is also always an hour of bliss since it is an hour lived in the calmness of God. My soul becomes silent before God. That means speak, Lord, for your servant is listening.[8]

My soul becomes silent before God, *who helps me.* God's hours are hours of succor and comfort. God has an answer for every distress of our soul, and this answer is always one and the same regardless of who receives it. To the man who rescues himself out of the frenzy and commotion of daily life, to the sick person who comes to God in misery, to the person lamenting the death of a loved one, to those burdened by guilt, to the man and the woman, the elderly and the child, God speaks the enticing words: I love you. Admittedly, the fire of God's love consumes all that is inauthentic and bad in human beings, and that hurts profoundly. Being silent before God means being small before him; it creates the pain of remorse, but also the joy of love and grace beyond all measure. My soul is silent before God, *who helps me.* If our soul has but found its way to God, he will help as surely as he is God. I listen attentively to God's word and drink deeply of it, the statement: It is you, you I love, abide with me, I am your real father.

[8.] Cf. 1 Sam. 3:10.

Well, of course, some might say, you're telling us all these wonderful things, but why is it that so few actually get this far? It must be something 483
that requires special power or grace.

There are two simple reasons. First, we are afraid of silence. We are so accustomed to commotion and noise that we are uncomfortable amid silence; we flee silence; we race from activity to activity to avoid having to be alone with ourselves for even a moment, to avoid having to look at ourselves in the mirror. We are bored with ourselves, and often the most desperate, wasted hours are those we are forced to spend by ourselves. Not only are we afraid of ourselves, of discovering and unmasking ourselves, but even more we are afraid of God, that he might disturb our aloneness [Alleinigkeit] and discover and unmask us, that God might draw us into partnership and do with us whatever he wants. Because we fear such unnerving, lonely encounters with God, we avoid them, avoid even the thought of God lest he suddenly get too close to us. Suddenly having to look into God's eyes, having to be accountable before him, is too dreadful a notion; our perpetual smile might fade, things might get completely serious in a way to which we are not at all accustomed. This anxiety characterizes our entire age. We live in perpetual fear of suddenly being seized and called to task by the infinite and would rather socialize or go to the movies or theater until we are finally carried to our grave, anything rather than having to bear a single minute before God. Let us examine ourselves and see to whom some of this does not apply. That is one reason. The other is that we are too lethargic and lazy in our religious lives. Maybe we once made a good start, but, ah, how quickly it lapsed. We protest that we are just not in the mood, that religion is a matter of mood and one must wait until that mood comes upon us; and then we wait, and often wait for years, maybe even to the very end of our lives until we are once again in the mood to be religious. But this position conceals a great deception. Fine, let religion be a matter of mood; but God is not a matter of mood; God is there even if we are not in the mood to come
together with him. Does this thought not worry us at all? Those who depend 484
on their moods become impoverished. A painter who paints only when in the mood will not get very far. In religion, as in art and science, times of high tension alternate with times of sober work and practice. Contact with God must be practiced; otherwise [we] can never find the right tone, the right word, the right language when God surprises us. We must learn the language of God, laboriously learn that language; we must work so that we, too, are able to speak with God. Prayer must also be practiced through serious work. Confusing religion with emotional daydreaming is a grievous, fateful error. Religion takes work, perhaps the hardest and certainly the most sacred work a person can undertake. It's pathetic to make do with

the assertion, "I'm just not religiously inclined"—when there is a God who wants us. That's just an excuse. No doubt, it's more difficult for some than for others. But we can be sure that no one has attained it without serious effort. And this is why silence before God, too, requires work and practice. Such silence requires the daily courage to expose oneself to God's word and allow oneself to be judged by it; it requires the spontaneity to rejoice in God's love every day. But this already brings us to the question: What are we supposed to do to penetrate through to this silence of God? Here I can say a bit to you based on my own modest experience. None of us is so rushed that we cannot find ten minutes a day during the morning or evening to be silent, to focus on eternity alone, allow eternity to speak, to query it concerning ourselves, and in the process look deeply into ourselves and far beyond ourselves, either by reading a couple of biblical passages or, even better, by becoming completely free and allowing our soul to travel to the house of the Father, to the home in which it finds peace. And those who seriously apply themselves to such exercises day after day will amply experience the golden abundance of the fruit such hours yield. Of course, it's always difficult at the beginning, and anyone who embarks on such an undertaking will feel rather funny, indeed perhaps even quite empty the
485 first few times. Before long, however, the soul is filled; it begins to come alive and feel stronger, experiencing the eternal silence residing in God's love, and the distress and worries, restlessness and haste, noise and commotion, tears and anxiety all are hushed within it, and it becomes silent before God, from whom its salvation comes. My soul is silent before God, who helps me.[9]

One law of the world is that there can be no rest and satisfaction in it. No passion is totally[10] quenched here. Fulfillment itself already contains the urge to move beyond what has been attained. The rich want to get richer, the powerful more powerful. The reason is that in this world nothing is whole, so that every success, be it ever so great, is still only a partial success. If peace and quiet are to be found anywhere, that can only be where the whole has already been attained; but that means in God. All human activity and searching is ultimately directed toward God and finds its ultimate fulfillment only in him. Only in God is there genuine peace and quiet, something the great church father Augustine superbly expressed in the

[9.] Cf. "On being alone," 3/19, p. 554.

[10.] [Literally, "finds its total stilling, or quenching," *findet hier ihre volle Stillung.* —CG] The reading is uncertain for "its," *ihre.*

words, "You have made us for yourself, and our soul is restless until it rests in you."[11] May God grant something of this rest to all of us, may God draw us into his stillness and solitude, and we will be grateful to him. Amen.

8. Sermon on 1 Corinthians 12:27, 26, Barcelona, Eighth Sunday after Trinity, July 29, 1928[1] 486

I Cor. 12:27, 26: Now you are the body of Christ and individually members of it. If one member suffers, all suffer together with it; if one member is honored, all rejoice together with it.[2]

There is a word that evokes tremendous feelings of love and bliss among Catholics who hear it, a word that stirs in them the most profound depths of religious feeling ranging from the awe and dread of judgment to the bliss of God's presence, but a word that assuredly also evokes feelings of home for them, feelings of the sort only a child feels in gratitude, reverence, and self-surrendering love toward its mother, the feelings that come over us when after a long time away we once again enter our parents' home, our own childhood home. And there is also a word that to Protestants has the sound of something infinitely banal, something more or less indifferent and superfluous, a word that does not make a person's heart beat faster, a word often associated with feelings of boredom, a word that in any event does not lend wings to our religious feelings—and yet a word that will seal our fate if we are unable to find in this word a new, or rather the original meaning. Woe to us if this word—the word "church"—does not soon acquire significance for us again, indeed if it does not become a matter with which our very lives are concerned. Yes, the word whose glory and greatness we want to examine today is "church."[3] Will we be able to behold in our service today something of the radiance and luster, the shining splendor that is

[11.] Augustine, *Confessions*, 1.1; see 3/2, ed. note 3.

[1.] *NL*, A 21,9 a; handwritten, with a note by Bethge: "8th after Trinity Barcelona." Previously published in *PAM* 1:165–75. Cf. also *NL*, A 21,9 b; typewritten copy by Bethge. Previously published with editorial changes in *GS* 5:439–46. According to Bonhoeffer's calendar (*NL*, A 18,2), twenty-five people attended. [Most of this sermon is cited, in a slightly different translation, in *DB-ER*, 63–65.—CG]

[2.] Bonhoeffer has accommodated Paul's sequence of verses (v. 26 following v. 27) in the internal development of his sermon.

[3.] Bonhoeffer first noticed this contrast in his experience of the church in Rome in 1924 (see *DBWE* 9:90–91 and 106–7), leading him to the theme of the *sanctorum communio*. His experiences in Barcelona sharpened this judgment.

487 the church? Ah, so much dust has settled on this word over the centuries that I hardly dare to hope. But it is perhaps the most urgent concern of the present that we properly understand what the church is, what was so infinitely important to Jesus in his own farewell discourses, what Paul already so eloquently discussed in his letter to the Ephesians—if I may ask but one thing of you, let it be to read a few chapters of this letter this afternoon; but not only do we want to understand all this, we also want to become the church ourselves. Just what that means is what we want to discuss today. This topic has nothing, absolutely nothing, to do with the church as an external political power, nor with any antithesis with the Catholic Church. No, being and becoming the church means something quite different, something indescribably more sublime and great. Paul calls it "being the body of Christ." Paul is writing to the congregation in Corinth, to people plagued by all sorts of questions who are themselves presenting considerable problems to Paul, people who in part deny the resurrection of Jesus, people in whose midst are some living in incest, a congregation in which sin is active just as today among us and dominated by weak faith. To such a congregation Paul now writes the words, "you *are* the body of Christ"; not "you should be," no, precisely that you "*are*." The most important thing to him is that they belong to the body of Christ, whether they are sinners or not. You are . . . apparently the text is saying this to us as well, "you are the body of Christ"; you need only to behold it; you need do nothing for it. God has already done everything; through God's free grace we are the body of Christ. But that also means that God has fused us together into a single life whose strength, breath, blood, and spirit is Jesus Christ. God has drawn us into his people, has chosen a community [Gemeinde] on earth whose Lord is Jesus Christ and to which we belong, a community whose life we experience together just as the leaf experiences the life of the tree or as a member of our own body experiences our life. God has accepted us into this church-community, and that means into his church. The body of Christ, the people of God on earth, the holy church-community that God has chosen—that is the church about which we will speak today. Not this or that building with the bell tower, not this or that organization or in any event only to the extent it is the earthly abode and home of the sojourning
488 people of God, the sanctified church-community, the holy church of Jesus Christ, the body of Christ whose members we are. Belonging to the church means belonging to the community of God, which is by no means the same as the congregation of our church; it means being deemed worthy by God to receive a portion in the gifts of eternity; it means embarking upon the pilgrimage of God's chosen people through the world under the banner of Christ; it means living from within Christ, and that means from within God

from eternity, though now no longer alone, but rather with all those who love Christ. Church means community [Gemeinschaft] with the people of God in God himself.

We have come to know various peoples; some of us have traveled widely in the world and have been exposed to different peoples and different customs. Today we hear about a people that only a few of us will have encountered, and yet a people whom any of us could have met even if we have never left our home town, and that is the people of God. Nor does this expression merely allude to the many individuals who seek and perhaps even find God throughout the world. No, it is a people in the true sense of the word, this people of God, with its own law and justice, a people whose members are connected through secret, mysterious relationships and who work quietly for one another and with one another, invisibly and yet with enormous power, a people that, like the knights of the Grail, is indiscernible to the eyes of mortals and remains invisible, a people that assembles and unites day after day, night after night, a people on a sojourn to its home, a home shimmering and shining in the far distance, a people walking in darkness that has nonetheless seen the light and knows the way, a people not of kings and princes, but in which every member must bear his or her own burden, a people burdened and weary and yet pardoned and liberated by God, a people bearing the cross but with blissful eyes, a people with a ruler who guides it with a sure hand even in the darkest night, a people whose members lift up and carry those who stumble along the way, a people—in a word—whose members love one another because God loves them. Not Germany and not
France and not America, but a people extending over the entire world, 489
whose members can be found here and there and everywhere—indeed, it also has and is yet seeking members among us! This is the people of God; this is the church of Christ.[4]

A people whose members love one another—this is unprecedented, transcending all human experience. How can someone say he knows of a people whose members love one another, a people in which every person

[4.] A comparison with Dibelius, *Jahrhundert der Kirche*, esp. 74–76 and 228, shows that the concept of "church" was a central theme at this time in Protestant Berlin and was empirically described in unmistakably similar terms as the transnational, ecumenical, and moral entity of the church. Nonetheless, Bonhoeffer's theological ("people of God") and eschatological ("on a sojourn to its home") response to the question of the church does differ from that position. [Here Bonhoeffer, not yet active in the ecumenical movement, states a position contrary to *völkisch* theologies developing at that time, which culminated in the German Christians—though Bonhoeffer himself was not entirely free of such sentiments at the time, as his congregational lecture shows. Cf. esp. 2/3, pp. 369–74.—CG]

is not ultimately concerned with personal gain, in which ultimately all its members are strangers; this assertion is singular in the world, namely, that there is an entire people whose members love one another, and it is to this people that God has assigned us as truly as we love Christ. We are living in this people perhaps without even knowing it, are carried and supported by it, live from its love, nor are we alone on this sojourn to our home; no, many others are standing alongside us, helping us, carrying us, supporting us, and showing us the way.

But just as miraculous as the people itself, as the church of God, as the body of Christ, are the means of its help. Three strengths are at work here that transcend all human capacity, gifts of God to every congregation that bestow the greatest power on earth upon Christians, upon us.[5] The first is that we are able to sacrifice ourselves for others with a joyous heart, that our life is a life only as a sacrifice offered to God and human beings, regardless of whether this sacrifice is visible or invisible. The strength of this sacrifice is the strength of community [Gemeinschaft], and because one sacrifices for the other within the people of God, that people is the most powerful people in the world. The other strength is—mysterious and strange, known to but a few, but a strength without which none of us would have even a glimmer of faith—that we are able to pray for one another, and that a million hearts pray every day for us as well, for our faith and for our strength. Consider what it means that the world is an altar at which millions of prayers
490 are offered to heaven, that not a second passes without this people lifting its hands and pleading for mercy for us, for each of us, that the hearts of the entire church-community quake and pray for our salvation, and that perhaps one or another from our own intimate circle of friends presents our soul before God day after day, interceding on its behalf. At such thoughts, who does not feel modest and small? Who knows whether this person or that person might even be the rescuer of our soul? Who knows whether someone has not kept a vigil for us through the night, kneeling before God, and that it is not our own merit that preserves us, but God's unfathomable grace and love for our neighbor and for us? All of us, however, need only for the congregation itself to pray for us daily, just as we do every Sunday in our great church prayer; and after all, in the Lord's Prayer we do not pray "my Father" but "our Father," and not "my debts" but "our debts." Paul and

---

[5.] [Here Bonhoeffer draws upon *Sanctorum Communio,* where he wrote that "being-for-each-other . . . through acts of love" takes the form of "*self-renouncing, active work for the neighbor; intercessory prayer; and, finally, the mutual forgiveness of sins* in God's name" (*DBWE* 1:184).—CG]

Moses, the prayer of both.[6] Like an invisible net, this intercession holds the church-community together throughout the world. None of us knows where we suddenly get the strength we did not have before, strength we did not even pray for. We need know only one thing, namely, that we owe such strength not least to the prayer of the congregation that represents us before God.

The third means, however, is the most sublime, most divine, most miraculous and mysterious and sacred one possible among human beings, namely, that we forgive one another's sins and take them away, I yours, you mine, in the name of God. That is the great mystery of confession, of the voluntary confession one person makes to the trusted other, to a mother, a spouse, a friend. The other person then removes the oppressive burden from our shoulders in the authority of faith and forgives all guilt in the name of God. The most profound and serious feature in the life of the Christian church-community is that we are able to take away one another's guilt. At the same time, the most forgotten aspect of all this is that you can and should become a Christ to me and I to you. Our congregations have forgotten what insuperable [strength] emanates from confession and the forgiveness of sins, in which one not only helps the other in [. . .][7] distress, nor merely prays
for the forgiveness of that person's sins, but redeems, reconciles that per- 491
son by acting in Christ's stead, by becoming Christ for that other person. Sacrifice, intercession, and the forgiveness of sins are the miraculous powers of the Christian church-community; all three can be summed up in the one word "love," the love God showed us, or "becoming Christ for the other person."[8] These three strengths are the blood of Christ's body holding everything together. *One* body, that means *one* life, and thus it is. All the members live *one* life, breathe the same air, are nourished by the same food, namely, by the word of God, and drink from the same drink, namely, from the blood of our Lord Jesus. Where one member is, there is the entire church-community. No one is alone, no one abandoned, no one homeless. The congregation is always there as well, in love, and that means in sacrifice, intercession, and the forgiveness of sins. No one is alone in joy; no one is alone in pain. "If one member is honored, all rejoice together with it." None of us is alone when we are carried to the baptismal font for the first time. None of us is alone when we experience God for the first time in our lives.

[6.] [This cryptic phrase is apparently a prompt for the preacher to ad-lib on prayers of Paul and Moses, perhaps referring to examples such as Acts 16:25–26 and Exodus 32:11–14.—CG]

[7.] Illegible.

[8.] Cf. Luther, *The Freedom of a Christian* (*LW* 31:367).

None of us is alone [in] the struggles of life, when we cry out on our sick bed, abandoned by all help, when we become old and lonely and homeless without our family, without comfort, when we struggle with death on our deathbed, when we cannot get a grip on ourselves in the face of grief and suffering—the church-community and the Lord of that church-community is with us. No matter how alone we are, it prays for us, stands with us before God, invisibly takes us by the hand and comforts us, makes misery our home by surrounding us, encompassing us in love. Text.[9] Hence, all you who grieve, who are sick, abandoned, homeless, dying—you are not alone; you are surrounded by a people that loves and supports you the way a mother loves her child, the way our home draws us to its bosom. Let yourselves be carried and loved, but also love and carry others yourself. If you bear one another's burdens, you will fulfill the law of Christ.[10] But the Lord is at work in the church-community; where that church-community is, there is Christ, there is God's love. Hence let us enter the congregation, let us enter
492 the people of God, with open eyes, see that you are surrounded by love. You *are* the body of Christ. You *are* the church of God. You *are* God's sanctified church-community. Behold and be astonished and give thanks.

There is but one remedy for our age, an age that is so feeble, so weak, so pathetically small and pitiful and homeless—back to the church, back to where one member bears the other in love, where one lives the life of the other, where there is community [Gemeinschaft] in God, where there is home because there is love. Our world should become part of the people of God; it should become church. But that is the goal and meaning of all our communities [Gemeinschaften], of marriage as well as of friendship. Only when a marriage is church, where each person sacrifices for the other, where each intercedes on behalf of the other, where each forgives the other's sins, where two live one life, there marriage has attained and fulfilled its deepest meaning.[11]

God has called us to be his children; God wants to be our loving Father, God our Father, the church our Mother, who supports and loves us. The church, that is our faith—I believe in a holy church—the church is the meaning of our human community [Gemeinschaft]; the church is our hope for this and for the coming age. In the words of an ancient church father:

[9.] That is, 1 Cor. 12:27 and 26.

[10.] Gal. 6:2.

[11.] Deleted: "But one more thing. Our small church seeks each Sunday to be an abode for the people of God. Let each of us consider this and then each decide how best to deal with it personally. An ancient church father spoke the words: Those who do not have God as their Father cannot have the church as their Mother. We will alter this

God our Father, the church our Mother, Jesus Christ our Lord—that is our faith.[12] Amen.

9. Sermon on Matthew 5:8, Barcelona, Tenth Sunday after Trinity, August 12, 1928[1] 493

Blessed are the pure in heart, for they will see God. Matt. 5:8

Just as in ancient Israel those who approached too near the ark of the covenant, the dwelling place of the God Yahweh, forfeited their lives because no person could endure the divine powers emanating from the ark,[2] so, too, must those who come too close to today's text lose their lives to it. Such strange powers emanate from it, such a strangely quiet radiance that we cannot tear our eyes away, like the merchant in Jesus's parable who could not tear his eyes away from the precious pearl he found and who sold all he had that he might behold that pearl his entire life.[3] So I bring you this text today in our sermon, knowing full well that the best thing we can do with regard to it is simply to be silent. To behold and be silent, to allow ourselves to be seized and conquered by this text, to lose our life to this text, to allow it to bear us upward to eternal heights and expanses.

---

statement slightly and say:" Here Bonhoeffer's later vehemently debated Cyprianic-Augustinian concept of the church ("*Extra ecclesiam nulla salus* [Outside the church there is no salvation]. The question of church fellowship is the question of the community of salvation") is explicated in this sermon for the first time. Cf. Staats, "Patristisches Erbe," 194–95. [Cyprian's actual words have a different logic from Bonhoeffer's version here: "You cannot have God for your Father if you no longer have the church for your mother" (*De Ecclesiae Catholicae Unitate,* 67 [chap. 6]). With regard to Bonhoeffer's 1936 statement—"Those who knowingly separate themselves from the Confessing Church in Germany are separating themselves from salvation" (DBW 14 [2/19], p. 676)—it is important to note that this is not an abstract, ahistorical general principle but a confessional statement made in the midst of the German Church Struggle, in response to the issue of the legalization of Confessing clergy by German Christian church administrations.—CG]

[12.] See ed. note 11.

[1.] *NL,* A 21,10 a; handwritten, with a note by Bethge, "10th after Trinity." Previously published in *PAM* 1:174–80. See also *NL,* A 21,10 b; typewritten copy by Bethge. Previously published in *GS* 5:446–52. As Bonhoeffer wrote to Rößler, he had never approached a sermon with such trepidation (see 1/40, p. 128). "The fantastic number of forty people" attended the sermon (letter to his parents, 1/42, p. 131; see also the calendar entry in *NL,* A 18,2). The sermon text is presumably taken from the Moravian Daily Texts for August 5, 1928 (Wendel, *Homiletik,* 24).

[2.] See 1 Sam. 5; 2 Sam. 6:6–7.

[3.] Matt. 13:45.

When the world fell away from God, when humanity turned away in creaturely willfulness from the will of the world,[4] when the creature began to grumble against [the] Creator, when night fell in the cosmos and over our earth, when the cold, icy wind of unkindness and envy began to blow through the world, making it shudder—our kindly God left one thing to humanity as a pale shadow of what it once possessed, namely, a *yearning*
494 *for its origin,* for its home, for God. Our eyes hurt from all the misery and suffering, all the dazzling lying and deception they have to see, and the shivering soul stretches and cries out with the words of the psalm, "When shall I come and behold the face of God?"[5] *Behold God*—that is what the world yearns for, as the night yearns for the day, the winter for the spring, evil for the good. We are all familiar with the hours of our lives when we grow tired of ourselves, when we are disgusted with ourselves, when we realize the whole pathetic weakness of the way we have led our life. We are all also familiar with the hours when we fall short, when we fail in what we want to accomplish, hours of defeat and humiliation, hours when we come to despise ourselves, when all the misery and shame become concentrated in Paul's words, "Wretched man that I am! Who will rescue me from this body of death?"[6] And the blessing of such hours is that in them, our yearning for God's countenance breaks forth, for the golden streets of the eternal city, for beholding God. Those not familiar with these hours, those who do not know this yearning, will not understand much of what Jesus has to say to us today.

Just like the individual person, so too the world itself experiences hours in which it cries out for God's countenance from within its godlessness and godforsakenness. The entirety of ancient Judaism is such a single cry: How can I come and behold the face of God? Socrates and Plato, Kant and German philosophy all join in this cry. And through our own age as well, this ancient question reverberates: How do we behold God? It is as if our gaze were fixed on the things and bustle of the world, on what is dreary, gloomy, gray, ugly, as if we were no longer able to lift our eyes or look in a different direction. And yet in all this darkness we still do sense that there must be something incomparably beautiful about the light. But who will give us the
495 eyes to see, eyes that do not immediately shut the moment a ray of light falls upon them? What must we do so that we not only sense or yearn for the light, for God, but genuinely behold God?

[4.] [*Weltwillen*, here meaning God's will for the world.—CG]
[5.] Ps. 42:2.
[6.] Rom. 7:24.

Jesus's words step into the midst of these questions: Blessed are the pure in heart, for *they* will see God. Nothing, absolutely nothing can empower us to behold God but a pure heart, the purity of our own being [Wesen]. "If the eye were not like the sun, it could not see the sun," Goethe wrote,[7] that is, if the eye were [not] something like the sun,[8] it could not behold the sun and would instead remain blind and unreceptive. Thus also our text says that if your soul is not something like the eternal divine, it will never behold God.[9] Just as a deep mountain lake reflects the cupola of heaven, as a clear crystal reflects every thing[10] in complete purity,[11] so too will our heart take in and reflect God, if it is a pure heart. Purity—this is a word that has a peculiarly beautiful, full, mature sound[12] for all of us, a word causing the heart momentarily to skip a beat, a word prompting a bit of melancholy to come over us—I recently read that an old scholar, after many years, read once more that particular passage in the Revelation of John that mentions those who stand before God in white robes; shaken and overwhelmed by the idea of purity, the old gentleman broke down in tears.[13] Clarity, purity—we experience it face to face with nature, under the starry heavens, when the sun rises from the sea in divine beauty and bathes the world in its gold, when we experience how the lily opens its calyx to the dew and the sun, we sense it in the child in quiet yearning and melancholy
retrospect, when the child plays, when it sleeps, when it lies in its mother's 496
arms, when beneath the lighted Christmas tree its eyes glow with the radiance of the soul and the Christmas lights. Purity—we are seized [. . .][14] by its beauty when we see a bridal couple extend hands to each other at the altar; purity—it radiates from the eyes of many mature people, lends such a strangely transfigured radiance to a person's countenance;[15] purity—it overwhelms us when we look into Jesus's eyes and heart.[16]

[7.] Goethe, *Zahme Xenien III* (*Werke*, 3:367; for other versions, see 3:681): "If the eye were not like the sun, it could never see the sun; if the spirit's power did not lie in us, how could we delight in the divine?" Cf. in this context *Act and Being* as well, *DBWE* 2:46. [The English translation here is that in *DBWE* 2.—CG]

[8.] Deleted: "if the eye were not clear and receptive to the light."

[9.] Deleted: "purity that is a."

[10.] Uncertain reading.

[11.] Concerning this imagery, cf. 3/19, pp. 552–53.

[12.] [See the alliteration of the two syllables of the word *Reinheit*, "purity."—CG]

[13.] Cf. Rev. 4; according to Otto Dudzus, the reference may be to Hermann Gunkel (*PAM* 1:177).

[14.] Illegible.

[15.] Marginal insertion: "Francis."

[16.] Deleted: "What is it about this word?"

What is it here that moves us so? It is that only where we see purity does the world itself become transparent and clear to us for what lends it meaning and beauty and life, that is, for God. It is only there that the dead matter of the corporeal world begins to shine, that we come to see vessels of God in that which is pure, and that we catch sight of God in what is human and transitory, in our own flesh and blood. And that shakes us to our very depths, we who are so far from it. "Blessed are the pure in heart."

Yes, here the misery begins anew. We are, after all, no longer pure; we carry the blemish and taint of sin in our soul. We are not God's transparent ones; we have darkened the light within us, have become impure through lies and deception and hypocrisy and passion. So we tighten up inside until it hurts when we hear that Jesus wants to help us and is saying to us, Blessed are the pure in heart, for they will see God.[17] We can summarize in one statement why this beatitude fades into space, into hopelessness: The world is playing masquerade. That is the bitter realization with which we must counter Jesus's own statement. We all adjust our masks according to our own tastes and ambitions, the masks in which we then go out among people to be acknowledged; we adorn ourselves with alien feathers, color and make up our faces, so that not a trace of our natural being is visible. And we avoid
497 stepping out into the bright light, preferring instead to remain in the shadows, where colors run together. And if someone gets too close and asks, Who are you, you who hide behind such a mask? we pull the mask more tightly around our face and flee. The world is playing masquerade, and now Jesus's words penetrate directly into the middle of this game: Blessed are . . . These words tear the masks from our faces, seeking to bring about clarity, honesty, to open our eyes to God. For we do know, after all, that our vision of God is obscured daily by the lack of clarity, the inauthenticity, and the unnaturalness of our being, that is, precisely by this masquerade. It is from this distress that Jesus seeks to extract us: Become simple, clear, genuine, natural, straightforward, pure, and your hearts will reflect God's own parental heart. Stop this costume party once and for all; be sincere toward yourselves and realize that you are nothing but God's creatures, that you have nothing to boast of that is your own, no unique rights, and that you should be God's transparent ones, pure, that you may capture God's own

[17.] Deleted: "Deception—that is the motto of the world; honesty, purity, and clarity—that is what the motto should be."

image within yourselves. Keep yourselves pure from the world, don't soil the white garments God has put on you. Blessed are the *pure* in heart.[18]

The most distressing realization in the life of every Christian is that we cannot remain pure, that day by day we fall down anew and night by night must cry out to God anew: Lord, I cannot do it alone; if you make me pure, then I am pure. May God create in me a pure heart.[19] I want so much to be pure. I want so much to behold God. And thus it is that as long as we sojourn on this earth, we never attain the full assurance of the promise: for they will see God.

Our gaze extends beyond the world of the transitory, beyond all ages, beyond the starry heavens to where a dear Father dwells,[20] where the light
is, where clarity and truth and purity are, where we stand before God with 498
new eyes and in white robes, where we behold God in the city with the gates of pearl and the golden streets, as the song describes.[21] To see God—that means to love the Father, to look him in the eyes the way we look a good friend in the eyes and are blessed. Blessed are the pure in heart, for they will see God. To see God means to drink in his light, his clarity like living water. It means to behold our home after wandering our whole life long, to throw ourselves on God's bosom and weep and rejoice the way a child does in its mother's arms. Blessed are the pure in heart, for they will see God. And yet seeing God is even more. It means recognizing God in his own life, recognizing him in the world, seeing him and understanding his will; it means climbing from one depth down to the other into the spirit of the deity; it means beholding in astonishment and childlike awe God's mysteries being revealed.[22] In this world all we have is a premonition of this. Here it remains merely piecework, whereas there we will behold God face to face.[23] To behold God means to become a piece of eternity ourselves

---

[18.] Deleted: "And now the promise: For they shall see God. Of course, we do know that we cannot remain pure in this world. We live and remain in defilement. But we do already sense here something of what it means to behold God."

[19.] Ps. 51:10. [The Luther Bible uses the word *rein*, "pure," in both the psalm and the beatitude, whereas English translations usually have "clean" in the psalm.—CG]

[20.] Allusion to the second verse of Friedrich Schiller's poem "Hymn to Joy": "Yes, the starry realms above / Hide a Father's smiling features" (*Schiller's Works*, 1:31).

[21.] Cf. esp. Philipp Nicolai, "Wachet auf, ruft uns die Stimme" ("Awake, the voice calls to us," *EKG*, no. 121, verse 3): "The gates are of twelve pearls . . . ," following Rev. 21:21. [The English translation by Catherine Winkworth, "Wake, awake for night is flying," reads in verse 3: "Of one pearl each shining portal. . . ."—CG]

[22.] Deleted: "before the power of the divine thoughts and."

[23.] [Cf. 1 Cor. 13:12.—CG]

in love, gratitude, purity. It means rejoicing along with the chorus of the redeemed in the white robes. Oh, what depth of wealth, both of wisdom and of the knowledge of God. From God and to him and through him are all things.[24]

For now, however, we still hear the uniform, dull steps of those who are yet wandering, and we wander and join in the cry that rises again and again to heaven: Make me pure of heart. Even louder[25] heaven calls us, Jesus himself calls us with his words: Blessed are the pure in heart, for they will see God.

499 **10. Sermon on 1 John 2:17, Barcelona, Twelfth Sunday after Trinity, August 26, 1928**[1]

1 John 2:17: The world and its desires are passing away, but those who do the will of God live forever.

The great philosopher of the ancient Greeks, Heraclitus of Ephesus, summarized his most profound insight regarding the world with the words: all things are in flux.[2] Nothing abides, nothing is secure, nothing is assured in the world. "It is not possible to step twice into the same river," he says elsewhere,[3] meaning that just when you want to seize life, it has already passed by, slipping through your hands, melting away like nothing. There's no stopping it.[4] Life does not live; it dies. To live means to die. During the same period in the Far East, Buddha taught the Indians about the deception and transitoriness of the world.[5] With irresistible claws, the enticing[6] world draws human beings in, pulling them from one passion to the next, not letting go, and yet it is all nothing but deception, illusion. It is not real, but a dream that torments us and then melts away.

[24.] Cf. Rom. 11:33–35.

[25.] Uncertain reading.

[1.] *NL*, A 21,11 a; handwritten, with a note by Bethge: "August 26, 1928, 12th after Trinity, Barcelona." Previously published in *PAM* 1:181–87. Cf. also *NL*, A 21,11 b; typewritten copy by Bethge; Previously published in *GS* 5:452–57. According to Bonhoeffer's calendar, thirty-eight people attended this sermon (*NL*, A 18,2).

[2.] Attributed to Heraclitus; see Diels-Kranz, *Die Fragmente der Vorsokratiker*, 1:145, line 27. [Plato has Socrates attribute the saying to Heraclitus in *Cratylus* 402 a.—CG]

[3.] See Sprague, *Older Sophists*, 56.

[4.] Deleted: "it is the fate of time that hangs over the world. Time."

[5.] Concerning Bonhoeffer's fascination with India, see *DB-ER*, 105; see also 1/153, p. 272, et passim.

[6.] Inserted later.

A bit later, the preacher Solomon[7] spoke the harsh words: "All is vanity."[8] The world is vain and its activities vain. The old song of the world is always telling about how pleasure passes away, about the trouble that comes, about the life one should sooner call death. All is vanity. "On sand, on sand, rests all that is built by human hand."[9] The misfortune hanging over the world, however, the misfortune that makes it so vain, is time. Time, a doubly frightful word. First because whatever happens remains something that happened; it can never be undone; not even the smallest bit of what hap- 500
pened can be brought back. Guilt remains guilt, omission remains omission. That is the reality that has and will cost us the most tears in our lives. What has happened, has happened for all time. The other terrible consideration is that nothing stands still, not even for a single moment, everything moves forward in eternal change and toward a specific goal, namely, death. The gods now are weeping, and weeping is every goddess that the beautiful wanes, that the perfect must die, as Schiller puts it.[10] Time marches mercilessly over the moment, the moment of bliss, of joy, of blessedness, of pleasure. "But all joy wants eternity—wants deep, wants deep eternity," Nietzsche wrote.[11] The puzzling, unfathomable contradiction in our lives is that only where we experience bliss do we want to be eternal, and yet nowhere are we more transitory than there. Joy in the world passes away because the world itself passes away. The world passes away with its joy, its beauty, its splendor, its humankind,[12] and its culture. Yes, but are these not all eternal? The works of a Beethoven, a Bach, a Goethe, a Michelangelo? The world passes away, and so also these works. What are a few centuries of fame in the history of God's world, compared to the ancient stars? What is all culture, all beauty, all human power, compared with the eternal beauty and infinite power of God? A speck of dust, a drop in the sea, a leaf blown by the wind, a nothing. To speak about the eternity of our culture, of our

[7.] [In the German Bible, Ecclesiastes is called *Der Prediger Salomo*, the preacher Solomon; in the NRSV the Hebrew *Qoheleth* is translated "teacher" rather than "preacher." —CG]

[8.] Eccl. 1:2.

[9.] Theodor Fontane, "The Bridge on the Tay," end of the first stanza, in Browning, *German Poetry*, 255. [Fontane wrote this poem after a disastrous collapse in December 1879 of the rail bridge over the Firth of Tay in Scotland. Bonhoeffer quotes exactly. —CG]

[10.] Friedrich Schiller, "Nenia," in Browning, *German Poetry*, 89. [This poem from 1800 takes its title from the Latin *naenia*, a funeral dirge. Quoted exactly.—CG]

[11.] Friedrich Nietzsche, *Thus Spoke Zarathustra*, "The Sleepwalker Song," section 12 (*Portable Nietzsche*, 436).

[12.] Uncertain reading.

philosophy, of our morality in view of all this is mere craziness of the sort only human foolishness and presumption can think up. The hour will come one day when the earth will be dashed to pieces, but despite knowing this the world will not change. The earth passes away, and the world passes away. Time rules over them all—or to speak more clearly: death. *Time and death are the same.* The world is a world of dying and of death. Everything that
501 happens in it is merely penultimate to the ultimate,[13] to death. Hence it is not life and joy and pleasure that is the final word concerning the world, but transitoriness and death. The law of death stands over the world, over the "evil world," to use an early Christian expression.[14] Here is the final boundary, the one that cannot be crossed.

If we consider all the limitless misery, the nameless pain this fate brings upon the entire world, then the misfortune of death acquires such powerful and frightening features that we begin to sense somehow that the creator of the world could not have intended it thus. The world must have fallen away from God's primal will. Some primal deed, a primal evil must have occurred in demonic rebellion against the creator God, and this primal evil is connected with this calamity, the primal evil that is still active and creative in us in contradiction to God, in rebellion and revolt against God's will as we all know it. And *that Old Testament myth intends to say* nothing other than this, the myth in which God imposes the fate of death over Adam and Eve, who disobeyed him: For out of dust you were taken, and to dust you shall return.[15] Like an evil spell, the fate of transitoriness hangs over the world, and only those who conquer the primal evil in the world, in us, can break that spell. Precisely because this fate of death is so tied to the evil in the world, it represents the most serious concern in the world for us.

The most serious thing in the world is death.[16] This seriousness begins where the world ceases, dies, where the world encounters its boundary; this seriousness begins where our lives cease, where we no longer exist, at the boundary of time. *The least serious thing in the world is the moment,* the penul-

---

[13.] Bonhoeffer's famous distinction appears here and in the following discussion for the first time. Cf. "Ultimate and Penultimate Things" in *Ethics* (*DBWE* 6:146–70). [In *Ethics* the ultimate is justification by grace, rather than death, while the penultimate is everything that precedes the ultimate, rather than the pleasures of the world (cf. also p. 519).—CG]

[14.] Cf. the New Testament documentation in his 1926 paper on John and Paul (*DBWE* 9 [2/13], p. 402). [There Bonhoeffer cites the Greek of Gal. 1:4 that refers to the "evil age."—CG]

[15.] Cf. Gen. 3:19.

[16.] Deleted: "the only thing that really is to be taken seriously in it; [two illegible words] i.e."

timate, the pleasure of the world, as John puts it.[17] It is up to each human being whether to live seriously or frivolously in the world, whether to persist in the penultimate or push through to the ultimate; whether, in the words of our text, to view the pleasure of the world as the ultimate or the transito- 502
riness of this pleasure.[18]

With Old Testament power, this text proclaims to us a memento mori:[19] Remember that everything ultimately comes to an end, that one day it will be time for you to take account of your life. And that then the moment of death will come upon you as assuredly as the world is a world of death and that nothing withstands the power of time except one thing—eternity, and that the end has come for you and for me. Lord, teach me that my days will end and that my life has a final goal and that I must then depart.[20] Do we wish to face this fact thoughtlessly? Do we wish to remain careless until the final hour? No, let us in God's name be serious about ourselves, and that means about the ultimate, about death, and then let us behold the miracle that has occurred. Let us think about the boundaries of the world, of time—and something miraculous will occur. Our eyes will be opened to the fact that the boundary of the world, the end of the world—is the beginning of something new, of eternity. Here time loses its power to eternity; the ultimate in the world, death, itself becomes something penultimate. All transitoriness is subsumed under the perspective of eternity. But this eternity is not far removed from us; no, from within eternity itself God has extended a hand into time in Jesus Christ; in the midst of transitoriness, in the midst of the world of death we can take God's hand and be drawn into eternity. This is the miracle of the revelation in Jesus Christ. Here amid all transitoriness and darkness stands a sign from eternity, serious and mighty, bathed in the radiance of the divine sun of grace and light—the cross. And there He[21] hangs, his arms outstretched as if to embrace the entire world in love and lead it to his Father. He who was God's love among human beings. Come to this cross, the sign of divine love, come into its light, cling 503

[17.] [See 1 John 2:16.—CG]

[18.] Deleted: "Depending on how we choose, our life will acquire different meaning, a different turn." The text breaks off here; the following manuscript page is probably lost.

[19.] ["Remember that you will die."—CG]

[20.] Cf. Ps. 39:4. [Bonhoeffer quotes the Luther Bible exactly; NRSV translation varies considerably.—CG]

[21.] [Departing from normal usage, Bonhoeffer capitalizes the personal pronoun, writing *Er*, He; but *Vater*, Father, as a German noun, is always capitalized and so we cannot tell if Bonhoeffer intended any special emphasis with that word.—CG]

to it, and it will shed its light on you as long you remain with it. And thus it has happened that you yourselves have now become eternal.

We said earlier that only the person who wipes out the primal evil in humanity can break the spell of death. That person is Jesus Christ. He hallows what is evil, turns the rebellious back to God, changes Saul into Paul. He cleanses sinners and calls out into eternity those whose fate is death. There stands the cross.

And now the most miraculous part of all. It is already here that he makes us eternal. We are no longer mortally transitory; we are eternal because God has called us; we are already eternal here in the midst of time itself, bearing eternity within our breast. Those who believe in him have eternal life; they can no longer die, and even though they die, they will live.[22] To be eternal in every moment[23] beholding God, that is the meaning of our lives. Now we have overcome death; it lies behind us like a nothing; we have pushed through from death to life. The world and its desires pass away, but those who do the will of God live forever.

But now the question is put clearly before us. Do you want to remain a person of death, someone who is blown along and passes away like grass,[24] or do you want to be a person of eternity, someone who was frightened by the idea of death and has now found eternity? There are only two choices. Remain careless and thoughtless and frivolous and a person belonging to the world of death,[25] or go forth now and take this matter seriously and you will become a person of eternity. Yes, of course, but how? Here Jesus offers an astonishingly simple answer: Do the will of God! And if I still am not familiar enough with that will, I can get the answer from Jesus: Go home and love your brothers and sisters, your wife, your children, your parents, and your friends. Get along with your neighbor, help those who need
504 help, give of what you have to those who do not have; be peace loving and compassionate, be pure of thought and word; you live in the world.[26]

[22.] Cf. John 11:25.

[23.] Perhaps an allusion to Schleiermacher, *On Religion*, 140: "to be one with the infinite in the midst of the finite, and to be eternal in a moment, that is the immortality of religion."

[24.] [Cf. Ps. 103:15.—CG]

[25.] Deleted: several illegible words.

[26.] What follows is an addendum that does not quite fit here and cannot easily be assigned a place: "Must I thus then flee from the world into solitude, become an ascetic, chastise myself, extinguish and smother all joy in the world within myself as something sinful, declare war on the sun and on joy and on happiness? And in this way become a person of eternity? This was the thinking of the Middle Ages and monasticism."

God put you into the world. In that world, in the midst of transitoriness, you are to do the will of God. Rejoice in what you can rejoice, but do not give your heart to the world; your heart belongs to eternity, to God. If the world demands your heart, declare war on the world; if it wants your strength, your help, your life, then give those things to the world to whatever extent you can, and where once you were a person of death you will become a person of eternity.

You will misunderstand this text and this sermon if you think that Christians are pessimists who think of nothing but their own transitoriness in everything they do and are resigned to this. Certainly, Christians are pessimists with regard to the world; they do not expect much from the world, nor are they cultural idealists, but they *are* optimists with regard to the divine in the world; they know that God has bequeathed them eternity and thus they are joyous, cheerful people, even if it's a cheerfulness that always has a touch of melancholy and weltschmerz. The Christian's field of activity is the world. It is here that Christians are to become engaged, are to work and be active, here that they are to do the will of God; and for that reason, Christians are not resigned pessimists, but are those who while admittedly not expecting much from the world are for that very reason already joyous and cheerful in the world, for that world is the seedbed of eternity. But those who do the will of God . . . eternity.[27]

The hour of decision is coming for us: eternal death or eternal life. Even if, as at the end of *Faust*, the evil spirit then pronounces "judged," if only the eternal, good spirit also pronounces "saved."[28]

11. Sermon on 2 Corinthians 12:9, Barcelona, 505
Fourteenth Sunday after Trinity, September 9, 1928[1]

2 Cor. 12:9: But he said to me, "My grace is sufficient for you, for my power is made perfect in weakness." So, I will boast all the more gladly of my weaknesses, so that the power of Christ may dwell in me.

When we find ourselves in the midst of guilt, of distress, of misery, when we are threatened with disaster as in that famous painting in which a fettered

[27.] Abbreviated repetition of the sermon text, 1 John 2:17.

[28.] Cf. Goethe, *Faust* (pt. 1, 4611–12), in *Collected Works*, 2:119: "Mephistopheles: She is judged! Voice (*from above*): She is saved!"

[1.] *NL*, A 21,12 a; handwritten, with a note by Bethge: "Barcelona, September 9, 1928." Previously published in *PAM* 1:188–96. See also *NL*, A 21,12 b; typewritten copy by Bethge. Previously published with editorial changes in *GS* 5:458–63.

man faces an approaching, horrible monster and yet can no longer defend himself, when the waters are rising ever higher and finally reach our neck, when the incubus weighs heavier and heavier upon us until we cannot even breath out of pure fear, cannot even cry out, then with our last energy we wrest a final cry from our breast, a cry for help: Lord God, come and help; I cannot go on; your waters are rising too high, I am going under, put a stop to this distress, pull me out of my misery, stem the tide, rescue me from my profound guilt.

Paul, too, once cried out in this way to God. Paul was a severely ill man, an epileptic. This terrible sickness repeatedly seized him and drained him of his strength and his courage for living and working. So he cried out three times to God in his distress: remove the thorn you have stuck in my flesh, and he hoped and prayed that God would comply—but he deceived himself, he remained sick, he was not helped, his hope had been in vain.[2] Instead, God gave him an answer that is greater than all earthly or physical help: My grace is sufficient for you, for my power is made perfect in weakness.[3]

506 ¶In order to understand this text, let us start with a completely different question: Why is there religion? What is its real meaning and purpose? If we pose this question to various religions around the world, we get one answer: to make human beings happy, both externally and inwardly. Happiness and religion belong together like brilliance and gold; religion that does not

[2.] 2 Cor. 12:5–9 is occasionally cited to support the notion that Paul was epileptic. Lietzmann rejects this argument (*An die Korinther,* 218–19).

[3.] Deleted: "Anyone who has seriously looked at the world has seen that there is much longing, much wishing, much hoping but little, very little, fulfillment, and that a tragic disparity obtains between hope and fulfillment. Resign yourself, simply resign yourself; that is the motto of the world; beautiful flowers bloom in the garden of the world, and golden fruits ripen; they entice and attract us, seek to draw us out of the grayness of daily life into the sweet dreamland of fulfillment, and deep within our breast there is something yearning and yearning for all sorts of goods, for health, for joy, for purity—and our wishes repeatedly crash against the rock-hard wall of reality. Here there is no fulfillment, here there is only longing; everything turns out differently than we wanted, above every moment of our lives the word 'resignation' is written; not only resignation with regard to the forbidden fruits [two illegible words], but also with regard to things that seem so good and even divine to us. Fatigued by being perpetually delayed and thwarted on the path of life, many flee to religion, hoping to get from it all that the world itself has denied: fulfillment of our wishes, both earthly and divine. And so people come before God with their wishes and longings, ah, but once to experience fulfillment, but once not to have to resign oneself. (What is the purpose of religion, if not to make life more bearable for people, if not now and then to grant to the pious something the unrighteous do not have? That's the way many people think. But how they err, how dreadfully they distort the truth)."

make a person happy is not religion. This means, however, that religion is conceived from the perspective of human beings and only in reference to human beings as the center of the world.[4] But what does the Bible have to say here? It puts its finger on one single event, one single sign, and leaves it to us to reflect: on the cross of Jesus. Here something unprecedented happened; the equation between religion and happiness is sundered once and for all on the cross, where God dies in love for human beings. Or does someone perhaps want to speak about inward[5] happiness, where Jesus, the emissary of God, dies with the cry, "My God, why have you forsaken me?"[6]
Religion and happiness, both internal and external, are sundered in this 507
moment, when heaven was torn open and over the cross appeared the new, unknown, incomprehensible word: grace, love, not as a new event on earth, but as a new word of God; and this word was not spoken over the imperial throne of a messianic world empire, nor over the heights of humanity, but over a hill of criminals, where a devout man dies with that godforsaken cry. This clearly distinguishes Christianity from all other religions from the outset. Here is grace, there happiness; here the cross, there the crown; here God, there the human being.

My *grace* is sufficient for you—that is the message of the cross. Seize happiness—that is the message of paganism.

What do you chose? God's grace, which bathes the hill of the cross in light and which you find wherever your own cross stands, in resignation, in renunciation of fulfillment of your pleasure, in renunciation of happiness? Or do you choose the happiness, both inward and external, that transfigures the world? Do you choose the religion of God or the religion of human beings? Here one cannot choose hastily; one must first become familiar with something of the reality of the two choices. It is doubtless not easy to find God where everything has failed us, to *see* grace, which one cannot see anyway, or genuinely to make do with grace where we find we must renounce something. (Who will take the burden from our shoulders? Who will bear our cross? Who will help when we are on the verge of despair?) Such beautiful flowers bloom and such golden fruit ripens in the garden of the world, which are nonetheless denied us as long as we live.

A dear friend, a spouse, or our only child lies sick in bed. We fall down on our knees and plead, Lord, please help, please spare us, please do not take the most precious thing we have in the world. But God does not listen.

[4.] Cf. Feuerbach, *Lectures on the Essence of Religion*, third lecture, and *The Essence of Faith according to Luther*, passim.

[5.] Uncertain reading.

[6.] Mark 15:34; Ps. 22:1.

Death sweeps through the room, and above the beloved deceased an invisible voice calls into our hearts: my grace is sufficient for you. We want to leap up in maddening pain; it is a mockery of our misery and woe, this word of grace, a word that as a matter of fact does not help when one cries out to
508 it—or is it perhaps the most profound truth and the most powerful, most regal gift to have this word spoken to us?[7]

This word has seen many a broken life, many a weeping eye and aching heart, has shone above many graves, come to many sickbeds, everywhere that God has commanded people to renounce something or to be resigned. Yes, it is certainly terrible when one day our life is shattered, breaks apart, and is turned completely upside down. But there is a reality in the world that is much, much more terrible, one arising from religion, from morality. The hardest thing [with] which God confronts us is not having to forgo the happiness of the world but having to forgo the good, indeed, having to forgo God; that is the most difficult thing to bear and is what casts us down to the ground again and again. Having to renounce the good, the pure, the divine—what does this mean? Only they can understand who have tried in their lives to take seriously the will of God, who have tried to take stock of their lives and make a change, who know what it means to collapse under the burden of evil they have loaded upon themselves, who have fully seen the ugliness and despicableness of their kind and then have tried, in tears, to turn back to the path of God. Then came the hope that things would turn out well and the way they were supposed to if only we wanted them to—and then, yes, then came the first relapse, and we were terrified to the depths of our beings; Lord God, this really is the last time, please forgive us just this one last time. And then it went further, and the great disappointment came, the greatest, most horrific we ever experienced in our lives, namely, that we are unable to be good, to be pure, that we constantly fall short of what we intended, and that the moment is stronger than our inten-
509 tions, that we cannot attain the good. We fall down on our knees before God: Please make me pure, make me good, and the very next day brings the distressing realization that we have become unfaithful. You're thinking that this description is exaggerated. Have a look, a serious look at God's will. Have a look at Jesus and then just as closely at yourself and you will

[7.] Deleted: "A father sits in a shabby room with his children, and the children cry because they are hungry. The father's heart aches, the pain gives him a lump in his throat, Holy God, please perform a miracle, a miracle—and the children remain hungry and continue to cry. My grace is sufficient for you. And here is someone else, someone who quite undeservingly has been slandered and has fallen into disrepute, has lost a job and all respect, and now this person, too, receives no other comfort than this word: My grace is sufficient. . . ."

shudder. This is how it is: evil, sin, what is base remains in control in us, and we remain in its spell as long we live—and we would surely despair of the good, of the sacred, of ourselves, and of God if we were not given this assurance: My grace is sufficient for you, for my power is made perfect in weakness.

Clearly, then, *religion* does not give us the fulfillment that the world denies us and does not create happiness on earth. No, it is in religion that unhappiness, unrest, renunciation have become powerful in the world. The message of grace confronts everything that happens in the world. My *grace* is sufficient for you. *What is grace?* It is something that cannot be seen, something we never directly perceive in our lives; quite the contrary, it is something completely improbable and incredible judged according to what we experience here. It speaks of an event beyond the world and seeks to pull us away from our own world to that other one. A dark abyss opens up, and a voice commands: "Jump across, I will catch you, I will hold you tight, I will stretch my hand out to you; now, go ahead, risk your very life, depend on me and on nothing else. My grace is sufficient for you; I am love, I have called you by name. You are mine."[8]

Indeed, if only things in the world looked differently, if only something suggested there really were a God of love, if only God would already fulfill my wishes here, then it would be easy to risk this step. But then God interrupts us: my thoughts are not your thoughts, nor are your ways my ways . . .[9] That is, we do not yet understand what happens in the world; the only thing we need to know is that it happens at God's initiative and that God wants what is best for us and, regardless of what happens, God is with us with grace. We will not understand God's thoughts about us. Nor will we feel 510
God's grace, will not touch it or see it, but only God's wrath—because God is God; and because he says it, even when everything is denied us, we can believe in God's grace. *Believe in God's grace.* But that means suddenly having the rug pulled out from under our feet,[10] means standing where actually no person can stand, means undertaking something infinitely absurd and infinitely courageous, means seeing God rather than the world, means seeing God's abundance rather than our own misfortune and guilt, means becoming extremely small and seeing God become great, means taking seriously the incomprehensible contradiction that God does indeed want to have something to do with the world—despite everything, and means

[8.] Isa. 43:1.

[9.] Cf. Isa. 55:8.

[10.] Cf. similar statements in 2/1, p. 326.

recognizing that God [is] greater than all distress and greater than our own hearts, which condemn us.[11]

Instead of wallowing in our own misery, in our own guilt, we should move beyond ourselves and behold the cross, where God took up and bore all misery and all guilt and in so doing poured out his love upon all who bear heavy burdens. Human misery and guilt, on the one hand, and God's grace, on the other—these belong together. Where there is much misery and much guilt, precisely there will you also find much of God's grace and certainly much of God's love. That is, where human beings become small and weak, God reveals divine glory. Not among the strong, among those already protected, the "righteous," do you find God's love, but among the miserable and guilty who cry out to him. God's power is made perfect in weakness; where I am weak, there I am strong. And that means that precisely because the world does not fulfill our longing, because it is a world of resignation and renunciation, a world of suffering in the most profound sense—I can be assured that God is with it. Where human hearts are shat-
511 tered, there[12] God moves in. Where a life is smashed against the rocks of reality, the light of divine help suddenly shines forth. Just when the sea is storming most furiously during the night, the sun rises. God does not want to be where human beings are trying to be great. Where human beings seem to be sinking in darkness, there God establishes the kingdom of divine glory and love, as John the Baptist said: "He must increase, but I must decrease."[13] The weaker human beings are, the stronger God is. This is as sure as that God's love and human misfortune meet on the cross of Christ, as sure as the cross of Christ has sundered the equation religion = happiness. My grace is sufficient for you, for my power is made perfect in weakness. Do not hope in this world for happiness, do not hope for fulfillment. Where the entire disaster of humanity, all its yearning and all its inevitable resignation become most clear, above the misery and guilt of the big cities, in the houses of the "tax collectors and sinners," above the institutions of human misery and suffering, above the graves of our loved ones, in the hearts of those who have lost their joy in life, in the breast of those who are unable to right themselves again because of their own guilt, there the message of divine grace triumphs; here unseen, invisibly, there in glory; here

[11.] Deleted: "means taking our own distress seriously, and certainly taking seriously God's help. Not always to look at ourselves and to think nothing more is left to do, that we are and will remain bad, that is, in death, but rather to focus on the one, unmistakable sign through which God has revealed grace in the world, namely, the cross."

[12.] Uncertain reading.

[13.] John 3:30.

improbably, there as reality; here as a lightning on the horizon of the ages, there as the flashing light of eternity.

We who live in the world of inevitable renunciation, who suffer because of our unfulfilled longings, in misery or guilt, we no longer behold ourselves, we look to the cross, where God can approach us in love, whether it be storming or thundering, whether the whole edifice of our lives be swaying and trembling, even when the distress of dying demands its victims, even if our own guilt mounts to the heavens—we take the hand of our Redeemer on the cross and cry out across the tossing waves to him: "I will not let you go, unless you bless me."[14]

12. Sermon on Romans 12:11c, Barcelona, 512
Sixteenth Sunday after Trinity, September 23, 1928[1]

Rom. 12:11c: Serve the time.[2]

Whether modern or not, this question stands today probably more than ever at the forefront of everyone's interests, not only in fashion or health matters, but in all areas of human interest, in science, literature, in religion.[3] And in this question, too, opinions diverge. Some subscribe straightaway to whatever is modern; others, those who are consciously unmodern, look back with a transfigured gaze to the good old days. To the question, Do you want to be a modern person? some answer as resolutely "yes" as others answer "no." What is the position of those who call themselves Christians?[4] What

---

[14.] Gen. 32:26.

[1.] *NL*, A 21,13 a; handwritten, with a note by Bethge: "September 23, 1928, 16th after Trinity, Barcelona." Previously published in *PAM* 1:196–202. See also *NL*, A 21,13 b; typewritten copy by Bethge. Previously published in *GS* 5:463–68. According to the calendar, fifty-eight people attended, including Bonhoeffer's parents (*DB-ER*, 114); hence Bonhoeffer may be consciously citing the motto of his great-grandfather Karl August von Hase in the middle and at the end of the sermon (see ed. note 16).

[2.] The text of Rom. 12:11c is cited according to Barth, *Epistle to the Romans*, 450, and against the primary witnesses of the Greek New Testament ("serve the Lord") and against Luther ("be appropriate to the times"). Bonhoeffer already characterized this verse in *Sanctorum Communio* as the "great motto of preaching" (*DBWE* 1:233). Cf. also Wendel, *Homiletik*, 24 and 51.

[3.] The original first sentence, which was deleted in favor of the present opening, read: "Like a powerful current from eternity to eternity, time [*Zeit*] runs, flows—a small excerpt of it."

[4.] Deleted: "Here, too, there are two camps: those who want to bring everything modern into the church simply because it is modern, and those who want to stay with what is traditional."

is their position with regard to the changing times? Should Christians think conservatively or progressively? Should they be unmodern or modern?

The basic question of every Christian is obviously the question regarding eternity. How do I attain eternity here in the midst of time? Here in the eternal flux of becoming and passing away, there is, after all, nothing eternal or abiding; here there is only one path—the path out of time, to become indifferent to everything that happens here, to live in eternity alone. The object is to escape the despot time.

513 By contrast, this text calls out:[5] If you want to find eternity, then serve the time. This text must strike us as an enormous contradiction. If you want what is intransitory, then focus on what is transitory. If you want what is eternal, focus on what is temporal. *If you want God, focus on the world.* It seemed as if we were just starting to get somewhere climbing out of the world and up to heaven on a ladder of virtues. The shore of the world was just beginning to disappear in the distance and we were already traveling about in eternal spaces, still only half human being, but already half god—when the world flung us back from our flight; we plunged downward from these great heights and now find ourselves in the world again. If you want to be eternal, then serve time, we are told. Serve time—but why? Because it is only within time that you will find God and eternity. It is the hidden will of God, who allows us to find him in time, that we find the will of God only in Jesus Christ.[6] Nothing existing in time is divine, absolutely nothing, not the church, nor even our religion. All of this is subject to transitoriness, and yet all the transitoriness of the individual contains a bit of God's will, a bit of eternity. Time is like an inexhaustibly deep fountain through whose water the gold of the ever-unreachable bottom shines; it is the mountain rock through which, unrecognized in the depths, the veins of gold run. All that is imperfect is at least a reflection of the perfect; all that is transitory a symbol of the intransitory. "Every moment is in direct relationship with God," a great historian wrote,[7] meaning that every moment conceals a bit of eternity that we must but find, and above every moment God reigns. The moment, the present, that is the decisive message at which this text is aiming. Serve time, that means every time, that means the present. In other words, the present is sacred, it stands under God's eyes, it is consecrated,
514 it is permeated by eternal light. The present, every present, is God's hour

[5.] Uncertain reading.

[6.] Corrupted sentence in the German original.

[7.] Cited from Ranke, *Theory and Practice of History*, 53. Bonhoeffer likes to cite it as "every moment" rather than Ranke's "every epoch"; cf. *LPP*, 230.

with us, an hour full of responsibility; today and tomorrow, the present in its entire reality and diversity. In all of world history, there is always only one genuinely significant hour—the present. Whoever flees the present is fleeing God's hour; whoever flees time is fleeing God. Serve time! The Lord of the ages is God; the turning point of the ages is Christ; the true spirit of the age [Zeitgeist] is the Holy Spirit.[8] Hence every moment conceals these three considerations: that I acknowledge God as the Lord of my life, that I bow before Christ as the turning point of my life from judgment to grace, and that [I] try to create space and energy for the Holy Spirit in the midst of the spirit of the world. Serve time; that means to serve God the Lord, Christ the Reconciler, the Spirit, the sanctifier of our world. Not until we grant to the present the fulfillment of its own[9] do we live Christian lives, do we serve time.

Serving time—and this brings us back to the initial question—does not mean becoming *slaves* to it, nor does it mean sanctioning whatever is *up to date* simply because it is up to date. Serving includes the strength of our own will and of our own thoughts, not the weakness of chasing after something or of just going along with something. *It does not mean to serve fashion*; it means to serve time. Fashion is what people do; it [can] be either good or despicable. Time is what God does, and serving time means serving God, not serving human beings. Hence Christians are neither modern nor unmodern; rather, they serve their own time, that is, they worry not about human beings but about God. And yet—they serve *their own time*, and that means they step into the midst of it with all its problems and difficulties, with it seriousness and its distress, and there they serve. Christians are people of the present in the most profound sense. Be it *political* and *economic* problems, *moral* and *religious* decline, concern for the present generation of young people—everywhere the point is to enter into the problems of the present, to enter with all the love and all the energy at your disposal. The water of the fountain of the time has become so murky that we can no lon- 515
ger see the gold of its eternal bottom; see to it that the fountain becomes pure and bright again, see to it that we are able to find a bit of eternity in the time, keep tunneling until you strike the eternal springs.

The most important part of serving is love. That means you must love your own time so that you can serve it. Do not remove yourselves from the

[8.] Punctuation corrected; cf. ed. note 16.

[9.] German text here is no longer readable. [Bonhoeffer means, as he often says later, give the present its due, do not flee the temporal world, serve God now and here.—CG]

events of modernity; all of us bear responsibility for the guilt and misery of us all. We must come to understand again *what solidarity is within humanity.* Keeping out of things and saying, "I have nothing to do with all these things today, it's too contemptible for me to get involved," means *not to serve, but to judge.* Be brotherly—serve the time.

The most profound insight, however, emerges only when we consider that not only does the world have its time and its hours, but our own life also has its time and its hour of God, and that behind the times of our own life God's traces become visible, that beneath our own paths lie the deep shafts of eternity, and every step generates a faint echo from eternity. If we but understand the deep, pure form of these times and how to represent them in the way we conduct our own lives, then we will encounter God's holy presence in the midst of our own time. "My times are your hand."[10] My childhood, my youth, my maturity, and my old age. Serve your time, the presence of God in your lives. God has sanctified your time; every time, properly understood, is immediate to God. And God wants us to be wholly what we are. *Be wholly a child* as long as you are a child, in play and joy, in receptiveness and gratitude, surrendering to the will of those you love. *Be wholly a young person,* in the independence and security, the courage and defiance accompanying this stage of life; in strength and yet in subordination[11] to the person you honor as your leader;[12] to the extent you fulfill the meaning of these, your own time given to you by God, you will be grounded in the depths of eternity. If you bear all the joys and sufferings
516 of your developmental years and fulfill the essence of what youth is in all its distress and in its freedom, then God will be pleased with you and you will have penetrated from time to eternity. *Be men and women,* both wholly and in their essence as created by God. Be human beings with your own wills, with your own passions and your own concerns, your happiness and your distress, your seriousness and your frivolity, your jubilation and your misery. God wants to see human beings, not ghosts who shun the earth itself. God loved the earth and made us from that earth; God made the earth our mother, God, who is our Father. We were created not as angels but as children of the earth with guilt and passion, strength and weakness, but as children of the earth whom God loves, children loved by God precisely in

[10.] Ps. 31:15.
[11.] Uncertain reading; perhaps "responsibility."
[12.] Cf. 3/7, p. 501.

our weaknesses, in our passions, in our guilt. Precisely in our defiant position on earth—within time, within our own time—God loves us; precisely in holding fast to our Mother Earth and to what she has given us, in solidarity with the human race, even where it is weak, in kinship with our own, small, weak times—God wants us, and something of eternity that destroys all time shines into our hearts.

An ancient Greek legend tells of the giant Antaeus, who was so strong that no one could conquer him.[13] Many tried and were defeated until one opponent lifted the giant up off the ground during the battle. Suddenly, the battle was over because the giant's strength abandoned him, since it flowed into him only when he was standing firmly on the ground. This legend of the giant Antaeus is profound.[14] Only those standing with both feet on the ground, who are and remain wholly children of the earth, who do not undertake hopeless attempts to flee to unreachable heights, who make do with what they have and gratefully hold fast to it, who have the full strength of human existence—those are the ones who serve time and thus also eternity. Then, however, it will happen that in the midst of time, we
again and again turn our eyes from its transitoriness to the time that comes 517
at the end of time itself. Serve time, serve the hour God wants to have with your people, with you yourselves; be people of the sacred present, a present that never returns, just as that compassionate Samaritan was a man of the present,[15] that you may become people of eternity.

The Lord of the ages is God. The turning point of the ages is Christ. The true spirit of the age [Zeitgeist] is the Holy Spirit.[16]

[13.] See 2/3, ed. note 44.

[14.] Although the text contains an insertion mark here, the text to be inserted is missing.

[15.] Cf. Luke 10:36–37.

[16.] The epigraph and leitmotiv of the famous church history textbook written by Bonhoeffer's great-grandfather, a book that influenced generations of Protestant theology students: "Everything has its time; the Lord of time is God, the turning-point of the ages is Christ. The true spirit of the age is the Holy Spirit" (Karl August von Hase, *History of the Christian Church*). Concerning the comparison between the spirit of the age [*Zeitgeist*] and the Holy Spirit, see also Bonhoeffer's memorial address for Harnack, 2/4.

13. Sermon on Luke 17:33, Madrid, Twentieth Sunday after Trinity, October 21, 1928[1]

Luke 17:33: Whosoever shall seek to preserve his soul shall lose it; and whosoever shall lose his life shall preserve it.[2]

Anyone who remembers his youth and his own coming of age, or who spends much time with young people of this age, knows that young people at this stage of their lives have only one question at the center of all their thinking and action. Young people differ from children in that their souls are divided, as it were; young people become the object of their own obser-
518 vation and come to perceive the full profundity of the riddle that each person is an ego, a separate self. They now stand as if before an abyss in which everything is seething and surging and raging; overwhelmed, they stare into all this wild and passionate activity and bustle and must recognize that all this is actually the self, the person's own ego. A new world opens up to them, the world of the soul, of one's own soul, a world greater and more impressive than the great external world. That is *my* self, *my* soul?! This uncannily strong, unpredictable, unbridled, demonic thing that assaults me—that's me? No, that's not me. It's something else, something dreadful that has put me under its spell; and yet—it *is* me, for in me, too, things are seething and surging like that. Why am I precisely an I? Indeed, what am I? Who am I? Why am I here? Where did I come from? What am I to do? Once these questions arise, they never again turn us loose. We feel assaulted by a superior power, by a whole world, by our own ego. And now we begin to look and search and ponder and stride from one discovery to the next in our own soul, and everything seems increasingly uncanny. We become anxious and frightened by our own selves, the misery of human existence seizes our heart for the first time and we ourselves seize up in our distress, in our unredeemed state, and we cry out for only one thing, for release from the

---

[1.] *NL*, A 21,14 a; handwritten, with a note by Bethge: "October 21, 1928, 20th after Trinity, Madrid." Previously published in *PAM* 1:202–7. See also *NL*, A 21,14 b; typewritten copy by Bethge with editorial changes. Previously published in *GS* 5:468–72. According to the calendar note (*NL*, A 18,2), Bonhoeffer delivered this sermon before eighty people in Madrid. This sermon presupposes various observations Bonhoeffer made regarding youth psychology, and his pedagogical efforts on behalf of the boy Karl-Heinz Köttgen probably influenced the sermon. [See esp. 1/83, p. 183; 1/87; and 1/91, pp. 191–92.—CG] In any event, the theme of the soul of the "young person" has been read into the sermon text. Participants in the service included young people addressed directly by Bonhoeffer. During this same period, Bonhoeffer was trying to establish religious instruction in the school (see 1/48, p. 144).

[2.] [Text follows Bonhoeffer's German, not the NRSV.—CG]

demon I, for control over it, for redemption. How do I save my ego? How do I become free? This is the fundamental question of all human thought and action. How do I form the formless, shape the shapeless? How do I master chaos? Those whose souls have not yet burned with this question or in whom it has been silenced by the power of habit will perceive not even a hint of what religion is and what it has to offer. The words γνῶθι σεαυτόν, "know yourself,"[3] stood above that ancient Greek temple, the idea being that only thus can you gain control of your ego, and yet one experience each of us can have is that throughout our lives we never get to know ourselves; we are 519
and remain unknown to ourselves—known only by God—and everyone experiences at least once that excessive self-brooding is self-flagellation. Despair instead of redemption.

Hence another path must be found for redeeming the self; self-control instead of self-knowledge, self-formation through the will.

Some genuinely believe they have found the will of God in this will to form the soul. So the life of many Christians consists solely in working toward the preservation and polishing of their souls. The primary focus is on one's own soul, the salvation of one's own soul. Everything I do, I do for the sake of my own soul—this seems to be the highest blossoming of Christian cultivation of the soul—and yet in reality it is nothing but ultimate egotism in its purest state, spiritualized and disguised and thus all the more dangerous. And now let us listen to our text. Whosoever seeks to preserve his soul shall lose it . . . This statement radically reverses the humanistic idea. Not a cultivation of the soul, not human culture, not moral polishing, but surrender of the soul to an other; not the soul as the center of the world but rather that to which the soul sacrifices itself.

It is the unmistakable experience for anyone who has ever been seized by a passion, be it a passion for thinking, a passion of intensely desiring something, a passion for one's vocation, a passion for another person—when we are caught up by such a passion, when we suddenly notice no longer even ourselves but rather only that other thing or other person, when our soul submerges in that activity or in the soul of the beloved, when we are no longer ourselves, there we suddenly know in some incomprehensible way that we have been created anew as another, new, better self. The God-willed meaning of every passion, a passion for one's vocation, for another person, is that in it our self submerges and by submerging is created anew, that the soul is cleansed where it is extinguished by something other than itself to which it surrenders itself. Here we find the inexhaustible blessing of our

[3.] Inscription in the forecourt of the temple of Apollo at Delphi.

vocational work, and here also the curse weighing upon the *machine*, which
520 turns those who must work at it day after day into part of the mechanism themselves, a mechanism with which they can never develop a personally passionate relationship.[4] It is from this perspective that the word "vocation"[5] reacquires its original religious, eternal, sacred meaning. Woe to the man and woman who have never sensed anything of this meaning, woe to the race that denies people the possibility of giving themselves and finding themselves in their vocation. From this perspective sources of eternity emerge within friendships, marriages, indeed, within every human relationship and family. Being able to surrender oneself, to forget and lose oneself, being able to bow beneath the claim of one's neighbor in the spirit of passionate sacrifice—and being able to find oneself again here on the altar of the most extreme surrender, that is our blessing, that is God's grace. Whosoever seeks to preserve his soul shall lose it . . . you boys / idea of the church. . . .[6]

Yes, but what becomes of my own soul if I surrender myself completely to the other? It will remain rough, unformed, unplanned! Well, then let your soul remain angular and rough, since even the most exquisite polish only helps for a while. Does it really matter all that much how your soul looks? Or is it more important that you do the will of God? That you enter into the cleansing process God lays upon you? Don't be so anxious about the salvation of your own soul; focus only on what God gives you to do, every moment anew and differently, and leave your soul to God, for he already knows better than you how to deal with it.

I wanted to speak to you about the redemption of the ego. Have we already thoroughly explained what that means from a Christian perspective? We have mentioned many things to which one can lose one's soul, but all that is included in the one thing, namely, losing one's soul to God, to the will of God. What a paradox: we do not preserve our soul for God, but rather lose it. But this means no longer focusing on our own soul at all, but rather only on God, it means leaving our soul in his hands. To lose my soul
521 means to lose my will, my plans, and my thoughts to God's will, plans, and thoughts. Here alone the drama of redemption reaches its culmination and

[4.] Bonhoeffer frequently levels such criticism at mechanization; see, e.g., 3/7, p. 500, and 3/18, ed. note 21.

[5.] Concerning the concept of vocation, see Holl, "History of the Word Vocation (*Beruf*)."

[6.] The phrases "you boys [*Euch Jungen*] / idea of the church" are a subsequent insertion.

conclusion. The passion of the self, this overwhelmingly frightening demon element, turns to God; in passion the ego surrenders to God, sacrifices itself to him, to his will. But it is like in Goethe's poem, where from the fiery altar of self-sacrifice of a human life a new human being emerges from the cloud of smoke.[7] The ego that has thrown itself away, that has sacrificed itself without any consideration of itself, for the salvation of the other, for God's honor, this self has entered into God and been touched by him; it has tasted eternity and has become new. It is redeemed—not through itself, only through God; not through maintaining itself or cultivating its soul or striving for perfection—but only through losing itself and forgetting itself, sacrificing itself, surrendering itself; not through beholding its own shortcomings and merits, but through beholding God's singular goodness. It is redeemed in the midst of the world, for only in the world can one live for God, only in the world can one sacrifice to God. In the world: that means precisely with one's neighbor. You who give yourself completely to your neighbor are giving yourself to God; through your neighbor, you will be redeemed by God. You have found the ego for which you have been searching since you were young; you—no, God has become Lord over your ego; you—no, God has torn you from the distress of the life of the ego and liberated you. You have lost your soul to God—no, God has lost his love to you; you have penetrated into God's—no, God has penetrated into your life. You have liberated yourself—no, God has bound you, bound [. . .][8]

[7.] Allusion to a passage from Goethe's 1797 poem, "The God and the Bayadere: An Indian Legend": "Thus increased her torments are / By the cruel, heartless quire / And with arms outstretching far / Leaps she on the glowing pyre. / But the youth divine outsprings / From the flame with heav'nly grace, / And on high his flight he wings, / While his arms his love embrace. / In the sinner repentant the Godhead feels joy; / Immortals delight thus their might to employ. / Lost children to raise to a heavenly place." See Goethe, *Poems of Goethe,* 71. See also Karl Viëtor's comment: "The loving union of God and creature, of the ego and the All, is here celebrated as the mystery which is at the heart of all great religions of redemption" (Viëtor, *Goethe the Poet,* 138).

[8.] The conclusion has been lost.

522 **14. Draft for a Liturgy, Barcelona, Remembrance Sunday,[1] November 25, 1928[2]**

But, in accordance with his promise, we wait for a new heaven and a new earth, where righteousness is at home.[3]

Lord, our faith and our hope are so weak. We do not dare to entrust our lives completely to your promise. We doubt your power. Lord, forgive the doubters and those without hope and give us today your promise anew. *Lord, have mercy on us . . .*

Those who sow in tears reap with shouts of joy. Those who go out weeping, bearing the noble seed, shall come home with shouts of joy, carrying their sheaves.[4] *Praise be . . . May the Lord be . . .*

Lord God, you make the waters rise around us. But look down upon your world. It is a terrible torment. Hunger and thirst, no home, no work, tears and despair; God, are these the children of your compassion? Is this the world you created? Ah, we must be frighteningly distant from you if your creatures must suffer so. We are soon at our end.[5] We no longer believe, and we no longer hope. But now come, O God, and end all this misery, all this suffering, and if it is your gracious will that we fall even deeper into the water, do not conceal your promise from us that you will create a new heaven and a new earth. That you have invited the poor and the miserable, the troubled and the suffering into your kingdom. Today we would still speak about this promise. God, make us happy again. Amen.

[1.] [Remembrance Sunday, *Totensonntag,* when Protestants remember their dead, is the last Sunday of the church year and therefore the Sunday before Advent; it corresponds to the Roman Catholic All Souls' Day, which is celebrated on November 2.—CG]

[2.] *NL,* A 21,19; handwritten. Previously published in *GS* 6:154. Draft for the opening liturgy (Kyrie, Gloria, Collect of the day), most suitable for the Sunday before Advent, November 25, 1928, since the prefatory antiphon 2 Pet. 3:13 belongs to this Sunday. By contrast, the citation from Ps. 126:5–6. fits the twenty-fourth Sunday after Trinity, November 18, 1928.

[3.] 2 Pet. 3:13. [NRSV translation altered.—CG]

[4.] Ps. 126:5–6.

[5.] Deleted: "We have become deaf."

15. Sermon (fragment) on Song of Solomon 8:6b, Barcelona, Remembrance Sunday, November 25, 1928[1] 523

Song of Sol. 8:6b: Love is strong as death.
Remembrance Sunday, November 25

We are standing by the sea; wave upon wave rolls in, breaks on the beach, and sinks away in the endless gray water; eternally one and ever another. And so it has been for hundreds of thousands of years; human life is but a moment before the ancient, primal sea; a wave that passes away even as it forms. And we are unable to turn our gaze away; for hours on end we stare over the foamy crests, outward—to where?—we hardly know ourselves, but it draws our gaze into the endless distance, out to where the sun sinks into the sea, where the waves rise, and the soul stretches out, wants to know what the eyes cannot sense—wants to know about what is beyond the gray sea—or whether it just continues on eternally like this, without an end, without a beyond, a process of becoming and passing away with neither measure nor goal—and yet as intensively as it searches, it always sees the same drama . . . no hope . . . eternal hiddenness. Then a powerful wave washes a strange, hitherto unknown fruit onto the island, wonderful to behold, a strange messenger from the longed-for distance, driven across the endless sea to the gray shore of our earth—from beyond the sea, from a blessed land.

We understand. The world rushes and roars incessantly in the same, eternal tempo; it is the rhythm of death, of eternal passing away pulsing in the world; it is the breath of putrefaction that the world breathes. And the soul stretches out, wants to move beyond the grayness, beyond the eternal sameness, the eternal meaninglessness, the eternally decomposable, and it searches for the messenger from the distance and finds it already in the midst of the world of dying, the guarantor of an island beyond the sea. It beholds the foreign fruit on earthly land where human beings are
able to love one another with all their souls and with all their hearts; here 524
something so phenomenal and different gleams and shines, something the world has never known; something incredibly new, unique, mighty, something superior to the world and its beings has appeared. Here in the love between human hearts God is found; here the world is overcome, death is conquered. For love is strong as death.

[1.] *NL*, A 21,15 a; handwritten, with a note by Bethge: "1928 Barcelona." See also *NL*, A 21,15 b; typewritten copy by Bethge. Sermon on the Sunday before Advent with draft for a liturgy (see 3/14). Cf. Bonhoeffer's letter to his parents on November 27, 1928 (1/58).

There is a battle going on in the world, a battle without equal, one into which we are all drawn, a war between the highest powers: the war of death against love, of love against death, two foes worthy of each other in majesty; but love is strong as death, for it is from God. Death, too, is from God, deriving its power not from within itself but through God, and that is the only reason it is able to defy love, but that is also why it must also succumb to love, since it is only the penultimate before the ultimate, because God is love, not death.[2]

Death is mighty in the world; it tears open wounds that never again completely heal; it reaps wherever it wants, and its scythe hums through both ripe and rotten fields. It takes the child from its mother's arms, seizes the young boy at play, abducts friend from friend, spouse from spouse, a brother from his brothers and sisters, mother, father from children, the aged from the circle of young people, gently or wildly, solemnly or horrifically, suddenly and peacefully—it is capable of the most monumental thing of all, namely, to separate loving hearts, to be victorious over love in this world. But love is strong as death. Death is strong over the world, but love is strong for eternity. Where there is love, there is eternity, and there is no more death. Where human hearts have met in the most profound, pure, sacred love, not even a thousand deaths have been able to separate souls from one another; there life is lived for eternity.

God created human beings and with them, in them, as the most gentle, profound, pure, purifying, mature element, the urge to be with other human beings, love for one's neighbor. Out of eternity God created human beings to complement one another. Friend and friend, spouse and spouse, God created them such that the one finds and purifies its soul through the other and such that they no longer live two but rather one life out of love [. . .]

525 **16. Homily for the Children's Service, Barcelona (?), Remembrance Sunday, November 25, 1928 (?)**[1]

Have you ever considered that in one thing we have absolutely the same fate as all the many animals and the great trees and beautiful flowers and butterflies and birds? Can you imagine what that is, why everything our loving

---

[2.] [Here it is love and God that are ultimate, not death as above; cf. 3/10, ed. note 13.—CG]

[1.] *NL*, A 21,18 a; handwritten, with handwritten notes by Bethge: "Sunday before Advent," "Barcelona-type paper," "children's service?" and "In Luther's *Hauspostille*" (*NL-Bibl.* 5 C 31). [This note by Bethge means that the manuscript of the address was found

God made, from human beings to the smallest bug, is the same and differs only from God? Well, it is that we must all die, that we cannot live forever on earth, that we are made from earth and must return to the earth. There has never been a human being or an animal that did not have to die, though certainly some trees live many hundreds or even thousands of years. You have doubtless already seen such trees, but look, someday they, too, must die; this is the way God wants it, and it has always been such that every small human child and every baby animal and every small flower born into the world has lived a while, has grown, and then, after it has lived long enough, has had to die. But you already know all of this. And you also know how sad we human beings are when our father or mother or brother or sister or a good boy or a good girl dies. Yes, we are sad and we weep because we will never see that person again, and we have a hard time getting used to the fact that that person's place at the table or in our classroom will be empty from now on, and that we will no longer see that person's loving face or hear that person's voice, that that person is now lying completely peaceful and silent in a coffin in the ground. And then we are quite sad, and we often think, "It's all over now," and we say, "Why has God done this to us?" And
then many poor souls cannot be comforted and instead weep again and 526
again, for weeks, months, and even years. For such saddened people, however, our God offers comfort, comfort in which they can find support. So that you can understand what kind of comfort this is, let me tell you a story that happened in the Great War.[2]

You see, in the Great War over a thousand Germans and even more French and Russian and British troops were killed every day. And every day over a thousand German families received a letter saying, "Your father or your brother was killed in action." And then again and again, mothers, children, and brothers and sisters wept many, many tears. Now once in the evening after heavy fighting, deep in winter, two soldiers lay next to each other on the battlefield, both of them severely wounded. Only one of them was still quite young; he had just turned seventeen and had volunteered for the army, had left his mother and his little brother, to whom he had always been nothing but a great joy, behind and saddened. The soldier next to him was already an older man, maybe fifty years old; he, too, had volunteered and now lay severely wounded in the cold snow. Worried and with tears in

---

in this 1846 edition in Bonhoeffer's library. Regarding *NL*, A 21,18 a, the German editors found that two manuscripts were cataloged under this number, pages 1–4 here published as 3/16 and pages 5–8 published as 3/20. A later typescript (*NL*, A 21,18 b) only transcribes pages 1–4.—CG] The dating to Barcelona 1928 is uncertain.

[2.] [The common name for World War I, before World War II.—CG]

his eyes, he looked at the younger man. But the younger man said quite cheerfully, "Stop, father, and don't be so sad; if God wills it, we will still manage to get home (they were somewhere deep inside France), but if God doesn't will it, then just think how beautiful it will be there when we are dead." And then they lay there a while longer, the son quite peaceful and glad, the father terribly worried, for he had a wife and mother and little boy at home who would be very sad and, indeed, who would now have nothing more to eat and no more clothes. The moon rose in the meantime, and both men were freezing cold, and both knew that they would not last much longer. Suddenly the young soldier called out, "Father, can you hear me? God is about to come get me, but I still quickly want to write mother a farewell letter." And with his last energy he pulled himself up, took a pencil and paper, and wrote something like this: "Dear Mother, When you hear that
527 we are dead, please don't cry, but rejoice as I rejoice, for we are then much better off than you, for we are with God. Say hello to everyone"—and then he had no more energy. Exhausted, he fell back and prayed softly; then he died.[3] Not long afterward, the father also died. When they found them the next morning, they buried them together and sent the letter to the mother, adding that both the father and the son had died. When the mother read this, she began to cry loudly and to lament, asking God repeatedly, "Why have you done this?" Then she pulled a terribly crumpled letter out of the envelope and read the son's letter, and read it again and again until, suddenly, she was quite happy, saying, "Pardon me, dear Lord, yes, you alone are right; you alone comfort us. Yes, my good husband and my dear son are with you. Why should I then weep? For with you there is no more suffering and no more death; there everything is wonderful and happy. You, God, will wipe away every tear from our eyes,[4] and even if things sometimes get hard here, in only a short time we are with you. Here we must suffer care and illness and many sad and ugly things, but it all passes so quickly. You yourself gave us your only son, and should I not let you have mine with joy? And just as you raised up the Lord Jesus, so you will also raise us up. Dear Lord, remind me often that I will one day come to you, remind me so that I may already be comforted and be peaceful here and hope in you alone!" That's what the mother said, and she still had to experience much unhap-

[3.] [Bonhoeffer could hardly write these words without deep feelings about the death in World War I of his brother Walter and the profound emotional effect this had on his mother.—CG]

[4.] Cf. Rev. 21:4.

piness. Her mother[5] died quickly one after the other following a serious illness. She herself had to work hard to support herself and her little boy till the boy, too, died. But the more misfortune befell her, the more resolutely she hoped in God, and when she noticed that she, too, had to die, she was glad and was not afraid to die at all.

But death is not the only suffering that God sends as a test for us. There is much, much other suffering as well, and perhaps you have already experienced some of it. Serious illness, either for us or for our parents or our brothers and sisters; concern for our daily bread; poverty; or maybe when 528
we feel unjustly neglected or punished by someone or maybe even hear that someone has said something nasty about us behind our backs. And when we are saddened by this because we did absolutely nothing to that other person, and perhaps in the evening we are crying in bed, then we should look to God and be glad that one day we will have it so good when we are finally with God. The Bible tells us about a rich, respected, pious man, Job, whose faith God tested with serious illness, poverty, and slander, but who did not turn away from God but rather trusted him. And God rewarded him for that trust. If we can already focus here on the goal, then just look, we receive a great power with which to bear suffering, and if we take all our worries to God, we become glad and can already see a bit of heaven even here.

Do you know that today, Remembrance Sunday, we are at the end of our church year? Next Sunday, the first Sunday in Advent, a new year begins. We conclude the year with two very serious holidays, namely, Repentance Day and Remembrance Sunday. On the day of remembrance for the dead, we want to direct all our thoughts toward those whom God has taken, though we will also remember that we, too, will have to die someday; and we will keep this in mind, for we, too, all want to come to God someday. And we don't want that day to frighten or surprise us.

We still want to discuss just how we will do all that.[6]

[5.] Deleted: "and her little boy."

[6.] Two words are listed for discussion beneath this sentence: "Sacrifice?" and an illegible word.

529 **17. Sermon on Revelation 3:20, Barcelona, First Sunday in Advent, December 2, 1928**[1]

Rev. 3:20: Behold, I stand at the door, and knock.[2]
First Sunday in Advent

Celebrating Advent means being able to wait. Waiting, however, is an art our impatient age has forgotten. It wants to pick the ripe fruit even though it has hardly finished planting the seedling. But greedy eyes[3] are all too often deceived because the apparently precious fruit is still green on the inside, and disrespectful hands ungratefully throw aside that which has disappointed them so. Those unfamiliar with the bitter bliss of waiting, of doing without while maintaining hope, will never experience the full blessing of fulfillment. Those who do not know what it feels like to wrestle anxiously with the most profound questions of life, of one's own life, and then to keep watch in anticipation and yearning until the truth is unveiled—cannot imagine how glorious is the moment when clarity emerges; and for those who do not know what it is like to court the friendship, the love of another person, to open up one's soul to the soul of that other person until it comes, till it arrives—for those people the profound blessing of the life of two intertwined souls will remain eternally concealed. We must wait for the greatest, most profound, most gentle things in life; nothing happens in a rush, but only according to the divine laws of germinating, growing, and becoming.

Of course, not everyone can wait, especially those who are sated, satisfied, and disrespectful. Only people who carry a certain restlessness around with them can wait, and people who look up reverently to the One who is great in the world. Hence only those whose souls give them no peace are able to celebrate Advent, who feel poor and incomplete and who sense
530 something of the greatness of what is coming, before which one can only bow in humble timidity, in anticipation till God inclines toward us—the Holy One, God in the child in the manger. God is coming, the Lord Jesus is coming, Christmas is coming, rejoice, O Christendom! This is what we hear today again for the first time. And already we want to hear in the distance

[1.] *NL*, A 21,16 a; handwritten, with a note by Bethge: "Barcelona, December 2, 1928." Previously published in *PAM* 1:207–13. See also *NL*, A 21,16 b; typewritten copy by Bethge. Previously published with editorial changes in *GS* 5:473–78. Cf. Bonhoeffer's letter to his parents on November 27, 1928 (1/58).

[2.] [The text of the Authorized, or King James, Version translates Bonhoeffer's German exactly.—CG]

[3.] Replaces "hands."

the song of angels about God's glory and about peace on earth;[4] but it is not yet time, we must still learn to wait and to wait properly. Make this time of waiting into a blessed time of preparation.

When Advent comes again and we hear and sing the traditional Christmas carols, a peculiar feeling secretly comes over us, and even the hardest hearts are softened; we sense something we felt as children when we were away from our mother, something like homesickness for past times, distant places, and yet such a blissful homesickness, without hardness, without grimness, and something in us yearns outward, farther than past years, farther than our childhood home, indeed, outward to our home beyond the clouds, to the eternal house of our Father. Something of the curse of homelessness descends upon us, the curse weighing upon the world itself, the curse of eternally having to sojourn without goal and without end. All around us we see wintry death and coldness, and we see within ourselves something uncanny, looking at us from a thousand terrible eyes, evil, evil that repeatedly banishes us to the world, evil we cannot get beyond no matter how hard we try. The two most real realities, about which we have spoken on the last two Sundays of the old church year,[5] now, at the beginning of the new year, lay themselves anew and with all their enormous weight upon the soul: evil and death. Who can offer help here? Who can offer redemption?

The one who redeems us from evil and from death should be our Lord. A groan wrests itself from our breast, "Come, God, Lord Jesus Christ, come into our world, into our homelessness, into our sin, into our death, come, you yourself, and share with us, be a human being as we are and conquer for us. Come into the midst of my evil, into my daily disloyalty, participate in my sin, the sin that I hate and yet cannot turn loose, be my brother, you holy God, become my brother—in the realm of evil and suffering and death. 531
Come along into my death, into my sufferings and struggles, and make me holy and pure despite this evil, despite death. And today his soft voice answers us: Behold, I stand at the door, and knock. And do we not quake at this word? The spirit we have summoned, the spirit of the redemption of the world, is not far; indeed, he is standing at the door, knocking, has already been standing there a long time, waiting for the door to be opened. The Lord is coming, God is coming, coming to us. Admittedly it is a soft voice we hear speaking there, and few people hear it. The market barkers and advertisers extol their rotten wares too loudly and noisily; everyone wants

[4.] Luke 2:14.

[5.] See the sermon fragment for November 25, 1928 (3/15).

to go through the door first, hastily and impatiently. And woe to those who do not pay attention to these gates, lest all sorts of well-groomed rabble fill up the house. And amid all that pushes itself upon us, the royal sojourner stands there patiently, unrecognized and quiet. That sojourner knocks very quietly. Can you hear it? Do you think the wanderer is not knocking on your door? Ah, let all these loud voices first be quiet and then listen closely to see whether there is not also someone knocking on the door of your heart, he who would make your heart his own, who would be your quiet guest. Jesus is knocking at your door and at mine. We must but open our ears and listen within ourselves. Jesus is coming most assuredly. Coming in this year too, coming also to us.

When early Christianity spoke about the return of the Lord Jesus, it was thinking first of all about a great day of judgment. And as alien to Christmas as this thought may seem to us, it derives from early Christianity and should be taken seriously. When we hear Jesus knocking at our door, the first thing that happens is that our conscience awakens: Are we properly prepared? Is our heart capable of becoming his dwelling place? Hence the time of Advent becomes a time of introspection for us. "With seriousness, O human souls, prepare your hearts,"[6] as the old hymn goes. It is quite peculiar how calmly we contemplate God's coming, whereas earlier peoples trembled before the day of God and the world quaked when Jesus Christ walked among us. It is so peculiar because we so often encounter God's
532 tracks in the world together with the tracks of human suffering, of the cross on Golgotha. We have grown so accustomed to the idea of divine love and of the coming at Christmas that we no longer sense the awe that God's coming should awaken in us. We have become dulled to the message; we only register what is welcome in it, what is pleasant, forgetting the powerful seriousness of the fact that the God of the world is approaching us on our small earth and now makes claims on us. God's coming is truly not merely a message of joy, but first of all horrifying news for every person with a conscience.

And not until we have perceived the terror of this matter can we then also appreciate the incomparable act of beneficence. God is coming, into the midst of evil, into death, judging evil in us and in the world.[7] And by judging it, God loves us, purifies us, sanctifies us, comes to us with grace and love. God makes us happy as only children can be happy; God is with us and now intends to be with us always, regardless of where we are, in our

[6.] Valentin Thilo, *EKG*, no. 9.

[7.] Deleted: "and [illegible] judging death."

sin, in our suffering and death. We are no longer alone; God is with us, we are no longer homeless, a bit of our eternal home has entered into us. This is why we adults can rejoice so profoundly in our hearts beneath the Christmas tree, more perhaps even than children can; we sense that God's goodness is once again coming near to us. We remember everything of God's goodness that we encountered during the past year, and we sense something of the strange home about which this strange tree is speaking. Jesus is coming in both judgment and grace. Behold, I stand at the door ... Lift up your heads, O ye gates.[8]

Christ is standing at the door, knocking. You are searching for him, would perhaps give anything to have him with you sometime, genuinely, actually with you, not just inwardly, but physically, in reality. But how could this be possible? Jesus was familiar with human beings and with their need to see, their desire for the tangible, and so he spoke of this need in a grandiose parable about how from day to day and in actual reality he is still wandering about on earth, and how we can indeed have him with us if we really 533
want to have him and not some image conjured by our imagination.[9] One day, at the Last Judgment, he will separate the sheep from the goats, and to those on his right he will say: Come, you that are blessed . . . "for I was hungry. . . ." To the astonished question . . . "just as you did it to one of the least of these. . . ."[10] But here we are confronted with the terrifying reality; Jesus is at the door, knocking, in reality, asking you for help in the figure of the beggar, in the figure of the degenerate soul in shabby clothes, encountering you in every person you meet. Christ walks the earth as long as there are people, as your neighbor, as the person through whom God summons you, addresses you, makes claims on you. That is the most serious and most blessed part of the Advent message. Christ is at the door; he lives in the form of those around us. Will you close the door or open it for him?

It may seem odd to see Christ in a countenance so close to us, but he did indeed say it. Those who avoid the serious reality of the Advent message cannot speak about Christ coming into their hearts. Those who do not learn from Christ's own coming that we are all brothers through Christ, through God, have understood nothing of the meaning of that coming.

Christ is knocking; but it is not yet Christmas, nor is it yet the great, final Advent, the final coming of Christ. And all the Advents of our lives, all the Advents we celebrate, are permeated by a yearning for that final Advent,

---

[8.] Ps. 24:7 (KJV).

[9.] Deleted: "something completely different."

[10.] Matt. 25:32–40; abbreviated using just key words [presumably to be spelled out by the preacher—CG].

the Advent of the words, "See, I am making all things new."[11] The time of Advent is a time of waiting, though our entire life is a time of Advent, a time of waiting for that final time when a new heaven and a new earth will emerge, when all human beings will be brothers and will rejoice with the words of the angels: Peace on earth and goodwill among people.[12] Learn to wait, for he has promised to come. Behold, I stand at the door. . . . And we call to him: Yes, come soon, Lord Jesus. Amen.[13]

534 **18. Sermon on Philippians 4:7, Barcelona, Sexagesima,[1] February 3, 1929[2]**

Phil. 4:7: May the peace of God, which surpasses all understanding, guard your hearts and your minds in Christ Jesus.

Whoever has felt but once how nature can embrace us and rob us of our senses, perhaps at a quiet forest lake in the evening, a lake that shines into our soul like the deep eyes of a child, perhaps before the simplicity of a beautiful forest flower we encounter like a pure greeting nature sends to its children; whoever has felt but once how creation, how Mother Earth seizes the heart—that person will know forever what he or she lacks. These people know what a bitter aftertaste such experiences leave behind; they know that tears of bliss, too, are salty. And one realization emerges for them that is great and profound and serious:[3] namely, that a rift runs through the world, a rift that is visible in nature where human beings are, and that disappears where human beings are no more. Human beings move through God's world as strangers, indeed as those who have been driven out, who have fallen. It is as if they see paradise before them and yet have been driven out and cannot enjoy its bliss; they bear the sign of Cain on their foreheads, the sign of human existence, the sign of outcasts.[4]

[11.] Rev. 21:5.
[12.] [Cf. Luke 2:14.—CG]
[13.] Cf. Rev. 22:20 et passim.

[1.] [The second Sunday before Lent.—CG]

[2.] *NL*, A 21,17 a; handwritten, with a note by Bethge: "February 3, 1929, last sermon prior to departing Barcelona in 1929." Previously published in *PAM* 1:213–20. See also *NL*, A 21,17 b; typewritten copy by Bethge with editorial changes. Previously published in *GS* 5:478–84.

[3.] Deleted: "in their hearts."

[4.] ["Outcasts" translates *Friedlosigkeit*, a medieval legal term applied to those whose crimes were so heinous that they were banned from human society, their goods confiscated, their wives considered widows, and who were liable to be killed by anyone without

A terrible, antidivine will has risen up in human beings and brought this gruesome fate of the outcast upon humankind. But it has left behind in the human soul a burning thirst, a tormenting longing for the peace that can only be peace with God. The message of peace has a strange sound for all of us, as if it had descended to us from another world and now wanted to tell us about that world. It touches us in the depths of our soul and has
something incredibly gentle and strong about it. It makes us blissful and 535
melancholy at the same time because we are a profoundly outcast [friedlos] race. We are torn apart and driven and worn down by our jobs, by our personal lives, we wrestle with questions we cannot answer, we fight for things we cannot attain, we argue with our fate and yet basically[5] are searching for but one thing, namely, to get beyond this demonic restlessness in us and enter into peace.[6] I am weary with contending! Why this desire and unrest? Come, sweet peace, oh come into my breast![7] But we must understand ourselves correctly. All our hurrying and chasing, working and striving, worrying and brooding longs not for the kind of peace that the fulfillment of some wish can bring us but for the peace only God can bestow upon our hearts, for the final, eternal peace of God. We sense the rift between us and the infinite and know that this rift, that is, our own godlessness and godforsakenness, is the basis of our weakness, our outcast state,[8] our restlessness; and all our activities are basically trying to do nothing other than to overcome this rift. Let us not deceive ourselves; we are unable to want anything but the peace of God, just as flowers are unable to want anything but the sun. God has oriented us to himself; in the ancient words of the church father: God, you have made us for yourself, and our hearts are restless until they rest in you.[9] The world thirsts for God's peace; it wants to see the rainbow of the peace of divine grace shine after the thunderstorm and yet cannot get past its own restlessness and haste. For it is a fallen world burdened with the unremitting fate of being outcast.

---

punishment. By using throughout the sermon variants of this term as the opposite of peace with God, Bonhoeffer highlights the radical alienation of the fallen human condition. Accordingly the usual translation of *friedlos* in this sermon is "outcast." Yet the German *friedlos* also means "without peace," and that is certainly a nuance that belongs here.—CG]

[5.] Deleted: "perhaps without knowing it."

[6.] Deleted: "not the peace that is the invention of this or that person [illegible], but the peace of God, which surpasses all understanding."

[7.] Bonhoeffer quotes Goethe's "Wanderer's Night Song" with slight variation; cf. the Longfellow translation in Goethe, *Selected Poems*, vol. 1 of the *Collected Works*, 58–59.

[8.] Deleted: "despondency."

[9.] Augustine, *Confessions* (1.1), 3; see 3/2, ed. note 3.

All humanity is like the Jew Ahasuerus who, according to the old legend,
536 blasphemed God and must now spend his life in eternal wandering, with no home, no rest, as an eternal outcast.[10]

With elementary force, however, the call for peace again and again breaks[11] out among humanity, first powerfully and mightily in the ancient prophets,[12] and now most recently again in the longing for world peace everywhere. But as beautiful and well-intentioned as all these hopes are, they fail to recognize that the peace we need is the peace that comes down to us from eternity, the peace of God with humanity, with every individual among us. As long as you do not know this peace, everything else is merely the semblance of peace, and you have not yet understood the depths of your own outcast life. Be reconciled with God, the New Testament calls out to us,[13] ask for God's peace for yourselves and for the world. Your life strives for unity, for harmony; where else can you find it but in God's peace? Your life is tormented by anxiety and restlessness; where else can it be calmed but in God's eternal peace?

If someone were to ask what exactly this peace is, I could only point to the transitory as a symbol of the intransitory.[14] Are you familiar with the peace of a sleeping child? With the peace a man finds far from all passion, when he looks into the eyes of his beloved wife? The peace the friend finds when he looks into the eyes of a loyal friend? The peace a son finds in the arms of his mother? The peace on many a mature countenance shortly before death? Are you familiar with the peace of the evening sun and of the night that covers all things and of the eternal stars? And are you familiar with the peace of the one who died on the cross—if you are, then take that
537 as a transitory sign, as a weak symbol of the peace of God. Having peace means feeling supported, loved, protected, means being able to be quiet, completely quiet; having peace with another person means being able to

---

[10.] Unlike anti-Semitic literature after the mid-nineteenth century, Bonhoeffer does not identify the legendary figure of Ahasuerus with the Jewish people. [The German editor means that in Bonhoeffer's text Ahasuerus is a symbol of "all humanity" and not of the Jewish people alone.—CG] He adopts the metaphor from the Romantic literary tradition; cf. Goethe's fragment "Der ewige Jude" (The eternal Jew), published posthumously in 1836, and his reference to the Ahasuerus legend in Goethe, *From My Life: Poetry and Truth, parts 1–3,* vol. 4 of *Collected Works,* 467–68.

[11.] Written above: "forces its way."

[12.] Cf. Bonhoeffer's first Barcelona lecture, 2/1.

[13.] 2 Cor. 5:20; deleted: "and comprehend that the peace God makes with you is a peace that surpasses all understanding."

[14.] Goethe, *Faust* II, 305 (part 2, act 5, 12104–5): "All that is transitory is only a symbol."

count with absolute certainty on that person's loyalty,[15] means being absolutely one with that person, means knowing oneself to be forgiven by that person. Having peace means having a home amid the restlessness of the world, means having solid ground beneath one's feet; and though the waves foam and rage ever so wildly, they can no longer rob me of my peace; my peace has made me free of the world, has made me strong against the world and ready for the other world. That we are to have such peace with God, however, is something transcending all human comprehension, all human understanding. The peace of God, however, is a peace that surpasses all understanding. Who can comprehend that with us, precisely with every one of us, we who have fallen away from God countless times, who are like a leaf blown away by the wind, like a grain of sand on the shore, one of many, one like all the rest, replaceable like every other part of the powerful machine—that God has made peace with each of us? That God says to each of us, Leave the rush and anxiety and restlessness of the world, come to me and to my peace. Give me your tormented, outcast heart, and I will heal your wounds and give your heart the peace of God. Come to me, all you that are weary and are carrying heavy burdens, and I will give you rest, and you will find rest for your souls.[16]

The peace of God is God's loyalty despite our own disloyalty. In the peace of God we are secure, protected, and loved. Admittedly, God does not completely eliminate our care, our responsibility, our unrest, but behind all this bustle and worry, the divine rainbow of peace has risen, and we find our lives supported and in unity with the eternal life of God. We know that the rift, of which we are always so painfully aware, is merely an ever-
new indication that God has closed that rift, has drawn us into his life just 538
as we are, as human beings of the earth,[17] as human beings with hearts and minds, in the language of the Bible: with passions and needs, caught up in the impressions of the world. The peace of God, which surpasses all understanding, protects our hearts and minds in Christ Jesus. May God tame our passions, take our thoughts and wills firmly in hand, and lead us to the peace of Jesus Christ, who spoke [the following words], who gave

[15.] Deleted: "But with regard to both human beings and God, the path to peace means—forgiveness. Only a marriage, a friendship, built on mutual forgiveness can have peace. But we are able to forgive only where we know that God forgives us; but that means that the most profound peace can obtain between human beings only when God has made peace with them."

[16.] Matt. 11:28–29.

[17.] Concerning the earthbound nature of human beings, see 2/3 and 3/12, pp. 530–31.

himself to us in that night of Golgotha: Peace I leave with you; my peace I give to you. I do not give to you as the world gives. Do not let your hearts be troubled, and do not let them be afraid.[18] The peace of God, however, is greater than anything we can say about it; it stands above all human will and thought, has reconciled the world, binding what was sundered, healing what was wounded, preserving our hearts and minds in Christ Jesus.

My dear friends, what greater wish could my heart have for you today, when I speak to you for the last time from this pulpit, than that this peace come upon you, move in with you, and dwell with you; that God make you into people of his own great peace, that you may rest in God in the midst of all the bustle of things in this world; that this peace clarify and prepare your souls that they themselves may radiate something of the brilliance and purity of the peace God puts into our hearts, radiate it into other outcast souls, so that each brings to the other this divine peace, friend to friend, spouse to spouse, mother to child. Though we still find ourselves in the midst of all the unrest of life, and though it is only in the quiet hours of our souls that we do receive, again and again, the peace of God, one day God will establish a kingdom in which peace itself rules, an eternal kingdom of peace, not of this world, but of the world from which that peace comes; and all who have already lived in the peace of God here, all whose lives are rooted in eternity will be invited to this kingdom. From within this eternal
539 kingdom, however, a ray of peace is shining through the clouds, and in this ray we already sense this kingdom. May this ray shine upon us, shine into us; may the peace of God descend upon you and keep your hearts and minds in Christ Jesus and lead you to the eternal kingdom.

My dear friends, the hour of my departure from your midst has arrived. A whole year of ministry in your congregation is now behind me, a year in which I wanted to give as much as I could. It was the first year in the practice of my ministry, and in it I came to sense all the beauty and all the seriousness of my vocation. Having to speak about God is indeed a great thing when one yet knows that with human words one can at best merely touch the hem of God's holy garment,[19] and that it is God's grace when God initiates something to his own glory. Many a time I have come to the pulpit with an anxious heart. Would I find the right words? In such cases, the message of God's peace has always helped, the peace that surpasses all understanding and works and creates in its own free way.[20] I hardly need

[18.] John 14:27.

[19.] [Cf. Matt. 9:20.—CG]

[20.] Here Bonhoeffer is alluding to the situation prior to the sermon; Phil. 4:7 is generally used as a vow following the sermon.

to tell you that I will never forget this congregation in which I have had such experiences, and that I am moved today by enormous gratitude for the past year. I owe it first of all to Pastor Olbricht that I was permitted to experience this year through him and with him; I would like to thank him and all of you for all the love, trust, cordiality, and loyal friendship you have bestowed upon me during this year, gifts that will make me wealthy for a lifetime. And though a different field of work now beckons me away from you, please accept as a symbol of our whole life, which is always a sojourning, my favorite verse, a verse with which I say farewell to you and which I have already cited several times here for you:

> Each day tells the other
> my life is but a journey
> to great and endless life. . . .[21]

19. Notes for a Young Man[1] 540

Two people met once on a country road. They didn't know each other. One had already traveled that way once before, not long before; the other didn't know where the road led. They understood each other without speaking; what[2] was then more natural than that they continued on together, the one who seemed to ask about the way, and the other who was so glad to be taking that road again. They continued along together—how long? only until the road led the one away from the side of the other?—or perhaps for a long time yet, a long time, perhaps without them even realizing it?

[21.] Beginning of the final verse of Gerhard Tersteegen's 1745 hymn, "Nun sich der Tag geendet" (Now the day is done) (*EKG*, no. 367); see 3/19, ed. note 3. A note inserted into the sermon manuscript contains the following addendum: "The machines roar and blare, the pulse of the world hammers away, wildly and frighteningly, cold passions have been aroused like the sea by a storm, humanity is like a severely ill person whose feverish eyes and hands, whose broken voice, utter but one greedy cry: business and world and advancement in the world. The world is without peace [*friedlos*], and our individual lives are without peace." Cf. also 3/7, ed. note 4, as well as 3/13, p. 534 and ed. note 4.

[1.] *NL*, A 21,20; handwritten draft, untitled; handwritten entry from Bethge: "Autumn 28, Spain paper"; the middle section uses different paper. Previously published in *PAM* 1:132–37. Most likely a fragment from Barcelona for a young man ("my dear young man," "but you are growing up"), presumably for his student and charge Karl-Heinz Köttgen.

[2.] Written above: "are words really needed?"

Along the way, one of them asks: Where is our journey taking us? The other: Each day tells the other . . .[3]

On Joy

You possess a fortunate talent, and I believe you can be glad. Be glad as much as you can; joy makes us strong, for it comes into us as a hand full of light from eternity. Being genuinely glad means seeing God in everything,
541 and his love, wherever things look cheerful and friendly but also wherever things are not quite as you would like them to be; and that is not very easy. Be glad as much as you can.

On Seriousness
On Growing — Difficult Hours
On Purity — On Being Alone
On Evil — On Prayer

Remaining Pure and Maturing[4]

You have no doubt seen a rock crystal before, or a clear mountain lake through whose water one can see all the way to the bottom. We call such things pure because light can penetrate and shine through the crystal, through the water. We call people pure if the light of God penetrates and shines through their entire being. Do you believe it is good to be pure? But do you also know that it is good to be mature? Remaining pure and becoming mature. . . . You already understand this now, and you will come to understand it ever more and ever more deeply. You know well that life is always trying to soil us, trying to make us base and common, and that it also often succeeds in doing this. You know that there are bad friends who drag sacred and serious things down into the dirt, friends who want you to hang out with them. They are in danger of losing the most precious gift human beings have, purity. Being pure means being clear, being upright, means taking control of one's thoughts so they cannot run away from us. Purity of body is also closely related to purity of the heart. One must take joy in purity; indeed, one must have a passion for what is pure so that one cannot

[3.] Ps. 19:3 [NRSV: v. 2]. Allusion to the final verse of Tersteegen's evening hymn that Bonhoeffer mentions as his "favorite verse" in his farewell sermon in Barcelona (see 3/18, p. 551, and ed. note 21 for that sermon). Life as a sojourn (cf. *LPP*, 142, where the verse is quoted) and attuning one's heart to what is eternal (*LPP*, 168–69) remain key eschatological images for Bonhoeffer.

[4.] "Remaining pure and maturing, that is the highest and richest life art," a key motif in the German Youth Movement; cf. Flex, *Der Wanderer zwischen beiden Welten*, 216.

be dragged down into the muck. Remaining pure means remaining a child, even after you have become a man. My dear young man, strengthen your 542
yearning for purity. Jesus says: Blessed are . . .[5]

Work

You believe that work is an unpleasant change from play; but you are growing up and must come to understand that we work for ourselves, not for someone else. Work is the means through which people make something out of themselves. Every work should basically be work on yourself. Do you know that in prison the most terrible punishment is for a prisoner to be deprived of work? Work gets you through difficult hours, comforts you and calms you; work is the last thing a sinking person can cling to. Woe to those who have not learned to work; be grateful to those who taught it to you.

Be hard toward oneself, gentle *toward* others; think of Jesus. Truth is from God; God loves truth. If you speak what is false, you are against God. Be clear and true. The struggle against untruth is difficult, and most people succumb; be better than most of those others and be victorious!

You know the picture of the knight with the defiant expression, proceeding well armed through a dark valley between death and the devil toward a bright castle of the sun. Be like this knight, who is intent on attaining life and purity, who takes up the battle against the powers of darkness, whose weapons[6]

Whoever would become a whole man must have been a whole child, a 543
whole boy. Everything you are, be totally; everything you do, do totally. Being a boy means being a young sculptor who is beginning to shape the image of his inner person, of his heart, who is chiseling the unhewn stone and giving it the shape he sees before him, a sculptor who is shaping himself. Before everyone there stands an image . . . take the chisel and begin cutting, even if it hurts.[7]

[5.] Matt. 5:8: "Blessed are the pure in heart, for they will see God." Concerning the previous sentence about remaining a child, cf. Matt. 18:2–3 and parallels: "Unless you change and become like children, you will never enter the kingdom of heaven." This notion, too, one that profoundly influenced the educated German middle class since the time of Schleiermacher (cf. *Christmas Eve*, 36, 53–55, 85–86), occurs repeatedly in connection with the German Youth Movement (see ed. note 4), including in connection with the experience of World War I. Cf. Stickelberger-Eder, *Aufbruch 1914*, 124–26, 158, 161, and 168.

[6.] This section of the text breaks off here. Albrecht Dürer's 1513 copper engraving *Knight, Death, and the Devil*, to which Bonhoeffer is alluding, was one of the most popular picture motifs in the middle-class German household.

[7.] Cf. the statement attributed to Michelangelo: "Sculptor God, begin! I am the stone," in Conrad Ferdinand Meyer's poem "In der Sistina," *Sämtliche Werke*, 1:250.

Being a boy means being a young smith who with all his energy forges the glowing iron; your heart is still malleable and glowing and soft. Don't miss the opportunity! Tomorrow may be too late! Forge the iron as long as it is hot. Be a strong boy against yourself.

You need a friend.[8] Seek him among your peers. If you want to have a friend and want to be a good friend yourself, you must be able to sacrifice, sacrifice some of your own will, some of your own wishes. You must be able to forgive, forgive when your friend does something harsh to you, when he hurts your feelings. You must be able to love your friend just as he is, with all his faults, to bear him up and support him with your love. You must be able to be loyal, in the face of gossip by those who like to blab, those who are envious, hateful, to be loyal to your friend no matter what. If you want to have a friend, you must be able to pray for him, to present his life along with your own before God and ask God to help your friendship, for your friend will need that. Only if your friendship has its basis in God can you call it "friendship."

You must be able to trust your friend; you must be able to confide in him completely, in both happy and difficult times. He will participate in your happiness and in your pain, will be glad with you and help you bear the bur-
544 dens that are too heavy for you. The one lives the life of the other, though you should both live your lives in God; *then you will be* friends.

Look people in the eye and you will know what they are about. Take note of how people laugh. Listen to how people speak about their parents. Listen to how they speak of God.

On Being Alone[9]

Every day, put a few minutes aside to be alone, and think about the coming day or the day that has just passed, about the people you have met. Also think about yourself and about what you are lacking. But never brood excessively by yourself; rather let the One who also knows your secrets participate in your solitude. Each of us has things we never utter, things we conceal like a beloved treasure within our solitude. Only God knows them; hence draw God into your solitude.

[8.] The theme of friendship remained decisive for Bonhoeffer till the end; cf. the poem "The Friend" (*LPP*, 388–91).

[9.] This theme, too, remains decisive; cf. "The Day Alone," in *Life Together*, *DBWE* 5:81–92.

On Prayer

The power of a human being is prayer. Accustom yourself to prayer already as a young boy. Prayer is drawing breath from God; prayer means surrendering and consecrating one's life to God; prayer means confiding in God. When you lie down to sleep in the evening, fold your hands and become quiet within and call on God to come to you, and then tell God how you have spent the day, whether it was sanctified or whether it tainted you, whether you spent it in love or anger, in peace or hatred, in good and evil, in purity and dirt. And then pray for your soul that God make it holy and pure; be ashamed of evil and rejoice in the good. Then before God's eyes mention the names of those who love you; thank God for giving you your mother and father, for giving you friends who love you, and ask God to abide with them all.

And if sometime you have something you don't want to confide in any- 545
one, then know that God does, after all, see everything and know everything, and go to him and pour out your restless heart to him at night, when everything is quiet and is sleeping, and God will give you rest. My dear boy, we have sometimes spoken about praying; do not forget it and don't be led astray. Through prayer you will become strong; *you* will become *a man.*

Tears are one of the most sublime things a person has. Hence don't waste them.

The beginning, the end.[10] Reverence.

20. Homily for the Children's Service, Berlin (?), Remembrance Sunday, November 24, 1929 (?)[1]

Have you ever considered that all the living things God created, the small bug, the butterfly, and the large animals, though also the beautiful flowers in the meadow and the tall trees in the forest, all actually have the same

---

[10.] Perhaps an allusion to the headstone inscription of Fritz Reuter: "The beginning, the end, O Lord, they are yours, the span between them, life, was mine. And if I was lost in the darkness, and didn't know where I was, with you, Lord, there is clarity, and light is your house." Cf. Meyer-Bothling, "Fritz Reuters 'Lowising,'" 218. [*Lowising* is the Low German nickname version of Luise, the name of Reuter's wife.—CG] Reuter, the nineteenth-century writer, was one of the authors whose work was read aloud during the evening readings in the Bonhoeffer family. Hence Bonhoeffer consciously cited Reuter and the inscription on his headstone even before his American diary entry of June 11, 1939 (*DBW* 15 [1/137], p. 219); cf. Bunners, *Fritz Reuter und der Protestantismus,* 67–70.

[1.] *NL,* A 21,18 a, pp. 5–8; handwritten. In *Nachlaß Dietrich Bonhoeffer,* 20, this manuscript is incorrectly viewed as a variant of the address in Barcelona (see 3/16, ed. note 1);

fate as we human beings do? Look, what is the same for everything, from
546 the smallest bird to human beings, is that we must all die, all of us, that we are able to live for only a short period of time on this earth and then we die and are buried; then we lie in the earth and become earth again ourselves. You and I and our parents and our brothers and sisters, everyone, all of us. Do any of you know what God said to Adam after expelling him from paradise and driving him out into the desolate earth? You were taken from the earth—(do you remember how human beings were made?)—and to the earth you shall return.[2] And that means that "you and your children and your children's children, you must all die one day," and that is no different for animals and plants. Of course, some trees live to be many hundreds of years old, but one day their strength, too, is gone, and they must die. Just why this is, only God knows, for God wanted it that way.

Look, children, nothing makes us sadder than for our dear father or mother or brother or sister or a good friend to die. All we can do is be sad, on and on, and cry, and we cannot be comforted. Indeed, why are we really so sad? Because we will no longer see our dear and good mother or father, or hear their voice, their place at the table will be empty, and in the evening we will have to pray all by ourselves in our bed. Then not only the children but the adults, too, are sad and weep. And when you go out into the street today, you will see many, many people with sad faces who are thinking today of their dear, deceased mothers, fathers, or children. A poor, sad woman with two small children goes to visit a grave; their father has died and left them in great poverty. Now the small children must go to work and earn money with their mother, and often they have very little to eat, and then the children cry, and the mother cries as well because the children are hungry and no one helps. And then the mother often asks God, "Why have you done this?" And once she even said, "Dear God, you will not help us anymore, and we are falling into ever more dire circumstances, so we don't
547 want to hear anything about you anymore." And then she cries on, for now she has lost the last thing she had, her God. Look, this poor woman had not heard the message we just heard: "God will wipe away every tear from their eyes."[3]

---

given the allusion to cemetery visits on this day (see below, "when you go out into the street today"), this address must have been delivered in Germany, probably on Remembrance Sunday, November 24, 1929, in the Berlin-Grunewald congregation (cf. also 1/114.2, p. 221).

[2.] Gen. 3:19.

[3.] Rev. 7:17; 21:4.

Let me tell you a bit about the very first Christians. Before there were many Christians, they were so weak that the Romans really persecuted them. The Christians built caves beneath the earth and held their services there so they would not be seen. Sometimes, though, some were caught, and then they either had to say that they no longer believed in their God and in their Lord Christ or they had to fight wild animals before the entire population and, though innocent,[4] be torn to pieces and killed. You see, Christians much preferred to die than to deny their dear God; indeed, they were even glad that they might die, for they knew that soon all their cares and worries would be over, and that they would soon be in heaven, where there are no more tears, but rather nothing but joy. So they sang beautiful songs of faith about their glorious hope in God and heaven; then the cages were opened, and the wild animals rushed in and tore them to pieces. All the other Christians, however, sang praises to God and thanked him for having given them men who were so brave in the face of death, and they returned home with glad hearts, for the others were, after all, now with God. But the Romans who saw these men and women were quite puzzled by them. And you know, even a few years ago, German pastors were shot to death by godless people in Russia[5] because they would not stop telling their congregations about God and about eternal life in heaven. They were held captive for months and received almost nothing to eat; women and 548
children were dragged off, but they all remained joyful in their hope in God and in his promises. All these men died gladly, for they had had much sorrow here on earth and now could finally get to God. When they were tormented and harassed, they did not cry, for they knew that this torment would only last a short while and that in heaven everything would be much more beautiful. They said, "If God sends us illness or hunger or war, it's because God is testing us to see whether our faith is firm, to see that we do not say, 'I don't want to have anything more to do with you,' but rather hold fast to God's promise that in heaven he will wash away the tears from our eyes and comfort us."[6]

They didn't complain and didn't cry, and when God took someone from their family, they were glad that that person was now much better taken

[4.] Uncertain reading.

[5.] Allusion to the "Baltic martyrs" of 1918–19. The best known among the thirty-two murdered pastors was Prof. Traugott Hahn, who was shot to death in Dorpat on January 14, 1919, together with the Russian Orthodox bishop Platon. Cf. Schabert, *Baltisches Märtyrerbuch*. These events strongly influenced anticommunist sentiment in the Protestant church during the Weimar Republic.

[6.] Deleted: "Just think, God has sent us a dear son, our Lord Jesus Christ, who was nailed to a cross for us, must we not then . . . to him."

care of with God. Just think, God gave his son to us human beings, and we want to complain when God takes one of us? "Just as God raised his own son, so also will God raise us." These are the words a good and only son wrote to comfort his parents in the hour of his death in a field hospital.

549 **21. Catechesis in the Second Theological Examination on the Fifth Petition of the Lord's Prayer, Berlin, June 29, 1930**[1]

Bibliography:[2]

H. Seebold, *Ausführliche Erklärung des kleinen Katechismus,* 1858.

J. Nissen, *Unterredungen über den kleinen Katechismus Luthers,* 1859.

J. Kolbe, *Der kleine Katechismus Luthers,* 1898.

A. Eckert, *Der Katechismusstoff des Konfirmandenunterrichts III.–V. Hauptstück,* 1905.

O. Hardeland, *Zweiundfünfzig Konfirmandenstunden,* 1910.

Meditation

An examination of the possibility of explaining the concept of debt or sin [Schuld][3] to children will determine whether they are capable in the larger sense of understanding the Christian message, for it is precisely here that one finds the heart of Christian piety. If children by nature prove to be inaccessible here, then all Christian instruction during the period of childhood would be pointless. The center of the gospel cannot be shifted with regard to the level of maturity of those to whom it is preached. The center of all proclamation is and remains the reconciliation that has occurred through Christ in the cross and resurrection. Only the path along which one leads

[1.] *NL,* D 11 (52/53); typewritten with handwritten title page: "Catechesis on the Fifth Petition of the Lord's Prayer. Dietrich Bonhoeffer," from the personal file. Concerning the context, see 1/116, ed. note 2; the catechism was given on June 29, 1930, in the children's service of the Grunewald congregation. The written version was evaluated by Paul Fahland (as reader; see 1/121.3), the trial instruction by Max Diestel (ibid.), though the latter apparently was not personally present and drew rather from the evaluation by Karl Meumann (see 1/122). As was already the case in the first examination (see *DBWE* 9 [1/114], pp. 185–86), the differences in the evaluations are significant. In the margins of the manuscript version of the catechesis, the reader made profuse use of the query "?" not all of which are noted here. As was customary at the time, Bonhoeffer also formulated the anticipated answers of the children; on the typewritten page these answers are found next to the questions, whereas here they are entered in italics at the end of each question.

[2.] [The first three books are on Luther's Small Catechism, and the other two are practical examples; titles are translated in the bibliography.—CG]

[3.] [The word *Schuld,* used in the German version of the fifth petition of the Lord's Prayer, has a range of meanings including debt, sin, guilt, (also offense, obligation), and

people to that reconciliation can vary. In the following catechesis, I will try
to find a path that children can travel and which leads to the main point 550
without displacing the center. In dealing with the fifth petition, one cannot simply presuppose that children already know what sin is, or, for example, that their conscience already informs them of it. A person's conscience, too, must be sharpened and directed, and the serious nature of guilt [Schuld] before God is not immediately clear to most children without further explanation. This seriousness would be the first thing one must explain to children; only then can they understand how great and necessary a thing the forgiveness of sin is, and then, in the manner of the unforgiving servant, the human being becomes a deterrent example and one's own forgiveness becomes a personal task. In this way, the connection between "forgive us our sins" and "as we also have forgiven those who have sinned against us" becomes unmistakably clear. There is no need to present to children the various explications this connection has undergone even by Luther. Here the simple exposition of the Small Catechism remains exemplary and substantively adequate. A discussion of the fifth petition in confirmation class, something one generally will undertake only when one has come to know the children better, will in such cases enjoy a considerable advantage over a catechesis such as the present one, insofar as one can then focus on concrete examples from the children's own lives.

Catechesis

Let's talk about the fifth petition of the Lord's Prayer.

What does it say? *And forgive us our debt [Schuld], as we also have forgiven our debtors [Schuldiger].*

Let's start with something completely external. What word begins the fifth petition?[4] *The word "and."*

When do we use the word "and"? *When we want to connect two thoughts together.*

What can we conclude from the fact that the fifth petition begins with 551
"and"? *We can conclude that the fifth petition is somehow connected with what comes before it.*

---

all three are used by Bonhoeffer in the catechism. The translation accordingly varies depending on the emphasis, and the word *Schuld* is given occasionally in brackets to indicate the consistency of the term. (When "guilt" is used, it is important to remember that the German *Schuld* refers to an objective reality rather than primarily to a subjective emotion.) In the Small Catechism, to which Bonhoeffer refers, the fifth petition uses *Schuld*, but Luther's commentary interprets it as *Sünde*, "sin." *The Book of Concord*, 358, translates *Schuld* as "debts," while the English text on the Web site of the Evangelical Church of Germany translates it "sin."—CG]

[4.] Bonhoeffer acquired this rhetorical "peg" from Nissen, *Unterredungen*, 623.

So we must try to understand the context in which the fifth petition occurs in the Lord's Prayer. What are we asking in the first petition? *That God's name be sanctified.*

What are we asking in the second petition? *That the kingdom of God come.*

What are we asking in the third petition? *That God's will be done.*

The first three petitions all have one word in common. What is that word? *The word "your."*

To whom does this "your" refer? *It refers to God.*

So about whom do we primarily think when we speak the first three petitions? *We think above all about God and his work.*

This is very important. Jesus tells us that when you want to pray to God, think first of all about God. Leave yourselves completely aside for a moment and see how much more important it is that we first learn to say: your name, your kingdom, your will. First you, and again you. Your name and not mine, your will and not mine. Only those who can pray in this way may then also come before God with other petitions. Now let's compare the petitions that follow. What are we asking from God in the fourth petition? *Our daily bread.*

About whom does Jesus now let us think in our prayer? *About ourselves.*

Which word shows us this? *The word "our."*

In which other petitions do the words "us" or "our" occur? *Our daily bread, our debt, do not bring us into temptation, rescue us from evil.*

So here we have a clear difference. Whereas at the beginning we always say "your," now after we have spoken this "your" from the bottom of our hearts we say "our." Now we are permitted to come to God with our own problems and needs. Just think about what it means to be able to come before God with our cares, the God who did, after all, create the world and all of us, the God who is infinitely great and mighty, and that God now agrees to accept our cares and worries and to listen to us when we approach him. What kind of concerns do we present to God in the fourth petition? *The concern for eating and drinking.*

552 What do eating and drinking mean for us? *They are absolutely necessary for our bodies.*

Why must we first ask God for them?[5] *Because it is God who makes the things grow and flourish that we need to eat and drink.*

Jesus says that God takes care of your bodies as well, and that you should at least have the bare necessity, bread. There is certainly something amiss

[5.] The reader underlined "why" and "for them."

in human society and the world when among Christian peoples there are those who have no daily bread! We said that the petition for daily bread is connected to the fifth petition by an "and," so there must be some connection between the two. Let's try to understand that connection now. Which concern do we bring before God in the fifth petition? *The petition that God forgive our sin.*

To which part of our whole being does the fourth petition refer? *To our body.*

To which part of our whole being does the fifth petition refer? *To our soul.*

So why does Jesus have us ask for forgiveness of our sins for our soul? *Because he believes it is important for our soul.*

Now we understand the connection between the fourth and the fifth petitions. What are we asking again in the fourth petition? *That which is necessary for our body.*

What are we asking in the fifth petition? *That which is necessary for our soul.*

This is why[6] these two petitions are connected by the little word "and." In the Lord's Prayer, the petitions are not just listed in some random order; rather the one belongs to the other, and only that way do we really understand it.

We see now that when Jesus has us ask for the forgiveness of our sin immediately after asking for our daily bread, he must have meant that this forgiveness represents something that is especially necessary for our soul, indeed, as necessary as bread is for our body. What happens when the body 553
gets no bread, nothing to eat? *The body dies.*

So the bread we petition from God is indeed that necessary. Life and death depend on it. So what will probably happen to the soul if its sin is not forgiven? *It will also die.*

And what will happen if its sin is forgiven? *It will live.*

So on what do its life and death depend? *On whether its sin is forgiven.*

Although this last point is probably correct as we have just described it, these are still merely our own thoughts on the matter and conclusions we have drawn. We have not yet really understood what it means to say[7] that the most necessary thing for the soul is the forgiveness of its sin, indeed, that the soul must die if its sin is not forgiven. There are many people today, and you probably know some, who have no idea that the soul, too, needs

[6.] The reader underlined this word and added the marginal remark "[illegible]?"

[7.] The reader marked the entire paragraph from this point forward and added the query "?"

something to stay alive, people who believe that the soul just takes care of itself somehow and that the main thing is for us to eat and drink and live well and that we have only a few obligations. But there are others who do indeed know that the soul, too, needs something to stay alive; it's just that they usually don't know what that is, and so they try to cultivate and keep their soul active in various ways. How do most people try to do this? *They read books, have discussions, go to the theater, to concerts, go on trips.*

And what do they hope to gain by doing these things? *They believe they are keeping their soul active and giving it what it needs most.*

And what is the disposition of the soul of people who believe they have everything they need? *Satisfied, happy.*

And so many people believe that the main thing is to satisfy their souls in the ways you have just described. And certainly it is often marvelous to read
554 a good book or to hear a beautiful concert. We wouldn't argue with that at all. But what would Jesus say to those who believe it is the most important thing of all? *He would say that they have not yet understood what the most important thing is.*

What is for Jesus the most important petition for the soul in the Lord's Prayer? *The petition that its debt*[8] *be forgiven.*

Of course, this is something quite different from what the people about whom we spoke earlier want and probably also quite different from what we ourselves have thought until now. But because Jesus said it, it is true, and for that reason we must try to understand it and to integrate it into our own lives if we want to live the way Jesus wants us to. Whom should we ask to forgive our debt? *We should ask God.*

And so who will grant us that which is the most important thing for us? *God will grant it to us.*

With whom must we thus especially remain in community if our soul is not to die? *With God.*

So the most important thing for people is thus that they come together with God and abide with God. Only God can give us what is most important for us. We cannot acquire it for ourselves; if we remain alone, we will not receive it. Only God, who made the soul, knows what it needs, and God alone is able to give it to the soul. That is the first thing we must remember. When we pray the Lord's Prayer in the evening at home or on Sundays in church, we are always speaking a confession when we speak the words "and forgive us our debt." What kind of confession? *A confession that we ourselves somehow have debt.*

[8.] [Bonhoeffer's argument that follows requires that *Schuld* be translated "debt" in this section.—CG]

To whom do we make this confession? *We make it to God.*

To whom are we thereby indebted? *We are indebted to God.*

Debt—this is a commonly used word; you have heard it often in church and in religious instruction. And precisely because it is so commonly used, it has become so hackneyed and worn out that we often use it as if it were just another word, a word like all others. Like a sword whose edge has
become dull. And[9] yet the serious nature of this notion has regenerated 555
and strengthened Christianity ever anew whenever it has seemed to become weary and weak. We need only think of Augustine or Luther, and even today there are again those[10] who can show us what this word is about, those who are whetting the sword once again. And if we do not understand this word again to be as sharp as it really is, then we have not understood it at all. All of you know words associated with debt. Name a few for me! *Debts, owing [schuldig]*[11] *excuse [entschuldigen].*

Let's look at the word debts. What does it mean if people have debts to others? *It means they still must give them something.*

Why must they still give them something? *Because it belongs to the others.*

What can I demand of those who owe me something? *I can demand that they return it to me.*

So I can demand it back; I have a claim to it because it belongs to me. What can happen if people don't pay their debts? *They can be punished.*

Then one says, "They are guilty," and punishes them because they have not returned something that belongs to someone else. That's the way it is among people. But what will likely happen if people do not give God what belongs to him? What must it mean for people to be indebted to God? *It must mean that people have something that belongs to God but do not return it.*

Now, admittedly we must consider whether it's even possible for human beings to have something that belongs to God. What we have does, after all, doubtless belong to us, and we can do with it as we please; we don't need to give God any part of it. Or what might there be that we all have and which nevertheless none of us have given ourselves? *We have not given ourselves life.*

Who gave us life? *God gave us our life.* 556

God gave life to our parents and through them to us. So to whom does our life belong? *It belongs to God.*

[9.] The reader marked the manuscript from here to the expression "who show us" and added the query "?"

[10.] Cf. Augustine, *Confessions*; Luther, esp. the Ninety-five Theses. Contemporary persons Bonhoeffer is considering probably include esp. Holl, perhaps also Barth and his commentary on Romans.

[11.] [Literally "being in debt." It also means "guilty." Bonhoeffer plays on the several nuances of the German word.—CG]

Now, instead of "life," we can also say "we ourselves." We ourselves belong to God. We are completely mistaken if we believe that we belong to ourselves. Throughout our lives, as long as we exist, we are God's possession. Now what follows from the fact that our life belongs to God? *It follows that we must return it to God, that we owe it to God.*

Now tell me everything that belongs to our life! *Our time (every day, every moment), our soul with its thoughts and wishes and fantasies, our body with all its members.*

All that belongs to life and so is God's property. Consider what it means to conduct our life in every moment as if it belonged to God, to guide our thoughts, rein in our wishes, keep our fantasy in check such that God remains Lord of them. Take very seriously the notion that our body, too, belongs to God. What should our eyes see and not see? What should our ears hear and not hear? Where should our feet lead us and not lead us? What should our hands grasp and not grasp, that is, if all this takes place before God's eyes?[12] Yes, the notion that we belong to God is meant just this simply and literally. There is no avoiding it and there are no exceptions. Everything is completely clear and definite, everything completely or not at all. It is also completely serious precisely because it is a matter of God, who allows none of his possessions to be purloined in any fashion; just think, the God who has power over our life in eternity. And now we go a step further. What must happen if people withhold from God something that belongs to him? *God's punishment must follow.*

From what disposition of God does this punishment emerge? *From God's anger.*

God's anger and God's punishment: These are the two frightening words
557 standing over those people who do not give their lives to God. God can genuinely become angry and mete out punishment; God is, after all, the holy God who wants to rule and govern alone and who wants human beings as children and not as disobedient rebels. The most fearful punishment from the angry God, however, is to be cast out by God to eternal death. This applies to all human beings, young and old. And even if you are still young, you must already realize today what a serious thing life is; for what can people expect if in their lives they have robbed God of something that belongs to God? *They can expect to be cast out into eternal death.*

What does the Lord's Prayer call the relationship such people have with God? *A relationship of debt.*

People are indebted to God, but why is all human debt a debt to God? *Because our life belongs to God alone.*

[12.] Underlined by the reader and marked with "?"

Hence debt[13] is the basis of the eternal death of the soul. Debt destroys the soul because it sunders community with God, because it makes God angry. Which word does Luther use in his explanation instead of debt? *Sins.*

Is the word "sins" singular or plural? *Plural.*

Is the word "debt" in the Lord's Prayer singular or plural? *Singular.*

What can we conclude from this? *That there are many sins, but only one debt.*

What does Luther say about our many sins? *"For we daily sin much."*[14] Here he is referring to all the individual bad deeds we do. So what is then our debt? *Something that is one time only.*

It cannot be an individual bad deed in our life, for then it would be called sin. Debt must concern one's entire life. So what is debt? *Debt is that we do not return our entire life to God.*

Debt is thus disobedience toward God in the broader sense, which makes God angry. Once we have understood what debt toward God is, however, we
hear within ourselves an unmistakable voice telling each of us that we our- 558
selves carry this debt around with us, that we ourselves have become guilty before God. What do we call this voice? *We call it conscience.*

In our conscience, we hear God talking with us in two ways. How does God speak prior to a bad deed? *God warns us.*

How does God speak after a bad deed? *God accuses us.*

Now God is angry; now we know with complete certainty that God can only cast us out, for God is just and wants what belongs to himself. And now the hours come in which we accuse ourselves. We are ashamed of ourselves, we detest ourselves, and we are afraid of God's anger and punishment. And now all the bad pictures and words rise up in us again, pursue us, do not let us go, and threaten and threaten us. Nothing can be put right again; everything remains as it was done. Where will all this lead? God gave you your life, your eyes, your hands, your thoughts, and you have abused them, have seen bad things, your hands have meddled in unjust affairs, you have had bad wishes and thoughts. Now God is distant and is angry with you, angry because your own sin now stands between you and God. Only under one condition can our soul be preserved from anger and death. What is that condition? *The condition that our sin be cleared away.*

[13.] [Here the argument highlights the "sin" dimension in the meaning of *Schuld.* —CG]

[14.] Luther, Small Catechism, explanation of the fifth petition (*Book of Concord*, 358).

So what should we try to attain with all our power? *To have our sin cleared away.*

For how must people be in order to receive new life from God? *They must be guiltless.*

In the Bible, God says, "You shall be holy, for I am holy."[15] Unholy people cannot live in community with God, for they are carrying guilt around with them; evil sticks tightly to them.

All of you know students from your classes at school who can do certain things particularly well. Some can jump well, others are especially strong, still others play the piano well, and yet another has the best grades in the class. What wish arises in you when you think of such students? *We would like*
559 *to do something as well as they do and to become good friends with them.*

We notice, then, that there is a big distance between us and the others. And how might we try to overcome this distance? *By trying to become similar to the others by also doing something particularly well.*

Now recall those hours in which, for example, you heard how Luther appeared at the Diet of Worms, or how joyfully martyrs went to their deaths.[16] What have we ourselves probably wished for many times? *That we might have just as much courage and faith as they.*

And when we now encounter Jesus and hear about his words and deeds, we are overcome by so much purity and holiness and love. We would probably like to be together with him always, and yet we know that an enormous chasm separates us from him and that we can overcome this chasm only if we ourselves are as holy, as pure, and as loving as he was. We hear God's own voice speaking in him: You shall be holy, for I am holy. And along with this voice, we recognize that we are not holy, but rather bear guilt, and that this guilt[17] must be removed from us if we are to come together with Jesus. But try as we may, we cannot ourselves undo what is already done; we cannot bridge the gap separating us from Christ and from God. Think about your life at home. We get into an argument about one thing or another, and during the argument we say something nasty to our mother or brother. We have really hurt our mother's feelings and made her sad. And now what we said stands there and turns against us, and we can neither get rid of it nor gloss
560 over it. It remains done. Now we try to become reconciled with our mother

[15.] Lev. 19:2; 1 Pet. 1:15–16.

[16.] Martyrs obviously were among Bonhoeffer's favorite examples of true discipleship; cf., e.g., *DBWE* 9:483; cf. also in the present volume his address on Remembrance Sunday, 3/20, p. 557.

[17.] [In German *Schuld* has a strong objective reference, as when a jury pronounces a "guilty" verdict, rather than the emphasis on subjective emotion so often found with the English word "guilt."—CG]

in all sorts of ways and to cheer her up again. We will do anything to please her. But what we said—remains said. We cannot make it disappear from the world, and we have not a single moment of peace as long as what we said still separates us from our mother. Only one thing can help now. From whom must such reconciliation come? *It must come from our mother.*

Not until our mother takes us in her arms again and tells us she will no longer hold against us what we said but will rather forget it, only then is what we said really eliminated, only then can we be glad again precisely because our mother is glad again. Now nothing separates us any longer; we are completely back together again. And now behold, just as it happens here, so also with God. We run around with a bad conscience, tormented by our guilt, separated from God, our soul tormented and fearful; the image of Jesus is always before us, and our soul wants to flee before it because it knows that it can do nothing to change what has happened. In such distress, Jesus himself comes to us and helps us, telling us that despite everything, we may still approach God. According to Jesus's own command, with which words may we approach God? *With the words: Forgive us our debt.*

What disposition does Jesus presuppose among those who can ask God for forgiveness? *A serious disposition, remorse.*

How can we express our remorse before God?[18] *By telling God the bad things we have done.*

Hence our prayer will not always have the same form or use the same words; we must ask God for forgiveness of our own sin in our own words. Such prayer requires not a lot of talk or long speeches but rather a petition from the heart. Which story of Jesus shows us that God prefers a short, sincere prayer rather than a long, dishonest discourse? *The story of the Pharisee and the tax collector.*[19]

With what words does the tax collector come before God? *With the words, "God, be merciful to me, a sinner!"*

And with what words does Jesus conclude the story? *With the words, "This* 561
man went down to his home justified rather than the other."

What does this mean? *It means that God forgave the tax collector's sins and that now the tax collector stands guiltless before God.*

Jesus himself prompts us to pray for the forgiveness of our sins. What may we conclude from this regarding God's response to our petition? *We can believe that God will fulfill our petition.*

[18.] The reader marked this statement with "?" and accompanied it with an illegible annotation.

[19.] Luke 18:9–14.

Jesus said: You who are tormented by guilt, you may come to God and ask him for forgiveness. God will accept you again and will remove what was separating you from him, your sin, your anger, and God's punishment, and will embrace you as his precious children. In which parable does Jesus tell us about a man who pours out his heart and asks for forgiveness from his father, toward whom he has behaved badly? *In the parable of the prodigal son.*[20]

Who is the father in the parable? *God.*

Who is the son in the parable? *Human beings.*

What feeling does the father have when he sees his son coming? *Sorrow at the son's misery.*

What does the father do then? *He approaches the son, embraces him, and kisses him.*

Why does he do that? *Because he loves his son despite everything, and because he sees that his son is remorseful.*

You see, that is how God acts toward all of us. God wants only that we bring our sin before him; then God will forgive us. What does the word "forgive" mean? *It means that God will not count our debt against us but rather will remit it.*

From what disposition does God do that for us? *From pure love.*

Now consider what kind of love that is. We do nothing but bad things toward God, and yet he requites it with pure love. God himself removes the obstacle separating us from him and makes us happy again and restores our good conscience. All that was separating us has been removed. What is our
562 relationship now again with God? *We are close to God again and can approach him again.*

Now think again about the example with our mother. We know that we have acted badly toward her and have really hurt her feelings. What do we try to avoid now? *We try to avoid crossing her path.*

We don't want to encounter her. Why not? *Because we have a bad conscience.*

So what does a bad conscience do? *It separates us from our mother.*

Imagine that at just this time you are supposed to take an excursion with your class at school and need to ask your mother for permission. How do you probably feel when you approach her? *That we really don't deserve to be asking for something else now.*

Things are quite the same and even more serious in our relationship with God. What will we do everything in our power to avoid when we have a bad conscience? *We will avoid approaching God.*

[20.] Luke 15:11–32.

What do we call it when a person approaches God? *We call it praying.*

So what is it that people with a bad conscience can no longer do? *They can no longer pray.*

They can no longer come before God, cannot ask anything of God; they have a bad conscience, and that separates them from God. They expect nothing from God but anger and punishment. How does Luther express this in his explanation? "*We are worthy of nothing for which we ask, nor have we earned it. Instead we ask that God would give us all things by grace, for we daily sin much and deserve only punishment.*"[21]

What do "of nothing" and "all things" refer to? *To the first four petitions.*

So Luther believes that if we have done something bad, we are not really permitted to approach God at all with these powerful first four petitions. We don't deserve that God grant us these gifts.[22] This is why we quickly 563
want to add the fifth petition to these first four and say: Lord, we do not deserve it, we have done many bad things toward you, but forgive us what we have done that is bad and grant us what is good.

Now think about Christmas. We know full well that we have not always given our parents only joy. But now Christmas Eve comes, and on our table we find something that we have wanted for a long time and many other wonderful things as well. Sometimes in such cases we are beside ourselves with joy and feel inundated with our parents' love. And now imagine that a neighbor's child were to come by whose parents were unable to buy gifts for it, and that child were to see our gifts. What would we wish for then? *We would like to give joy to that other child as well.*

Why do we probably have this wish? *We want to share something of our own joy.*

What would you think of a child who never had such a wish? *We would think the child was hardhearted and doesn't deserve love.*

Now, if instead of anger and punishment a person experiences nothing but love from God, that person will have one great wish. What is that wish? *To share that love.*

How can one do that? *One can also show other people love instead of anger and punishment.*

How can we show that? *By not holding against people the evil they do toward us.*

How does the fifth petition in the Lord's Prayer express that? *We forgive our debtors.*

[21.] Luther, Small Catechism, explanation of the fifth petition (*Book of Concord*, 358).

[22.] The reader underlined this sentence and queried, "Does God grant us gifts in the first three petitions?"

What would we think about people who don't do that? *We would think they don't deserve God's love.*

Jesus thought so, too. In which parable does Jesus tell us about such a man? *In the parable of the unforgiving servant.*[23]

What did the servant's lord do for the man? *He forgave him a great debt.*

564 What did the servant then do? *He left, found a person who owed him money, and demanded the debt be paid; when he could not pay, the servant threw him into prison.*

What does Jesus say about this? *Jesus says that just as the man acted toward his debtor, so also would his lord now act toward him.*

What does that mean for us? *It means that if God forgives our sins, so also should we forgive our debtors their*[24] *sins against us.*

This parable represents a great threat to us if we do not act accordingly. We have all had the experience of someone doing something unjust to us. What feelings did we have then? *Feelings of anger.*

Jesus now says we should forgive that injustice because God also forgives our injustices. What kind of will within us resists forgiving that other person's evil? *We want our rights.*

We are too proud to forgive. Against what does the other's injustice toward us transgress? *Against our honor.*

We believe we owe it to ourselves to preserve and demonstrate our honor and our pride. That is why forgiving is so difficult. But do you think God has no honor? After all, we have transgressed against God's honor, and God, too, finds it difficult not to consider that honor. God is willing to pay something; it costs the death of his own Son. But now the miraculous occurs. God finds honor by giving and forgiving without end or measure. So we, too, should seek our honor by forgiving others, by thinking not of ourselves but of them. Luther once noticed how his wife, Käthe, reproached and accused some young girls, and he called to her: "Have you already prayed the Lord's Prayer?"[25] Why did Luther ask this question? *To tell his wife she should remember that all of us do a lot of bad things toward God and yet experience only good, and that she should act accordingly.*

Certainly at first it seems difficult to forgive. But it ceases to be difficult
565 when we consider how much love God pours out upon us. And it becomes

[23.] Matt. 18:23–35.

[24.] Bonhoeffer mistakenly wrote "his" instead of "their."

[25.] Bonhoeffer adopted this story from Johann Nissen, *Unterredungen*, 627.

easier each time. What does Luther say about this in his explanation? *"So, on the other hand, we, too, truly want to forgive heartily and to do good gladly to those who sin against us."*[26]

In what frame of mind should we then forgive others? *Warmly and gladly.*

What does Luther add to forgiving? *Doing good.*

Here it is quite clear then. Precisely the way God acts toward us, so also should we act toward others. Then that which separates us also disappears and we belong together just as we belong together with God.

What word in the fifth petition shows us that we human beings belong together in the larger sense? *The word "our."*

We say not "my debt" but "our debt." Who is to speak this "our"? *The Christian congregation.*

What does this "our" mean? *It means that we share the debt.*

We must also remember that we are all in the same distressful situation, that one also shares the debt of the other. Just think how the evil words we have spoken or the evil things we have done have continued to have an effect in the hearts of our comrades, and how much evil they may have caused, how many souls they may have corrupted!

Think seriously about that. In the Lord's Prayer, an entire, guilty people calls upon and entreats God, not just we alone. And we want to do our best to ensure that this people receives help. We can do this precisely by forgiving those who sin against us. Only then are we praying the Lord's Prayer seriously.[27]

[26.] Cf. Luther, Small Catechism, explanation of the fifth petition (*Book of Concord*, 358).

[27.] The following passage from the Finkenwalde homiletics lectures reveals much about Bonhoeffer's experiences with the Lord's Prayer catechesis: "Be forewarned about preaching sermons on the Lord's Prayer because of the high demands this daily prayer makes on sermons based on it. Also one should not mangle the Lord's Prayer in catechetical instruction" (*GS* 4:271; cf. Fant, *Bonhoeffer*, 160, as well as the passage in *Discipleship* (*DBWE* 4:154–58). [These sentences are not found in *DBW* 14 (2/10), pp. 491–92. In Bonhoeffer's time catechizing was a highly formalized process, and he felt that the Lord's Prayer had such a unique place in Christian practice as "the essence of prayer" that it should not be degraded by taking it apart and quizzing it in catechesis.—CG]

566 **22. Sermon for the Second Theological Examination on 1 Thessalonians 5:16–18, Teltow, July 20, 1930**[1]

1 Thess. 5:16–18
Meditation

The text: Although verse 18b might be construed as referring to verse 18 alone, word order and rhythm seem to require it to refer to verses 16–18. All three imperatives are to be understood only in connection with God's revelation in Christ. In Christ we learn that God's will for human beings is that they rejoice always, pray without ceasing, and give thanks in all circumstances. This becomes understandable if God's will in Christ is understood as gospel, as good news. From this perspective, the ordering of the first imperative as the most general becomes clear. Joyfulness as the living response of human beings to the good news and as the basic attitude of Christian life before God is based on turning one's life to God in prayer, which in its own turn is based on gratitude for receiving all life and all goodness from God, gratitude that as receptivity toward God thus resembles faith. Here the Christian attitude toward life is directed back to faith in the good news. An understanding of the nature of joyfulness, prayer, and gratitude is followed by reference first to its foundation, which resides in Christ, in God's nearness in Christ, in the good news, in the message of God's will to us in Christ, and then to its strength, which is capable of supporting the "always," "without ceasing," "in all circumstances." The three superscriptions of the sections in the following outline attempt to summarize the overall content of nature, foundation, and strength. Keeping this
567 message of the joyful Christian life alive today in the congregation is as necessary as it is difficult. It seems possible to me only if the sermon also clearly emphasizes the contrast over against the weariness, moroseness, and resignation in our contemporary life.

[1.] *NL*, D 11 (48/49); typewritten; for the evaluation of this sermon by Schlabritzky and Diestel, see 1/121.4. This text must have been especially appealing to Bonhoeffer, since he had already preached on it on May 13, 1928, in Barcelona (according to the calendar *NL*, A 18,2; cf. also the letter to Rößler, 1/40). However, that sermon has not been preserved. "Rejoice always" as the theme of the "first imperative" and thus as a guiding theme had appealed to Bonhoeffer's great interest, already evident in 1926 during his university years, in "Joy in Early Christianity" (see *DBWE* 9, 2/11).

Bibliography.[2]
Pank, *Ich schäme mich des Evangeliums nicht*, 1910, p. 464
Uckeley, *Lebenskräfte*, 1924, p. 101ff.
Hirsch, *Der Wille des Herrn*, 1925, p. 41ff.
Naumann, in the *Postille* of Petersmann-Borsdorff, 1927, p. 176f.

Disposition
Christian Life under the Good News

The good news that enters into our daily life seeks to lead us to

I. Joyfulness as the basic Christian attitude toward life under the good news of God's nearness in Christ
   a) nature of joyfulness
   b) foundation of joyfulness
   c) strength of joyfulness

   Joyfulness lives from

II. Prayer as an orientation of one's life toward God
   a) nature of prayer
   b) foundation of prayer
   c) strength of prayer

   and from

III. Gratitude as the reception of life from God
   a) nature of gratitude
   b) foundation of gratitude
   c) strength of gratitude

Sermon: 568
1 Thess. 5:16–18

Rejoice always, pray without ceasing, give thanks in all circumstances; for this is the will of God in Christ Jesus for you.

Anyone returning to our homeland today from an extended stay in a foreign country immediately notices that today's Germans look different from other peoples and probably also different from the way they themselves looked earlier. The distress of the last fifteen years has left its mark on their faces. In their expressions one sees something like a reproach against a life that has treated them roughly and then also something like dull resignation over against some unavoidable pressure. Anyone with open eyes can easily

[2.] [The titles are translated in the bibliography. Naumann's article on Lutheran joyfulness (cf. 1 Thess. 5:16, "Rejoice always") is in a volume of homilies edited by Petersmann-Borsdorff and Otto.—CG]

see in our faces that we are a people with a heavy, frightful burden on our backs, a people that takes its steps forward only slowly and with great effort. There is one slogan and one only: Work. And again: Work unless you want you or your children to fall on bad times. Such knowledge oppresses a person, turns work into a curse and life into care and anxiety. Is it surprising that dissatisfaction and grumbling soon arise, that pessimism and melancholy fetter people like chains to the earth, that their mouths go silent and their hearts become bitter? And all of us gathered here for God's word, are not most of us among these people as well? We come from all kinds of work and toil in our workaday worlds, we struggle for our daily bread, and in our free time all that is then left is concern about our future and our children's future. The past week has brought worry, care, or sorrow to each of us who has not become completely blunted. We see the myriad forms of distress around us and see the numerous forms of help that would have to exist to possibly alleviate any of it. We believe we know something about life and have a right to view things pessimistically

569 And now, despite everything, we are here to call upon God and to ask for his word. We hear the apostle's word, and it seems to come from some distant, unknown land: Rejoice always, pray without ceasing, give thanks in all circumstances. What kind of words are these? Words of a man who knew nothing of life? For whom everything was gentle and peaceful and friendly? Not at all; they are the words of a man who was shaken and beaten by the storms of life quite differently than we are, a man who though persecuted and pursued, stoned and beaten, caught in shipwrecks and prison, wanted only one thing, namely, to be the messenger of God's will as delivered to us in Christ Jesus, the messenger of the gospel, that is, of the good news to human beings. Doesn't that make you stop and think for a moment?

But we hear different words. We are men and women whom life has hardened; we have seen more than enough distress and misery, including in our own personal lives. Such words are not for us; they are of no use to a manly [männlich] life that consists of seriousness and work and duty and nothing else. Of course, if we were children, things would be different, perhaps we could still live that way; but today?—Indeed, if only we were children! That is the melancholy cry we hear today. But don't we hear this, as it calls to us repeatedly from the mouth of Jesus and the apostles: You are in fact children, indeed, you are children of your Father in heaven. And as such children you should heed God's voice and do his will. Listen to the message, the good news to God's children as sent through Christ Jesus and transmitted to us by Paul: *Rejoice always.*

So let us try to open our ears now—for God's word to us is not what seems self-evident but that which seems alien and strange. And indeed,

these words are certainly strange: Rejoice always. Are we to rejoice in the manner of that crowd of people we see searching for "gaiety" each evening in the great streets of Berlin? Certainly not; they are like moths that dance and flutter around the light at night until it burns them up. Christian joyfulness has nothing to do with such gaiety. Nor does Christian joyfulness have anything to do with some pleasant diversion after a gray workday. Everything we generally call joyfulness, even joyfulness that is not entirely illegiti- 570
mate, is prompted by things that are transitory like everything else in the world, things that in their very transience take our joyfulness away from us when they pass away, leaving behind only melancholy recollection. Where is all that joyfulness that our personal or professional life has brought us in pleasant hours? Irrevocably gone. "Forget the past; beautiful as it may have been, it can never return again the way it was."[3] Today's text, however, speaks about a happiness that abides, one that lasts a lifetime, one that does not dissipate when those happy times are over, one that endures because it has its foundation where there is no more growth or decline, namely, in the fatherly heart of God. Here you find anything but wild boisterousness and desire, which, after all, are merely the anxious grasping for things in this transitory world. Here we stand as whole persons before God the Father; our hearts are filled with a happiness never known before, a happiness that seeks to seize and change our lives from within. This joyfulness has only one enemy,[4] namely, the care and sorrow that subjugate people to this world and make them fearful. A person should be joyful, not fearful, since above all that happens there is a heaven, an eternity, a Father.

But with my tormented, heavy heart, where does my joyfulness come from, where do I find it? Go outside and see how children play and rejoice and are happy; see how the birds of the field fly high up to heaven and are joyous in the sun. Watch them, and then watch them again and again, and then rejoice with them, become like them, like a child that is joyous in its father's garden. Above all, however, turn to him who loved the children and birds and flowers and who himself was a joyous child of his Father and who has become your redeemer: to Jesus Christ. In him the Father himself encounters you; in him God comes close to you, and in him one thus 571
finds the foundation and source of all joyfulness. Rejoicing means enjoying God's nearness in Christ Jesus.

Here, of course, joyfulness knows neither measure nor goal; here one must rejoice always, even when things get tough and quite serious, when everything seems to be teetering and about to fall. For God is there. God

[3.] Citation source unidentified.

[4.] The reader underlined "only one enemy" and added the query "?"

extends a hand to me in Christ, holds me and makes my heart firm and strong. God and Christ the Redeemer make me glad amid all suffering, all tears, glad in community with them. Even if our path becomes so dark that we no longer see where to step, even if the clouds grow heavy and dark, in the distance we nonetheless have already caught a glimpse of our home; we know that our sojourn in this world will come to an end, we have a presentiment of the future of our Lord Jesus Christ, who will redeem us from all anxiety and toil, and we rejoice. Today we Christians are still running around with heavy countenances, with heads hung low, and with anxious hearts. Some sorrow is oppressing us; our conscience is tormenting us. And we even believe that things must be this way, that it is part of a serious life, instead of seeing that in Christ God has given us a glad heart, that God's strength is greater than our distress, his grace stronger than our conscience, and that we children can approach the Father and live in community with God. Away with all fears and worries, away also with all the ponderous piety; instead, let us speak along with the poet: May we become simple, and may we be devout and joyous like children before you here on earth.[5]

This one, great, inner joyfulness that should be the undercurrent of Christian life is based on two powerful life utterances of the Christian heart. Paul finds them actualized in view of God's will as revealed in Christ.

Pray without ceasing. That is the first thing. But even as we hear these words, we sense opposition stirring within us. We really don't want to hear much about such things. We want people to work and to fulfill their obligations, and whether there is time afterward for praying as well—that just
572 doesn't seem so important. Today we can no longer establish monasteries as in former times whose sole purpose is to ensure that prayer never ceases in them, that an eternal chain of prayers is always ascending to heaven. But not just that; it has become all too clear that our age has little room at all for prayer. Prayer has become alien to us, and for that very reason things look so frightening around us. But let us not speak about others. What about us? How much weariness and lethargy, apathy and fatigue are we dragging around with us? How often do we find it difficult to utter even a few words from within our lukewarm hearts? How often would we like to pray and yet simply cannot? And how wonderful is it when occasionally our hearts genuinely do warm up in prayer to God, when we sense that God really does still live and speak and is just waiting and waiting for us to speak a word

[5.] See the 1779 hymn of Matthias Claudius, "Der Mond ist aufgegangen" (The moon has risen), *EKG*, no. 368, verse 5.

from within the depths of our being, for us to cry out so that God can hear us? How many of us suffer from this poverty of prayer and alienation from prayer? And yet one thing is certain: the Christian cause lives or dies—and yet that's impossible—with prayer; prayer is the heart of Christian life. Precisely today this must be emphasized again in all simplicity and seriousness. Luther said that as a shoemaker makes shoes and a tailor clothes, so also must a Christian pray.[6] Whoever does not pray is not a Christian. That so few people know this today derives simply from the fact that they no longer understand what praying means. Praying is not just asking, nor is it just giving thanks—in today's text, Paul does not speak about giving thanks until later—praying means first all to become so quiet that we perceive God's word to us, and then it means to respond to that word either in words or in deeds. Praying means to turn one's life to God and to his word as revealed to us through Christ, to surrender, entrust our lives completely to God, to throw ourselves into God's arms, to grow together with God, to sense God's life in our own lives. Praying means wanting to approach and remain close to God because God has come close to us.

We are able to pray only because Christ is there. In Christ, our prayer has its foundation, for through Christ we have God as our Father. 573

Pray without ceasing can thus only mean: let your entire life be a prayer, let it be turned toward God and be a response to God's word in Christ.

Christ, however, is also the strength of our prayer, and only with this strength can we pray without ceasing. But precisely because Christ is our strength, the strength that leads us to the Father, prayer makes us joyous and strong, and thus a person who prays will no longer be afraid and will no longer be sad. In prayer Christ is close to us, God is close to us. And often when we bring our guilt before God with trembling and hesitation and only want to call on him from afar, we nonetheless experience again and again that, if we but call on God correctly, God does not remain distant from us, but rather draws us close, indeed quite close, enclosing us in his heart, comforting all our sadness, dispelling all our sorrow, and gladdening our heart. We become joyous in prayer. Hence pray without ceasing, give your life to God, turn your life toward God. If you draw near to God, God will draw near to you.

But how can we do all this if we do not receive our entire life ever anew from God's hand? If we do not have the assurance that God does indeed support and guide and protect our life?

[6.] *WA.Tr* 6:162 (no. 6751).

That is, how can we do all this if we are not basically grateful human beings? Here we encounter the other powerful root that secures the life of the joyous Christian to God's foundation: *Give thanks in all circumstances.*[7]—Here the most important element is the last one: "in all circumstances." For all of us have had times when our hearts, full of gratitude, have looked up toward God, high points in our lives, moments that seem to remove us from the entire world and bring us so close to God. But these are not the times in which our gratitude proves itself.

Even pagans thank their gods for beneficent gifts. No, "giving thanks in all circumstances" is precisely where one finds the miraculous, Christian element. In times when it seems like nonsense to the normal person, when sorrow and distress pile up, in times of degradation, hurt feelings, and humiliation to bow and to accept life anew from God's hand and thus abide with God: that is what it means to give thanks in all circumstances.

574 As has been related regarding the great church father of the East whose life concluded with tribulation and prison and from whose mouth came the final words: Thanks be to God for all things.[8]

Here gratitude is just another word for the faith that remains unshaken even when God seems to be concealed for a short moment, faith that is joyous amid tears because it knows about Christ the redeemer, has its foundation completely in Christ, and holds fast to his good news. "Though I at first feel nothing of your power, you nonetheless lead me to the goal even through the night."[9] "Thanks be to God for everything"—here we see how things stand, here we see what kind of Christian spirit we have, here the unsealed source of joyfulness is opened that receives the good news, the gospel, ever again and ever anew, even where it is strangely hidden.

We often believe that gratitude degrades us, makes us dependent, and for that very reason we basically remain ungrateful. Yet precisely the opposite is the case. Gratitude makes us rich and gives us energy because it makes us receptive. If we are grateful, we make room for God in our hearts, let him in completely, receive him in faith, get so close to him, and in this way we become rich and strong, inexhaustible energy flows into us which, because it comes from God, directs our entire life. We rejoice in our God

[7.] [Cf. also Eph. 5:20.—CG]

[8.] The last words of the church father John Chrysostom, who died on September 9, 409, on his way into exile: "Glory to God for all things"; cf. Palladius, *Dialogue on the Life of St. John Chrysostom*, 73.

[9.] From Julie von Hausmann's 1862 hymn, "So nimm denn meine Hände" (*EKG* (addendum), verse 3). ["Lord , take my hand and lead me" (*Lutheran Book of Worship*, no. 333) contains in verse 3 some of the quoted words.—CG]

in Christ, not merely here and there, but always and without ceasing and in all circumstances.

The words that have spoken to us today Paul wrote to a congregation he called the model of all believers, his joy, his crown, his boasting, his glory.[10] He might well ascribe such words to such a congregation. But to us? Amid all the sublime words we have uttered, we should not forget that we ourselves are in any event not such a congregation. Each of us should 575
go, alone and quietly, and confess that we are far removed from this goal. What do we know of such Christian joyfulness, of such a life that is actually a prayer, of such gratitude that receives God in faith? What do we know of the good news, and how much of it do we integrate into our own lives? We are mired deep in anxiety and in the cares of life. Yet for that very reason we probably also sense something of what the apostle means when he speaks about God's will, the will that is to make us glad such that we can pray in the words of the hymn: May the eternally rich God give us in our lives an ever-joyous heart and noble peace.[11]

And even if we are yet too weak and weary, we must let such words work on us; we must get down to work but must do so just as one goes about God's work in the larger sense, namely, with our eyes on the good news to us and by praying that God may bring us to the point that we might speak with pure, joyous hearts:

> My heart leaps
> And cannot be sad.
> Full of joy and singing,
> It sees nothing but sunshine.
> The sun that shines so brightly for me
> Is my Lord Jesus Christ;
> What makes me sing
> Is what is in heaven.[12]

[10.] Cf. 1 Thess. 2:19–20.

[11.] Martin Rinckart's 1636 hymn, "Nun danket alle Gott" (*EKG*, 228, verse 2). [Cf. "Now thank we all our God" (*Lutheran Book of Worship*, 533); in Catherine Winkworth's translation a version of the words quoted is in verse 2.—CG]

[12.] From Paul Gerhardt's 1653 hymn, "Ist Gott für mich, so trete" (*EKG*, no. 250, verse 13). The choice of these stanzas may have been influenced by their use in Naumann's "Lutherische Fröhlichkeit," 176. [Cf. verse 4 of "If God himself be for me" (*Lutheran Book of Worship*, 454).—CG]

576 **23. Sermon on 1 John 4:16, New York, Armistice Day Sunday, November 9, 1930**[1]

God is love; and he that dwelleth in love dwelleth in God, and God in him.[2]

It is indeed a strange feeling for me just coming over here from Germany to stand now on an american pulpit and before an american christian congregation. It occurs anew to my mind in this hour the world wide extent of our faith and hope. I am overwhelmed in considering the idea of God, the father, who dwells beyond the stars and looks down upon his children in the whole world in America and Germany, in India and in Africa, there is not any difference before God, as Paul sais: there is neither Jew nor Greek, there is neither bond nor free, there is neither male nor female, for ye are all one in Christ Jesus.[3] God has erected a strange, miraculous and wonderful sign in the world, where we all could find him, I mean, the cross of Jesus Christ, the cross of the suffering love of God. Under the cross of Christ we know that we all belong each to another, that we all are brethren and sisters in the same need and in the same hope, that we are bound together by the same destiny—namely being a human being with all his suffering and all his joys, with sorrows and with desires, with disappointments and fulfilments—and most important a human being with his sin and guilt, with his
577 faith and hope. Before the cross of Christ and his inconceivable suffering disappear all our external differences, we are no more rich or poor, wise or simple, good or bad, we are no more Americans or Germans, we are one large congregation of brethren, we recognize, that nobody is good before God, as Paul sais: for all have sinned and come short of the glory of God,

[1.] *NL,* A 25,6 b; handwritten, variant of the "address" above (see 2/9); in original English, including errors. The printed invitation to this service has been preserved; see *NL,* A 27,6 (3). It reads: "Memorial Methodist Church, 21 Tuckahoe Road, November 6, 1930. Dear Friend, Your [*sic*] are cordially invited to attend the Armistice Day Service to be held in our Church next Sunday November 9 at 11:00 A.M. Dr. Dietrich Bonhoefier [*sic*], a Professor of the University of Berlin, will speak. From the heart of Germany he will bring us a message on 'WAR'. Did you ever wonder what the German People are thinking about war? This is an unusual opportunity to find out. Don't miss it! Sincerely, Rev. George Yoxthiemer, Minister." [Written in English. The church was in Yonkers and in 1965 merged with several other congregations to form The Church of the Master. Armistice Day commemorates the end of World War I at "the eleventh hour of the eleventh day of the eleventh month" in 1918 and was a national day of remembrance in many countries; after World War II it was renamed Veteran's Day in the United States.—CG]

[2.] 1 John 4:16b.

[3.] Gal. 3:28.

beeing justified freely by his grace.[4] Let us look at the love of Christ, who without guilt bore the cross, who gave his life as a sacrifice, who suffered on the cross—why? because he had loved his people more than himself. And then let us consider our own feebleness and our own want of courage, our anxiety when sorrow and grief threaten, our selfish desire to live a comfortable and careless[5] life. In profound and serious abashment we Christian people must confess, that we are not worthy of such great love of God. If you ask me what is Christendom? I answer: Christendom is the great congregation of people, who humble themselves under God and who put all their hope and faith on the love and the help of God. Christendom is the community, in which man and man stand each for one, as a brother stands for his brother. Christendom is one great people composed of peoples of every country, in concord in his faith and his love, because there is One God, One Lord, One Spirit, One Hope.[6] That is the marvellous mystery of the people of God. Above all differences of race, nationality, custom there is an invisible community of the children of God. Here each one prays for the others, he might be American or German or African, here each one loves the others without reservation. Let us in this hour gratefully consider that we all belong to this church, that God has called us to his children and made us brethren, that there cannot be any hate and enmity, but only the best will to understand each other—otherwise we would not be worth to bear the name of Christ, we would offend the glory of God, who is a God of love and not of hate.

Now I stand before you not only as a Christian but also as a German, who loves his home the best of all, who rejoices with his people and who suffers, when he sees his people suffering, who confesses gratefully, that he received from his people all that he has and is. So I bring you this morning 578
a double message, the message of Germany and the message of the Christianity in Germany. I hope, you will hear this message with a christian heart, with the readiness of a christian soul to understand and to love, wherever and whomever it might be. The 11. of November 1918 brought to Germany the end of a frightful and unparalleled time, a time, which we pray, if God wills, will never return. For four years German men and lads stood for their home with an unheard of tenacity and intrepidity, with the imperturbable consciousness of their duty, with an inexorable selfdiscipline and with a glowing love for their fatherland and with the belief in its future. For weeks

[4.] Rom. 3:23.
[5.] [Bonhoeffer presumably means "carefree."—CG]
[6.] Cf. Eph. 4:4–5.

and months these people suffered privations of every kind, they persevered in hunger and thirst, in pain and affliction, in craving after the home, after mothers and wifes and brothers and children. In the country did not cease the stream of tears, of old and young people. Every day the message came to more than 1000 familys, that the husband, the father, the brother had died in the foreign country. Hardly any family was spared. Death stood at the door of almost every house and called for entrance. Once came the message about the death of many thousand seventeen and eighteen year old boys killed in a few hours. Germany was made a house of mourning. The break down could not be delayed longer. Famine and enervation were to powerful and destructive. I think, you release me from talking about our feeling in Germany in those days. The recollection of this time is gloomy and sad. Very seldom will you hear today in Germany anybody talking about these days. We will not reopen an old and painful wound. But however we felt, the war and its dreadful killing and dying was finished. Our minds were still too confused and bewildered, we could not yet conceive and quietly consider the meaning of all the events of the last years and months. But gradually we saw more and more clearly; and christian people in Germany, who took the course and the end of the war seriously, could not help seeing here a judgment of God upon this fallen world and especially upon our people. Before the war we lived too far from God, we believed too much in our own power, in our allmightiness and righteousness. We attempted to be
579 a strong and good people, but we were to proud of our endeavours, we felt too much satisfaction with our scientific, economic and social progress and we identified this progress with the coming of the Kingdom of God. We felt too happy and complacent in this world, our souls were too much at home in this world. Then the great disillusionment came. We saw the impotence and weakness of humanity, we were suddenly awakened from our dream, we recognized our guiltiness before God and we humbled ourselves under the mighty hand of God. When I was just speaking here on "guiltiness", I added on purpose: guiltiness "before God." Let me tell you francly, that no German and no stranger, who knows well the history of the origine of the war, believes, that Germany bears the sole guilt of the war, a sentence which we were compelled to sign in the treaty of Versailles.[7] I personally do not believe on the other hand that Germany was the only guiltless country, but

[7.] Bonhoeffer wrote down the wording of Article 231 in his notebook (*NL*, A 25,6 a); cf. 2/9, note 7. [Having rejected the view that Germany was the only guilty country, in the next sentence Bonhoeffer states that, on the other hand, he does not believe that Germany was guiltless.—CG]

I as a Christian see the main guilt of Germany in quite a different light.[8] I see it in Germany's complacence, in her belief in her allmightiness, in the lack of humility and faith in God and fear of God. It seems to me, that this is the meaning of the war for Germany: we had to recognize the limits of man and that means: we discovered anew God in his glory and allmightiness, in his wrath and his grace.

The same 11. of November 1918, which brought to us the end of the war, was the beginning of a new epoch of suffering and grief. The first years after the war showed to us the corruption in our public life. The general poverty caused by the hungerblockade had dreadful consequences. Germany was starved out. In the street you could see the undernourished people, the pale and sickly children. The number of suicides increased in a terrifying way. Everyone who is familiar with the conditions in Germany today, 12 years after the war, knows, that in spite of some changes in their external aspect social conditions are almost as unhappy as 10 or 12 years ago. The debts of the war press us not only in regard to our financial standard but likewise in regard to our whole behaviour, we see the hopelessness 580
of our work; it is impossible for us to provide social and economic conditions for our children in the future, in which we can trust for security. The Germans are a suffering people today, but they will not despair. They will work for building up a new and better home, they will work for peace in their country, they will work for peace in the world. When I came over here, I was astonished on being asked again and again, what German people think about a future war. I tell you the truth: German people do not speak at all about that, they don't even think of it. You almost never would hear in Germany talk about war and much less about a future war. We know what a war means for a people

I have been accustomed once in every year since my boyhood to wander on foot through our country and so I happen to know many classes of German people very well. Many evenings I have sat with the familys of paysants[9] around the big stove talking about past and future, about the next generation and their chances. But always when the talk happened to touch the war, I observed, how deep the wound was, which the past war had caused to everyone. The German people needs and wants above all peace. As a christian minister I think, that just here is one of the greatest tasks for our church, to strengthen the work of peace in every country and in

[8.] The next sentence was deleted: "The guilt of which I speak is something deeper than political responsibility."

[9.] Bonhoeffer means "peasants."

the whole world. It must never more happen, that a christian people fights against a christian people, brother against brother, since both have one Father. Our churches have already begun this international work.[10] But more important than that is, it seems to me, that every christian man and woman, boy and girl takes seriously the great idea of the unity of Christianity, above all personal and national desires, of the one christian people in the whole world, of the brotherhood of mankind, of the charity, about which Paul says: "Charity suffers long and is kind; charity envieth not; char-
581 ity vaunteth not itself, is not puffed up; beareth all things, believeth all things, hopeth all things, endured all things. Charity never faileth."[11] Let us consider, that the judgement comes for everyone man and woman, boy and girl, in America and Germany, in Russia and in India; and God will judge us according to our faith and love. How can the man, who hates his brother, expect grace by God? That is my message as a German and as a Christian to you, let us love each other, let us build in faith and love one holy christianity, one brotherhood, with God, the Father, and Christ, the Lord, and the Holy Spirit as the sanctifying power. Nobody is to little or to poor for this work; we need every will and force. I address now especially you, boys and girls of the U. St., future bearer and leader of the culture of your country. You have brothers and sisters in our people and in every people, do not forget that. Come what may, let us never more forget, that our christian people is the people of God, that if we are in accord, no nationalism, no hate of races or classes can execute its designs, and then the world will have its peace for ever and ever. Let us remember the prayer of Christ spoken shortly before his end: I pray for them, which shall believe on me: that they all may be one; as thou, Father, art in me, and I in thee, that they also may be one in us.[12]

And the peace of God, which passeth all understanding shall keep your hearts and minds through Christ Jesus.[13] Amen.

[10.] Especially through Max Diestel, Bonhoeffer was already aware of the peace efforts of the World Alliance for Promoting International Friendship through the Churches, in which he was to work as a youth secretary beginning in 1931; cf. *DB-ER*, 98–99, 175, et passim.

[11.] 1 Cor. 13:4–7.

[12.] John 17:20b, 21a.

[13.] Phil. 4:7.

24. Sermon (fragment) on Deuteronomy 32:48–52, Havana, Cuba, Fourth Sunday in Advent, December 21, 1930[1] 582

Deut. 32:48–52: On that very day the LORD addressed Moses as follows: "Ascend this mountain of the Abarim, Mount Nebo, which is in the land of Moab, across from Jericho, and view the land of Canaan, which I am giving to the Israelites for a possession; you shall die there on the mountain that you ascend and shall be gathered to your kin, as your brother Aaron died on Mount Hor and was gathered to his kin; because both of you broke faith with me among the Israelites at the waters of Meribath-kadesh in the wilderness of Zin, by failing to maintain my holiness among the Israelites. Although you may view the land from a distance, you shall not enter it—the land that I am giving to the Israelites."

Deut. 32:48–52 *Fourth Sunday in Advent*

This is a very serious matter. But Advent, too, is a serious matter; in fact, it is an enormously serious matter. You know, we are strange people. When Advent season comes around again, we sing maybe a couple of Christmas
carols at home with our children, we hurry and rush to complete our Christ- 583
mas shopping, write a couple of Christmas cards, and then after we have finished with all the Christmas celebrations in clubs and groups, smiling and merry we enter the promised land, Christmas land.

But Moses dies on the mountain, from which he was permitted to greet the promised land only from a distance. Whenever the Bible talks about God's promises, it is always a matter of life and death. Whenever we talk about them, we are generally referring to a couple of happy days with our

[1.] *NL*, A 25,5 a; handwritten, in part on the stationery of "Mrs. Harold Boericke, 5953 Drexel Road, Overbook, P.S."; with a note by Bethge: "December 21, 1930, in USA, Cuba." Previously published in *PAM* 1:220–26. See also *NL*, A 25,5 b; later typewritten copy (incomplete). Previously published in *GS* 5:485–90. The conclusion to the sermon has been lost. This sermon dates to a time of personal crisis: "I have rarely had this much trouble getting into the Christmas spirit" (to Rößler, December 11, 1930, see 1/148). In a letter to Maria von Wedemeyer on August 20, 1943, Bonhoeffer recalled, "The sun has always attracted me, and I've often been reminded by it that human beings were taken from the earth and don't just consist of thin air and thoughts. So much so that once, when I went to Cuba to preach there at Christmas, and exchanged the ice of North America for its luxuriant tropical vegetation, I almost succumbed to sun-worship and could hardly remember what I was really supposed to preach. It was a genuine crisis, and a hint of it assails me every summer when I get to feel the sun" (*Love Letters from Cell 92*, 68). Concerning this situation, cf. also *DB-ER*, 151–52. The sermon on Gen. 32:25–32 and 33:10 on March 13, 1932 (*DBW* 11, 3/6) is structurally and thematically similar, cf. Wendel, *Homiletik*, 217–18. Concerning this topic see also the 1944 poem, "The Death of Moses" (*DBW* 8 [4/197], p. 590).

family. God spoke to Moses: Ascend this mountain of the Abarim and die on the mountain in view of the promise. And Moses was God's prophet, the man God had chosen to lead his people out of the house of bondage, out of fear and terror and onward to freedom. Moses had once stood in the rock cleft where he was permitted to behold the mystery of God's glory; he had brought the tablets of the covenant down from thunderous Sinai to the unfaithful people. Ever since God had called him, he had known and wanted only one thing, namely, to lead the people to God's promise. His life was a journey to the promise, a journey in hope through disappointments, tribulations, defeats, through apostasy and unfaithfulness; but he had a hunger for the promised land that drove him ever onward. Now he is an old man, and only one thing still keeps him going, namely, God's word about the promised land. He is full of hope. And then, finally, the hour comes when all these things are to be fulfilled. Everything he has believed so far is to be justified and acquire its ultimate meaning. And now the Bible recounts with the simplest conceivable words: On that very day the Lord addressed Moses as follows . . . Then Moses died at the Lord's command.

Isn't that disturbingly serious? We know from our own small daily lives what small unfulfilled hopes are. Each of us could say something about such things, even our children. Some of us may even be familiar with great unfulfilled hopes; I'm referring to hopes worthy of being hoped, like the hope that we might overcome secret weaknesses or disavow concealed sins. How many despairing attempts we often make, how fervently we pray in such distress, and how difficult it is when our hopes are not fulfilled: "My
584 grace is sufficient for you"[2] is the answer Paul received when he called upon God during acute suffering; live in hope and die in hope. Your hopes will not be fulfilled. If we reflect earnestly on such things in our own [lives], we can sense how seriously the Bible is speaking here. But things become even more disturbing. Why must Moses die in view of the promise? Here we hear all the expressions that are so important in the world of the Bible: disobedient, unholy, sin, death. There are connections here we no longer see. The sinner dies before the promise. Moses belongs to his people, hence [he] dies. If we had composed this story, we would have made him the first to enter the promised land with rejoicing. But God says: Ascend the mountain and die. He had hoped and believed; he was homesick for a home he had never seen. Jesus says, "Blessed are those who hunger and thirst

[2.] 2 Cor. 12:9.

for righteousness . . . "[3] But Moses dies on the mountain in view of the promise.

The language this ancient story is speaking is quite clear. Whoever has seen God must die; the sinner dies before God's promise. Let us understand what this means for us so close to Christmas. At Christmas, God's great promise is to be fulfilled, a promise infinitely more momentous than that of the promised land. God promised to come near to the earth personally, to come near to us; God promised to lead us to redemption, to salvation, to blessedness. But we know of this promise and, like Moses, we sojourn; and yet we must know that if Moses had to die, we, too, would certainly have to die if God were to deal with us according to his own prerogative. Yet as Christians, we also know that we are not to die but rather are to live in the promise, and that the promise is to be ours.

But we can't help it, we cannot on our own initiative first climb up to Moses on the mountain and in all humility wait for God's command: Die on the mountain, die at Advent, you shall no longer behold the fulfillment. But if we have genuinely considered all this, would we really want to enter the promised land in such an uninhibited and clueless fashion? Maybe children can. In any case we no longer can. In view of this fact, the seriousness of the 585
Advent season becomes clear to us. Great things are being promised and are already under way, unprecedented events are being proclaimed, things no human ear has ever heard,[4] unrevealed mysteries are being revealed, and already the earth and humanity is quaking at what is approaching, and the voice of a prophet cries out into the anxious world: the kingdom of heaven has come near, God the Lord is coming, the Creator and Judge is approaching humankind in love and will take us home to the eternal festival meal. God is coming. Are you prepared? Here that one great question appears, the question with which the New Testament begins and ends, the only decisive question for the entire world and for our entire life: Are you prepared for God? This is how the Bible sees the world. Stay awake, for it is night, and you would like to sleep; but God's glory will burst into the night; did it not happen in just this way in Bethlehem? Be dressed for action and have your lamps lit,[5] for the Lord intends to come, and woe to the servant whom the Lord finds sleeping. Of course, it is certainly understandable that we are tired and that our eyes close during the night of the world; fill your lamps with oil nonetheless that you may go through the night to meet the

[3.] Matt. 5:6.

[4.] Here and in the following paragraph, Bonhoeffer is drawing on motifs from Philipp Nicolai's hymn, "Wake, awake, for night is flying" (*Lutheran Book of Worship*, 31).

[5.] Luke 12:35.

bridegroom,[6] put on your wedding robe lest you be expelled [from the] festival meal.[7] Hence the entire message of Advent becomes a disturbing penitential sermon to us. Before Jesus stands John the Baptist, whom we are not to skip over. Throughout early Christendom, the Advent season was a time of penitence, not a time of joy; indeed even all the songs we just sang speak about this, and justifiably so, it seems to me.

(But in three days now Christmas really will be here again. The great transformation is to take place again. God wills it thus. The hoping, expectant, yearning world is to become a world to which the promise is given. All
586 lament is to go silent; no tears are to flow; no more lonely suffering is to suffocate or threaten us. He who will help is here; he who will never leave us alone is here.)

Let us work out our own salvation with fear and trembling.[8] Beyond all this, however, the Bible is full of the proclamation that this great miracle has occurred as God's own deed without any help from human beings. According to the divine decree in eternity, the Son went out from the Father, and at the same hour a small baby boy was born in a manger in Bethlehem. The ox and the ass and a couple of shepherds from the fields celebrated the first Christmas. Above this manger, however, heaven was torn open. Angels and stars sang joyfully into the sacred night, and God's love looked down upon this child and his believers. It was God personally, however, who lighted the Christmas tree during this consecrated night, the starry heavens of the eternal Father. What had happened? God had seen the misery of the world and had come personally to help. Now God was there, not as a powerful God, but concealed in humanity, where what is sinful, weak, pathetic, and miserable is found in the world; precisely there is where God appears and can be found by every human being. And this proclamation makes the rounds anew through the world each year and is also coming again this year to us.

Each of us approaches Christmas with different personal feelings. Some approach it with pure joy in anticipation of this day of rejoicing, friendship, and love. So children . . .[9] Others try to find a moment of peace from routine daily life beneath the Christmas tree; they want to dream of past days and times full of sunshine, want to forget what is all around them when they look into the lights on the Christmas tree and hear the old Christmas carols; they yearn for this blessed forgetting. Still others approach Christ-

[6.] Cf. Matt. 25:1–13.

[7.] Cf. Matt. 22:11–13.

[8.] Cf. Phil. 2:12.

[9.] [Incomplete sentence beginning "So ist Kinder . . ."—CG]

mas with much trepidation. Instead of being a pure festival of joy for them, disturbing thoughts of separation awaken in them; it is precisely on this day that they become particularly aware of their personal misery, of their loneliness. Human hearts are so different beneath [the] Christmas tree. And it is probably correct to say that each of us who has looked around a bit in the world perhaps finds it particularly strange to be celebrating Christmas 587
this year. Hoards of unemployed stand before our eyes, millions of children throughout the world are hungry and miserable, people are starving in China, the oppressed in India and in other unhappy[10] countries, and in everyone's eyes one sees an expression of despairing perplexity. And despite all this, Christmas comes. Whether we want it to or not, whether we are in the mood for it or not, we must hear again that Christ, the savior, is born,[11] precisely the saving world is our lost world, and just as God [. . .] Christ [. . .][12]

[10.] Uncertain reading.

[11.] Cf. the 1818 Christmas carol of Franz Gruber, "Silent Night," verse 2.

[12.] The manuscript breaks off here; the conclusion has been lost.

Hans Christoph von Hase

"Turning Away from the Phraseological to the Real" A Personal Recollection

"I don't think I've ever changed very much, except perhaps at the time of my 588
first impressions abroad, and under the first conscious influence of Papa's personality. It was then that a turning away from the phraseological to the real ensued." This was what Dietrich Bonhoeffer wrote from prison on April 22, 1944, in response to Eberhard Bethge's question whether he had ever experienced a break in his life. "Continuity with one's own past is actually a great gift."[1]

Hence for Bonhoeffer, who rarely spoke about his innermost experiences and even then only with great reserve, a decisive change and maturation process must have commenced during these years between Barcelona and New York, 1928–31. These changes are worth tracing within the wealth of material offered in this volume. As Bonhoeffer's cousin, and as someone who three years later received the same scholarship to Union Theological Seminary in New York and was similarly able to immerse himself in the world of American churches and their theology, I have agreed to comment on the veritable forest of materials in this present volume. I will now try to delineate and note some of the key points. In so doing I hope to encourage the reader not to shy away from examining this volume, a volume in which there is still so much to discover.

[1.] *LPP*, 275–76, letter of April 22, 1944. Translation from *DBWE* 8, forthcoming.

Points of Orientation

Those seeking theology in this volume should immerse themselves in the letters, letters that are of cultural as well as personal interest, and in which questions of faith and life that concerned Dietrich Bonhoeffer during this period are expressed with great originality. For orientation the reader is referred to
589 Eberhard Bethge's biography[2] and to Hans-Richard Reuter's afterword to the new edition of *Act and Being*.[3] The following points can provide additional orientation. For the time Bonhoeffer served as vicar in Barcelona, from 1928 to 1929, see the "Continuation of the Curriculum Vitae" (after 1927),[4] Pastor Olbricht's reports,[5] and a personal characterization of the supervising pastor in Bonhoeffer's diary.[6] For the period covering Bonhoeffer's *Habilitation*, qualifying for university teaching, and his second theological examination, from 1929 to 1930, see the postdoctoral dissertation *Act and Being*,[7] including the inaugural lecture accompanying *Act and Being*, "The Anthropological Question in Contemporary Philosophy and Theology,"[8] contained in the present volume. Also, the final correspondence with Adolf von Harnack deserves special attention,[9] as does the memorial address[10] for Harnack on June 15, 1930. For the year of study at Union Theological Seminary in New York, 1930–31, see the two extensive critical reports,[11] including one to the Church Federation Office in Berlin, which provide an analysis of American church life and piety as well as of pragmatic theology.

Why Theology?

If one's concerns are to be understood, it may be easier to reveal one's most secret inner drives to complete strangers than at home. One of the most striking and revealing documents in this volume is a manuscript, revised several times, for a lecture on the theme of "war."[12] During the initial months of his year of study in the autumn of 1930, including on Armistice Day (November 11, 1930),[13] Bonhoeffer delivered this lecture to groups

[2.] *DB-ER*, 97–169.
[3.] *DBWE* 2:162–83.
[4.] 1/114.2.
[5.] 1/66 and 1/74.
[6.] 1/75.
[7.] *DBWE* 2.
[8.] 2/7.
[9.] 1/93 and 1/95.
[10.] 2/4.
[11.] 1/181 and 1/182.
[12.] 2/9, 2/10, 3/23.
[13.] [Cf. 3/23, ed. note 1. The Armistice Day sermon was actually given in a church service observing the day on Sunday, November 9, 1930.—CG]

of students and young people, to several congregations, and once in front of a thousand high school students. For the students at Union Theological Seminary, all of whom worked in one form or another in congregations, the 590
over thirty foreign students were a treasure trove of speakers for the groups of the International Fellowship of Reconciliation, where the Union students also worked. The German theme in 1930 was the Young Plan. This replaced the reparations payments stemming from the Treaty of Versailles with the sum of 112 billion gold marks.[14] In view of the global economic crisis this generated a mood of despair and provided the National Socialists, who until that point had been merely a splinter party, with one hundred representatives in the national parliament. I had to deliver similar lectures in New York myself in 1933, albeit on the topic of the Church Struggle and the persecution of the Jews.

In these lectures, Bonhoeffer strikes a passionate tone that evokes a sympathetic reaction among his listeners, a tone quite different from his otherwise reserved manner and one that shows how the wounds of war in a nine- to twelve-year-old boy still burned with undiminished intensity twelve years later:

> The 11. of November 1918 brought to Germany the end of a frightful unparalleled time, a time, which we pray if God wills, will never return. . . . In the country did not cease the stream of tears, of old and young people. Every day the message came to more than 1000 familys,[15] that the husband, the father, the brother had died in a foreign country. Hardly any family was spared. . . . two brothers of mine stood on the front. The older one 18 years old was wounded, the younger one 17 years old was killed. 3 first cousins of mine were also killed. . . . Although I was then a small boy, I never can forget those most gloomy days of the war. Death stood for the door of almost every house and called for entrance.[16]

Bonhoeffer continues by describing the famine and starvation, including a critical discussion of the question of war guilt, and then concludes: "Christian people in Germany . . . could not help seeing here a judgment of God upon this fallen world and especially upon our people. Before the

[14.] [The Treaty of Versailles imposed heavy reparation payments on Germany, which defaulted in 1923. In response the Dawes Plan was adopted in 1924 with a new payment schedule that the Weimar Republic still could not meet. Consequently the Young Plan was adopted in January 1930, setting reparations at $26.35 billion to be paid in fifty-eight and one-half years at the rate of about $473 million per year.—CG]

[15.] Actually it was two thousand.

[16.] See 2/9, p. 412; Bonhoeffer's English.

591 war we lived too far from God, we believed too much in our own power, in our almightiness and righteousness. . . . Then the great disillusionment came. . . . we were suddenly awaked from our dream, we felt the wrath of God upon us, and we recognised our guiltiness before God."[17]

This text refers us directly back to Bonhoeffer's early childhood, about which his twin sister Sabine recounts:

> From eight to ten years old Dietrich and I slept in the same room and when we were in bed at night we used to have earnest discussions about death and eternal life. The war of 1914 had broken out, and we heard of the deaths of our older cousins and some of our classmates' fathers. And so in the evenings, after prayers and hymn singing, in which our mother always took part when she was in the house, we used to lie awake for a long time and try to imagine what it must be like to be dead and to have entered eternal life. We used to make special efforts . . . to think only of the word *eternity* and not admit any other thought to our minds. This eternity seemed to us very long and uncanny. . . . We staunchly kept up this self-imposed exercise for a long time. . . . All this was an absolute secret between us twins.[18]

The death of his brother Walter, whom everyone loved, in the field hospital on April 28, 1918, was probably the most powerful shock ever suffered by the family, as it was for my own childhood as well. Sabine describes this shock in her memoirs.[19] In a brief curriculum vitae for his "Hedgehog" student fraternity in Tübingen, Dietrich wrote: "From the time that I was thirteen years old it was clear to me that I would study theology."[20]

As for myself, I was surprised that Dietrich had already decided by his confirmation in 1921 to study theology, a notion that to me as a pastor's son was utterly remote. He was already borrowing leather-bound theological books from my father, his godfather (some of these came from the library of our great-grandfather, Karl August von Hase); these books did not interest me at all. Bethge recounts how Dietrich's brothers tried to convince the fourteen-year-old what a feeble institution the church was, and that he was
592 taking the path of least resistance. To this he confidently responded: "In that case I shall reform it!"[21]

[17.] See pp. 415–16.
[18.] Leibholz-Bonhoeffer, *Bonhoeffers,* 32–33.
[19.] [Ibid., 17–19.—CG]
[20.] *DBWE* 9:55.
[21.] *DB-ER,* 36.

Even as a child I already wondered how Dietrich was able to decide so early to study theology and then remain unswervingly true to that decision. Most of our generation who decided during the 1920s to pursue theology were seeing the end of an epoch taking place and were watching religion collapse along with the world of their fathers; as a result, they had to go through long inner struggles before genuinely deciding on theology. I myself, similarly moved by this "crisis" like Dietrich, began at the University of Göttingen with the goal of studying nuclear physics; but I then met Karl Barth, who motivated me to turn my attention to helping perplexed human beings and thus to study theology.

From Phraseology to Reality

Bonhoeffer's "primal experience" [Urerlebnis][22] motivated him to become a theologian so that he might (1) understand the wrath of God, (2) comprehend the reality of God's gracious presence in the church (*Sanctorum Communio*), (3) work for peace, and (4) live with death and renounce marriage in anticipation of coming persecution. All these themes not only appear in this volume; they also permeate Bonhoeffer's entire life and work. All exhibit a very real connection to reality and in no way resemble the kind of phraseology of which he accuses himself. These themes remain with him until the end.

(1) The Wrath of God

At that time it was difficult to proclaim the wrath of God in German theology and impossible to do so in America. But the German and European reality had been shaped by the catastrophe of war, and the question of guilt was bitterly debated, including within the nascent ecumenical movement.
Moreover—and this was perhaps even more important—the catastrophe 593
of World War I was perceived to be a judgment on European Christendom. Karl Barth's commentary on Romans provided the first response. I can still hear him say: "God is in heaven and you are on earth!"[23] It was in the spirit of Barth that Bonhoeffer composed and delivered his first congregational lecture in 1928 in Barcelona, "The Tragedy of the Prophetic and Its Last-

[22.] [This allusion to Luther to describe an adolescent experience of Bonhoeffer can be read as referring to the death of his brother Walter in 1918 or to the decision to study theology in 1919, or to both as a single experience; but see also the reference to a later experience in Bonhoeffer's letter to Bethge of April 22, 1944, quoted in the title of Hase's memoir.—CG]

[23.] [Barth, *Epistle to the Romans*, 10; for his explication of this slogan see, e.g., *The Humanity of God*, 38–46.—CG]

ing Meaning";[24] he also defended the whole Barth before the astonished faculty and students at Union Theological Seminary in 1930. Although at that time he still lamented the utter lack of understanding for Barth, three years later I found that people there, especially Reinhold Niebuhr and John Baillie, were already more open to this new theology.

The frequent discussions we had after Sunday noon dinners at the Bonhoeffer home addressed Luther's primal experience and his monastic struggles (the Lectures on the Psalms of 1513 and the Lectures on Galatians of 1516–19), Kierkegaard's *Sickness unto Death*, Georges Bernanos's *Star of Satan* and *The Diary of a Country Priest*, Dostoyevsky and the Russian philosophers of religion. We also discussed our own contemporary teachers: in addition to Karl Barth also Friedrich Gogarten, Emil Brunner, Rudolf Bultmann, and the philosophers Martin Heidegger, Erich Przywara, and Eberhard Grisebach; all of them were searching for the "reality" of revelation or for meaning in the contemporary world. Many open-minded students were searching for something similar, as demonstrated by their doctoral dissertations. To mention but three examples from many among my immediate acquaintances: Bonhoeffer's own *Sanctorum Communio* (1930), Franz Hildebrandt's *EST: Das lutherische Prinzip* (1931), and Hans Christoph von Hase's *Die Gegenwart Christi in der Kirche* (1933).

So what does Bonhoeffer mean with his abrupt judgment "phraseology"? We young theologians discovered that our teachers had constructed their theological "system" more or less on the "academic" presuppositions of
594 Kantian or Hegelian philosophy. These presuppositions could not, however, be brought into agreement with the biblical doctrine of God and Christology and certainly not with biblical anthropology. Darwinism was inexcusably ignored at that time by theology; in 1933 Darwinism took thinking people by surprise. We slaved away at the many interpretations of existence. Bonhoeffer's *Act and Being* is a comprehensive attempt to engage with what are in part rather ingenious preliminary attempts offered by the philosophers of our time. In his inaugural lecture he comes to the conclusion that they are all useless,[25] since "theological thought . . . belongs solely to the church."[26] "Jesus, the one for others," does not fit into any system.

[24.] See 2/1.
[25.] [For a more nuanced view, see p. 14.—CG]
[26.] See 2/7, p. 408.

(2) The Reality of Revelation

The assertion that the reality of revelation could be discovered only in the actual existing congregation, and that Christ must be comprehended as "existing as church-community," as implied in his first book, now had to prove itself for him in two contexts: a foreign German congregation that had experienced little of the war, and in American churches in which, at least to a certain extent, people were no longer speaking about Christ and Christ's sacrificial death. Piety was a private mater, and the community was to provide a social setting for believers. That these congregations concretely represented Jesus Christ, the crucified and resurrected, demanded tremendous faith[27] that contradicted liberal theological thinking. The lack of Christological substance in the American proclamation profoundly shocked Bonhoeffer, as demonstrated by his concluding report.[28] Nonetheless his engagement in the same congregations—as well as the engagement of other students—in the charitable activities of metropolitan New York did prompt him to reflection. In the seminary itself the ethicists Ward and Niebuhr addressed theological and "ethical viewpoints in modern literature,"[29] and each week Professor Webber took his seminar to visit one 595
of the social hotbeds and its aid agencies that Christians, Jews, or Chinese kept going. Was the presence of Christ revealed here, too?

Bonhoeffer acquired his most profound impression of a living congregation in the Abyssinian Baptist Church of his friend Frank Fisher in nearby Harlem, where he participated intensively for six months in both the Sunday school and worship. The strong impression of the deep piety, Christian love, and community of these African Americans stayed with Bonhoeffer for the rest of his life.[30] His friend Paul Lehmann wrote: "What was so impressive was the way in which he pursued the understanding of the [Negro] problem to its minutest detail through books and countless visits to Harlem, . . . but even more through a remarkable kind of identity with the Negro community, so that he was received there as though he had never been an outsider at all."[31]

The realization that the African American issue was a touchstone for the faith and credibility of the church never again left Bonhoeffer. It prepared

[27.] The Barcelona lecture "Jesus Christ and the Essence of Christianity" (2/2) reveals something of this problem.

[28.] See 1/181, p. 313.

[29.] See 2/11.

[30.] See *DB-ER*, 154–55; 1/181; 1/182.

[31.] See *DB-ER*, 155.

him to summon the Confessing Church after 1933 to defend persecuted Jews, not just those who had converted to Christianity,[32] and to become engaged at great risk to himself in rescuing individuals.

(3) Peace Ethic

Bonhoeffer found yet another friend among the exchange students, the Frenchman Jean Lasserre, in whom for the first time he encountered a rigorous pacifist, someone who professed obedience to the prohibition against violence in the Sermon on the Mount.[33]

In his Barcelona congregational lecture "Basic Questions of a Christian Ethic" in January 1929, Bonhoeffer dealt from a different perspective with what was for him the extremely pressing topic of peace.[34] Following the
596 commandment of the Sermon on the Mount, he developed an ethically contextual alternative for the case of hostile attack: "If ever I find myself in the distressing situation of having to decide whether to expose my biological brother, my biological mother to the hand of the attacker, or to raise my own hand against the enemy, then the moment itself will doubtless tell me which of these two is and must be my neighbor, including before the eyes of God."[35] Here Bonhoeffer is following the ethical affirmation of a defensive war as was still customary in conservative middle-class circles and churches after 1918. Indeed, he went a dangerous step further: "Every people, however, has within itself a call from God to create its history, to enter into the struggle that is the life of nations. . . . Now, should a people experiencing God's call in its own life, in its own youth, and in its own strength, should not such a people also be allowed to follow that call even if it disregards the lives of other peoples?"[36] Here the voice of the "people without space" [Volk ohne Raum][37] is still speaking, a voice probably also

---

[32.] [See, for example: "The church has an unconditional obligation to the victims of any ordering of society, even if they do not belong to the Christian community" ("The Church and the Jewish Question," in *NRS*, 225).—CG]

[33.] See *DB-ER*, 154; see also ed. note 73 in the editor's afterword of this volume. [Bonhoeffer's close friend Franz Hildebrandt was a lifelong pacifist, as was Paul Lehmann and faculty members such as Reinhold Niebuhr and Harry Ward at the time of Bonhoeffer's postdoctoral year at Union (see Green, *Bonhoeffer*, 338).—CG]

[34.] See 2/3.

[35.] 2/3, p. 371.

[36.] 2/3, p. 373.

[37.] [Hase alludes to the title of the 1926 book by Hans Grimm, *Volk ohne Raum*, which reflects the fact that German nationalist discourse about *lebensraum* (living space) that began in the late nineteenth century had become widespread by the 1920s, a decade in which the Nazi movement also grew. Cf. 2/3, ed. note 34.—CG]

kept alive by the years of hunger but also the voice that was to justify the assault on the Soviet Union in 1941. Today I still know people my own age in whom the traumatic fear lives on that Germany must die of starvation.

Two years later, beginning in November 1930, Bonhoeffer became the spokesperson for the German peace movement, which he estimated to be an "enormous power," and issued the passionate summons: "It must never more happen, that a christian people fights against a christian people, brother against brother, since both have one Father. . . . the last judgement comes for everyone, in America and Germany; and God will judge us according to our faith and love. . . . Today as never before nations of Europe—except Germany—are preparing for war. . . . We must no longer waste time."[38] After returning home from America just one year later, Bonhoeffer was elected at the conference in Cambridge to be youth secretary of the World Alliance for Promoting International Friendship through
the Churches for central and northern Europe. A stormy period of activity 597
began for him on behalf of peace and disarmament—despite those who raged in protest against it, even German professors of theology.[39] He summarized this activity on August 30, 1934, at the conference of the World Alliance and "Life and Work" at Fanø in Denmark, in words that caused both sensation and protest: Christians "cannot take up arms against one another, since they know that by doing so they would be taking up weapons against Christ himself."[40] His next decision was one fraught with consequence, namely, to refuse military service if things got serious, a step that inexorably would have been punished by death; this decision was carried forward by his resolve to bear even the most extreme consequences under the Hitler regime.

(4) Living with Death

"I will not grow old; I'll die when I'm forty years old." Even today I can still remember my horror when Bonhoeffer, sitting at the window of his study in his parents' home, interrupted our conversation and very quietly spoke these words. I objected that, quite the contrary, he ought to give thanks to God for his robust health and energy. "Yes, that's how it is"—was all he could say in response. That was in 1929, but he repeated it later a number of times to other people as well. In what was already a more dangerous period, in 1937, according to Sabine, her husband, Gert Leibholz, visited Dietrich when the latter was sick; during the visit, Dietrich suddenly said, "You and

[38.] 2/9, pp. 417–18. [Bonhoeffer's English.—CG]

[39.] See *DB-ER*, 193–200.

[40.] *NRS*, 290 [trans. altered].

I will not live long lives."[41] Gert Leibholz died in 1984 at the age of eighty, Dietrich in his fortieth year on the gallows, shortly before his camp was liberated. When he decided to return home from America in 1939, shortly before war broke out, to share Germany's fate with his brothers, he also responded to his former teacher Baillie's invitation to deliver guest lectures in Scotland, suggesting the topic "Death in the Christian Message."[42] After the war began and then certainly while in prison, beginning in 1943, Bonhoeffer thought constantly about death, and he had the strength to reflect
598 seriously upon it. The childhood meditations of the ten-year-old remained influential throughout his life, ultimately finding mature expression in the literary attempts (novel and drama) of *Fiction from Tegel Prison* and in the correspondence of *Letters and Papers from Prison*.[43] Martin Heidegger's thesis that human Dasein is differentiated from objective presence-at-hand [Vorhandensein] by a provisional [vorlaufend] anticipation of death accurately describes the sense of time during those years, as well as Bonhoeffer's own thinking and decisions. His undeveloped topic "Death in the Christian Message" still awaits theological-biographical examination.

This context probably also includes the sentence Bonhoeffer spoke often during these years, namely, that "pastors should not be permitted to marry at all in our times so that, regardless of what difficulties the church encounters, they can work on behalf of their congregations without having to think about the welfare of their own families."[44] Even though not a few extremely intelligent and delightful young women from his extended circle of friends were indeed interested in the charming twenty-two-year-old, he was extremely reserved in this matter and was even more so after the emergence of Hitler's Reich. Even though there was no war in 1929 and no National Socialist regime on the horizon, he would not accept my objections that marriage is, after all, God's gift and commandment. In these times pastors must be prepared to make free decisions. And yet, what beautiful wedding sermons he delivered! What profound respect for marriage they express!

[41.] Leibholz-Bonhoeffer, *Bonhoeffers*, 43.

[42.] *DB-ER*, 661.

[43.] In the indexes of the two volumes, the term "death" occurs twenty-eight and thirty-one times, respectively.

[44.] [Hase is reporting from personal memory. The opinion is also reported by others; see, e.g., Arnold, "Conversations with Dietrich Bonhoeffer," 4.—CG]

Truth Has an Effect

With a brilliant *Habilitation* and a good second theological examination "for church service," but inwardly dissatisfied, Bonhoeffer departed for New York on September 6, 1930. After a thorough analysis in *Act and Being* of transcendentalists and ontologists, his search for a philosophy in which one could accommodate the Christian doctrine of God and Christian anthropology to academic thinking and to his contemporaries came to a negative
conclusion. He was standing on the threshold of a new direction. His inau- 599
gural lecture concluded with the words: "My attempt to provide guidelines for a genuine theological anthropology . . . [is possible] only if this theological undertaking is itself incorporated into the reality of the church in which Christ is present. . . . Therefore, every theological problem not only points back to the reality of the church of Christ, but theological thought in its entirety also recognizes itself as something that belongs solely to the church."[45]

With regard to the American churches, Bonhoeffer was interested in what the "reality of the church" there might include in the way of piety but equally in its engagement in the needs of the world; he was also interested in a theology whose liberal and pragmatic philosophical background seemed to contradict the message of the gospel. Regarding the first point, the congregations and their social engagement in the big city provided the right place to study. Regarding the second, Union Theological Seminary provided a similarly appropriate setting as one of the first independent theological seminaries in the United States, as it was located near Columbia University in the center of New York and near the huge African American community of Harlem. Union was an old, endowed institution, supported only by endowments and contributions from its former students. It was open to all denominations, had a first-class faculty composed of lecturers open to contemporary thinking, and had many foreign students and guest professors. As such, it cultivated an incredibly open ecumenical tradition. Even today, Union maintains lifelong contact with its graduates. For example, at the World Council of Churches assembly in Amsterdam in 1948, Union president Van Dusen invited all the Union graduates who were present to a dinner; sixty-three former students, representing all continents, attended. Interdenominational, not bound to any particular church administration, its influence extends into most of the churches in the United States, though also in Asia and South America. On campus, where approximately three

[45.] 2/7, pp. 407–8; cf. *NRS*, 68–69.

hundred postgraduate students lived at that time, ecumenical friendships
are forged. Frank Fisher and Jean Lasserre have already been mentioned as
some of the friends Bonhoeffer made there. Other lifelong friends included
600 the Swiss student Erwin Sutz, who later introduced him to Barth and helped
him during the most difficult times of the war, and the American Paul
Lehmann, with whom Bonhoeffer could engage in intensive discussions
of theological and ethical problems, and who tried with all means at his
disposal to keep him in the United States in 1939 so that Bonhoeffer, a con-
scientious objector,[46] would be safe during the coming war.

With a faculty-student ratio of 1 to 8, contact with professors was naturally quite close. Students chose a professor as a tutor who would then spend one hour a month with them and keep abreast of the students' course of study. Bonhoeffer gratefully acknowledges the "lack of professional constraint in personal contacts."[47] The professors whose courses and seminars Bonhoeffer chose were Reinhold Niebuhr and Harry Ward as social ethicists; John Baillie, a Scot, as a systematician who also conducted a seminar together with the philosopher of religion Eugene Lyman on "philosophical theology." Lyman helped Bonhoeffer understand the regnant philosophy, the pragmatism of William James and John Dewey, by conducting a personal tutorial with him every two weeks for which Bonhoeffer read the complete works of James. Bonhoeffer never ceased to emphasize how rewarding for him this private tutorial was.

It is not the task of this afterword to reconstruct Bonhoeffer's lively theo-
logical debates and experiences during this year. He did this himself best
in his thorough and insightful "Report on My Year of Study at Union Theo-
logical Seminary in New York, 1930/31" for the Church Federation Office
in Berlin, which is found in this volume.[48] At the end of this report, he
mentions that theologically he did not learn a great deal in the United
States. Yet precisely in his attempt to understand the only school of thought
still lacking in his debate with philosophy, namely, pragmatism and behav-
601 iorism, he learned more than he realized; for he learned something that
was missing from German theology—the grounding of theology in real-
ity—and he learned the genuine theological questions that stood behind
the churches' ethical challenges to society. And for their part, his friends at
Union learned that the "theology of crisis" did indeed represent a genuine

[46.] [Bonhoeffer never formally registered as a conscientious objector, but there is documentation from 1932 to 1943 that this was his personal attitude, and his cousin is presumably referring to this attitude; see the editor's introduction, p. 27, note 130.—CG]

[47.] 1/181, p. 306.

[48.] 1/181.

challenge for American theology as well. When I arrived at Union Theological Seminary in the autumn of 1933, the global situation already looked far more threatening. In the United States, the global economic crisis had plunged 12 million people into unemployment, and in Germany Hitler had come to power. Belief in progress was wavering, and one spoke once more about sin. Hence upon my arrival, I encountered a lively interest in Karl Barth and his friends.

What Bonhoeffer himself owed to his American experiences, experiences that had in the meantime matured, we learn from a second, thirty-page report. He wrote it following his decision to return to Germany from New York at the end of July 1939 after a stay of only four weeks and despite the immediate threat of war, a decision to return even though it would bring mortal danger for him as a conscientious objector.[49] During the four weeks between the end of July and the end of August 1939, weeks in which every German secretly prepared for the worst, it would hardly have occurred to anyone to compose long travel reports unless he was urgently concerned with documenting—in the fashion of a last will and testament, as it were—an extremely important ecumenical task on the basis of his experiences. Bonhoeffer's portrayal of his experiences in America served to open his brethren in the Confessing Church, who were fixated on confessions and confessional writings, to the possibility of ecumenical unity with the 220 "denominations" in America and to take this "Protestantism without Reformation" seriously. American Protestants, who as refugees had "already made their confession"[50] and were now dependent on the tolerance of those who had taken them in, no longer had any claims on the Reformation. Bonhoeffer shows that for this Protestantism, it is not confessional writings but rather ritual, liturgy, community life, and constitution that secure the identity of the church. But: "Where ten years ago interest was predominantly centered on the 'social gospel,' today an explicitly dogmatic interest has been aroused, and particularly at the most significant place of theological education in the country, Union Theological Semi- 602
nary in New York."[51] "Reinhold Niebuhr, one of the most significant and creative contemporary theologians in America, whose primary works one must know, if one is to have an overview of the theological situation . . . , [and] the sharpest critic of contemporary American Protestantism and of

[49.] [See ed. note 46.—CG].

[50.] [*DBW* 15:442; the essay "Protestantism without Reformation" is in DBW 15, 2/6. All translated passages from this essay are from the forthcoming *DBWE* 15.—CG]

[51.] *DBW* 15:456.

the contemporary social order, has for years made a profound impression through his strong emphasis on the cross as the center and the end of history, coupled with a strong political theology."[52] Bonhoeffer concludes his report: "The decisive task for today is the dialogue between Protestantism without Reformation and the churches of the Reformation."[53]

When Bonhoeffer writes in Tegel prison on June 8, 1944, "The question is: Christ and the world that has come of age,"[54] he has incorporated into this statement important experiences and insights from his stay in America. Following up on these experiences and insights is a task worthy of the effort.

[52.] *DBW* 15:457–58.
[53.] *DBW* 15:460
[54.] *LPP*, 327.

Reinhart Staats

Editor's Afterword to the German Edition

Dietrich Bonhoeffer's writings from the years 1928–31 include private texts, 603
theological and scholarly texts, and texts relating to practical church matters. Although all these texts are, of course, significant for Bonhoeffer's own external and internal biography, the sheer scope of their intellectual and indeed their geographical horizon, which extends from Barcelona to New York to Berlin, permits the texts to function simultaneously as documents of the contemporary history of the period, particularly of Germany during the waning years of the Weimar Republic (see section I of this afterword). They document the general history of the church during this period (section II) as well as a theological upheaval that in the German Protestant context can be understood as a shift from a liberal Protestant theology to a more church-oriented dogmatic theology, and which ultimately led to the articulation of the theology of the Confessing Church (section III). Finally, these writings from 1928 to 1931 also document Bonhoeffer's initial attempts at a consistent position on church and theology. Occasionally we already find in these writings formulations that emerge in Bonhoeffer's better-known later works in a more fully developed, mature form (section IV).

I

During these years, Bonhoeffer worked more intensively with children and young people than he ever would again. Every section of the present volume confirms a remark he made in his curriculum vitae: "Since I had already become especially interested and engaged in youth work during my period of study in Berlin, it was a great pleasure for me that in Barcelona I could

devote myself particularly to this branch of practical work as well."[1] Young people apparently found him to be an exciting, enthusiastic storyteller. In
604 the children's services in Barcelona, he gathered experiences that were important for his sermons, and for six months he regularly conducted Sunday school lessons for young African Americans in the Abyssinian Baptist Church, one of the large Baptist churches in Harlem. In this young church of the African American working class, he encountered a form of Christianity that was exemplary in its focus on preaching and on church life. "For indeed, God is closer to children than to adults. In this sense, Jesus becomes the discoverer of the child."[2] This sentence, from one of Bonhoeffer's lectures, functions as the guiding principle with which he sets out on the path that would lead him to young people. His experiences with children in Barcelona even prompted him to plan a larger work on "the problem of the child in theology";[3] although he never carried this out, it does resonate at the conclusion of his postdoctoral dissertation, *Act and Being*, where he briefly addresses the "eschatological possibility of the child."[4]

Bonhoeffer's engagement with children and young people during these years was part of a larger process of socialization in Germany at the time that, for many of the children of solid, middle-class families, began in the German youth movement. Indeed, this background often resonates in Bonhoeffer's own dialogue with young people. The guiding moral slogan of Walter Flex's 1917 book, *Der Wanderer zwischen beiden Welten*, which had become the guidebook for idealistic hikers and nature lovers among the postwar youth and for Bonhoeffer as well, was: "Remain pure and come to maturity." In this context, Bonhoeffer's "Notes for a Young Man" also give the impression of a conversation with himself: "Remaining pure means remaining a child, even after you have become a man."[5] This impression is especially strong when Bonhoeffer interprets the travels of the young man in a theological sense as expressed in his favorite verse, "Each day tells the other / my life is but a journey / to great and endless life"; this verse will accompany him the rest of his life.[6]

605 Although this proximity to the German Youth Movement is certainly not everywhere as evident within the larger corpus of Bonhoeffer's work, until

[1.] 1/114.2, p. 220; cf. Feil, *Theology of Dietrich Bonhoeffer*, 68.

[2.] 2/2, p. 351.

[3.] 1/40, p. 128; concerning this entire topic, cf. *DBWE* 2:3.

[4.] Cf. the section in *Act and Being* on "The Definition of Being in Christ by Means of the Future: The Child," (*DBWE* 2:157–61, esp. 159).

[5.] 3/19, p. 553.

[6.] Ibid., p. 551. This verse by Gerhard Tersteegen appears again in 1943 at the conclusion to Bonhoeffer's evening prayer for his fellow prisoners (*LPP*, 141–42).

1931 he was still very much a child of his own German social history in this regard.[7] The Bonhoeffer household, of course, was not really very profoundly affected by the characteristic features of organized youth associations. Members of the family could certainly poke fun at the uniforms, banners, camps, and indeed at the entire emotionalism. Yet even the Bonhoeffer children had gone hiking with one another, relatives, and friends, and had engaged in the accompanying youth rituals of spending the night in some farmer's barn or in youth hostels. Such memories probably provided the background to Bonhoeffer's initial disappointment in Barcelona when he remarked that "the era of the youth movement in Germany passed by without leaving a trace here."[8] In America, too, he immediately sought out activities with young people and enthusiastically recalled his own, decidedly German memories, especially of one particular summer evening singing folk songs around a campfire "with a group of young people from our German youthmovement."[9]

Bonhoeffer's socialization also included a certain cultural disinterestedness that was probably typical of the time and is doubtless more noticeable to those already familiar with the cultural upheaval in Germany that took place during the 1920s and especially in Berlin. Bonhoeffer enthusiastically read good religious literature (Bernanos, Wittig), then in Spain naturally familiarized himself with *Don Quixote* (which would continue to be of significance for him even into his *Ethics*). His lectures and sermons also reveal an excellent familiarity with nineteenth-century German literature (especially with Goethe, Conrad F. Meyer, Fritz Reuter); at the same time, however, he apparently had no interest at all in Hermann Hesse,[10] Thomas Mann, or Alfred Döblin. His reading of Shaw leaves him with the unmistakable impression that Shaw is completely "shallow."[11] He purchased a painting 606
by Picasso in Barcelona more to satisfy his brother Klaus's wishes than his own.[12] By contrast, to the extent Bonhoeffer's political views are evident at all, they were immune to an ideological nostalgia about historical events

[7.] One of Bonhoeffer's contemporaries remarked that although "Bonhoeffer loved and engaged in the various forms of the youth movement, as early as 1925 he already 'didn't like it anymore.'" (Robert Held, personal communication to Hans Pfeifer, August 10, 1985; *DBWE* 9:568, ed. note 40 [trans. altered]); this remark probably applies, however, only to what are being called the "forms" associated with the youth movement.

[8.] 1/5, p. 63.

[9.] 2/10, p. 418.

[10.] Bonhoeffer apparently would have answered no when asked by a Berlin student whether he was familiar with Hermann Hesse's latest publication in 1930, *Narcissus and Goldmund* (Victor Goldschmidt to Bonhoeffer on March 1, 1931; *NL*, C 20).

[11.] See 2/11.4.

[12.] See 1/23.

or achievements. For example, he was disturbed by the originally idealist notion, now applied to secular and political circumstances, that God is identical with historical development, which is also why in America he ultimately criticized the ideologically grounded concept of democracy.[13] The Barcelona sermon "Serve the Time" (*kairos*)[14] clearly expresses Bonhoeffer's understanding of history, an understanding that does, of course, have certain political implications. This sermon consciously addresses the theme of time in connection with the Luther Bible and with Karl Barth's *Epistle to the Romans* and thus does not read "serve the Lord" with the original text in Rom. 12:11, though neither does it subscribe to any historical-theological understanding of *kairos*.[15] Many of Bonhoeffer's contemporaries, however, did indeed experience their own era as a turning point, and in 1933 many nationalist theologians thought they were experiencing a salvific moment, a *kairos*, in the present historical moment.[16] By contrast, even as early as this sermon, which is typical of Bonhoeffer's understanding of history, he believed that such a turning point in history could be brought about only by Christ himself: "The Lord of the ages is God. The turning point of the ages is Christ. The true spirit of the age [Zeitgeist] is the Holy Spirit." This was also the motto of his great-grandfather, Karl August von Hase, the famous nineteenth-century church historian.[17] Bonhoeffer accordingly says of history in the larger sense that "every moment is in immediate relation to God," thus incorporating into the center of his own understanding of history a slightly altered version of Leopold von Ranke's assertion that "every epoch is in immediate relation to God."[18]

607 One might point out that, after his return from Barcelona, Bonhoeffer's political ethics in 1930/31 in Berlin and New York was filled with an emotionalism about peace that was likely influenced by the basic pacifist undercurrent that dominated various German cultural circles at the time. It was, after all, the era of the democratic peace politics of foreign minister and Reich chancellor Gustav Stresemann (who died on October 3, 1929).[19] Bonhoeffer, too, based his own peace ethics, which he was already clearly

---

[13.] Cf. "Das Social gospel" (*DBW* 12, 2/4).

[14.] 3/12.

[15.] Cf. "Das Social gospel" (*DBW* 12:204–5, 210–11). Although Bonhoeffer composed this text [drafted by Lehmann; cf. *DBW* 17:112–13, 115—CG] only after returning from America, it does reflect his American experience.

[16.] Cf. Hirsch, *Die gegenwärtige geistige Lage.*

[17.] See 3/12, p. 531 and ed. note 16.

[18.] See Feil, *Theology of Dietrich Bonhoeffer,* 110–11.

[19.] It was also a time of emergent antiwar literature, beginning with the book *All Quiet on the Western Front,* by E. M. Remarque, which unleashed a flood of literary antiwar

formulating during his early days in America, on his German and specifically Berlin experiences. His call to peace among the nations, however, is always accompanied by apologetic-patriotic recollections about Germany's fate in World War I and by a sharp rejection of the Versailles treaty, with its ascription of guilt solely to Germany (article 231).[20] Hence his thinking from the summer of 1929 on was shaped less by genuinely pacifist than by "semi-pacifist" ideas, even though such ideas could, in fact, be understood as wholly pacifist during that particular period. In this Bonhoeffer was certainly not alone within the political, cultural, or even church circles.[21] This situation may also explain why Bonhoeffer did not see, or did not want to see, "how during the last years of the Weimar Republic the balance of power in German Protestantism shifted again considerably toward an aggressive nationalist sentiment."[22] At least in the extant texts, Bonhoeffer never really comments on the reports he received from Ger-
many[23] about the sudden ascent of the Nazis after the parliamentary elec- 608
tions on September 14, 1930, and about the accompanying surge of the "brown tide." Nor does he take notice of the increasing anti-Jewish sentiment among the German public. In Barcelona, he compared humanity at large to the legendary, eternally wandering Jew Ahasuerus.[24] He did not become aware of the gospel's opposition to racism until he was personally confronted with the "situation of negroes" in America. Bonhoeffer still naively writes, "especially since we don't really have an analogous situation in Germany."[25] Indeed, in 1931 Bonhoeffer's brother Karl-Friedrich still considered the "Jewish question" to be a "joke" compared to the "negro problem" in America.[26]

Of course, these texts become more easily accessible to readers today if we consider not only Bonhoeffer's social milieu but also the change our own system of values underwent under the influence of the momentous subsequent periods in German history. One is much less likely to expect too

---

polemic. See 2/11.1, the bibliographical report "War Literature." Cf. Stickelberger-Eder, *Aufbruch 1914*, 24.

[20.] See 2/9, pp. 412–13 and 414–15.

[21.] Concerning the concept of "semi-pacifism," see Nowak, *Evangelische Kirche und Weimarer Republik*, 193. Concerning pacifism in the larger sense during the Weimar period, see Holl and Wette, *Pazifismus in der Weimarer Republik*.

[22.] Nowak, *Evangelische Kirche und Weimarer Republik*, 193.

[23.] Cf. 1/164, pp. 282–83.

[24.] Cf. 3/18, p. 548, and ed. note 10.

[25.] 1/168, p. 293.

[26.] 1/157.

much of these texts if one considers not only the political but also the cultural changes associated with Hitler's seizure of power in 1933, the division of Germany after 1945, and even the university and educational reforms in Germany after 1968. These and other events and changes now separate us from Bonhoeffer's texts from 1928–31, texts that precisely as documents of contemporary history sometimes seem to have an enormous historical distance from us. At the same time, however, Bonhoeffer's "old fashioned" characteristics occasionally seem not merely reflective of his own time but also quite human in a more universal sense. Hence we never hear anything about Bonhoeffer reading newspapers,[27] or rather, we do so only once in connection with America; yet even then, Bonhoeffer only reads a certain
609 article because it was required as homework for a seminar.[28] This remoteness from contemporary politics can sometimes be taken quite far. Why do we hear nothing about the military dictatorship under General Primo de Rivera (minister president from 1925 to 1930) supported by the Spanish king Alfonso XIII? Or about the serious student unrest that occurred just after Bonhoeffer arrived in Spain and that ultimately caused the universities in Madrid and Barcelona to be closed down in March 1928?

Bonhoeffer's "medium" was personal dialogue with friends and relatives, and in this context one must remember that personal letters as a form of communication have in our own time not necessarily always been replaced by more human forms. Thus this volume also documents an increasingly rare literary genre that at one time played an important role in shaping theological, philosophical, cultural, and even political opinions and which in the larger sense represented an important cultural form of ordinary life, namely, letter writing as a form of daily meditation.

Bonhoeffer was accustomed to form his opinions within his immediate surroundings and within immediate human experiences and reflection. In this connection, we also encounter lovely and accurate descriptions of places and landscapes, especially from his excursions in Spain, in New York, in Cuba, and in Mexico, often even accompanied by theological interpretations as in his assertion that the bullfight, as the "Sunday corrida[,] constitutes the necessary counterpart to Sunday mass,"[29] or in his description of a Corpus Christi procession.[30] One can almost speak of a "theological geography" in this regard. Because the media tend to prevent a person

[27.] Cf. also 1/35; Bonhoeffer searches the newspapers to find out what the weather is like in Germany!

[28.] See 2/12.3, 2/12.7.

[29.] 1/19, p. 83.

[30.] Cf. 1/26.

from experiencing and judging in an immediate, direct fashion, Bonhoeffer was disinclined to let himself be dependent on them. Indeed, he viewed a church based on the media or on advertisement as a Christian scandal. Though he first articulates such fundamental criticism in America, his words could easily be applied to church circumstances today in Europe: "One can hear sermons on almost anything in New York; there's only one thing on which one cannot hear a sermon, or can do so only very rarely, at least I have not managed to, namely, on the gospel of Jesus Christ, on the cross, on sin and forgiveness, on death and life. In New York, they preach about virtually everything; only one thing is not addressed, or is addressed 610
so rarely that I have as yet been unable to hear it, namely, the gospel of Jesus Christ."[31] Bonhoeffer becomes genuinely angry in the face of the weekly programs supported by the larger New York churches "with their daily, indeed almost hourly events, teas, lectures, concerts, charity events, opportunities for sports, games, bowling, dancing for every age group. . . . All these things, of course, take place with varying degrees of tactfulness, taste, and seriousness; some churches are basically 'charitable' churches, others have primarily a social identity. One cannot avoid the impression, however, that in both cases they have forgotten what the real point is."[32]

Bonhoeffer later incorporated similar criticism into his *Ethics*, basing it on the Lutheran doctrine of two kingdoms. The phenomena associated with secularization in the Anglo-Saxon countries, he suggests, have resulted from a lack of the appropriate distinction among the offices and spheres of the state and the church. "The claim of the church-community of believers that it is building up the world with Christian principles ends, as a look at New York church bulletins amply shows, in the complete collapse of the church into the world."[33] In December 1930 Bonhoeffer sadly recounts to Helmut Rößler how difficult he finds it to get into the spirit of Christmas in America; "one feels like one is standing on an observation tower looking out over the whole world, and no matter where one looks, most of what one sees is infinitely depressing." This infinite watching from a distance, from the "observation tower" America offers him, makes him miss the reassuring presence of good friends, the "cloud" of true Christian witnesses. "Then there is also the situation of the church here, which, without suspecting it, is now only smiling in desperation. The almost frivolous attitude here

[31.] 1/181, p. 313. Bonhoeffer considered sermons in the African American Baptist churches to be an exception; cf. 1/181, p. 315.

[32.] 1/181, pp. 313–14.

[33.] *DBWE* 6:127.

is unprecedented, and my hope of finding Heb. 12:1[34] fulfilled here has been bitterly disappointed."[35] This criticism of America recurs in the *Eth-*
611 *ics,* only this time from a more theological perspective: "The godlessness remains concealed. This also means, however, that the blessings of suffering . . . are withdrawn from the church."[36]

Although Bonhoeffer's criticism of American cultural life is probably typical of the German understanding of America prior to 1945, especially where it focuses on the "threat that America does represent for us,"[37] that same criticism has probably still not been overcome in lay and intellectual circles in Europe even today. The same does not hold true with regard to the criticism Bonhoeffer levels at the American educational system. Here he is still presupposing circumstances in Germany that the sociologist Helmut Schelsky portrayed in 1963 in his swan song for the old German university titled *Einsamkeit und Freiheit*[38] and which since the 1960s at the very latest have utterly disappeared. Hence today, too, Bonhoeffer's criticism can seem quite relevant in Germany, in the West as well as in the East, and probably everywhere in Europe precisely because the European educational system no longer radically differs from the American. At the same time, however, one can discern a criticism of Germany's own earlier university system even at this distance, insofar as Bonhoeffer unreservedly acknowledges the possibilities for building one's character within the American educational system. "The unreserved nature of living together prompts one person to be open to another." He does miss the "impetus for developing one's own thoughts that is fostered at German universities by the more reclusive life of individuals. Hence there is little intellectual competition and little intellectual ambition, as a result of which seminars, lectures, and discussions tend to assume a rather harmless character. . . . Although high-school and college preparation for seminary study does indeed teach students a great deal, there is one thing it does not teach them, namely, to work independently. The textbook method and the professors' treatment of students as utter children have disastrous results."[39]

612 Finally, a consideration of the changes in sexual ethics since the 1960s can also facilitate an understanding of Bonhoeffer in the context of

---

[34.] ["Therefore, since we are surrounded by so great a cloud of witnesses, let us also lay aside everything that burdens us." Bonhoeffer's version differs slightly from the NRSV.—CG]

[35.] 1/148.

[36.] *DBWE* 6:127.

[37.] 1/181, p. 320.

[38.] Schelsky, *Einsamkeit und Freiheit.*

[39.] All quotations here are from 1/181, pp. 305–7.

his own time. Social behavior was determined not by "relationships" or "partnerships," as one describes such things today, but by friendships: in Barcelona with Detlef Albers and Hermann Thumm; in Germany with Helmut Rößler and Franz Hildebrandt; and in America with Frank Fisher, Jean Lasserre, Erwin Sutz, and Paul Lehmann. Nicolaus Sombart, son of the well-known sociologist Werner Sombart, recently described his own youth[40] in Berlin-Grunewald with interesting sociological and psychological observations that allow comparison with Bonhoeffer's situation. Sombart, too, recalls the sexual ground rules that applied to middle-class youth: "Romantic relationships at that time were quite chaste."[41] Here we also encounter the model of the "charismatic young man" who becomes a leader for other, generally younger persons. In the noisy "age of machines, of economic competition, of the dominance of fashion and sports,"[42] one needs divine quietude, which Bonhoeffer still dares to describe in enthusiastic analogies drawn from nature typical of the period: "like the young boy who is speechless gazing upon his hero and leader, . . . like the man . . . calmed by the gaze of his beloved woman . . . like all of us who are silenced in reverence and awe at the heart of nature, under the starry heavens."[43] Later, however, Bonhoeffer recognized too well the dangers of the German *Führer* myth, as we see in his radio broadcast of February 1, 1933, "The Führer and the Individual in the Younger Generation,"[44] which touches on a fundamental psychosocial problem of more recent German history as well, namely, the yearning for a youthful male leader.[45] On the other hand, Sombart also recalls the homoerotic milieu surrounding some male 613
organizations during those years. Bonhoeffer's own effect on young men seems to have been free of such undertones. Albrecht Schönherr recalls that "perhaps it was because people saw in him a completely harmonious person, even a 'simple' person in the sense of Matt. 6:22. I myself never sensed anything low or licentious or common in him. Although he could be easygoing, he never 'let himself go.' Young people are attracted to integrated personalities or models of this sort. Bonhoeffer loathed tying people to himself, and perhaps that is precisely why so many were attracted to him."[46]

[40.] Sombart, *Jugend in Berlin*, 17, 20, 166–68.

[41.] Ibid., 17.

[42.] 3/7, p. 500.

[43.] 3/7, p. 501–2.

[44.] *NRS*, 190–204, the expanded form of March 1933.

[45.] Ibid., esp. 196–98.

[46.] In Zimmermann, *I Knew Dietrich Bonhoeffer*, 126 [trans. altered].

II

During these years when Bonhoeffer was an assistant pastor, an academic assistant preparing for his *Habilitation*, and an exchange student in America, his position was still determined by financial and professional dependence, especially on the Church of the Old Prussian Union and its High Church Council in Berlin. Nonetheless, it is impossible to ignore the fact that Bonhoeffer enjoyed a certain preferential treatment. Here and there, these texts also provide a bit of amusing insight for the reader. Even though Bonhoeffer was the successful director of a preachers' seminary in Finkenwalde in 1935, he himself was never required to attend such an institution. The church administration recognized his previous scholarly training, evidenced especially in his postdoctoral dissertation, and as a result excused him from the requirement.[47] Bonhoeffer himself understood the vicar's position in the German Protestant congregation in Barcelona, which lasted a mere eleven months, as a favorable distinction. His supervising pastor, Pastor Olbricht, gave the young doctor of theology considerable freedom, which Bonhoeffer put to good use. He began to work independently on a lecture series on "Crisis and Hope in the Contemporary Religious Situa-
614 tion,"[48] and saw to it that each week the children's services grew increasingly popular until they finally represented a genuine attraction in that congregation. On his own initiative he set up religious instruction for the older classes in the German school located next to the church and as a substitute pastor also conducted services on Majorca and in Madrid. Pastor Olbricht was absent for months, doubtless taking advantage of his assistant's industriousness for a bit of private vacation and offering Bonhoeffer the opportunity for trying out his own theological and ecclesiastical independence.

Back in Berlin, Bonhoeffer clearly missed the freedom he had enjoyed in Spain. His work as an assistant to the systematic theologian Wilhelm Lütgert, during which he not only worked on his postdoctoral dissertation but also had to grade "excruciatingly dumb seminar papers,"[49] seemed like musty, dull confinement. "The air is close in Germany, close and musty enough to suffocate you, and everywhere it smells like sweat. . . . Only one thing is important now: never to forget that this kind of life is unworthy, regardless of whether one is able to overcome it or not."[50] His later negative assessment of his own postdoctoral dissertation, *Act and Being*, ("in the

[47.] Cf. 1/115 and 1/117.
[48.] See 2/1–3.
[49.] 1/87.
[50.] 1/76.

meantime this product has become rather disagreeable to me")[51] suggests that his displeasure with his position as an academic assistant may also have affected his attitude toward his postdoctoral dissertation. Unlike the subsequent history of the dissertation, *Sanctorum Communio,* the work *Act and Being* has not really made much of a mark in Bonhoeffer scholarship, even though it represents an important building block for the development of Bonhoeffer's later, independent theological positions.[52] Because Bonhoeffer lived with his parents and other family members in Berlin from February 1929 till September 1930, his experiences in Berlin during this period are only sparsely documented by letters. His sense of inner freedom from church supervision is evident insofar as he was permitted on several occasions to miss the evening sessions for ministerial candidates held by his 615
church superintendent.[53] The Evangelical High Church Council and the consistory for Mark Brandenburg, a decidedly Prussian bureaucracy that had jurisdiction over Bonhoeffer, did not, however, give Bonhoeffer any preferential treatment in his second theological examination. His overall grade of "fairly good" would correspond in Germany today to a grade of 2+ or "good+" on a scale where the highest score of 1 = "very good." Considering that "very good" was rarely bestowed at that time, Bonhoeffer certainly received a better-than-average overall grade. He received "very good" only in "Dogmatics and Ethics." The only rather puzzling grade is his unremarkable "passed" in catechetical studies even though his supervising pastor, Meumann, with whom he had completed his practical requirements in children's worship, wrote that Bonhoeffer had "considerable experience with church instruction and understands how to adapt to children."[54] It is also striking that on August 23, 1930, the High Church Council rejected, "because of considerations of principle," the application for Bonhoeffer's early ordination, which would have bestowed on him all the rights of a minister, including that of administering the sacraments.[55] At twenty-four years of age, Bonhoeffer was indeed still too young for ordination. Since the time of the early church, the "canonical age" had been fixed at twenty-five, though there had always been exceptions, something explicitly permitted by the law of the Church of the Old Prussian Union.[56] Although it was only

---

[51.] See the letter to Erwin Sutz of February 28, 1932 (*DBW* 11 [1/39], 63).

[52.] Cf. the German editor's introduction to *DBW* 2:12.

[53.] Cf. 1/81 and 1/89, though also already 1/3.

[54.] 1/122.

[55.] 1/129.

[56.] See the "Church Law regarding Training and Employability of Clerics" of March 5, 1927, section 1, paragraph 3: "The Evangelical High Church Council has the authority to excuse a candidate from the age requirement."

after his return from America that Bonhoeffer was ordained on November 15, 1931, at St. Matthias Church in Berlin, there is no indication that the postponement vexed him in any way. Indeed, the correspondence between Berlin and New York shows that Bonhoeffer's church superiors, especially superintendent Max Diestel, were quite supportive of his activities abroad.

As interesting as these texts are with their insights into administrative matters involving the church and the university, they are certainly no less
616 interesting with regard to church life in Barcelona, Berlin, and New York in which Bonhoeffer not only participated but which he also actively tried to shape. Indeed, he never really "takes a vacation" from his church engagement. It seems he is engaged in all its activities, though always without affectation and without being ostentatiously "clerical." He always takes as his point of departure his own theological understanding of the nature of the church, an understanding he always seeks in church praxis itself; although he usually doesn't find it, he doesn't become resigned. It is only in America that he finds church life among whites to be utterly depressing and that among African Americans to represent true Christianity. He viewed this experience as "one of the most important and gratifying events of my stay in America"[57] "I heard the gospel preached in the Negro churches."[58] Anyone familiar with Bonhoeffer's style knows how reserved he was with emotional assessments. In this context, however, in various reports to Berlin, he does indeed speak in superlatives. He was also deeply moved at that time by Negro spirituals and even brought some back to Germany with him; years later he was still impressed enough by these spirituals to introduce them to the candidates in Finkenwalde. Bonhoeffer was probably one of the first Protestant theologians from Germany to recognize and appreciate this music as genuine church music.

Hence one should not mistake Bonhoeffer's practical engagement in and for the church, engagement beginning with his period as a vicar in Barcelona, as an uncritical partisanship for ecclesiastical regulations and institutions. Even his dissertation, *Sanctorum Communio,* with its famous assertion that the "church is Christ existing as church-community,"[59] was basically an ecclesiology, that is, a theory of the church, "half-historical and half-systematic,"[60] which understands itself as a "theological [dogmatisch]" rather than as an empirical "study of the sociology of the church."

[57.] 1/181, p. 315.

[58.] Ibid.

[59.] *DBWE* 1:211 et passim.

[60.] 1925, *DBWE* 9:148.

Well equipped as he was with the Augustinian concept of the church as presented in Harnack's seminar,[61] Bonhoeffer was fully capable of distinguishing between the empirical church and its hidden and future essence. The wheat and the chaff have not yet been separated. Hence there is no Christian basis for fleeing into an understanding of the church that, as is largely the case in neo-Protestantism, is enraptured by the notion of an essentially invisible church. A review written prior to the trip to America emphasizes once again that only "genuine theological concepts" can adequately understand and articulate social phenomena within the Christian church.[62] This rediscovery of a theological understanding of the church was evident elsewhere in Protestant Germany as well during the waning years of the Weimar Republic, as is shown by the studies of Paul Althaus and Hans Christoph von Hase.[63] This theme, however, could be employed both in criticism and in defense of the historical heritage in the concrete church of the present. Both positions are expressed in one particular book that was widely read in Protestant circles at the time, namely, *Das Jahrhundert der Kirche*,[64] by Otto Dibelius, one of Bonhoeffer's superiors and supporters. By contrast, Bonhoeffer himself believed that the tension between the empirical church, on the one hand, and the community of saints, on the other, was a theological truth that was to be fully maintained within theological scholarship as well. 617

In Barcelona, Bonhoeffer was able, as it were, to test in real practice the theological premise presented in his first published work, *Sanctorum Communio*. Never again would he experience so intimately and personally the peculiar character of the German *Volkskirche*. Congregations in foreign countries generally foster the home-church ideal with exceptional dedication: nativity plays, choral clubs, "Relief Agency for Impoverished and Needy Germans in Spain," and so on. Bonhoeffer participated in all such activities, and his sermons and lectures, with their erudite and empathetic ability to draw from the wealth of classical German culture, must be read 618
against this background as well. But something is missing. Today vicars generally have their most enduring or impressive experiences with the *Volkskirche* while performing what are known as their "official duties." The texts in this volume say absolutely nothing about such things, probably because

[61.] Cf. Staats, "Das patristische Erbe."

[62.] 2/8, p. 409.

[63.] Althaus, *Das Erlebnis der Kirche*; idem, *Communio Sanctorum: Die Gemeinde im lutherischen Kirchengedanken*. Hans Christoph von Hase had been working on this topic since 1930; see his *Die Gegenwart Christi in der Kirche* and 1/143, p. 253.

[64.] "The century of the church," published in 1926; 6th ed., 1928.

Bonhoeffer was not permitted to perform marriage ceremonies or funerals. Pastor Olbricht says nothing of such things in his own reports; Bonhoeffer himself writes that during the lengthy absences of Pastor Olbricht he represented him "entirely on my own, and depended only on special occasions on the help of the Spanish Protestant pastor."[65]

In Barcelona, Bonhoeffer encountered a well-situated congregation of businessmen, which not only the German Youth Movement but also World War I apparently passed by without leaving a trace. He writes that the young people "have experienced nothing, or very little, of war, revolution, and the painful aftermath of this period, they live well and comfortably, enjoy perpetually good weather."[66] It is against this background that one must understand Bonhoeffer's occasional justification of war, which in one instance culminates in the dreadful thesis that "love for my people will sanctify murder, will sanctify war."[67] After Bonhoeffer's return to Berlin in 1929, statements such as this and the broader assertion that ethics is "a matter of earth and blood"[68] never recur in his work. It is also worth noting that even in these Barcelona texts, texts deriving from a period in which the young vicar was still very much a participant in the "neo-Lutheran religious revaluation of the idea of the '*Volk*,'"[69] one finds nothing racist, even though the senior pastor of this German congregation, Fritz Olbricht, is
619 depicted in a photo taken after 1933 with the National Socialist party insignia on his lapel.[70]

Back in Berlin, Bonhoeffer also came into contact with the new peace movement in his church, a movement substantively shaped by his general superintendent, Otto Dibelius. Dibelius's book *Friede auf Erden?* was a manifesto condemning war in a fashion that would today be self-evident but at that time was one of extreme courage, so much so that he was openly attacked as a "pacifist" by many Protestants. What Dibelius was actually advocating was a genuinely "Christian pacifism" "with no ifs, ands, or buts, with no limitations and no compromise. . . . *There should be no war because*

[65.] 1/114.2, p. 220. Actual circumstances as documented here seem to contradict Olbricht's remark to the Berlin church administration that the Spanish Protestant pastor was not really a welcome guest at funerals (1/27).

[66.] 1/5, pp. 62–63.

[67.] 2/3, p. 372.

[68.] 2/3, p. 376.

[69.] See Heinz Eduard Tödt, in his essay "Dietrich Bonhoeffer's Ecumenical Ethic of Peace," in *Authentic Faith,* 118 (trans. altered).

[70.] See the *Festschrift zum 100jährigen Bestehen der Deutschsprachigen Evangelischen Gemeinde in Barcelona* (1985), 12.

God does not want war."[71] The church peace efforts of those years cannot have passed Bonhoeffer by without leaving a trace, though the rather modest documentation of the Berlin period 1929–30 offers no direct statements in this regard. He did, for example, know of the Berlin pastor Günther Dehn, who was reviled as a pacifist. Indeed, Bonhoeffer valued Dehn's sermons quite highly.[72] As already suggested, immediately after arriving in America and reflecting on his own Berlin experiences, Bonhoeffer emphasized the yearning for peace in Germany.[73] Around the same time, the Berlin superintendent Max Diestel, his direct church superior, encouraged Bonhoeffer to familiarize himself not only with the world of Christian ecumenism in America but in connection with that, after September 1931, to become involved in the World Alliance for Promoting International Friendship through the Churches, a largely Protestant-influenced ecumeni- 620
cal association advocating peace and reconciliation among nations, where Bonhoeffer ultimately became youth secretary.[74]

Bonhoeffer's inclination to expand his own experience into more distant Christian and non-Christian spheres alike, an inclination his academic supervisors in Berlin encouraged, represented the kind of ecumenical initiative that was still rare in those days. Hanns Lilje, later well known as the bishop of Hanover, though theologically less close to Bonhoeffer, made a similar trip to India after his plans to study in America did not come through and remarked in a retrospective on the years 1927–29 that "this move into the oikumene was inevitable."[75] By contrast, Bonhoeffer's planned trip to India did not come through, a plan he made on three different occasions (1928, 1931, and 1934).[76] Just how strong this yearning for India was in Protestant and ecumenical circles during the 1920s can be seen in the enthusiastic reception of the Indian-Christian itinerant monk "Sadhu" Sundar Singh in Protestant Germany in 1922, and certainly in the

[71.] Dibelius, *Friede auf Erden?* 181; italics in original. (Dibelius's book about "peace on earth," published in 1929, was already in its 3rd ed. in 1930). See also Stupperich, *Otto Dibelius*, 174–82.

[72.] See 1/106. Cf. Scholder, *Churches and the Third Reich*, 1:172–78.

[73.] See ed. note 21. Because Bonhoeffer's peace ethic was already decisively influenced by his Berlin experiences during the years 1929–30, one should not overestimate the influence of the French pacifist Jean Lasserre in America. Bonhoeffer's recollection of a conversation "in America thirteen years ago with a young French pastor" (letter to Bethge, July 21, 1944, *LPP*, 369) is quite critical of Lasserre and is referring to the topic of "a saint" rather than directly to pacifism. Cf. *DB-ER*, 153–54; and *DBWE* 4: 291–93.

[74.] *DB-ER*, 142, 175, and 193–202.

[75.] Lilje, *Memorabilia*, 17.

[76.] *DB-ER*, 105, 327, 406–9.

discussion during the subsequent years among well-known ecumenists such as Friedrich Heiler and Nathan Söderblom.[77] In 1928, while Bonhoeffer was in Spain, his grandmother had encouraged him "to get to know this contrasting world in the East," which included "India, Buddha, and his world."[78] Hence it was not just sympathy for Gandhi's nonviolent resistance and pacifism that prompted this initial plan to travel to India. When the third India plan almost succeeded in 1934, with Bonhoeffer wanting nothing more than to go "straight to Gandhi," his grandmother was again the first to learn of the plan. Now it was apparently the themes of "community life as well as methods of training" that were to secure him an invitation to the great Mahatma through Bishop Bell's mediation. Instead Bonhoeffer decided to go, not to India, but to Pomerania, "where he would have to form his own ashram—the seminary—without prior experience in the
621 Far East."[79] These initial plans to travel to India and America were thus prompted mainly by an early yearning for structured "community life."[80] Regarding the period shortly after Bonhoeffer's return from America, Robert Stupperich, assistant pastor in Potsdam, recalls that in 1931 Bonhoeffer visited him with several students and during a subsequent walk in the forest spoke about the necessity of a *vita communis* for Protestant theologians.[81]

The ideas that will inform Bonhoeffer's later work so decisively—Christian peace ethics and a Christian understanding of the Oikumene, based on the experience of life together in discipleship of Christ—begin to emerge already during these initial years of church work. In February 1930 in Berlin, Bonhoeffer finds himself yearning for his old congregation in Barcelona, "of which I am very fond, and I feel in general that academic work will not hold me for long."[82] Ten months later he writes from America, "I am drawn more and more to the ministry."[83] This present volume thus documents within Bonhoeffer's engagement in the church the inner reserve he developed toward traditional academic theology, a reserve that only after 1933, under altered circumstances, became a farewell.

[77.] Biehl, *Der Fall Sadhu Sundar Singh*.
[78.] Letter of February 20, 1928 (*NL*, C 2); unpublished.
[79.] See *DB-ER*, 406–9, esp. 409.
[80.] See *DB-ER*, 105.
[81.] See Staats, "Das patristische Erbe," 182.
[82.] 1/106, p. 205; see also *DB-ER*, 128.
[83.] 1/150, p. 267; see also *DB-ER*, 167.

III

Among the great theological personalities at the Berlin university still accompanying Bonhoeffer's development during these years, only one really steps into the foreground during the summer of 1930: Adolf von Harnack. The texts in this volume offer few details documenting how, for example, Bonhoeffer's overall understanding of Luther continued to be determined by the church historian Karl Holl, who died in 1926, or how he was otherwise influenced theologically by the historian of dogma Reinhold Seeberg, who was his dissertation supervisor, and by the systematic 622
theologian Wilhelm Lütgert, as whose assistant he worked. He mentions Holl only as an aside and even then already with noticeable distance in his academic inaugural lecture in Berlin, though his critical comment ("peculiarly meager estimation of Christology in Luther")[84] does indeed focus on precisely the weak point in the interpretation of Luther represented by Holl and his school. Bonhoeffer's relationship with Seeberg and Lütgert seems to have been more on a professional level. While he criticizes Seeberg once as a preacher,[85] he views Lütgert as being under Seeberg's theological influence: "Lütgert will have even less understanding of my work than does Seeberg."[86] By contrast, Bonhoeffer maintained a close teacher-pupil relationship with "his Excellency" Harnack, the universally learned church historian who as the first president of the Kaiser Wilhelm Society[87] was respected far beyond the discipline of theology.[88] In the margin of his own copy of his theses defended at his doctoral examination in 1927, Bonhoeffer wrote an emotional and thus extremely revealing "address" to Harnack, insisting that "what I have learned and understood in your seminar is too closely bound to my entire person for me ever to forget it."[89] In a letter from Barcelona, he confesses that his own "theological foundation" was laid in Harnack's seminar.[90] Harnack himself dedicated one of his last writings to his private seminar and in the foreword added a cordial reference to Bonhoeffer's participation; the work of the true theologian, he says, should be an undertaking filled with "joy"! Bonhoeffer alludes to 623

[84.] 2/7, p. 401.

[85.] See 1/106. In Seeberg's seminar, Bonhoeffer misses not so much the teacher, that is, the personal relationship, as the "shared scholarly work"; see 1/36, p. 119.

[86.] 1/70, p. 169; see also *DB-ER*, 121.

[87.] Today it is called the Max Planck Society.

[88.] Concerning this relationship and the following discussion, see Kaltenborn, *Adolf von Harnack als Lehrer Dietrich Bonhoeffers*, as well as Staats, "Adolf von Harnack"; idem, "Das patristische Erbe."

[89.] *DBWE* 9 (2/16), p. 439.

[90.] Cf. 1/93.

this assertion a few months later when he delivers a memorial address for Harnack, who died on June 10, 1930, to Harnack's last circle of students and a distinguished audience: "Non potest non laetari, qui sperat in Dominum."[91] In his address, Bonhoeffer emphasizes that Harnack's legacy included not only the freedom of research, which was a basic principle of liberal theology, but also the fact that Harnack was a "theologian"—"this was the greatest thing for us."[92]

This assessment of Harnack as a "theologian" rather than as a historian, philologist, and socially conscious and active cultural politician must have seemed like a rather daring assertion at that time, when a deep theological chasm already separated Barth and Harnack. By contrast, Otto Dibelius, who for years had himself been a senior student in Harnack's seminar, was echoing a widespread opinion when he asserted that although he had learned a great deal from Harnack, he had not learned any theology.[93] Bonhoeffer's public championing of Harnack as a theologian, however, did not imply an uncritical acceptance of Harnack's theology. As early as the Barcelona sermons and lectures in which Bonhoeffer touches on the critique of religion articulated by "dialectical theology," a critical relationship with Harnack emerges in which Bonhoeffer is searching for his own, independent insights. Yet precisely the independence and freedom of the theologian "who formed his own free judgment each and every time, and expressed it clearly whatever the anxious inhibitions of the crowd" is what characterizes Harnack's inheritance, namely, the realization that theological truth comes about in joy and freedom and is thus bound only by "the eternal ground
624 of all thought and all life."[94] It is thus not so much individual theological positions as Harnack's own theological understanding of the "world" and of "human beings," that is, Harnack's own methodology, concealed in all his scholarly activity, that Bonhoeffer retained in memory, as he wrote in 1936, "with a peculiar, doubtless extremely 'fleshly' [sarkischen] love."[95] Shortly before his death in 1930, Harnack had outlined a model of the "stages of scholarly and scientific knowledge" according to which the high-

[91.] Cf. 2/4, p. 381, and ed. note 9. Harnack's dedication of his *Einführung in die Alte Kirchengeschichte* (see 1/93, ed. note 2) refers, by way of several allusions to the theme "joy," to Bonhoeffer's active participation in the senior seminar; Bonhoeffer was in charge of the joint project on the theme of "joy" that ultimately became a celebratory gift for Harnack on his seventy-fifth birthday in 1926 (*DBWE* 9 [2/11], pp. 370–85).

[92.] 2/4, p. 381.

[93.] Stupperich, *Otto Dibelius*, 37.

[94.] 2/4, pp. 380–81.

[95.] Postcard from Bonhoeffer to Helmut Goes in July 1936; unpublished (*NL* addendum 15).

est stage of any discipline consists in the understanding of human beings with their ideas, standards, and values. It is here that one finds the ultimate ethics of scholarly and scientific knowledge: "Scholarly and scientific disciplines seek to determine, for the sake of purposive action, a knowledge of what is real."[96] This succinct statement also reflects an understanding of the theologically comprehensible relationship between a knowledge of reality and Christian ethics that will ultimately distinguish Bonhoeffer's own life work.

In Seeberg's seminars, but particularly in Harnack's, which Bonhoeffer attended most frequently, a patristic baseline was drawn that constantly reemerges in Bonhoeffer's later theology. Indeed, it was probably also Bonhoeffer's extremely intimate familiarity with the theology of the church fathers that later prompted him to seek dialogue with Anglican theologians, since patristics was part of the fundamental theological training of all Anglicans. Between 1928 and 1931 Bonhoeffer comes to a positive appreciation of the church fathers Cyprian, Augustine, and John Chrysostom, as well as of the Constantinian shift in the assessment of Eusebius.[97] One particularly good example is the Cyprianic ecclesiology Bonhoeffer invokes in a rather Catholic-sounding sermon in Barcelona on the essence of the church. This sermon concludes with an invocation of Cyprian's words, "God our Father, the church our Mother, Jesus Christ our Lord—that is our faith."[98] Harnack would never have preached in such a way. In the larger 625
sense, Bonhoeffer's independence over against Harnack (which Harnack himself wanted!), as well as his ultimate shift toward a theological understanding of the church of the sort he encountered in Barth's circle, can be discerned quite well in Bonhoeffer's ecclesiology during these years. Quite early, in fact, already in his dissertation, *Sanctorum Communio*, Bonhoeffer altered Harnack's question regarding the "essence of Christianity" into the question regarding the "essence of the church." In 1932 Bonhoeffer quite deliberately gave one of his first lecture courses this title.[99] This shift toward a new understanding of the church also becomes evident in one of the Barcelona lectures Bonhoeffer gave that is closely related to Harnack, not only in its title but also in its terminology: "Jesus Christ and the Essence

[96.] Harnack, "Stufen wissenschaftlicher Erkenntnis," 202; cf. Staats, "Adolf von Harnack," 102–4.

[97.] See the subject index; concerning this entire issue, see Staats, "Das patristische Erbe."

[98.] 3/8, p. 511.

[99.] "The Essence of the Church." See *DBW* 11, 2/9; previously published in *GS* 5:227–75.

of Christianity." Here, however, the decidedly liberal Protestant notion that "Christianity conceals within itself a germ hostile to the church" is balanced by the additional remark, "yet Christianity needs the church." Ultimately even direct opposition to Harnack emerges in the contentions that "the assertion of the infinite value of the soul is un-Christian" and "Christianity is neither congenial to culture nor does it have faith in progress."[100] As such statements show, although Bonhoeffer's relationship to Harnack was indeed characterized by loyalty and continuity, it was also informed by critique and an inclination to make a new beginning.

Bonhoeffer's former teacher John Baillie recalled in 1956 that the recipient of a German Academic Exchange Service [DAAD] fellowship was "the most convinced disciple of Dr. Barth."[101] For his own part, Bonhoeffer encountered in American theologians an utter lack of understanding of Paul, Luther, and the Reformation doctrine of justification, and found their thinking everywhere characterized instead by a "Pelagianism" based on justification by works.[102] Would this not have driven him to become a "Barthian" in America? That is, doesn't his transatlantic experience
626 relativize his partisanship somewhat?[103] One striking feature is that in his assessment of Luther's *De servo arbitrio* during his stay in America, Bonhoeffer draws heavily from Harnack's work on the history of dogma.[104] Similarly, Bonhoeffer's emphasis in America on God's self-revelation "in history," his emphasis on the incarnation ("God really entered history"), and the remark that revelation takes place in historical facts rather than in ideas

[100.] 2/2, pp. 354–55.

[101.] *DB-ER*, 158.

[102.] See 1/181, p. 311.

[103.] The files of the Evangelical Central Archives in Berlin (EZA 5/196) contain a position paper of the Berlin mission scholar Julius Richter, whose responsibilities included evaluating the reports of returned theological fellowship recipients (besides Bonhoeffer at Union Theological Seminary, recent returnees included Decke-Cornell and Klingenberg in Hartford, Gerber and Kandler in Chicago, and Luecken in Frankfort). Richter remarked that of all the reports that year, "only the one presented by Dr. D. Bonhoeffer had any depth." Although Richter found his own observations in the United States confirmed by Bonhoeffer's report, he also thought the latter's report too one-sided and suggested that "one cannot judge the entire United States from the vantage point of New York alone." Bonhoeffer himself anticipated this objection in a letter to Max Diestel on April 25, 1931 (1/170). The late date of Richter's own remarks (December 10, 1931) shows that they were made in connection with Bonhoeffer's work with the World Alliance (which began in early September 1931). Along with Diestel, Dibelius, Deißmann, and others, Richter probably welcomed Bonhoeffer's entry into the peace work of the World Alliance even if he was not personally involved in assisting Bonhoeffer in the process. See *DB-ER*, 191.

[104.] See 2/14, p. 443.

all accord rather poorly with a pure Barthian position.[105] Nonetheless, in his New York seminar presentations Bonhoeffer clearly distances himself from the Ritschlian school in Berlin in which he himself had grown up;[106] he speaks a clear yes to the forensic doctrine of justification ("the coming grace") and, quite in the sense of Karl Barth, rejects any and all psychologically based doctrines of justification.[107] Of course, such positions could only provoke courteous repudiation from his American teachers, as shown by one of Reinhold Niebuhr's critiques.[108] Eberhard Bethge drew attention to this situation quite early, pointing out that "the interpretation of Barth in Bonhoeffer's work at Union Theological Seminary encountered an audience that was simply not prepared to turn down this particular path in theological history."[109] Hence when reading these texts, which were 627
doubtless of considerable importance for Bonhoeffer's intellectual development, readers today should keep in mind their original *Sitz im Leben* and remember the context in which they occurred. Texts concerning contemporary themes of practical ethics, for example, originally also functioned as brief reports on the writings of other authors. In providing such concentrated reports on these writings and only cautiously inserting his own evaluations, Bonhoeffer was following the methodology of scholarly indices he had learned from his Berlin teachers. Hence the great apologia for Barth in the lecture "The Theology of Crisis" is first of all an objective presentation that seeks to do justice to Barth's position; hence it is probably best not to generalize its introductory sentence, "Coming . . . to a man like K. Barth I confess that I do not see any other possible way for you to get into real contact with his thought, than by forgetting at least for this one hour everything you have learned before concerning this problem."[110] Given its context, this sentence is probably better understood as "you ought to forget what has been said in the preceding seminar classes on the relationship between philosophy and science."

The significance for theological history of the texts in this volume, a volume covering such a wide geographical and biographical horizon, cannot be assessed adequately in this afterword. Between Harnack and Barth, Bonhoeffer also encountered the American philosophy of pragmatism,

---

[105.] See 2/17, 458. Hans Pfeifer and Eberhard Bethge both believe that in America Bonhoeffer tended to "mingle his own propositions with those of Barth and actually attribute them to him, no doubt without realizing it" (*DB-ER*, 159 and note 38).

[106.] See 2/17, p. 469.

[107.] See 2/15, pp. 416–17.

[108.] 2/15, ed. note 13.

[109.] *GS* 3:8.

[110.] 2/17, p. 463; see also *DB-ER*, 159.

on the one hand, and even before that the philosophy of existentialism in Berlin. One might, however, draw attention especially to Bonhoeffer's Berlin inaugural lecture, "The Anthropological Question in Contemporary Philosophy and Theology,"[111] a piece closely related to his postdoctoral dissertation, *Act and Being*. Bonhoeffer's critique of Martin Heidegger, the philosophical head of existentialist theology, contains a harsh warning: he "has been accused of being petit-bourgeois."[112] The danger here, Bon-
628 hoeffer suggests, is that of philosophical individualism. "Ultimately the person himself answers the question about the human being. . . . And precisely by grasping his own existence completely in this world, the human being ultimately is able to do violence to the world."[113] By contrast, Bonhoeffer then explicates "what is really new" in the dialogical philosophy of Eberhard Grisebach, who "cannot conceive the human being apart from the concrete other person." "In reality, existence is only in an encounter with a You." Hence Bonhoeffer is also initially quite in accord with the theological premise of Friedrich Gogarten, especially in the latter's corrective of Barth, to the extent "the theology of revelation excludes individualistic thinking." In conceding to one's fellow human being God's own absolute claim, however, Gogarten ultimately calls into question God's divine nature, and theology becomes innerworldly ethics.[114] In retrospect, it is regrettable that Bonhoeffer did not perceive "what is really new" in Grisebach also in the theology of Martin Buber.[115]

IV

Finally, let us now try, as far as possible, to view the colorful collection of texts in this volume against the larger backdrop of Bonhoeffer's collected works. The most promising point of departure is probably the evaluation of this period in his life he himself composed in his prison cell on April 22,
629 1944. Hans Christoph von Hase has quite appropriately introduced his own account with this recollection in which Bonhoeffer remarks, "I don't think

[111.] See 2/7.

[112.] 2/7, p. 396.

[113.] Ibid. I believe that Bonhoeffer's critique of Heidegger coincides with the critique Hans Jonas formulated decades later regarding Heidegger's reception among theologians: "The being whose fate Heidegger ponders, is the quintessence of this world; it is *saeculum*. Against this, theology should guard the radical transcendence of its God" (Jonas, "Heidegger and Theology," 248).

[114.] Cf. 2/7, p. 402.

[115.] Although Martin Buber taught in Frankfurt from 1923 to 1933, German Protestant theology took notice of him only after 1945. Cf. Buber, *I and Thou*, and "Dialogue," in *Between Man and Man*, 1–39; cf. also Feil, *Die Theologie Dietrich Bonhoeffers*, 31.

I have changed very much, except perhaps at the time of my first impressions abroad, and under the first conscious influence of Papa's personality. Then a turning away from the phraseological to the real ensued."[116] The question remains open whether Bonhoeffer is including his experiences in Rome in 1924. In any event, the enduring impressions accompanying his experiences in Spain in 1928–29 and America in 1930–31 are doubtless to be included here. Bonhoeffer articulated the significance of these years in three other statements as well whose contexts are thus certainly worth examining here. For in these few statements one can discern, as if in a magnifying glass, not only the larger significance of these years themselves but also elements that will ultimately endure and come to fruition in Bonhoeffer's later work.

1. After the vicar had spent a few weeks getting settled in Barcelona, he made a diary entry on March 8, 1928, that breaks off with the following words: "My theology is beginning to become humanistic; what does that mean? I wonder whether Barth ever lived abroad? Wittig's *Leben Jesu* is making a very strong impression on me. Tomorrow I am to preach here for the first time. I decided on Rom. 11:6 as my text, after having begun to work on many other texts."[117] This statement should be understood within its proper context. What he comes to see more clearly is not what separates him from Barth but rather what he fails to find in the leader of the theology of revelation, namely, a humanistic theology focused on the whole world in its history. "Humanistic theology" also refers specifically to classical antiquity, whose open questions Christianity itself answers. In Barcelona he picks up the legendary motif from antiquity: "The great Pan is dead"; "it represents a pagan counterpart to the message of Good Friday" to which the Christian Easter message responds: "Not 'the great Pan is dead,' but rather God lives, and we with God."[118] Yet another motif from antiquity that Bonhoeffer transfers into humanistic theology is the legend of the giant Antaeus, who 630
was invincible as long as his feet were touching the earth. In the symbol of Antaeus, Bonhoeffer appropriates Nietzsche's insistence that we develop in ourselves the kind of loyalty to the earth so characteristic of antiquity; he then develops that symbol into an understanding of a Christianity that is itself bound to the earth, a Christianity that orients itself toward the incarnation of the God of the Christians and thence comes to an understanding

[116.] Letter of April 22, 1944, *LPP*, 275. [For a discussion of this statement, see the editor's introduction, pp. 4, 38–41. Translation is from the forthcoming English edition of *DBW* 8.—CG]

[117.] 1/5, p. 64.

[118.] 3/3.1, pp. 488–89.

of reality in the larger sense.[119] The symbol of Antaeus will accompany Bonhoeffer even into his very last conversations concerning the ethics of this-worldly responsibility.[120] In a letter to Barcelona written from Berlin in 1930, Bonhoeffer writes that "perhaps today as never before, 'spirit' really is to be found in the particular, that is, precisely in the 'material,' in concretely given reality—and precisely not in 'intellectuality' [Geistigkeit]; viewed from this perspective, I really do find in Barcelona life something like an unconscious search for truth being expressed."[121]

Josef Wittig's book *Leben Jesu in Palästina, Schlesien und anderswo,* which strongly influenced Bonhoeffer at that time, can also help explain this shift toward a "humanistic" theology. Wittig was a patristics scholar and Catholic writer who was for a time condemned by the Roman Curia for his "modernism." In this book he presents a modern example of what discipleship to Jesus means, giving the Sermon on the Mount a central role and attesting Christianity's openness to the world with the inclusion of antiquity: "The priest who is to become a new Paul must have been with Paul in Jerusalem, Athens, and Rome if he is to know how Paul would preach in Berlin."[122] Finally, even Bonhoeffer's first sermon in Barcelona on the freely
631 chosen passage Rom. 11:6 can help explain his diary remarks. This sermon addresses one of the basic Christian beliefs regarding grace (Bonhoeffer's famous book *Discipleship* will first address the notion of "costly grace" in 1937):[123] It is in God's own goodness that "our gaze is opened to the entire world."[124] "Only one thing remains, namely, that God comes to human beings and bestows grace[,] the path from eternity into time, the path of Jesus Christ."[125] The critique of an ethic of principles that occurs for the first time in the Barcelona texts is thus also to be understood in connection with Bonhoeffer's new personal experiences. This is "the great moral renewal Jesus brought about, the dismissal of principles."[126] The attendant critique of an unclear understanding of "religion" does admittedly correspond largely to Karl Barth's critique of religion. Still, after Barcelona Bonhoeffer's own theology is more humanistic, which also means that it is

[119.] See 3/12, p. 351, and 2/3, pp. 377–78.

[120.] See the 1943 drama fragment, *DBWE* 7:67–70; see also Feil, *Theology of Dietrich Bonhoeffer,* 112.

[121.] 1/83, p. 182.

[122.] Wittig, *Leben Jesu,* pt. 2. Bonhoeffer also expresses his high appreciation of this book in a letter to his parents, saying that he is "finding Wittig really excellent" (1/13).

[123.] *DBWE* 4:43–56.

[124.] 3/2, p. 481.

[125.] Ibid., p. 484.

[126.] 2/3, p. 365.

more ecumenical without imposing on his understanding of the Oikumene any institutional ecclesiastical elements.

2. One of the pupils from the Thursday group in the Berlin Grunewald congregation wrote to Bonhoeffer in New York on June 19, 1931: "I also think I have understood what you wrote about yourself, especially about the renewal of your philosophy and theology through your new perspectives."[127] Unfortunately, the letter in which Bonhoeffer might have mentioned such "new perspectives" has not been preserved. The texts in this volume relating to his time in America only permit us to speculate whether Bonhoeffer was positively influenced by the American philosophy of "pragmatism," which was the main issue in this regard. We do indeed read in Bonhoeffer's summarizing report that he "read almost the entire philosophical works of William James, which really captivated" him; other well-known empirical thinkers also played a role, including Dewey, Russell, Watson, and Whitehead. In the final analysis, however, the critique predominates; Bonhoeffer still insists that in such a context religion inevitably turns into pure social ethics; among epigones, pragmatism becomes 632
"radical immanent ethical humanism."[128] His letters to Max Diestel speak even more unequivocally about the betrayal of real theology, insisting that "the Jamesean notion of the finite God is rooted deep within most of the theologians and pastors here. They find it to be profound and modern and do not sense at all the impertinent frivolousness in all such talk. Despite all this, I am nonetheless grateful to have been so thoroughly introduced to these basic questions again. Indeed, here one once again understands what important questions really are and how much one owes to our own theology."[129]

Hence it is precisely American theology that leads Bonhoeffer back again to European theology. Bonhoeffer himself presents an example of this situation in his *Ethics*, where he recalls a horrific example of false judgment leading to a false verdict, the famous "Scottsboro case," which was handed down in 1931 against nine young African American men and which provoked a storm of indignation among respected Europeans as well. "A Christian, disturbed by these events, asked a leading church official in Germany to consider raising his voice also in protest against this case. For his refusal to do so, the official cited the 'Lutheran' understanding of vocation, that is, the limitation of the extent of his responsibility."[130] In this context

[127.] Letter from Victor Goldschmidt to Bonhoeffer on June 19, 1931 (*NL*, C 20).

[128.] 1/181, pp. 310, 311; cf. *DB-ER*, 161.

[129.] 1/150, p. 266. Cf. also 1/170.

[130.] *DBWE* 6:295. See Carter, *Scottsboro*.

Bonhoeffer is criticizing the kind of strict interpretation of Lutheran vocational ethics that was loudly proclaimed precisely among National Socialist Lutheran theologians toward the end of the Weimar Republic. According to Paul Althaus, for example, every nation had its "very own vocation."[131] It is interesting to see how in his *Ethics* and on the basis of his experiences in
633 America, Bonhoeffer wishes to keep the "boundaries" of vocational ethics open over against the neo-Lutheran tradition, since the "responsibility in a vocation follows the call of Christ alone."[132] It is similarly striking how Bonhoeffer provides a surprising Christian interpretation to the call of the European philosopher Friedrich Nietzsche not only, as already seen, regarding loyalty to the earth but also in the commandment "to love those farthest away."[133] Hence it was primarily from his experiences in the church itself that Bonhoeffer acquired the new theological views in America that he would then try to develop more fully in debate with the European tradition. His recollection that it was only in the black churches that he heard the gospel preached remained ineradicable. In America he thus continues and strengthens the development of the ecumenical understanding of the church on which he first embarked in Barcelona. For it is precisely in the church itself that the gospel must retain its radical nature so that discrimination against distant nations and races comes to an end.

3. One of Bonhoeffer's new theological views is apparently also associated with a personal crisis around Christmas 1930. On a hot August day in 1943, Bonhoeffer writes to his fiancée from his prison cell: "The sun has always attracted me, and I've often been reminded by it that human beings were taken from the earth and don't just consist of thin air and thoughts. So much so that once, when I went to Cuba to preach there at Christmas, and exchanged the ice of North America for its luxuriant tropical vegetation, I almost succumbed to sun-worship and could hardly remember what I was really supposed to preach. It was a genuine crisis, and a hint of it assails me every summer when I get to feel the sun."[134] It was during this crisis that he wrote the letter to Helmut Rößler in which he speaks of depressing
634 experiences and of how he misses the warm closeness of friends and the

[131.] See Nowak, *Evangelische Kirche und Weimarer Republik*, 229. Bonhoeffer's lost letter from 1931, to "a leading church official," was thus presumably addressed to Althaus (after 1926 president of the Luther Society) or to a church figure closely associated with him; Bethge suspects it was Otto Dibelius; see *DBWE* 6:295, ed. note 181).

[132.] *DBWE* 6:293.

[133.] Ibid., 294. Cf. Nietzsche, *Thus Spoke Zarathustra*, especially the chapter "On Love of the Neighbor" (*Portable Nietzsche*, 172–74).

[134.] *Love Letters from Cell 92*, 68.

"cloud" of true Christian witnesses.[135] The sermon delivered in Havana on the fourth Sunday in Advent 1930 does indeed contain traces of this personal insecurity.[136] At least in its original manuscript, this sermon is incomplete and breaks off before the end. Its theme is "the death of Moses" (Deut. 32:48–52), a theme that, as shown by the prison poem he composed in September 1944, Bonhoeffer could never quite shake.[137] The life of Moses was "a journey to the promise, a journey in hope through disappointments, tribulations, defeats, through apostasy and unfaithfulness."[138] And yet not even Moses reaches the promised land; up to the bitter end he must experience only the penultimate in order to get to the ultimate: "Ascend this mountain . . . and die!"

What resonates in these sentences is the inevitability of the experience of death. As early as the first lecture in Barcelona, "The Tragedy of the Prophetic and Its Lasting Meaning," Bonhoeffer emphasizes the enduring Christian truth expressed in the Old Testament wisdom found in the prophetic oracle in Jeremiah 45: "I am going to break down what I have built, and pluck up what I have planted—that is, the whole land. And you, Jeremiah, wanted to desire great things for yourself."[139] Bonhoeffer will return to this theme in prison: "We will not bemoan the fragmentariness of our life, but rather rejoice in it. I can never get away from Jeremiah 45."[140] In the lecture "The Theology of Crisis,"[141] which Bonhoeffer wrote about the same time as the crisis in Cuba, the necessity of the experience of death ultimately issues in what is also a theological insight, one that through the same form as Jesus's own death cry, "My God, my God, why have you forsaken me?" (Mark 15:34), becomes an insight into true human existence.[142] As is well 635
known, Bonhoeffer's prison thoughts prompt him to evoke this cry from the cross when he writes, "The God who is with us is the God who forsakes us. The God who lets us live in the world without the working hypothesis of God is the God before whom we stand continually."[143] This statement, too, may distantly derive from Bonhoeffer's first experiences abroad.

[135.] See 1/148, especially the reference to Heb. 12:1, and also the letter to his friend Rößler, 1/78.

[136.] 3/24.

[137.] "The Death of Moses," in *Dietrich Bonhoeffer's Prison Poems.* [In the *DBW* series, the poem is in *DBW* 8, 4/190.—CG]

[138.] 3/24, p. 586.

[139.] Jer. 45:4–5 [NRSV trans. altered]; cf. 2/1, p. 340.

[140.] February 23, 1944, *LPP*, 219; cf. also *LPP*, 105, 297, 370.

[141.] 2/17.

[142.] 2/17, p. 465.

[143.] Letter of July 16, 1944, *LPP*, 360.

Addendum[144]

(1) In the wake of the historical changes following the fall of the Berlin Wall in 1989, Holger Roggelin found two letters from Klaus Mehnert to the Church Federation Office in the Archives of the Evangelical Church of Germany in Berlin (Evangelische Zentralarchiv) (inventory EZA 5/2865) that confirm our suspicion that it was Mehnert, as secretary of the German Academic Exchange Service, who took the initiative with regard to Bonhoeffer's fellowship in America. In the first, dated January 10, 1930, Mehnert mentions a phone call with Bonhoeffer in which he encouraged the latter "by all means to apply" even though he did not yet know of any open positions "in New York and Chikago [*sic*]." In the second letter, dated March 10, 1930, Mehnert writes, " Contrary to expectation, we have succeeded in securing Dr. Bonhoeffer a position to study at Union Seminary in New York. We just received the following telegram from Miss Dybwad: 'Bonhoeffer accepted Union.'"

At the beginning, however, it was the farsighted academic and intellectual concern of Berlin church figures, most notably Max Diestel, who stood behind the practical engagement of the German Academic Exchange Service on Bonhoeffer's behalf and behind Union Theological Seminary's acceptance of Bonhoeffer's application. In a letter written on November 5, 1942, commemorating Diestel's seventieth birthday, Bonhoeffer recalls two momentous phone calls with Diestel. In the first, in December 1927, Diestel asked him whether he wanted to go to Barcelona as an assistant pastor—an event that, as Bonhoeffer writes, "set my entire thinking on a track from
636 which it has not yet deviated and never will." In the second call, in May 1930, Diestel offered him the fellowship at Union Theological Seminary in New York, where he experienced a year "that has been of the greatest significance for me up to the present day" (*DBWE* 16:367–68). It might be noted that Bonhoeffer did, however, err regarding the second phone call, since a handwritten marginal note in Mehnert's March 10, 1930, letter indicates it was the Church Federation Office that informed Bonhoeffer on March 14, 1930, at the latest about his acceptance to Union Theological Seminary.

[144.] [This addendum reports three documents, two letters from Mehnert and one from Deißmann, that were discovered while the German edition of this volume was already in production. The Deißmann letter was squeezed into an editorial note, and the second Mehnert letter was published in DBW 17; it was also already in production, and there was only room for the one letter considered more significant. In this translation the Mehnert letter is 106a and the Deißmann letter 135a. For additional new material in this volume discovered since DBW 10 and DBW 17 were published, see the editor's introduction, pp. 43–44.—CG]

In the letter to Diestel, Bonhoeffer also says that the time between 1928 and 1931 was "of fundamental importance for my entire manner of thinking and for the direction my life has taken"—an assessment readers will doubtless find confirmed in this volume.

(2) Bonhoeffer's letter to Adolf Deißmann of September 23, 1930, was also discovered only after the political changes of 1989 and could not be incorporated into the sequence of part 1 of the German volume. The editors are indebted to Prof. Günter Wirth, Berlin, for finding this letter.

APPENDICES

Appendix 1. Chronology 1928–1931

1928	January 18	Prior to departing for Barcelona, Bonhoeffer meets one last time with the children's worship assistants at Pastor Meumann's; final meeting of the Thursday circle.	639
	January 22	Last children's service in Berlin, text: Matt. 9:1–8 (the forgiveness of sins).	
	February 8–15	Journey to Barcelona via Paris.	
	February 19	Installation service in Barcelona.	
	March 11	First sermon, on Rom. 11:6.	
	April 7–June 1	Bonhoeffer's brother Klaus visits.	
	April 8	Easter sermon on 1 Cor. 15:17.	
	April 15	Sermon on Matt. 28:20.	
	April 23–ca. May 10	Tour of Spain with Klaus (as far as Madrid with Pastor Meumann, who stays in Spain till May 13). Continues on to Toledo, Cordoba, Seville, Algeciras, Spanish Morocco, Granada.	
	May 13	Sermon on 1 Thess. 5:17.	
	June 3	Sermon on Luke 12:49.	
	June 7	Attends Corpus Christi procession.	
	June 24	Sermon on Matt. 7:1.	
	June 27	Vacation begins, Bonhoeffer substitutes for Pastor Olbricht; Olbricht and virtually the entire German colony depart Barcelona. Bonhoeffer begins working on his postdoctoral dissertation. Weekly children's services.	
	July 15	Sermon on Ps. 62:2.	

July 29 Sermon on 1 Cor. 12:26–27. Two-day car trip with Dr. Krebs and a German teacher.

August 12 Sermon on Matt. 5:8.

August 26 Sermon on 1 John 2:17.

September 9 Sermon on 2 Cor. 12:9.

September 19 Bonhoeffer's parents visit (till October 8).

September 23 Sermon on Rom. 12:11c.

October 1 Trip with his parents through southern France (Costa Brava, Nimes, Avignon).

640 October 10 Postdoctoral dissertation plan takes shape after publication revisions for the dissertation *Sanctorum Communio* are almost complete.

October 17–28 Substitutes for Pastor Lahusen in Madrid.

November 1–7 Bonhoeffer falls ill.

November 13 Beginning of the lecture series "Crisis and Hope in the Contemporary Religious Situation." First lecture: "The Tragedy of the Prophetic and Its Lasting Meaning."

November 25 Remembrance Sunday; sermon on Song of Solomon 8:6b.

November 27 Pastor Olbricht departs on a journey and leaves his vicar in charge of the congregation until just before Christmas. Dialogue circle with the secondary school seniors begins.

December 2 Sermon on the first Sunday of Advent on Rev. 3:20.

December 11 Second lecture: "Jesus Christ and the Essence of Christianity."

December 23 Nativity play performance.

December 25 Christmas sermon on John 1:14 (lost).

1929 January 1 Sermon (lost).

January 10 Trip to Majorca on church business.

January 13 Two services on Majorca.

February 3 Farewell sermon on Phil. 4:7.

February 8 Third lecture: "Basic Questions of a Christian Ethic."

February 17 Departure for Geneva; spends a week there with his brother Klaus.

February 27 Arrival in Berlin.

	Beginning summer semester 1929	Academic assistant in systematic theology with Wilhelm Lütgert in Berlin.	
	June 28	German Evangelical Church day of mourning commemorating the tenth anniversary of the Versailles treaty.	
	July 2	Serves as an opponent at the doctoral defense of P. W. Gennrich.	
	October 3	Reich Chancellor and Foreign Minister Gustave Stresemann dies.	
	October 24	Collapse of the New York stock market ("Black Thursday").	
	December 18	Bonhoeffer thanks Adolf von Harnack for his words of farewell. Further development of plans to go to America.	
1930		Number of unemployed in Germany climbs from 3.2 million (January) to 4.38 million (December).	641
	January 11	Application for a fellowship from the German Academic Exchange Service (DAAD).	
	January 28	Conversation with German National People's Party representative Reinhard Mumm in the parliament (concerning financing the publication of *Sanctorum Communio*). Parliament accepts the Young Plan, against vehement nationalist opposition. Implementation of the plan is halted in 1931.	
	March 14	*Act and Being* submitted for postdoctoral degree.	
	March 28	Doctoral dissertation manuscript with Trowitzsch publishers.	
	April	Bonhoeffer visits the congregation in Barcelona.	
	April 8	Delivers lecture in the church.	
	April 15	Lütgert's report on *Act and Being*.	
	April 19	Arrival in Berlin.	
	May 15	Confirmation of the U.S.A. fellowship.	
	May 22	Petitions to be excused from the preachers' seminary.	

	June 15	Delivers address at the memorial service for Adolf von Harnack.
	June 29	Catechetical examination in the Grunewald church children's service under Pastor Meumann.
	July 5–8	Second theological examination.
	July 12	Trial lecture. Postdoctoral degree for systematic theology.
	July 20	Worship service with sermon exam in Teltow.
	July 31	Public inaugural lecture: "The Anthropological Question in Contemporary Philosophy and Theology."
	August 7–22	Vacation in Friedrichsbrunn.
	August 29	Denial of early ordination request, since Bonhoeffer had not reached the required age of twenty-five.
	September 1	Meeting of the U.S.A. exchange students.
	September 2	Delivery of the first copies of *Sanctorum Communio.*
	September 5	Departure for the U.S.A. on the *Columbus.*
	September 15	Spends a week visiting the Boerickes in Philadelphia.
642	October 5	Bonhoeffer's grandmother writes to him concerning the results of the September 14 parliamentary elections (National Socialists go from 12 to 107 seats).
	October 25	Attends the Negro Center in Harlem.
	November 9	Delivers Armistice Day sermon in the Memorial Methodist Church ("A Message on War") on 1 John 4:16.
	End of November	Car trip to Washington D.C. (till December 6).
	November 28–December 1	Visits the Boerickes in Philadelphia.
	December 1–4	Attends Federal Council of Churches meeting and visits Howard University in Washington, D.C.
	December 13	Travels to Cuba (till January 2, 1931).
	December 21	Sermon on the fourth Sunday in Advent in Havana on Deut. 32:48–52.

	End of 1930	Otto Dibelius's 1930 book on peace, *Friede auf Erden?* already in its 3rd edition.
1931	January	The "Dehn case" intensifies.
	January 20	Bonhoeffer's mother writes about her fear that "a government of Nazis is coming."
	January 31	Karl Barth delivers his lecture "The Crisis of the Protestant Church" before 1,400 listeners; sharp attack on Otto Dibelius.
	February 7	Otto Dibelius responds with the lecture "The Responsibility of the Church: A Response to Karl Barth." On the same day, Dibelius writes a letter to Bonhoeffer presenting the possibility of his assuming the position of student chaplain at the Technical College in Berlin.
	May 5	Begins a car trip with Lasserre to the Midwest, New Orleans, and Mexico; Lehmann accompanies them to Chicago and Sutz to New Orleans.
	June 20	Departs New York by ship for Europe.

Appendix 2. Bonhoeffer's Courses at Union Theological Seminary[1]

First Semester 643

Philosophy of Religion 13: The philosophy of the Christian religion; Professor Lyman

The essence of Christianity; the meaning and validity of the leading Christian ideas; Christianity and the religion of the future. Lectures, reports, discussions, and group conferences under the direction of the instructor.

Philosophy of Religion 19: Religion and ethics; Associate Professor Niebuhr

Two hours weekly throughout the year.[2] Advanced course. Is ethics autonomous? Is religion more than ethics? What validity have the leading philosophical theories as to the relation between religion and ethics? What do the typical historical connections and divergencies between them teach? What is the most constructive interpretation of their connection?

Systematic Theology 91: Seminar in philosophical theology; Professor Baillie cooperating with Professor Lyman and Assistant Professor van Dusen

The seminar in the Department of Systematic Theology will be held in cooperation with the Department of the Philosophy of Religion, the subject for the current year being "The bearing of recent cosmological theories on theology."

[1.] [From the Union Theological Seminary Announcement (1930), which contained detailed course descriptions, and the Catalogue (1931); cf. also Bethge's notes, *GS* 6:190, and Green, "Bonhoeffer's Courses." Course numbers indicate the level of the course and the semester in which it was given.—CG]

[2.] [Bonhoeffer did not take the continuation of this course in the second semester. —CG]

Practical Theology 55: The minister's work with individuals; Prof. Coffin, assisted by special lecturers

Conferences upon pastoral visitation and consultation, the treatment of various spiritual difficulties such as unbelief, indifference, and various sins against society, sickness, sorrow, poverty, and problems arising out of social maladjustments and nervous diseases.

Missions 11: The present expansion of Christianity; Prof. Fleming

The aim of this course is to consider the fundamental factors that concern the world-wide mission of the Christian faith and spirit. The conditions, problems, aims, and agencies of the work will be treated in such a way as to afford a background for further missionary thinking. The course is intended for those who do not expect to go abroad for service. Lectures, discussions, readings.

Second Semester

Philosophy of Religion 18: Religious aspects of contemporary philosophy; Prof. Lyman

Advanced course. From the standpoint of the philosophy of religion topics like the following will be investigated: pragmatism; the philosophy of Bergson; modern realism; the reinterpretation of idealism; the new naturalism; the personalist philosophy; the new cosmology. Lectures, discussions, papers.

Systematic Theology 92:[3] Seminar in philosophical theology; Professor Baillie cooperating with Professor Lyman and Assistant Professor Van Dusen

Christian Ethics 42: Ethical issues in the social order; Professor Ward

A discussion of the ethical issues involved in (1) the basic problems of the social order—disease, crime, war, sex relations; (2) methods and ideals of social organizations. Lectures, readings, reports and individual conferences. Undergraduate courses in labor problems and in elementary economics are a profitable introduction to this course.

Christian Ethics 52a:[4] Ethical viewpoints in modern literature; Professor Niebuhr

A critique of selected examples from modern essayists, novelists, and poets. Readings, discussions, lectures.

[3.] [See description under *Systematic Theology 91*.—CG]

[4.] [This course, and the following one, are continuations of *Christian Ethics 51a* and *51b* given in the first semester. They each met for one hour per week and could be taken separately or together. Bonhoeffer did not take the first-semester courses.—CG]

Christian Ethics 52b: Ethical interpretations; Professor Ward

An evaluation of current events, in light of the principles of Christian ethics. Lectures, assigned readings, and discussions.

Practical Theology 56: Parish administration; Professor Coffin

Conferences upon methods of church finance and benevolence, the church's work for men, for women, for young people, for children, the pastor and social problems, the church and social classes, church discipline, evangelism, etc.

Church and Community 16: The cooperation of the church with social and character-building agencies; Mr. Webber

This course is designed to acquaint students for the ministry with the ideals, programs, and methods of such social and character-building agencies as the settlements, the Boy Scouts, Girl Scouts, Pioneer Youth, the YMCA, the YWCA, the American Social Hygiene Association, the Playground and Recreation Association, the Big Brother and Big Sister Federation, and the Child Study Association. The need for further cooperative efforts between the churches and these organizations in the common task of building character and creating community welfare will be examined, as will the possibilities for the elimination of overlapping and competition. Consideration will also be given to the responsibility of the minister and of his church for the fostering of social agencies.

Appendix 3. Unpublished Material from Bonhoeffer's Literary Estate 1928–1930

1. Letters, Diaries, Documents (without letters from others) 644

Addressee or contents	Date	*NL* number
Calendar 1928	1928	A 18, 2
List of clothing items	n.d.	A 18, 3 (1)
Landlady's bill	n.d.	A 18, 3 (2)
Calling cards	n.d.	A 18, 3 (3)
Dialogue between "a German" and "Son"	n.d.	A 18, 3 (4)
Guest ticket for Mardi Gras	February 18, 1928	A 18, 5 (3)
Information about parish events	March/April 1928	A 18, 4 (1)
Newspaper clippings	n.d.	A 18, 4 (2)
Membership card, sports club	n.d.	A 18, 5 (4)
To Hans von Dohnanyi	November 6, 1928	A 19, 3 (7)
Applications to the DAAD	January 9, 1930	A 26, 3 (1)
Application to Union Theological Seminary	February 12, 1930	A 26, 3 (2)
Confirmation of fellowship	March 11, 1930	A 26, 3 (10)
Bonhoeffer's library card at Union Seminary	n.d.	A 26, 3 (10)
Exam questions, Second Theological Examination	May 20, 1930	A 30, 1 (2)
Summons to Second Theological Examination	June 25, 1930	A 30, 1 (3)

Announcement of inaugural lecture	July 22, 1930	A 30, 2 (9)
Assistantship year	July 24, 1930	A 30, 1 (5)
Acceptance of the *Habilitation*	August 31, 1930	A 6 (10)
Recommendation from J. Douglas	September 1, 1930	A 26, 3 (8)

2. Papers, Lecture Notes

	Topic	Date	*NL* number
	Lecture notes, Niebuhr, Religion and Ethics	First semester 1930/31	A 24, 2
	Francis Xavier	First (?) semester 1930/31	A 24, 3
645	Lecture notes, Lyman, Contemporary Philosophy	Second semester 1930/31	A 24, 4
	Lecture notes, Ward, Christian Ethics	Second semester 1930/31	A 24, 5
	Lectures notes, Webber, Church and Community	Second semester 1930/31	A 24, 8
	Materials concerning the “Negro problem”	First semester 1930/31	A 24, 9
	Newspaper clippings	October 13/27, 1930	A 24, 10 (2)
	Invitation	October 25, 1930	A 24, 20 (3)
	Information sheet on Riverside Church	November 16, 1930	A 24, 10 (1)
	YMCA membership card	n.d.	A 24, 10 (4)

3. Sermons

No additional material

Appendix 4. Texts Published in *Gesammelte Schriften* and in *DBWE* 10

GS	*DBWE* 10
1:17	256–57
1:51–53	126–28
1:54	204–5
1:54	226–27
1:54–55	261
1:55–60	281–87
1:66–74	411–18
1:74–75	418–19
1:75–79	265–67
1:79–81	294–96
1:81–83	296–97
1:84–103	305–20
3:15	119–22
3:16–17	142–43
3:17–18	144–45
3:18	115–16
3:18–19	194–95
3:20	196–97
3:20–21	280–81
3:22–23	291–92
3:59–61	379–81
3:62–84	389–408
3:85–90	440–44
3:91–99	445–51
3:100–109	451–61
3:110–26	462–76
3:127–29	438–40
3:130–32	408–10
5:116–34	325–42
5:134–56	342–59
5:156–80	359–78
5:416–17	479–80
5:417–23	480–85
5:423–28	485–89
5:428–34	490–95
5:434–39	500–505
5:439–46	505–11
5:446–52	511–16
5:452–57	516–21
5:458–63	521–27
5:463–68	527–31
5:468–72	532–35
5:473–78	542–46
5:478–84	546–51
5:485–90	585–89
6:99–108	57–64
6:109	65
6:109–10	65
6:110	66
6:110–11	66–67

6:111–12	67–68
6:112–15	68–70
6:115–16	71–72
6:116–18	72–74
6:118–19	74–76
6:119	78
6:120–21	80–82
6:121–22	83–84
6:122–24	88–90
6:124–25	93
6:125	91–92
6:125–26	94–96
6:127–28	96–97
6:128–30	98–100
6:130–31	103–5
6:132–34	109–12
6:135	112–13
6:135–37	115–16
6:137	117
6:138–39	118–19
6:139–43	119–22
6:143–44	122–24
6:144	124–25
6:144–45	125–26
6:145	129–30
6:145–47	130–32
6:147	132–33
6:148	133–35
6:148	138–39
6:149	143–44
6:150	147
6:150–51	148–49
6:151	151
6:152	149–50
6:152–53	152–53
6:154	536
6:155–56	154–55
6:156–57	155–56
6:157–58	158–60
6:158–59	160–62
6:159	163–64
6:160	165–66
6:160–61	166–68
6:161–63	168–69
6:163	170
6:164	170–71
6:165–67	171–73
6:167–68	174–75
6:169–71	177–78
6:171	141–42
6:173	222
6:174	224
6:174–75	227–28
6:175	236
6:175–76	238
6:176–77	237
6:178–79	241–42
6:179	243
6:179–80	251–52
6:180–81	257–58
6:181–82	259
6:182–84	268–70
6:185–87	270–72
6:187–88	293–94
6:188–89	298
6:189	299
6:191–93	320–22
6:193–97	429–38
6:198–202	420–27
6:211	279
6:234	303n2
6:235	303–4

Bibliography

1. Archival Sources and Private Collections

Dietrich Bonhoeffer's papers and personal library, as well as correspondence from others and relevant material in other archives, have been cataloged in the *Nachlaß Dietrich Bonhoeffer* volume compiled by Dietrich Meyer and Eberhard Bethge. All such citations in *DBWE* are indicated by *NL*, followed by the corresponding reference code within that published index. Not all this material is part of the actual Bonhoeffer Nachlaß in the Staatsbibliothek in Berlin; footnote citations of *NL* material from other archives also give the numbering from the respective archive. All the material listed in the Meyer and Bethge catalog, however, has been included on microfiches now located at the Staatsbibliothek in Berlin (previously at the Bundesarchiv in Koblenz) and in the Bonhoeffer collection at Burke Library, Union Theological Seminary, New York. The designation *NL-Bibl.* in some bibliographic records indicates that a copy of the book was found in Bonhoeffer's personal library.

Evangelisches Zentralarchiv, Berlin (EZA)
  Bestand 5 (Kirchliches Außenamt)/196; 1890; 1891; 2865
  Bestand 29 (Superintendentur Berlin Kölln-Land I)/G 264/I; G 442
Geheimes Staatsarchiv Berlin, Bestand Preußischer Kulturbesitz
Humboldt-Universität Berlin, Universitätsarchiv
  Bestand Theologische Fakultät
Staatsbibliothek zu Berlin
  Nachlaß Dietrich Bonhoeffer (Nachlaß 299)
Zentral- und Landesbibliothek Berlin (ZLB)
  Historische Sammlungen: Nachlaß Adolf Deißmann

Private Collections (locations at the time of German *DBW* publication)
  Ruth-Alice von Bismarck
  Emmi Bonhoeffer

Klaus Bonhoeffer
Anne Doerr
Walter Dreß
Hans Christoph von Hase
Sabine Leibholz

2. Literature Used by Bonhoeffer

Althaus, Paul. *Communio Sanctorum: Die Gemeinde im lutherischen Kirchengedanken* (The communion of saints: The congregation in the Lutheran understanding of the church). Munich: Chr. Kaiser Verlag, 1929. *NL-Bibl.* 3 B 2.

Barth, Karl. *Die christliche Dogmatik im Entwurf.* 1: *Die Lehre vom Worte Gottes: Prolegomena zur christlichen Dogmatik* (Christian dogmatics in outline. 1. The doctrine of the Word of God: Prolegomena to Christian dogmatics). Munich: Chr. Kaiser Verlag, 1927. *NL-Bibl.* 3 B 9. Also published in *Gesamtausgabe* (Collected works), vol. 2, edited by Gerhard Sauter (Zurich: Theologischer Verlag, 1982).

"The Birth Control Revolution." *Commonweal,* April 1, 1931, 589–91.

Blakely, Paul L., SJ. "A Picture of Prohibition: A Series of Quotations Paints a Vivid Picture." *America* 44, no. 18 (February 7, 1931): 432–34.

Bonhoeffer, Karl. *Ein Beitrag zur Kenntnis des großstädtischen Bettel- und Vagabundentums: Eine psychiatrische Untersuchung* (A contribution to the understanding of urban beggars and vagabonds: A psychiatric study). Berlin, 1900.

Brunner, Emil. *Der Mittler: Zur Besinnung über den Christusglauben.* Tübingen: J. C. B. Mohr (Paul Siebeck), 1927. *NL-Bibl.* 3 B 15. Translated by Olive Wyon as *The Mediator* (New York: Macmillan, 1934).

Bultmann, Rudolf. "Die Geschichtlichkeit des Daseins und der Glaube: Antwort an Gerhardt Kuhlmann." *Zeitschrift für Theologie und Kirche,* n.s., 11 (1930): 339–64. Also published in *Heidegger und die Theologie,* edited by G. Noller, 72–94 (Munich: Chr. Kaiser Verlag, 1967). Translated as "The Historicity of Man and Faith," in *Existence and Faith: Shorter Writings of Rudolf Bultmann,* edited by Schubert M. Ogden, 92–110 (Cleveland: World, 1960).

Čapek, Karel. *R.U.R.* Prague: Aventinum, 1920. Translated by Claudia Novack as *Rossum's Universal Robots,* with an introduction by Ivan Klíma (New York: Penguin, 2004).

Chafee, Zechariah, Jr. "After Prohibition—What?" *Forum and Century* 85, no. 1 (January 1931): 4–9.

Chamberlain, William Henry. "Russia and the World Crisis." *New Republic* 66, no. 846 (February 18, 1931): 8–10.

Chase, Stuart. "Our School Burns Down." *New Republic* 66, no. 848 (March 4, 1931): 71–72.

Christian Century 38, no. 5 (February 4, 1931): 159–61 (editorial article).

"The Churches and Birth Control." *Federal Council Bulletin* 14, no. 4 (April 1931): 19–20, 25. New York: Federal Council of the Churches of Christ in America, 1931.

Cullen, Countee. *Copper Sun.* New York: Harper & Brothers, 1927.

Dehn, Günther. *Der Gottessohn: Eine Einführung in das Evangelium des Markus (Die urchristliche Botschaft)* (The Son of God: An introduction to the Gospel of Mark: The primitive Christian message). Berlin: Furche Verlag, 1929. *NL-Bibl.* 1 D 8.

Dewey, John. "The Need for a New Party. I: The Present Crisis." *New Republic* 66, no. 850 (March 18, 1931): 115–17.

———. "The Need for a New Party. II: The Breakdown of the Old Order." *New Republic* 66, no. 851 (March 24, 1931): 150–52.

Dostoyevsky, Fyodor Mikhaylovich. *Die Brüder Karamasoff.* Translated by Dmitry Merezhkovsky and E. K. Rahsin. 2 vols. Munich: R. Piper, 1908. *NL-Bibl.* 8 C 11. Translated and introduced by David McDuff as *The Brothers Karamazov* (London: Penguin, 2003).

———. *Schuld und Sühne [Raskolnikow].* Leipzig, 1926. Translated by Constance Garnett as *Crime and Punishment* (New York: Heritage Press, 1938).

Dreiser, Theodore. *Free, and Other Stories.* New York: Boni & Liveright, 1918.

Du Bois, W. E. B. *The Souls of Black Folk: Essays and Sketches.* Chicago: A. C. McClurg, 1928.

Duhm, Bernhard. *Israels Propheten* (Israel's prophets). 2nd ed. Tübingen: J. C. B. Mohr, 1922. *NL-Bibl.* 1 C 7.

Eckert, Alfred. *Der Katechismusstoff des Konfirmandenunterrichts* (Catechetical materials for confirmation instruction). Leipzig: Strübig, 1905.

"Federal Council on Birth Control." *The Outlook and Independent: An Illustrated Weekly of Inquiry* 157, no. 13 (April 1, 1931): 458–59.

Fendt, Leonhard. *Der Wille der Reformation im Augsburgischen Bekenntnis: Ein Kommentar für Prediger und Predigthörer* (The will of the Reformation in the Augsburg Confession: A commentary for preachers and the sermon audience). Leipzig: H. G. Wallmann, 1929. *NL-Bibl.* 5 B 2.

Finney, Ruth. "The Power Fight Goes On." *Nation* 131, no. 3416 (December 24, 1930): 697–99.

Flex, Walter. *Der Wanderer zwischen beiden Welten: Ein Kriegserlebnis* (The wanderer between two worlds: A war experience). Vol. 1 of *Gesammelte Werke* (Collected works). Munich: Beck, 1925.

Gilfond, Duff. "The Muscle Shoals Lobby: How the Cyanamid Company Has Hoodwinked the Farmers." *New Republic* 62, no. 802 (April 16, 1930): 234–36.

Gogarten, Friedrich. "Das Problem einer theologischen Anthropologie" (The problem of a theological anthropology). *Zwischen den Zeiten* 7 (1929): 493–511.

Graves, Robert. *Good-bye to All That: An Autobiography*. New York: Blue Ribbon Books, 1930.

Grisebach, Eberhard. *Gegenwart: Eine kritische Ethik* (The present: A critical ethic). Halle an der Saale: M. Niemeyer, 1928.

Der gute Kamerad: Illustriertes Knaben-Jahrbuch (The good comrade: Illustrated yearbook for boys). Edited by O. Hohenstatt. Stuttgart: 1886–.

Hall, Thomas C. *The Religious Background of American Culture*. Boston: Little, Brown, 1930.

Hardeland, Otto. *Zweiundfünfzig Konfirmandenstunden: Ein Handbuch für Geistliche nach des Verfassers gleichzeitig in 40. Aufl. erscheinendem Konfirmandenunterricht* (Fifty-two confirmation lessons: A handbook for ministers concurrent with the author's 40th edition of his confirmation instruction). 4th ed. Dresden, 1910.

Harnack, Adolf von. *Aus der Werkstatt des Vollendeten* (From the workshop of a completed life). Edited by Axel von Harnack. Gießen: A. Töpelmann, 1930. *NL-Bibl.* 2 B 6.

———. *Einführung in die Alte Kirchengeschichte: Das Schreiben der römischen Kirche an die korinthische aus der Zeit Domitians (1. Clemensbrief), übers. und den Studierenden erklärt* (Introduction to ancient church history: The writing of the Roman church to the Corinthian church from the time of Domitian [1 Clement], translated and explained for students). Leipzig: J. C. Hinrich, 1929.

Hase, Karl August von. *Kirchengeschichte*. 12th rev. ed. Leipzig: Breitkopf & Härtel, 1899–1900. *NL-Bibl.* 2 B 6. Translated by Charles E. Blumenthal and Conway P. Wing as *A History of the Christian Church* (New York: D. Appleton, 1875).

Heidegger, Martin. *Sein und Zeit*. Halle an der Saale: M. Niemeyer, 1927. Translated by Joan Stambaugh as *Being and Time: A Translation of* Sein und Zeit (Albany: State University of New York Press, 1996).

Hesse, Hermann. *Narziß und Goldmund*. Berlin: Suhrkamp, 1949. Translated by Ursule Molinaro as *Narcissus and Goldmund* (New York: Farrar, Straus & Giroux, 1968).

Hirsch, Emanuel. *Der Wille des Herrn: Predigten* (The will of the Lord: Sermons). Gütersloh: Bertelsmann, 1925.

Ibsen, Henrik. *Brand: Ein dramatisches Gedicht*. Leipzig: P. Reclam, 1923. Translated by Inga-Stina Ewbank as *Brand*, edited by Geoffrey Hill (London: Penguin, 1996).

Insull, Martin J. "The Real Power Problem." *Forum* 83, no. 2 (February 1930): 88–94.

James, William. *The Varieties of Religious Experience: A Study in Human Nature.* New York: Longmans, Green, 1928. Reprint, New York: Simon & Schuster, 2004. (Gifford Lectures, Edinburgh, 1901–2).

Johnson, James Weldon. *The Autobiography of an Ex-Coloured Man.* 1927. Introduced by Carl Van Vechten. New York: Knopf, 1927. Reprint, 1979.

———. *The Book of American Negro Spirituals.* New York: Viking, 1929. *NL-Bibl.* 8 C 6.

———. *God's Trombones: Seven Negro Sermons in Verse.* New York: Viking, 1927. *NL. Bibl.* 5 C 19.

Johnson, James Weldon, and Herbert Seligman. "Legal Aspects of the Negro Problem." *Annals of the American Association of Political and Social Sciences* (November 1928): 1–8.

Kellogg, Arthur. "The Eleven Wickersham Reports." *Survey* 65, no. 10 (February 15, 1931): 539.

Kolbe, Johannes. *Der kleine Katechismus Dr. M. Luthers in ausgeführten Katechesen: Für den Lehrer der Oberklasse der Volksschule und im Konfirmandenunterricht nach den neuern Grundsätzen der Methodik bearbeitet* (The Small Catechism of Dr. M. Luther in complete catecheses: Prepared for the teacher of the upper class of the Volksschule according to the more recent principles of methodology). 3rd ed. Breslau: Carl Dülfer, 1898.

Lewis, Sinclair. *Babbitt.* London: Jonathan Cape; New York: Harcourt, Brace, 1922. Reprint, New York: Random House, 2002.

———. *Elmer Gantry.* New York: Grossett, 1929. Reprint, Oxford: Oxford University Press, 1983.

Lewisohn, Ludwig. *Mid-channel: An American Chronicle.* New York: Harper & Brothers, 1929. Reprint, New York: Arno Press, 1975.

———. *Stephen Escott.* New York: Harper, 1930.

Locke, Alain Le Roy. *The New Negro: An Interpretation.* New York: A. & C. Boni, 1925. Reprint, New York: Simon & Schuster, 1997.

Ludwig, Emil. *Lincoln.* Berlin: E. Rowohlt Verlag, 1930. Translated by Eden and Cedar Paul as *Lincoln* (Boston: Little, Brown, 1930; reprint, New York: Fawcett, 1962).

Metropolitan Life Insurance Company. *Unemployment Insurance: A Summary of Some Existing Governmental and Private Plans.* New York: Metropolitan Life Insurance, 1931.

"Missouri Heads 1931 Lynching Parade." *Literary Digest* 108, no. 5 (January 31, 1931): 17–18.

Moton, Robert Russa. *What the Negro Thinks.* Garden City, N.Y.: Doubleday, Doran: 1929.

NAACP. *First Line of Defense: A Summary of 20 Years of Civil Rights Struggle for American Negroes.* New York: NAACP, 1930. *NL* A 24,9.3.

Naumann, Friedrich. *Briefe über Religion—mit Nachwort "Nach 13 Jahren"*

(Letters on religion—with an Afterword "After 13 years"). Berlin: Georg Reimer, 1917. *NL-Bibl.* 7 B 14.

———. "Lutherische Fröhlichkeit 1 Thess 5:16" (Lutheran joyfulness 1 Thess. 5:16). In *Postille: Predigtrufe aller Zeiten an unsere Zeit in kurzen Lesungen für Wochen-, Schul- und Hausandachten: Mit einem Geleitwort von Rudolf Otto* (Sermon addresses from all ages to our time in brief readings for weekly, school, and house devotionals: With a comment by Rudolf Otto), edited by Gertrud Petersmann-Borsdorff and Rudolf Otto. Gießen: A. Töpelmann, 1927.

New York Public Library. *The Negro—A Selected Bibliography.* 1930. *NL* A 24,9.1.

Nietzsche, Friedrich. *Also sprach Zarathustra: Ein Buch für alle und keinen.* Leipzig: A. Kröner, 1927. *NL-Bibl.* 7 A 58. Translated and with a preface by Walter Kaufmann as *Thus Spoke Zarathustra* (New York: Viking Press, 1966).

———. *Jenseits von Gut und Böse: Vorspiel einer Philosophie der Zukunft—Zur Genealogie der Moral.* Leipzig: A. Kröner, 1924. Reprinted as *Jenseits von Gut und Böse* [together with *Zur Genealogie der Moral*], edited by Giorgio Colli and Mazzino Montinari. Berlin: Walter de Gruyter, 1988. Translated and edited by Marion Faber as *Beyond Good and Evil: Prelude to a Philosophy of the Future,* with an introduction by Robert C. Holub (Oxford: Oxford University Press, 1998).

Nissen, Johann. *Unterredungen über den kleinen Katechismus Luthers: Ein praktisches Handbuch für Schullehrer* (Discussions on Luther's Small Catechism: A practical handbook for school teachers). Kiel: Ernst Homann, 1859.

Oehler, Richard, comp. *Nietzsche-Register: Alphabetisch-systematische Übersicht über Friedrich Nietzsches Gedankenwelt, nach Begriffen und Namen aus dem Text entwickelt* (Nietzsche index). Stuttgart: A. Kröner, 1943.

Ovington, Mary White. *How the National Association for the Advancement of Colored People Began.* New York: NAACP, 1914. *NL* A 24,9.5.

Pank, Oskar. *Ich schäme mich des Evangeliums nicht: Ein Jahrgang Predigten* (I'm not ashamed of the gospel: Sermons for the course of a year). Halle an der Saale: R. Mühlmann, 1910.

Parpert, Friedrich. *Das Mönchtum und die evangelische Kirche: Ein Beitrag zur Ausscheidung des Mönchtums aus der evangelischen Soziologie.* (Monasticism and the Protestant church: Contribution to the exclusion of monasticism from Protestant sociology). Aus der Welt christlicher Frömmigkeit (From the world of Christian piety) 10. Edited by Friedrich Heiler. Munich: Ernst Reinhardt, 1930.

Pickens, William. "The Suppressed 'Sensational Story.'" *The World Tomorrow* 14, no. 2 (February 1931): 47–48.

Ranke, Leopold von. *Über die Epochen der neueren Geschichte*. Munich: Duncker & Humblot, 1917. *NL-Bibl.* 2 A 21. Translated as "On Progress in History," in *The Theory and Practice of History*, edited by Georg G. Iggers and Konrad von Moltke (New York: Irvington, 1993).

Rauschenbusch, Walter. *For God and the People: Prayers of the Social Awakening*. Boston: Pilgrim Press, 1910.

Remarque, Erich Maria. *Im Westen nichts Neues*. Berlin: Propyläen Verlag, 1929. Translated by A. W. Wheen as *All Quiet on the Western Front* (London: Putnam, 1930).

Renn, Ludwig [Arnold Friedrich Vieth von Golßenau]. *Krieg*. Frankfurt am Main: Frankfurter Societäts-Druckerei, Abteilung Buchverlag, 1929. Translated by Willa and Edwin Muir as *War* (New York: Dodd, Mead, 1929).

———. *Nachkrieg*. Frankfurt am Main: Frankfurter Societäts-Druckerei, Abteilung Buchverlag, 1930. Translated by Willa and Edwin Muir as *After War* (New York: Dodd, Mead, 1931).

Rubinow, I. M. "How Big Shall the Big Brother Be?" *Survey* 65, no. 12 (March 15, 1931): 652–53.

Schmidt, Hans Wilhelm. *Zeit und Ewigkeit: Die letzten Voraussetzungen der dialektischen Theologie* (Time and eternity: The ultimate presuppositions of dialectical theology). Gütersloh: Bertelsmann, 1927.

Seebold, Hermann. *Ausführliche Erklärung des kleinen Katechismus Dr. Martin Luthers, in Fragen und Antworten verfaßt und mit Zeugnissen der heiligen Schrift und Liederversen versehen: Ein Hülfsbuch für evangelisch-lutherische Lehrer und Hausväter* (Thorough explanation of the Small Catechism of Dr. Martin Luther, composed in questions and answers and accompanied by witnesses of holy Scripture and hymn verses: An aid for Protestant-Lutheran teachers and family heads). 3rd ed. Göttingen: Vandenhoeck & Ruprecht, 1858.

Shaw, George Bernard. *Androcles and the Lion: A Fable Play*. London: Constable, 1929.

———. *The Apple Cart: A Political Extravaganza*. London: Constable, 1930. Translated by Siegfried Trebitsch as *Kaiser von Amerika: Eine politische Komödie in drei Akten* (Berlin: S. Fischer, 1929).

———. *Candida: A Mystery*. London: Constable, 1913.

———. *Major Barbara: In Three Acts*. London: Constable, 1909.

———. *The Man of Destiny: A Trifle*. London: Constable, 1929.

———. *St. Joan: A Chronicle: Play in Six Scenes and an Epilogue*. London: Constable, 1921.

———. *You Never Can Tell: A Comedy in Four Acts*. London: Constable, 1928.

Sherover, Miles M. "An American Loan to Russia?" *New Republic* 65, no. 837 (December 17, 1930): 127–30.

Sherriff, Robert C. *Journey's End: A Play in Three Acts.* London: V. Gollancz, 1929. Reprint, London: Penguin, 2000.

Slocombe, George. "India and the Round Table Conference." *Nation* 132, no. 3424 (February 18, 1931): 173–74.

Soule, George. "National Planning: The Problem of Creating a Brain for Our Economy." *New Republic* 66, no. 850 (March 4, 1931): 61–65.

———. "Will the Five Year Plan Succeed?" *New Republic* 65, no. 835 (December 3, 1930): 61–64.

Spates, Thomas G. *Unemployment as an International Problem.* Geneva Special Studies, vol. 2, no. 3, March 1931. Geneva: Geneva Research Information Committee, 1931.

Stewart, Edith Ann. *The Life of St. Francis Xavier: Evangelist, Explorer, Mystic.* Containing Xavier letters translated by David MacDonald. London: Headley Bros., 1917.

Thomas, Norman. "The Banks of New York." *Nation* 132, no. 3423 (February 11, 1931): 147–49.

———. "Socialism: The Way Out for America." *World Tomorrow* 14, no. 3 (March 1931): 72–74.

Tillich, Paul. *Religiöse Verwirklichung* (Religious realization). Berlin: Furche Verlag, 1930.

Toller, Ernst. *Die Maschinenstürmer: Ein Drama aus der Zeit der Ludditenbewegung in England in fünf Akten und einem Vorspiel.* Leipzig: E. P. Tal, 1922. Translated by Ashley Dukes as *The Machine-Wreckers: A Drama of the English Luddites in a Prologue and Five Acts* (New York: Knopf, 1923).

———. *Masse-Mensch: Ein Stück aus der sozialen Revolution des 20. Jahrhunderts.* Potsdam: G. Kiepenheuer, 1921. Translated by Louis Untermeyer as *Man and the Masses: A Play of the Social Revolution in Seven Scenes* (Garden City, N.Y.: Doubleday, Page, 1924).

Troeltsch, Ernst. *Die Soziallehren der christlichen Kirchen und Gruppen.* Vol. 1/1 of *Gesammelte Schriften.* Tübingen: J. C. B. Mohr, 1912. Translated by Olive Wyon as *The Social Teaching of the Christian Churches* (New York: Macmillan, 1931; reprint, Louisville: Westminster/John Knox, 1992).

Uckeley, Alfred. *Lebenskräfte: Predigten für Gebildete aus den akademischen Gottesdiensten der Albertus-Universität zu Königsberg i. Preußen* (Life forces: Sermons for the educated from the academic worship services of the Albertus University in Königsberg in Prussia). Berlin, 1923.

Von Kühlmann, Richard. "The Permanent Bases of German Foreign Policy." *Foreign Affairs* 9, no. 2 (January 1931): 179–94.

Ward, Harry F. *Which Way Religion?* New York: Macmillan, 1931. *NL-Bibl.* 7 B 27.

Washington, Booker T. *Up from Slavery: An Autobiography.* New York: Association Press, 1901.

Witkop, Philipp, ed. *Kriegsbriefe gefallener Studenten.* Munich: Georg Müller, 1928. Selected and translated by Annie F. Wedd as *German Students' War Letters* (London: Methuen; New York: Dutton, 1929).

Wittig, Josef. *Leben Jesu in Palästina, Schlesien und anderswo* (Life of Jesus in Palestine, Silesia, and elsewhere). 2 vols. Gotha: L. Klotz, 1927. *NL-Bibl.* 8 C 50.

Zweig, Stefan. *Jeremias: Eine dramatische Dichtung in neun Bildern.* Leipzig: Insel Verlag, 1920. Translated by Eden and Cedar Paul as *Jeremiah: A Drama in Nine Scenes* (London: Allen & Unwin, 1929).

———. *Sternstunden der Menschheit: Zwölf historische Miniaturen.* Frankfurt am Main, 1928. Translated and with an afterword by Lowell A. Bangerter as *Decisive Moments in History: Twelve Historical Miniatures* (Riverside, Calif.: Ariadne Press, 1999).

3. Literature Mentioned by Bonhoeffer's Correspondents

Althaus, Paul. *Der Geist der lutherischen Ethik im Augsburgischen Bekenntnis* (The spirit of Lutheran ethics in the Augsburg Confession). Munich: Chr. Kaiser Verlag, 1930. *NL-Bibl.* 4.1.

Barth, Karl. "Die Not der evangelischen Kirche" (The crisis in the Protestant church). *Zwischen den Zeiten* 9 (1931): 89–122. *NL-Bibl.* 3 A 4. Reprinted in Barth, *"Der Götze wackelt": Zeitkritische Aufsätze, Reden und Briefe von 1930 bis 1960* ("The idol teeters": Contemporary essays, speeches, and letters from 1930 to 1960), edited by Karl Kupisch, 33–62. Berlin: K. Vogt, 1961.

Bernanos, Georges. *Die Sonne Satans: Ein Roman.* Translated by Fr. Burschell. Hellerau: Jakob Hegner, 1927. Translated by J. C. Whitehouse as *Under Satan's Sun* (Lincoln: University of Nebraska Press, 2001). Originally published as *Sous le soleil de Satan* (Paris: Plon-Nourrit, 1926).

Dibelius, Otto. *Die Verantwortung der Kirche: Eine Antwort an Karl Barth* (The responsibility of the church: A response to Karl Barth). Berlin: Kranzverlag, 1931.

Das evangelische Deutschland: Jahr- und Adreßbuch der kirchlichen Behörden und der gesamten evangelischen Geistlichkeit Deutschlands (Protestant Germany: Annual and address book of church administrative offices and all Protestant pastors in Germany). 10th ed. Leipzig, 1927–28.

Fendt, Leonhard. "Christus in der Verkündigung" (Christ in the proclamation). *Monatsschrift für Pastoraltheologie zur Vertiefung des gesamten pfarramtlichen Wirkens* (Monthly periodical for pastoral theology to deepen all facets of pastoral ministry) 27 (1931): 78–89.

Harnack, Adolf von. *Possidius: Augustins Leben.* Eingeleitet und übersetzt (Possidius: Augustine's life; introduced and translated). Abhandlungen der preußischen Akademie der Wissenschaften: Philosophisch-historische Klasse (Studies of the Prussian Academy of Science: Philosophical-historical class), 1930, no. 1. Berlin: Akademie der Wissenschaften, 1930.

Hase, Hans Christoph von. *Die Gegenwart Christi in der Kirche* (The presence of Christ in the church). Beiträge zur Förderung christlicher Theologie (Contributions to the promotion of Christian theology), vol. 38, no. 1. Gütersloh: C. Bertelsmann, 1934.

Hildebrandt, Franz. *EST: Das lutherische Prinzip* (EST: The Lutheran principle). Studien zur systematischen Theologie (Studies in systematic theology) 7. Göttingen: Vandenhoeck & Ruprecht, 1931.

John of Salisbury. *Metalogicon*. Edited by C. C. J. Webb. Oxford: Clarendon, 1929.

Kinderharfe: Liederbuch für evangelische Kindergottesdienste (Sonntagsschulen) (Children's harp: Hymnal for Protestant children's worship services [Sunday schools]). Berlin, 1912.

Lütgert, Wilhelm. *Die Religion des deutschen Idealismus und ihr Ende* (The religion of German idealism and its end). Vol. 4: *Das Ende des Idealismus im Zeitalter Bismarcks* (The end of idealism in the age of Bismarck). Gütersloh: C. Bertelsmann, 1930.

Macholz, Waldemar. "Grundsätzliches zur Gottesdienstgestaltung" (Basic considerations for creating worship services). *Monatsschrift für Gottesdienst und kirchliche Kunst* (Monthly periodical for worship and church art) 26 (1931): 3–25.

Müller, Hans Martin. "Zur Verständigung über Sozialethik" (On coming to an understanding regarding social ethics). *Die Eiche* 19 (1931): 40–61.

Piper, Otto. "Adolf von Harnack gestorben: Ein Leben für die Wissenschaft" (Adolf von Harnack has died: A life dedicated to scholarship). *Hannoverscher Courier* 267 (June 11, 1930).

Przywara, Erich. *Kant heute: Eine Sichtung* (Kant today: An examination). Munich: Oldenbourg, 1930.

Schmidt, Hans Wilhelm. "Die ersten und die letzten Dinge" (The first and the last things). *Jahrbuch der theologischen Schule Bethel* (Yearbook of the Bethel theological school) 1 (1930): 177–237.

Seeberg, Reinhold. *Lehrbuch der Dogmengeschichte.* Vol. 4/1: *Die Entstehung des protestantischen Lehrbegriffs* (The origins of Protestant doctrine). Rev. 4th ed. Leipzig: A. Deichert, 1933. Abridged translation by Charles E. Hay as *Textbook of the History of Doctrine,* 2 vols. in 1 (Grand Rapids, Mich.: Baker Book House, 1956). (The English translation was originally made in 1905 from a modified version of the first German edition; it does not correspond in organization and pagination to the third German edition used by Bonhoeffer.)

Wirth, Herman. *Aufgang der Menschheit: Untersuchungen zur Geschichte der Religion, Symbolik und Schrift der atlantisch-nordischen Rasse* (Rise of humankind: Investigations on the history of the religion, symbolism, and writing of the Atlantic-Nordic race). Jena: E. Diederichs, 1928.

4. Literature Consulted by the Editors

Adams, Frank T. *James A. Dombrowski: An American Heretic, 1897–1983.* Knoxville: University of Tennessee Press, 1992.

Ahlfeld, D. Friedrich. *Sermons on the Catechism, Volume Four: The Sacraments and the Word.* Translated by J. W. Richard. Burlington, Iowa: Lutheran Literary Board, 1924. Originally published as *Katechismuspredigten* (Halle: R. Mühlmann: 1852–).

Aland, Kurt, ed. *Glanz und Niedergang der deutschen Universität: 50 Jahre deutsche Wissenschaftsgeschichte in Briefen an und von Hans Lietzmann (1892–1942)* (Glory and demise of the German university: Fifty years of the history of German scholarship in letters to and from Hans Lietzmann [1892–1942]). Berlin: De Gruyter, 1979.

Althaus, Paul. *Das Erlebnis der Kirche* (The experience of the church). 2nd ed. Leipzig: Dörffling & Franke, 1924.

———. *Evangelium und Leben: Gesammelte Vorträge* (Gospel and life: Collected lectures). Gütersloh: C. Bertelsmann, 1927.

———. *Die letzten Dinge: Entwurf einer christlichen Eschatologie* (The last things: Outline of a Christian eschatology). Gütersloh: C. Bertelsmann, 1926.

———. *Religiöser Sozialismus: Grundfragen der christlichen Sozialethik* (Religious socialism: Basic questions of Christian social ethics). Gütersloh: C. Bertelsmann, 1921.

———. *Die Theologie Martin Luthers* (The theology of Martin Luther). Gütersloh: Gütersloher Verlagshaus Gerd Mohn, 1975. Translated by Robert C. Schultz as *The Theology of Martin Luther* (Philadelphia: Fortress Press, 1988).

Angell, James W. *Der Wiederaufbau Deutschlands: Von Versailles bis zum Young-Plan.* Veröffentlichungen des Instituts für Finanzwesen an der Handelshochschule Berlin (Publications of the Institute for Financial Studies at the Berlin Trade School) 2. Munich: Duncker & Humblot, 1930. Originally published as *The Recovery of Germany.* Published for the Council on Foreign Relations. New Haven, Conn.: Yale University Press, 1929.

Arnold, Hardy. "Conversations with Dietrich Bonhoeffer." *Plough,* no. 6 (September 1984): 4–6.

Augustine, Bishop of Hippo. *Dreizehn Bücher Bekenntnisse.* Translated by C. J. Perl with annotations by A. Holl. 2nd ed. Paderborn: Ferdinand

Schöningh, 1964. Translated with an introduction and notes by Henry Chadwick as *Confessions* (Oxford: Oxford University Press, 1991).

Barth, Karl. "Der Christ in der Gesellschaft." In Moltmann, *Anfänge der dialektischen Theologie, Teil I,* 3–37. Translated by Douglas Horton as "The Christian's Place in Society," in *The Word of God and the Word of Man,* 272–327 (London: Hodder & Stoughton, 1928).

———. *Die christliche Dogmatik im Entwurf* (Christian dogmatics in outline). Vol. 1: *Die Lehre vom Worte Gottes: Prolegomena zur christlichen Dogmatik* (The doctrine of the Word of God: Prolegomena to Christian dogmatics). Munich: 1927. Also published in *Gesamtausgabe* (Collected works), vol. 2, edited by G. Sauter (Zurich: Theologischer Verlag, 1982).

———. *Die kirchliche Dogmatik.* Zurich: Evangelischer Verlag, 1932–67. Translated by G. W. Bromiley as *Church Dogmatics,* edited by G. W. Bromiley and T. F. Torrance, 4 vols. (Edinburgh: T & T Clark, 1956–77). Vol. 1, pt. 1: *Die Lehre vom Wort Gottes: Prolegomena zur kirchlichen Dogmatik.* Erster Halbband. Translated as *The Doctrine of the Word of God: Prolegomena to Church Dogmatics,* vol. 1/1, rev. ed. Vol. 1, pt. 2: *Die Lehre vom Wort Gottes: Prolegomena zur kirchlichen Dogmatik.* Zweiter Halbband. 6th ed. Zurich: Evangelischer Verlag, 1975. Translated as *The Doctrine of the Word of God: Prolegomena to Church Dogmatics,* vol. 1/2. Vol. 3, pt. 3: *Die Lehre von der Schöpfung,* Dritter Teil. 2nd ed. Zurich: Evangelischer Verlag, 1961. Translated as *The Doctrine of Creation,* vol. 3/3.

———. *Die Menschlichkeit Gottes.* Theologische Studien 48. Zurich: EVZ Verlag, 1956. Translated by John Newton Thomas and Thomas Weiser as *The Humanity of God* (London: Collins; Atlanta: John Knox, 1976).

———. *Der Römerbrief.* 10th printing of the new, revised edition of 1922. Zurich: EVZ Verlag, 1967. Translated from the sixth edition by Edwyn C. Hoskyns as *The Epistle to the Romans* (London: Oxford University Press, 1933, 1960).

———. "Schicksal und Idee in der Theologie." *Zwischen den Zeiten* 7 (1929): 309–48. Also published in Barth, *Theologische Fragen und Antworten,* vol. 3 of *Gesammelte Vorträge,* 54–92 (Zollikon: Evangelischer Verlag, 1957). Translated and edited by H. Martin Rumscheidt as "Fate and Idea in Theology," with an introduction by Stephen W. Sykes, in *The Way of Theology in Karl Barth: Essay and Comments,* 25–61 (Allison Park, Pa.: Pickwick, 1986).

———. "Das Wort Gottes als Aufgabe der Theologie." In Moltmann, *Anfänge der dialektischen Theologie, Teil I,* 197–218. Translated by Douglas Horton as "The Word of God and the Task of the Ministry," in *The Word of God and the Word of Man,* 183–217 (London: Hodder & Stoughton, 1928).

———. *Das Wort Gottes und die Theologie.* Munich: Chr. Kaiser Verlag, 1925. Translated by Douglas Horton as *The Word of God and the Word of Man* (London: Hodder & Stoughton, 1928).

Die Bekenntnisschriften der evangelisch-lutherischen Kirche. Edited and published in the anniversary year of the Augsburg Confession, 1930. Göttingen: Vandenhoeck & Ruprecht, 1930 [1952]. Translated by Charles Arand, Eric Gritsch, Robert Kolb, William Russell, James Schaaf, Jane Strohl, and Timothy J. Wengert as *The Book of Concord: The Confessions of the Evangelical Lutheran Church,* edited by Robert Kolb and Timothy J. Wengert (Minneapolis: Fortress Press, 2000).

Besier, Gerhard. *Krieg—Frieden—Abrüstung: Die Haltung der europäischen und amerikanischen Kirchen zur Frage der deutschen Kriegsschuld 1914–1933; Ein kirchenhistorischer Beitrag zur Friedensforschung und Friedenserziehung* (War—peace—disarmament: The position of the European and American churches regarding the question of German war guilt 1914–1933; a church historical contribution to peace research and peace education). Göttingen: Vandenhoeck & Ruprecht, 1982.

Bethge, Eberhard. *Bekennen und Widerstehen: Aufsätze, Reden, Gespräche* (Confessing and resisting: Essays, speeches, conversations). Munich: Chr. Kaiser Verlag, 1984.

———. *Dietrich Bonhoeffer: Theologe—Christ—Zeitgenosse; Eine Biographie.* Munich: Chr. Kaiser Verlag, 1967. Translated by Eric Mosbacher, Peter Ross, Betty Ross, Frank Clarke, and William Glen-Doepel as *Dietrich Bonhoeffer: A Biography,* under the editorship of Edwin Robertson, revised and edited by Victoria Barnett, based on the seventh German edition (1st Fortress Press ed., Minneapolis: Fortress Press, 2000).

———. "Dietrich Bonhoeffers Weg vom 'Pazifismus' zur Verschwörung" (Dietrich Bonhoeffer's path from "pacifism" to conspiracy). In *Frieden—das unumgängliche Wagnis: Die Gegenwartsbedeutung der Friedensethik Dietrich Bonhoeffers* (Peace—the unavoidable risk: The contemporary significance of Dietrich Bonhoeffer's peace ethic), edited by Hans Pfeifer, Internationales Bonhoeffer Forum: Forschung und Praxis 5, 119–36. Munich: Chr. Kaiser Verlag, 1982.

Bethge, Eberhard, Renate Bethge, and Christian Gremmels, eds. *Dietrich Bonhoeffer: Sein Leben in Bildern und Texten.* Munich: Chr. Kaiser, 1989. Translated by John Bowden as *Dietrich Bonhoeffer: A Life in Pictures* (Philadelphia: Fortress Press, 1986). Translated by Brian McNeil as *Dietrich Bonhoeffer: A Life in Pictures,* edited by Renate Bethge and Christian Gremmels, 2006 centenary ed. (Minneapolis: Fortress Press, 2006).

Biehl, Michael. *Der Fall Sadhu Sundar Singh: Theologie zwischen den Kulturen* (The case of Sadhu Sundar Singh: Theology between cultures). Studien zur interkulturellen Geschichte des Christentums 66 (Studies on the intercultural history of Christianity 66). Frankfurt am Main: Lang, 1990.

Bizer, Ernst. "Der 'Fall Dehn'" (The "Dehn Case"). In *Festschrift für Günther Dehn,* edited by W. Schneemelcher, 239–61. Neukirchen: Kreis Moers, 1957.

Bloch, Ernst. *Atheismus im Christentum: Zur Religion des Exodus und des Reichs.* Vol. 14 of *Gesamtausgabe* (Collected works). Frankfurt am Main: Suhrkamp, 1968. Translated by J. T. Swann as *Atheism in Christianity: The Religion of the Exodus and the Kingdom* (New York: Herder & Herder, 1972).

Bonhoeffer, Dietrich. "Christ and Peace." In *A Testament to Freedom: The Essential Writings of Dietrich Bonhoeffer*, edited by Geffrey B. Kelly and F. Burton Nelson, rev. ed., 93–95. San Francisco: HarperSanFrancisco, 1995.

———. *Christ the Center.* New translation by Edwin Robertson. San Francisco: Harper & Row, 1978.

———. "Concerning the Christian Idea of God." *Journal of Religion* 12, no. 2 (April 1932): 177–85.

———. "The Death of Moses." In *Dietrich Bonhoeffer's Prison Poems*, edited and translated by Edwin Robertson, 95–103. Grand Rapids, Mich.: Zondervan, 2005. Previously published as *Voices in the Night: The Prison Poems of Dietrich Bonhoeffer*, 97–106 (Surrey, England: Eagle, 1998; Grand Rapids, Mich.: Zondervan, 1999).

———. *Dietrich Bonhoeffer: Einführung in seine Botschaft* (Dietrich Bonhoeffer: Introduction to his message). Edited by the Presseverband der Evangelischen Kirche im Rheinland. Düsseldorf: "Verlag Kirche in der Zeit," 1955.

———. *Dietrich Bonhoeffer Werke.* 17 vols. Edited by Eberhard Bethge et al. Munich: Chr. Kaiser/Gütersloher Verlagshaus, 1986–99. Translated as *Dietrich Bonhoeffer Works,* Victoria J. Barnett, Wayne Whitson Floyd Jr., and Barbara Wojhoski, general editors. 17 vols. (Minneapolis: Fortress Press, 1996–).

Vol. 1: *Sanctorum Communio: Eine dogmatische Untersuchung zur Soziologie der Kirche.* Edited by Joachim von Soosten. Munich: Chr. Kaiser Verlag, 1986. Translated by Reinhard Krauss and Nancy Lukens as *Sanctorum Communio: A Theological Study of the Sociology of the Church*, edited by Clifford J. Green (Minneapolis: Fortress Press, 1998).

Vol. 2: *Akt und Sein: Transzendentalphilosophie und Ontologie in der systematischen Theologie.* Edited by Hans-Richard Reuter. Munich: Chr. Kaiser Verlag, 1988. Translated by Martin Rumscheidt as *Act and Being: Transcendental Philosophy and Ontology in Systematic Theology*, edited by Wayne Whitson Floyd Jr. (Minneapolis: Fortress Press, 1996).

Vol. 3: *Schöpfung und Fall: Theologische Auslegung von Genesis 1–3.* Edited by Martin Rüter and Ilse Tödt. Munich: Chr. Kaiser Verlag, 1989. Translated by Douglas Stephen Bax as *Creation and Fall: A Theological Exposition of Genesis 1–3*, edited by John W. de Gruchy (Minneapolis: Fortress Press, 1996).

Vol. 4: *Nachfolge*. Edited by Martin Kuske and Ilse Tödt. Munich: Chr. Kaiser Verlag, 1989; 2nd ed., Gütersloh: Chr. Kaiser/Gütersloher Verlagshaus, 1994. Translated by Barbara Green and Reinhard Krauss as *Discipleship*, edited by Geffrey B. Kelly and John D. Godsey (Minneapolis: Fortress Press, 2001).

Vol. 5: *Gemeinsames Leben: Das Gebetbuch der Bibel*. Edited by Gerhard Ludwig Müller and Albrecht Schönherr. Munich: Chr. Kaiser Verlag, 1987. Translated by Daniel W. Bloesch and James H. Burtness as *Life Together* and *Prayerbook of the Bible*, edited by Geffrey B. Kelly (Minneapolis: Fortress Press, 1996).

Vol. 6: *Ethik*. Edited by Ilse Tödt, Heinz Eduard Tödt, Ernst Feil, and Clifford Green. Munich: Chr. Kaiser Verlag, 1992; 2nd ed., Gütersloh: Chr. Kaiser/Gütersloher Verlagshaus, 1998. Translated by Reinhard Krauss and Charles West, with Douglas W. Stott, as *Ethics*, edited by Clifford J. Green (Minneapolis: Fortress Press, 2005).

Vol. 7: *Fragmente aus Tegel*. Edited by Renate Bethge and Ilse Tödt. Gütersloh: Chr. Kaiser/Gütersloher Verlagshaus, 1994. Translated by Nancy Lukens as *Fiction from Tegel Prison*, edited by Clifford J. Green (Minneapolis: Fortress Press, 2000).

Vol. 8: *Widerstand und Ergebung* (Resistance and submission). Edited by Christian Gremmels, Eberhard Bethge, and Renate Bethge, with Ilse Tödt. Gütersloh: Chr. Kaiser/Gütersloher Verlagshaus, 1998.

Vol. 9: *Jugend und Studium: 1918–1927*. Edited by Hans Pfeifer, with Clifford Green and Jürgen Kaltenborn. Munich: Chr. Kaiser Verlag, 1986. Translated by Mary Nebelsick, with the assistance of Douglas W. Stott, as *The Young Bonhoeffer: 1918–1927*, edited by Paul Matheny, Clifford J. Green, and Marshall Johnson (Minneapolis: Fortress Press, 2001).

Vol. 10: *Barcelona, Berlin, Amerika: 1928–1931*. Edited by Reinhard Staats and Hans Christoph von Hase, with Holger Roggelin and Matthias Wünsche. Munich: Chr. Kaiser Verlag, 1991. 2nd ed., Gütersloh: Chr. Kaiser/Gütersloher Verlagshaus, 2005. Translated by Douglas W. Stott as *Barcelona, Berlin, New York: 1928–1931*, edited by Clifford J. Green (Minneapolis: Fortress Press, 2008).

Vol. 11: *Ökumene, Universität, Pfarramt: 1931–1932* (Ecumenical, academic, and pastoral work: 1931–1932). Edited by Eberhard Amelung and Christoph Strohm. Gütersloh: Chr. Kaiser Verlagshaus, 1994.

Vol. 12: *Berlin: 1932–1933*. Edited by Carsten Nicolaisen and Ernst-Albert Scharffenorth. Gütersloher: Chr. Kaiser/Gütersloher Verlagshaus, 1997.

Vol. 13: *London: 1933–1935*. Edited by Hans Goedeking, Martin Heimbucher, and Hans-Walter Schleicher. Gütersloh: Chr. Kaiser/Gütersloher Verlagshaus, 1994. Translated by Isabel Best as *London: 1933–1935*, with supplementary material translated by Douglas W. Stott, and edited by Keith Clements (Minneapolis: Fortress Press, 2007).

Vol. 14: *Illegale Theologenausbildung: Finkenwalde 1935–1937* (Theological education at Finkenwalde: 1935–1937). Edited by Otto Dudzus and Jürgen Henkys, with Sabine Bobert-Stützel, Dirk Schulz, and Ilse Tödt. Gütersloh: Chr. Kaiser/Gütersloher Verlagshaus, 1996.

Vol. 15: *Illegale Theologenausbildung: Sammelvikariate: 1937–1940* (Theological education underground: 1937–1940). Edited by Dirk Schulz. Gütersloh: Chr. Kaiser/Gütersloher Verlagshaus, 1998.

Vol. 16: *Konspiration und Haft: 1940–1945*. Edited by Jørgen Glenthøj, Ulrich Kabitz, and Wolf Krötke. Gütersloh: Chr. Kaiser Gütersloher Verlagshaus, 1996. Translated by Lisa E. Dahill as *Conspiracy and Imprisonment: 1940–1945,* with supplementary material translated by Douglas W. Stott, and edited by Mark S. Brocker (Minneapolis: Fortress Press, 2006).

Vol. 17: *Register und Ergänzungen* (Index and supplements). Edited by Herbert Anzinger and Hans Pfeifer, assisted by Waltraud Anzinger and Ilse Tödt. Gütersloh: Chr. Kaiser/Gütersloher Verlagshaus, 1999.

———. *Gesammelte Schriften* (Collected writings). Edited by Eberhard Bethge. 6 vols. Munich: Chr. Kaiser Verlag, 1958–74.

———. *No Rusty Swords: Letters, Lectures and Notes 1928–1936 from the Collected Works of Dietrich Bonhoeffer.* Edited and introduced by Edwin H. Robertson. Translated by Edwin H. Robertson and John Bowden. New York: Harper & Row, 1965.

———. *Predigten—Auslegungen—Meditationen 1925–1945* (Sermons, exegeses, meditations). 2 vols. Edited by Otto Dudzus. Munich: Chr. Kaiser Verlag, 1984–85.

———. Review of Friedrich Parpert, *Das Mönchtum und die evangelische Kirche: Ein Beitrag zur Ausscheidung des Mönchtums aus der evangelischen Soziologie* (Monasticism and the Protestant church: A contribution on the exclusion of monasticism from Protestant sociology). *Deutsche Literaturzeitung,* no. 50 (December 13, 1930): 2356–58.

———. *Widerstand und Ergebung: Briefe und Aufzeichnungen aus der Haft.* Edited by Eberhard Bethge. Munich: Chr. Kaiser, 1951; expanded ed., 1970, 1985. Translated by Reginald H. Fuller as *Letters and Papers from Prison,* edited by Eberhard Bethge, translation revised by Frank Clark et al., additional material translated by John Bowden for the enlarged edition published in London (London: SCM, 1971; New York: Macmillan, 1972; New York: Simon & Schuster, 1997).

Bonhoeffer, Dietrich, and Maria von Wedemeyer. *Brautbriefe Zelle 92: Dietrich Bonhoeffer–Maria von Wedemeyer, 1943–1945.* Edited by Ruth-Alice von Bismarck and Ulrich Kabitz. Munich: Beck, 1992. Translated by John Brownjohn as *Love Letters from Cell 92: The Correspondence between Dietrich Bonhoeffer and Maria von Wedemeyer, 1943–45* (Nashville: Abingdon Press, 1995).

Bonhoeffer, Klaus. *Die Meistbegünstigung im modernen Völkerrecht* (Most-favored nation status in modern international law). Berlin: J. Springer, 1930.

"Bonhoeffer's Lectures on Preaching." See Fant, Clyde.

Brecht, Martin. *Martin Luther*. Vol. 2: *Ordnung und Abgrenzung der Reformation, 1521–1532* . Stuttgart: Calwer, 1986. Translated by James L. Schaaf as *Martin Luther: Shaping and Defining the Reformation 1521–1532* (Minneapolis: Fortress Press, 1990).

———. *Martin Luther*. Vol. 3: *Die Erhaltung der Kirche, 1532–1546*. Stuttgart: Calwer, 1987. Translated by James L. Schaaf as *Martin Luther: The Preservation of the Church, 1532–1546* (Minneapolis: Fortress Press, 1993).

Browning, Robert M., ed. *German Poetry from 1750 to 1900*. Foreword by Michael Hamburger. New York: Continuum 1984.

Brunstäd, Friedrich. *Die Idee der Religion: Prinzipien der Religionsphilosophie* (The idea of religion: Principles of the philosophy of religion). Halle an der Saale: Max Niemeyer, 1922.

Buber, Martin. *Ich und Du*. Leipzig: Insel Verlag, 1923. Translated by Ronald Gregor Smith as *I and Thou* (New York: Scribner, 2000).

———. *Zwiesprache*. Berlin: Schocken Verlag, 1932. Translated by Ronald Gregor Smith as "Dialogue," in Buber, *Between Man and Man*, introduced by Maurice Friedman, 1–39 (New York: Macmillan, 1966).

Büchmann, Georg. *Geflügelte Worte: Der Zitatenschatz des deutschen Volkes* (Familiar quotations: A treasury of citations of the German people). Completely revised and edited by G. Haupt and W. Hofmann. 32nd ed. Berlin: Haude & Spener, 1972.

Bunners, Christian. *Fritz Reuter und der Protestantismus: Theologische Beiträge zu Fritz Reuter, seinem Werk und dessen Rezeption* (Fritz Reuter and Protestantism: Theological contributions to Fritz Reuter, his work and its reception). Aufsätze und Vorträge zur Theologie und Religionswissenschaft (Essays and addresses on theology and religious studies) 82. Berlin: Evangelische Verlagsanstalt, 1987.

Burggraf, Julius. *Goethepredigten* (Goethe sermons). Gießen: A. Töpelmann, 1913.

Cancik, Hubert, and Helmuth Schneider, eds. *Der Neue Pauly: Enzyklopädie der Antike*. Stuttgart: Metzler, 2001–. Translated as *Brill's New Pauly: Encyclopedia of the Ancient World* (Leiden: Brill, 2002–).

Carter, Dan T. *Scottsboro: A Tragedy of the American South*. Rev. ed. Baton Rouge: Louisiana State University Press, 1979.

Casel, Odo. *Das christliche Kultmysterium.* Regensburg: F. Pustet, 1932. Translated as *The Mystery of Christian Worship,* edited by Burkhard Neunheuser, introduced by Aidan Kavanagh (New York: Crossroad, 1999).

———, ed. *Jahrbuch für Liturgiewissenschaft* (Annual of liturgical scholarship). Münster, 1921–41.

Cresswell, Amos S., and Maxwell G. Tow. *Dr Franz Hildebrandt: Mr Valiant-For-Truth.* Leominster: Gracewing, 2000.

Cullen, Countee. *The Black Christ and Other Poems, by Countee Cullen, with Decorations by Charles Cullen.* New York: Harper & Brothers, 1929.

Cyprian, Bishop of Carthage. *De lapsis* and *De Ecclesiae Catholicae Unitate.* Latin and English. Text and translation by Maurice Bévenot. Oxford: Clarendon Press, 1971.

Daix, Pierre, and Georges Boudaille. *Picasso: Blaue und Rosa Periode.* Munich: Bruckmann, 1966. Translated by Phoebe Pool as *Picasso: The Blue and Rose Periods: A Catalogue Raisonné of the Paintings, 1900–1906* (Greenwich, Conn.: New York Graphic Society, 1967).

Delitzsch, Franz. *System der biblischen Psychologie.* Leipzig: Dörffling & Franke, 1855. Translated by Robert Ernest Wallis as *A System of Biblical Psychology* (Edinburgh: T. & T. Clark, 1890).

Deutschsprachige Evangelische Gemeinde Barcelona, 1885–1985 (German-speaking Protestant congregation in Barcelona, 1885–1985). Barcelona: privately printed, 1985.

Dibelius, Otto. *Friede auf Erden? Fragen, Erwagungen, Antwort* (Peace on earth? Questions, reflections, answer). Berlin: Furche Verlag, 1930.

———. *Das Jahrhundert der Kirche: Geschichte, Betrachtung, Umschau und Ziele* (The century of the church: History, examination, observation, and goals). Berlin: Furche Verlag, 1926; 6th ed. 1928.

The Didache: Text, Translation, Analysis and Commentary. Edited by Aaron Milavec. Collegeville, Minn.: Liturgical Press, 2003.

Diels, Hermann, and Walther Kranz. *Die Fragmente der Vorsokratiker.* 12th ed. 3 vols. Zurich: Weidmann, 1966. Translated and edited by Rosamond Kent Sprague as *The Older Sophists: A Complete Translation by Several Hands of the Fragments in Die Fragmente der Vorsokratiker, edited by Diels-Kranz . . . with a New Edition of Antiphon and Euthydemus* (Columbia: University of South Carolina Press, 1972).

Dietrich Bonhoeffer's Prison Poems. See Edwin Robertson, ed., under Bonhoeffer.

Dombrowski, James A. *The Early Days of Christian Socialism in America.* New York: Columbia University Press, 1936.

Dostoyevsky, Fyodor Mikhaylovich. *Die Brüder Karamasoff.* Darmstadt, 1960. Translated by David McDuff as *The Brothers Karamazov* (London: Penguin, 2003).

Dreß, Walter. *Die Mystik des Marsilio Ficino* (The Mysticism of Marsilio Ficino). Berlin: W. de Gruyter, 1929.

———. *Die Theologie Gersons: Eine Untersuchung zur Verbindung von Nominalismus und Mystik im Spätmittelalter* (Gerson's theology: An investigation of the connection between nominalism and mysticism in the late Middle Ages). Gütersloh: C. Bertelsmann, 1931. *NL* Bibl. 2 C 2.3.

Drews, Arthur. *Die Christusmythe.* Jena: E. Diederichs, 1924. Translated from the 3rd ed. (rev. and enlarged) by C. Delisle Burns as *The Christ Myth* (Chicago: Open Court, 1911).

Duke, David Nelson. "The Development of an Ethic of (Racial) Justice: The Formative Experiences of Bonhoeffer's American Education." Archives of the Burke Library at Union Theological Seminary, New York, Bonhoeffer Secondary Papers, series 1A, box 3.

———. *In the Trenches with Jesus and Marx: Harry F. Ward and the Struggle for Social Justice.* Tuscaloosa: University of Alabama Press, 2003.

———. "The Radical Social Gospel of Harry F. Ward and Dietrich Bonhoeffer's American Education." Archives of the Burke Library at Union Theological Seminary, New York, Bonhoeffer Secondary Papers, series 1B, box 4, IBS 92, DUKE.

———. Response to Josiah Ulysses Young, "'Is the White Christ Distraught by These Dark Skins His Father Wrought?'" Paper presented to the Bonhoeffer Group, American Academy of Religion Annual Meeting, 1998. Archives of the Burke Library at Union Theological Seminary, New York, Bonhoeffer Secondary Papers, series 1A, box 3.

Dumas, André. *Dietrich Bonhoeffer: Theologian of Reality.* Translated by Robert McAfee Brown. New York: Macmillan, 1971.

Dürer, Albrecht. *Forty-eight Metal Engravings.* With an essay by Ivan Marazov. London: MacDonald Orbis, 1988.

Ehrenreich, Barbara. *Dancing in the Streets: A History of Collective Joy.* New York: Metropolitan Books, 2007.

Erdmann, Karl Dietrich. *Die Zeit der Weltkriege* (The time of the world wars). Vol. 4 of *Handbuch der Deutschen Geschichte* (Handbook of German history), edited by Bruno Gebhardt and Herbert Grundmann. Stuttgart: Klett-Cotta, 1978.

Ermenc, Joseph. J. "Where the Action Was: Reminiscences of a Peer Chemist. An Interview with Aristid von Grosse." In *Atomic Bomb Scientists: Memoirs, 1939–1945,* edited by Joseph J. Ermenc, 263–318. Westport, Conn.: Meckler, 1989.

Eusebius. *The Life of Constantine.* Vol. 1 of *Nicene and Post-Nicene Fathers,* edited by Philip Schaff and Henry Wace, 2nd series, 481–559. Reprint, Peabody, Mass.: Hendrickson, 1994.

Evangelisches Kirchengesangbuch in den Gliedkirchen der Evangelischen Kirche in Deutschland, seit 1951 (Protestant church hymnal for use in the member churches of the Protestant churches in Germany since 1951).

Fant, Clyde E. *Bonhoeffer: Worldly Preaching.* Nashville: Thomas Nelson, 1975. (Contains "Bonhoeffer's Lectures on Preaching.")

Feil, Ernst. *Die Theologie Dietrich Bonhoeffers: Hermeneutik, Christologie, Weltverständnis.* 2nd ed. Gesellschaft und Theologie: Systematische Beiträge 6. Munich: Kaiser Verlag; Mainz: Matthias-Grünewald-Verlag, 1979. Translated by H. Martin Rumscheidt as *The Theology of Dietrich Bonhoeffer* (Philadelphia: Fortress Press, 1985).

Fendt, Leonhard. *Die religiösen Kräfte des katholischen Dogmas* (The religious powers of Catholic dogma). Munich: Chr. Kaiser Verlag, 1921.

Festschrift zum 100jährigen Bestehen der deutschsprachigen evangelischen Gemeinde in Barcelona (Festschrift on the occasion of the 100-year anniversary of the German-speaking Protestant congregation in Barcelona). 1985.

Feuerbach, Ludwig. *The Essence of Christianity.* Translated by George Eliot. New York: Harper, 1957.

———. *Das Wesen der Religion, 30 Vorlesungen.* Leipzig: A. Kröner, 1923. Translated by Ralph Mannheim as *Lectures on the Essence of Religion* (New York: Harper & Row, 1967).

———. *Das Wesen des Glaubens im Sinne Luthers: Ein Beitrag zum "Wesen des Christentums."* Libelli series 280. Darmstadt: Wissenschaftliche Buchgesellschaft, 1970. Translated by Melvin Cherno as *The Essence of Faith according to Luther* (New York: Harper & Row, 1967).

Fischer, Fritz. *Griff nach der Weltmacht: Die Kriegszielpolitik des kaiserlichen Deutschland 1914/18.* Düsseldorf: Droste, 1961. Translated with introductions by Hajo Holborn and James Joll as *Germany's Aims in the First World War* (New York: W. W. Norton, 1967).

Floyd, Wayne Whitson, Jr. *Theology and the Dialectics of Otherness: On Reading Bonhoeffer and Adorno.* Lanham, Md.: University Press of America, 1988.

Freyer, H. *Antäus: Grundlegung einer Ethik des bewußten Lebens* (Antaeus: Foundation of an ethic of conscious living). Jena: E. Diederichs, 1922.

Gerstenmaier, Eugen. *Die Kirche und die Schöpfung: Eine theologische Besinnung zu dem Dienst der Kirche an der Welt* (The church and creation: A theological reflection on the service of the church to the world). Berlin: Furche Verlag, 1938.

Goethe, Johann Wolfgang von. *The Poems of Goethe: A Selection with Introduction and Notes.* Edited by Ronald D. Gray. Cambridge: Cambridge University Press, 1966.

———. *Werke.* Edited by Erich Trunz. Hamburger Ausgabe. 7th ed. 14 vols. Munich: C. H. Beck, 1975. Translated as *Goethe's Collected Works,* 12 vols. (Cambridge, Mass.: Suhrkamp, 1983–89).

Green, Clifford J. *Bonhoeffer: A Theology of Sociality*. Grand Rapids, Mich.: Wm. B. Eerdmans, 1999.

———. "Bonhoeffer's Courses and Ethics Readings at Union Theological Seminary." *Dietrich Bonhoeffer Yearbook 3*. Gütersloh: Gütersloher Verlagshaus, 2008.

———. "Pacifism and Tyrannicide: Bonhoeffer's Christian Peace Ethic." *Studies in Christian Ethics* 18, no. 3 (2005): 31–47.

Grimm, Hans. *Volk ohne Raum* (People without space). 2 vols. Munich: A. Langen, 1928.

Guthrie, William Norman. *Seven Oracles from the Cross*. London: Longmans, Green, 1935.

Handy, Robert T. *A History of Union Theological Seminary in New York*. New York: Columbia University Press, 1987.

Harnack, Adolf von. *Ausgewählte Reden und Aufsätze* (Selected speeches and essays). Edited by A. von Zahn-Harnack und A. von Harnack on the occasion of the author's one hundredth birthday. Berlin: W. de Gruyter, 1951.

———. "Fünfzehn Fragen an die Verächter der wissenschaftlichen Theologie unter den Theologen." *Die christliche Welt* 37, no. 1–2 (January 11, 1923): cols. 6–8. Translated by Keith R. Crimm and Louis De Grazia as "Fifteen Questions to Those among the Theologians Who Are Contemptuous of Scientific Theology," in *The Beginnings of Dialectic Theology*, edited by James M. Robinson, 165–66 (Richmond: John Knox, 1968).

———. *Lehrbuch der Dogmengeschichte*. Vol. 3: *Die Entwicklung des kirchlichen Dogmas*. 4th ed. Tübingen: J. C. B. Mohr, 1910; Darmstadt: Wissenschaftliche Buchgesellschaft, 1983. Translated by J. Millar as *History of Dogma*, vol. 3 (New York: Russel & Russel, 1958).

———. *Marcion: Das Evangelium vom fremden Gott: Eine Monographie zur Geschichte der Grundlegung der katholischen Kirche*. Leipzig: J. C. Hinrichs'sche Buchhandlung, 1921. Reprint, Darmstadt: Wissenschaftliche Buchgesellschaft, 1960. Translated by John E. Steely and Lyle D. Bierma as *Marcion: The Gospel of the Alien God* (Durham, N.C.: Labyrinth, 1990).

———. "Stufen wissenschaftlicher Erkenntnis" (Stages of scientific knowledge). In *Reden und Aufsätze* (Speeches and essays), n.s., 5. Gießen: A. Töpelmann, 1930.

———. *Das Wesen des Christentums*. Leipzig: J. C. Hinrichs, 1900. Translated by Thomas Bailey Saunders as *What Is Christianity? Sixteen Lectures Delivered in the University of Berlin during the Winter Term, 1899–1900*. New York: Harper, 1957. Reprint, with an introduction by Rudolf Bultmann, Gloucester, Mass.: Peter Smith, 1978.

Hase, Hans Christoph von. *Die Gegenwart Christi in der Kirche* (The presence of Christ in the church). Beiträge zur Förderung christlicher Theologie

(Contributions to the advancement of Christian theology), vol. 38, no. 1. Gütersloh: C. Bertelsmann, 1934.

Heidegger, Martin. *Sein und Zeit.* Halle: M. Niemeyer, 1927. Translated by Joan Stambaugh as *Being and Time: A Translation of Sein und Zeit* (Albany: State University of New York Press, 1996).

Hennecke, Edgar, and Wilhelm Schneemelcher, eds. *Neutestamentliche Apokryphen in deutscher Übersetzung.* Vol. 1: *Evangelien.* Tübingen: J. C. B. Mohr, 1959. Translated by A. J. B. Higgins et al. as *The New Testament Apocrypha,* vol. 1: *Gospels and Related Writings,* edited by R. McL. Wilson (Philadelphia: Westminster, 1963).

Heussi, Karl. *Kompendium der Kirchengeschichte* (Compendium of church history). Tübingen: Mohr, 1928.

Hirsch, Emanuel. *Die gegenwärtige geistige Lage im Spiegel philosophischer und theologischer Besinnung: Akademische Vorlesungen zum Verständnis des deutschen Jahres 1933* (The contemporary intellectual situation as reflected by philosophical and theological thought: Academic lectures for understanding the German year 1933). Göttingen: Vandenhoeck & Ruprecht, 1934.

Holl, Karl. *Gesammelte Aufsätze zur Kirchengeschichte* (Collected essays on church history). 3 vols. Tübingen: J. C. B. Mohr, 1928–32.

———. "Die Geschichte des Wortes Beruf." In *Der Westen* (The West), vol. 3 of *Gesammelte Aufsätze zur Kirchengeschichte* (Collected essays on church history). Translated by Heber F. Peacock as "The History of the Word Vocation (*Beruf*)," in *Review and Expositor* 55. no. 2 (April 1958): 126–54.

———. "Der Neubau der Sittlichkeit." In *Luther,* vol. 1 of *Gesammelte Aufsätze zur Kirchengeschichte,* 131–244. Tübingen: J. C. B. Mohr, 1923. Translated by Fred W. Meuser and Walter R. Wietzke as *The Reconstruction of Morality,* edited by James Luther Adams and Walter F. Bense (Minneapolis: Augsburg, 1979).

———. "Tolstoi nach seinen Tagebüchern" (Tolstoy according to his diaries). In *Der Westen,* vol. 3 of *Gesammelte Aufsätze zur Kirchengeschichte,* 433–49.

———. "Was verstand Luther unter Religion." In *Luther,* vol. 1 of *Gesammelte Aufsätze zur Kirchengeschichte,* 1–90. Tübingen: J. C. B. Mohr, 1923. Translated by Fred W. Meuser and Walter R. Wietzke as *What Did Luther Understand by Religion?* edited by James Luther Adams and Walter F. Bense (Philadelphia: Fortress Press, 1977).

Holl, Karl, and Wolfram Wette, eds. *Pazifismus in der Weimarer Republik: Beiträge zur historischen Friedensforschung* (Pacifism in the Weimar Republic: Contributions to the history of the peace movement). Sammlung Schöningh zur Geschichte und Gegenwart (Schöningh series on history and the present). Paderborn: Schöningh, 1981.

Horton, Myles, with Judith Kohl and Herbert Kohl. *The Long Haul: An Autobiography*. New York: Doubleday, 1990.

Hultsch, Friedrich. *Pappus Mathematicus* (Pappas [of Alexandria] the mathematician). Berlin, 1876–78.

James, William. *The Varieties of Religious Experience: A Study in Human Nature*. New York: Longmans, Green, 1928. Translated, edited, and with an afterword by Eilert Herms as *Die Vielfalt religiöser Erfahrung: Eine Studie über die menschliche Natur* (Darmstadt, 1979).

Jonas, Hans. "Heidegger und die Theologie" (1964). In *Heidegger und die Theologie: Beginn und Fortgang der Diskussion* (Heidegger and theology: Beginning and continuation of the discussion), edited by G. Noller, Theologische Bücherei (Theological library) 38, 316–40. Munich: Chr. Kaiser Verlag, 1967. Translated as "Heidegger and Theology," in Jonas, *The Phenomenon of Life: Toward a Philosophical Biology*, 235–61 (New York: Harper & Row, 1966).

Kaltenborn, Carl-Jürgen. *Adolf von Harnack als Lehrer Dietrich Bonhoeffers* (Adolf von Harnack as a teacher of Dietrich Bonhoeffer). Theologische Arbeiten (Theological studies) 31. Berlin: Evangelische Verlags-Anstalt, 1973.

Kaufmann, Walter A., ed. and trans. *The Portable Nietzsche*. New York: Penguin, 1982.

Kautsky, Karl. *Der Ursprung des Christentums*. Stuttgart: J. H. W. Dietz Nachfolger, 1921. Translated by Jacob Wittmer Hartmann as *Foundations of Christianity: A Study in Christian Origins* (London: Orbach & Chambers, 1925, 1973).

Kegel, Martin. *Los von Wellhausen! Ein Beitrag zur Neuorientierung in der alttestatmentlichen Wissenschaft*. Gütersloh: Bertelsmann, 1923. Translated by Marian Nolloth as *Away from Wellhausen: A Contribution to the New Orientation in Old Testament Study* (London: J. Murray; Nashville: Publishing House of the Methodist Episcopal Church, South, 1924).

Kelly, Geffrey. "An Interview with Jean Lasserre." *Union Seminary Quarterly Review* 27, no. 3 (1972): 149–60.

Keynes, John Maynard. "Causes of World Depression." *Forum and Century* 85 (January 1931): 21–25.

Kierkegaard, Søren. *Purity of Heart Is to Will One Thing: Spiritual Preparation for the Office of Confession*. Translated by Douglas V. Steere. New York: Harper & Row, 1967.

Knittermeyer, Hinrich. "Transzendentalphilosophie und Theologie: Eine kritische Erinnerung zum 22. April 1924" (Transcendental philosophy and theology: A critical recollection on the occasion of April 22, 1924). *Christliche Welt* 38 (1924): 220–26, 258–67, 354–61, 408–13.

Kunze, Gerhard. *Die gottesdienstliche Schriftlesung* (Scripture reading in worship). Part 1: *Stand und Aufgabe der Perikopenforschung* (Status and task of pericope research). Veröffentlichungen der evangelischen Gesellschaft für Liturgieforschung (Publications of the Protestant Society for Liturgical Research) 1. Göttingen: Vandenhoeck & Ruprecht, 1947.

Lasserre, Jean. "Lasserre's Memoir of Bonhoeffer at Union Seminary, 1930–31." *Newsletter,* International Bonhoeffer Society, English Language Section, no. 31 (1986): 1–4. Translated by Allen Hackett from *La Vie Chretienne* (October–November 1981).

Lehmann, Paul Louis. "A Critical Comparison on the Doctrine of Justification in the Theologies of Albrecht Ritschl and Karl Barth." ThD diss., Union Theological Seminary, New York, 1936.

Leibholz, Gerhard. *Christianity, Politics and Power.* London: Sheldon Press; New York: Macmillan, 1942.

———. *Das Wesen der Repräsentation unter besonderer Berücksichtigung des Repräsentativsystems: Ein Beitrag zur allgemeinen Staats- und Verfassungslehre* (The nature of representation with special consideration of the representative system: A contribution to the general doctrine of state and constitution). Beiträge zum ausländischen öffentlichen Recht und Völkerrecht (Contributions to foreign civil and international law) 11. Berlin: W. de Gruyter, 1929, 1966.

Leibholz-Bonhoeffer, Sabine. *Vergangen, erlebt, überwunden: Schicksale der Familie Bonhoeffer.* 4th ed. Gütersloh: Gütersloher Verlagshaus Gerd Mohn, 1983. Translated as *The Bonhoeffers: Portrait of a Family* (Chicago: Covenant, 1994).

Lietzmann, Hans. *An die Korinther I/II* (To the Corinthians I/II). Handbuch zum Neuen Testament (New Testament handbook) 9. Tübingen: J. C. B. Mohr (Paul Siebeck), 1907.

Lightfoot, Joseph Barber. *The Apostolic Fathers: Clement, Ignatius, and Polycarp.* Edited and translated by J. B. Lightfoot. Vol. 1. Reprint, Peabody, Mass.: Hendrickson, 1989.

Lilje, Hanns. *Memorabilia: Schwerpunkte eines Lebens* (Memorabilia: The central points of a life). Nuremberg: Laetare, 1973.

Lincoln, Abraham. *The Collected Works of Abraham Lincoln.* Edited by Roy P. Basler. 9 vols. New Brunswick, N.J.: Rutgers University Press, 1953–55.

Lütgert, Adolf, and Adolf Schlatter, eds. *Beiträge zur Förderung christlicher Theologie* (Contributions to the advancement of Christian theology). Serial publication. Gütersloh: Bertelsmann, 1921–28.

Luther, Martin. *Archiv zur Weimarer Ausgabe der Werke Martin Luthers* (Archive of the Weimar edition of the works of Martin Luther). Vols. 1–2: *Opera-*

tiones in Psalmos, 1519–1521 (Psalms 1–10 [Vulgata]). Edited by Heino Gaese, Hans-Ulrich Perels, and Ursula Stock. Cologne: Böhlau, 1981.

———. *D. Martin Luthers Hauspostille* (Martin Luther's house postils). Berlin: Evangelischen Bücher-Verein, 1846.

———. *Kirchenpostille.* Translated as *Sermons of Martin Luther: The Church Postils,* edited by John N. Lenker (Charlottesville, Va.: InteLex, 2000). Available at http:www.nlx.com.

———. *Werke: Kritische Gesamtausgabe.* 58 vols. Weimarer Ausgabe. Weimar: H. Böhlau, 1883–. Translated as *Luther's Works,* vols. 1–30 edited by Jaroslav Pelikan, vols. 31–55 edited by Helmut Lehmann, complete works on CD-ROM (Minneapolis: Fortress Press; St. Louis: Concordia, 2002).

Lutheran Book of Worship. Minneapolis: Augsburg, 1978.

Marsh, Charles. *Reclaiming Dietrich Bonhoeffer: The Promise of His Theology.* New York: Oxford University Press, 1994.

Mehnert, Klaus. *Ein Deutscher in der Welt: Erinnerungen 1906–1981* (A German in the world: Recollections 1906–81). Stuttgart: Deutsche Verlags-Anstalt, 1981.

Meier, Kurt. *Der evangelische Kirchenkampf: Gesamtdarstellung in drei Bänden* (The Protestant Church Struggle: Complete account in 3 vols.). Vol. 1: *Der Kampf um die "Reichskirche"* (The struggle over the "Reich church"). Göttingen: Vandenhoeck & Ruprecht, 1976.

Meyer, Conrad Ferdinand. *Huttens letzte Tage.* (Hutten's last days). Stuttgart: Reclam, 1988.

———. *Sämtliche Werke: Historisch-kritische Ausgabe* (Complete works: Historical-critical edition). Edited by H. Zeller and A. Zäch. Vols. 1 and 8. Bern: Benteli, 1963, 1970.

Meyer, Dietrich, and Eberhard Bethge, eds. *Nachlaß Dietrich Bonhoeffer: Ein Verzeichnis; Archiv, Sammlung, Bibliothek* (Dietrich Bonhoeffer's literary estate: A bibliographical catalog; archive, collection, library). Munich: Chr. Kaiser Verlag, 1987.

Meyer-Bothling, Hans-Peter. "Fritz Reuters 'Lowising': Zur Biographie Luise Reuters" (Fritz Reuter's "Lowising": Concerning the biography of Luise Reuter). In *Vom Reichtum des Erzählens: Fritz Reuter 1810–1874* (From the richness of the tale: Fritz Reuter 1810–1874), edited by U. Bichel, F. Minssen, and H. de Voss, 210–25. Munich: Langen Müller, 1985.

Moeller van den Bruck, Arthur. *Das dritte Reich* (The Third Reich). Edited by Hans Schwarz. Hamburg: Hanseatische Verlagsanstalt, 1931.

Moltmann, Jürgen, ed. *Anfänge der dialektischen Theologie, Teil I: Karl Barth. Heinrich Barth. Emil Brunner.* (The beginnings of dialectical theology. Part 1: Karl Barth, Heinrich Barth, Emil Brunner). 5th ed. Theologische

Bücherei: Systematische Theologie (Theological library: Systematic theology), vol. 17, no. 1. Munich: Chr. Kaiser Verlag, 1985.

Müller, Gerhard. *Die Rechtfertigungslehre: Geschichte und Probleme* (The doctrine of justification: History and problems). Studienbücher Theologie: Kirchen- und Dogmengeschichte (Studies on theology: The history of church and dogma). Gütersloh: Gerd Mohn, 1977.

Die Mündige Welt (The world come of age). Vol. 2. Part. 1: *Weißensee.* Part 2: *Verschiedenes* (Various items). Edited by Eberhard Bethge. Munich: Chr. Kaiser Verlag, 1956.

Die Mündige Welt (The world come of age). Vol. 5: *Dokumente zur Bonhoefferforschung 1928–1945* (Documents on Bonhoeffer research 1928–1945). Edited by Jørgen Glenthøj. Munich: Chr. Kaiser Verlag, 1969.

Nelson, F. Burton. "The Relationship of Jean Lasserre to Dietrich Bonhoeffer's Peace Concerns in the Struggle of Church and Culture." *Union Seminary Quarterly Review* 40, no. 1–2 (1985): 71–84.

Neumann, Peter. *Die Jungreformatorische Bewegung* (The Young Reformation movement). Göttingen: Vandenhoek & Ruprecht, 1971.

Niebergall, Friedrich. *Die moderne Predigt: Kulturgeschichtliche und theologische Grundlage. Geschichte und Ertrag* (The modern sermon: Cultural-historical and theological foundations. History and findings). Tübingen: J.C.B. Mohr, 1929.

Nietzsche, Friedrich. *The Antichrist.* Translated by Walter Kaufmann. In *The Portable Nietzsche,* 565–656. New York: Penguin Books, 1954, 1982.

———. *Werke* (Works). Kritische Gesamtausgabe (Complete critical edition). Edited by G. Colli and M. Montinari. Parts 5 and 6. Berlin: De Gruyter, 1971.

———. *The Will to Power.* Edited by Walter Kaufmann. Translated by Walter Kaufmann and R. J. Hollingdale. Reprint, New York: Vintage Books, 1967, 1968.

Nowak, Kurt. *Evangelische Kirche und Weimarer Republik: Zum politischen Weg des deutschen Protestantismus zwischen 1918 und 1932* (Evangelical Church and Weimar Republic: The political path of German Protestantism between 1918 and 1932). Göttingen: Vandenhoeck & Ruprecht, 1981.

Orwell, George. *1984.* 1949. Reprint, New York: Harcourt, 2000.

Otto, Rudolf. *Das Heilige: Über das Irrationale in der Idee des Göttlichen und sein Verhältnis zum Rationalen.* Breslau: Trewendt & Granier, 1917. Translated by John W. Harvey as *The Idea of the Holy: An Inquiry into the Nonrational Factor in the Idea of the Divine and Its Relation to the Rational* (London: Oxford University Press, 1929).

Palladius. *Dialogue sur la vie de Jean Chrysostome.* Vol. 1. Paris: Les Éditions du Cerf, 1988. Translated and edited by Robert T. Meyer as *Dialogue on the Life of St. John Chrysostom*, Ancient Christian Writers 45 (New York: Newman Press, 1985).

Pauly, August Friedrich von. See Cancik and Schneider, *Der Neue Pauly*.

Pfeifer, Hans. "Die Bedeutung der Jugendbewegung für Dietrich Bonhoeffer" (The significance of the youth movement for Dietrich Bonhoeffer). *Dietrich Bonhoeffer Jahrbuch/Dietrich Bonhoeffer Yearbook 2003*, edited by Victoria Barnett et al., 74–92. Gütersloh: Chr. Kaiser/Gütersloher Verlagshaus, 2003.

———. "Learning Faith and Ethical Commitment in the Context of Spiritual Training Groups: Consequences of Dietrich Bonhoeffer's Post-Doctoral Year in New York City, 1930/1931." *Dietrich Bonhoeffer Yearbook 3*. Gütersloh: Gütersloher Verlagshaus, 2008.

Plato. *Cratylus*. Translated by Benjamin Jowett. In *The Collected Dialogues of Plato*, edited by Edith Hamilton and Huntington Cairns, 421–74. Pantheon Books. New York: Bollingen Foundation, 1961.

Przywara, Erich. "Drei Richtungen der Phänomenologie" (Three directions of phenomenology). *Stimmen der Zeit* 115 (1928): 252–64.

Rasmussen, Larry L. *Earth Community, Earth Ethics*. Maryknoll, N.Y.: Orbis Books, 1996.

Die Religion in Geschichte und Gegenwart (Religion in history and the present). 5 vols. Tübingen: Mohr, 1909–13; 3rd newly revised ed., 1957–65.

Rieger, Julius. *Bonhoeffer in England*. Berlin: Lettner Verlag, 1966

Ritschl, Albrecht. *Die christliche Lehre von der Rechtfertigung und Versöhnung*. Vols. 1 and 2, 2nd rev. ed. Bonn, 1882. Vol. 3, 2nd rev. ed. Bonn: A. Marcus, 1883. Vol. 1 translated by John S. Black as *A Critical History of the Christian Doctrine of Justification and Reconciliation* (Edinburgh: Edmonston & Douglas, 1872). Vol. 3 translated as *The Christian Doctrine of Justification and Reconciliation: The Positive Development of the Doctrine*, edited by H. R. Mackintosh and A. B. Macaulay (Edinburgh: T. & T. Clark; New York: Charles Scribner's Sons, 1900; reprint; Clifton, N.J.: Reference Book Publishers, 1966).

Röhm, Eberhard. *Sterben für den Frieden. Spurensicherung: Hermann Stöhr (1898–1940) und die ökumenische Friedensbewegung* (Dying for peace. Tracing the path: Hermann Stöhr (1898–1940) and the ecumenical peace movement). Stuttgart: Calwer, 1985.

Rumscheidt, H. Martin. *Revelation and Theology: An Analysis of the Barth-Harnack Correspondence of 1923*. Cambridge: Cambridge University Press, 1972.

Schabert, Otto. *Baltisches Märtyrerbuch* (Baltic book of martyrs). Berlin: Furche Verlag, 1926.

Scheler, Max. *Der Formalismus in der Ethik und die materiale Wertethik: Neuer Versuch der Grundlegung eines ethischen Personalismus*. Halle an der Saale:

M. Niemeyer, 1921. *NL-Bibl.* 4.42. Also published as vol. 2 of *Gesammelte Werke,* 4th ed. (Bern: Francke Verlag, 1954). Translated by Manfred S. Frings and Roger L. Funk as *Formalism in Ethics and Non-formal Ethics of Values: A New Attempt toward the Foundation of an Ethical Personalism,* 5th rev. ed. (Evanston, Ill.: Northwestern University Press, 1973).

Schelsky, Helmut. *Einsamkeit und Freiheit: Idee und Gestalt der deutschen Universität und ihrer Reformen* (Solitariness and freedom: Idea and structure of the German university and [of] its reforms). 2nd ed. with "Addendum 1970." Wissenschaftstheorie, Wissenschaftspolitik, Wissenschaftsplanung (The theory, politics, and planning of scholarship) 20. Düsseldorf: Bertelsmann Universitätsverlag, 1971.

Schiller, Friedrich. *Musenalmanach für das Jahr 1797* (Almanac of the Muses for the year 1787). Neustrelitz: Michaelis, 1797.

———. *Sämtliche Werke.* Stuttgart, 1759–1805. Translated as *Schiller's Works,* edited by J. G. Fischer, with a biographical introduction by Hjalmar H. Boyesen, 4 vols. (Philadelphia: George Barrie, 1883).

Schleiermacher, Friedrich Daniel Ernst. *Über die Religion: Reden an die Gebildeten unter ihren Verächtern.* In *Schriften aus der Berliner Zeit 1796–1799,* vol. 1/2 of *Kritische Gesamtausgabe,* edited by G. Meckenstock. Berlin: W. de Gruyter, 1984. Translated and edited by Richard Crouter as *On Religion: Speeches to Its Cultured Despisers* (Cambridge: Cambridge University Press, 1996).

———. *Die Weihnachtsfeier: Ein Gespräch.* Halle an der Saale: Schimmelpfennig & Kompagnie, 1806. Translated with an introduction and notes by Terrence N. Tice as *Christmas Eve: Dialogue on the Incarnation.* (Richmond: John Knox Press, 1967; reprint, San Francisco: EM Texts, 1990).

Schmid, Heinrich. *The Doctrinal Theology of the Evangelical Lutheran Church.* Translated by Charles A. Hay and Henry E. Jacobs. 3rd ed. Minneapolis: Augsburg, 1961.

Scholder, Klaus. *Die Kirchen und das Dritte Reich.* Vol. 1: *Vorgeschichte und Zeit der Illusionen 1918–1934.* Frankfurt: Propyläen Verlag, 1977. Translated by John Bowden as *The Churches and the Third Reich,* vol. 1: *Preliminary History and the Time of Illusions, 1918–1934* (Philadelphia: Fortress Press, 1988).

Schweitzer, Albert. *Geschichte der Leben-Jesu Forschung.* 4th ed. Tübingen: J. C. B. Mohr, 1926. Translated by W. Montgomery, J. R. Coates, Susan Cupitt, and John Bowden as *The Quest of the Historical Jesus* (Minneapolis: Fortress Press, 2001).

———. *Kultur und Ethik.* Special edition with the inclusion of *Verfall und Wiederaufbau der Kultur.* Munich: Beck, 1960. Translated by C. T. Campion as *Civilization and Ethics* (London: A. & C. Black, 1929).

Sellin, Ernst. *Einleitung in das Alte Testament.* Leipzig: Quelle & Meyer, 1929. Translated by David Green and completely revised and rewritten by Georg Fohrer as *Introduction to the Old Testament* (London: SPCK, 1976).

Seneca. *Moral Essays.* Translated by John W. Basore. 2 vols. Loeb Classical Library, Latin and English. Cambridge, Mass.: Harvard University Press, 1998.

Siegmund-Schultze, Friedrich. *Die Wirkungen der englischen Hungerblockade auf die deutschen Kinder.* Special issue of *Die Eiche,* edited as a special publication at the initiative of the Working Group for the Politics of Justice. Berlin: F. Zillessen, 1919. Translated as *The Effect of the Hunger Blockade on Germany's Children* (n.p., 1919).

Sombart, Nicolaus. *Jugend in Berlin, 1933–1943: Ein Bericht* (Youth in Berlin, 1933–1943: A report). Frankfurt: Fischer, 1984.

Spengler, Oswald. *Der Untergang des Abendlandes: Umrisse einer Morphologie der Weltgeschichte.* Munich: Beck, 1923. Translated by Charles Frances Atkinson as *The Decline of the West* (New York: A. Knopf, 1926, 1999).

Staats, Reinhart. "Adolf von Harnack im Leben Dietrich Bonhoeffers" (Adolf von Harnack in the life of Dietrich Bonhoeffer). *Theologische Zeitschrift* 37 (1981): 94–122.

———. "Das patristische Erbe in der Theologie Dietrich Bonhoeffers" (The patristic legacy in the theology of Dietrich Bonhoeffer). *Berliner Theologische Zeitschrift* 5 (1988): 178–201.

Staats, Reinhart, and Matthias Wünsche. "Dietrich Bonhoeffers Abschied von der Berliner 'Wintertheologie'—Neue Funde aus seiner Spanienkorrespondenz 1927" (Dietrich Bonhoeffer's farewell to the Berlin 'Winter Theology'—New documents from his 1927 Spanish correspondence). *Zeitschrift für Neuere Theologiegeschichte/Journal for the History of Modern Theology* 1 (1994): 179–200.

Steiner, Robert Philipp. "Bonhoeffer lesen in Südafrika: Die 'theologische Geographie' der Grenze." In *Dietrich Bonhoeffer lesen im internationalen Kontext* (Reading Dietrich Bonhoeffer in the international context), edited by Ralf K. Wüstenberg, 63–116. Frankfurt: Peter Lang, 2007.

———. "From Phraseology to Reality: A 'Theological Geography.' Bonhoeffer's Early Travels and the Notion of the Boundary." PhD diss., University of Cape Town, 2004.

Stickelberger-Eder, Margrit. *Aufbruch 1914: Kriegsromane der späten Weimarer Republik* (1914, a time of change: War novels of the late Weimar Republic). Züricher Beiträge zur deutschen Literatur- und Geistesgeschichte (Zurich contributions to German literary and intellectual history) 56. Zurich: Artemis Verlag, 1983.

Stier, Ewald. "Kirche und Politik: Von der Tagung der Jungevangelischen in Magdeburg" (Church and politics: The conference of young Protestants in Magdeburg). *Christliche Welt* 44 (1930): 749–52.

Stupperich, Robert. *Otto Dibelius: Ein evangelischer Bischof im Umbruch der Zeiten* (Otto Dibelius: A Protestant bishop in an age of upheaval). Göttingen: Vandenhoeck & Ruprecht, 1989.

Tietz, Christiane. *Bonhoeffers Kritik der verkrümmten Vernunft: Eine erkenntnistheoretische Untersuchung.* Tübingen: Mohr Siebeck, 1999.

Tillich, Paul. *On the Boundary: An Autobiographical Sketch.* New York: Scribner, 1966.

———. *The Religious Situation.* Translated by H. Richard Niebuhr. New York: Meridian Books, 1956. Originally published as *Die Religiöse Lage der Gegenwart* (Berlin: Ullstein, 1926).

Tödt, Heinz Eduard. "Dietrich Bonhoeffers ökumenische Friedensethik" (Dietrich Bonhoeffer's ecumenical peace ethic). In *Frieden—das unumgängliche Wagnis: Die Gegenwartsbedeutung der Friedensethik Dietrich Bonhoeffers* (Peace—the unavoidable risk: The contemporary significance of Dietrich Bonhoeffer's peace ethic), edited by Hans Pfeifer, Internationales Bonhoeffer Forum 5, 85–117. Munich: Chr. Kaiser Verlag, 1982. Also in Tödt, *Authentic Faith: Dietrich Bonhoeffer's Theological Ethics in Context,* translated by David Stassen, 112–42 (Grand Rapids, Mich.: Wm. B. Eerdmans, 2007).

———. "Judendiskriminierung 1933: Der Ernstfall für Bonhoeffers Ethik" (Discrimination against Jews 1933: The test case for Bonhoeffer's ethics). In *Ethik im Ernstfall: Dietrich Bonhoeffers Stellung zu den Juden und ihre Aktualität* (Ethics in an extreme situation: Dietrich Bonhoeffer's position regarding the Jews and its relevance), edited by Wolfgang Huber and Ilse Tödt, Internationales Bonhoeffer Forum 4, 139–83. Munich: Chr. Kaiser Verlag, 1982. Also in Tödt, *Authentic Faith: Dietrich Bonhoeffer's Theological Ethics in Context,* translated by David Stassen, 73–111 (Grand Rapids, Mich.: Wm. B. Eerdmans, 2007).

Toomer, Jean. *Cane.* Introduced by Darwin T. Turner. New York: Liveright, 1993.

Traub, Gottfried. *Aus suchender Seele* (From a searching soul). Berlin: Buchverlag der Hilfe, 1906.

Troeltsch, Ernst. *Die Absolutheit des Christentums und die Religionsgeschichte.* 3rd ed. Tübingen: J. C. B. Mohr, 1929. Translated by David Reid as *The Absoluteness of Christianity and the History of Religions* (Richmond: John Knox Press, 1971).

Tryon, Harold H., ed. *Union Theological Seminary: Alumni Catalogue 1836–1947.* New York: [Union Theological Seminary], 1948.

Union Theological Seminary Announcement (1930).

Union Theological Seminary Catalogue (1931).

Very, Francis G. *The Spanish Corpus Christi Procession: A Literary and Folkloric Study*. Valencia: Tip. Moderna, 1962.

Viëtor, Karl. *Goethe: Dichtung, Wissenschaft, Weltbild*. Bern: Francke, 1949. Part 1 translated by Moses Hadas as *Goethe, the Poet* (Cambridge, Mass.: Harvard University Press, 1949). Parts 2 and 3 translated by Bayard Q. Morgan as *Goethe, the Thinker* (Cambridge, Mass.: Harvard University Press, 1950).

Vries, Jan de. *Altgermanische Religionsgeschichte* (History of the ancient Germanic religion). Vol. 2: *Die Göttervorstellung über den Kosmos* (The gods' understanding of the cosmos). 2nd, completely rev. ed. Grundriß der germanischen Philologie (Outline of Germanic philology), vol. 12, no. 2. Berlin: W. de Gruyter, 1957.

Webber, Charles C. "A History of the Development of Social Education in the United Neighborhood Houses of New York."

Weber, Max. "Politik als Beruf." In *Gesammelte politische Schriften*, 396–450. Munich: Drei Masken Verlag, 1921; in 2nd ed., edited by Johannes Winckelmann, 493–548. Tübingen: Mohr, 1958. Translated, edited, and with an introduction by Hans H. Gerth and C. Wright Mills as "Politics as a Vocation," in *From Max Weber: Essays in Sociology*, 77–128 (New York: Oxford University Press, 1946).

———. *Die protestantische Ethik und der Geist des Kapitalismus*. In vol. 1 of his *Gesammelte Aufsätze zur Religionssoziologie*. Tübingen: J. C. B. Mohr, 1934. Translated by Talcott Parsons as *The Protestant Ethic and the Spirit of Capitalism* (New York: Charles Scribner's Sons; London: George Allen & Unwin, 1958, 1976).

Wedemeyer, Maria von. "The Other Letters from Prison." *Union Seminary Quarterly Review* 23 (1967): 23–29.

Wehler, Hans-Ulrich. *Das deutsche Kaiserreich 1871–1918*. Edited by J. Leuschner. Deutsche Geschichte (German history) 9. Göttingen: Vandenhoeck & Ruprecht, 1983. Translated by Kim Traynor as *The German Empire, 1871–1918* (Oxford: Berg, 1997).

Wendel, Ernst Georg. *Studien zur Homiletik Dietrich Bonhoeffers: Predigt—Hermeneutik—Sprache* (Studies on the homiletics of Dietrich Bonhoeffer: Sermon—hermeneutics—language). Hermeneutische Untersuchungen zur Theologie 21. Tübingen: J. C. B. Mohr, 1985.

White, Walter F. *Rope and Faggot: A Biography of Judge Lynch*. New York: Alfred A. Knopf, 1929.

Wright, Jonathan R. C. *"Above Parties": The Political Attitudes of the German Protestant Church Leadership, 1918–1933*. London: Oxford University Press,

1974. Translated as *"Über den Parteien": Die politische Haltung der evangelischen Kirchenführer 1918–1933* (Göttingen: Vandenhoeck & Ruprecht, 1977).

Young, Josiah Ulysses III. "'Is the White Christ, Too, Distraught by These Dark Skins His Father Wrought?' Dietrich Bonhoeffer and the Problem of the White Christ." *Perspectives in Religious Studies* 26, no. 3 (1999): 317–30.

———. *No Difference in the Fare: Dietrich Bonhoeffer and the Problem of Racism.* Grand Rapids, Mich.: Wm. B. Eerdmans, 1998.

Zahn-Harnack, Agnes von. *Adolf von Harnack.* 2nd ed. Berlin: W. de Gruyter, 1951. Translated by William Henry Allison and William Henry Walker as "Adolf von Harnack," typewritten MS, Harvard Divinity School, 1941, 1949.

Zerner, Ruth. "Dietrich Bonhoeffer's American Experiences: People, Letters, and Papers from Union Seminary." *Union Seminary Quarterly Review* 31, no. 4 (Summer 1976): 261–82.

Zimmermann, Wolf-Dieter, ed. *Begegnungen mit Dietrich Bonhoeffer.* 4th ed. Munich: Chr. Kaiser Verlag, 1969. Translated by Käthe Gregor Smith as *I Knew Dietrich Bonhoeffer* (New York: Harper & Row, 1966; London: Fontana Books, 1973).

Zorilla y Moral, José. *Don Juan Tenorio.* Madrid: Ediciones Cátedra, 2005. Translated and introduced by Robert G. Trimble as *A Translation of José Zorilla's Don Juan Tenorio* (Lewiston, N.Y.: Edwin Mellen Press, 2003).

Zündel, Friedrich. *Jesus in Bildern aus seinem Leben* (Jesus in pictures from his life). 2nd ed. Munich: Chr. Kaiser Verlag, 1923. *NL-Bibl.* 1 D 37.

Index of Scriptural References

Index of Names

This index lists people mentioned in this volume, including authors and editors of literature cited in the notes. It provides brief profiles of the people listed and differs from the German edition by also including information about those whose work began after 1945, as well as additional information of interest to readers of the English edition. It does not include personal names that appear in book titles or only in the bibliography. When possible, dates of birth and death have been provided.

Index of Subjects

Editors and Translators

Victoria J. Barnett (MDiv, Union Theological Seminary, New York) is general editor of the *Dietrich Bonhoeffer Works,* English edition, and director of church relations at the United States Holocaust Memorial Museum. She is the author of *Bystanders: Conscience and Complicity during the Holocaust* (Greenwood Press, 1999) and *For the Soul of the People: Protestant Protest against Hitler* (Oxford University Press, 1992) and the editor and translator of the new revised English edition of *Dietrich Bonhoeffer: A Biography,* by Eberhard Bethge (Fortress Press, 2000), as well as *And the Witnesses Were Silent: The Confessing Church and the Jews,* by Wolfgang Gerlach (University of Nebraska Press, 2000). In addition to numerous book chapters and articles, she is the author of the essay on Bonhoeffer on the U.S. Holocaust Memorial Museum Web site.

Clifford J. Green (PhD, Union Theological Seminary, New York) is executive director of the Dietrich Bonhoeffer Works, English edition, and professor emeritus of theology, Hartford Seminary. A native of Australia, he received his education at Sydney University, Melbourne College of Divinity, the University of London (Richmond College), and the World Council of Churches' Graduate School of Ecumenical Studies (University of Geneva). His main teaching appointments were at Wellesley College, Goucher College, and Hartford Seminary. He was the founding president of the International Bonhoeffer Society, English Language Section, from 1972 to 1992. He is the author of *Bonhoeffer: A Theology of Sociality* (Eerdmans, rev. ed., 1999), translated as *Freiheit zur Mitmenschlichkeit: Dietrich Bonhoeffers Theologie der Sozialität* (Gütersloher Verlagshaus, 2004); coeditor of *Ethik* and *Jugend und Studium* in the German *Dietrich Bonhoeffer Werke*; editor of *Sanctorum Communio, Fiction from Tegel Prison,* and *Ethics,* and coeditor of *The Young Bonhoeffer: 1918–1927* in the *Dietrich Bonhoeffer Works,* English edition; and author of numerous articles and bibliographical works on Bonhoeffer. His other publications include *Karl Barth: Theologian of Freedom* (Collins, 1989;

Fortress, 1991); *Churches, Cities, and Human Community* (Eerdmans, 1996); and chapters on Tillich, Marx, Cone, and Gutierrez in *Critical Issues in Modern Religion* (Prentice-Hall, 1973, 1990).

Douglas W. Stott is a freelance editor and translator. A graduate of Davidson College, Northwestern University, and Emory's Candler School of Theology, he also studied in Germany at the Philipps University in Marburg and at the University of Stuttgart. His translation credits include several volumes of the *Theological Dictionary of the Old Testament* and the *Exegetical Dictionary of the New Testament*; commentaries for the Old Testament Library; *DBWE* 10, *Barcelona, Berlin, New York: 1928–1931*, and *DBWE* 14, *Theological Education at Finkenwalde: 1935–1937*; and F. W. J. Schelling's *Philosophy of Art*. He was also on the translation team of volume 1 of *Religion Past and Present*. He is currently preparing an annotated English edition of the correspondence of Caroline Schlegel-Schelling.

Barbara Wojhoski studied art history at New York University, ancient history at the Philipps University in Marburg, Germany, and anthropology at Georgia State University, and has participated in archaeological excavations of Late Woodland Period sites in Arkansas. She has been a fulltime freelance editor since 1995 for academic and denominational presses and has worked on projects ranging from a dictionary of the Miami-Illinois language to contemporary fiction translated from German to theological commentaries and philosophical works.